# Confronting Capitalism

Confronting Capitalism:
Dispatches From a Global Movement
Edited by Eddie Yuen, Daniel Burton-Rose,
and George Katsiaficas,
Soft Skull Press 2004

Cover Art by Eric Drooker (www.Drooker.com)
Back Cover Photograph/Frontispiece by Mike Fox, ThinkFirst Media/SIPA PRESS
Book Design by David Janik

Published by
Soft Skull Press
71 Bond Street
Brooklyn, NY 11217

Distributed by
Publishers Group West
www.pgw.com
1.800.788.3123

Printed in Canada

Cataloging in Publication Data is on file with the Library of Congress

# Table of Contents

**Introduction** Eddie Yuen . . . . . . . . . . . . . . . . . . . . . . . . . . . . . . . . . . . . . . . .vii
**Internationalism Against Globalization: A Map of Resistance**
     James Davis, Paul Rowley, and Eddie Yuen . . . . . . . . . . . . . . . . xxx
**A Protestography** Thatcher Collins . . . . . . . . . . . . . . . . . . . . . . . . . . . .xxxiv

## Part I:  Roots of the Movement
**Seattle Was Not the Beginning** George Katsiaficas    . . . . . . . . . . . . . . . . . .3
**Zapatismo and Global Struggle** Manuel Callahan . . . . . . . . . . . . . . .11
**Photographs** Emily Abendroth . . . . . . . . . . . . . . . . . . . . . . . . . . . . . .19
**Scaling the Heights to Seattle** David Kubrin . . . . . . . . . . . . . . . . . . .21

## Part II:  Crashing the Summits
**World Trashed Organization!** Schnews . . . . . . . . . . . . . . . . . . . . . . . .31
**A Global Carnival of the Dispossesed** Katherine Ainger . . . . . . . . . . . . . . .33
**The Globalization of Resistance** Mark Laskey . . . . . . . . . . . . . . . . . .36
**In Praise of the Seattle Coalition** Eliot Katz . . . . . . . . . . . . . . . . . . .46
**Seattle Diary** Jeffrey St. Clair . . . . . . . . . . . . . . . . . . . . . . . . . . . . .48
**Anarkids and Hypocrites** Barbara Ehrenreich . . . . . . . . . . . . . . . . . .72
**Seeds of a Movement** Stanley Aronowitz . . . . . . . . . . . . . . . . . . . . .75
**Color Blind** Andrew Hsiao . . . . . . . . . . . . . . . . . . . . . . . . . . . . . . . .82
**Prague 2000: The People's Battle** Boris Kagarlitsky . . . . . . . . . . . . . . .86
**Art** Eric Drooker . . . . . . . . . . . . . . . . . . . . . . . . . . . . . . . . . . . . . . .102
**Infernal Pain in Prague** Pol Potlatch . . . . . . . . . . . . . . . . . . . . . . . . .104
**Holidays in the Sun** Ramor Ryan . . . . . . . . . . . . . . . . . . . . . . . . . . .109
**Photographs** Leticia Velasquez . . . . . . . . . . . . . . . . . . . . . . . . . . . . .115
**The Charming Outcome of the Cancun Peace Talks** Writer's Bloc . . . . . . .117
**Cancun: The Collapse of the Neoliberal Offensive** Immanuel Wallerstein .122
**Something Did Start in Quebec City** Cindy Millstein . . . . . . . . . . . . . . . . . .126
**And Balanced With This Life, This Death** Ramor Ryan . . . . . . . . . . . . . . .134
**Genoa and the Antiglobalization Movement**
     Silvia Federici and George Caffentzis . . . . . . . . . . . . . . . . . . . . .142
**Growing Through Daring, Forgetting Through Fear** Carwil James . . . . . . .154
**Contra Cumbre in Quito** Daniel Burton-Rose . . . . . . . . . . . . . . . . . . .159

## Part III: We are Everyone? NGOs, Social Forums, and
       Problems of Representation
**This Is What Bureaucracy Looks Like** James Davis . . . . . . . . . . . . . . .167

**Another Forum is Possible** Ezequiel Adamovsky . . . . . . . . . . . . . . . . . . . . . . .180
**On Populism and the Antiglobalization Movement**
      James O'Connor . . . . . . . . . . . . . . . . . . . . . . .183
**Seattle '99** Eric Krebbers and Merjin Schoenmaker . . . . . . . . . . . . . . . . .196
**Fascists for Che** Nick Mamatas . . . . . . . . . . . . . . . . . . . . . . . . . . . . . .202
**Shutting Us Out** Kristine Wong . . . . . . . . . . . . . . . . . . . . . . . . . . . . . .204
**Peoples' Global Action** Sophie Style . . . . . . . . . . . . . . . . . . . . . . . . . .215
**Anti-Europeanism and Anti-Americanism** Michael Hardt . . . . . . . . . . . .222
**Interview with Barbara Epstein**
      Douglas Bevington and Chris Dixon . . . . . . . . . . . . . . . . . . . . . . . . .224

# Part IV: Facts on the Ground—The Hidden Topography of Revolt
**Why Not Show Off About the Best Things?** Wu Ming . . . . . . . . . . . . . . .235
**Confronting Empire** Arundhati Roy . . . . . . . . . . . . . . . . . . . . . . . . . . .243
**Out of the Ordinary** Naomi Klein . . . . . . . . . . . . . . . . . . . . . . . . . . . .247
**Resistance in Peru** Eric Schwartz . . . . . . . . . . . . . . . . . . . . . . . . . . . .261
**Standing Challenges to Capitalism in the Balkans**
      Shon Meckfessel . . . . . . . . . . . . . . . . . . . . . . . . . . . . . . . . . . . . . . .266
**Apology for the Algerian Insurrection** Jaime Semprun . . . . . . . . . . . . . .275
**Flare Up!** Erin Volheim . . . . . . . . . . . . . . . . . . . . . . . . . . . . . . . . . . . .278
**Testimonies and Declarations** Women Speak Out . . . . . . . . . . . . . . . . .282
**Rattling the Chains of Global Apartheid** Jeff Conant . . . . . . . . . . . . . . .286
**Insurgent Chinese Workers and Peasants** John Gulick . . . . . . . . . . . . . .292

# Part V: Articulating Resistance
**Activistism: Left Anti-Intellectualism and Its Discontents**
      Liza Featherstone, Doug Henwood, and Christian Parenti . . . . . . . . . . . .309
**Art** Josh MacPhee . . . . . . . . . . . . . . . . . . . . . . . . . . . . . . . . . . . . . . .315
**The Meaning of Seattle** Noam Chomsky . . . . . . . . . . . . . . . . . . . . . . .317
**Carnival to Commons** Dorothy Kidd . . . . . . . . . . . . . . . . . . . . . . . . . .328
**The Direct Action Dividend** Rachel Brahinsky . . . . . . . . . . . . . . . . . . . .339
**Neither Their War Nor Their Peace** Retort . . . . . . . . . . . . . . . . . . . . . .343
**The Revenge of the Concept** Brian Holmes . . . . . . . . . . . . . . . . . . . . .347
**Art** Kevin Harris . . . . . . . . . . . . . . . . . . . . . . . . . . . . . . . . . . . . . . . .367
**Spiritual Warfare** Hakim Bey . . . . . . . . . . . . . . . . . . . . . . . . . . . . . . .369
**A Short Personal History of the Global Justice Movement** L. A. Kauffman . .375
**Glossary** Iain Boal . . . . . . . . . . . . . . . . . . . . . . . . . . . . . . . . . . . . . . .389
**Contributors** . . . . . . . . . . . . . . . . . . . . . . . . . . . . . . . . . . . . . . . . . .405

# Introduction
## Eddie Yuen

This book is an updating of *The Battle of Seattle: the New Challenge to Capitalist Globalization,*which was published by Soft Skull Press in February 2002. In the four years since the Seattle protests, so much has happened to both the project of capitalist globalization and the movement against it that it has been nearly impossible for activists and scholars to keep pace with events. This volume is a way station on the road to understanding this phenomenon, a series of snapshots and critiques from an unfinished history.

At the time of this writing, the people of the world are besieged by war, terror, and repression. In these grim times, it is important to remember that the choices facing humanity are not between "free markets" and "totalitarianism," as was argued during the cold war, nor between Western consumerism and religious fundamentalism, as many pundits now have it. It must be remembered, at all costs, that there is another force in the world today, a "second superpower" as the *New York Times* has dubbed it, which has powerfully challenged the logics and practices of capitalism, war, corporate democracy, and commodity identity and which thrives and grows still, despite everything.

This "superpower" is a movement that can be likened to a "storm of history" that sprang from the shantytowns of Algiers, Kingston, and Caracas to the Lacandon jungle and the Narmada river valley. It touched down in Seattle in 1999, a portent of climate change, shocking the complacent victory celebration of free-market fundamentalists. From there trade winds spread the movement across the North Atlantic world, arcing, in a remarkable two-year period, through London, Washington DC, Nice, Prague, Naples, Quebec City, Gothenburg, and Genoa. After the twin assaults of Genoa and 9/11/01[1] many, particularly in North America, might have thought the storm over—but this was not the case. The tempest returned, stronger than ever, to the South—Asia, Africa and, especially, Latin America. The struggles in places like Argentina, Bolivia, South Africa, and South Korea, and the potential of a deepening global network of workers, students, farmers, youth, indigenous people, immigrants, and "marginals," is the greatest source of hope in the world today.

This volume is an attempt to gather together some of the liveliest debates and commentaries from within this evolving global movement. Although the material is organized into five parts, this book, like the movement it describes, is perhaps best read as a network or rhizome rather than as a linear train of information. Thus, while the essays are organized topically and chronologically whenever possible, the authors inevitably range over a variety of issues that intersect in an unruly yet hopefully productive way. For example, many authors deal with the question of racial diversity within the movement, but we have not (as is tempting) "ghettoized" them into one chapter, on the grounds that this question is so important that it must be a constituent part of all internal discussions.

This book focuses primarily on the history, composition, tactics, and politics of the new movements against global capitalism; it does not include in-depth analysis of neoliberalism or the shift towards war and domestic repression within the world system. All of these subjects deserve far more detailed treatment than space allows here, and readers are encouraged to pursue the many excellent books on these subjects.[2]

Before going any further, it is necessary to say a few words on terminology. While there is a wide consensus amongst activists that "antiglobalization" is a particularly simplistic and misleading name for the movements discussed in this book, proposed alternatives, like the struggle itself, are multiple. Among the proposed labels currently in circulation are: "no global," "counterglobalization," "global justice movement," "globalization movement," "movement against global apartheid," "antisystemic movement," and "anticapitalist movement."[3] Although I have my preferences as an editor, this book is not the right place to impose a consistent set of terms for the movement, as this must come organically from a kind of international consensus of the streets. In this introduction, I will usually use the terms "the movement" and "the globalization movement" (if for no other reason than that they are the shortest phrases), and each article will employ whatever terminology its authors see fit. It is also important to remember that "the movement" is always a plurality—the famous "movement of movements"—so that to speak of it in the singular is an inevitable grammatical fiction. Finally, we must remember that more important than the terms themselves are the ideas behind them, since even the most eloquent of phrases is no substitute for in-depth analysis. To this end there is a glossary of keywords by Iain Boal at the end of the book to help decode whatever terminology, jargon, clichés, or ideology the reader may encounter in the book and in media coverage of the movement.

## Chiapas, Seattle, Genoa—Reprazent

One of the many hip-hop terms to enter the lexicon over the last twenty-five years, the idea of "representing," of shouting out to proclaim your community or locale, captures perfectly the spirit of the recent globalization and antiwar protests. On February 15, 2003, to name just the most dramatic instance, the millions of people marching in hundreds of cities around the world were not solely petitioning their rulers; they were also representing themselves directly as local citizens of a networked global polity. In bypassing the mediation of politicians, the people made clear the distinction between the *inhabitants* and the *governments* of nation-states. This distinction is so elementary as to be obvious, but it must be insisted on against the wartime conflation of leaders and populaces that serve Bush and bin Laden so well. By simply declaring, "We are here!" through massive street demonstrations, the antiwar movement has humanized Americans in the eyes of the rest of the world. An argument could truthfully be made, in fact, that the antiwar movement and the globalization movement (especially at Seattle) have genuinely created goodwill for Americans, while the belligerence of the Bush administration has effectively endangered Americans (and white people in general) everywhere in the world. The greatest achievement of the movement, though, lies not in salvaging national identities but in producing new kinds of political communities through its activity. This is what this volume seeks to describe.

Part I, "Roots of the Movement," documents some of the sites of resistance and communities that "reprazented" themselves prior to the movement's explosion into the global consciousness at Seattle. The single most important point here is that the recent upsurge against capitalist globalization has its origins not in Seattle but amongst the peoples of the global South. This is illustrated by the graphic "Internationalism Against Globalization: A Map of Resistance," which enjoins us to think of these struggles in a unified (though not totalizing) way. George Katsiaficas, in "Seattle Was Not the Beginning," traces a line between the protests against IMF structural adjustment programs (SAPs) that have rocked the world from the late '70s, peaking perhaps in the uprising in Caracas in 1989, to the demonstrations in Seattle, Melbourne, Prague, and Genoa. Manuel Callahan, in "Zapatismo and Global Struggle," focuses on the inspiration that Chiapas has given to the form and content of the new movement. By understanding these antecedents to Seattle, the movement in the overdeveloped world may be less seduced by illusions of its own centrality and recognize that the global majorities are not merely passive victims of "free trade" and structural adjustment.

Part I continues with a contribution by David Kubrin on the roots of the globalization and antiwar movements in the USA. This piece, along with later contributions by Barbara Epstein on American radical movements of the '30s and '60s and Andrew Hsiao on recent movements of people of color, are intended to counter the deep historical amnesia that afflicts most people in the US, including many activists. Despite the novelty appeal of such angles as "A new generation takes to the streets" or "Turtles and teamsters united in protest," the media have on the whole characterized both the globalization and antiwar movements as shallow and anachronistic echoes of the '60s. In this narrative, the rich history of American dissent, ranging from the wildcat strikes and G.I. resistance of the '70s, through the AIDS activism and Central American solidarity of the '80s, to the wilderness defense and environmental justice movements of the '90s, are all effectively erased. Worst of all, '60s comparisons will always be spurious for the simple fact that the '60s *did* happen, with one result being a deep and widespread distrust of corporate and government authority. In the early '60s (the benchmark of comparison whenever antiwar movements are rekindled in America) the overwhelming majority of white Americans actually trusted the government and media. Such a consensus is no longer the case today as, ironically, eight years of right-wing Clinton bashing has finished the job of discrediting the political system and media initiated by the New Left.

Movements today emerge from societies that are as much cynical as they are ignorant and brainwashed. While activists often condescendingly assume the latter orientation, the rulers of empire understand that it doesn't matter so much whether or not their subjects believe their lies as long as they feel overwhelmed and disempowered. But cynicism need not inevitably work in the interest of power—it can be "weaponized" into activism as much as apathy. There are tremendous possibilities for politicization in the fact that virtually every institution of society—electoral politics, corporate capitalism, neo-liberal ideology, the Catholic Church, the fast food, health care and music industries—is in the throes of a legitimation crisis. At their best, social movements offer a compelling analysis of these crises while at the same time presenting alternatives in the form of prefigurative politics, counterinstitutions, and dual power.[4]

While it is hard to measure the success of the movement in affecting institutional power, there is no denying that it has partially transformed the global political climate of passive disgust and withdrawal into an atmosphere of rebellion.[5] The movement has set an example that has been observed and emulated by diverse sectors of global society. As Callahan documents, the Zapatistas galvanized Mexican students, farmers, and workers to take action on issues that affect their everyday lives. In Seattle and Quebec City, many trade unionists were inspired by the militant environmentalists and the direct action movement to question the timid politics of their own bureaucracies. In Italy, huge sections of society were roused into action by the police atrocities against the movement in Genoa, as Wu Ming document in their piece, "Why Not Show Off About the Best Things?" In western Europe generally, the "No Global" movement has invigorated the enormous political strikes that have taken place since 1995 against attempts by the governments of Italy, Germany, Portugal, Spain, Austria, and France to impose neoliberal austerity measures.[6] In all of these cases, the atmospherics of dissent and critical inquiry produced by the globalization movement have enhanced and expanded already existing struggles. Rather than concentrating solely on the successes or failures of their stated goals, activists should remember what authorities never forget: that "the movement is the message."[7]

Recognizing the atmospherics of rebellion is also significant because it represents a cultural coup for anticapitalist forces. As has been widely remarked upon, rebellion (especially that of youth) is one of the most sought-after commodity signifiers by marketers.[8] The movement has given young people a chance to own their rebellion again, to wrest the sign of rebellion from the demagogues and shock jocks that lead the charge in scapegoating the weak.[9] Amidst the superficiality of stylistic rebellion, the movement's insistence on mass direct action does create experiences that are not easily commodified. It is no surprise then, that the image of the rebel, while still a coveted signifier for product marketing, is increasingly being crafted by authorities into something sinister—the school shooter, the serial killer, and, above all, the terrorist.

## Summits of Resistance

Part II, "Crashing the Summits," surveys the cycle of summit disruptions in the overdeveloped world that commenced at Seattle 1999 and were truncated by state terrorism at Genoa and by the advent of a new era of aggressive US imperialism after the terrorist attacks of September 11, 2001. The opportunities presented for the movement during this period will not soon come again, as capitalism in 1999 had reached such a state of ideological overreach that it dared to speak its name (after decades of the disingenuous euphemisms—"free enterprise," "the market," and "democracy") and to stage high-profile gatherings in accessible cities. Seattle sent out a powerful message that neoliberal capitalism was being rejected even at the time and place of its greatest triumph. Faced with the withering criticism of the movement and a multifaceted global crisis, the "Washington Consensus" was replaced in Washington by the open advocacy of old school imperialism (supplanting decades of the cold war lingo of "emerging markets" and "fledgling democracies"). The movement must now confront this resurgent imperialism and all of the racism, nationalism, and fear mongering.

This is not to say that summit demonstrations have ceased after the escalation of police violence at Genoa and the militarization of American society after 9/11/01. The demonstrations against the Word Bank and EU summits in 2002 in Spain were the largest yet (500,000 in Barcelona, 150,000 in both Madrid and Seville), the protests against the G8 in Evian, France, in June, 2003 were immense, and the anti-WTO demonstrations in Cancun in 2003 were singularly effective. Yet the combination of state preparedness, overwhelming police repression, and media blackouts and slander have rendered direct action and blockades much more difficult to effectively pull off. Moreover, the retreat of the summits to remote locales like Qatar and the Canadian Rockies have convinced many in the Northern movement to make local organizing and solidarity the focus of their energies.[10] In this context, the essays in this section provide an opportunity to evaluate the lessons and contributions of this phase of the movement.

Some of the high points include:

- The experiential proof that radical critiques can escape subcultural ghettos and connect with vast numbers of people.

- The return of "the People" to the stage of history. As Michael Hardt puts it in his essay "Anti-Europeanism and Anti-Americanism:" "One of the great achievements of the globalization protest movements...has been to put an end to thinking of politics as a contest among nations or blocks of nations."

- An extraordinary collective learning curve, as movement ideas ricochet around the world and evolve in unexpected ways. Some examples include Cacarolozeros from Argentina, tripods from Sarawak, snake dances from Japan, the Black Bloc from Germany, overalls and padding from Italy, ropes and grappling hooks from Korea, Copwatch and Critical Mass from San Francisco, Reclaim the Streets from England, Food Not Bombs from the Black Panther Party (via the Diggers), and encuentros and social forums from the Zapatistas.[11] The velocity with which these ideas have circulated and mutated must be attributed not principally to the Internet but to the flesh-and-blood networks that materialize most concretely at the countersummits.

- The discovery of new ways to inhabit urban space. The insertion of carnival, potlatch, and jubilee, not the semiotics of supplication, into the architecture of power.

- The use of music, dance, sexuality, and humor to de-commodify pleasure and liven up resistance. The movement has been successful at exorcizing the legacy of the hairshirt left while simultaneously critiquing the empty satisfactions of consumer culture.

- Learning to respond to repression by communicating, expanding, and opening up the movement, rather than turning inward to clandestinity and subculture. Capital would like nothing more than for activists to withdraw from mass organizing, but this is yet another instance where the movement has learned from the mistakes of the '60s and '70s.

- The role of the summits in the Indymedia phenomenon and the delinking of tens of thousands of people around the world from corporate media.

- A refusal to accept masculinist definitions of politics and power and a general refusal of instrumentalist and utilitarian logics.

- The shift from static to flexible demonstration tactics that has became one of the signature qualities of the movement, particularly at London on June 18, 1999; Seattle in 1999; Prague in 2000; and San Francisco in the antiwar demonstrations of April 2003. Since "flexibility" is rivaled only by "globalization" as a buzzword of neoliberalism, it is fitting that the tactics of the movement are as nimble as the flows of finance capital.[12]

As the element of surprise has waned, however, the state has violently attempted to set up barriers to "swarming," "smart mobbing," and "just-in-time" mobilizations.

- The necessity of connecting the globalization movement with local communities. At their best, the days of action have had a long-term politicizing impact on the summit host cities (notably Seattle, Genoa, and, to a lesser extent, Prague). On a related note, we may observe with hindsight that the militancy of the protests is largely determined not by the intentions of the demonstrators but by the amount of participation of the local population, particularly working-class youth. In Seattle, for example, much of the rioting and looting was committed by white "street kids" and disenfranchised African-American youth, respectively. In Quebec City, some of the most serious street fighting was conducted by Quebecois youth, who drew upon a history of militant struggle going back to the '60s, while in Genoa, which has some of the highest unemployment and heroin addiction rates in Italy, hundreds of local youth turned out to battle the hated *carabinieri*. The lesson here is that the most disruptive elements of summit demonstrations are often local youth, whose degree of politicization and manner of expression may be quite different from the predominantly middle-class globalization protestors. The detonation effect of the movement on oppressed local communities is clearly one of the reasons why the era of capitalist summits in central or historical cities has probably come to an end.

## Militarization and Antiviolence

Many of the authors in this section deal with the tactical debates that have preoccupied the movement since Seattle. In fact, these debates have largely died down, as a rough consensus around the idea of diversity of tactics (discussed in this book by Millstein and Katsiaficas) has provided a basis of unity for pacifists, militants, and everyone in between. Even more significantly, though, the escalating military response of the system has compelled the movement to rethink its strategies of confrontation. As Genoa, Geneva, and Gothenburg in Europe and the Port of Oakland, Sacramento, and St. Louis in the US have shown, Northern white activists are increasingly being treated like their counterparts in Argentina, the Philippines, or Harlem. Capitalist globalization is now characterized by a race to the bottom for basic freedoms and civil liberties as well as for environmental and working conditions.

The task facing the movement, then, is to continue to take direct action against unjust authority without mimicking the militarization of the state. As David Graeber has pointed out, activists have had some success in exploding the pacifist/militant dichotomy by ritualizing or parodying (as the white overalls did) the violence of the state while at the same time creating genuinely disruptive situations.[13] A parallel effort to unwind this dichotomy can be found in the grassroots initiatives to end self-destructive gun violence among urban communities of color in the USA.[14] These "Stop the Violence" campaigns have had some success in rejecting the American fetishization of violence and guns by invoking, counterintuitively, the autonomist spirit of Malcolm X as much as the healing spirit of Martin Luther King. The sensibility of antiviolence rejects the deep-rooted logic that firepower is redemptive and problem solving while maintaining a commitment to the empowerment and self-defense of oppressed communities. Such a stance of antiviolence could be instructive for globalization activists as it refuses the kind of escalation of rhetoric that swept through the movement during the Seattle-to-Genoa period. Other examples of struggles that have de-escalated the confrontation with compulsively violent states while at the same time remaining effective and militant include the mass actions in Nigeria, China, and Mexico described in this volume. Given the current global climate of escalating repression and terror, it is imperative that the movement distinguish itself from the states and right-wing fundamentalists who communicate solely through violence.

## Direct Democracy and Network Organizing

Another topic that surfaces repeatedly in Part II is the movement's commitment to radical democratic processes and network models of organizing. Even the corporate media have acknowledged the efficacy of the decentralized and horizontal organizational structure of the movement, and how utterly distinct it is from the rigidly hierarchical economic institutions and civil authorities that it challenges. As Dorothy Kidd, Brian Holmes, and Sophie Style observe in their pieces, radical democratic networks did not originate in Seattle any more than the movement itself did—they have deep histories all over the world.

The postwar tradition of direct democracy in the US can be traced to the African-American civil rights movement and the early New Left,[15] but was sustained principally by radical counterculturalists and feminists from the late '60s on. In Europe, it is rooted in anarchism and council communism, particularly the workers' and soldiers' soviets of the Russian revolution, the affinity groups of the Spanish revolution of the '30s, and the worker and student councils of Paris in 1968 and Italy in 1969.[16] In the global South, elements of radically democratic self-organization have been present in countless struggles, ranging from the Iranian revolution of 1979 and the Kwangju uprising in South Korea in 1980 to the first Palestinian intifada and the South African township uprisings of the '80s. In the South, democratic self-organization draws upon residual pre-capitalist community formations—the collective "soil of cultures" of which the Zapatistas speak.[17] For activists from hyperalienated Western societies, communities of struggle are often consciously created, with ideas patched together from neopaganism and non-Western political theory (particularly that of indigenous people[18]), although at times these elements are thrown together in problematic or even culturally imperialist ways. What all these diverse traditions share, however, is an understanding that popular power is too important to be delegated to bureaucracies or surrendered to leaders.[19]

Although it is empowering, prefigurative, and effective, radical democracy is not without its problems. Before activists become too self-satisfied with their antiauthoritarian process, they should consider the fact that much of the rhetoric of radical democracy, networking, and decentralization has been co-opted by decidedly nonradical political and social forces. Examples include business school jargon, the adoption by some neo-Nazis of the anarchist-inspired "leaderless resistance,"[20] and an influential RAND Corporation report that identifies "netwar" as a style of organizing favored by demonstrators, criminals, and terrorists[21]. This RAND analysis is especially pernicious as it does not make the distinction that, for the globalization movement, networks are self-consciously utilized *precisely because* they are thought to be consistent with antiauthoritarian goals, while for fascists, gangsters, and theocrats, networks are seen as merely a convenient method for attaining their ultra-authoritarian ends. It is up to the movement to make clear the politics of its process, since it can no longer be assumed that decentralization, networks, and participatory democracy are inherently liberatory.

Another problem facing the political process of the movement is the "tyranny of structurelessness,"[22] the criticism that radical democracy is tacitly exclusionary towards nonwhite and working-class people due to the fact that it is excessively time consuming, privileges bourgeois oratorical conventions, and is characterized by an insular subculture. These problems may not be as intractable as they seem, however, since many young activists of color are increasingly interested in reclaiming their traditions of participatory democracy.[23]

## Keeping It In the Streets

Part III, "We Are Everyone? Organization and Representation Within the Movement," presents articles on four other key internal issues that confront activists: first, the problem of sectarianism; second, the relationship between the street movement and nongovernmental organizations (NGOs); third, the question of racial diversity within the movement; and fourth, the problem of right wing antiglobalization and antiwar groups.

The re-emergence of sectarianism (anarchist, autonomist, and liberal as well as Marxist-Leninist) has been an annoying problem since the twin crises of Genoa and 9/11/01 put the movement in an introspective mode. This necessary time of reflection was exploited by sectarians, whose dogmatic certainty is so contrary to the movement's spirit of inquiry and whose retrograde organizational forms mirror those of the state and capital. After sleeping on Seattle and the vibrant new anticapitalist energy afoot in the world, those sectarians who survived the '80s now retroactively seek to be the vanguard of this new "locomotive of history."

The influence of sectarian authoritarianism should not be exaggerated, since direct democracy and participatory forms of organizing are foundational, not incidental, to the movement. Nevertheless, two aspects of sectarianism are potentially harmful to the movement. The first, as Barbara Epstein points out in this collection, is that they tend to recruit and burn out young activists who are seduced by their avowed omniscience and then disillusioned with radical politics altogether when contradictions inevitably emerge. The second is that sectarians are often more committed to building their organizations than building the movement. If they are committed to mass actions at all, it is only to actions that they *control*, a destructive attitude that sets a terrible example for the movement.

A far more serious issue is the tension between the street movement and the nongovernmental organizations (NGOs). NGOs are of course extremely diverse, but all have been greatly empowered by the globalization movement and the social forums. As Ezequial Adamovsky, Jeff Conant, Dorothy Kidd, and Jeffrey St. Clair all warn in their articles, many NGOs view street demonstrations as a bargaining chip rather than a site for the development of popular power. As James Davis warns in his piece, "This is What Bureaucracy Looks Like," the professionalization of activism may have a similar effect to the ritualization of direct action that Barbara Ehrenreich describes earlier: it can rob movements of their vitality and edge. The lesson here is that the movement is more than the sum of its organizations, however important they may be, and that to broker mass political participation for "a seat at the table" will probably result in a weakening of both the street movement and the NGOs.

## Race and the Movement

The glaring whiteness of the globalization and antiwar movements in the US has been probably the greatest source of self-examination and regret within its ranks. The movement's lack of racial diversity stands in sharp contrast to its deep engagement with patriarchy and homophobia or even its tentative negotiations with representative organizations of the working class (i.e. unions). But neither seeking to "recruit" people of color into the preexisting movement (a strategy that Kristine Wong and Carwil James both discuss in their essays) nor retroactively creating a mythology that mass demonstrations in the US are, in fact, racially diverse are adequate responses to this dilemma. A more promising starting point would be a recognition that there are, parallel to the highly visible globalization and antiwar movements, a complex of struggles which are led by people of color and which continue to thrive even in the post 9/11/01, climate. These include, as Hsiao documents in his essay "Color Blind," campaigns against institutional racism, the prison-industrial complex, and police brutality. Moreover, it is simply not true, as some white activists assume, that capitalism, globalization, and foreign policy are too abstract for working-class communities of color to connect to their daily lives. After all, American inner cities were among the first laboratories for "structural adjustment" during the fiscal crises of the '70s and African Americans have been disproportionately affected by capital flight and de-industrialization over the last three decades.[24] Furthermore, millions of the new immigrants to the USA and other rich countries are effectively refugees from the "civil" wars of recolonization, asset stripping, privatization, and enclosures demanded by the economic experts.[25] Many of these immigrants also bring with them militant labor traditions (as European immigrants did in the last century) and, increasingly, direct experience with struggles against the IMF and neoliberalism. In short, people of color in the overdeveloped world provide an experiential link with the raw violence of capitalist globalization (including war). These communities, along with a militant rank-and-file labor movement, are the social forces that the politicians and managers would least like to see at the forefront of the globalization and antiwar movements.

· While activists have made some progress in acknowledging "the diversity question," the "whiteness" of the movements' culture and organizational forms is often alienating to working-class people of color. Although cultural rebellion in the US and western Europe has been co-opted to the point where it is no longer nearly as polarizing as it was in the '60s,[26] it may still, as Hsiao and Wong point out, strike other constituencies as self-indulgent acting out by white kids. A corrosive aspect of this gap is the "common sense" understanding that middle-class white activists have an affinity for decentralization, direct democracy, and anarchism while people of color are dependent on charismatic leadership and enamored of hierarchical organizations. This assumption relieves white activists of the responsibility of interrogating the power imbalances produced by their white skin privilege while at the same time reinforcing the hegemonizing claims of some nonwhite leaders and NGOs to represent their entire communities. As scholars such as Robin Kelley[27] and George Lipsitz[28] have pointed out, the political practices of communities of color are every bit as diverse and sophisticated as those of predominantly white social movements; these practices cannot be reduced to their formal organizations.

The greatest obstacle to the inclusiveness of the movement, however, is the fact that participation in direct action politics is much riskier for people of color than for whites. African Americans and Latinos in particular have borne the full brunt of the police state that white activists have briefly tasted in Seattle, Philadelphia, and the Oakland docks, and are unlikely to be persuaded to join in demonstrations that seem foolhardy or sacrificial. The legacy of the massive prison expansion of the last two decades cannot be overestimated, not only in terms of the 2 million–plus people who are locked up, but also when we consider the chilling effect on millions more who are on probation or parole, have "two strikes," or are subject to deportation.[29] The escalating repression of immigrants, Arabs, South Asians and Muslims in Europe as well as the US has created a climate in which millions of people have been stripped of the possibility of any public political expression.

## Beyond Left and Right?

While the Southern Poverty Law Center is wrong in asserting that the globalization movement in the US has been significantly infiltrated by far-right elements, it is true that some neofascists do see the movement as a potential site for recruiting and spreading their hatred. To understand this phenomenon, the movement would do well to reject the "centrist/extremist" model that is used by many liberal hate-crime watchdog groups,[30] and instead develop a nuanced critique of the versions of "antiglobalization" on offer. James O'Connor, in his piece, "On Populism and the Antiglobalization Movement," provides a taxonomy of populisms Left and Right, North and South, which clarifies some of the more confusing corners of this debate. In the US, far-right forces often advocate for the working class (as long as it is white, male, and American) and sometimes even cast themselves as Green, thereby making themselves alarmingly congruent with much of the rhetoric of the "antiglobalization" movement. Meanwhile, in the global South, religious fundamentalists seek to hijack the language of anti-imperialism while pursuing their reactionary goals of patriarchal capitalist theocracy. The best response to these spurious oppositions is, of course, a genuinely diverse movement, one committed to combating racism, sexism, homophobia, nationalism, and terrorism wherever they may be found. Although some on the left may be weary of the more narcissistic and superficial forms of identity politics that have emerged in recent years, this doesn't mean that it is possible to return to speaking of "universal" class and environmental subjects unmarked by race, gender, and sexuality. As long as xenophobia, white supremacy, and patriarchy are normative for American society they must always be overtly and even stridently denounced. Finally, the presence of right-wing arguments compels the movement to sharpen its understanding of capitalism and war. As Nick Mamatas,Erin Schoenmaker, and Mervin Krebbers point out, a vacuum of analysis provides fascists, racists, and anti-Semites a space to attempt to smuggle in their poison, usually disguised as insider conspiracy information divulged by experts. The danger of this is not so much the *specifics* of the particular conspiracy theory (which may ultimately prove to be true), but the *logic* of conspiricism as a way of understanding the world. Conspiracy thinking is fundamentally disempowering as it projects omnipotence onto authority, while disregarding historical contingency and contradiction and downplaying the agency of social movements.

## Solidarity without Illusions

*"We are in the interregnum between the death of the old world and the birth of the new, and in this interregnum there are many morbid symptoms."—Antonio Gramsci*

The existence of right-wing "antiglobalization of fools" challenges the movement to reflect critically on the age-old questions of solidarity and internationalism. In Part IV, "Facts on the Ground," we present a cluster of articles on struggles from around the world, which, to a greater or lesser degree, can be seen as part of the "movement of movements." It is up to the movement to develop its own theoretical criteria for deciding which aspects of these struggles to solidarize with, as many scholars make no distinction between the various popular responses to capitalist globalization. Manuel Castells, for example, argues that "from an analytical perspective, there are no 'bad' and 'good' social movements" and makes the case that the Zapatistas, the American militias, and the Aum Shirikyo cult in Japan share a common adversary in the "new global order."[31] The RAND Corporation, as already mentioned, bundles together Zapatistas and anarchists with criminal gangs and al Qaeda on the basis of their "network" organizational structure. While both of these approaches have merits from an academic standpoint, they do not help activists solve the very practical question of how to distinguish the "morbid symptoms" of settler colonial resentment or millenarian nihilism from movements with a potentially universal vision of compassion and dignity.

Peoples' Global Action (PGA), which Sophie Style discusses in this book, is a concrete example of the new networks of solidarity that characterize the globalization movement. PGA is attempting to move beyond the "Third World-ism" that enraptured much of the Western left from the '60s to the '80s by creating a critical space for diverse non-Western voices to dialogue. The challenge for Northern activists is to navigate between the Scylla of paternalist disdain for actual subaltern voices and the Charybdis of unconditional support for the most visible and connected leadership of non-Western movements. The disastrous consequences of unconditional solidarity extended to *organizations*, not *peoples*, should by now be evident. In the first place, the resources and legitimacy conferred by well-intentioned denizens of the North on autocratic non-Western leaders often translate into catastrophic betrayal of the very ideals of the liberation struggles.[32] Secondly, when the inevitable revelations of bad behavior occur (as happened with the USSR, the Chinese Cultural Revolution, and countless other "gods that failed") a furious reaction amongst the formerly "illusioned" often takes place. The Trotskyist origins of the neoconservatives currently wielding power in Washington should be a strong caution concerning the virulence of these backlashes.

This section, in many ways the heart of this book, considers popular struggles that will generally be recognized as "progressive"; they confront a common enemy (whether it be named neoliberalism, capitalism, or empire) and employ methods not incommensurable with their liberatory goals. Needless to say, each one of the struggles documented here has its own unique history, and this is of course the primary motivation and understanding for its participants. At the same time, the power of the movement lies in its ability to think as globally as capital and consider each struggle as a potential example of what Raymond Williams called "militant particularism."[33]

Part IV begins with Wu Ming's commentary on recent events in Italy, a society rightfully considered to be one of the multiple centers of the movement. From Europe, we proceed south to some of the recognized fulcrums of the movement—Argentina, Peru, Nigeria, and South Africa. The section concludes with pieces on two struggles that lie on the outer horizon of the movement's imagined borders. The movement of unemployed Chinese workers and the Berber uprising in Algeria are two struggles that are in no way networked with the globalization movement yet have much to teach (and learn from) it. The former represents the greatest potential challenge to global capitalist production, while the latter is an apparent refusal of both the brutal Algerian state and the equally brutal Islamic fundamentalism that had presented itself as the only alternative. What direction these struggles evolve in remains to be seen, but both display resemblances to some of the practices and sensibilities of the movements in Chiapas, Italy, or Argentina, despite their seeming incommunicability.

Part V, "Articulating Resistance," presents a set of pieces interrogating various aspects of theory and practice in the movement. Although there is a newfound curiosity among activists about history and political economy, Liza Featherstone, Doug Henwood, and Christian Parenti argue in their essay, "Activistism: Left Anti-Intellectualism and Its Discontents," that the movement in the US is woefully weak in its theoretical development. While this may be a controversial assertion, there is no doubt that, in the global circulation of activist skills, the US has been strongest in tactical innovation and democratic process while lagging behind with regard to serious discussion of economic and political theory. In the US, activists routinely endure six-hour meetings on logistics and process, while their counterparts in Europe, Africa, Latin America, and Asia spend the same grueling sessions engaged in heated debates on the nature of globalization, capitalism, and other political questions. While American pragmatism has its advantages, it is hampered by an inability to deal with complexities—this is why 9/11/01, and the shift from globalization to imperialism has left so many activists scrambling. While the globalization movement was able to communicate successfully in Seattle by simplifying that which appeared to be complex (the WTO, neoliberalism, economics), in its new incarnation as an antiwar movement it must complexify that which appears to be simple (good vs. evil, civilization vs. barbarism, security vs. terror). The propensity to seek monocausal explanations leads to weak arguments that in turn may lure some activists to the safe havens of sectarian dogma or conspiracy theory.[34] Lack of analysis can also lead to the kind of moral self-righteousness and Manichean reductionism that has been thoroughly staked out by Bush, Ashcroft, and Fox News. History is made neither by great men nor "evil-doers," and it is up to the movement to offer an alternative to the apocalyptic dualism that is engulfing the world.

How then is the movement to understand the shift from capitalist globalization to permanent war? In the first place, it must rediscover the historical fact that "free markets" and imperialism have ever been intertwined. In the era in which we have periodized the current globalization movement, from the late '70s/early '80s to 9/11/01, the preferred instruments of wealth redistribution from South to North were "free trade" and debt, the collection of which was administered by the IMF and the World Bank. The necessary violence to enforce this asset stripping was usually outsourced to nominally independent Third World elites, with military hardware and training provided by the Northern metropoles. Over time, however, the collective movements of the South succeeded in exposing and delegitimizing this process, and the cycle of demonstrations from Seattle to the present heralded the accelerating political awakening of millions of people in the North as well. 9/11/01 thus occurred at a time when a new ideology was sorely needed by the world system to rationalize and disguise its accumulation. In particular, a new way to form legitimized violence, always the ideologically weak link of the "globalization" process, was desperately needed to contend with the increasingly articulate resistance to capitalism that was sweeping the planet. The war against Iraq represents the full realization of this project—"armed privatization" as Naomi Klein has dubbed it—and it is thus vitally important that the movement understand both the continuities and ruptures of this transition.

The second point to note here is that neoliberalism and neofascism are fully compatible and in fact complementary, as the economic "miracles" in Chile in the '70s and China since the '80s should prove. Arundhati Roy and Klein describe this connection in chilling detail in their pieces on India and Argentina, respectively. This insight presents an urgent challenge to the movement, as repression is the immediate barrier to any possibility of struggle for change. We must remember that the mid- to late-twentieth-century "dirty wars" against the Left in the Middle East, Southeast Asia, and Latin America were often dubbed "wars on terror" by their perpetrators.

Part V also contains much discussion on how the movement should theorize itself. This is important, for as Chris Dixon and Douglas Bevington have argued,[35] writings by the corporate media,[36] the RAND Corporation, and other intelligence agencies have been far more useful for activists than academic social movement theory.[37] Clearly, the movement must seize the initiative in defining the stakes of its struggle, since other theoretical entrepreneurs are waiting to fill the void.

One of the myriad theoretical approaches which has proven to be helpful to the movement is the concept of "commons," which informs the work of several authors in this volume. In this framework, all of the struggles documented in this book, and countless others, can be understood as battles against the enclosure of commons, whether they be geographical spaces (homelands, housing, neighborhoods), communities (the "iron rice bowl" in China, welfare states in Europe), natural resources (seeds, genomes, water, oil, clean air, oceans, wilderness), or information (cyberspace, cultural production). By expanding our understanding of commons to include all social, political, technological, and cultural resources that are being threatened by privatization or commodification, we can begin to understand the struggles of communities outside of the narrow boxes of "political activity" and "representation."[38] For tens of millions of people in the world, including the Argentinean *piqueteros*, unemployed Chinese workers, and indigenous people of Mexico and Nigeria described in this book, the commons are the very precondition for existence!

## More Power Than We Know

Understanding the centrality of commons greatly expands the concept of prefigurative politics that is one of the defining characteristics of the movement. If it can be shown that commons, gifting, and mutual aid are present everywhere, even in the most fully capitalist societies on earth, then the project of the movement is to recognize, claim, and above all, politicize them. This is the gist of Naomi Klein's observation that the Argentinean generals in the '70s "understood that their true obstacle to complete social control was not leftist rebels, but the very presence of tightly knit communities and civil society." In the global South and some communities in the North, movements appear to be organic extensions of society, since they draw their power from vast reserves of as yet uncommodified social solidarity. By contrast, for many activists from the hyperalienated North the first discovery of meaningful community comes through participation in social movements and feels like a complete rupture from everyday life.

An experiential proof of the latent power of this solidarity can be found wherever a disaster ("natural" or "man made") strikes. Contrary to the "common sense" expectation that a Hobbesian war of each against all will erupt as soon as state authority breaks down, the immediate response of ordinary people to such occurrences is spontaneous solidarity and mutual aid.[39] In fact, the experience of collective power in the face of the failure of the state and capital to respond to disaster has sometimes spawned revolutionary movements— notably in Nicaragua after the 1972 earthquake and Mexico after the 1985 earthquake.

Elites understand this dynamic far better than traditional leftists, and go to great lengths to ensure that ordinary people never realize their own power. An example that the movement would do well to reclaim occurred in New York City after September 11, 2001, when thousands of people spontaneously gathered in Union Square. The speed with which Mayor Giuliani cleared the square of people and memorials while President Bush enjoined the nation to go shopping as a means of fulfilling civic duty illustrates how threatened these authorities were by an outbreak of autonomy and genuine democracy.

It is no mystery, then, why many of the most rooted and articulate strands of the movement come not from the "labor aristocracy" or privileged students of the North but rather from the most seemingly marginal peoples of the planet—the farmers and indigenous peoples of the Niger Delta, Papua New Guinea, India, Korea, and Latin America. Their poverty of commodities is proportional to their wealth of commons—their ancestral lands, hybridized local knowledges, and enduring traditions of exchange based on reciprocity rather than the market. Brian Holmes offers a theoretical analysis of these dynamics in his piece, "Artistic Exchanges, Networked Resistance," and the Writers Bloc collective describe an instance of their actualization in their piece, "The Charming Outcome of the Cancun Trade Talks."

## The Power of Negative Thinking

It is a longstanding self-criticism on the left that there is a lack of a concrete positive vision of what real alternatives to capitalist globalization should look like. While most authors in this collection would agree on some level with this sentiment, it is important for the movement not to abandon the powerful stance of *refusal* in favor of abstract debates over hypothetical futures. The movement so far has helped to precipitate a crisis in the affirmative ideology of capitalist globalization (e.g. the mantra that market democracy represents the "end of history") by maintaining a broadly "negative" position—"one no, many yeses." The commodity utopia of neoliberalism was countered with the "anticommodities" of the gift and carnival, the ubiquitous violence of the state was at times neutralized by the movement's "antiviolence," and the claim to legitimate representation by the G8 and capital was forcefully negated by the movements' mobilizations of neighborhood, watershed, and globe. In short, the movement should acknowledge the tremendous rhetorical power that accompanies a stance of negation and refusal, and not feel pressured into excessively diverting its energies towards hammering out blueprints which are unrealistic at best and divisive at worst.

## They Say TINA, We Say NOTA

When George W. Bush famously declared "you're either with us or against us," it is unlikely that he anticipated the way in which he would be correct. The majority populations of virtually every country in the world are now united against US policy—a level of global consensus not attained since Vietnam (that word that wakes the elites at night "with their pacemakers knocking," as Retort says). Crucially, the media and politicians have been unsuccessful, even in the US, at slandering antiwar protestors as being supportive of either Saddam Hussein or al Qaeda. In fact, this argument has in many cases backfired, as millions of people are now aware of the US role in producing both of those entities. By rejecting this false opposition, the people of the world have in fact performed an impressive theoretical move—they have spurned the Thatcher/Reagan ideology of TINA (There is No Alternative) on the level of geopolitics.[40] By asserting the ability to say NOTA (None of The Above), the movement has paved the way for the rejection of any number of false binaries and bullying ultimatums that power presents to us (freedom vs. security, liberty vs. equality, race vs. class, jobs vs. trees, local vs. global, theory vs. practice).

## The Importance of Claiming Victories

The movement must remind itself of its victories, even at this grim moment. As happens so often with radical social movements, the "no globals" have not acknowledged or celebrated the many partial victories and rhetorical coups they have collectively gained in the whirlwind years since Seattle. There are two major reasons for this. The first is that Power ("*La Pouvre*," as dissidents in Algeria so succinctly describe their system) will never credit oppositional forces with forcing them into concessions or defeats. The second is that the movement reinforces this narration by disdaining the reformist or rhetorical victories it *actually* achieves, as its power stems from its uncompromising ambition to *radically* change the world. The resulting erasure of popular struggle from history has led many to believe that labor laws, civil rights, and environmental protections were all spontaneously granted by benevolent elites after thoughtful consideration. One purpose of this collection, then, is to bear witness to the partial victories of the movement.

What are these victories? The discrediting of the authority of government, capital and media is a major achievement, although the movement must do much more to create alternatives. With regard to capitalist globalization, the WTO, the World Bank, and especially the IMF have been very resistant to the demands of the movement, even the meager debt relief endorsed by the Pope and Bono. This lack of concessions, however, may be a sign of systemic weakness not strength within the system, however—as Silvia Federici has observed, "they have nothing to give." Nevertheless, it is clear that the project of "trade liberalization," considered a *fait accompli* before Seattle, has suffered serious setbacks, although inter-elite conflicts account for a large part of this crisis.

With regard to the US wars in Afghanistan and Iraq, too many in the movement believed their own rhetoric that they could stop the wars from happening, leading to a premature demobilzation once the wars commenced. As with Watergate in the '70s, the antiwar movement abdicated the stage of history at precisely the moment of its vindication, as all of its critiques and predictions were confirmed. While the movement undoubtedly raised the cost of empire and possibly placed some restraint on the overt commission of war crimes, its disappearance from the streets squandered much of the power it had generated. Nevertheless, if some of the energy of the spring of 2003 can be channeled into campaigns and counterinstitutions, the movement will not have been a failure.

The movement has won its most clear-cut victories, however, on the plane of ideas. The globalization movement has had devastating success in exposing the savagery, hypocrisy, and insanity of neoliberalism, so much so that John Kenneth Galbraith has stated that there has been a "nearly complete collapse of the prevailing economic theory."[41] Unfortunately, the movement has not sufficiently taken credit for this ideological collapse. Turncoat critics from within the system—John Gray, George Soros, Jeffrey Sachs, and Joseph Stiglitz—have effectively co-opted and diluted the critiques of capitalism that had emerged collectively from the peoples of the world.[42] Just as Monsanto and the other biotech companies seek to privatize and commodify the collective ancestral wisdom of the world's farmers with their transgenic and "terminator" technology, so too do these specialists in rehabilitation seek to claim for their own purposes the critical insights that the movement has discovered.

But this dance of co-optation plays against the backdrop of mounting carnage, and the totality of capitalism's conquest of the world is ultimately the bitter source of the movement's strength and perseverance. At the midpoint of the last century, Max Horkheimer and Theodor Adorno wrote: "the fully enlightened world radiates disaster triumphant."[43] Now the dawn of the new century offers us disasters undreamed of. As the apologists of capital celebrate the billions spent on bioengineering research to "improve nutrition and medicine," they silently watch the depopulation of the African continent by preventable diseases such as AIDS, malaria, and dysentery due to the absence of an "effective market" (money) on the part of the Africans.[44] Everything imaginable is considered to be a commodity, with the only disputes being over price. An elite team of population biologists, economists, and geographers has calculated that the earth is greatly undervalued; they estimate that the real worth of the combined ecosystems (excluding the moon and satellites) to be $28 trillion. Meanwhile, as the diversity of consumer choice has never been greater for the world's rich; with all manners of world cuisine, world music, world travel, or world literature available to the discerning customer, actual lived diversity is ground to dust. One telling symptom is the extinction rate of human languages; according to best estimates, every two weeks on average one of the world's 6,000 remaining languages dies somewhere,[45] while the ones we use are so degraded as to make speaking of compassion or love seem a banal joke. Each year, thousands of species go extinct and millions of "units" of forest, fishery, and other "resources" are harvested for the market.[46] Endless warfare and the degradation of formal democracy seem likely to increase as the system spirals deeper into crisis. Worst of all, in the absence of radical democratic visions, countless oppressed people around the world are turning to self-destructive despair and religious fundamentalism, further compounding the crisis.

In the face of all this, it is well to recognize that the globalization movement is a reality. This book bears witness to the movement's practice and theory from below, while acknowledging the calamities that make its project so urgent.

1. As George Caffentzis points out, September 11 should also be remembered as the anniversary of another act of terrorism—the CIA coup in Chile in 1973.

2. Some examples include William Tabb, *The Amoral Elephant: Globalization and the Struggle for Social Justice in the 21st Century* (Monthly Review Press, 2001); Joel Kovel, *The Enemy of Nature*, (London: Zed Books, 2002); and Immanuel Wallerstein *The Decline of American Power* (New York: The New Press, 2003).

3. All of these are clearly an analytic improvement over the once popular "movement against corporate globalization" since, as James O'Connor has pointed out, corporations are a form that capital takes, not capital itself. Since the terms "capitalism" and "imperialism" have been rehabilitated by their advocates, they may again be used descriptively by radicals without feeling like strident jargon.

4. Ironically, radical extraparliamentary politics often create the possibility for institutional openings and successful reformist politics.

5. Aufheben, "'Anti-Capitalism' as Ideology . . . and as Movement," *Aufheben* #10 (2002).

6. Kolya Abramsky, ed., *Restructuring and Resistance: Diverse Voices of Struggle in Western Europe*, 2001. Email: resresrev@yahoo.com.

7. For example, in the US outside of San Francisco, the antiwar movement set itself up for demoralization and demobilization by focusing too much on an unrealistic appeal to authorities to stop the invasion of Iraq rather than an attempt to build communities of long-term resistance.

8. See Robert Goldman and Steven Papson, *Sign Wars* (Routledge, 1997) and Thomas Frank and Matt Weiland, eds., *Commodify Your Dissent: Salvos from the Baffler* (W. W. Norton and Co., 1997).

9. R.W. Connell, *Moloch Mutates: Global Capitalism and the Evolution of the Australian Ruling Class, 1977–2002* (Overland ,.2002).

10. The Republican National Convention scheduled for New York City in August 2004 looms as a monumental exception to this pattern.

11. For a multimedia history of Critical Mass and many other instances of dissent in San Francisco, see the CD-ROM *Shaping San Francisco* (www.shapingsf.org).

12. See David Harvey, *The Condition of Postmodernism* (Oxford: Basil Blackwell, 1989) and Emily Martin, *Flexible Bodies* (Beacon, 1994) for insights on "flexible accumulation" and its implications.

13. David Graeber, "The New Anarchists," *New Left Review* 13 (January–February 2002): 61–73.

14. John Brown Childs on gang truces in *Global Visions: Beyond the New World Order*, edited by Jeremy Brecher, John Brown Childs, and Jill Cutler (South End Press, 1993).

15 Especially SNCC (Student Nonviolent Coordinating Committee).See Clayborne Carson, *In Struggle* (Harvard University Press, 1981). For a succinct and clear theoretical discussion of participatory democracy, see Hannah Fenichel Pitkin and Sarah M. Shumer, "On Participation," *democracy* (Spring, 1981).

16. Richard Gombin, *The Radical Tradition: A Study in Modern Revolutionary Thought* (New York: St Martin's Press, 1979).

17. Gustavo Esteva and Madhu Suri Prakash, *Grassroots Postmodernism: Remaking the Soil of Cultures* (London: Zed Books, 1998).

18. Harold Barclay, *People Without Government: An Anthropology of Anarchy* (Kahn & Averill and Cienfuegos Press, 1982).

19. This is not to underestimate the many consequential cultural and historical differences between the forms of radical democracy North and South. One of the most important of these is that movements in the South operate on an incomparably larger *scale.* See Tom Mertes, *Grass-Roots Globalism* in New Left Review 17, September-October 2002.

20. James Ridgeway, *Blood In the Face: The Ku Klux Klan, Aryan Nations, Nazi Skinheads, and the Rise of a New White Culture* (Thunder's Mouth Press, 1995).

21. John Aquilla and David Ronfeldt, eds., *Network and Netwars: The Future of Terror, Crime and the Military* (2001).

22. Jo Freeman, *The Tyranny of Structurelessness* (Dark Star Press, 1984).

23. This has perhaps been most evident at recent demonstrations in the US in which some Latino, African-American, and Asian-American student activists organized themselves into affinity groups based on the Seattle model.

24. Ron Rucker, "People of Color Represented in Small Numbers," *Street Sheet*, September

2000.

25. Midnight Notes Collective, *Auroras of the Zapatistas: Local and Global Struggles of the Fourth World War* (Autonomedia Books, 2001).

26. In contrast to most countries in the global South: in Mexico City during the Zapatista march of 2001, for example, the presence of nude demonstrators under the banner of "We Have Nothing to Hide" was profoundly controversial.

27. Robin D. G. Kelley, *Race Rebels: Culture, Politics, and the Black Working Class,* (New York: Simon & Schuster, 1996).

28. George Lipsitz, *A Life in the Struggle: Ivory Perry and the Culture of Opposition* (Philadelphia: Temple University Press, 1995).

29. Christian Parenti, *Lockdown America: Police and Prisons in the Age of Crisis* (Verso, 2000).

30. "This centrist/extremist model, as we call it, obscures the rational choices and partially legitimate grievances that help to fuel right-wing populist movements, and hides the fact that right-wing bigotry and scapegoating are firmly rooted in the mainstream social and political order." Chip Berlet and Matthew N. Lyons, *Right-wing Populism in America: Too Close for Comfort,* (Guilford Press, 2000), 15

31. Castells goes on to say, "I like the Zaptistas, I dislike the American militia, and I am horrified by Aum Shinrikyo. Yet, they are all . . . meaningful signs of new social conflicts, and embryos of social resistance and, in some cases, social change." Manuel Castells, *The Power of Identity* (Blackwell, 1997), 70.

32. Oppressed peoples of the North, such as African-Americans, have also experienced disillusionment following excesses of uncritical Third World solidarity. See Robin Kelley: "Roaring From the East: Third World Dreams" in *Freedom Dreams: The Black Radical Imagination* (Beacon, 2002)..

33. David Harvey, *Spaces of Capital: Towards a Critical Geography* (Routledge, 2001), 173..

34. An example is the assertion that the invasion of Iraq is solely about oil as *fuel* as opposed to, at the very least, that it is also about oil as *power*. See Michael Klare, *Resource Wars,* (Metropolitan/Owl, 2002).

35. Chris Dixon and Douglas Bevington, "An Emerging Direction in Social Movement Scholarship: Movement-Relevant Theory," unpublished paper, 2003.

36. The *Financial Times* special report of September, 2001: http://specials.ft.com/counter-cap/index.html. See also "Globalization and Its Critics," [supplement] *The Economist* (September 29, 2001).

37. Canadian Security Intelligence Service, "Anti-Globalization—A Spreading Phenomenon,"

2001, http://www.csis-scrs.gc.ca/eng/miscdocs/200008_e.html.

38. Olivier De Marcellus, "Commons, Communities & Movements," http://info.interactivist.net/article.pl?sid=03/01/28/1518256&mode=nested&tid=9.

39. Sociologist Lee Clark, cited in Claudia Dreifus, "Living One Disaster After Another, and then Sharing the Experience," *New York Times*, May 20, 2003. Another example is the 1989 Loma Prieta earthquake in the San Francisco Bay Area, after which California Highway Patrol officers forcibly prevented working-class African-Americans from risking their lives to rescue predominantly white commuters trapped under the Cypress freeway in Oakland.

40. The hegemony of this phrase is demonstrated by the fact that the movement slogan "Another World Is Possible" resonates so strongly around the world. In another era, such a self-evident phrase would not have been seen as subversive.

41. Cited in A Postscript for the Global Anti-Capitalist Movement, in *Que Se Vayan Todos*, 2002, anonymous publication.

42. John Walton and David Seddon, *Free Markets and Food Riots: The Politics of Global Adjustment*, (Blackwell, 1994).

43. Theodor Adorno and Max Horkheimer, *The Dialectic of Enlightenment* (Allen Lane, 1973).

44. To cite just one statistic, the UN estimates that 11 million children die of preventable causes each year. *New York Times*, March 14, 2002.

45. David Crystal, *Language Death* (Cambridge University Press, 2000).

46. Environmental News Service reported on August 23, 2001, that Kenyan conservationist Richard Leakey estimates that 55 percent of all species will go extinct in the next 50–100 years.

# Internationalism Against Globalization

## A Map of Resistance

# James Davis and Paul Rowley
# Text: Eddie Yuen

Capitalist globalization is of course nothing new (see glossary), but if we periodize the current moment of "globalization" as beginning in the early '80s, corresponding to the implementation of IMF structural adjustment programs (SAPs) in the Third World and former Second World, a distinct pattern of resistance emerges. This map is an effort to depict this resistance graphically, to give shape and gravity to events that are generally portrayed by the corporate media as random, inchoate singularities (when they warrant mentioning at all).

This map is not intended to be a comprehensive account of struggle and unrest around the world, even of those events that can unambiguously be claimed as anti-capitalist. Instead, we have limited ourselves here to demonstrations, riots, and events that are specific responses either to SAPs or summits/fulcrums of capitalist globalization. Even allowing for these limitations, the density of events on this map (especially in the global South) suggests that a matrix of antiglobalizing practices has been steadily taking shape over the last twenty years. The fact that it has only been "discovered" as a worldwide movement after Seattle in 1999 is an indication more of Eurocentric blindness in the North than of theoretical underdevelopment in the South.

The differing icons represent the qualitatively different nature of resistance between the underdeveloped and overdeveloped world. The crosshair icon represents rebellions, ranging from spontaneous uprisings to general strikes, against the neoliberal policies that have been described by critics as "the third world war." These policies include the displacement of communities due to the privatization of land and water, the clearcutting of forests to pay off foreign debt, the murderous immiseration of urban populations through fuel and food-staple price increases, and the dismantling of public health care and education. The global majorities have courageously resisted these measures, and have developed increasingly sophisticated theories and practices in the process.

The coffin icon represents fatalities, the numbers of people known to have been killed by government forces (serving the interests of the IMF and capital generally) in these struggles. While we have not quantified the number of people killed by the governments of the South in the name of globalization, even the incomplete tally depicted in the map numbers in the thousands (topped by the more than 600 slaughtered by Venezuela in 1989) and shows no signs of abating. (Needless to say, the amount of deaths directly attributable to SAPs and neoliberalism number in the millions, but would show up in UN statistical registers as due to "natural causes" such as starvation, disease, and crime).

There is only one coffin icon beside the icon of antiglobalization demonstrations in the overdeveloped world. This should serve as a sobering reminder that, as egregious as state repression has been in Prague, Quebec City, Gothenborg, Genoa, and Geneva, it does not compare in savagery to the social liquidation faced by the global majorities. This is not to diminish the significance of the growing resistance in the North, but simply to underline the fact that, as the Zapatistas put it, globalization is a question of life and death.

But another difference separates the antiglobalization protests of the North and South. In the South, demonstrations are usually directed at the immediate effects of a specific neoliberal policy, such as the privatization of water in Bolivia or the raising of fuel prices in Nigeria. In the North, demonstrations typically target the entire project of capitalist globalization, and consequently appear to operate on a higher level of theoretical abstraction than the "primal outbursts" of the South. It is our hope that this map will undermine such a mind/body duality by demonstrating the potential unity of the movement North and South. As the World Social Forums at Porto Allegre have shown, there are many around the world who are seeking to connect the seemingly fragmented struggles depicted here.

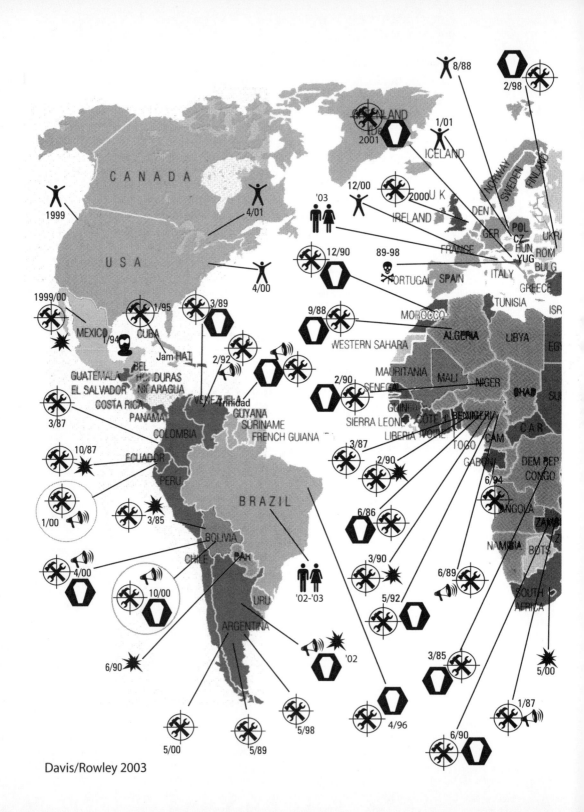

Davis/Rowley 2003

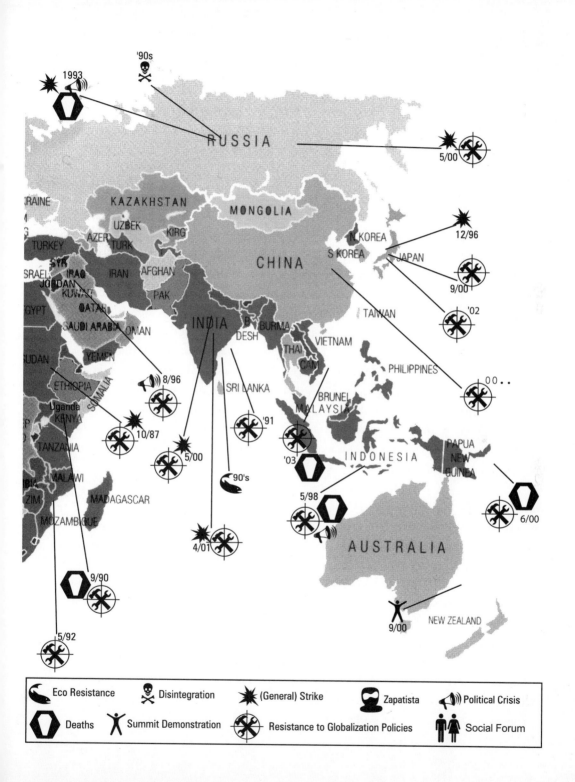

'90s

1993

RUSSIA

5/00

KAZAKHSTAN
MONGOLIA

UZBEK
KIRG
AZER
TURK

RAINE

TURKEY
SYR
ISRAEL
IRAQ
JORDAN
KUWAIT
QATAR
EGYPT
SAUDI ARABIA
SUDAN
YEMEN
ETHIOPIA
SOMALIA
Uganda
KENYA
TANZANIA
MALAWI
ZIM
MOZAMBIQUE
MADAGASCAR

IRAN
AFGHAN
PAK
OMAN

INDIA
DESH
BURMA
SRI LANKA
THAI
CAM
VIETNAM
TAIWAN

CHINA

N. KOREA
S. KOREA
JAPAN

12/96

9/00

'02

00..

PHILIPPINES

BRUNEI
MALAYSIA

INDONESIA

PAPUA
NEW
GUINEA

8/96

10/87

5/00

'91

90's

'03

5/98

4/01

6/00

9/90

AUSTRALIA

5/92

9/00

NEW ZEALAND

| | Eco Resistance | | Disintegration | | (General) Strike | | Zapatista | | Political Crisis |
|---|---|---|---|---|---|---|---|---|---|
| | Deaths | | Summit Demonstration | | Resistance to Globalization Policies | | | | Social Forum |

# A Protestography
## Thatcher Collins

By 1994 several new organizations came to power: the WTO, the EU, NAFTA, and APEC. At the same time, the Karnataka Farmers of India (1993), the Zapatistas of Mexico (1994), and the Landless Campesino Movement of Brazil (1995) changed the form and intensity of resistance to the economic power of elites. The end of South African Apartheid by 1994 also awakened a new economic justice movement in South Africa, as with the Soweto Electricity Crisis Committee, a group of guerrilla electricians and plumbers.

The dates below give the first day or the main event of a chain of protests from 1993 to the present. This list is *not* complete—there are many more protests, especially in the South. The 1980s saw many protests against structural adjustment. Also unincluded are protests against militarism and environmental issues, plus numerous distantly related strikes. What is listed are protests against meetings by the major economic institutions or protests sparked directly by their policies. There are a few exceptions to this rule that are a major part of the story, such as the protests that reversed a coup in Venezuela.

The list does not always give the reason a protest or strike happens. The definitions and descriptions of the organizations should help clarify who does what and why. Understanding the organizations helps explain the relative frequency (over all and over time) of protests against them.

## World Trade Organization (WTO)
The International Trade Organization (ITO) was initiated in Washington DC in the mid 1940s. The US used loan conditions and aid conditions to bring European nations into the negotiations. A portion of the ITO agreement, the General Agreement on Tariffs and Trade (GATT), was the only part to survive after the US Congress failed to ratify the ITO with the two-thirds majority as needed for an international treaty. The WTO passed in 1994 since it needed only a simple majority. It is now in the form of a US law (as with the IMF and World Bank in 1945).

The WTO is a system of trade rules with a dispute-resolution body and organizes negotiations for mutual reduction of tariff trade barriers. Those rules cover public (government) trade barriers, but not private (business) trade barriers like monopolies and monopsonies (businesses with workers that lack alternative employers). The WTO does not make rules on debt or development. However, development aid is the carrot, and debt the stick, that brings weaker nations into line with the economically powerful nations (i.e. the G7 nations) during negotiations. Many industries are permitted. For example, elementary schools in the US are not under WTO jurisdiction because their administration is not part of the international market; so even though these schools are, in a way, WTO-illegal, they are "grandfathered in" until they become privatized. However, schools built by international development programs are more likely to be under WTO jurisdiction.

Consensus is the basic decision-making structure, one nation with one vote, and anyone theoretically can veto an agreement or expansion. Yet in practice economic pressure, often via development aid, debt, and the IMF, makes the negotiations follow the familiar economic hierarchy, only implicitly.

The WTO is self-enforcing. If a nation feels that another nation has violated the WTO rules, it can use countervailing measures, usually in the form of a tariff, or the threat of a different retaliation. The initial determination is by the violated nation, and proves its case with economic data. The technical skills used to determine or prove such violations are to be found in, or afforded by, large or rich nations. Whole industries and thousands of jobs can hang on such retaliation. In some cases the effects of the tariff, even if illegal from the onset, still serve to punish that industry in the short term during months of dispute resolution. The WTO works for industry in two ways: 1) striking down domestic laws, including environmental and labor laws; and 2) shifting the burden of trade protection and regulation to private industry, indirectly, in the form of economic power in a deregulated marketplace. The second goal is shared by the IMF and World Bank. The dispute resolution process is closed to the public and decided by representatives drawn from business.

An important but nearly distinct negotiating area is the trade-related aspects of intellectual property (TRIPs) agreement. This agreement regulates everything from music to GMO corn to airplane parts, and it is fundamental to success in global industry—especially in the pharmecuetical, biotech, and transportation industries.

## International Monetary Fund (IMF)

Established in 1944 in Bretton Woods, New Hampshire, along with the World Bank. An IMF loan or program is typically a necessary first step to gaining access to major sovereign nation loans. Membership in the IMF is required for membership in the World Bank. Members act like investors, where the number of votes each nation receives depends on the amount of capital invested in the IMF (as for the World Bank, too). The US, the UK, France, Germany, and Japan have the most invested and each get to appoint a representative to the IMF board of directors and another for the World Bank. The rest of the members elect nineteen board members for each organization.

The debt conditions—called structural adjustment programs, or austerity measures—are set by the IMF on debtor nations and include ending of subsidies, devaluing currency, changing labor and environmental laws, privatizing state industries and services, budget cuts, tax increases, and deregulation. Small economies, small business, and low-income people are most vulnerable to the resulting unpredictable price increases and potential swings between shortages and surplus.

The IMF works to solve balance of payment differences—when a country imports more than it exports—through monetary policies that reduce consumption in the form of structural adjustment. On the other side, debtors nations try to raise hard currency (US dollars, yen, euros) through commodities that sell on the international market; important examples include oil, steel, lumber, agriculture, coffee, tourism, textiles, and electronics.

As nations compete for hard currency, they typically overproduce these products—as most of the major commodities have near-perfect competition, the price drops and this puts downward pressure on wages and profits. The IMF is now working on a dispute resolution system to formalize a process for nations that default or change governments. Sovereign debt is held by some combination of domestic debt (in local currency or hard currency), private foreign debt, bilateral foreign debt (including the Paris Club), and multilateral debt (including the IMF, World Bank, European Bank for Reconstruction and Development (EBRD), Arab Monetary Fund, Inter-American Development Bank (IADB), Asian Development Bank (ADB), etc.). An IMF loan is typically a precondition for all the other loans; an IMF loan is more like a security deposit to prevent capital flight—acting as an insurance policy for investors. Thus, the IMF mostly advises and affects debtor nations. More and more, sovereign debt is held by private investors as bonds (including World Bank bonds), the bondholders' collective rights against the sovereign debtor are somewhat untested.

## World Bank

The World Bank originally helped rebuild western Europe after WWII along with the US Marshall Plan, the set of development plans that made the US the world's largest international creditor, and raised it to its peak of economic power. By the 1970s, the Bank evolved into a development organization for the South.

The bank funds specific projects, usually development oriented and capital intensive—like dams and bridges—projects built by corporations from creditor nations. The conditions on these loans augment or replace IMF structural adjustment programs, which in turn affect the tariff reduction negotiations at the WTO. Many of these projects have failed and hurt investors, people, governments, or all three.

## North American Free Trade Agreement (NAFTA)

Canada and the US implemented a Free Trade Agreement in 1989, then added Mexico with NAFTA in 1994. In 2002, Chile joined a bilateral trade agreement with the US (as with Canada in 1997), effectively adding Chile to NAFTA. And currently, CAFTA, a Central America trade block, and CARICOM, a Caribbean community trade block (minus Cuba), are set to be added to NAFTA. These are steps toward the Free Trade Area of the Americas (FTAA or ALCA), which would include all of North and South America (minus Cuba). These trade blocks compete with the WTO by setting statutory precedents and by giving the US a unified negotiating block. But unlike the WTO, corporations in NAFTA countries can sue governments directly (called a Chapter 11 lawsuit). Also, certain employees of companies can get "TN status," a type of work visa specific to that job but does not allow the employees' family to work in the host country. NAFTA is also the testing ground for agricultural trade liberalization, which so far has seen the Mexican market flooded by cheap subsidized US corn. The Organization of American States (OAS) helps to organize FTAA negotiations. And Plan Puebla Panama is a series of World Bank and Inter-American Development Bank financed development projects for Central America, created under the hope of producing export commodities and energy. Success of the FTAA is often linked to US aid and drug-eradication packages (including fumigation and military aid) in South America: Plan Colombia, Plan Dignidad (Bolivia), and the Andean Regional Initiative.

Closely tied to these agreements is dollarization, where a nation adopts the US dollar as its currency. Ecuador, El Salvador, and Panama now use the dollar, and Argentina's peso was pegged to the dollar before the economic collapse. These nations have some significant aspect of their economy and banking dollarized: Chile, Mexico, Costa Rica, Honduras, Nicaragua, Peru, Bolivia, Uruguay, the Bahamas, Cambodia, Haiti, Laos, Afghanistan, and Liberia. This gives the US Treasury Department some limited control over the monetary policy of these nations, namely the interest rates, which nations usually use to affect inflation and growth. That control is not on their behalf, but is tied to the needs of the US economy. Dollarization of the Americas may follow passage of the FTAA.

## Asia Pacific Economic Cooperation (APEC) and Asia Europe Meeting (ASEM)

These two interregional economic groups are of rather minor importance, but remain as an alternative grouping in case of another collapse or set back at the WTO, and thus a WTO negotiating tool. APEC, formed in 1989, is pursued also as a way to prevent an all-Asia trade block that could compete with the EU or FTAA/NAFTA. Within it, the US is negotiating bilateral free-trade agreements with Australia, the Phillippines, Singapore (2002), Vietnam (2001), Jordan (2001), and Sri Lanka. Israel already has Free Trade Agreements with the US and Canada.

## Multilateral Agreement on Investment (MAI)

Organized by the Organization for Economic Cooperation and Development (OECD) in 1997 and organized under draft WTO additions under the name, trade-related investment measures (TRIMs), these proposals empower a corporation to sue governments (federal, regional, local) whose public policies reduce their profits. TRIMs would also ban capital controls (currency exchange rules) as a tool of public policy, a tool with which a nation can stop capital flight during a financial crisis. Capital controls might eventually become the jurisdiction of the IMF during a financial crisis, further lessening the control of capital by a national government. Most foreign investment passes between developed nations, but the impact of foreign investment on developing nations is significant, and risky, but potentially very profitable. Thus the exclusion of the developing nations from the MAI negotiations at the OECD meetings killed a major purpose of the MAI (the ratification of the developing nations), as did the public pressure and developing nation outrage stemming from a leak of the draft text. Investor rights are still planned for the FTAA and the expansion of the WTO TRIMs.

## World Economic Forum (WEF)

This group of business leaders spawned the Uruguay trade round that created the WTO—the US government threw its political will behind the Uruguay Round and an expanded multilateral system, and then Canadian Trade Minister John Crosbie made the actual proposal for a WTO. The WEF has no official power, but is a brainstorming session by the business elites that ultimately have the most influence on global and regional financial institutions.

## Group of Eight (G8) and Group of Seven (G7)

These are distinct groups that work in tandem. The Group of Seven economic powers—the US, UK, France, Germany, Italy, Canada, and Japan—forms the most important trade negotiating meeting, one that usually drafts the leading WTO negotiating documents. The G7 is known within the WTO negotiations as the Quad: the EU, US, Canada, and Japan. The Group of Eight political powers simply add Russia for security and political meetings to the list of G7 nations. The G7/G8 meetings each year are important because they bring together eight heads of state.

Each administrative area (security, foreign affairs, et cetera) has its own ministerial of the seven or eight relevant cabinet ministers in the runup to the main meeting. The IMF and World Bank are typically represented at the G7 finance ministers meeting. The G20 is a group of friendly developing nations that advise the G7.

The G7 has also initiated the New Partnership for African Development (NEPAD), as part of an EU-inspired African Union, organized to help reduce trade barriers between African nations, and opened up Africa to more foreign investment and privatization.

## European Union (EU)

The EU is a union of political, economic, legal, and immigration policies for member states that started in 1946. Beyond that, the EU has somewhat weaker free-trade agreements with states in the queue for membership (like the former Soviet republics along the Baltic) and with southern Mediterranean nations. Travel and immigration within the EU is less restrictive, but entry into and out of the union by non-EU citizens is difficult. The EU Commission began as a customs union in 1956, then as a common market in 1994. In 2002 Europe's single currency, the euro, was launched for universal use by member nations that chose to join the monetary union of the EU—this centralizes control of European monetary policy in the European Central Bank and forces Europe to balance the monetary needs of one nation with the others.

Britain, Sweden, and Denmark have not yet adopted the euro. The 2003 war in Iraq has encouraged some skeptical Europeans to join the euro as a way of counterbalancing the economic power and political power of the US (the dollar is the primary currency of international banking, savings, loans, and oil trading). The EU also has a parliament and negotiates at the WTO as a block.

## 1993

October 2, *Bangalore, India* | Uruguay Round (WTO) Protests against the WTO began at its birth with half a million Karnataka farmers.
October, *Russia* | IMF

## 1994

January 1, *San Cristobal de las Casas, Mexico* | NAFTA Mexican soldiers were hung over from New Year's Eve and off-guard the day NAFTA went into effect. The Zapatistas, an indigenous movement from the jungles of Chiapas, took over the state capital, San Cristobal de las Casas, and eight other towns with masks, boots, uniforms, and machine guns. The 3000 men and women of the Zapatista Army of National Liberation (EZLN) were pushed back by 14,000 government soldiers. The Zapatistas then turned to the internet as way to build on the international attention from the takeover. They started their own schools and public services in an autonomous zone that was surrounded by the Mexican military. Vicente Fox's campaign promise of a peace agreement with the Zapatistas helped bring him to power and bring an end to over seventy years of one-party rule in Mexico. Fox, a former Coca-Cola executive, has not reached such a peace agreement, and in many ways has escalated the conflict. Indigenous protests and resistance against their military occupation go back hundreds of years, especially 1712 and 1869.

May, *Uganda* | IMF The government layed off 48,000 in the civil service.

June, *Gabon* | IMF

## 1995

July, *Ecuador* | IMF

September, *Madrid, Spain* | World Bank 10,000 people protest.

November, *Kenya* | IMF

## 1996

April 17, *Para, Brazil* | IMF At the massacre at Eldorado de Carajas, nineteen *campesinos* were killed by police in a protest, bringing the four year total to 163.

August, *Karak, Jordan* | IMF

August 26, *Brasillia, Brazil* | IMF 100,000 demonstrate against export-driven land reform, and launch the Landless Campesino Movement (MST) as a major political force after a full year of escalating occupations of unproductive lands. It was a protest that included other left opposition parties such as the Workers Party (PT), whose leader, Lula da Silva, would become president in 2002. The MST would win elections in the south and begin participatory budgeting and the World Social Forum.

September, *Argentina* | IMF Carlos Menem is elected in 1989, introduces an IMF austerity program, and pegs the peso to the US dollar in 1992. A general strike during Menem's second term as president begins in 1996. Menem fires his finance minister, Domingo Cavallo, and the economy worsens.

## 1997

February, *South Africa* | IMF & World Bank

June 9, *Amsterdam, Netherlands* | EU

September 21 | MAI & OECD A public relations war led by Northern NGOs, started by a leaked draft of the MAI

November 25, *Vancouver, Canada* | APEC Demonstrators knocked down a fence, surrounding the Indonesian president Suharto and the rest of the summit. Police arrested forty-two. In 2001, a commission found that the police had not displayed "professionalism" in its use of pepper spray; the report also claimed that Prime Minister Jean Chretian was involved in directing the police. On the twenty-fifth Chretian declared: "For me, pepper, I put it on my plate."

December 15, *Seoul, South Korea* | IMF

## 1998

January 29, *Davos, Switzerland* | WEF

April 16–May 20, *Indonesia* | IMF President Suharto falls after public protests against the IMF. The Vietnam war was waged in large part to protect the economic and political power of Indonesia, the site of a CIA-backed coup in 1965.

May 8, Kiev, *Ukraine* | European Bank of Reconstruction & Development (EBRD)

May 16, *Birmingham, UK* | G8/G7 See "World Trashed Organization!"

May 17, *Geneva, Switzerland* | WTO See "World Trashed Organization!"

June 15, *Cardiff, Wales* | EU

October, *Algiers, Algeria* | IMF

November 28, *Sindhanoor, India* | GMOs (and WTO) Karnataka farmers burned three fields of GMO trial crops in "Operation Cremation Monsanto." The crop locations were only revealed by the government by November 26.

December 14, *Vienna, Austria* | EU

## 1999

January 28, *Davos, Switzerland* | WEF

February, *Romania* | IMF & World Bank

March 8, *Ecuador* | IMF

April 9, *Mexico City* | IMF National Autonomous University of Mexico (UNAM) students sought to stop the imposition of tuition, another result of government budget cuts, over a series of strikes and protests lasting months.

April 26, *Christcurch, New Zealand* | APEC

May 1 | May Day

May 10, *Argentina* | IMF

May 29 *Millau, France* | 1999 WTO A new McDonald's is dismantled by French farmer José Bové and nine others.

June 3, *Cologne, Germany* | EU

June 18, *Cologne, Germany* | G8

July, *Ecuador* | IMF

July 27, *Brazil* | IMF A caravan by the MST.

August, *Brasilia, Brazil* | IMF 15,000 *campesinos* protest against personal debt from their failed farms, in part from cheap food imports and government budget cuts; hundreds of thousands of *campesinos* occupy land in large camps.

September 4, *Karachi, Pakistan* | IMF

September 12, *Auckland, New Zealand* | APEC

September 15, *Mexico City* | UN Conference on Trade & Development (UNCTAD)

October 15, *Tampere, Finland* | EU

October 29, *Berlin, Germany* | Trans-Atlantic Business Dialogue (TABD)

November 1, *Toronto, Canada* | FTAA

November | IMF World Bank economist and former Clinton advisor, Joseph Stiglitz, quit his job at the bank, and in the coming months sided with the protesters. He reportedly has a non-aggression agreement to not criticize the World Bank, but continued his outspoken comments against the IMF. A year later, he became a corecipient of the Nobel Prize in Economics for his work on how unequal information causes market inefficiencies and market failures (market theory assumes that buyers and sellers have the same information).

November 30, *Seattle, US* | WTO 50,000 prostest. See "Seattle Diary."

## 2000

Ongoing, *Argentina* | IMF Strikes and fuel-tax protests. Soybean exports dropped after the European and Asian markets reject GMO soy. Foot-and-mouth disease hits the beef industry.

January 29, *Davos, Switzerland* | WEF

January 29, *Quito, Ecuador* | IMF The IMF and the national government imposed a structural adjustment program and dollarized the economy, prompting indigenous people and young military officers to take the parliament building. A young military engineer, Lucio Gutiérrez, participated in the indigenous-led protests and coup and became the officially elected president in November 2002.

February 12, *Bangkok, Thailand* | UNCTAD

March, *Costa Rica* | IMF 10,000

April 16, *Washington DC, US* | IMF & World Bank

April 23, *Cochobamba, Bolivia* | World Bank Hundreds of thousands of mostly indigenous or poor demonstrated against the US company Bechtel, which had just won a contract for the privatized public water service in and around Cochobamba. The plan was organized and financed by the World Bank, an epitome of the Bank's new direction toward financing privatization. The protest began when Bechtel hiked water rates for its new water monopoly. Bechtel, the Bank, and the Bolivian government withdrew from the deal, probably at the request of the Bolivian government since Bechtel is suing Bolivia in the International Center for the Settlement of Investment Disputes (a part of the World Bank, closed to the public). One of the protest leaders, Oscar Olivera, would go on to run for president; but coca-growers union leader Evo Morales would come in second in 2002 running on an anti-US antiprivatization platform.

May 1 | May Day

May 4, *Nairobi, Kenya* | IMF

May 7, *Chiang Mai, Thailand* | Asian Development Bank (ADB)

May 10, *South Africa* | World Bank 200,000 protest in several cities amid a general strike of about half the workforce.

May 11, *India* | IMF 20 million go on strike.

May 15, *Mun River, Thailand* | World Bank

May 22, *New York, US* | UN Millennium Forum

May 31, *Buenos Aires, Argentina* | IMF

June, *Port-au-Prince, Haiti* | IMF

June, *Nigeria* | IMF Bond strike against raising local oil prices and the visit of US Treasury Secretary Laurence Summers.

June 21, *Paraguay* | IMF

June 4, *Windsor, Ontario, Canada* | OAS

June 6, *Bucharest, Romania* | IMF

June 12, *Bologna, Italy* | OECD

June 30, *Salzburg, Austria* | WEF

June 30, *Millau, France* | Millau Ten Convictions José Bové and nine others are convicted of wrecking a McDonald's under construction, Bové is also sentenced for destroying GMO crops. A protest rallies in support of the ten French farmers.

July, *Washington DC, US* | World Bank A vigil outside the bank helped bring attention to China's application for assistance to resettle more Chinese in Tibet, and China withdrew the application. Many World Bank shareholding nations also opposed the loan.

July 20, *Okinawa, Japan* | G8 African leaders appeared in their first of three meetings with the G8, who thank the Seattle protests for giving them a seat at the table. Promises for debt relief are subsequently renewed at the next two G8 meetings.

July 25, *Seoul, South Korea* | IMF

August, *Colombia* | IMF strikes

August, *Honduras* | IMF strikes

September, *Bolivia* | IMF

September, *Brazil* | IMF

September 8, *New York, US* | UN Millennium Summit, a development summit

September 11, *Melbourne, Australia* | WEF 10,000

September 23, *Pakistan* | IMF The Awami Caravan

September 26, *Prague, Czech* | IMF & World Bank 10,000 protest. See "Prague 2000" and "Infernal Pain in Prague."

October 18, *Seoul, South Korea* | ASEM

October 24, *Montreal, Canada* | G20

November, *El Salvador* | IMF A four- month strike begins, protesting the privatization of the health sector.

November, *Ghana* | IMF Students protest undisbursed student loans with blockades and government office occupations.

November 16, *Cincinnati, US* | TABD

November 30, *Seattle, US* | WTO Every year since Seattle, the anniversary protest ritually re-enacts the days of action, including ritual glass-breaking and not-so-ritual arrests.

December 6, *Nice, France* | EU


# 2001

January 8, *Angola* | IMF National strike.

January 17, *Bhopal, India* | World Bank & ADB

January 27, *Davos, Switzerland* | WEF

January 29, *Quito, Ecuador* | IMF Indigenous groups occupy the IMF offices in Quito and demonstrate for two weeks, ending with reversals of some austerity measures.

February 18, *Istanbul* | G20

February 19, *Bamako, Mali* | IMF

February 26, *Cancún, Mexico* | WEF 400 protest. See "Holidays in the Sun."

March, *Mexico* | Zapatista Caravan A proactive protest; instead of reacting to a particular meeting, the Zapatistas forced a meeting with the government to reinstate *campesino* rights nixed under NAFTA and to pull back the military occupation of Chiapas; the caravan drew people from all over the world, and especially from all over Mexico.

March 12, *Peru* | IMF

March 15, *Naples, Italy* | OECD

March 18, *Santiago, Chile* | IADB

March 22, *Argentina* | IMF

March 27, *Chiang Mai, Thailand* | WTO

March 31, *Turkey* | IMF

April 6, *Buenos Aires, Argentina* | FTAA

April 11, *Ankara, Turkey* | IMF

April 14, *Istanbul, Turkey* | IMF

April 15, *Quebec City, Canada* | FTAA 25,000 protest. See "Something Did Start in Quebec City"

April 17, *Karnataka, India* | WTO

April 21, *Malmo, Sweden* | EU

May, *Argentina* | IMF 80,000 protest, and by June 7.2 million go on strike for twenty-four hours.

May 1 | May Day

May 9, *Honolulu, US* | ADB

June 6, *Durban, South Africa* | WEF

June 7, *Colombia* | IMF

June 14, *Gothenburg, Sweden* | EU This protest was soon eclipsed by Genoa. But the 25,000 demonstrators received similar treatment—a pre-emptive raid on activists by police the day before and live ammunition. Three demonstrators were shot by police and one of them died. The protest was also fueled by the presence of George W. Bush.

June 18, *Jakarta, Indonesia* | IMF

June 25, *Barcelona, Spain* | World Bank When the bank canceled their meeting the protest became a victory march.

June 26, *Papua New Guinea* | IMF & World Bank Three protesters shot dead

July, *Nepal* | World Bank & ADB

July, *India* | IMF National Strike by public service employees

July 1, *Salzburg, Austria* | WEF

July 18, *Argentina* | IMF General strike

July 20, *Genoa, Italy* | G8/G7 See "And Balanced With This Life, This Death" and "Genoa and the Anti-Globalization Movement"

August, *Angola* | IMF National Strike

September 28, *Washington DC, US* | IMF & World Bank The protest and the meeting were cancelled because of September 11th. Instead an antiwar march takes place.

October 2, *Bangalore, India* | WTO

October 7, *Miami, US* | WEF

October 12, *Singapore* | ASEM

October 12, *Stockholm, Sweden* | TABD

October 18, *Tokyo, Japan* | APEC

October 19, *Gent, Belgium* | EU

October 29, *Hong Kong* | WEF

November 7, *Delhi, India* | WTO

November 9, *Doha, Qatar* | WTO Protests were legalized for the week of the WTO ministerial, but only fifty or so NGO leaders were allowed into the country, and Qatar's majority, the foreign noncitizen workers, faced deportation if they protested. NGOs claimed a victory in new language in the TRIPs agreement, ostensibly allowing poor nations to produce AIDS drugs without paying the patent holders. In later negotiations, the US changed the language to only include "extreme urgency."

November 16, *Ottawa, Canada* | G20 The IMF meeting was essentially rescheduled and folded into this meeting.

December 13, *Brussels, Belgium* | EU

December 19, *Argentina* | IMF The economy collapses, and the government freezes bank accounts and delays pension checks. Meanwhile looting and daily protests lead to the resignation of several ministers and two presidents.

## 2002

January 31, *New York, US* | WEF See "Growing Through Daring, Forgetting Through Fear"

March 14, *Fortaleza, Brazil* | IADB

March 16, *Barcelona, Spain* | EU 400,000

March 18, *Monterray, Mexico* | UN International Conference on Financing for Development

March 20, *Guatemala* | Plan Puebla Panamá

April 11, *Caracas, Venezuela* | IMF (indirectly) In 1989, the IMF imposed structural adjustment on Venezuela, and by February 27 that year a major protest ended in the killing of 4000 demonstrators—the *Caracazo*. Nearly three years later, the Bolivar Revolutionary Movement 200 (MBR-200), including Lt. Hugo Chávez, fails to take over the government in a coup to end the IMF policies. More years of protest and more structural adjustment end with Chávez becoming the new president nearly ten years after *Caracazo*. A new constitution, a new public assembly, and a major new presidential election are won by Chávez. Then, a US-supported coup on April 11 nearly succeeds, but protests from the nation's poor and military bring Chávez back to power twenty-four hours later. Unusually, OAS condemns the coup.

April 19, *Washington DC, US* | IMF & World Bank 40,000 protest

April 25, *Montreal, Canada* | G8 Labor Ministers

May 1 | May Day

May 17, *Madrid, Spain* | EU-Latin America Summit

May 21, *Santiago, Chile* | US-Chile Free Trade Agreement (FTAA)

May 22, *South Korea* | IMF Strike

May 29, *Barcelona, Spain* | EU-Mediterranean Summit A group working for an FTA between the EU and the southern Mediterranean nations of North Africa and the Levant (except Libya).

June 6, *Brussels, Belgium* | European Business Summit

June 17, *Argentina* | IMF Two protesters killed at a road block.

June 10, *Rome, Italy* | World Food Summit

June 11, *Boston, US* | World Bank President speaks at MIT.

June 13, *Peru* | IMF Three killed in five days of protests.

June 17, *Halifax, Canada* | G7

June 21, *Seville, Spain* | EU

June 24, *Oslo, Norway* | World Bank

June 25, *Dhaka, Bangladesh* | IMF

June 26, *Kananaskis (near Calgary) & Ottawa, Canada* | G8/G7 Canada's Terrorism Bill C36 was largely written for economic events and economic disruption. The security operation surrounding the meeting was the largest peacetime military operation in Canadian history; many activists reorganized themselves to protest in Ottawa instead of facing the military zone. African leaders attended the meeting, and here NEPAD and the new African Union received financial and political backing from the G8 nations. Before the summit, significant attention landed on the Kyoto Protocol for reducing greenhouse gas emissions. The oil-rich province of Alberta reminded the federal government that provinces have legal jurisdiction over natural resources, and thus for enforce (or fail to enforce) Kyoto-mandated emission cuts.

June 28, *Amman, Jordan* | IMF Jordan's first female member of Parliament, Toujan Al-Faisal, goes on a twenty-nine-day hunger strike to protest the IMF.

July 15, *San Salvador Atenco, Mexico*

July 23, *Managua, Nicaragua* | PPP

August 8, *Fortaleza, Brazil* | IADB

August 31, *Johannesburg, South Africa* | World Summit on Sustainable Development (WSSD) Though development politics are often treated separately from trade politics—the WSSD meeting, also known as Rio + 10 Earth Summit, demonstrated how far development and trade had become linguistically and politically linked. The WTO's new trade round was a "Development Round" and the goal of many of the government and industry participants of the UN sponsored meeting was reach sustainable development through the WTO's Development Round. One of the biggest polluters in the world, the US, objected to the already weak agreement. Protests, walk outs, and alternative summits followed the week long event. See "Rattling the Chains of Global Apartheid."

September 15, *Salzburg, Austria* | WEF

September 16, *Colombia* | FTAA

September 19, *Copenhagen, Denmark* | ASEM

September 23, *Paraguay* | IMF

September 28, *West Coast of the US* | ILWU (longshoreman) lockout and strike. The most direct action–oriented union that participated in the Seattle protests gets trouble from the shipping industry and the Bush administration, ultimately leading to a stalemate and returning to the status quo.

September 28, *Washington DC, US* | IMF & World Bank

October 12, *Central America* | Plan Puebla Panamá. PPP was condemned for years by the Zapatistas among others, but here, on the 510th anniversary of the arrival of Christopher

Columbus and the beginning of the genocide of indigenous people, demonstrators coordinated protests throughout Central America, at the same time facing the imminent passage of CAFTA and its conjoinment with NAFTA.

October 19, *Seoul, South Korea* | ASEM

October 24, *Colombo, Sri Lanka* | IMF

November 1, *Quito, Ecuador* | FTAA see "*Contra Cumbre* in Quito"

November 7, *Chicago, US* | TABD

November 14, *Sydney, Australia* | WTO Before this WTO mini-ministerials went more or less unprotested. Mini-ministerials are where WTO draft texts are negotiated by the most powerful countries in order to drive consensus at the official venues.

November 20, *Rio de Janeiro, Brazil* | WEF

December 15, *Copenhagen, Denmark* | EU

December 20, *Buenos Aires, Argentina* | IMF Anniversary of the protests that toppled successive government administrations.

## 2003

January 23, *Davos, Switzerland* | WEF

January 28, *Honduras* | FTAA

January 31, *Mexico City* | NAFTA The full effect of NAFTA's agricultural policies went into effect on January 1, 2003, and Mexican farmers face more subsidized agricultural goods flooding their markets, which could lead to losing their land.

February 11, *Bolivia* | IMF Starting back on January 8, coca growers, pensioners, campesinos, and workers started a month of protests and road blocks, with at least twenty-three people dead, and at one point included a police strike. The Congress expelled one of its members: coca grower, union representative, protest organizer, Evo Morales. The government wanted to raise taxes to decrease the budget deficit, under the urging of the IMF.

May 1 | May Day

September 10–13, *Cancun, Mexico* | WTO See "The Charming Outcome of the Cancun Trade Talks" and "Cancun: The Collapse of the Neoliberal Offensive."

November 17–21, *Miami, US* | FTAA

November 20, *London, UK* | State visit by George W. Bush

# Part I:
# Roots of the
# Movement

# Seattle Was Not the Beginning
## George Katsiaficas

In the months subsequent to the now-legendary battle of Seattle, the leaders of the World Bank, the International Monetary Fund, and the Trilateral Commission all defined the antiglobalization upsurge as having begun in that city—and therefore as following in the glorious tradition of Microsoft and Starbucks. No less an authority on world economic affairs than Alan Greenspan, chair of the Federal Reserve Board under four US presidents, recently commented that " . . . the arguments against the global trading system that emerged first in Seattle and then spread over the past year arguably touched a chord in many people . . . "[1]

Did the current wave of antiglobalization protests begin in Seattle? No, the movement emerged first outside the United States—in Venezuela, South Korea, India, Germany and dozens of other countries. Even if we define the movement narrowly, as Greenspan has—i.e., as only being against the global trading system and not against the entirety of the capitalist world system—it is hardly of American origin. In fact, the Seattle protests themselves involved some thirteen hundred civic, social movement, and trade union organizations from over eighty countries. And furthermore, on N30, there were major demonstrations in fourteen US cities; twenty thousand people marched in Paris, eight thousand in Manila, three thousand in Seoul, and thousands more around the world. In Mexico City a few days later, ninety-eight people were arrested and tortured for demanding the release of arrested Seattle demonstrators. Yet US activists don't include those people as part of the "Seattle" action. The Mexicans who demonstrated in solidarity with the arrested protesters in Seattle acted because they felt it was the best thing to do. For us not to recognize their actions as part of our movement is to fly in the face of the solidarity they demonstrated. Our blindness is conditioned by media silence and a host of other conditions. We need to make more of an effort to overcome the systematic fragmentation of our movement.

The anti-WTO protests in Seattle have had an immense impact on the antiglobalization movement around the world. Yet in our celebration of this action, several problems arise. I notice blindness to pre-Seattle forerunners; a failure to pose international solidarity as an alternative to globalization; and underestimation of the efficacy of tactical diversity.

As a symbol for the hundreds of thousands of people around the world who have demonstrated against the neo-liberal agenda of the institutions of global capital, Seattle is vitally significant. But disregarding antiglobalization movements in other countries, particularly those at the periphery of the world system, reproduces the biases and distortions of the very system being opposed. Such disregard slyly reinforces one of the world system's central ideas: the life of a human being in the United States or Europe is worth more than the life of a Third World person. For the IMF, World Bank, and giant multinational corporations, an American life is far more valuable than the life of a Venezuelan or a Vietnamese—hence in their view the protests against globalization began in Seattle. But progressive and radical history must be qualitatively different than the history of the neoliberalist champions and their corporate masters. Our history must reflect the notion that all human life is of equal value.

The best known of Seattle's precursors is the Zapatista uprising in Chiapas, Mexico. The preponderant influence of the Zapatistas on the activists in Seattle was evident in the many protesters who carried their flag, and their posters and wore masks. The Zapatistas have been key organizers of the Peoples' Global Action Against "Free" Trade, an umbrella for movements on five continents including the Landless Peasants' Movement of Brazil and India's Karnataka State Farmer's Movement. Besides these organizations, antiglobalization uprisings in dozens of Third World countries predated the Seattle confrontation. Of these many popular responses to conditions of economic hardship dictated by global institutions, the Venezuelan uprising in 1989 was the most significant. In a few days beginning on February 27, thousands of people rose up against the imposition of IMF-ordered austerity measures. The police and army shot to death more than three hundred people and wounded thousands of others. More than two thousand people were arrested. Because of its importance, let me take a closer look.

## Venezuela

Consider the following: the structural imperatives of the existing world system have resulted in poor Latin American countries paying billions of dollars in interest *each year* to rich countries' banks. Total indebtedness of the region was approximately 420 billion dollars in 1989. Of all the countries in Latin America, Venezuela had long enjoyed one of the highest standards of living, no doubt because of the exploitation of its vast oil reserves. When president Carlos Andres Perez, a longtime social democrat, came peacefully to power, few suspected he would preside over a bloody imposition of IMF-dictated austerity measures. Yet in order for the IMF to grant his government the power to avoid an economic meltdown (i.e., $1.5 billion in badly needed credit so he could lift the ceilings on interest rates and let the currency float), they required him to raise prices for food, gasoline and bus fares. On February 16, the new austerity program was announced and on February 27, it was to take effect. That day, however, rather than peacefully submitting to hardship and misery, poor people in the shantytowns that ring Caracas's modern center rose up to smash the imposition of the IMF's orders.

All at once, everywhere there was resistance. In the eastern shantytown of Petare, seventeen people were killed in pitched battles with the forces of order. Shotguns and even machine guns were used by the government against rocks and an occasional sniper—not much of a match, but a heavily contested one. Snipers in the El Valle neighborhood south of Caracas killed an army major; in response, at least twenty people were shot and killed. In sixteen other Venezuelan cities, including Maracaibo, San Cristobal, Valencia, Puerto LaCruz, Barquisimeto, Carora, Merida, Puerto Ordaz, and Guarenas, the poor rose up. For days they refused to submit. On March 3, troops were still looking for snipers. On the ninth, the *New York Times* reported up to 375 deaths; the Venezuelan media counted more than six hundred throughout the country. Even after calm had apparently been restored, the insurgency reappeared in other forms. In April thousands of high school and university students protested against the withdrawal of government subsidies. In May, the first national strike in thirty-one years erupted. In the wake of the uprising, Venezuelans reconfigured their country's political system and swept Hugo Chavez into power.

The rulers of the world economy can hardly plead ignorance of the Venezuela events. Greenspan had already begun his tenure in office and world financial institutions were directly involved. Indeed, within days of the fighting, on March 9, the US government began to shift its policy, easing repayment provisions on the debt. In concert with the IMF, World Bank, and a cluster of other governments and global institutions, the U.S. loaned more than the amount Venezuela needed (some $2 billion in emergency loans).

Although protests in the periphery are mounted against specific grievances in their own national territory, their character is as much against capitalist globalization as the protests in Seattle. They arise against the global system and their institutional masters—economic dictators who make slaves of entire countries and regions. The free market model imposed on Venezuela in the '80s and '90s left eighty percent of the population living in slums and on the threshold of utter poverty. They turned to Chavez to pull them out of their collective misery. In 1998, his newly formed party won fifty-six percent of the vote.

Why is this international precursor of Seattle unknown to North Americans? In the US, we pride ourselves on our free press. How could such an uprising occur and leader after leader profess to know nothing about it? Similarly, food riots in the Dominican Republic in 1985, Brazil in 1986, and dozens of countries have been wiped from memory. What of the seventy-five thousand people who marched in Berlin in 1988 when the World Bank and International Monetary Fund held their meetings? Protesters there were very powerfully influenced by the outbreak of earlier riots in the Third World, and their massive and militant presence compelled thousands of bankers and monetary experts to depart Berlin a day earlier than planned.

The attempt to depict the antiglobalization movement as a US phenomenon is the other side of the more general invisibility of the rest of the world for many Americans. Setting Seattle as the starting point of a new global upsurge is part of the system's counteroffensive. Instead of seeking simply to repress and condemn the movement, leaders of the world's major financial institutions are seeking to turn the protests into socially acceptable and even systemically beneficial avenues of action. (This apparent openness from the institutions of power does however present the opportunity for the development of inside-outside strategies.)

Paying attention to the protests of young people in the capitalist metropolis while rendering invisible activists in other countries is one way of maintaining the superiority of the wealthy countries of the world. Maintaining the hegemony of the USA is also critical to the maintenance of the existing order. For a long time now, defining social movements along national lines is one way in which historians and world leaders have stripped activists of their radical antisystemic politics. Our alternative to the top-down globalization of huge multinational corporations and their militarized nation-states is an internationalism founded upon autonomous nuclei of popular participation. Protests against the meetings of the leaders of globalization concretely enunciate our critique of their policies. Clarifying the internationalism of autonomously organized revolts helps develop the self-conscious formulation of a planetary alternative to globalization.

## Eros and Internationalism

As is becoming increasingly clear, militant antisystemic actions build upon one another, a phenomenon I have elsewhere described as the eros effect.[2] Through the power of exemplary peoples' actions leading to involvement by others, small groups are able to detonate social explosions in which millions of ordinary people unexpectedly take the direction of society into their own hands and make long overdue changes. Ordinary people acting together can force a president of a country, even a brutal and long entrenched dictator, out of office. They can neutralize the armed forces. Last year, for example, a few days after the Serbian people overthrew Slobodan Milosevic, the people of the Ivory Coast overthrew their dictator, Robert Guei, when he attempted to stop the counting of votes in an election he was losing. Thousands of Ivorians took to the streets, and although Guei's presidential guard fired on them and killed hundreds of people, the crowd refused to disperse. Instead they continued marching on the presidential palace. Guei fled and "people power" (a term that originated in the Philippines in 1986 after the overthrow of Marcos by thousands of people who refused to leave the streets) won another victory. The *New York Times* quoted one student, Alfred Tohouri, saying: "The mistake Guei made was to let us watch scenes from Belgrade."[3]

Because of the power of the media and the global village character of the world today, the eros effect has become increasingly important. Social movements are less and less confined to one city, region or nation; they do not exist in isolation in distant corners of the globe; actions are often synchronically related. Social movements in one country are affected sometimes more by events and actions outside their own national context than they are by domestic dynamics. The international embeddedness of N30 is evident enough in the autonomously organized global wave of resistance events in the year after it. The protests in Seattle helped define and motivate the antiglobalization movement. Inspired by N30, protests erupted in the streets of Bangkok in February 2000, Washington DC in April, and subsequently in Melbourne, Prague, and Davos. In the Czech Republic, one of the most popular chants was "Prague, Seattle, Continue the Battle!" (Although it is not as well known, activists in Prague were as successful as their Seattle predecessors in compelling leaders of the world's financial architecture to change their meeting plans.)

We speak so often of internationalism. But then why do we define antiglobalization struggles nationalistically? Greenspan, Wohlfenson, the Trilateral Commission, and the World Bank have characterized the upsurge against globalization as parochial, as nationalistic, while portraying themselves as progressive and global. Are progressives against globalization because we are nationalists? In Venezuela today, the answer might be yes. The Chavez government embodies the antiglobalization impulse but Chavez has to relate to his national context since he is president of a country. His activism has been global— he organized OPEC to raise world oil prices and thereby bring a greater share of the world's economic output to the oil-producing countries. Ominously, US intervention in Colombia and the regionalization of that war loom on the horizon of globalization's future for Venezuela.

Should progressives in the US also think and act nationalistically? Do we share anything with the Pat Buchanans and other US nationalists who oppose globalization? No. In opposition to the globalization of corporate control by the IMF, World Bank, WTO, and their governments, our internationalism calls for grassroots, autonomous political participation and mutually agreed connections between people, not connections dictated by the market or the political demands of those with power and money. The progressive antiglobalization movement is not against international ties; it wants to see ties that are fair and decent. It is against ties that force people off land, against the kinds of global economic relations that make it possible for the corporations to profit greatly from degrading the world. Billions of people must struggle mightily and suffer daily simply to obtain the bare necessities of life.

The *Intelligence Report,* a publication of Morris Dees' Southern Poverty Law Center, wrote that the neo-Nazis and WTO protestors in Seattle are cut from the same cloth.[4]

Because the Seattle protests focused only on global institutions and not on the US government's role in all of this, the movement is open to that charge. So putting forth internationalism as our politics—not just opposition to globalization—is critical to differentiating us from the antiglobalization forces that are pro-US.

## South Korea, the Power of Autonomy, and the Dialectic of Social Movements

Diversity of tactics, organizations, and beliefs is one of the great strengths of autonomous social movements. Using a creative variety of tactics—including militant street demonstrations—as a part of our arsenal, we can change societies in ways that parliamentary efforts or more established movements cannot. In South Korea, autonomous movements overthrew a repressive military dictatorship and established democracy. Autonomous trade unions not tied to the *chaebols*—huge corporate concentrations such as Hyundai and Daewoo—were also won, and both governments of Korea were pushed toward reunification.

The Kwangju uprising of 1980—an upheaval in which as many as two thousand people were killed—was the pivot around which these movements ascended. After the brutal imposition of martial law by thousands of elite paratroopers and police, the people of Kwangju drove the military out of the city and held it for almost a week. Although many people were massacred when the army retook the city, Kwangju has become a symbol motivating action in many other countries.[5]

South Korean social movements can teach us significant lessons. In the past few years, the IMF has intoned that South Korea will have lower economic growth if it doesn't break up the chaebols. Ironically, South Korean President and Nobel Peace Prize winner Kim Dae Jung, once held on death row by the military dictatorship for his alleged role in the Kwangju uprising, is now leading the neoliberalist penetration of the Korean economy. Winning democracy and getting Kim Dae Jung elected were amazing feats that we can attribute to the power of millions of ordinary people who took to the streets. Subsequently with some kind of democratic structure in place and autonomous trade unions struggling for more rights for working people, the Kim government used repression against its former allies, breaking up workers' protests with helicopters and police violence. When Kim Dae Jung, hero of the last phase of popular struggles in South Korea, turns into his opposite, history's dialectical character is revealed. No doubt, his opening to North Korea and defusing of the half-century state of war on the Korean peninsula are historic accomplishments; his government's more recent repression of workers' demonstrations speak to history's rapid pace and inner irony.

While in Korea force has been widely used for decades to maintain the status quo, in the US media manipulation and consumerism have largely been sufficient to assure corporate rule. Nonetheless, as in Korea, today's activists are often tomorrow's authorities.

Both the mayor and police chief of Seattle were sixties people. While the mayor prides himself on having been an antiwar activist during the Vietnam war, police chief Norm Stamper was a product of San Diego State University's humanistic police training program. The program distilled the sixties model of community policing, which came about in response to demands for community control of the police. Such co-optation of the sixties—i.e., its use to provide new ideas and leaders for the system—is very common in Europe. The Greens in Germany are but one example of leadership inside governments who are used to legitimize a new military role for Germany as well as to repress militant movements (because that's the role they are compelled legally to play as part of the government).

The aura of the sixties is being used against the antiglobalization movement in another way. An exaggerated sixties diminishes contemporary movements. Movements today are written off as shadows, imitations or lesser siblings. Seattle is recognized as highly significant, but movements between the sixties and the present are forgotten. Glorification of decades (or of great events and individuals) diminishes the importance of continuity and everyday activism in the life of social movements. As a social construction, the myth of the sixties functions thereby to discourage people from having authentic movement experiences now, in the present.

Finally, sixties activists themselves, speaking as representatives of those halcyon days of yesteryear, intervene today as critics of militant popular struggles. Using their legitimacy as sixties activists, they interject the authority of the sixties into the current movement. Sixties veterans were valuable and significant parts of the Central American antiintervention movement in the '80s. Thirty years ago, we paid dearly for the absence of sufficient elders. However, when the legitimacy of the past is used as a weapon to argue for a particular position rather than to inform a discussion, the effect can be deleterious, often undermining creative exploration and fresh thinking. I think here of the some of the post-Seattle debates around violence. (Some are reprinted in this book.)

For me, Seattle was a chance to connect with people from different generations of activists. I was invited to come and talk during the protests by Daniel, whom I had never met, and whom I think of today as a friend. Ironically, my scheduled speech at Left Bank Books the night after N30 had to be cancelled because of the declaration of martial law.

Thanks to the "No Protest Zone," we had the space to go off and get acquainted, and as a result we decided to work together on this book.

Ho Chi Minh City
January 31, 2001

This is a revised version of a talk given at Evergreen State College in Olympia, Washington on November 17, 2000. Thanks to Daniel Burton Rose, Billy Nessen, and Eddie Yuen for their comments.

1. *New York Times*, November 15, 2000, C2.

2. I first developed this concept in relation to an understanding of the global imagination of 1968. See *The Imagination of the New Left: A Global Analysis of 1968* (South End Press, 1987).

3. *New York Times*, October 26, 2000, 14.

4. "Morris Dees' New Scam," *Counterpunch,* (March 16–31, 2000): 2.

5. For an analysis of this vitally important event, news of which has largely failed to enter the consciousness of most Americans (activists included), the best source is *Kwangju Diary: Beyond Death, Beyond the Darkness of the Age* by Lee Jae-eui (UCLA Asian-Pacific Monograph Series, 1999). Also see my article, "Remembering the Kwangju Uprising," *Socialism and Democracy* Vol. 14, No. 1 (Spring–Summer 2000). This article and more of my work is avaialble at www.eroseffect.com.

# Zapatismo and Global Struggle:

## "A Revolution to Make Revolution Possible."

# Manuel Callahan

June 27, 20031

*What I've heard as answers generally seem to respond to a particular model of academic inquiry that leaves out what I believe is central: how do you empower an oppressed and impoverished people who are struggling against racism, militarism, terrorism and sexism too? I mean, how do you do that? That's the real question.*

—Kathleen Cleaver, 1999.[2]

*We Indian peoples have come in order to wind the clock and to thus ensure that the inclusive, tolerant, and plural tomorrow which is, incidentally, the only tomorrow possible will arrive. In order to do that, in order for our march to make the clock of humanity march, we Indian peoples have resorted to the art of reading what has not yet been written. Because that is the dream which animates us as indigenous, as Mexicans and, above all, as human beings. With our struggle, we are reading the future which has already been sown yesterday, which is being cultivated today, and which can only be reaped if one fights, if, that is, one dreams.*

—Subcomandante Marcos, 2001.[3]

Increasingly activists and intellectuals have begun to analyze the future possibilities of the radical democratic experiment that gained momentum with the coordinated festivals of resistance such as J18 and N30 of 1999. Yet, the astonishing success of what many describe as a globally networked resistance against neoliberalism has been confronted by a number of equally profound challenges. Many, for example, have begun to express doubt regarding the effectiveness of serial protests driven by the meeting schedules of the WTO, World Bank, and IMF. Still others have raised an important alarm regarding the bureaucratization of the movement, especially in the form of a well-funded NGO presence opportunistically attempting to proffer a "respectable face of dissent."[4] One of the most compelling challenges to the movement is producing a "space of non-militarized contestation," as Eddie Yuen clearly posits in the introduction to this volume.

In the course of this introspection many have acknowledged the impact the Ejército

Zapatista Liberación Nacional (EZLN) and their support base have on globalized struggle.[5] For some the Zapatista influence in the "many-headed street movement" was heard
in the *Ya Basta!* shouted in Seattle and echoed in the rumblings during the protests that
followed. In many respects the Zapatista uprising is the moment when the movement
against globalization found its global audience, and it is perhaps the place where the tactics of that movement began. The international mobilizations facilitated by Peoples'
Global Action (PGA) had a direct link to the Zapatistas. "PGA is an offshoot of the international Zapatista movement," explains Olivier de Marcellus, "founded in a meeting that
prolonged the Second Encuentro in southern Spain, and drawing a lot of its European
support from people who also support the Zapatistas."[6] In addition, the Independent
Media Center, a critical space for the movement to circulate struggle, also owes a debt to
the Zaps. "The Zapatistas," according to Jeff Perlstein, "provided a model for this mode of
operation: affirm local struggles while simultaneously inviting an exploration of larger networks of struggle."[7] While the role of the EZLN as catalysts for convergence has been critical, even Subcomandante Marcos has admitted, "the EZLN has reached a point where it
has been overtaken by Zapatismo."[8]

The EZLN shocked the world by presenting a guerrilla that did not seek state power.
Although the Zapatista refusal of state power has won the respect of an emergent movement, little has been said about their political practice on the ground. The political work
of the EZLN is all the more profound given that it has been carried out in the face of
extreme daily repression in the form of the low-intensity war conducted against the communities in rebellion throughout Chiapas. Zapatismo as a political practice has transformed the politics of refusal, the *Ya Basta!*, into *encuentro*, a politics of space and a politics of listening. It has been through the number of *encuentros* or gatherings that the EZLN
have convened and hosted since they declared *Ya Basta!* that they have had the most profound influence. "The audacity of the Zapatistas," the Midnight Notes Collective reminds
us, "was to open a clearing in the forest heavily patrolled by the Mexican Army and to
allow others to come to speak to each other about capitalism and revolution."[9]

The Zapatistas are only one of a number of important struggles in Chiapas, southern Mexico more generally, and the nation as a whole. The Zapatistas are equally indebt-
ed to the "revolutionary prefiguration" discussed throughout this volume. The Zapatistas
are not unique in their claims or commitment to such political practices as consensus or
radical democracy. Nor were the Zapatatistas the first to protest the negative impact of
neoliberal structural adjustments or unique in making the struggle more militant. The
Zapatistas have never claimed any special or unique role for themselves in the "movement." On the contrary, the Zapatistas have consistently called for civil society to organize
itself and resist in its own locale in its own way. Refusing to dictate or direct the movement

they have sought to pose questions, to open a space for encounter. They have been consistent in keeping with what they have argued is the task of an armed movement: to "present the problem, and then step aside."[10] It is crucial that Zapatismo and some of its most profound statements, e.g. "lead by obeying," "never again a world without us," and "one world where many worlds fit," be understood as something more than slogans. Zapatismo may be an "intuition," as Subcomandante Marcos suggests, but it also contributes new theory. Thus, we are not only interested in how Zapatismo is generated, but also in how it is deployed.

The Zapatista struggle has produced new theoretical frameworks for political analysis, practices, and objectives. Subcomandante Marcos recently made the Zapatista contribution explicit when he explained their "effort at *encuentro*." "It is not," he argues, "an attempt to establish political and programmatic agreements, nor to attempt a new version of the International. Nor does it have to do with unifying theoretical concepts or standardizing conceptions, but with finding, and or building, common points of discussion. Something like constructing theoretical and practical images which are seen and experienced from different places."[11] The "tendencies" of Zapatismo do not suggest a set political program or ideological dogma, but rather these statements continue to take on added meaning as the Zapatista struggle, in particular, and the antiglobalization movement, more generally, unfolds.

The Zapatista model of *encuentro* does not rely on ideology, organizational affiliation, or even identity. *Encuentro* is not a political rally, radical academic conference, or activist forum, struggling to claim for itself activist market share. Rather, it is a political space convened for dialogue, analysis, and direct action that deliberately and creatively acknowledges and respects difference, i.e., different political proposals and cultural practices that emerge from a variety of subject positions, histories, and political commitments. The model of *encuentro—as strategy, process, space, gathering, event*—depends on the mutual recognition of the dignity of the participants in order to collectively imagine new horizons. While affirming local struggles and at the same moment animating larger networks of struggle against neoliberalism, *enceuntro* as a radical template for "circulating struggle" creates a political opening that makes it possible to bridge the gap between the "first" and "third" worlds without implying either a radical or liberal tutelage. The Zapatista provocation challenges the movement to collectively protect the space of encounter as a "commons of wealth not yet lost."[12]

Beginning on August 8, 1994, the EZLN convened the National Democratic Convention (CND) to build "a new political relationship . . . based not in the confrontation of political organizations among themselves, but in the confrontation of their political proposals with different social classes." In the proposal for the CND the Zapatistas demonstrated their resolve to struggle for "free and democratic space for political struggle."[13] To provide a space for that encounter the Zapatistas constructed Aguascalientes, invoking the 1914 meeting when revolutionary leaders also sought a peaceful transition through dialogue. It was, Subcomandante Marcos declared:

> no more no less than a celebration of a fear broken, of the first teetering step towards the possibility of offering the nation a ya basta that not only has an indigenous and campesino voice, a ya basta that adds, that multiplies, that reproduces, that triumphs, that can be the celebration of discovery: that of knowing ourselves, not now with a vocation for defeat, but of thinking that we have the possibility of victory on our side.[14]

In August 1995 the Zapatistas responded to the government's intransigence and duplicity by proposing the Consulta Nacional e Internacional in which 1.2 million Mexicans and more than one hundred thousand international supporters participated. In December 1995, the Zapatistas began the construction of additional Aguascalientes (La Realidad, Oventic, La Garrucha, Roberto Barrios, Morelia) as new sites for the expanding dialogue between civil society and the EZLN to take place, the original site having been maliciously destroyed during the Mexican military's February 1995 offensive. A month later the EZLN convened the National Indigenous Forum, later to become a more formal and federally recognized body as the National Indigenous Congress (NIC), in October 1996.

The most notable and profound encounter began with the "First Declaration of La Realidad" in January 1996. The Zapatistas initiated a series of gatherings that would further a worldwide movement of resistance to neoliberalism. The convening of the First Continental Encounter for Humanity and Against Neoliberalism in April 1996 paralleled similar gatherings in Europe and other parts of the world, examining the economic, political, social, and cultural aspects of "how one lives under neoliberalism, how one resists, how one struggles and proposals of struggle against it and for humanity."[15] Immediately following the continental gatherings, over three thousand grassroots activists and intellectuals from forty-two countries arrived at La Realidad in July 1996 for the First Intercontinental Gathering For Humanity and Against Neoliberalism. In his closing statement Subcomandante Marcos asked, "who can say in what precise locale, and at what exact hour and date this intercontinental encounter for humanity and against neoliberalism began?" To which he answered, "We don't know. But we do know who initiated it. All the rebels around the world started it. Here, we are only a small part of those rebels, it's true. But to all the diverse fences that all the rebels of the world break every day, you have added one more rupture, that of the fence around the Zapatista reality." A second intercontinental *encuentro*, with the theme of "one world where many worlds fit," was organized by a sophisticated and well-linked network of Zapatista supporters and activists and held throughout Spain in August 1997.

On February 25, 2001, twenty-three *comandantes* and Subcomandante Marcos began the March for Indigenous Dignity, passing through twelve states and arriving in Mexico City to a crowd of over two-hundred-fifty on March 11. The March for Indigenous Dignity was yet another strategic direct action that kept the Zapatistas and the indigenous struggle for autonomy on the nation's political agenda, much like the march of 1,111 Zapatistas to Mexico City in September 1997. Prior to the march, the Zapatistas insisted that negotiations with the Mexican government could not resume unless President Vicente Fox freed all Zapatista political prisoners, dismantled 7 of the 259 military installations in the conflict zone, and implemented the San Andrés Peace Accords. The EZLN's trek to the nation's capital established an important forum to make transparent the extent of the president's political will to pursue peace, control the military, and influence Congress. It was a nothing less than a rolling *encuentro*.

This brief overview of some of the most notable events the Zapatistas initiated illustrates their consistent effort to construct political spaces for dialogue between a guerrilla and an increasingly organized civil society. This overview by no means represents fully the framework, contradictions, and successes of the space they have convened, omitting, for example, the number of organizational and institutional links that sustain the encounter. Here we would note, for example, the EZLN's strategic use of advisors as well as the development of such political formations as the Frente Zapatista Liberacion Nacional and Enlace Civil. In the *encuentros, consultas,* and *marchas* that opened vital political spaces, Mexican and international civil society could remain in solidarity while at the same moment engage in a dialogue with the Zapatistas. More importantly, civil society increasingly engaged in an emerging dialogue with itself. "Our blood and our word," the Zapatistas declared, "have lit a small fire in the mountain and we walk a path against the house of money and the powerful. Brothers and sisters of other races and languages, of other colors, but with the same heart now protect our light and in it they drink of the same fire."[16]

Beyond their own community the Zapatistas have not organized, rather they have convened with a profound moral authority. The combined success of the Aguascalientes that host a persistent flow of collaborative projects, delegations and visitors are equally noteworthy in this context. The "zapatours"—groups, delegations, and organizations traveling to Chiapas in caravans, serving as human rights activists, or living in the communities as peace observers—provide not only aid, support, and increased visibility for the Zapatista struggle, but serve as important opportunities to witness the commitment and practice of Zapatismo. Activists and intellectuals who observe the struggle of the base communities experience firsthand a rebel community resisting a military siege and low-intensity war through dialogue, consensus, and direct action. Most travelers return to their communities profoundly inspired to intensify their solidarity efforts and embrace strategies that emphasize dialogue and consensus.

A new concept of solidarity inspired by the Zapatistas, "respect for local autonomy and differing motivations for struggle," exposes the limits of solidarity activism.[17] Zapatismo reveals the limits of building a movement based only on a single issue, raising resources and aid through a single campaign, and producing networks based on short-lived and fragile coalitions. Often traditional solidarity projects define, represent, and speak for the struggle(s) of others, insisting on the progress of those being aided. An uncritical solidarity effort can lead to the unfortunate facilitation of development projects resulting in a new form of imperialism. Moreover, professional well-funded NGOs "can become shadow bureaucracies parallel to Southern Nation State administrations."[18]

Ultimately, a bureaucratic model of social change without a respect for social relations is not able to prioritize and facilitate the transformation of those providing the aid. *Encuentro* as a model of political work presupposes individual and collective transformation that results from dialogue. A space that allows for the possibility of individual and collective transformation into a community with purpose—"One No, Many Yeses!"[19] David Graeber persuasively argues that the movement, heavily influenced by anarchism, has been able to respond to the inspiration of the Zapatistas and other struggles from the global South as it seeks to "invent what many call 'a new language' of civil disobedience, combining elements of street theatre, festival and what can only be non-violent warfare."[20] The Zapatistas, serving as a link between traditional solidarity strategies and more radical alternatives, provide an important example of the possibilities of an unarmed guerrilla operating in sites of privilege, a resistance that makes direct action and disciplined formations central elements of their political practice without abandoning dialogue.

The bridge that has been established is manifest in a new international, not an international based on rigid party doctrines or dogmas of competing organizations but "an international of hope." The new international is defined by dignity, "that nation without nationality, that rainbow that is also a bridge, that murmur of the heart no matter what blood lives it, that rebel irreverence that mocks borders, customs and wars."[21] Essential is the recognition of diversity, resisting the homogenization that results, as Subcomandante Marcos suggests, from the competing hegemonies of the twentieth century.[22] "Instead of a new bureaucratic apparatus, for the world coordination of a political movement expressing universal ideals and proposals," Gustavo Esteva explains, "the International of Hope was created: a web constituted by innumerable differentiated autonomies, without a center or hierarchies, within which the most varied coalitions of discontents can express themselves, to dismantle forces and regimes oppressing all of them."[23]

1 The author would like to thank Eddie Yuen, Ramor Ryan, Jim Davis, and Vik Bahl for their suggestions on earlier drafts.

2 Kathleen Cleaver, "Women, Power, and Revolution," *New Political Science* 21:2 (1999): 233.

3 Speech given at the "Paths of Dignity: Indigenous Rights, Memory and Cultural Heritage" intercultural meeting, Mexico City, March 12, 2001.

4 Jim Davis, "This Is What Bureaucracy Looks Like," in Eddie Yuen, Daniel Burton Rose, George Katsiaficas, eds., *The Battle of Seattle: The New Challenge to Capitalist Globalization* (New York: Soft Skull Press, 2001): 176.

5 For analytical purposes it is important to distinguish between the Zapatistas and Zapatismo. The EZLN is the army that serves the base communities. Zapatistas are comprised of the EZLN and their supporters from the base communities. Zapatismo is a political strategy claimed by those who share a set of political commitments and a political identity. Supporters beyond Chiapas include those who limit their activity to traditional solidarity strategies as well as those who link their local struggles to an expanding global network with a renewed sense of urgency and analytical coherence.

6 Olivier de Marcellus, "Peoples' Global Action: Dreaming Up An Old Ghost," in Midnight Notes collective, *Auroras of the Zapatistas: Local and Global Struggles of the Fourth World War* (New York: Autonomedia, 2001): 103.

7 Jeff Perlstein, "The Independent Media Center Movement: An Experiment in Media Democracy," *Media File* 20: 1 (January/February 2001), http://www.media-alliance.org/mediafile/20-1/perlstein.html.

8 Subcomandante Marcos, "The Punch Card and the Hour Glass," *New Left Review* 9 (May-June 2001): 70.

9 "The Hammer and . . . or the Sickle? From the Zapatista Uprising to the Battle of Seattle," in *Auroras of the Zapatistas,* 10.

10 Subcomandante Marcos, "La entrevista insólita," interview by Julio Scherer García, *Proceso* 1271 (11 Marzo 2001): 15.

11 Subcomandante Marcos, "The World: Seven Thoughts in May of 2003," *Rebeldia #7* (May 2003).

12 "The Hammer and . . . or the Sickle? From the Zapatista Uprising to the Battle of Seattle," in *Auroras of the Zapatistas,* 9.

13 "Second Declaration from the Lacandona," in EZLN, *Documentos y comunicados* (México, D.F.: Ediciones Era, 1994): 273.

14 "Marcos to Democratic National Convention," in EZLN, *Documentos y comunicados* (México,

D.F.: Ediciones Era, 1994): 307-08.

15 "First Declaration of La Realidad," in EZLN, *Documentos y comunicados 3* (México, D.F.: Ediciones Era, 1997): 126.

16 "Fourth Declaration of the Lacandon Jungle," in EZLN, *Documentos y comunicados 3* (México, D.F.: Ediciones Era, 1997): 80–1.

17 Brian Holmes, "Revenge of the Concept."

18 Davis, "This Is What Bureaucracy Looks Like."

19 This summation comes from Gustavo Esteva. For an insightful analysis of global resistance making use of the phrase, see "One No, Many Yeses," *Midnight Notes* 12 (December 1997).

20 David Graeber, "The New Anarchists," *New Left Review* 13 (January-February 2002): 61–73.

21 "First Declaration of La Realidad," in EZLN, *Documentos y comunicados 3* (México, D.F.: Ediciones Era, 1997): 126. For an exceptional discussion of dignity as a concept for social analysis in a capitalist context as the "struggle against subordination," and as such speaks to the social antagonism that constitutes how "human social practice is organized" linked to the Zapatista struggle, see John Holloway, "Dignity's Revolt," in John Holloway and Eloína Peláez, eds. *Zapatista! Reinventing Revolution in Mexico* (London: Pluto Press, 1998): 159–198.

22 Subcomandante Marcos, "La entrevista insólita," interview by Julio Scherer García, *Proceso* 1271 (11 Marzo 2001): 12–13.

23 Esteva, "People's Power," 162.

# Emily Abendroth

# Scaling the Heights to Seattle
# David Kubrin

The one thing we were denied in Seattle was a vision of what the downtown area must have looked like from above—intersection after intersection immobilized in a crazy-quilt pattern of different kinds of lockdowns, standing lines of arm-linked militants, giant inflatables, and other large structures that for one reason or another proved too difficult to move. The State owned the air space, having issued new regulations prior to November 30 reserving for itself the right to fly overhead and look down on us. No one from our media or theirs apparently thought to take an elevator to some central thirty-third floor to take a picture of the streets from above. Hence, no media images. So the glorious sight of a city under siege from the globalized forces of outrage during the Battle of Seattle was seen only by the spy satellites and various other agents of the State.

For a great many observers, of course, the obvious question was how all this had come to pass? What precedents, what processes, what essential pieces had to be in place to account for the fact that after boasting since at least 1970 that we were going to "stop business as usual," we actually did? How did we come to know what had to be done?

What follows is a prehistory of Seattle, looking at some of the principal themes and elements of the direct action and nonviolence that formed the core of the Seattle actions of November 30 and after. It reflects my experiences as an activist in the Bay Area for the past thirty years and what I was able to find out about campaigns and actions in other critical arenas over the past several decades. Given the brevity of my essay, I will necessarily focus almost exclusively on events and patterns in the United States.

Although 1960s activism was firmly rooted in both direct action and nonviolence, by the end of the decade a sharp fall-off of both could be seen. A recently developed movement dynamic of establishing an individual's or group's revolutionary credentials by continually raising the ante of militance was part of it, and so too the widespread feeling that purposely courting incarceration, in the circumstances of large numbers of activists being setup, entrapped, or assassinated, was perhaps not wise. This was especially true for black activists, even though nonviolent direct action had been responsible not only for the first of the lunch counter sit-ins at the beginning of the decade, but by the middle had created, in the Mississippi Freedom Summer, the first substantial fissure in the critical edifice of black belt racism. In Northern cities, too, by the late '60s the Black Panther Party—and Malcolm X earlier—were disparaging the notion that one should love one's racist oppressor.

Not least, large numbers of New Left activists turned to many older models of Leninist organizing, which made the traditional arguments advanced to justify civil disobedience appear naive. A professional revolutionary certainly did not hope, as Southwestern Georgia Student Nonviolent Coordinating Committee field workers in 1963 had, to establish a "beloved community," nor did the Ghandhian notion of breaking the law as a form of *sàtyagraha*, or truthforce, make much sense to cadre who, in most instances, were convinced that they had to keep any revolutionary affiliations hidden. Establishing in COINTELPRO a systematic way of targeting—and hopefully eliminating— left activists, the government in the late '60s and early '70s had reacted to the movement's mounting militance with ever-increasing use of court injunctions, stretching out of sentences, and sustained efforts to dry up the cultural ponds in which the would-be US insurgent guerrilla freely swam.

In the face of government repression and the splintering of the left, many activists in the early '70s turned to project-based organizing, reflecting the plethora of issues and oppositions the early black liberation and antiwar movements had inspired in their wake: women's liberation, Native American and Latino liberation, free health clinics and food co-ops/conspiracies, prison support collectives and printing coops, gay liberation and legal collectives, back-to-the-land communes and anti-rape projects. As the movement began to lay down the infrastructure of resistance, if not revolution, less energy seemed available for direct action or jail time.

Despite these many obstacles, centers from which a politic of civil disobedience and direct action radiated had existed from the 1940s on, especially among veterans of the World War II conscientious-objector camps and in parts of the movement based on forms of religion or spiritual beliefs. Through the American Friends Service Committee (AFSC), Quakers maintained their tradition of radical pacifism, in, for example, their sailing a small ship, the Golden Rule, into the Pacific nuclear test site in 1958. Catholic Workers similarly engaged in defiant actions to disrupt public air-raid drills in New York City in the mid-'50s. Other groups doing radical direct action in the '50s included the Committee for Nonviolent Action, the Fellowship of Reconciliation (which for two years held vigils at Fort Detrick, where the US perfected chemical, biological, and radiation weapons and warfare), and the anarchist-inspired War Resisters' League.

Movement for a New Society (MNS), an organization with roots in Quaker activism, arose in the turmoil of the '60s and emphasized the central role of consensus decision making and nonviolence in direct action. MNS was to play particularly significant roles in the early organizing efforts around nuclear power and weapons in the mid and late '70s.

A strong tradition of direct action was evident among Native American and Latino activists in the late '60s. Early American Indian struggles around issues of sovereignty and land, such as the Long Walk, the occupation of Alcatraz in 1969, and support work for Big Mountain, must have particularly alerted government officials to very deep strategic implications, for during the 1973 occupation of Wounded Knee, the federal government quickly demonstrated their eagerness to respond to such challenges with a military siege. Though not perhaps expressed in the language of consensus politics, there was a tendency in these struggles to pay close attention to how the issues were framed not just by the militants, but by elders or women in the community. In New Mexico, important land struggles and protests in relation to uranium mining involved establishing road blocks, among other tactics; here, too, self-defense against armed attacks was found necessary.

Reliance on direct actions, such as boycotts, vigils, and fasting as mobilizing techniques, and on the principles of nonviolence was instrumental in the successful organizing of migrant workers by the United Farm Workers in the late '60s and early '70s. From early on the struggle for justice and organizing among the farmworkers involved the larger community and frequently featured agitation by radical theater performances; it also built on a long tradition in that community of pilgrimages and processions. For both Native American and Latino struggles, protests often began with ceremonies or prayers.

In urban areas, housing struggles erupted in squats and occupations in the mid-'70s and early '80s. In San Francisco, many hundreds of activists from the Asian community and other organizations across the city mobilized on numerous occasions to show support for the elderly, mostly Filipino tenants of the International Hotel when its owners threatened to raze it; they put in place a plan to establish a (symbolic) human barrier against the sheriff when the expected eviction actually occurred. Militant struggles around public housing in Boston resulted in the establishment of a tent city.

Some of the actual political and ideological trends, and a great deal of the spirit that was so central in Seattle, were already manifesting themselves in the antinuclear campaigns that emerged in the mid and late '70s. A big push to bring online or begin actual construction of a wave of new nuclear power facilities across the country caused some of the scattered embers of long-standing local opposition to flare up. In 1976 a handful of local activists in New Hampshire, impressed by the occupation of a nuclear construction site in Germany by opponents and inspired by '60s civil rights direct actions, cut the fence surrounding the future site of the Seabrook nuclear facility, entering and climbing a construction crane. Moved by their civil disobedience, a couple of thousand protesters converged a year later for a Clamshell Alliance–sponsored sit-in at the Seabrook site. Participants at Seabrook were organized by affinity groups and had received training in nonviolence before the sit-in. About fourteen hundred of them were arrested by the New Hampshire police.

As the Seabrook opposition rapidly grew, a serious conflict arose, some activists proposing to turn towards large legal rallies as a way of demonstrating the breadth of opposition to the facility, while others argued that abandoning direct action at that point would be a critical mistake. This latter group, which eventually would become the Coalition for Direct Action at Seabrook(CDAS), demanded that civil disobedience continue as the focus of their opposition. They called for massive civil disobedience for the fall of '79, and over six thousand people arrived, prepared to assault the fences around the Seabrook site. Many beatings, gassings, macings, and assaults with high pressure water hoses, along with attack dogs held at the ready by State Police, however, kept activists at a standoff.

In the face of such State repression, the CDAS was persuaded that complete autonomy of affinity groups could not always work. Coordinating committees and decision making by an eighty-percent (by 1980, this was down to seventy percent) "consensus" were introduced for actions. Even so, neither the CDAS nor the larger original Clamshell Alliance were able to sustain the high numbers and determination of the earlier actions. Some of those originally mobilized around Seabrook, on the other hand, broadened their aim, a number of them shifting to the related issue of nuclear weapons, now seen as bigger, more global dangers. They went on to organize direct actions at the Pentagon. Still other veterans of Seabrook organized mass civil disobedience on Wall Street, targeting banking, energy, and manufacturing firms, the real beneficiaries of nuclear power.

Around the same time as the mobilizations at Seabrook, a parallel antinuclear movement was sprouting up in the Midwest. As if the nightmare visions of mushroom clouds in our skies evoked a metaphorical mushrooming of resistance, opposition sprang up in scattered locations, notably in the mountainous terrain around Denver. As in New Hampshire, some of the early opposition to the Rocky Flats nuclear facility, where plutonium triggers for US thermonuclear warheads were produced, was led by longtime nonviolent activists and veterans of the '60s protests against racism and the Indochinese War. Over several years, '60s activists and some Vietnam veterans organized local opposition to the facility. Early in 1978, a mass rally was scheduled at Rocky Flats, which was to end in symbolic direct action and arrests. When authorities made no arrests, a spontaneous move to establish a long-term occupation of the railroad tracks leading to the plutonium facility drew wide support. It was only after a week of continuous presence that police began arresting the occupiers, but their places were taken by others. Support from the Denver area, at least initially, was strong. As at Seabrook, those intent on building a broad-based movement, particularly among the Rocky Flats workforce, were opposed to the occupation; this pitted the AFSC and Mobilization for Survival, which had both done some of the initial organizing against the Rocky Flats facility, against the Rocky Flats Truth Force. Nonetheless, a continuous presence on the tracks, punctuated by periodic arrests and temporary removals by periods of particularly foul weather, continued for a number of years.

On the West Coast, several other nuclear sites became staging grounds for direct actions, sometimes with the groups sponsoring protests at one site emerging out of prior actions at another nuclear facility, as was the case with the Livermore Action Group(LAG), which mobilized activists against the lab where nuclear weapons are designed. Initially it was among those jailed after an action at Diablo Canyon Nuclear Power Facility that LAG began.

Though there were differences in the actions at Diablo Canyon (led by the Abalone Alliance), Vandenberg Air Force Base (Vandenberg Action Group), Livermore National Laboratory (LAG), and the Nevada Test Site (American Peace Test), the similarities were more striking. As at Seabrook and Rocky Flats, protests were organized around affinity groups, participants were required to take nonviolence training prior to the action, and action handbooks were issued describing the politics, history, logistics, legal matters, first aid, etc., of the upcoming action. A strong commitment to decision making by consensus persisted, unlike at Seabrook, where it unraveled as activists were unable to resolve the serious political differences between advocates of moderate forms of protest and those insisting on continued civil disobedience. Though tensions over these differences continued, for the most part they were not as divisive as they had been at Seabrook.

In 1983, a blockade of the Livermore Lab by several thousand protesters on Summer Solstice ended with over a thousand activists under arrest. Prior to the action, activists had debated a strategy of "jail solidarity" as a way of demanding equal treatment of all those arrested. Thus, most of the one thousand arrestees refused for two weeks to go to their arraignments until the court finally agreed, with great reluctance, to sentences that were equal for all (first, second, or multiple offenders alike) and did not include probation.

Here, however, a characteristic dynamic emerged. In the face of this tremendous political victory, the Bay Area antinuclear movement was plagued by strategic confusion, unclear where its priority should now be, whether to plunge ahead or shift to a new route. By then, however, the Reagan administration had pushed other matters to the fore. The heating up of the cold war by the rhetorical and strategic posturing of President Reagan refocused much of the energy of activists against his counterrevolutionary policies in El Salvador, Nicaragua, Hondurus, and Grenada. The liberation theology that was such a potent weapon in the Latin American liberation movements inspired many US Christian activists to take very active roles in the solidarity actions in support of the Salvadoran and Nicaraguan uprisings and in the establishment of sanctuaries for those fighting deportation from the US back to homelands where their lives were in danger. Witness for Peace worked among Nicaraguan villages as a form of protection for them and to bear witness against US policies. The Pledge of Resistance in 1984 solicited public commitments to engage in civil disobedience should US troops invade Nicaragua. Even earlier, Catholic militants had begun "Plowshare" actions involving the destruction of military weapons and lengthy periods of imprisonment, and Christian activists had been responsible for direct actions aimed at the nuclear submarines, missiles, and other forward weapons of nuclear war.

In the mid-'80s labor militants, students, and black activists engaged in a variety of direct actions, including the building of shanty towns on university campuses to call attention to their institutions' support of apartheid in their investment policies, so as to isolate and economically and politically cripple the South African apartheid regime. The same fight was taken up by communities that pressed public institutions to divest.

The war of aggression against Iraq by US and allied forces in the early '90s evoked a storm of opposition in the first phases of the Gulf War, including, in California, huge marches and rallies and many instances of activists blocking bridges and interstate thoroughfares. One Bay Area anarchist group blocked downtown streets on several occasions with funereal processions consisting of activists dragging "dead" automotive parts.

Certain strategic bridges also were erected. A critical gap was crossed when Greenpeace and others began emphasizing the vital import of environmental justice issues. Another was the opportunity that the fights against NAFTA, GATT, and MAI offered to establish vital connections between environmental groups, NGOs, and trade unionists.

Activists had begun experimenting with reshaping protests into forms of processions, incorporating pageant, dance, costumes, and types of theater, building on traditions begun in the '60s by Bread and Puppet Theater, El Theatro Campesino, and the San Francisco Mime Troupe. A San Francisco Three Mile Island Memorial March in 1980 ended with a tug-of-war between marchers representing Air, Water, Fire, and Earth elements, pulling apart a cooling tower nuclear float that had been the focus of an ongoing skit during the procession, depicting a nuclear facility undergoing a meltdown. A couple of years later, an anarchist "Hall of Shame" tour of the San Francisco headquarters of the corporate benefactors of nuclear weapons and power sent small roving groups from corporate site to corporate site during lunch hour for simultaneous teach-ins, where indictments, theater, or corporate histories were presented. Incantations, spells, and other forms of magical power raising were woven into many of these actions by the increasing numbers of self-identified pagan and witch activists, similarly at Diablo Canyon, Vandenberg, and Livermore; at the women's actions at the Pentagon in 1980 and '81; and at the Seneca Women's Peace Camp in 1983. Comparable approaches were used by activists as part of the 1984 protests at the Democratic Party national convention in San Francisco.

In the course of these varied actions, the movement was to change its scope and its vision, as if all the mushrooms and LSD consumed by many activists in the '60s and later were now having a delayed effect, leading militants to branch out, and eventually up, taking protest to new levels and domains and giving it wholly unpredictable shapes and textures. As early as the Diablo blockade, a Peace Navy was afloat so that the blockade might truly encircle the site. As with the Sea Shepherds, Greenpeace, and others, the boats blockaded ports and sealanes to nuclear transport or later, whaling expeditions.

It was perhaps in taking to the skies that the direct action movement was able to transcend former ideological constraints and overcome earlier limitations. Earth First!'s defense of ancient trees brought many activists up into the branches, and from that perspective it was a simple step to begin hanging the giant banners bearing slogans and images from the trees and bridges, skyscrapers, dams, or cranes, reclaiming the use of the "airways" accessible to those without capital. Greenpeace, Rainforest Action Network, and then the Ruckus Society perfected the tactics of a "Peace Airborne," considered somewhat of an elite division as in the US Armed Forces. Greenpeace also experimented with variations of lockdown devices that could enable a few determined activists to immobilize strategic locations for hours at a time.

The build-up to the Gulf War also brought giant puppets into play on a more prominent scale, embodying phantasmagorical images of the oppressors and their puppets and depicting the multifaceted forces increasingly arrayed against them, thus able to project the many-sided opposition to global capital large against the sky and powerful in our imaginations. Building on traditions, techniques, and images from Bread and Puppets and the Women's Actions at the Pentagon, the giant puppets presented allegorical motifs in outrageous imagery and helped provide the flavor of a street festival, bringing out activists' senses of play and fantasy and turning the new mobilizations into spontaneous theaters of resistance. Prior to the 1996 Democratic Party convention in Chicago, a weekend workshop to train activists in puppet making and related aspects of street protests was given by Wise Fool Puppet Intervention and other organizers and led to the formation of the first of the Art and Revolution Convergences.

Had she been alive, Emma Goldman could easily have danced at these kinds of actions.

In the final analysis, however, we have capital itself to thank for our successes. Since the splintering of the left in the late '60s, legions of organizers have been relentlessly preaching that salvation was ours if only we could achieve unity. Though coalitions were assembled on numerous occasions, often the groups entered into agreements with others not much deeper than the willingness to share a common sound system and some of the flyers advertising the event on issue. Capital, however, was able to force us to overcome many previous hurdles.

Everywhere, "the market" trumpeted its victories—over communism, over history, and, with biotech, over life itself. In a word, capital overreached itself. Its triumphant claim to have now integrated every activity in the most remote villages into the overall global marketplace revealed a critical weakness: highly integrated structures are not only highly intrusive, but also extremely vulnerable. Perturbations that might readily be absorbed in a more flexible structure can readily result in system-threatening crises in rigid ones, so that the collapse of the Thai economy can bring chaos to the markets of Brazil and Mexico and threaten havoc even in the economies of the rich, industrialized countries. The unprecedented extent of capital's present reach has stretched thin the fabric of mystification that in normal times has been used to hide the realities of capitalism—stretched it to the point of transparency. Globalization has revealed not only the global aspirations of capital, but its inexorable drive to transform all things, all processes, and all relationships into commodities. In so doing, it created for us the material conditions for our coming together in a spectacular orgy of global opposition.

*My thanks to Jim Haber, Marian Daub, Bob Thawley, Steve Nadel, David Creighton, Starhawk, K. Ruby, Kelly Quirke, Mishwa Lee, and Iain Boal for many fruitful and provocative conversations.*

# Part II: Crashing the Summits

# World Trashed Organization!

## Festivals and Riots Against the G8 and the WTO

# SchNEWS

May 1998
Revised by editors for clarity.

### Birmingham, UK

People dance in a ten-thousand-strong street party in front of a canary yellow army of con-scripted police. Tripods tower against the Birmingham skyline. Only blocks away, inside the secure walls of Birmingham's G8 conference hall, Clinton, Blair and the global sum-mit team are dancing away to "All you need is love."

### Geneva, Switzerland

By Monday the G8 globalization tour has moved to the Palais des Nations in Geneva for World Trade Day. On the street, hundreds of protesters are being arrested, beaten, and deported by the Genevan authorities.

For four days this small city is under siege as the leaders of the 132-nation World Trade Organisation meet at the United Nations building. Clinton, Blair, Castro, Mandela, and other attendees leave the city in shock after the worst riots here since 1932. The opposition is led by Peoples' Global Action (PGA).

The city erupts before the ministers even step off their planes. Five thousand peo-ple come to Saturday's Street Party: by midnight it's a full scale riot. One car is set alight and thousands of police charge the main encampment of protesters, firing tear gas into the crowd. The demonstrators smash hundreds of windows, mainly of banks and corporate offices, until 5 A.M. They cause over half a million pounds damage.

Genevans awake on Sunday to a city resembling a warzone. On pavement, phone boxes, and walls the graffiti message is clear: "WTO ASSASSIN." . . "WTO vs. THE PEO-PLE." . . "REVOLUTION '98." From the moment the world leaders sit down on Monday morning to the conclusion on Wednesday evening the streets are filled with riot police and demonstrators, with the constant noise of sirens and low-flying helicopters.

## May 18

The offices of Lockheed, a multinational arms trader, are occupied by one group while a spontaneous street demo stops traffic and sets off smoke bombs. By lunchtime the United Bank of Switzerland is forced to close and police keep back while road after road is blockaded by protesters. The group continues up to the UN building, which is surrounded by armed police. The crowd chants in French, Spanish, and English. By nightfall there's a highly charged stand-off as a party kicks off next to the university.

## May 19

Activists from Colombia, India, South Korea, Mexico, Nicaragua, Argentina, Aotearoa/New Zealand, and across Europe continue to network and organize direct action under the banner of PGA. In a deliberate display of nonviolence, hundreds march gagged and bound through town to call attention to the global muting of human rights that the WTO regime imposes. At a prominent statue of Rousseau they enact a burial of his "social contract" between people and their rulers. Meanwhile, the director of the WTO, Renatto Ruggiero, tells the conference that everyone must drive faster towards globalization, or face the danger of crashing. His Mercedes is later overturned.

As darkness descends, so do the people. A crowd of around five hundred, many "L'Hiphop" kids from nearby council estates, confront police at Plain Palais. Protestors systematically trash the nearby McDonald's and Pizza Hut. Police fire CS gas, so the angry mass smash more shops, overturn cars, and run through the city in diffuse groups. Plainclothes police on mopeds give chase to troublemakers. At 1 AM police surround Artamis, a huge squatted alternative center, and arrest everyone they can. Between Monday and Tuesday 287 are detained.

## May 20

Hundreds assemble outside the UN for a final push. They attempt to enter the building and stop the General Assembly. They walk, Gandhi-style, headlong into a line of riot police. There's a blur of truncheons and the ambulances begin to arrive. According to hospital staff over sixty people are treated that day, some for major injuries.

## May 23

The squatters organize a demonstration against police brutality and the inhumane treatment of those arrested (strip searches, medical neglect, and psychological abuse). The conference is over, and for now Geneva is quiet.

"This is without doubt a popular uprising against the issue of globalization," one activist told SchNEWS. "Not just in Geneva but in cities all over the world people are beginning to realize the consequences of this crazy process and the *importance of resisting by any means necessary.*"

# A Global Carnival of the Dispossessed
## Katherine Ainger

*Z Magazine*, September 1999

As G8 leaders met to shape the agenda for the global economy at the summit in Koln, Germany on June 18 this year, five thousand protesters carrying signs saying "We ate the G8" and "It's Stupid, the Economy" were turning London's financial district upside down in a Carnival Against Capital. Bankers and traders watched from behind tinted windows as protesters played volleyball with inflatable globes and danced to samba rhythms in the spray of a waterspout from a damaged fire hydrant.

The protest—the most dramatic London had seen in ten years—seemed to come out of nowhere. By the end of the day a group of the protesters had invaded and trashed the ground floor of the London International Financial Futures Exchange, three McDonald's had their windows broken, two people had been run over by police vans, and riot police were charging in. The sight of anarchy hitting the world's largest financial center prompted newspaper headlines that denounced the protesters as "evil savages," an ignorant "unwashed horde" hell-bent on turning a "carnival into a riot."

Many of the scenes were undoubtedly ugly. But in dismissing the protesters as an inarticulate British subculture, the media were missing the biggest story of the day. The carnival-goers in London—the majority of whom had been nonviolent in actions and intent—were members of a far larger, invisible but international constituency organizing around a common enemy: globalization. The events in London were only one of many during the June 18 "international day of action, protest and carnival aimed at the heart of the global economy," when simultaneous protests against global capitalism, the international financial system, and corporate power took place in forty-three countries around the world.

The response to globalization has resulted in some extraordinary new coalitions. For example, this summer four hundred Indian farmers invited by local antiglobalization activists went on a month-long protest tour around centers of power in Europe. The president of the All India Farmers Union, Vijay Jawandia, said, "Those in the North have to understand our struggle and to realize it is part of their own. Everywhere the rich are getting richer, the poor poorer, and the environment is being plundered. Whether in North or South, we all face the same future."

New communications technology such as the Internet and email has played an integral part in the process of economic globalization, but it has also fueled a parallel globalization of resistance. The idea for June 18 was proposed by British eco-activists Reclaim the Streets, who organize illegal street parties against car culture and capitalism. Circulated on international email lists and through the Internet, the proposal caught on and gathered momentum.

The June 18 events were as diverse as the groups taking part. In Barcelona "street reclaimers" invoked the slogan of the rebellious Paris students of 1968, "Sous les paves, la plage" ("Under the sidewalk, the beach") and, dressed in swimming costumes, put out towels and sunbathed on the road, handed out French fries to commuters in their cars, and later took part in a seven-hundred-strong street party. Music and dancing also hit the streets of San Francisco with "art attackers" who, armed with giant puppets and candy, lobbied those working for multinationals that exploit sweatshop workers to take the day off work and "join the revolution." In Melbourne, Australia, Kim Beazely, leader of the opposition, received a custard pie in the face for speaking at a global trade conference sponsored by Shell, while thousands of partygoers in Sydney held up traffic as a massive street festival got underway.

The National Alliance of People's Movements in India, a coalition of two hundred grassroots organizations, made a statement declaring they were taking part because so many in India have "been marginalized by the market economy and World Trade Organization policies," while in Pakistan union leaders risked their lives to come out of hiding to protest for "bread, not nuclear bombs."

Most dramatically, ten thousand people in Port Harcourt, Nigeria gathered to welcome Dr. Owens Wiwa, younger brother of the executed Ogoni activist Ken Saro-Wiwa, back from a four-year exile. The crowd, led by a coalition of indigenous activists, held a Carnival of the Oppressed against corporate imperialism and the military dictatorship, during which they unofficially renamed a main street Ken Saro-Wiwa Road and blockaded the Shell office headquarters. The singing and dancing in the streets brought the petroleum capital of Nigeria to a standstill for the day.

A "virtual sit-in" on behalf of the Zapatistas, prompted by a group called Electronic Civil Disobedience, led to thousands of hits "flooding" the website of the Mexican embassy in the UK. Meanwhile in Montevideo, Uruguay, protesters took part in a parade through the Stock Exchange and McDonald's, accompanied by a PVC jockey riding a giant Pollution Plastisaurus made of plastic rubbish, and ending with the ritual burning of a cardboard television as the "agent of consumer-culture." A diverse coalition of religious groups took to the streets in Brazil as part of the June 18 network to call for the cancellation of Third World debt.

Street protests of various kinds—many targeting corporate headquarters and stock exchanges—also took place in Tel Aviv, Minsk, Madrid, Valencia, Prague, Hamburg, Koln, Milan, Rome, Siena, Florence, Ancona, Amsterdam, Madrid, Glasgow, Edinburgh, Lancaster,

Zurich, Geneva, Toronto, Vancouver, Ottawa, Washington, New York, Los Angeles, Austin, Boston, and Eugene. The website for June 18, which streamed live video images from Australia and London, declared, "Our resistance is as transnational as capital."

These new coalitions have been building since 1996, when Mexican Zapatistas held an international *encuentro* in Spain. Social and environmental movements in the North and South met and were strengthened by their common rejection of their assigned role as the "expendable members of the global economy."

By February 1998 an international meeting in Geneva had attracted over four hundred people from seventy-one countries involved in grassroots activism, from Argentinean teachers hunger-striking against privatization to Canadian Postal Union workers to landless peasants in Brazil to Indian farmers to indigenous groups such as the U'wa to European antiroad protesters. Together they launched a loose network called Peoples' Global Action Against Free Trade and the World Trade Organization. They wrote, "Despite the huge material differences, struggles in privileged and under-privileged parts of the corporate empire have more and more in common, setting the stage for a new and stronger sort of solidarity . . . Scattered around the world again, we will not forget. We remain together. This is our common struggle."

The energy gained from that meeting was tremendous. A global street party took place in twenty different countries during the G8 summit in Birmingham in May last year. Two days later, eight thousand people erupted onto the streets of Geneva in an anti-World Trade Organization protest, fifty thousand Brazilians participated in a "Cry of the Excluded" march, and two hundred thousand Indian farmers and fisher folk took to the streets of Hyderabad demanding India's withdrawal from the WTO.

By September that year, John M. Weekes, chair of the General Council of the WTO, was pointing out that "trade is no longer seen as an arcane subject of no interest to the public," and the chair of Nestle, Helmut Maucher, was criticizing "single-issue" protest groups afflicted with "globaphobia."

The United States has so far not witnessed the kind of mass antiglobalization protests that have taken place in Europe and the Third World. But all eyes are now on the millennium meeting of the World Trade Organization in Seattle, November 30 to December 3. Pirellis Perissich stressed at the Geneva Business Dialogue last year that the next round of trade liberalization "is going to be very difficult—resistance will be bigger than before." One US trade official predicts that Seattle 1999 will be "like Chicago in 1968." As the agenda of free trade and liberalization comes into increasing conflict with realities of job insecurity, exploitation, unemployment, and social and environmental breakdown, more and more of the dispossessed will have little to lose in joining the insurgent carnival.

# The Globalization Of Resistance
## N30 International Day Of Action
# Mark Laskey

### N15

*Amsterdam, Netherlands:* Dutch activists from the Mayday Action Group occupy a replica of a seventeenth-century Dutch East India ship. They hang a giant banner reading "Stop the WTO" between the masts.

### N16

*Geneva, Switzerland:* The world headquarters of the WTO is occupied by twenty-seven people aided by three dozen supporters blocking traffic outside. One group chains themselves to the staircase that leads to Moore's office. They unfurl a banner that reads: "No Commerce, No Organization: Self-management!" Another group makes it to the roof and drops two huge banners. They read: "WTO kills people—Kill the WTO !" and "Moore aux tyrants!" (a pun meaning "Death to the Tyrants" and "Moore to the Tyrants "). One of the protesters beams pictures of the occupation directly onto the Internet from a portable installation. Another faxes a communiqué from WTO HQ. In the third hour of the occupation, police purge the building without making any arrests or recording people's identities.

### N22

*Ankara, Turkey:* From November 22–30 peasants, environmentalists, and trade unionists from the Working Group of Turkey Against the MAI and Globalization march over 2,000 miles in protest of the WTO and global capitalism.

### N24

*New Delhi, India:* More than 300 indigenous people from Madya Pradesh storm the World Bank building. They cover it with posters, graffiti, cow shit, and mud while they chant slogans and sing traditional songs. They leave the area only after the country director for the World Bank in India meets the demonstrators and receives an open letter signed by all their member organizations.

*Manila, Philippines:* Protesters against the Association of Southeast Asian Nations (ASEAN) gather outside the Philippine International Convention Center, where they're beaten by riot police and sprayed with a water cannon. ASEAN is holding its third informal summit and preparatory meeting.

## N27

*New York City:* A Buy Nothing Day demonstration is held against the WTO at 44th Street/Times Square. The protesters erect a two-story tripod, bringing traffic to a standstill and drawing a large crowd.

*Geneva, Switzerland:* Two large columns of demonstrators—2000 farmers and 3000 city dwellers—meet to march on WTO headquarters. The farmers are answering a call made by all of the Swiss farmers' associations (the Union des Producteurs Suisses, as well as the Union des Paysans Suisses and the Chambers of Agriculture). The city people were called out by a coordination against the Millennium Round. They gather in front of the United Nations building and in the heart of the banking district.

## N30
### United States

In solidarity with groups protesting WTO policies, over 9,000 workers from the International Longshore and Warehouse Union (ILWU) shut down ports from San Diego to nearly Canada. About three dozen ports take part in the twelve-hour work stoppage. It is estimated that almost half of US trade carried on ships goes through West Coast ports.

*Atlanta, GA:* A varied group of activists from the Rainforest Action Network, IWW, AIM, Food Not Bombs, Dogwood Alliance, and Earth First! gather in Woodruff Park in downtown to tell people what the WTO is all about. There are a couple of musicians and some disjointed chanting. Food Not Bombs serves a meal.

*Amherst, MA:* Over 100 demonstrators meet on the town common to protest the WTO. As a diverse group of speakers addresses the crowd, a theater troupe, dressed in business suits, marches solemnly around the assembly carrying a huge chained globe. At the end of the demonstration, protestors huddle around a phone to hear an Amherst resident in Seattle describe the day's events. When they learn of the success of their co-protesters, they erupt in cheers of joy.

*Austin, TX:* In a demonstration organized by the ad hoc Just Say No To WTO Coalition!, over 500 antiglobalization activists gather at Republic Square and march through downtown. Art & Revolution carry a giant WTO/octopus puppet, the radical cheerleaders entertain the crowd with some anticorporate cheers, and a Critical Mass bicycle ride (accompanied by a number of hostile police on motorcycles) blocks intersection after intersection during the rush-hour commute.

*Baltimore, MD:* A demonstration starts around 4:30 P.M., but doesn't pick up speed until after 5 P.M., when Critical Mass and a black bloc join, bringing the number of participants to around 125.

*Louisville, KY:* In protest of "increasing poverty and cuts in social services, low wages, sweatshops, meaningless jobs, more prisons, deforestation, gridlocked cities, global warming, genetic engineering, gentrification, and war," a number of anti-WTO activists meet in Jefferson Square Park for a day of celebration and resistance.

*Montpelier, VT:* More than three dozen activists from Bread and Puppet, Vermont Anarchist Black Cross, Institute for Social Ecology, and the Vermont Livable Wage Campaign assemble in front of the court house in solidarity with the people of the world protesting the global capitalist free market. Demonstrators perform street theater, hold signs, march, and hand out literature to passersby.

*Morgantown, WV:* Over two dozen people from the Morgantown Anarchist Group, West Virginia branch of the Sierra Club, and others gather in front of the West Virginia University student union in protest against the WTO. People chant, hand out leaflets, juggle, and carry signs attacking the WTO.

*Nashville, TN:* About forty-five protesters gather in front of Al Gore's presidential campaign headquarters. At one point, protesters enter the reception area and serenade some bemused members of Gore's campaign staff with "No, no, no WTO . . . "

*Philadelphia, PA:* One hundred and fifty activists rally outside the Banana Republic Superstore. When the weather gets too cold, they go inside the store and hold their news conference. Stunned Banana Republic workers and Philly police look on.

*Santa Cruz, CA:* About one hundred people gather at the town Clock Tower, a traditional spot for protests, to voice their opposition to the WTO. It is well covered by the local press.

*Washington, DC:* One hundred or so protestors turn out at Lafayette Park, and again at the USIA Building, to express solidarity with the Seattle protesters and their displeasure with corporate greed and the FDA's inaction with regard to genetically engineered foods.

## Canada

*Edmonton, Alberta:* About one hundred people hold a demonstration outside Canada Place in downtown Edmonton over the noon hour. The demonstration is sponsored by the People's Action Network.

*Halifax, Nova Scotia:* A Citizen's Tour of the downtown area is very successful. Protesters chant anti-WTO slogans, distribute pamphlets, and perform street theatre (including an appearance by WTO-man!). There is decent media turnout.

*Ottawa, Ontario:* One-hundred-twenty to one-hundred-fifty people gather around the Eternal Flame on Parliament Hill. Good music, lively banners and interested media make the event a success.

*Peterborough, Ontario:* Approximately 150 people attend the the Anti-WTO Discussion Night.

*Toronto, Ontario:* In solidarity with the Seattle protesters, several hundred protesters march through the streets of Toronto's financial district. They tour downtown, stopping at a number of corporations who gave financial support to the Seattle host committee for the WTO. Earlier in the month, on November 4, anti–free trade "goblins" disrupted a negotiating meeting of the Free Trade Area of the Americas in Toronto. They loosed stink bombs made from shit and rotten eggs.

*Winnipeg, Manitoba:* Over 300 people rally against the WTO at the intersection of Portage and Main. They shut down Portage Avenue during rush hour and march to the University of Winnipeg. The action is organized by the Manitoba Coalition Against the World Trade Organization, which has also organized a month of panel discussions on the WTO. Organizations mobilizing for the rally include: CUPE Manitoba, Canadian Auto Workers, Postal Workers, Food Not Bombs, the Greens, Industrial Workers of the World, Canadian Association of the Non-Employed, and the Manitoba Young New Democrats.

## Iceland

*Reykjavik:* Anti-American protesters target a US military base and the embassy. They demand "Yanks Out" (a promise the US has left unkept since WW2).

## England

*Halifax:* A Nestle factory is occupied and a banner is dropped outside. Sixteen are arrested.

*Leeds:* In the city center around fifty protestors face over three hundred cops. The protesters mill around and hand out leaflets outside of scummy companies.

*London:* Over 2,000 people gather at Euston Station to support striking public transportation workers and to highlight the links between the free trade agenda of the WTO and the privatization of public transport in the UK. The rally becomes more militant when about 500 people try to block a main traffic artery. They are pushed back by lines of riot police using tear gas. Some protesters fight back, using bottles and stones. They overturn a police van and set it on fire, then scatter and spread throughout the city. Occasional skirmishes continue. Thirty-eight people are arrested; both protesters and police report injuries.

*Manchester:* Lloyds Bank on Cross Street is occupied and shut down by about fifty activists, who then proceed to block the street outside.

*South Devon:* A disused garage and an old Toll House slated to be turned into "luxury flats" are squatted in Totnes to draw local people's attention to the WTO.

## Ireland

*Limerick:* Twenty people hold a festive protest in the center of the city outside of a McDonald's, a HMV, a Burger King and a Penny's.

## Wales

*Bangor:* Over forty people attend a demonstration. There is good press coverage.

*Cardiff:* An anti-WTO procession marches through the center of town.

## Portugal

*Lisbon:* Nearly 300 people with giant puppets march through the streets and block traffic. During different stops there is fire breathing and street theatre. The city Christmas tree and a McDonald's are covered in graffiti.

## France

*Dijon:* Over forty people chain themselves to the doors of the Chamber of Commerce and occupy the Industry and Business Institute. Activists wearing shirts reading "Enslaved By Money?" use U-locks and arm-tubes to block the entrances of the two buildings. Others throw fake blood and money on the pavement. They also glue posters on walls and shops, display banners, play drums, scream, and give out free tea and coffee as well as flyers about capitalism, anarchism, and alternative culture.

*Paris:* Over 20,000 people march through the streets denouncing the WTO. In two Parisian suburbs, 800 miners clash with police, ransack a tax office, and burn a number of cars. Five days earlier, 5,000 French farmers with their sheep, ducks and goats feast on regional products under the Eiffel tower in protest of the impact of trade liberalization enforced by the WTO.

*Toulouse:* Protesters invade the town's commercial district with a large sound system. They hang large anti-WTO signs on street lights. anticapitalist Father Christmases give rotten fruit—the fruit of capitalism—to passersby.

## Switzerland

*Geneva:* The WTO's world headquarters are again the target of direct action. In a pre-dawn move, saboteurs trigger an explosion in a small power supply building. They damage electrical transformers and wipe out HQ's computer links to the ministerial meeting in Seattle. For over two hours the WTO is entirely without power; computer servers are down for most of the morning. The Swiss news agency ATS reports that it has received a statement claiming responsibility for the act from a group calling itself "Green Apple."

## Netherlands

*Amsterdam:* Over 100 activists unfurl banners in the departure hall of Amsterdam's Schipol Airport, targeting official WTO sponsors Lufthansa, Northwest Airways, and United Airlines. The demonstrators hold a sit-in, demanding free flights to Seattle from the offending airlines. They maintain the sit-in for several hours, accompanied by dozens of press people and the police.

## Germany

*Berlin:* A satirical march is held, raising banners calling for more order, more security, and more police. Riot police, formed in lines in front of borgeoisie restaurants and shops, exude confusion, as if they are wondering why demonstrators aren't attacking property. The demonstration ends with a slide show on the WTO policies projected on the side of a building.

*Tuebingen:* Around twenty people dress as WTO delegates and show up in the pedestrian area of the town's shopping center. A big globe is enthusiastically kicked about. Some folks dressed as Death speechify about the lethal policies of the WTO. A few banners are dropped, one reading "Globalize Solidarity not the Economy." Police are obnoxious, performing identity checks on protesters. They seize film from a participant and destroy it.

## Italy

*Milan:* Members of the Tutti Blanche ("white overalls") group lock themselves to a McDonald's, and hang enormous banners denouncing neoliberalism from it. An informational tent against the WTO is set up in the central square of Largo Cairoli. The day ends with a debate at the Social Center Leoncavallo. Andres Barreda Marin, a professor at Mexico City's UNAM, speaks on the influence of US economy on capitalist globalization and on the situation in Chiapas.

*Padau:* A peaceful demonstration in front of a genetics exhibition is attacked by police. Top managers of companies that use genetically modified organism technology are in attendance at the exhibition.

*Rome:* A direct action group occupies the headquarters of the National Committee for Biosafety. They hang banners against GMOs and the WTO. The action had been promoted by various squats and grassroots unions.

## Greece

*Athens:* Protestors clash with riot police throughout the day and into the night, following demonstrations outside the US embassy. Demonstrators protest a wide range of issues, including the tyranny of the capitalist free market and neoliberal trade policies.

## Czech Republic

*Prague:* Earth First! Prague joins the N30 and Buy Nothing Day actions with banners, music, and masks at the city's Tesco Supermarket, while Food Not Bombs provides a meal. The event lasts two hours and is attended by about seventy people. It is covered by all the major TV stations and newspapers of the Czech Republic.

## Turkey

*Bergama:* Protests take place against the Eurogold Corporation, which plans to operate a gold mine in the area that would use cyanide-based extraction methods. The protests are also against planned thermal and nuclear power plants.

## Israel

*Tel Aviv:* Around thirty people demonstrate outside the US embassy in protest of the WTO. Those present include Women in Black, members of an anarcho-communist collective, and direct action Greens.

## Pakistan

*Muzafer Ghar:* More than 8,000 people demonstrate against the WTO.

## India

*Bangalore:* Several thousand peasant-farmers from all the districts of Karnataka province gather to protest the WTO at the central train station, then make their way to Gandhi's statue. At the end of the demo protesters issue a "Quit India" notice to Monsanto. The document is an ultimatum: the company must leave the country or suffer direct action against its installations. Another notice is issued to the Indian Institute of Science, which opened its research facilities to Monsanto, demanding that the school expel the transnational corporation from its campus.

*Narmada:* More than 1000 people from sixty different villages participate in a colorful procession protesting agreements and institutions that are roping India and the rest of the world into the downward spiral of globalization.

*New Delhi:* Hundreds of indigenous people blockade the World Bank building. Many others participate in a three day sit-in at Raj Ghat (where Gandhi's ashes are buried). At the latter location protesters burn a statue symbolizing the WTO. These actions have two specific targets: forces trying to build a massive, devastating dam in Maheshwar—Indian industrial interests, multinational corporations and the German state—and the WTO regime, for the equally vandalistic and insidious dispossession that it creates globally. Speakers at the rallies state their commitment to Gandhi's vision of a self-reliant, sustainable, solidarity-based India composed of village republics.

## Korea

*Seoul:* Korean People's Action Against Investment Treaties and the WTO New Round hold a demo in front of government offices in Seoul. Over two dozen progressive organizations, including the KCTU and the National Farmer's Union are represented; over 3,000 workers, students, and activists take part.

## Philippines

*Bacolod:* Thousands attend a rally against President Estrada's plans to amend the Constitution to allow for greater foreign investment.

*Manila:* Militants from the Proletarian Revolutionary Army perform a drive-by on Shell's headquarters, opening fire with automatic weapons and a grenade launcher. The PRA members shatter the windows and metal façade of the large shimmering building. Elsewhere in the city, roughly eight thousand union members and activists rally against Philippine membership in the WTO in front of the US embassy and near the Malacanang presidential palace. Their slogans angrily state that the WTO's latest meeting could lead to unneeded food imports and a drop in local farmers' incomes.

## Australia

*Brisbane:* Activists protest against the WTO in front of the Stock Exchange.

*Melbourne:* The offices of public relations firm Burson-Marsteller are occupied, in an effort to link the spin doctors of consumerism with the neoliberal agenda of the WTO.

## D1

*Boston, MA:* Over six hundred antiglobalization protesters gather outside of the Boston Federal Reserve Building. A feeder march of about two hundred starts at the Park Street subway station and winds its way through the Downtown Crossing shopping district, blocking traffic during rush hour. Large puppets lead the way to the Federal Reserve. The crowd has tripled in size by the time the rally begins at 5 P.M. Persevering in the face of biting winds and subzero temperatures, participants listen to speeches from community organizers and labor leaders, while others maintain a steady stream of cheers, jeers, and creative chants.

## D2

*Ljubljana, Slovenia:* In solidarity with all people struggling for a better world, one hundred people gather in front of the Presern Monument to demonstrate against the tyranny of the WTO and the globalization of neoliberal capitalism.

## D3

*Tucson, AZ:* Over fifty demonstrators gather at McDonald's near the university in solidarity with the Seattle protesters. Many protesters have plungers, illustrating the theme of the demonstration: "Flush Out Corporate Greed."

*Manila, Philippines:* Protesters try to force their way into the US Embassy for a "lightning rally" against the violent dispersal and arrests of protesters at the WTO conference in Seattle, Washington.

## D11

*Mexico City, Mexico:* Hundreds demonstrate in front of the US Embassy demanding the release of the protesters arrested in Seattle, as well as political prisoner Mumia Abu-Jamal. Rocks and fireworks are thrown at the embassy, resulting in several broken windows. Police charge the crowd, clubbing people and chasing them across the fourteen-lane Paseo De la Reforma Boulevard.

Ninety-eight protesters are arrested. Nineteen of the prisoners are minors and though told they would be released after twenty-four hours, they are held in prison for three days. At the same time that the minors are released a special police force transports the rest of the prisoners. The protesters are made to lay face down, and are beaten and told that they're being moved to Military Camp #1, infamous for supposedly being the burying grounds of the massacred students of October 2, 1968. The police threaten to kill them and make their bodies disappear. The prisoners are shipped to the Reclusorio Norte (Northern Penitentiary), but initially believe that they are in Military Camp #1. Prison guards employ humiliation and torture tactics, including forcing prisoners to walk in "duck formation"—a squatting position and accompanied by quacking sounds. Those who do not comply are kicked and dragged. Prisoners are also forced to hold their hands in the air for an unendurable amount of time. In the beatings, guards try to not leave marks.

A bail of 2,803,200 pesos (approximately $285,000 USD) is set for the release of the prisoners. Unions, student unions, and the general public, raise the money, and the protesters are released on December 15. Those arrested were accused of rioting, property damage, and "aggressions."

# In Praise of the Seattle Coalition
# Eliot Katz

They came from around the globe to change the shape of the globe
They formed a human chain and sidewalks declared their support
They led labor down unpaved roads and mountain ranges from all sides
    tipped their peaks in salute
They wore turtle caps and the Pacific roared its approval
They chanted "This is what democracy looks like" so that we who could
    not be in Seattle could watch TV & see what democracy looks like
They called for human rights and were gassed with inhuman chemicals
They insisted the food be kept clean of genetic experiment and were shot
    with rubber bullet pellet red meat welts
They demanded an end to worldwide sweatshops and were treated
    to the best nightsticks multinational business could buy
It was a coalition for the ages, of all ages, of all stages, of varying degrees
    of calm and rages
After curfew, the skies lit up & birds flew across continents to celebrate
Ancient redwood trees shook their leaves to prevent WTO delegates
    from being received
The town salmon agreed to wear union windbreakers for the week
When the mayor outlawed public gasmasks, the air sucked up to help out
It was the audible applause of the quantum that drove the police chief mad
A dog ran across the road to dispose of pepper spray containers
Stampeding cops were stopped by dolphins swimming in mid-street
I saw this every hour on the hour behind the CNN lens
In a thousand tongues, even the internet logged on the side of the young
O friends, you have jumpstarted this nation and revealed an America
    with a million human faces
Of course the corporations were defeated, any objective observer
    could see they were outmatched from the opening bell
Now come the subtle somersaults and the internationalist flips
Now the courageous maneuvers that follow a win

# Seattle Diary
## Jeffrey St. Clair
*Counterpunch*

Seattle has always struck me as a suspiciously clean city, manifesting a tidiness that verges on the compulsive. It is the Singapore of the United States: spit-polished, glossy, and eerily beautiful. Indeed, there is perhaps no more scenic setting for a city: nestled next to Elliot Bay on Puget Sound, with the serrated tips of the Olympic Mountains on the western skyline and hulking over it all the cool blue hump of Mt. Rainier.

But Seattle is also a city that hides its past in the underground. It is literally built on layers of engineered muck, a soggy Ilium. The new opulence brought by the likes of Microsoft, Boeing, Starbucks, and REI is neatly segregated from the old economic engines, the working docks and the steamy pulp mills and chemical plants of south Seattle and Tacoma. It is a city that is both uptight and laid back, a city of deeply repressed desires and rages. It was the best and the worst of places to convene the WTO, that Star Chamber for global capitalists. On this week Seattle was so tightly wound that it seemed primed to crack. The city, which practiced drills to prepare itself against possible biological or chemical warfare by WTO opponents, was about to witness its own police department gas its streets and neighborhoods. By the end of the week, much of Seattle's shiny veneer had been scratched off, the WTO talks had collapsed in futility and acrimony and a new multinational popular resistance had blackened the eyes of global capitalism and its shock troops, if only for a few raucous days and nights.

## Sunday

I arrived in Seattle at dusk and settled into the King's Inn, my ratty, noisy hotel on Fifth Avenue two blocks up from the ugly Doric columns of the Westin, the HQ of the US trade delegation and on Tuesday and Wednesday nights the high-rise hovel of Bill Clinton. On the drive up from Portland, I had decided to forego the press briefings, NGO policy sessions, and staged debates slated at dozens of venues around Seattle. Instead, I was determined to pitch my tent with the activists who had vowed in January to shut down Seattle during WTO week. After all, the plan seemed remotely possible. The city with its overburdened streets and constricted geography does half the job itself. And, in an act of self-interested solidarity, the cabbies, who held festering grudges against the city on a variety of claims, had just announced plans to time a taxi strike to coincide with the protest.

Around 10 P.M., I wandered down to the Speakeasy Café, in the Belltown District, which I'd heard was to be a staging area for grassroots greens and anarchists with modems. On this warm late November night, there were stars in the Seattle sky, surely a once a decade experience. I took it as an omen. God knows of what strange portent.

The Speakeasy is a fully wired redoubt for radicals: it serves beer, herbal tea, vegan dishes and, for a ten-dollar fee, access to a bank of computers where dozens of people checked their email and the latest news, from *Le Monde* to the BBC, from WTOwatch.com to the *New York Times*. I ran into Kirk Murphy, a doctor who teaches at the UCLA medical school. I'd gotten to know Murphy slightly during the great battles to fight DreamWorks and its ill-fated plan to bury the Ballona Wetlands in Los Angeles under acres of concrete, glass, and steel. The doctor was wearing an Earth First! t-shirt and drinking a Black Butte Porter, the microbrew of choice for the radical environmental movement. Dr. Murphy knows a lot about treating victims of police brutality and he had prepared a handbook for protesters on how to deal with tear gas, pepper spray, rubber bullets, and concussions. Hundreds of copies had been printed and would be passed out to volunteer medics and protesters before the big march on Tuesday.

"Do you think it will come to that?" I asked. "Well, I hope not," Murphy said. "But if it doesn't, we probably won't have accomplished much, eh?"

Murphy said that the direct action crowd was assembled at a warehouse on East Denny, up toward Seattle Community College. It was a twenty-minute walk and I arrived at midnight to a scene of dizzying and cheerful chaos. The Denny Street warehouse was far more than a meeting place; it was part factory, part barracks, part command and control center, part mosh pit. Later on it would become an infirmary.

Inside so-called affinity groups were planning their separate direct actions; others were constructing giant street puppets, bearing the likeness of corporate titans and politicians, such as Clinton and Maxxam chieftain Charles Hurwitz. Another group, led by Earth First!ers from Eugene, Oregon were putting the finishing touches on what one referred to as the Trojan Horse, a twenty-foot-tall armored siege tower on wheels, capable of holding fourteen people. The bulky contraption was meant to be rolled up near the convention center, allowing the people inside to climb out a hatch in the roof and scale over tops of the Metro buses, which the security forces had parked as barricades near the building.

I knew the chief architect of this creation and asked him if he wasn't wasting time and money on such an easy target, as Saddam Hussein had done with his giant, billion dollar cannon destroyed in the first air strike of the Gulf War. "Just wait," he said, a spark of mischief in his eye.

## Monday

And the revolution will be started by: sea turtles. At noon about 2,000 people massed at the United Methodist Church, the HQ of the grassroots NGOs, for a march to the convention center. It was environment day and the Earth Island Institute had prepared more than 500 sea turtle costumes for marchers to wear. The sea turtle became the prime symbol of the WTO's threats to environmental laws when the WTO tribunal ruled that the US Endangered Species Act, which requires shrimp to be caught with turtle excluder devices, was an unfair trade barrier.

But the environmentalists weren't the only ones on the street Monday morning. In the first showing of a new solidarity, labor union members from the Steelworkers and the Longshoremen showed up to join the march. In fact, Steelwoker Don Kegley led the march alongside environmentalist Ben White. (White was later clubbed in the back of the head by a young man who was apparently angry that he couldn't complete his Christmas shopping. The police pulled the youth away from White, but the man wasn't arrested. And White later played down the incident.) The throng of sea turtles and blue-jacked union folk took off to the rhythm of a chant that would echo down the streets of Seattle for days: "The people united will never be divided!"

I walked next to Brad Spann, a Longshoreman from Tacoma, who hoisted up one of my favorite signs of the entire week: "Teamsters and Turtles Together At Last!" Brad winked at me and said, "What the hell do you think old Hoffa thinks of that?"

The march, which was too fast and courteous for my taste, was escorted by motorcycle police and ended essentially in a cage, a protest pen next to a construction site near the convention center. A small stage had been erected there hours earlier and Carl Pope, the director of the Sierra Club, was called forth to give the opening speech. The Club is the nation's most venerable environmental group. It's often on the right side of issues, such as old-growth preservation and trade. But in the past decade it has become increasingly captured by the Democratic Party, willing to forgive nearly every failing. For example, the Club was adamantly opposed to NAFTA, and helped lead a feisty coalition of green and labor groups in opposition to the treaty. But when Bill Clinton and Al Gore stuffed NAFTA down their throats, there was barely a bleat of protest and they endorsed the free-trade team for a second term in 1996.

I'd never met Carl Pope before and was surprised by what I encountered. He is a tiny man with a shrill and squeaky voice who affects the look and hair-flipping mannerisms of RFK circa 1968. Nearing ninety, Dave Brower, Pope's more militant predecessor, still has the look of a mountain climber; Pope gives the impression that the only climbing he does is on a StairMaster. I couldn't follow much of what Pope had to say, except that he failed to utter any harsh words about Clinton or Gore, the architects of more than 200 environment-shredding trade deals since 1993. The speech was delivered with a smugness that most of the labor people must have heard as confirmation of their worst fears about the true nature of environmentalists in suits.

Standing near the stage I saw Brent Blackwelder, the head of Friends of the Earth. Behind his glasses and somewhat shambling manner, Blackwelder looks ever so professorial. And he is by far the smartest of the environmental CEOs. But he is also the most radical politically, the most willing to challenge the tired complacency of his fellow green executives. I told him: "Brent, you're the Chomsky of the environmental movement." He chuckled, evidently pleased at the comparison.

He was slated to give the next talk and I asked him what he thought of following Carl Pope, a Gore promoter, whose staffers had just plunged a few knives in Blackwelder's back following Friends of the Earth's endorsement of Bill Bradley in the Democratic primaries. He shrugged. "We did our damage," Blackwelder said. "Our endorsement of Bradley stung the Sierra Club almost as much as it did Gore." But Blackwelder isn't under any illusions about Bradley, either. "Bradley's a free trader," Blackwelder said. "We pleaded with him to at least make a strong statement in opposition to the US position on the timber tariff issue. But he wouldn't budge. There was a real opportunity for him to stick it to Gore and prove himself as the better green."

Blackwelder's speech was a good one, strong and defiant. He excoriated the WTO as a kind of global security force for transnational corporations whose mission is "to stuff unwanted products, like genetically engineered foods, down our throats." Afterwards, I asked Blackwelder what would happen if Clinton announced some environmental sideboard, another meager trust-me pledge. "The plague of Clinton is to say one thing and do another,"

Blackwelder said. "He talked this line before with NAFTA. But even with the sideboards, everything we said about NAFTA has come true, only worse." I told Blackwelder that I had heard Clinton was going to meet in Seattle on Wednesday with the heads of the National Wildlife, World Wildlife Fund, and the Sierra Club. "That's what I hear, too," Blackwelder said. "But he won't meet with us, because he knows we'd call his bluff."

After the speechifying most of the marchers headed back to the church. But a contingent of about 200 ended up in front of McDonald's where a group of French farmers had mustered to denounce US policy on biotech foods. Their leader was Jose Bove, a sheep farmer from Millau in southwest France and a leader of Confédération Paysanne, a French environmental group. In August, Bove had been jailed in France for leading a raid on a McDonald's restaurant under construction in Larzac. At the time, Bove was awaiting trial on charges that he destroyed a cache of Novartis' genetically engineered corn. Bove said his raid on the Larzac McDonald's was prompted by the US' decision to impose a heavy tariff on Roquefort cheese in retaliation for the European Union's refusal to import American hormone-treated beef. Bove's act of defiance earned him the praise of Jacques Chirac and Friends of the Earth. Bove said he was prepared to start a militant worldwide campaign against "Frankenstein" foods. "These actions will only stop when this mad logic comes to a halt," said Bove. "I don't demand clemency but justice."

Bove showed up at the Seattle McDonald's with rounds of Roquefort cheese, which he handed out to the crowd. After a rousing speech against the evils of Monsanto and its bovine growth hormone and Round-up Ready soybeans, the crowd stormed the McDonald's, breaking its windows and urging the customers and workers to join the marchers on the streets. This was the first shot in the battle for Seattle.

Moments later the block was surrounded by Seattle police, attired in black body armour and Darth Vader-like helmets. Many of them arrived on armored personal carriers, black military trucks referred to affectionately by the TV anchors on the nightly news as "the Peacekeepers." But this time cops held their distance, merely making a show of their fire-power and potential to cause havoc. They cordoned off a four-block area until the crowd dribbled away in about an hour. At this point, there was still lightness in the air. A big Samoan cop cracked a smile as a protester waved a hunk of stinky cheese in front of his face.

I returned to my hotel early that night. Too exhilarated and exhausted to sleep, I fell back on the bed and flipped on the television. A newscaster was interviewing Michael Moore, the pudgy-faced director of the WTO. "I've always been on the side of the little guy," Moore proclaimed.

## Tuesday

Fewer than twelve hours later, Seattle was under civic emergency, a step away from martial law. National Guard helicopters hovered over downtown, sweeping the city with search-lights. A 7 P.M. curfew had been imposed and was being flouted by thousands—those same thousands who captured the streets, sustained clouds of tears gas, volleys of rubber bullets, concussion grenades, high-powered bean cannons and straightforward beatings with riot batons. The bravery of the street warriors had its tremendous triumph: they held the streets long enough to force the WTO to cancel their opening day. This had been the stat-ed objective of the direct action strategists, and they attained it.

The predicted scenario had been somewhat different. There was to be the great march of organized labor, led by the panjandrums of the AFL-CIO, with James Hoffa Jr. in a starring role. Labor's legions—a predicted 100,000—were to march from the Space Needle to the Convention Center, clogging the streets and peacefully prevent the WTO delegates from assembling.

This never happened. Instead the labor chiefs talked tough but accepted a cheap deal. They would get a Wednesday meeting with Bill Clinton, with the promise that at future such WTO conclaves they would get a "seat at the table." So instead of joining the throngs bent on shutting down the opening of the WTO, the big labor rally took place at noon around the Space Needle, some fifteen to twenty blocks from the convention center where the protesters on the front lines were taking their stand. Speaker after speaker took to the podium to address the crowd. None of them mentioned that only blocks away the cops were battering hundreds of demonstraters who had risked their lives to keep the WTO from launching its meetings. When the labor march finally got under way around 1 P.M. it's marshals directed most of the marchers away from the battle zones down by the convention center. They didn't want to add fuel to the fire or put their members at risk.

For the direct action folks, the morning began in the predawn hours, in a light rain, a thick fog rolling in off Puget Sound. More than 2,000 people amassed in Victor Steinbrueck Park, on the waterfront north of Pike's Place market. Once again, steelworkers and Earth First!ers led the way, carrying a banner with the image of a redwood tree and a spotted owl. The march featured giant puppets, hundreds of signs, the ubiquitous sea turtles, singing, chanting, drumming and nervous laughter. There was an atmosphere of carnival to the gathering. New Orleans during Mardi Gras. Juarez on the Day of the Dead. A carnival with an ominous edge.

As the sky finally lightened, I found myself walking next to a group of black men and women trailing a white van. They turned out to be one of the more creative groups in the march, a collection of hip-hop artists from across the country. The van, dubbed the Rap Wagon, carried a powerful sound system capable of rocking the streets with a convoluted and improvized rap called "TKO the WTO." Walking with me up Pine Street to the Roosevelt Hotel was an eighteen-year-old from South Central LA named Thomas. I asked him why he was here. "I like turtles and I hate that fucker Bill Gates," he said. Good enough for me. Thomas and I held hands, forming part of a human chain at the intersection of Seventh and Pine, intent on keeping the WTO delegates from reaching their morning meetings.

A British delegate was prevented from entering the convention center after he left the Roosevelt Hotel. He tried to bust through the human chain and was repulsed. Angered, he slugged one of the protesters in the chest and ran down the block towards us. When he reached the corner a small black woman confronted him, shouting: "You hit somebody! I saw you." Whack. The delegate punched the woman in the face, sending her sprawling back into Thomas and me. The scene could have turned ugly, as protesters rushed to protect the woman. But the lead organizer at the corner took control, ushering the delegate into a nearby bookstore.

Meanwhile, a block down the street another frustrated WTO delegate pulled a revolver from his coat pocket and aimed it at protesters blocking the entrance to the Paramount Hotel, where the opening ceremonies were scheduled. The police rushed in with their clubs and jabbed the protesters away from the gun-wielding man, who was neither detained nor stripped of his weapon.

Around 10 A.M., I ran into my friend Michael Donnelly, a veteran Earth First!er from Oregon. Donnelly and I walked up to Sixth and Union, where we heard that a group of forest activists had taken control of an intersection. The site was to become the first violent attack by police on protesters. A band of about 200 protesters had sat down in the street. They were playing music. Others were dancing. A squad of riot cops approached. The sergeant mumbled something over a megaphone. "Fifteen minute warning," Donnelly said."We've got fifteen minutes and then these guys are going to try to clear us out. "

About ten minutes later, a Peacekeeper vehicle arrived, more cops clinging to its side. The back of of the truck was popped open and dozens of tear gas canisters were unloaded. And, then very suddenly, a tear gas can was launched into the sitting demonstrators. It oozed a grey-green smoke. Then seconds later another one. And then five or six more of them were fired into the crowd. One of the protesters nearest the cops was a young, petite woman. She rose up, plainly disoriented from the gas, and a Seattle policeman, crouched less than ten feet away, shot her in the knee with a rubber bullet. She fell to the pavement, grabbing her leg and screaming in pain. Then, moments later, one of her comrades, maddened by the unprovoked attack, charged the police line, Kamikaze-style. Two cops beat him to the ground with their batons, hitting him at least twenty times. As the cops flailed away with their four-foot-long clubs, the crowd chanted, "The whole world is watching, the whole world is watching." Soon the man started to rise. Somehow he got on his hands and knees and then he was shot in the back by a cop who was standing over him. His hands were cuffed behind him and he was dragged away across the pavement.

The so-called rubber bullets are meant to be fired at areas of the body with large muscle mass. Like the thighs or the ass. But over the next two days Seattle cops would fire off thousands of rounds without exhibiting any caution. Dozens of people, none of them threatening the cops with harm, were shot in the back, in the neck, in the groin, and in the face. All places that the ammunition's manufacturers, ever conscious of liability questions, warn could cause severe trauma or death.

By now another volley of tear gas had been throw into the crowd and the intersection was clotted with fumes. At first I was stunned, staring at the scene with the glazed look of the freshly lobotomized. Then my eyes began to boil in my head, my lips burned, and it seemed impossible to draw a breath. When it's raining, the chemical agents hug close to the ground, taking longer to dissolve into the air. This compounds the tear gas' stinging power, it's immobilizing effect. I staggered back up Sixth Avenue toward University, where

I stumbled into a cop decked out in his storm trooper gear. He turned and gave me a swift whack to my side with the tip of his riot club. I feel to my knees and covered my head, fearing a tumult of blows. But the blows never came and soon I felt a gentle hand on my shoulder and woman's voice say, "Come here."

I retreated into a narrow alley and saw the blurry outline of a young woman wearing a Stetson cowboy hat and a gas mask."Lean your head back, so that I can wash the chemicals out of your eyes," she said. The water was cool and within seconds I could see again. "Who are you?" I asked. "Osprey," she said, and disappeared into the chemical mist. Osprey. The familiar, totemic name of an Earth First!er. Thank god for Edward Abbey.

But the battle going on at Sixth and University was far from over. The police moved in on a group of protesters from Humboldt County who had locked themselves with cement casts on their arms, thus immobilizing themselves in the middle of the intersection. They were ordered to evacuate the area, which of course they couldn't and wouldn't do. Then after this obligatory warning the cops attacked ferociously, dousing them in the face with spurts of pepper spray and then dropping searing tear gas canisters on top of them. After a few minutes valiant police fell upon the helpless protesters with their batons. Two of the dozen or so protesters were knocked unconscious, the rest were bloodied and bruised. But the group held its ground for hours and by 2 P.M. the cops had backed off. The University intersection had been held.

Pepper spray has a nasty history. But it is becoming more and more popular with police departments as part of their arsenal of "safe" weapons. Of course, pepper spray is often used in situations where cops could otherwise handle the situation without violence. In Seattle the cops were using a 10 percent solution, carted around in containers that looked link mini-fire extinquishers. Pepper spray this potent has been linked to more than 100 fatalities in the US and Canada, often from allergic reactions or suffocation after being sprayed, tackled, and cuffed. Despite this, law enforcement agencies have done almost no scientific studies on the effects of pepper spray on human health. And there's no federal or state agency that regulates the manufacture or use of the chemical.

The Seattle cops used MK-46 First Defense Red Pepper manufactured by Defense Technologies (Def-Tech) in Caspar, Wyoming. Pepper spray (oleorsin capscium) is made from extracts of capscium peppers mixed with an alcohol solution that causes intense burning of the skin, nose, mouth, and eyes. Def-Tech cautions that the toxin is meant only to be used for defensive purposes, to protect the safety of a cop, and shouldn't be sprayed on people at a distance of less than three feet. This warning was routinely ignored by the Seattle police who liberally sprayed the stinging solution directly into the face and even on the genitals of demonstrators.

Who were these direct action warriors on the front lines? Earth First!, the Alliance for Sustainable Jobs and the Environment (the new enviro-steelworker alliance), the Ruckus Society (a direct action training center), Jobs with Justice, Rainforest Action Network, Food Not Bombs, Global Exchange, and a small contingent of anarchists, the dreaded Black Bloc.

There was also a robust international contingent on the streets Tuesday morning: French farmers, Korean greens, Canadian wheat growers, Mexican environmentalists, Chinese dissidents, Ecuadoran antidam organizers, U'wa tribespeople from the Colombian rainforest, and British campaigners against genetically modified foods. Indeed earlier, a group of Brits had cornered two Monsanto lobbyists behind an abandoned truck carrying an ad for the Financial Times. The detained the flacks long enough to deliver a stern warning about the threat of frankencrops to widlife, such as the monarch butterfly. Then a wave of tear gas wafted over them and the Monsanto men fled, covering their eyes with their neckties.

By noon, around the convention center, the situation was desperate. The Seattle police, initially comparatively restrained, were now losing control. They were soon supplemented by the Kings County sheriffs' department, a rough mob, which seem to get their kicks from throwing concussion grenades into crowds, with the M-80-like devices often exploding only inches above the heads of people.

Around 12:30 someone smashed the first storefront window. It could've been an anarchist. It could have been an agent provacatuer or a stray bullet or concussion grenade. What's clear, though, is that the vandalism—what there was of it—started more than two hours after the cops had attacked nonviolent protesters amassed at Sixth and Union. Protesters who had offered themselves up for arrest. At most, the dreaded Black Bloc, which was to become demonized by the press and some of the more staid leaders of labor and green groups, amounted to fifty people, many of them young women. Much of the so-called looting that took place was done not by the anarchists, but by Seattle street gangs.

As the day ticked away the street protesters kept asking, "Where are the labor marchers?" Many expected that at any moment thousands of longshoremen and Teamsters would reinforce them in the fray. Those absent masses never came. The marshals for the union march steered the big crowds away from the action. The isolation of the street protesters allowed the cops to get far more violent.

Even in the run-up to WTO week in Seattle, the genteel element—foundation careerists, NGO bureaucrats, policy wonks—was raising cautionary fingers, saying that the one thing to be avoided in Seattle this week was civil disobedience. The Internet was thick with tremulous admonitions about the need for good behavior, the perils of playing into the enemies' hands, the profound necessity for decorous—i.e. passive—comportment. Their fondest hope was to attend in mildly critical posture—not only the WTO conclave in Seattle, but all future ones. This too became the posture of big labor. On Tuesday, in answer to a question from CNN's Bernard Shaw on whether labor wanted to kill the WTO, James Hoffa Jr. replied, "No. We want to get labor a seat at the table."

Eventually, several phalanxes of union marchers skirted their herders and headed up Fourth Avenue to the battlegrounds at Pine and Pike. Most of them seemed to be from the more militant unions: the Steelworkers, IBEW, and the Longshoremen. And they seemed to be pissed at the political penury of their leaders. Randal McCarthy, a Longshoreman from Kelso, Washington, told me: "That fucker, Sweeney. No wonder we keep getting rolled. If he were any dumber, he'd be in management."

For a couple hours there had been an eerie lull in the tear gas assaults. Out on streets no one knew that the cops had run out of gas and had had to send a supply plane to Montana, where they picked up 3,300 pounds of more toxic CN gas, known to chemists as 1-cholorace-tophenol and to police bureaucrats as a "less lethal" munintion. Less lethal indeed.

Now reloaded the cops went on a rampage. A report by the Washington chapter of the American Civil Liberties Union crisply summed up the sadistic behavior of the cops that afternoon: "Officers struck or pepper sprayed people who posed no physical threat, were not resisting arrest, or were not being allowed to leave the scene. Some officers singled out people who questioned police authority or said things uncomplimentary to the police, and bystanders who were simply walking down the street."

At 3:24 P.M. the mayor of Seattle, egged on by a furious Madeleine Albright, who had spent the morning boiling in rage over being locked down in her hotel, declared a civic emergency, the equivilent of martial law in heart of America's most self-consciously liberal city. A rigid curfew was imposed. People were to be off the streets from 7 P.M. to 7 A.M. One immediate effect was to give the cops, whose ranks were now swollen with raw recruits from across the state of Washington, a greenlight to bully and slash their way across the streets of downtown. By 4 P.M., Seattle had become a free-fire zone for cops and nearly everyone—protesters, workers, shoppers, and even other cops—were targets. A few hours later the city banned the sale, purchase, and possession of gas masks. The initial order was so sweeping that it later had to be amended to exempt police and military personnel.

These emergency orders and closures came rapidly. It's stunning to experience how quickly a city can be turned into a police state. The decisions were made by executive fiat from the mayor. Ultimately, the Seattle city council ratified all the repressive measures—but not until December 6, a week after the initial declaration of a civic emergency.

By darkness on Tuesday the 2,000 or so street warriors had won the day, even though they were finally forced to retreat north and east out of the city center and into the neighborhood of Capitol Hill. The opening ceremonies for the WTO ministerial had been cancelled. But suppose 30,000 union people had reinforced them? Downtown could have been held all night, and the convention center sealed off. Maybe even President Clinton would have been forced to stay away.

Oh, yeah, what about that siege tower? Well, it turned out to be an excellent diversionary tactic. When the Seattle police's SWAT teams converged to disable the Earth First!er's strange contraption, it gave the direct action groups time to secure their positions, successfully encircling the convention center, the nearby hotels, and WTO venues. It an odd way it may have been a key to the great victory of the day.

## Wednesday

Wednesday was the turning point of the week. After the vicious crackdown of Tuesday night, where even Christmas carolers in a residential area were gassed, many wondered who would show up to confront the WTO, Bill Clinton, the police, and the National Guard the next morning. More than a thousand, it turned out. And the numbers grew as the day wore on. The resistance had proved its resilience.

Our presence in downtown was no longer wanted. In fact, it was illegal. The mayor had ordered twenty-five square blocks of downtown cordoned off. The heart of the city was a "no protest zone" with entry controlled by the police. The mayor made a few exceptions: Seattle was open to WTO delegates; business owners and workers; downtown residents; security and emergency personnel; and, tellingly, holiday shoppers. The closure itself was a stark violation of the US constitution and a Supreme Court case called Collins v. Jordan, which compels municiple governments to permit protests close enough so that they can be heard and seen by the intended audience.

But the Seattle officials, under the lash of the Clinton security team, went further. Their goal was to suppress political speech, not riots or looting or even civil disobedience. The cops were told to bar any visible signs of protest against the WTO or dissent against police tactics, including signs, leaflets, buttons, and even t-shirts. This situation soon became dangerously absurd. About 10 A.M. on Wednesday a gang of cops body-slammed a protester who was standing on Sixth Avenue handing out leaflets. The text was far from incendiary. It was merely a copy of a *New York Times* story from that morning on the cops' rampages of the day before. Another squad of censors with guns detained a man who was handing out paper to passersby on the sidewalk sheets of containing the text of the Bill of Rights. His stash of papers was confiscated.

The morning's first march headed down Denny Street from Seattle Community College toward downtown. The 250 marchers were met at about 7 A.M. by a line of cops in riot gear at Eighth Avenue. A sobering sign that things had become more serious was the sight of cops armed with AR-15 assault rifles. Some brave soul went up to one of the deputies and asked, "Do those shoot rubber bullets?" "Nope," the cop replied through a Darth Vader-like microphone embedded in his gas mask. "This is the real thing." Dozen of protesters were arrested immediately, placed in plastic wrist cuffs, and left sitting on the street for hours–more than were arrested all day on Tuesday.

Watching all this were attorneys from National Lawyers Guild (NLG). The NLG had sent dozens of legal observers to Seattle to record incidents of police brutality and to advise demonstrators on how to act after being arrested. On Denny Street that morning I met Marge Buckley, a lawyer from Los Angeles. She was wearing a green t-shirt with "NLG Legal Observer" printed across the front and was furiously writing notes on a pad. Buckley said she had filled several notepads on Tuesday with tales of unwarranted and unprovoked shootings, gassings, and beatings.

"Look! " Buckley said, as we trotted down the sidewalk to catch up with the marchers who had abandoned Denny Street, seeking another entry point into city center."How weird. The people are obeying traffic signals on their way to a civil disobedience action." A few moments later I lost track of Buckley, when the police, including a group mounted on horses, encircled the marchers at Rainier Square. I slipped through the line just as the Seattle police sergeant yelled,"Gas!" Someone later said Buckley had been arrested.

I wouldn't be surprised if she had been nabbed. The police had begun targeting the "command-and-control" of the demonstrators—people with cellphones, bullhorns, the known faces and suspected organizers, medics, and legal observers.

The NLG folks were near the top of the list. At 7:56 on Wednesday morning, the following message went out over police radios to Seattle street cops: "Heads up! FYI! We are having some legal observers probing our lines, taking notes on our posts. So if any officer around the Convention Center sees these folks, wearing green, legal observers—they're taking notes. Take the notes from them and get 'em outta here."

Several of the plainclothes cops at the Denny Street encounter had photos in their hands and were scanning them to identify the lead organizers. As the marchers occupied the intersection singing "We Shall Overcome," about twenty police formed into a wedge and quickly attacked the protesters, seized a bald-headed man talking on a cellphone (it seemed nearly everyone in Seattle had a cellphone and a camera), and dragged him back to the police line. The man was John Sellers, director of the Ruckus Society. Sellers was held for an hour, then released.

Later the police hierarchy grappled for excuses, even claiming that they had been taken outmanuevered by the protesters' "sophisticated use of cellphones and walkie talkies."

On Wednesday afternoon, I encountered Kirk Murphy, the doctor. His Earth First! t-shirt had been replaced by a business suit and a rain jacket. I raised my eyebrows at him. He said, "I'm trying hard not to look like part of the support team. They've arrested a lot of our medics and I need to stay out of jail to help the injured."

These targeted arrests may have been meant to turn the protests into the chaotic mess the city's PR people were characterizing it as to the media. But it didn't happen. The various groups of protestors, sometimes in the hundreds, huddled together and decided their next course of action by a rudimentary form of consensus. Everyone was given a chance to have a say and then a vote was taken on what to do next and, usually, the will of the majority was followed without significant disruptions. The problem was that it slowed down the marches, allowing the police and National Guard troops to box in the protesters, most tragically later Wednesday evening at Pike's Place Market.

As the march turned up toward the Sheraton and was beaten back by cops on horses, I teamed up with Etienne Vernet and Ronnie Cummings. Cummings is the head of one of the feistiest groups in the US, the PureFood Campaign, Monsanto's chief pain in the ass. Cummings hails from the oil town of Port Arthur, Texas. He went to Cambridge with that other great foe of industrial agriculture, Prince Charles. Cummings was a civil rights organizer in Houston during the mid-sixties. "The energy here is incredible," Cummings said. "Black and white, labor and green, Americans, Europeans, Africans, and Asians arm-in-arm. It's the most hopeful I've felt since the height of the civil rights movement."

Vernet lives in Paris, where he is a leader of the radical green group EcoRopa. At that very moment the European Union delegates inside the convention were capitulating on a key issue: the EU, which had banned import of genetically engineered crops and hormone-treated beef, had agreed to a US proposal to establish an scientific committee to evaluate the health and environmental risks of biotech foods, a sure first step toward undermining the moratorium. Still Vernet was in a jolly mood, lively and invigorated, if a little bemused by the decorous nature of the crowd. "Americans seem to have been out of practice in these things," he told me. "Everyone's so polite. The only things that're on fire are dumpsters filled with refuse." He pointed to a shiny black Lexus parked on Pine Street, which the throngs of protesters had scrupulously avoided. In the windshield was a placard identifying it as belonging to a WTO delegate. "In Paris that car would be burning."

Somehow Vernet and I made it through four police barricades all the way across town to the International Media Center, a briefing area hosted by Public Citizen in the Seattle Center, a cramped Greek Revival-style structure. I was there to interview my old friend, Dave Brower, and Steelworker David Foster. The Daves were late and to pass time I sat down in front of a TV. There was Bill Clinton speaking at the Port of Seattle. His verbal sleight-of-hand routine was in masterful form. He denounced Tuesday's violence, but said the WTO delegates should listen to the "legitimate" protesters. He said he disagreed with most of their views, but said that some should at least be permitted to observe the proceedings. Later that day Clinton met with the obeisant green leaders, including National Wildlife's Mark van Puten, the Sierra Club's Carl Pope, and World Resources Institute chairman

William Ruckleshaus. Ruckleshaus is also a longtime board member of Weyerhaeuser, the Seattle-based transnational timber company. On Thursday, environmentalists held a large demonstration outside the downtown offices of the timber company's realty wing. Needless to say, the leaders of the big green groups didn't show up for that one.

Clinton talked about having the WTO incorporate environmental sidebars into its rulemaking. But then the administration didn't back away from its Global Logging Amendment, an accelerated reduction in tariffs on the global timber trade. George Frampton, head of the Council on Environmental Quality and former head of the Wilderness Society, appeared at a press conference later in the day and stiff-armed the greens. "Knowledgeable environmentalists shouldn't have anything against the measure," Frampton said. His voice reeked with condescension. In fact, this was the one issue on which all the big groups were united in opposition to the US position.

"This follows the tried and true Clinton formula: kiss 'em, then fuck 'em over, " Steve Spahr, a bus driver, computer repairman, and ancient forest defender from Salem, Oregon, told me.

Clinton called the events outside his suite in the Westin "a rather interesting hoopla." The president expressed sympathy for the views of those in the streets at the very moment his aides were ordering Seattle Mayor Paul Schell (aka "Mayor Shellshocked") to use all available force to clear the streets. There is now no question but that the most violent attacks by the police and the National Guard came at the request of the White House and not the mayor or the police chief. And, in fact, CNN has reported that Clinton has once again flouted the Posse Comitatus Act by sending in a contingent from the US military to the scene. More than 160 members of the Domestic Military Support Force were sent to Seattle on Tuesday, including troops from the Special Forces division and the Delta Force. Clinton, of course, has been quite happy to blame Mayor Schell, the Seattle police, and the WTO itself for both the chaos and the crackdown, while offering himself as a peacemaker to the very battle he provoked.

While Clinton was jabbering on, Victor Menotti became the latest victim of police brutality. Menotti is an environmental trade specialist for the International Forum on Globization and a fierce critic of the WTO. Victor's a policy wonk and a good one. He was also a credentialed WTO observer. Menotti had been attending a briefing by Clinton administration reps and other WTO officials on a global logging initiative. The meeting had taken a bad turn. Menotti, carrying a sheaf of papers, took a break from the dismal session inside the convention center and went outside to brief his colleagues out on the street. "It looks like your worst fears have been realized," Menotti said. In other words, the Clinton administration had once again caved into the pressures of the multinational timber giants. Then there was a sudden flurry of activity at the nearby corner of Fifth and

Pike. "I saw the crowd in front of me reel back and turn and run, and I just looked over my shoulder and saw black ponchos flying and the sticks in the air, and I just fled myself," Menotti said. Menotti recalls scooting down the street for about a block. He negotiated his way around a parked car and then it dawned on him that the police were after him for some reason. "I just thought, `There's no reason to run,'" Menotti said. Menotti was arrested, his papers siezed, and he was hauled off to jail. "I kept thinking: who was it that targeted me for arrest."

The police report says Menotti was arrested for "obstructing an officer." But he was never charged. Even so, he spent the night in the King County Jail. It was in that jail cell that Menotti met Gezai Yihdego, a thirty-five-year-old black Seattlite who had been born in war-torn Etitrea. It immediately struck Menotti that Yihdego didn't look like the typical WTO protester. He wasn't. Yihdego was a cab driver. On Wednesday morning he was cruising past the Madison hotel when he was flagged down by a woman. He picked her up and pulled back into traffic, but was almost immediately thereafter halted by a policeman. The cop reached into the Yihdego's window and sharply pulled the steering wheel to the left.

"'Sir, I have a passenger,' Yihdego told the cop. 'And you may put our life in danger. Don't pull this. It's my car. You have no right to touch my car, my property.' But he opened the door and tried to push me hard to the right. I resisted that and I said, 'This is my car. Get out.' Then he started to drag me out."

Yihdego's frightened passenger wasn't an ordinary citizen, but a member of the Clinton administration and an official WTO delegate. She later told the *Seattle Times* that she had objected to the treatment of Yihdego, but she was still so frightened that she wanted to remain nameless. "The policeman opened the door, grabbed the cab driver, threw him to the ground, and there were six other officers that surrounded him," she said. "I'm just stunned."

The Clinton administration official told the cops that the cab driver had done nothing wrong and that they should leave him alone. They didn't. One of the cops jerked Yihdego up off the pavement and shouted, "Where are you from?"

"Hell, look, man, what does that have to do with anything?" Yihdego said. "Are you arresting me for being foreign? For having an accent? For being black? For being a taxi driver?"

Over the protest of the Clinton administration official, Yihdego was carted off to jail. Neither he nor Menotti were ever charged with a crime.

Eventually, Clinton shut up and Brower and Foster walked into the room. Brower was breaking new ground once again by pulling together a new group of trade unionists and greens. At eighty-seven-years-old, Brower, the arch druid, is finally beginning to show his age. He walks with a cane. A pacemaker regulates his heartbeat. He is fighting bladder cancer. And he can't drink as many dry martinis as he used to. But his mind is still as agile as an antelope, his intellectual vision startlingly clear and radical. "Today, the police in Seattle have proved they are the handmaidens of the corporations," said Brower. "But something else has been proved. And that's that people are starting to stand up and say: we won't be transnational victims."

Brower was joined by David Foster, director for District 11 of the United Steelworkers of America, one of the most articulate and unflinching labor leaders in America. Earlier this year, Brower and Foster formed an unlikely alliance, a coalition of radical environmentalists and Steelworkers called the Alliance for Sustainable Jobs and the Environment, which had just run an amusing ad in the New York Times asking "Have You Heard the One About the Environmentalist and the Steelworker." The groups had found they had a common enemy: Charles Hurwitz, the corporate raider. Hurwitz owned the Pacific Lumber Company, the northern California timber firm that is slaughtering some of the last stands of ancient redwoods on the planet. At the same time, Hurwitz, who also controlled Kaiser Aluminum, had locked out 3,000 Steelworkers at Kaiser's factories in Washington, Ohio, and Louisiana. "The companies that attack the environment most mercilessly are often also the ones that are the most antiunion," Foster told me. "More unites us than divides us."

I came away thinking that for all its promise this tenuous marriage might end badly. Brower, the master of ceremonies, isn't going to be around forever to heal the wounds and cover up the divisions. There are deep, inescapable issues that will inevitably pit Steelworkers, fighting for their jobs in an ever-tightening economy, against greens, defending dwindling species like sockeye salmon that are being killed off by the hydrodams that power the aluminum plants. When asked about this potential both Brower and Foster danced around it skillfully. But it was a dance of denial. The tensions won't go away simply because the parties agree not to mention them in public. Indeed, they might even build, like a pressure cooker left unwatched. I shook the thought from my head. For this moment, the new, powerful solidarity was too seductive to let such broodings intrude for long.

If anything could anneal the alliance together it was the actions of the Seattle cops and National Guard, who until Wednesday afternoon had displayed a remarkable reluctance to crackdown on unionists. The Steelworkers had gotten permission from the mayor for a sanctioned march from the Labor Temple to the docks, where they performed a mock "Seattle Steel Party," dumping styrofoam steel girders into the waters of Elliot Bay, then, showing their new-found green conscience, fishing them back out.

When the rally broke up, hundreds of Steelworkers joined with other protesters in an impromptu march down First Avenue. As the crowd reached Pike Place Market, they found paramilitary riot squads waiting for them and were rocked with volleys of military-strength CN gas, flash bombs, and larger rubber bullets, about a half-inch in diameter. The carnage was indiscriminate. Holiday shoppers and Metro buses were gassed. In an effort to jack up the intimidation, the cop squads were marching in almost goose-stepping fashion, smacking their riot clubs against their shin-guards to create a sinister sound with echoes back to Munich. This was the most violent of the street battles that I witnessed, involving hundreds of police and more than twenty tear gas attacks.

That night repeated volleys of concussion grenades were launched over the crowd, sending many people diving down onto the pavement and others scurrying into store-fronts for safety. After a tremendous explosion a Seattle cop was caught on the depart-ment's videotape exclaiming, "That was sweet!"

There is a certain species of pacifist who finds any outward expression of outrage embarrassing. Thus it was that demonstrators at nearly every corner and barricade where being cautioned "not to retaliate" against police attacks. They were even warned not to throw the tear gas cans back toward the police lines. But, of course, that was the safest place for them. They weren't going to hurt the cops, who were decked out in the latest chemical warfare gear.

That night at Pike Place Market a can of tear gas landed at my feet. Next to me were a young woman and her four-year-old son. As the woman pulled her child inside her rain-coat to protect him from the poison gas, I reached down, grabbed the canister and heaved it back toward the advancing black wall of cops. The can was so hot it seared by hand. Expecting to be shot at, I dove behind the nearest dumpster and saw a familiar face. It was Thomas, one of the rappers I'd walked with on Tuesday morning. We huddled close together, shielding our eyes from the smoke and gas. "Now all these muthafuckas up here have a taste of what it's like in Compton nearly every night," Thomas screamed.

When the cops are on the streets in force, black people always pay the price. As Thomas and I were ducking flash bombs and rubber bullets, Seattle police were busy harassing Richard McIver, a black Seattle city councilman who was on his way to a WTO reception at the Westin Hotel. Even though McIver flashed the police with his embossed gold business card identifying him as a councilman, the police denied him entry. They roughly pulled him from his car and threatened to place him in handcuffs. Rep. Dennis Kucinich, the Democrat, witnessed this scene from Ohio. "I'm fifty-eight-years-old," McIver said. "I had on a four-hundred-dollar suit, but last night I was just another nigger."

Seattle had become a proving ground for what defense theorists have dubbed "asymmet-rical warfare," urban assaults against a city's own citizens. The Seattle officials claimed they were caught off-guard, hamstrung by a city ordinance that prevented them from doing covert investigations. But the organizing for the Seattle protests weren't much of a secret.

What hadn't already been reported by the *New York Times* and *Wall Street Journal* was available for the cops to study on numerous web sites. Even the irrascible Ruckus Society attempted to negotiate mass arrests with the police. But the deputy chief told John Sellers that they simply didn't have the manpower to handle it in such a coordinated fashion. Sellers smiled and replied, "We can live with that."

The moaning from the cops was a weak attempt to cover their ass and to strike a hated restriction on their police powers, the Seattle Police Investigations Ordinance. The measure prohibits Seattle police from infiltrating and spying on individuals and groups based solely on their political affiliations and opinions, an entirely sensible law that was passed in 1979 after it came to light that Seattle police had amassed thousands of dossiers on people and groups because of their politics, not any evidence of wrongdoing.

Seattle police said they responded aggressively only when their officers were hit with rocks, bottles, and Molotov cocktails. Well, frankly, this is bullshit. Seattle isn't Beirut. There's no rocky rubble on the streets of the Emerald City. In fact, there weren't any glass bottles, either. In the eight or nine confrontations I witnessed, the most the cops were hit with were some half-full plastic water bottles and a few lightweight sticks that had been used to hold cardboard signs.

Despite the fearmongering by the police and Clinton administration flacks, the evidence of a civilian riot was nonexistent. With tens of thousands of demonstrators on the streets for a week, under near-constant assault by cops, there were no firearms confiscated, no Molotov cocktails discovered, and no police officers seriously injured—though many later claimed disabilities for stress, anxiety, and exhaustion. Most of the fifty-six officers who filled out injury reports were victims of friendly fire—hit by concussion grenades, overcome from tear gas and pepper spray, burns from mishandling tear gas cannisters, hearing loss from grenades and gunfire. One officer even claimed that a tight-fitting gas mask cracked several of his teeth.

In the end, what was vandalized? Mainly the boutiques of Sweatshop Row: Nordstrom's, Adidas, the Gap, Bank of America, NikeTown, Old Navy, Banana Republic, and Starbucks. The expressions of destructive outrage weren't anarchic, but extremely well targeted. The manager of Starbucks whined about how "mindless vandals" destroyed his window and tossed bags of French Roast onto the street. But the vandals weren't mindless. They didn't bother the independent streetside coffee shop across the way. Instead, they lined up and bought cup after cup. No good riot in Seattle could proceed without a cup of espresso.

These minor acts of retribution served as a kind of Gulf of Tonkin incident. They were used to justify the repressive and violent onslaughts by the police and the National Guard. Predictably, the leaders of the NGOs were fast to condemn the protesters. The

*World Trade Observer* is a daily tabloid produced during the convention by the mainstream environmental groups and the Nader shop. Its Wednesday morning edition contained a stern denunciation of the direct action protests that had shut down the WTO the day before. Pope repudiated the violence of the protests, saying it delegitimized the position of the NGOs. He did not see fit to criticize the actions of the police.

But even Carl Pope was outdone by Medea Benjamin, the diminutive head of Global Exchange, who her sent her troops out to protect the facades of NikeTown and the Gap from being defaced by protesters. Benjamin told the *New York Times*: "Here we are protecting Nike, McDonald's, the Gap, and all the while I'm thinking, 'Where are the police? These anarchists should have been arrested.'" Of course, Nike is used to police intervening to protect its factories from worker actions in places like Indonesia and Vietnam and it's depressing to see Benjamin calling for such crackdowns in Seattle.

The assault on NikeTown didn't begin with the anarchists, but with protesters who wanted to get a better view of the action. They got the idea from Rainforest Action Network activists who had free-climbed the side of a building across the street and unfurled a huge banner depicting a rattlesnake, coiled and ready to strike, with the slogan, "Don't Trade on Me."

Occupying the intersection in front of NikeTown was a group of Korean farmers and greens, several dressed in their multicolored traditional garb. It's no secret why they picked this corner. For decades, Nike has exploited Korean workers in its Asian sweatshops. These folks cheered wildly and banged their copper kettles when a climber scaled the façade of Nike's storefront, stripped the chrome letters off the NikeTown sign and tossed them to crowd, as Nike store managers in the window a floor above ate their lunch. The action should have warmed the hearts of nearly everyone, even the Seattle Downtown Beautification Association. For one brief moment, the city of Seattle had been rid of an architectural blight. As Harper's magazine reported a few years ago the black-and-silver neo-noir stylings of NikeTown outlets bear an eerie resemblance to the designs concocted by Albert Speer for the Third Reich.

The cops finally overreached that night when they backed us up into the Capitol Hill district, the densest residential neighborhood north of San Francisco. The area was far outside the curfew zone and the no-protest area. But more than a hundred cops came anyway, claiming that the protesters might take over the East Precinct building.

Brian Derdowski had a different recollection. Derdowski is a member of the King County council. When he saw the TV coverage of the cops driving the protester up into the Capitol Hill district, he went there himself. For the next four hours he tried to mediate between the cops and the protesters and residents. But he was gassed himself and took down accounts of police driving vans directly into the crowd. "The police were going around in vans, approaching groups of demonstrators and residents, jumping out of vehicles, using tear gas and rubber bullets on people, then jumping back into the vehicles and driving away," Derdowski recalled.

People watching TV late that night saw a cop accost a man on the sidewalk, poke him in the chest with his baton, kick him in the groin and then, for good measure, shoot him in the neck with a rubber bullet. The man wasn't a WTO protester, but a resident who had been gassed out of his home.

Another strange story of that night was recorded by a National Lawyers Guild attorney from a worker trapped in his downtown office building on Wednesday afternoon: "The witness states that he left his downtown work at 3:30 that day. Aware of what had been going on, he states he asked an officer if it was safe to leave. The officer reportedly stated that it was a peaceful protest and no tear gas would be fired. The worker states he had walked a few blocks and was hit with CS gas. As he turned to leave, he was disoriented by concussive grenades, and hit again with gas. He then returned to his place of work and disposed of his ruined contact lenses. He tried to leave again at 5 P.M., but was gassed. Later that evening, he returned to his home at Capitol Hill. Here he witnessed police shooting rubber bullets and tear gas at residents and into a business. Standing near his house he was shot with rubber bullets."

Around midnight a woman got off work at a restaurant in Capitol Hill. Her boyfriend had come to escort her home through the battle-strewn streets. She later told her story to investigators with ACLU: "We just hit the street when an officer said, 'Get the fuck out of here.' Then he hit my boyfriend with his nightstick. My boyfriend said, 'We are not protesters, we are just walking home.' And the officer hit him again. By then there was another officer and they pushed us up against the storefront and frisked us. An officer said, 'You've no idea what we've been through today.' They then sprayed my friend with pepper spray and handcuffed him. As they hauled him off to the squad car, I started back to the restaurant to get my boss. When I turned back to look at him again, an officer sprayed me in the face with pepper spray."

It was a little after 2 A.M. There were less than a hundred of us left on the street. We faced even more cops. Someone began to sing Silent Night. And the final assault of gas and grenades is launched. I stumble back to the King's Inn and finally go to sleep with the words of John Goodman, a locked-out steelworker from Spokane, ringing in my head. "The things I've seen here in Seattle I never thought I'd see America."

## Thursday

The next morning I was coughing up small amounts of blood, 600 demonstrators were in jail, the police were on the defensive over their tactics, and the WTO conference itself was coming apart at the seams.

The arrested had been hauled off to the old Sand Point naval base, where many of them sat for hours in crowded buses. In most cases, the arresting officers didn't write individual arrest reports. Many of the arrestees were offered a deal: they would be released on the condition that they not re-enter the downtown area. It was a deal few took. They were essentially tortured for their refusal. Most were held for more than seventy-two hours without being arraigned, allowed medical attention or contact with their attorneys.

And some were savagely beaten. Take the case of Keith Holm. Holm is a thirty-five-year-old construction worker who was arrested on misdemeanor charges on Wednesday. He was taken to King County Jail, where he was almost immediately roughed up by deputies. "Right as I went in, I was singled out off the bus, along with five others," Holm later told the Seattle Weekly. "I was passed around like a hackey sack. They stamped on my back and the backs of my knees. They busted my face through a steel door and then through a glass door. There were clumps of my hair in their fingers. There was nonstop screaming and profanity. They kept asking my name and saying they were going to kill me, going to fuck me up." There were more than 300 reports of brutality against protesters inside Seattle's jails.

In the end there were 631 arrests, all but 24 on misdemeanor charges such as obstructing pedestrian traffic or failure to disperse. The charges against 511 of the arrestees were dismissed. Only 14 cases actually went to trial and there the Seattle DA's record was far from impressive: 10 plea bargains, 2 guilty verdicts, and 2 acquittals.

Inside the WTO, the African nations had shown the same solidarity as the protesters on the streets. They refused to buckle to US demands and coaxed from US Trade Rep.resentative Charlene Barshevsky a blunt threat: "I reiterated to the ministers that if we are unable to achieve that goal I fully reserve the right to also use an exclusive process to achieve a final outcome. There's no question about my right as a chair to do it or my intention to do it, but it is not the way I want this to be done." Despite the heavy-handed bluster, the African delegates hung together and the WTO talks collapsed.

I walked out on the street one last time. The acrid stench of CN gas still soured the morning air. As I turned to get into my car for the drive back to Portland, a black teenager grabbed my arm. "Hey, man, does this WTO deal come to town every year?" I knew how the kid felt. Along with the poison, the flash bombs and rubber bullets, there was an optimism, energy, and comraderie that I hadn't felt in a long time.

## Seattle and Beyond

Beyond the wildest hopes of the street warriors, five days in Seattle have brought us one victory after another. The protesters initially shunned and denounced by the respectable "inside strategists," scorned by the press, gassed and bloodied by the cops and National Guard shut down the opening ceremony; prevented Clinton from addressing the WTO delegates at Wednesday night gala; turned the corporate press from prim denunciations of "mindless anarchy" to bitter criticisms of police brutality; and forced the WTO to cancel its closing ceremonies and to adjourn in disorder and confusion, without an agenda for the next round.

In the annals of popular protest in America, these have been shining hours, achieved entirely outside the conventional arena of orderly protest and white paper activism and the timid bleats of the professional leadership of big labor and environmentalists. This truly was an insurgency from below in which all those who strove to moderate and deflect the turbulent flood of popular outrage managed to humiliate themselves. The contradiction between the demur agenda of the genteel element and the robust, tear-it-all-down approach of the street legions was already apparent by Tuesday.

Here's a might-have-been for you. All day long, Tuesday, November 30, the street warriors in downtown Seattle vindicated their pledge to shut down the first day of the WTO talks, in itself a rousing victory. Locked-down Earth-First!ers, Ruckus Society agitators, anarchists, and other courageous troublemakers sustained baton charges, tear gas, and rubber bullets, hopefully awaiting reinforcement from the big labor rally taking place around the Space Needle, some fifteen or twenty blocks from downtown. As the morning ticked away and the cops got rougher, the street warriors kept asking, "Where are the labor marchers?", expecting that at any moment thousands of longshoremen and teamsters would reinforce them in the desperate fray.

But the absent legions of labor never showed. Suppose they had. Suppose there had been 30,000 to 40,000 protesters around the convention center, vowing to keep it shut down all week. Would the cops have charged such a force? Downtown could have been held all night, and perhaps President Bill would have been forced to make his welcoming address from SeaTac or from the sanctuary of his ardent campaign funder, the Boeing Company. That would have been a humiliation for imperial power of historic proportions, like the famous greeting the Wobblies organized to greet president Woodrow Wilson after the breaking of the Seattle general strike in 1919 when workers and their families lined the streets, block after block, standing in furious silence as the President's motorcade passed by. Wilson had his stroke not long thereafter.

This might-have-been is not posed out of churlishness, but to encourage a sense of realism about what is possible in the struggle against the trading arrangements now operative in the WTO.

Take organized labor, as embodied in the high command of the AFL-CIO. As these people truly committed to the destruction of the WTO? Of course they aren't. It was back in February of this year that the message came down from AFL-CIO HQ that rallying in Seattle was fine, but the plan was not to shut down the WTO. Labor's plan was to work from the inside. As far as any street action was concerned, the deals were cut long ago. Labor might huff and labor might puff, but when it comes to the WTO what labor wants, in James Hoffa's phrase, is a seat at the table.

And what does this seat at the table turn out to be? At Seattle those labor chieftains were willing to settle for a truly threadbare bit of window dressing, in the shape of a working group which will, in the next round of WTO talks, be sensitive to labor's concerns. Here's the chronology. The present trade round will ponder the working group's mission and composition and make recommendations for the next round of trade talks. Then, when the next round gets under way, the working group will perhaps take form. Guess what? It's at least 2014 A.D. before the working group is up and running.

There are unions—the autoworkers, steelworkers, teamsters, machinists, UNITE—that have rank-and-file members passionately concerned about "free trade" when, as a in the case of Teamsters, it means Mexican truck drivers coming over the border at two dollars an hour. But how many of these unions are truly ready to break ranks and holler "Death to the WTO!" For that matter, how many of them are prepared to think in world terms, as the capitalists do? Take the steel workers, the only labor group which, in the form of the Alliance for Sustainable Jobs and the Environment, took up position in downtown that Tuesday morning (and later fought with the cops and endured tear gas themselves). But on that same day, November 30, the *Moscow Tribune* ran a story reporting that the Clinton administration has effectively stopped all cold-rolled steel imports from Russia by imposing penalty duties of 178 percent. Going into winter those Russian working families at Severstal, Novolipetsk, and Magnitogorsk are facing tougher times than ever. The reporter, John Helmer, wasn't in doubt why: "Gore must try to preserve steel company and steel worker support."

As the preceding item suggests, there's no such thing as "free trade." The present argument is not about trade, for which (except for maybe a few bioregionialists in Ecotopia) all are in favor in some measure. The argument is about how trade is to be controlled, how wealth is to be made and distributed. The function of the WTO is to express in trade rules the present balance of economic power on the world held by the big corporations, which see the present WTO round as an opportunity to lock in their gains, to enlist its formal backing in their ceaseless quest for cheap labor and places to dump their poisons.

So ours is a worldwide guerilla war of publicity, harassment, obstructionism. It's nothing simple, like the "Stop the War" slogan of the 1960s. Capitalism could stop that war and move on. American capitalism can't stop trade and survive on any terms it cares for.

We truly don't want a seat at the table to "reform" trade rules, because capitalism only plays by the rules if it wrote those rules in the first place. The day the WTO stipulates the phase-in of a world minimum wage of three dollars an hour is the day the corporations destroy it and move on. Anyone remember those heady days in the 1970s of the New World Economic Order when Third World countries were going to get a fair shake for their commodities? We were at a far more favorable juncture back then, but it wasn't long before the debt crisis had struck, the NWEO was dead, and the mildly progressive UN Commission on Trade and Development forever sidelined. Publicity, harassment, obstructionism . . . Think always in terms of international solidarity.

Find targets of opportunity. South Africa forces domestic licensing at cheaper rates of AIDS drugs. Solidarity. The Europeans don't want bioengineered crops. Fight on that front. Challenge the system at the level of its pretensions. Make demands in favor of real free trade. Get rid of copyright and patent restrictions and fees imposed on developing nations. Take Mexico. Dean Baker, of the Center for Economic and Policy Research reckons that Mexico paid the industrial nations last year $4.2 billion in direct royalties, fees, and indirect costs. And okay, let's have real free trade in professional services, with standardization in courses and tests so that kids from Mexico and elsewhere can compete with our lawyers, accountants, and doctors.

A guerilla war, without illusions or respectable ambitions. Justice in world trade is by definition a revolutionary and utopian aim.

# Anarkids and Hypocrites
## Barbara Ehrenreich

*The Progressive*, June 2000

In retrospect, it looks like a case of false advertising. Posters for the April 16 anti-IMF actions in Washington, DC, promised a "nonviolent demonstration." But what actually happened was that thousands of demonstrators were teargassed, pepper-sprayed, and/or beaten with police batons.

The Midnight Special Legal Collective, which provided legal support for the demonstrators, reports that one protester had three ribs broken during his arrest. Another was beaten bloody, then tossed into a paddy wagon with the instruction that he be driven around for a few hours before being taken to a hospital. In jail, hundreds of protesters were denied food or water for twenty-four hours, leading in at least one case to a severe hypoglycemic reaction. According to the legal collective:

> One group of men was taken into a basement, put into a cage, and told by a U.S. marshal, 'There are no cameras here. We can do whatever we want.' Anyone who looked up while the marshal was speaking was punched in the face. People were being released from prison in the middle of a cold, rainy night, without jackets, shoes, in some cases without shirts, and without any money to take a bus or cab anywhere—all had been taken from them by officials.

If this is nonviolence, you'd be better off taking up extreme boxing.

The anti-IMF posters were, of course, promising that the demonstrators themselves would behave in a nonviolent fashion, but nonviolence on one side is, at least in theory, connected to nonviolence on the other. If the protesters are civil and predictable in their actions, then, it is generally hoped and believed, the police will be moved to emulate them. And if the police should fall short of perfect nonviolence, then—the reasoning goes—the poor, martyred demonstrators will at least have the moral upper hand. Hence, in no small part, the excessive reaction by organizers of the Seattle anti-WTO protests to the black-clad anarchists who threw rocks through the windows of NikeTown, Starbucks, the Gap, and a few other chain stores last November.

No humans were harmed in the rock-throwing incidents—the stores were closed at the time. Yet anti-WTO organizers from the Direct Action Network reacted as if their protest had been taken over by a band of Hell's Angels. Instead of treating the young rock-throwers like sisters and brothers in the struggle—wrongheaded, perhaps, but undeniably enthusiastic—protest organizers swept up the broken glass.

Will somebody please call Hypocrisy Watch? The same people who administered a public spanking to the anarkids featured, as one of the anti-WTO's honored guests, one José Bové, the French farmer who famously torched a McDonald's. The double standard for what counts as "violence" was never explained.

Seattle organizers also fretted that the anarkids' actions would upset the unions, although no union leaders issued a peep of complaint. It would have been odd if they had, since America has one of the most violent labor histories of any industrialized nation in the world, and not every little bit of that violence was perpetrated by the Pinkertons. Nor did the rock throwing demonstrably "ruin" the Seattle protests in the eyes of the public. In fact, it probably doubled the media attention, with most press accounts carefully distinguishing between the fifty thousand rock-less protesters and the twenty or so window smashers.

And it would be interesting to know how many of the anarkid-bashers ever took the time to denounce the riot that swept Los Angeles just after the Rodney King verdict in 1990. Yes, I said "riot"—including attacks on people as well as property, much of it belonging to merely middle-class, mostly Korean-American, citizens. But the oh-so-politically-correct, whose numbers no doubt include some of today's self-righteously nonviolent protesters, prefer to call that an "uprising."

The events in Seattle and DC are in many obvious ways enormously heartening, but they also illustrate how absurdly ritualized left-wing protests have become, at least on the side of the protesters. Once, back in the now-prehistoric sixties, a group would call for a demonstration, with or without a police permit, and the faithful would simply show up. If you were fortunate or fleet of foot, you got away unscathed. Otherwise—well, everyone knew there were risks to challenging the power of the state.

Sometime in the early 1980s, demonstration organizers started getting smarter—or, you might say, more scientific and controlling—about the process of demonstrating. In the anti-nuclear power and antiwar movements of the day, they carefully segregated protesters who wished to be arrested from those who did not and insisted that the potential arrestees be organized into "affinity groups" that had been trained for hours or even days in the technology of "nonviolent civil disobedience." It made sense at the time. Affinity groups provided a basis for consensual decision making among large numbers of people. The training—in linking arms, going limp, and "jail solidarity"—helped assure minimal bodily harm to the arrestees. Besides, everything gets professionalized sooner or later: why not the revolution?

But there are problems with the new liturgy of protest. For one thing, not everyone has a master's degree in nonviolent civil disobedience, and many potential protesters, even quite militant ones, would be put off by the countercultural atmosphere of the trainings. I can remember almost being turned away from an antinuclear action in 1982 until one of my companions had the wit to lie and claim that we had indeed gone through extensive training.

Then there is the numbingly ritual quality of the actions: protesters sit down in a spot prearranged with the police, protesters get carried off by the police and booked, protesters get released. Sometimes safely ritualized protests can be effective, as when, in March 1999, almost twelve hundred people—including dignitaries like former New York City Mayor David Dinkins—got themselves arrested to protest the shooting of Amadou Diallo. But even one of the organizers of that protest, longtime activist Leslie Cagan, points out the irony in the protesters' harmonious relationship with the very police force whose homicidal behavior they were protesting.

Worst of all, nonviolence on the part of protesters does not guarantee nonviolent behavior on the part of the police. In Seattle, as well as in DC, many protesters were rewarded for their civility with pepper spray, beatings, and gas. These are not crossing guards we are up against, but some of the most highly militarized police in the world. In a few decades, they have moved from terrorizing communities of color to deploying torture as a tactic against anyone, of any color, who steps out of line: starving detainees in DC, rubbing pepper spray in the eyes of antilogging protesters in California, confining prisoners to potentially lethal restraint chairs . . .

Clearly the left, broadly speaking, has come to a creative impasse. We need to invent some new forms of demonstrating that minimize the danger while maximizing the possibilities for individual self-expression (sea turtle costumes, songs, dancing, and general playfulness). We need ways of protesting that are accessible to the uninitiated, untrained, nonvegan population as well as to the seasoned veteran. We need to figure out how to capture public attention while, as often as possible, directly accomplishing some not-entirely-symbolic purpose, such as gumming up a WTO meeting or, for that matter, slowing down latte sales at a Starbucks.

Rock throwing doesn't exactly fit these criteria, nor did the old come-as-you-are demos of the sixties. But neither do the elaborately choreographed rituals known as "nonviolent" civil disobedience. The people at Direct Action Network, Global Exchange, and other groups were smart enough to comprehend the workings of the WTO, IMF, and World Bank. Now it's time for them to figure out how large numbers of people can protest the international capitalist cabal without getting clobbered—or trashed by their fellow demonstrators—in the process.

# Seeds of a Movement
## From Seattle to Washington and Beyond
# Stanley Aronowitz

From the moment we stepped out of the Metro and began walking toward the demonstration I had a feeling that organizers' predictions of about ten thousand protesters were a little overstated. When we arrived at the Ellipse early on a hot April Saturday morning the area was sparsely filled and my heart sank. Is there a new movement being born or was the Seattle march in December 1999 a fluke whose success was made possible only by union members who were mainly interested in protecting their jobs? Getting closer to the epicenter of the event it became clear that the emblems of labor presence, banners, t-shirts, and hats were largely missing.

With few exceptions the labor movement had not shown up to oppose the many insults visited on the planet and upon its populations by the IMF and the World Bank. Trade is one thing: what the WTO does to labor is crystal clear. It puts it in competition with itself on a world scale, and unions, particularly in the manufacturing sector, are ready to fight against free trade that would export their jobs to low-wage areas of the globe. But the complex activities of these international financial institutions are something else. Often their interventions damage the physical environment, reduce or obliterate the sovereignty of struggling nation-states and determine patterns of global investment, resulting in the expansion of low-wage industries here and starvation and joblessness there. These issues touch the hearts of rain forest defenders and tree huggers, students who morally condemn corporations that subject women and children to long hours and slave wages. But the attempt to broaden the struggle against capitalist globalization has not (yet) gripped American working men and women. Except for the embattled garment and other low wage workers, the direct connection between the shop and the new global economic and physical environment is simply not evident in the same way that the Mexican *macquiladores* or Chinese TV and computer factories are. In these instances plants in economically disadvantaged countries threaten the relatively high wages and benefits of workers in this country. What enrages union members is the Husky case where the company pulled up stakes in Ohio to escape seventeen-dollar-an-hour union wages and set up shop in China to pay twenty-five cents. What was left at the Washington demonstration was a band of individuals, most of them inspired by the anti-WTO Seattle days, by antisweatshop sentiments, and by their intellectual grasp of how dangerous these agencies are. It was clear though, despite many union endorsements for the Washington rally, that, unlike Seattle, the event had inadequate organization and even fewer resources.

An hour later more people started streaming into the area and by early afternoon it was plain that the slim ranks had swelled, if not to ten thousand, at least to respectability. Many quickly filled the spaces under the trees that surrounded the nearly unbearably hot open field where thousands strained to hear the steady stream of barely audible speakers recite the litany of IMF calamities. Announcing their attendance a small band of black, Asian, and Latino marchers circled the periphery, as if to rebuke an earlier report, published in the *Wall Street Journal,* that this was to be virtually an all-white convocation. Their spirited rebuttal only highlighted the accuracy of the *Journal's* prediction. For there was little doubt that if the organizers had made a serious effort to attract racialized minorities to the event they had failed abysmally. But of course they did not. The fact is the incipient movement, reflected in the crowd, was composed largely of an agglomeration of student Nike haters, environmentalists, the small but growing group of anarcho-ecologists (themselves split eight ways to Sunday), and old and new leftovers, almost all of whom were middle-class whites.

I had a moment of nostalgia for another spring day in Washington thirty-five years ago when an unprecedented twenty-five thousand people—mostly students—filled the same precincts to mount the first significant national protest against the Vietnam War. Far from suffering the absence of organized labor, that demonstration faced the almost united opposition of a prowar labor movement, the liberal wing of the Democratic Party, and cold war intellectuals. Like the earlier insistence of the militant wing of the civil rights movement that the regular, segregationist delegation of the Mississippi Democratic Party to be unseated at the 1964 Atlantic City Democratic convention, the resolve of Students for a Democratic Society to set its face against the wheel of American foreign policy and its friends in the liberal establishment had been greeted with alarm by those allied to the Johnson administration's New Deal–ish domestic policies that, by the standard of the period, were considered very progressive. The war opponents persisted and, in time, put millions into the streets, forcing a sitting president out of office and changing the complexion of American politics. The images of that struggle flashed and then flickered. The two moments, then and now, were sufficiently different to suppress comparison. This new movement had to be taken on its own terms as well as in the context of the last two decades of retreat and regroupment, decades that witnessed the virtual disappearance of a political opposition worthy of the name in every developed capitalist nation.

In an ironic twist, we who made the insurgent politics of the 1960s—movements of black freedom, second-wave feminism, students, the "new" public- and service-sector labor unions, the poor, the disabled, antiwar, and those associated with consumers—were helped as much as hindered by the politics of the cold war. As long as the Soviet Union, despite its warts, remained an alternative, world capitalism's ability to roll back the great postwar compromise between labor and capital was severely restricted. The compromise, according to which, in return for political and ideological loyalty, capital agreed to a series of regulations and to social welfare programs, had weathered conservative Eisenhower and Nixon presidencies and the exigencies of full wartime mobilization that all but halted Johnson's own resolve to produce a New Deal for blacks. The social movements of the 1950s and 1960s operated well within the boundaries created by the global stalemate: through mass pressure—including civil disobedience—the black freedom movement and its allies held up to world scrutiny the tacit and overt state policies of black oppression, which became intolerable even for the ruling elites (in the 1960s blacks actually narrowed the wage gap considerably and gained increased access to education, health care, and other services); radicals prodded liberals in the feminist movement to take up the social and cultural, as well as the economic position of women and brazenly asked how the United States could maintain inequality with respect to abortion rights, opportunities for higher education, and for day care services when these were available in Communist countries; and after Caryl Chessman was executed in 1967, a movement for prison reform, in the first place against the death penalty, made unprecedented strides. Berkeley students demanded that their education be something different from what their leader, Mario Savio, termed a knowledge factory. Even the Reagan administration, which ruthlessly fired eleven thousand air traffic controllers for striking against the government and did everything it could to weaken and to devalue all manner of public goods, was unable to abolish welfare and to privatize social security, a hesitance which led David Stockman to resign in disgust.

The collapse of the Soviet Union and the transformation of China into a state capitalist society unquestionably changed the terms of global political engagement. Driven by neoliberal economic ideology which proclaimed the "free market" the best guarantee of prosperity for all, the IMF, the World Bank, and a gaggle of consultants trained in the Milton Friedman school of economic policy flooded both the former Communist countries and the Third World. They counseled governments to dismantle their state-run welfare programs, tear down tariff barriers, and open their markets to Coca-Cola and other consumer products. In order to minimize the political turmoil that might result from such policies they were advised to build their police and military forces, even at the cost of increasing their already bloated debt to Western banks. Beneath the advice was the news that World Bank loans to pay for reconstruction and the huge debt already accumulated would be contingent upon slashing budgets, removing state regulation of investment, and opening the veins of their natural and human resources to international capitalist exploitation. All in the name of *development*. To an eerie silence, in the United States a Democratic president signed the Welfare Reform Act and condemned millions to work at minimum wages on penalty of losing their meager public allowances. And, falsely warning that funds would soon dry up without "reform," heeding their Wall Street patrons, conservatives once more beat the drum for schemes to allow holders of social security accounts to invest all or part of their savings in the skittish stock market.

When a reluctant Bill Clinton launched his presidency in 1993 by backing the North Atlantic Free Trade Agreement and driving it through a Democratic Congress it was apparent to many, including a mostly somnolent but suddenly partially revived AFL-CIO, that globalism was now more than slogan; it had become the basis for a major turn in American foreign economic policy. The United States and its network of Western European partners were, through the governing boards of newly strengthened international trade and financial organizations, forcing into existence a New World Order. National sovereignty was a thing of the past for many struggling countries of the South and East. The national context for collective bargaining and for environmental legislation was seriously eroded by the removal of production industries from the advanced industrial societies to low-wage regions, especially Asia, and by IMF sanction for the wholesale destruction of ecosystems in raw material–rich regions of Latin America and Africa. For many activists the nation-state was regarded as no more than one among many sources of contestation. Recognizing that power had been massively displaced to new institutions constructed in the service of a host of recently created transnational corporations, in the 1990s activists began a fervent search for new targets and for new levers.

Prior to the Seattle demonstrations, environmentalists and other non-governmental organizations eagerly attended a series of mostly UN-hosted summits in which the major powers solemnly pledged a new course and the IMF and World Bank echoed these false promises of substantial concessions to the NGOs. By the middle of that decade it was apparent that some once-militant groups such as the Sierra Club had entered an alliance with the "reformed" transnationals and the United States government. Others were not so convinced and began to focus on trade policy, one of the main arenas for the free marketeers.

Seattle was a miscalculation for the Empire on more than one count. When a coalition emerged to protest a major meeting of the World Trade Organization, not a few unions were among the endorsers, but the federal and local governments really did not expect that more than the usual suspects would show up. After all, John Sweeney, the AFL-CIO president, was tied by the hip to Gore's presidential campaign and did not relish the prospect of the embarrassment from massive trade union participation in the protest. Yet the Steelworkers, which accused the WTO of encouraging dumping low-priced foreign steel on the domestic market, and UNITE, the union of garment, textile, and shoe workers, showed uncharacteristic independence when they boldly declared their full support of the event. Sweeney had to be cajoled and ultimately dragged to condemn the administration's trade policy and eventually to support the march and rally. Nor did the authorities anticipate the West Coast Longshore Workers Union, which closed all Pacific coast ports for a day. And the authorities surely did not prepare for the more than thirty thousand demonstrators outside of labor's ranks who showed up to join more than twenty thousand union members. Among these were a relatively large contingent of proponents of direct action and civil disobedience who, upon entry into the city, promptly overwhelmed the local police and together with other demonstrators, effectively shut the city down. By the end of the days of protest Seattle's mayor had egg on his face. Politically shy of clamping down on protesters in the relatively liberal city, he was forced at the eleventh hour by the Feds to come out swinging. Conservatives condemned him for too little and too late and the labor and liberal groups yelled police brutality.

The Seattle debacle was a wake up call to Washington law enforcement officials. They would not be caught napping. Washington police chief Charles Ramsey hired the former FBI official charged with containing and otherwise breaking up the 1960s demonstrations. The former FBI official had handled the obstreperous crowd at the 1968 Democratic convention. Shortly before April 15 he told an interviewer that Washington authorities would take a zero-tolerance policy, meaning they would crack down hard on disobedient demonstrators. As we marched down Constitution Avenue past the IMF and World Bank headquarters it was hard to miss the presence of hundreds of cops assigned to the peaceful activities. On a pretext of health and safety hazards the authorities had already shown their hand by shutting down the hastily erected headquarters of the anti–IMF/World Bank coalition. Not visible were hundreds more police and other government security authorities assigned to break the extralegal activities of demonstrators who were attempting to block the streets leading to the IMF and World Bank headquarters. Hundreds of direct actionists were beaten and arrested in the side streets away from the TV cameras and from public view. Weeks later more than one hundred of them were still in jail.

As the boisterous demonstrators shouted and sang their demands, one could hear a note that almost never passed the lips of earlier movements. To be sure there was that elliptical enunciation by SDS president Paul Potter at the 1965 antiwar rally of the "system," but here on the banners it was named: capitalism. Instead of emanating from tired leftist sects, these flags were hoisted by sixteen-, eighteen- ,and twenty-year-olds. And then the scales fell from my eyes. I was in the midst of a parade of young people and with the exception of some who were there literally in wheelchairs, I was among the oldest participants in the event. This was no Socialist Scholars Conference where, at times, perhaps half the attendees were over fifty. This was a march led and dominated by people well under thirty. The new movement against global capitalism was a youth movement.

For that reason there was a welcome absence of the signs of the old left. Sure they sold their papers and stuck out in the crowd. But they were not the driving force of the movement. The first SDS president, Al Haber, now more than sixty, strode alongside me with eyes shining and a big grin almost dwarfing his huge gray beard. He said, "maybe it's starting again." I nodded my agreement, hoping against hope that what we were witnessing was the energy of a generation rather than a raggle-taggle group of inveterate antis. We knew a fair number of participants but could not have known the veterans of anti-sweatshop campaigns who succeeded in persuading their university administrations to join workers-rights coalitions, the brigades of anarchist youth in their black hats and armbands, and the greens of many stripes who were fighting to preserve wildlife and clean water. As I came away from that day, I was half convinced that, finally, a new breed of radicals was emerging and that it had a fair chance to spread to a generational movement. I had seen high school as well as college students and it reminded me of my own teen activist days.

On Monday after the march, writers for the *Legal Times* reported that the police were taking a hard line against the protesters: "The DC police, armored and with visors down, marched in formation toward the barricade separating them from 500 protestors clustered at the intersection of 20th Street and Pennsylvania Avenue on Monday morning. As they marched, the officers slapped their batons against their shinguards in rhythm." They showered pepper spray at the protesters who, according to the reporters "recoiled in agony their eyes swollen and closed. Other protesters surrounded them, rinsing their eyes with bottled water . . . Meanwhile the crowd chanted 'Sit Down, Sit Down,' and more than a hundred protesters [did] so settling down in the middle of Pennsylvania Avenue. It worked: the spraying stopped. The atmosphere lightened."

Having said all this, it's still not a genuine social movement. I returned from DC to an email from L. A. Kaufman, a former editor of *Socialist Review,* whose newsletter extolled the network that provided the sinews of organization and the larger forces that are straining to forge a new alliance against global capitalism. She praised their lack of ideologies and programs and urged her online readers to concentrate on direct action tactics. While I would not want to see the incipient alliance adopt a sterile ideological framework of, say, socialism in its current permutations, I would want to see a vigorous debate over *ideas.* If anticapitalism is the leading edge, what are the alternatives? Is resistance enough to persuade more than an elite of semiprofessional organizers to stay the course of opposition? Or does the movement need a rich address to the cultural, educational, and social dimensions of life? Do we need to consider running candidates as one tactic without sinking into electoralism? Or is direct action the bottom line against which all else is mere tinkering?

In a time when the imagination is stultified and rechanneled into the dead end of practical reform, rechanneled by the pervasive pessimism that has overcome those still encapsulated in the prisonhouse of defeat, what we need now is a healthy dose of utopian thought. Socialism carries too much baggage, not only that of the discredited communist version but also the severely compromised social-democratic variant. Socialism equals the welfare state and perhaps anarchism—the endgame of any genuine radical movement—and ignores the mediations. Yet, somewhere between is the beginning of a solution. For what we have learned in the last decade is that we have little or no wiggle room, leading some to conclude that all that remains is direct confrontation with Empire and with capital. Capital and its supplicants provide little space for compromise because the forces of the opposition are still incipient. Does this justify all-out confrontation? Clearly many who made the alliance that produced Seattle and Washington—and not only the trade unions—are still caught in the logic of incremental reform. They believe the nation-state still has enough juice to yield concessions. So the problem is to think and debate the alternatives, to experiment with reform even if it yields very little or nothing, and to craft a new politics of internationalism that takes into account the still-potent force of national states and their identities. The hardest work is thinking.

# Color Blind

## Activists of Color Bring the Economic War Home, But Is the Movement Missing the Message?

# Andrew Hsiao

*Village Voice,* July 25, 2000

One weekend last summer, Jia Ching Chen found himself in the bucolic Santa Monica hills, dispensing advice to a roomful of young activists on some of the finer points of occupying a corporation's headquarters. For Chen, the talk itself was not all that new—as a longtime trainer for the Ruckus Society, the Berkeley-based group that in the last four years has schooled a couple of thousand activists in the arts of direct action protest, the twenty-eight-year-old Chen had led many similar workshops. Still, he says, he had never been more excited by a Ruckus event because, for the first time Chen could remember, he was not one of the only people of color in the room.

Indeed, that weekend's Democracy Action Camp—staged on the eve of the August 2000 Democratic convention in LA—brought together more than forty African American, Latino, and Asian American activists with an equal number of white organizers, and was mirrored by a similar camp held on the East Coast to prep for the Republican convention in Philadelphia. For Chen, who has also raised hell with the Third Eye Movement—Bay Area "hip-hop organizers"—it was a rare instance when activist worlds collided. And the camps were "a transforming moment" for the notoriously hippy-hairy Ruckus, he says, a measure of how "we're really trying to address the racial and class divides."

He was talking, of course, about divides that were uncomfortably evident during the spectacular mass protests in Seattle and Washington DC against the WTO, the World Bank, the IMF, and global corporate domination. While the demonstrations electrified radicals across the country, the fact that the ranks of protesters were overwhelmingly white—especially pronounced after organized labor's early withdrawal at A16 (and the arrest of hundreds of young activists of color on the first day of the DC demos)—itself sparked months of internal protest. Many organizers working in black, Latino, and Asian communities were at once elated and disappointed by the demonstrations. Radical black scholar Robin D.G. Kelley spoke for many when he said, "The lack of people of color involved in those protests is a crisis." And for a time, discussion of the racial cast of the protests took on the tones of crisis management, confrontation, and denial. As Mark Rand, executive director of San Francisco's JustAct, noted last summer, "The e-mails have been flying, the listservs have been burning up." Widely circulated articles in *ColorLines*, the publication of the Oakland activist institute the Applied Research Center, prompted expansive—and often angry— electronic exchanges by posing the question, "Where was the color at A16?," and cataloguing "the reasons the Great Battle [of Seattle] was so white."

For many activists of color, those reasons began with the notion that "structural adjustment" abroad can seem abstract to people who "are getting our asses kicked daily," as Van Jones, the director of the Bay Area's Ella Baker Center for Human Rights, says. Meager resources certainly kept some people of color away from Seattle and Washington. And direct-action tactics have a different meaning in communities where many are undocumented or already have a perilous relationship with the police. Some activists of color who went to Seattle or DC came home complaining of an insider's culture of privileged militancy, while others pointed to the racial disconnect in movement ideologies. Activist-academic Vijay Prashad, who helps organize New York's annual Youth Solidarity Summer, for example, argues that the anarchist vibe of the antiglobalization movement turned off people of color, given how the state "is still seen as the arbiter of justice for our communities."

Meanwhile, some white organizers groused that communities of color were simply missing the movement, and perhaps—in their insistence on local, racial issues—the global economic point itself. Others said racial criticisms were based in an outmoded identity politics that has been transcended by the all-inclusive politics of economics. Besides, noted one lead organizer of A16, after Seattle the Mobilization for Global Justice made a number of efforts to diversify the ranks, hiring an outreach coordinator (the group's only paid staffer), visiting African-American churches in Washington, and paying for buses of mostly black ACT UPers from Philadelphia. Njoki Njoroge Njehu, the US director of the international 50 Years Is Enough Campaign, concluded an email defense of A16 outreach efforts with this pointed question: "For me, the question is to my sisters and brothers of color. Where were you on April 16?"

Framing the issue this way, however, as a matter of failed outreach (or of the limitations of activists of color) only sharpened for many the sense that the antiglobal folks just didn't get it—and heightened the sense of missed opportunities. For if the last few years has brought an explosion of radical organizing against globalization, these same years have also featured a concurrent resurgence of activism among young people of color—around issues like police brutality, juvenile justice, and the death penalty. In California, for example, the fight against the draconian juvenile justice measure Propisition 21—designed to funnel teens into adult prisons by giving prosecutors the power to charge fourteen-year-olds in adult court—galvanized an array of multiracial youth groups, especially in the spring months of 2000 leading up to A16. But even in the Bay Area, home to antiglobalization stalwarts like Global Exchange and the Rainforest Network, "these two movements—antiglobalization and anti–prison industrial complex," as Mark Rand puts it, "have been like two ships passing in the night."

Ultimately, the antiglobalization movement's distance from communities of color led many to miss what's distinctive about new activism in these communities. Increasingly, young critics of the criminal-justice system recognize that the prison boom is connected to cuts in social spending and that more aggressive policing of schools, streets, and borders is the toxic by-product of neoliberalism. "They take an anticorporate cut on the criminal-justice issue," says Van Jones. In March 2000, just before Prop. 21 passed, black, Latino, and Asian youth activists designed a campaign that involved storming the headquarters of corporations like Chevron, Pacific Gas & Electric, and Hilton, which had bankrolled the ballot initiative. One hundred seventy-five young people organized by the Third Eye Movement were arrested at the San Francisco Hilton in what Jones calls "the first hip-hop generation sit-in."

Hip-hop also provided the soundtrack for the Prison Moratorium Project's forty-city "No More Prisons" raptivists tour, whose targets include multinational Sodexho Alliance, a major underwriter of the private prison industry (and through its subsidiary, Sodexho-Marriott Services, a purveyor of cafeteria food on some 900 US campuses). Meanwhile, to cite just one more example, L.A.'s immigrant-led Bus Rider's Union has wedded "an explicitly anticorporate analysis," as lead organizer Cynthia Rojas puts it, to its campaign against "'transit racism.' We've done solidarity work with the Zapatistas and connected our struggle to the enormous rise of money for prisons. Basically you're talking about capitalism."

These movements bring the economic war home, and by largely missing that message, the American antiglobalization movement has been fighting with one arm tied behind its back. As Van Jones puts it, "Outreach is a false issue, because the point isn't to make the movement look like a Benetton ad. The question is: How will this convergence actually change the movement?" Following Seattle and A16, movement groups retooled for R2K and D2K, trying to get the different currents of protest to meet at the Republican and Democratic conventions. There were plenty of unlikely and welcome convergences. In Philly, for example, out-of-town antiglobalists got a good taste of the Kensington Welfare Rights Union, one of the country's most creative and flat-out kick-ass movements of poor and homeless people, and—through its multistate marches, world summits, and international lawsuits—a pioneer in connecting the global corporate agenda to local battles. Meanwhile, says Philly organizer Amadee Braxton, cochair of the Black Radical Congress, R2K organizing, beginning with the Democracy Action Camp, helped young activists of color "struggling to find the language to describe structural adjustment at home" broaden their vocabulary. After all, it's not as if national black, Latino, and Asian leadership has taken an anticapitalist, anti-imperialist turn: just as big labor's critique of globalization was blunted by its embrace of Al Gore, so did the NAACP's fondness for the ex-vice president put it inside the Democratic convention, not outside with young protesters of all colors.

Still, for some, there was a disconnected, menu-like quality to the protests at the conventions, partly exacerbated by the decision to devote particular days to specific themes. And it's unclear how activist groups have changed. That they will have to change, probably profoundly—if they truly want convergence—is unquestionable. Consider the road traveled by JustAct. Just a few years ago, JustAct was known as the Overseas Development Network, founded by two brothers from Bangladesh but the very image of what Rand describes as "a mildly progressive organization of mostly white, middle-class students that came into its own in the era of 'We Are the World.'" Then, Rand jokes, he made the mistake of hiring "some young rabble-rousers—working-class youth of color who were very engaged in survival struggles in their communities." Now the organization has been transformed (beginning with its full moniker, JustAct: Youth Action for Global Justice). It has twin concerns: global youth organizing and the more than 70 percent of American young people who don't attend four-year colleges.

The metamorphosis has been painful, involving "bitter arguments and many tear-filled meetings"—and not a few stormy resignations—says Rand, but it has wrought an impressively diverse staff interested in linking local and global struggles. The group helped mobilize multiracial contingents at Seattle, A16, and D2K. Jia Ching Chen, who traveled a similar route from international human rights issues into criminal-justice activism, is now one of JustAct's organizers. A one-man bridge between movements, he was arrested at the San Francisco Hilton, in Seattle, and in L.A.

But even as the antiglobalization movement could learn from JustAct's difficult evolution, organizers in communities of color could gain by studying the struggles of radical outfits like New York's CAAAV: Organizing Asian Communities, which from a mid-'80s origin as an antibias group has added a transnational class analysis to its grassroots presence—and which was one of the groups that sent a contingent of activists of color to A16 and R2K. Both currents could gain from an enlarged sense of each other's movements—and, perhaps, a less diminished understanding of shared histories. As Robin Kelley points out, the rise of people-of-color-led international efforts in the supposedly identity-heavy '80s and '90s—like Central American solidarity groups and the South African divestment campaign—are seemingly forgotten by many today.

Teamsters, turtles—and raptivists? "Our capacities have been weakened because of our blind spots," Van Jones notes. "If we can bring both currents together, we'll have a flood. And the corporations will have a big problem."

# Prague 2000: The People's Battle
# Boris Kagarlitsky

- *Do not wear your Annual Meetings ID badge in public.*

- *Be prepared to display your Annual Meetings ID badge at police checkpoints or when entering the Prague Conference Centre (PCC), and wear it at all times in the PCC and at official Annual Meetings events.*

- *Do not take taxis on the street—ask the hotel or restaurant to call one for you.*

- *Avoid demonstration sites.*

- *Leave in the opposite direction if one is encountered.*

- *Do not engage in debates with demonstrators.*

- *Take leaflets or brochures without comment.*

- *If obstructed by demonstrators, do not try to force your way through, seek help from the nearest police officer.*

- *You are advised not to display jewelry, or wear ostentatious clothing such as furs.*

—From a memorandum to participants in the meeting of the World Bank and the International Monetary Fund.

**September 20** Ordinary Prague citizens have been issued instructions that recall warnings of a nuclear attack. The police have put leaflets in people's letter-boxes appealing to everyone not to go out onto the street, and if possible, to leave the city altogether for the period of the summit. School holidays have been extended. Meanwhile, radical left groups have attached posters to the walls of buildings, calling on Prague residents to come into the streets, and in this way to express their disagreement with the people who are "violating our social rights and freedoms."

The truth is that in Prague, an opponent of the IMF and a critic of capitalism who decides to join in the demonstrations faces an unexpected problem—there are too many demonstrations and other actions. Each group has come up with its own initiative. Left intellectuals have refused to go to communist meetings, and non-government organizations have vied with one another. The antifascists for the most part have held independent actions, without informing anyone else. The humanists have been unwilling to collaborate with anyone either.

**September 21** The more established NGOs are conducting their seminars under the aegis of the group Bankwatch, which, as its name indicates, monitors the actions of the international banks. Some of the participants in these deliberations are turning up in ties. People constantly stress their professionalism, and call for discussions with the heads of the IMF and the World Bank. More radical groups have united around the Initiative Against Economic Globalisation (IAEG). Here the atmosphere is quite different, with men in torn jeans and women with tattoos. Each group regards the other ironically.

Nevertheless, they stress: we have common goals, and we are not going to quarrel. There are reports that in response to the actions of the left and of the "informals," a demonstration has been called by the ultra-right. Quite spontaneously, a new dominant idea is beginning to take hold of the left-wing youth, an idea formulated in the simple slogan, "Beat up the skinheads!"

Putting this into practice would not be particularly hard, considering the huge numerical superiority of the left, strengthened by reinforcements in the form of German anarchists, for whom the week would be wasted if there were no fights with fascists. Fortunately, the police have kept the demonstrations of the left and of the nationalists far enough apart to avoid street fighting. A few fascists have nevertheless been beaten up.

**September 22, Afternoon** We are received by World Bank director James Wolfensohn. He reminds me of Gorbachev. The same goodwill, the same desire for dialogue, and the same helplessness when it comes to the practical question of carrying out reforms.

Even his nickname—Wolfie—is similar. A wonderful man, no doubt, with whom to go to the opera or dine.

Wolfie reassures the representatives of civil society, and tries to justify himself. As proof of the changed character of the bank, he cites what seems to him to be a very convincing figure. Earlier, the bank had two employees working on the problems of civil society: now there are several dozen. New departments and new posts have been created.

The news of a massive growth in the bureaucracy fails to arouse the representatives of civil society. "Give us a chance," Wolfensohn repeats. I begin to feel sorry for him.

Everyday political life was terribly like that in Moscow in the late 1980s. Informal organizations, perestroika . . . The same stormy meetings, the queues for the microphone, the cacophony of demands behind which lies a general discontent, understood and formulated in different ways, with the way life is organized. And the same helpless promises from the authorities, who already understand that carrying on as before is impossible, but who cannot manage anything new. The international financial institutions are just as unreformed as the Soviet bureaucracy. And just like the Soviet party system when it felt the challenge of the times and of society, they are trying somehow or other to reform themselves. Everyone knows how perestroika ended in the Soviet Union. It is quite possible that for the IMF and the World Bank, the consequences of reform will be just as dismal. And even fewer people will regret this than mourn for the USSR.

**September 23, 09:00** I am travelling across the city by tram. At eleven o'clock President Havel is to lead a discussion in the castle between participants in the movement and the heads of the IMF. The city is still almost empty. But sometimes groups of young people are to be seen on the streets, their appearance leaving not the slightest doubt as to why they are here. T-shirts with pictures of Che Guevara and threadbare jeans. Closer to the centre of town, little herds of confused tourists are visible. Making their way through the streets are cavalcades of Audi cars, protected by police cars with flashing lights; inside the Audis are the conference delegates. Meanwhile, the police are taking up their positions. Helicopters circle over the city. Blue uniforms are everywhere. On the flanks of many of the uniforms I notice sickeningly familiar canvas bags containing gas masks, the same as used to be given to us in school during elementary military training exercises. The gas masks have evidently not been used since 1989. The thought strikes me: they are firing off "cherry" gas. It feels as though a war is about to break out.

The sun has emerged, the embellishments on the medieval spires have begun to shine, and the Charles Bridge lies revealed in all its loveliness. Prague during these days is so beautiful you feel like crying.

I ask a middle-aged policeman the way. He starts speaking Russian cheerfully enough, but immediately apologizes. He doesn't know a short route to the castle. He and the other police standing there have been brought in from Moravia. Police have been brought from the whole country, and the armed forces have been put on alert.

I am now in the castle. There is an unexpected call on my mobile phone; my wife in Moscow is worried. I explain that there is no reason to be concerned. In my pocket I have a card identifying me as a participant in the meeting of the IMF and the World Bank, together with an invitation from Havel. On the cover of my passport the police have stuck a special hologram affirming my loyalty. None of this strikes her as especially convincing. "They don't hit you in the passport, they hit you in the face."

The meeting with Havel recalls the last talks before the outbreak of armed hostilities. The sides are still meeting for negotiations, although the troops are already taking up their positions.

We go up to the castle. There are numerous stops for document checks and checks with metal detectors. Soldiers of the presidential guard are in booths, standing just as in London, only their bearing isn't as erect, their uniforms don't fit especially well, and to judge by everything, they're not particularly well fed. In a medieval hall built for ball games, about a hundred representatives of NGOs are assembling, together with a similar number of functionaries of international financial organizations. And television cameras, television cameras . . .

Now Havel arrives. In front of the podium, a small military band has appeared. Guards in red uniforms start playing something like the overture to a Viennese operetta, but an unshaven saxophonist strikes up as well. For several minutes the theme of power and the theme of discontent alternate, but then the guards and the dissident saxophonist begin to play in unison, and all the instruments merge into an optimistic coda. This is evidently meant to reflect Havel's idea of the reconciliation of the authorities and the dissidents.

The reconciliation does not happen.

The first address is from Katarina Lizhkova, speaking in the name of the demonstrators gathering on the streets. A striking young woman from Brno, she speaks impeccable English. "There will not be any dialogue. You talk about dialogue, but the police have already prepared water cannon and tear gas. Thousands of people have been illegally held up at the border, and here in Prague thousands more are being subjected to police persecution simply because they want to exercise their legal right to protest. But we will not stop until the antidemocratic institutions of the financial oligarchy are abolished." The left side of the hall applauds, while the right maintains a gloomy silence.

Walden Bello, one of the movement's most popular ideologues, takes the microphone. "The international financial institutions are a danger. They aren't answerable to anyone. Don't believe what they say. They talk of fighting against corruption, but they supported Yeltsin in Russia! They talk about democracy, but they gave money to the dictator Suharto in Indonesia.

"Now that you've lost your authority, you start talking about social justice. But the words and the deeds part company. If you want changes, then cancel the debts of Russia, cancel the debts of Indonesia. You've made your loans conditional on policies that have brought these countries to ruin and collapse. The programs that are being implemented under the dictates of the IMF almost invariably fail. What right do you now have to demand this money back?" The leftists applaud, while the rightists keep silent.

Trevor Manuel, a one-time communist and revolutionary, and now the South African finance minister, objects to Bello: "Without the international financial institutions, things would be even worse for poor countries." The right wingers applaud. Someone among the leftists mutters: "Traitor!"

In the hall the atmosphere of confrontation is even stronger than on the street. Encountering a hostile audience, Wolfie has become completely self-effacing. Crushed, he hangs his head, again trying to justify himself. By contrast, new IMF director Koler holds forth aggressively. "I have spoken with Third World leaders, and they have had a mass of questions, but no one has demanded that the fund be dissolved. On the contrary, they want to work with us!" "You mean they want to thieve together," mutters the British journalist Alex Kallinikos, who is sitting next to me.

George Soros takes the stand, and unexpectedly, begins to expound the general positions of Marxism on the nature of the capitalist system. Then, just as unexpectedly, he declares: "So long as the rules are as they are, we are going to play by these rules. You should not expect anything else from us financiers. I don't want to lose."

He finishes up with an appeal for reform of the system while there is still time.

Bello once again flings himself on Koler. "Why are you unwilling to reorganize the administration of the IMF? The structure is completely undemocratic. Where are your promised reforms?" Koler replies that the fund is making efforts and improving its work.

"That's not a reply," Bello shouts. "I asked a concrete question. You are simply not willing to reorganize the system of administration! So what is there for us to discuss with you?"

Havel thanks all the participants in the dialogue. The two sides go their separate ways.

**14:00** The first demonstrations begin. We go to look at the communists. There are not especially many people, and the speeches are dull. Surrounding the platform is a solid bank of grey heads.

Further along, young Trotskyists, anarchists, Greeks, and Kurds are gathering and talking. I discover two American students from Madison. A year and a half ago I delivered a lecture to them. What are they doing at a communist meeting? "This is a warm-up. Like a bad rock group before a good concert. You have to start with something."

**September 24, 14:00** A seminar on problems of globalization, conducted by the IAEG. The hall is full of a polyglot crowd. The only ones missing are Russians—no "suspicious elements" have been granted visas. The average age in the auditorium is about twenty-five. Someone has come with a baby. People laugh, applaud, come out to the microphone and make wordy declarations. The chairperson grows nervous. "Let's have fewer declarations and more discussion. We have to show the gentlemen from the establishment an example of real democracy!"

A small group of young women from Latvia have come, and sit in a corner on the floor. They chew gum, speaking a mixture of Russian and Latvian, and enthusiastically applaud the speeches on the tyranny of the transnational corporations. Various Americans arrive late; they are coming directly from the airport, some with rucksacks and bags. They exchange remarks—who was allowed in, who was taken from the plane. It turns out that the FBI gave the Czech authorities "blacklists" of citizens of its own country who, it recommended, should not be allowed to get to Prague.

The word *nevyezdnye*—in Soviet times, people denied the right to travel abroad—flashes through my head.

A report arrives saying that a further thousand or so people have been held up at the border by the Czech authorities. Bello interrupts his speech; he is backed up by Kallinikos: "Eleven years ago in Prague, the people came out onto the streets demanding freedom of movement, and at that time President Havel was on our side. Now his police are illegally closing the border!"

It is announced that a spontaneous demonstration against the illegal actions of the police is under way at the Interior Ministry. But the protesters are few: two hundred at most. The chairperson of the meeting appeals to everyone who has nothing else to do to join the picket line. With a clatter of chairs, people from the back rows get up and head for the exit. Fortunately, I have already delivered my speech.

On the border, it is obvious, total confusion reigns. Some people are being held up, while whole columns of others are getting through without the slightest hindrance. The border guards are searching each car thoroughly, rummaging in suitcases and leafing through printed material.

Queues have appeared, and the honest burghers have got stuck in them. Meanwhile, the demonstrations are continuing. Today about two thousand people form a living chain in support of Jubilee 2000, a movement demanding the writing off of the debts of the Third World and the former communist countries. A similar number of people gather for a meeting of the Humanist Alliance. The main events, however, are expected on Tuesday, when a protest march is due to take place. Reports come through that the march has been partially banned. Some districts of the city are closed to the demonstrators. Lawyers for the protesters argue that the ban is illegal. But this is no longer the main thing. The general mood has taken on a definite shape: we know that we will go there anyway, and that no one will stop us.

Walden Bello is like Lenin in October. Since the demonstrations in Seattle, he has been transformed from an academic into a real leader. Now he is on the platform. "Everything is decided on the streets! All available resources must be mobilized. We need living strength, you understand, everything depends on living strength! We need bodies!"

"Living strength" continues to arrive. Everywhere there are groups of young people, speaking in every imaginable language from Hungarian to Basque. The language of international communication is, of course, the same as among the bankers—English. Alongside the Lidensky Bridge is the convergence center, the organizational headquarters for the march and the workshop where placards and effigies are made. Here as well, instruction sessions are held, maps of Prague are distributed, and suggestions are made as to where people should go in order to find places to stay. This is important, since the youth hostels are full to bursting. People are told how to give first aid to the wounded, and what to do if they are affected by tear gas. When the work ends an improvised concert begins. Along with the activists, rock groups are arriving, and street theatre troupes from throughout Europe. Elsewhere, a "Festival of Resistance" is also underway. Here about a dozen groups from the Czech Republic, Holland, Britain, and Italy are playing.

Dusk has already fallen, and people are still coming, in jeans and carrying rucksacks. Some are carrying placards. A group of young Germans are seated directly on the grass next to the tram stop, and are discussing something. The Swedes have already held an instruction session. There were several hundred of them, and they were discussing how to act in the case of a clash with police, how to act if arrested, and where to phone in Stockholm, since every third one of them has a mobile telephone. One woman is returning to Sweden; on Tuesday she will have to spend the whole day at home by the telephone.

The tension is growing. The feeling is like before a battle. Everyone is waiting for reinforcements. News reaches the "Standart" and the convergence center: three hundred Austrians are already on the way, and will arrive tomorrow. It is unclear where the Hungarians are; they are expected any minute. The Slovaks have already arrived, but fewer of them than were expected. The Spaniards and Greeks are due to come on special trains.

The advance guard of the Italian contingent appears on the Charles Bridge. More than a thousand of them have come. Four people were not admitted. The rest sat at the border for several hours, demanding that their comrades be admitted, before deciding in the end to carry on to Prague. Now the most active of them, a hundred or so people, are sitting directly on the Charles Bridge, singing "Bandiera Rossa" and partisan songs from the Second World War. On the bridge, activists of the protest movement are mingling with people in respectable suits who have come for the IMF meeting. Everyone wants to feast their eyes on Prague.

**September 25** In the Standart, the seminars and discussions are continuing. The World Bank and the IMF are also holding their meetings in the Congress Centre. The two sides, of course, are behaving quite differently; the officials of the World Bank are still trying to justify themselves, meeting with representatives of the non-government organizations, promising to investigate matters and to put them in order. The IMF ignores the protests. Larry Sommers, the US treasury chief, has already warned the heads of the World Bank that he will not permit any serious concessions to the developing countries or to critics of the system.

By Monday evening, around 8,000 activists from various countries are in Prague. Most of the Czechs are coming from Brno; they appear at the last moment. The police are preparing to meet the demonstrators on the bridge that leads to Visegrad, where the conference center is located. In the neighborhoods nearby, residents are being asked to remove their cars from the streets. The ambulances and hospitals are preparing to receive casualties. The schools have already been shut for a week. In all, 11,000 police and riot troops have been mobilzed. Around 12-15,000 demonstrators are expected.

In the convergence center, a battle plan is worked out. When the demonstrators approach the bridge, they will split into three columns. One will go onto the bridge, while the two others will try to outflank the police on the sides. One of the Britons observes that for such a maneuvre, you cannot do without cavalry.

The column going onto the bridge is not supposed to get into a fight with the police; its job is only to stand and chant slogans. The Italians advance; this decision does not suit them. "We're going to force our way across the bridge," they declare. "We're not here to pay compliments to the police." The Italians were not in Seattle (save the four detained at the border) and they want to show what they're capable of. A few French people of the older generation share their experience, explaining how in Paris in 1968 they built barricades. There is just one question: in those days demonstrators had cobblestones to use for these purposes, but what are you supposed to do with asphalt?

The leaders of the groups are given maps of the city with the traffic routes marked on them. On the reverse side, a brief plan of action is printed in several languages. The proposal is that irrespective of the outcome of the fight at Visegrad, in the evening the protesters will blockade the opera, where the bankers and bureaucrats will be assembling. First the protesters will try to stop them getting into the hall, and if they do get in, then not to let them out again until morning. Other groups go to the expensive hotels where the delegates have installed themselves, and will keep up a barrage of noise the whole night. Around a dozen rock groups and bands will take part in the action.

Sleepless nights are nothing new for the protesters. I see Martin Brabec, one of the ideologues of the IAEG. He looks totally exhausted, but happy. "Martin, do you ever sleep?" "About three hours a night."

There is to be a meeting at nine o'clock. After the meeting, at eleven o'clock, the march on Visegrad will begin.

**September 26, 08:00** At the entrance to the metro there are police patrols. Over the radio comes the announcement that Visegrad metro station is closed.

**08:30** I have breakfast with Petr Uhl, an old friend from the dissident movement of the '80s. Petr himself is not going to the demonstration, but his daughter has already set off for Peace Square, where the participants are assembling. His apartment in the centre of Prague is like the yard of an inn. Staying with him have been members of the French movement ATTAC, which calls for new rules for international finance and for the defense of debtor countries. Last night Petr was host to a group of German teenagers—their hair green, rings in their noses, ears and lips. Catherine Samary, who teaches economics in Paris, laments: "In one night, these kids ate everything in the fridge!"

**09:00** We are on Peace Square. The area where the protesters are gathering in front of a church is like a Tower of Babel. About ten thousand people are speaking all the languages of Europe at once. Turks, Greeks, Kurds, Spaniards and Basques are standing next to one another. A huge balloon, symbolising the IMF, rolls over the crowd, and everyone can push it. Among the crowd are comic effigies and revolutionary placards. From time to time new columns arrive, often accompanied by small bands or musical groups. Here there are Scandinavians, and behind them, Britons and Spaniards. In the back rows are a dozen Dutch people in white coats painted with pictures of a huge tomato—the symbol of the Socialist Party. Trade union activists from northern Europe carry their banners, looking like the icons carried in old-time church processions. The Italian column, with its banners unfurled, surges onto the square. Heading the column is a minibus, and behind it are members of the Ya Basta! movement, which has already distinguished itself by breaking up several international gatherings. The Italians have a menacing air. All of them are wearing helmets, are carrying shields, and are dressed in white coats of the type worn by chemical clean-up squads. Some are wearing homemade body armor of fibreglass or cardboard. And of course, there are protective masks, in some cases gas masks. The people on the square applaud them.

**11:00** The action gets under way. On the plan, the three columns are marked in different colors—blue, yellow, and pink. The strangest of the columns is the pink one. Here there are very few political placards, and party banners or ideological symbols are totally absent. Many participants are dressed in pink, and have even painted their faces pink. In place of banners, there are pink balloons. In the middle of the column is a pink cardboard tank, with flowers sticking out of its make-believe guns.

On the recommendations of the police, the shops and cafes along the route to be taken by the column are closed. I recall a line from the poet Blok: "Fasten the shutters, now there is going to be looting!" For a while I march with the pink column, but then I decide to join the yellow column, which has the menacing-looking Italians at its head. In the yellow column are around three hundred Hungarians, French, Americans, and Turks. From time to time someone encounters a friend, and rushes to embrace them. We swap stories with Hungarian friends, and hear the latest news from New York. Here there are more journalists than anyone else. They are following the Italians, not concealing the fact that they are hoping to see and to photograph clashes with the police. I have other motives: I prefer the yellow column because here it is obviously safer. No surprises are expected, and no one will attack us until the approach to the bridge. In the two other columns it is still not clear what might happen.

The final turning before the bridge: the column stops. From a loudspeaker on the Italian minibus there are orders and instructions; the main thing is not to do anything without coordinating it with the organisers. The orders are given in Italian, then repeated in English, Spanish, Czech, and French. Drums begin beating. A group of people in blue protective jackets appears, wearing armbands with the red cross. Many demonstrators don gasmasks. Someone communicates with the other columns over a mobile phone, trying to work out what is happening with them. We approach the bridge.

The bridge has been blockaded by the police in a highly effective fashion. Behind metal barriers stands a front rank of police, all in body armor, with shields and clubs. The most modern equipment has been got ready especially for this encounter, to the order of American specialists. The feeling arises that what we are faced with is perhaps a troop of medieval samurai warriors, perhaps several dozen Darth Vaders.

Behind the backs of the first rank of police, there are armored personnel carriers (APCs)! The bridge is totally blocked, but to judge from everything, not even armored vehicles seemed to the police commanders to be enough. Behind the APCs, along the whole length of the bridge, police cars, trucks, and minibuses are parked bumper-to-bumper. There is no possibility of getting through here, but neither are the police going to attack.

On the bridge, the police feel confident, but who knows what might happen if they have to fight these fearsome Italians on the streets? Both sides push and shove one another a little with their shields, but do not shift from their positions. An order to disperse immediately is read out to the demonstrators in Czech and English, but no one moves. The police try shooting off a little tear gas, but this does not make the slightest impression on the protesters. The gas quickly dissipates. From behind the backs of the Italians, young Czechs taunt the police, reminding them that not even the Communists used APCs against unarmed demonstrators. Instructions come from the minibus: everyone who does not have a gas mask is to go to the rear of the column, but not to leave the vicinity. If there is a clash, it is important for the front ranks to have a rear guard.

The standoff continues. The journalists are getting bored. Behind the column, the demonstrators have set up a field kitchen, where they give a bowl of soup and an apple to all who want them. Everyone can decide for themselves whether to pay or not. I pay twenty kronas, but the soup isn't worth that much. . . .

**14:20** The standoff at the bridge continues. The demonstrators are bored, and the police in their armor are getting hot in the sunshine. Meanwhile, a real battle is under way further north. It seems that someone from the blue column has started throwing rocks at the police. Other people speak of a truck being driven at full speed into a crowd of demonstrators. They also speak of police provocateurs (the next day I see four of them, still dressed like anarchists, returning to police headquarters). One way or another, a real battle has broken out. Shots can be heard occasionally, through the screeching of sirens and the clattering of helicopters. From time to time, ambulances drive past. There are wounded on both sides. The police are using tear gas, and from time to time are firing their weapons simply in order to frighten people. The demonstrators are building barricades, have burnt several cars, and are throwing stones. The Poles and Germans throw themselves into the fight with particular fury. A number of anarchists prepare Molotov cocktails. Later, it would emerge that they even managed to set fire to a police APC, but that the flames were promptly extinguished. The police drive the blues out of one street, but regrouping, they immediately appear on another.

The yellow column does not move. Several young Englishmen approach me; from the look of it, they are students. They complain that they are wasting their time here. Obviously, they too would rather be fighting the police. For some reason I recall a phrase from *War and Peace*: "Prince Andrey's regiment was in reserve."

I attach myself to a group of French protesters; here, the people are older, and the conversations are more interesting. Olga, an ATTAC staff member, explains to me that she has never joined a political party, and that ATTAC is something quite different—a real movement, radical but not sectarian. Two more French people from a "contact group" appear unexpectedly. The pink column has managed to reach the Congress Center along a side street, and has blocked the exits, but there are not enough people, and reinforcements are urgently needed. The French group moves off, and I follow them.

It has been discovered that the police barriers are not so difficult to break through. We go down under the bridge by footpaths, cross a street—and there we are at the Congress Center! The police observe with amazement how our detachment has appeared behind their barricades. A helicopter flies above.

The exits from the Congress Center are blockaded by groups of a few dozen people. They sit directly on the pavement, singing and chanting slogans. Street theater troupes perform in the "no man's land" between the police and demonstrators. Here there are French, Israelis, and a mixed group from Eastern Europe. People exchange news. It turns out that a Belarussian detachment has formed here spontaneously. The Belarussian students doing courses in Prague have turned out for the demonstrations to a man and woman.

The Czechs sing some doleful song, and along the police barriers the French stretch out ribbons like those that are used to mark danger zones on a building site. The police are no longer blockading the demonstrators; rather, they are themselves blockaded. A number of bankers in dark suits, who have gathered to the accompaniment of shouts and whistles, pass through to the Congress Center. One of the organizers of the column, a huge young Austrian with long hair, comes running up. He shouts: "Why did you let them through? Have you forgotten why we're here?" Now, men in expensive suits are no longer allowed through. Journalists in jeans pass through without impediment, as does an ambulance. So too do several local residents whose doors are beyond the police barrier. From beyond the barriers, another group of men in ties and expensive suits appears. The demonstrators link arms and block their path. The police start beating demonstrators, and a melée breaks out. The crowd screams: "Shame!" "Down with the IMF!" The bankers run back in fright. A few minutes later some very important gentleman emerges from the conference center. A number of police immediately rush to clear a way for him with their clubs. The police have almost broken through, but at that moment, from around the corner there appears a new group of demonstrators. They are singing something as they march, and have raised pink balloons. Despite the group's thoroughly peaceful appearance, the police hide behind their shields, and begin retreating. The banker flees. Singing all the while, the demonstrators carry on marching.

**16:30** A column of around a thousand people marches around the hill, following exactly the same route as a French group shortly before. Once again there are shouts, the beating of drums, and singing. At the end of the column, a group of very youthful Britons in ski masks is assembled around their banner—a smiling green skull on a black background. We are already next to the bridge. Where the police had earlier drawn up their lines, overturned barriers are lying. The police are retreating up the path toward the Congress Center. These are ordinary police, without helmets, shields, or armor. They are clearly not anxious for a fight.

Pursuing the police, the demonstrators charge up the hill. Everything recalls the storming of a medieval castle. The police on the hill draw up their ranks and throw themselves into the attack, but from down below comes a hail of stones. These are from the Britons. The police turn and run. With shouts of "Hurrah!" and "Down with the IMF!," several dozen people rush onward and upward. They have now reached the gallery on the ground floor of the Congress Center. Others, forming ranks, begin moving up the path that by this time has been cleared of the enemy. Over the building, as a sign of victory, soars a pink balloon. A placard reading "Stop the IMF!" is attached to the balcony of the Congress Center. To help the assault force, reinforcements—Italians, Britons, and

Dutch—come down from the direction of the bridge. To block the way of police vehicles, they build a barricade of overturned rubbish containers and police barriers. There is the sound of drums, whistles, and rattles. Beneath the walls of the Congress Center, young women in pink gas masks are dancing. The upper balconies are full of people watching the assault, some in horror and others in curiosity.

I realize that the battle has been won.

The Congress Center is not taken by storm today, but this has not been part of the plans of the demonstrators. The riot police who rush to the scene clear the balcony and the entrances to the building, and then release tear gas. The gas disperses quickly, without causing much harm to the attackers, but a certain amount of it drifts up and penetrates the building of the Congress Center, causing discomfort to the delegates and officials. After this, the demonstrators retreat in organized fashion to nearby streets, and continue the siege.

By five o'clock, the spirit of the defenders has been broken once and for all. The blockade has succeeded. For two and a half hours not a single car, and not a single bus, has been able to leave the besieged building. The police have had to evacuate particularly important people by helicopter. The rest, after somehow or other managing to break out of the building, reach their hotels by evening, using public transport. Half of the stations of the Prague metro, however, are not working. The delegates to the summit try to force their way onto crowded trams, elbowing Prague residents aside. The residents hit back. Wolfensohn too is forced to travel by metro, evidently for the first time in his life.

On the tactical level, the battle went brilliantly. The American instructors who trained the Czech police were expecting a repeat of Seattle, where the demonstrators first blockaded the hotels, and then tried to march along the main street in a single large crowd. The organizers of the Prague protest decided to do everything differently, and although the police undoubtedly knew of the plans of action, they could not understand them. In Seattle, the demonstrators had tried to stop the delegates from getting into the conference hall. In Prague, they did not let the delegates out, and this proved even more effective. Secondly, the demonstrators, in the best traditions of the military arts, carried out the tactical maneuvre of dispersing their forces. While the main brunt of the special police attacks was diverted onto the blues, and while the yellows blocked the bridge and disrupted traffic movements, the pinks were able to make it through to the building by breaking up into small detachments. Once there, they regrouped, and the circle was closed. Each column had its own national and political peculiarities. The people who were mainly looking for a fight finished up in the blue column. In the yellow column were the most disciplined and organized elements; this was where most of the members of left political groups were to be found. The Italians looked extremely threatening, but when they clashed with police, would break off the engagement relatively quickly. On the bridge, however, they made the necessary impression on the enemy.

What happened at the bridge was not a pointless waste of time. To use military terminology, this was a "demonstration." The APCs, trucks, large numbers of police cars, and riot squad units were kept there as though paralyzed. By five o'clock the yellow column had marched off in a body to the opera house, but the police themselves could no longer unblock the bridge, which remained closed to traffic. The pinks seemed the most inoffensive and even absurd, but behind this absurdity were cunning and persistence. It was no accident that the dominant forces here were the Czechs and British. It was they who decided what the day's outcome would be.

**18:00** The Opera House. Several thousand people surround the Opera on all sides, blocking the entrances. There are no police anywhere, and groups of demonstrators roam about the center of the city unhindered. On many streets, traffic is closed off. The demonstrators stop a Mercedes full of "new Russians," whom they have taken for conference delegates. At first, they want to overturn the car, but on hearing that the owners are "mere businessmen," they leave them be.

At the Opera, an impromptu meeting is under way. Speakers are addressing the crowd over a megaphone, in several languages. Sometimes there is translation, sometimes not. "The Prague Spring of 1968 was the beginning of the end for Soviet totalitarianism. Prague in 2000 is the beginning of the end for the dictatorship of the international financial oligarchy!" The crowd chants a new slogan: "Prague, Seattle, continue the battle!"

It is announced that the operatic performance scheduled for the summit delegates has been cancelled. The crowd applauds, and one of the speakers suggests organising "our own alternative opera." The Britons and Americans break into "We Shall Overcome!" On the balcony of the opera house, the Austrian Erich Probsting appears. "Today Prague has belonged to us. We have won a victory over global capitalism. We have united people from Eastern and Western Europe, people from north and south. We are forcing them to respect our rights. We want to decide our fate for ourselves! Tomorrow we shall go out onto the streets again, to show that the struggle is continuing!"

**22:30:** Wenceslas Square. While we are sitting in a pizza shop discussing the day's events, a new fight breaks out a few dozen metres away. A group of Germans and Poles are sacking a McDonald's outlet. These restaurants are favorite targets of all the protest actions. Anticipating trouble, the managers of the restaurant have put safety glass in the windows, but this merely excites the young radicals further. They use police barriers as rams. When we go out onto the square, there is no longer a McDonald's. The windows are broken, and the sign has been smashed. Over the square hangs the sharp smell of tear gas. People are having their photographs taken against a backdrop of shattered glass.

Police and demonstrators mingle chaotically on the square. No one understands anything, or controls anything. A bus appears, full of participants in the summit. Its safety glass windows have been cracked by stones, and the windscreen is smeared with something white. The faces of the passengers display terror. The crowd hisses and whoops. Police appear in body armor, with dogs. The dogs are extremely savage, so savage that they start attacking one another. They are taken away.

By the end of the day, the police are starting to behave far more viciously, not only against people who are using violence, but also against peaceful demonstrators. The blockade on the Congress Center has somehow been broken, and many of the protesters have been beaten and arrested. The total number of those detained is more than four hundred; of these, about a hundred are foreigners, and the rest Czechs. More than sixty people have been injured on both sides. The convergence center has been seized by the police. Before the demonstration began, the participants were given a map with the telephone number of a lawyer who could be called in case of arrest, as well as the telephone numbers of the fire and ambulance services. The law notwithstanding, the detainees have not been given the right to contact a lawyer. The Czechs are having a particularly bad time. The foreigners, as a rule, are being deported from the country within a few hours. The other detainees are being taken to Plzen, where they are beaten, denied anything to eat or drink, and prevented from sleeping.

**22:30** The press center of the IAEG. Work is going ahead on collecting information. The press center's telephone line was cut off several days ago, but mobile phones are still working. While we are making our inquiries about the day's events, an uproar resounds from the entrance. With a crash, a metal grille closes in front of the door. The neo-Nazis are attacking the press center. I realize to my horror that the building does not have an emergency exit. The attack, however, is beaten off. The episode has lasted no more than three or four minutes.

**23:00** The Charles Bridge. Several dozen weary young people have gathered beneath the statues, and are eating ice cream. Several of them have torn clothes and bruised faces. All are indescribably happy.

**September 27** The events of the previous day have provoked differences within the movement. Many American intellectuals are shocked by what has happened. Chelsea, the American press secretary of the IAEG, is almost crying. "We aren't violent people, we're peaceful, all this is terrible." The German press secretary Stefan takes a quite different attitude: the violence was inevitable. The police tactics were all aimed at ruling out any possibility of a successful nonviolent action. Those who wanted violence most of all were the press. "If there hadn't been barricades and broken windows, they wouldn't have shown anything at all. The police intended to disperse us from the very first. In West Berlin, clashes like this are commonplace. So what's all the discussion about?"

The demonstrations are continuing in various places, and from time to time they are broken up. The main demand is for the release of the detainees, but the number in custody is constantly growing. On Peace Square, most of those who have assembled are Czechs and Germans. Riot police are dragging a young Czech activist along the ground. The crowd screams "Fascists!"

**18:00** Young people are walking about the Old Place with placards declaring: "I am an activist too—arrest me!" A jazz band is playing beneath the medieval clock, and the crowd chants, "The IMF must go!" Demonstrators go onto the Charles Bridge. On the other side of the bridge, police in body armor are drawn up. "There's a McDonald's there, and they're scared we're going to storm it," explains an Australian journalist working for an environmental organisation.

People question one another on the details of what happened on the previous day, who marched in which column. Maksim, a Ukrainian television journalist, tries to obtain an interview from the young Portuguese woman who we thought at first was British because of her impeccable London accent. She and a few friends bought tickets to Prague just three days ago, setting off, as she puts it, "to war." She laments that there are almost no Portuguese present. "We're so unorganized!" Maksim suggests that she repeat this on camera, but she refuses and makes off, declaring, "I hate the television!"

**22:30** A bar in Old Place. I drink beer with Maksim, one of his colleagues, and a number of activists from Germany. The Ukrainians have just completed a direct broadcast in which Maksim was asked to comment on a rumor that the IMF meeting would be cut short. We phone colleagues from the BBC, who confirm it. Yes, the summit will end a day ahead of schedule, and there will be no concluding press conference. The reasons are not announced. The triumphant closing ceremony has been cancelled; in the press release something vague is said to the effect that all the speeches by the participants have been unexpectedly short. There are also some general comments about the uprising in Prague.

We order another round of beer. At the neighboring tables, British and Dutch protesters shout with joy and embrace one another.

"What the hell," says one of the German women. "It turned out to be so easy!"

# Eric Drooker

Quebec City

DROOKER

# Infernal Pain In Prague
# pol potlatch as told to fran harris and daniel burton-rose

*The Infernal Noise Brigade (INB) is an insurrectionary drum corps and performance unit with a primary drive towards street action. They travelled to Prague to provide the soundtrack for popular rage against the World Bank and the International Monetary Fund. Formed for the N30 WTO protest and based in Seattle, the INB is a mélange of black and green uniforms, twirling batons, rifles, fire chains, snares, bass drums, and metal percussion. They have been seen marching with gas masks through clouds of tear gas and backlit by flaming barricades. Gigs have included San Francisco's and Portland's May Days of 2000 and 2001 respectively, the Black Rock Desert Burning Man Festival, and several rowdy street events.*

*After the crazy day of S26, with anticapitalist activists contesting control of our global future, state forces attacked with violent rage as night fell. The vengeful state apparatus consumed over 800 activists, citizens, and ethnic minorities. Two INB members were unfortunate enough to be counted among these numbers. The following is an account by bass drummer, pol potlatch. Notably, pol was one of a handful of brown activists in Prague for the convergence.*

Everyone in the marching band was exhausted from having played all day. We split into groups so everyone could do what they wanted. I went off with two other members of the INB to get something to eat and try to meet up with other activists.

There is an amazingly large and aggressive police presence. They're shooting off so many concussion grenades that the sky overhead is lighting up. Everyone on the streets is being corralled and hauled to jail. We're thinking, "Wow. Things are really getting crazy here all of a sudden."

We try to pretend that we have nothing to do with the protests to get past the police lines. Soon a crowd comes running towards us. Someone is yelling, "Oh my god, run away. It's the fascists." People grab and drag us to get us moving.

Our majorette starts yelling that a man is getting the shit beat out of him by a gang of thugs. I turn around, see that no one is chasing us, and so I yell, "Hey, stop running." As we look back a man emerges from the shadows covered in blood. His fingers are broken and shattered, sticking in wrong directions. He's dazed and disoriented. The crowd has dispersed by now. We are trying to help this guy get home.

Every direction we go in, people yell, "You can't go down this street; the fascists are coming." We're getting hemmed in to a smaller and smaller area. Gangs of thugs are running through the streets of Prague armed with medieval weaponry: maces and clubs, long stakes and halberds. The police allow and encourage them to attack anyone who looks like an anarchist. Over the next couple of days we also find out that they were encouraged to attack gypsies, Jews, and anyone who was brown-skinned.

All of sudden a tram pulls up in front of us. This Irish guy comes up from behind and pushes the four of us onto it. He yells, "Get the fuck on the tram! The fascists are right behind you. We've got to get out of here." On the tram he says, "Okay. Don't say anything. We don't know who is on this tram or who might turn us in." Then he asks us, "Where do you need to be? I can help you get home." We decide on the spot we can trust this guy. We tell him where we need to be and he tells us how to get there. But we misunderstand his directions and end up in a big, dark intersection where we don't want to be.

Police are driving all around us. Our majorette has giant, silver serpents climbing out of her hair. Her lover, an INB support person, has facial piercings and is wearing a lot of anarchist paraphernalia. I am black. We obviously stand out to them.

As I'm looking at my map trying to get back to base ("Commie Bloc") someone yells, "Oh my god! They're right behind you! Look out! Run!" Before I can even turn something hits me in the head and in the back, in the head again, and in my arms.

Ninja-garbed soldiers are screaming at me in Czech and pummeling me with sticks. I'm thrown on the ground, punched and kicked, and hogtied. They pull a hood over my head. I receive a very intense beating. I blackout repeatedly.

I guess my legs are unbound at some point because I'm standing though I'm still handcuffed. I'm being held up by a billyclub. The military police remove the hood. I don't see my people anywhere. I think, 'Good they got away . . . boy, I guess I'm fucked.'

Two of the military police that have been working me over turn me around. I see one of my companions, the majorette, across the street, handcuffed as well. She already had a broken arm, which was in a cast. The police refrained from beating her. I don't see her lover which I hope means he got away so that the rest of the Brigade can find out what happened to us.

Police are everywhere. I'm on the verge of blacking out and I'm trying not to hyperventilate. The soldiers drag me across the street and stand me up next to my friend. I try to talk to her. A soldier presses a club into my throat and barks, "Shut up! Shut up!"

We demand an English-speaking lawyer and state clearly that we are not to be separated. I also tell them I'm going to faint and need to throw up. As I start to fall over a cop throws me against the wall and shouts that I'm not allowed to faint. A bunch of British kids had come out of a bar and were watching me get brutalized. The police arrest them for watching.

Police cars arrive to take us away. The police try to separate my bandmate and me. I yell at them and demand that my companion and I be taken in together. They throw me in the back of a car with a bunch of white boxes full of donuts and pastries. As the car tries to drive off, one of the soldiers who had been working me over whacks the hood of the car to stop it. In a strange lapse into humanity, he opens the back door and gently seats my friend next to me. He slams the door and yells in English, "Go! Get out of here!"

As we fly though the city we see people being stomped everywhere. State police, military police, riot cops, Special Forces are on a rampage. I think that the driver is showing us these scenes intentionally.

We are taken to a torture chamber/detention center in the heart of the city. It is the place where state enemies, Jews, gypsies, and politicos were tormented before the revolution. Now it's a jail. As we are dragged into the station a cop throws me down the stairs; the driver of the car catches me and tells the other officer to stop.

In the processing area detainees are spread around the room with cops pressing their faces against the concrete. They are all handcuffed and some have their feet cuffed as well. The police are jamming billyclubs into the spines and kidneys of the arrestees and bouncing their faces off walls. They are kneeing the males in the nuts. And for their amusement, they're intimating raping the women by rhythmically stabbing their billyclubs at them from behind. I turn to see them doing this to my friend. My face is slammed against the wall. The sexually assaulting officer is female.

I see one of the British kids who is on the streets when we were arrested. He had been a loudmouth then and he was a loudmouth now. A cop smashes his face into the concrete. He staggers back with blood flowing from his mouth and nose. He quips, "Thank you, sir. May I have another?" The cop bashes his head into the wall several more times. The Brit's eyes roll into the back of his head. "You think you're a tough guy now? Wait'll I get these handcuffs off . . . ," he taunts the cop.

For processing they dig through our pockets, take our IDs and all our belongings. We're led into a room with two giant cages on either side. Each cage is divided into four cells. The one to our left is full: three cells of men, one of women. The cage to our right holds a gang of Czech fascists; they sport shaved heads, black flight jackets, and swastika tattoos, and are yelling obscenities at the women in the cage across from them. The guards line us up, put little numbers on us, and photograph us. I'm put in a cell with the men; my friend is put in a cell with the women. The cops are really nice to the fascists, smiling brightly at them like, "Hi! How's it going?" All the cops are white; the Czech Republic is a white country. Some of the cops and Nazis know each other by name.

The cops bring the skinheads hot chocolate and let them go to the bathroom whenever they ask. When the cops walk past our cages they yell and scream at us, jab sticks through the bars, and threaten to come in and beat us more. They refuse to give us water.

The police start to release the fascists. The cops tell us they can't process us because we are foreigners and we must wait for the Special Police. We are incensed by our treatment, but people are maintaining beautiful spirits.

The cell is stuffed. We take turns sitting and standing. The people who are really fucked up lie beneath the benches. The police come by with photographs looking for specific individuals. We hide them with our bodies.

The guards refuse to bring us food and are recalcitrant in taking us to the bathrooms. The women start to chat them up the, trying to make friends so we can get food and water. A small collection of stashed money is quietly passed to a sympathetic guard. What comes back is the best apple I ever tasted, the most refreshing water and herbal tea I've ever drank. We get a pack of smokes as well.

Every now and then people are taken out of their cages. Some are beaten. I hear that a group of women are taken into a back room and are forced to do exercises in their underwear. I'm taken out and a statement is extracted from me. I lie outrageously. After being photographed I am returned to the cage, though some folks never return. At some point—I have no idea if it is day or night—the Greek ambassador comes and takes all the Greek activists with him. He pays off the cops. I think that is brilliant.

I'm fainting continuously. I remember the sun coming up at some point. The Special Police arrive and begin moving people in large numbers to a different holding center. My friend the majorette and I are reunited. We are pulled out, handcuffed again, and thrown into a truck. It is dark again. We get all of our belongings back except for our IDs. Men and women in black suits are yelling at us through the back of the truck asking if we have been tortured. We don't know if they are activists, reporters, or legal support. We find out later that they are the legal delegation for INPEG, the group that called for the Prague convergence. We are trying to let them know that we have been totured.

The police take us to an apartment building. On the way to the main lobby black suits ask us about our condition. The police shove us past them quickly. We realize we are in an old folks home; elderly people in bathrobes and slippers are scratching their heads as we are marched through.

We're taken to an upstairs room. We're some of the first to arrive. More people slowly filter in. A bunch of the cops are dressed head to toe in black leather, looking like SS officers. Regular cops shove us into chairs and open all the windows, letting in freezing air.

The sun is coming up again; intense bright white. We're in really uncomfortable chairs, but we're glad to be sitting down. Some people are sitting on the floor. We're only allowed to whisper. Someone moves to close a window and a cop makes a motion to strike him. The cops laugh and joke about it in Czech.

More people are showing up. It seems like every group is in worse shape than the one before. Folks are hobbling in with broken ankles, feet, arms, collarbones, missing teeth. This is the most insane collection of bruises I've ever seen in one room. The dark-skinned people have the worst of it.

Another funny cop joke was at the point of a knife. A cop would draw a knife and approach toward your throat. With a sudden lunge they would dive over your body and slice off your handcuffs. Each new group gets to experience this. We're punished if we try to let them know it's coming.

We still haven't been charged with anything. I have cracked ribs, broken fingers, the tendons of my left ankle are ripped, and I have a concussion.

Eventually there are over a hundred of us in this space. They separate us by gender. People are taken away. Some come back and tell us they've been strip-searched or cavity-searched on a higher floor. Some come back really shook up and they tell us they had the shit beaten out of them. Others don't come back.

The cops start telling some people, "Get the fuck out and don't come back." These people are allowed to leave for real. The crowd is getting smaller.

Finally they call my name and my friend's. I think it's our turn to get beat (again). The police start handing out IDs; they give us our passports. They tell us we have twenty-four hours to leave the country. If we don't leave, we're informed, they'll throw us back in jail.

"You really don't want that," one cop admonishes. We think, "You're right. You people are fucking terrifying."

# Holidays In The Sun
## A Little Atrocity On The Mayan Riviera
# Ramor Ryan

### Neoliberal Paradise Found

There is a bus that leaves the indigenous town of Altamirano, Chiapas, near the Zapatista headquarters at Morelia, that sets out for Cancun full with temporary construction workers. The workers, Tseltal and Tojolabal *campesinos*, work six or seven days a week for twelve hours a day, for the paltry sum of forty pesos a day, about four dollars. They labor to construct the ever- expanding hotel industry and elite tourist playground. There are over 20,000 rooms in Cancun and the average price is around $100 a night.

Twenty-five years ago Cancun was a sleepy fisherman's village looking out over the beautiful Caribbean. Today it is more like a US colony modeled after Disneyland or a Hollywood movie set. The graceful shoreline is now choc-a-bloc with astonishingly ostentatious hotels of enormous proportions. Some are postmodern representations in the style of ancient Mayan pyramids, others are more reminiscent of gangster-run Havana casinos of bygone eras; all cater to the rich, the vast majority of clients foreigners from the US and Europe. The sweeping avenue down the peninsula is a veritable wet dream for American shopping mall fanatics, with every brand store and logo commodity represented in abundance.

Jose Alfredo, a young Zapatista from a village near Altamirano returned a few months ago from his first stint of work at Cancun. "I thought I had left Mexico!" he commented, "I thought I was in another country." And he is right in one sense; Cancun is a model of a new kind of global space. It is an embodiment of the global village as neoliberals would have it. A sanctuary for the wealthy where poverty does not exist. A utopia without hunger or illiteracy, or any of the everyday realities of life for the majority, not because there is some fine neoliberal solution, but because they are excluded. Cancun is a world of illusion where everything is shiny and happy, nothing can disturb the idea of this fanciful paradise. And just in case anybody is foolish or crazy enough to disagree or raise their voice in dissent, a huge security apparatus, both private and public, maintains a high profile. It is quite apt that the World Economic Forum chose this location for their latest reunion to discuss the liberalization of Latin American markets and the consolidation of the neoliberal economic strategy for this region.

## Enter the Clowns . . .

Globophobics are everywhere. Everywhere the globalizers have gone since the breakdown of the Seattle round in November of 1999, they have been pursued and harrassed by a plethora of protestors. The Cancun meeting continues with this successful strategy on behalf of the antiglobalization movement. A diversity of people have come to this absurd resort to organize and demonstrate, and possibly blockade and disrupt the proceedings. By their presence alone, the globophobics have affected the meeting. Various mouthpieces for the Economic Forum dispatch their press releases in defense of their doctrine, and try desperately to disarm the dissenting voice by engaging them in vacuous dialogue.

But what is to be done? How to effectively achieve the goal of disrupting the meeting? On the other side of southern Mexico the Zapatistas have been in rebellion since NAFTA came into force in '94. In many respects the Zapatista uprising is the moment when the movement against globalization found its first global audience, and it is perhaps the place where the tactics of that movement began. If agility, imagination, and cunning are tactics the movement has embraced with success, then the Zapatistas are the template. The Zapatistas have renovated revolutionary action by using daring strategy, righteously and poetically serenading the populace and media while striking a pose with their guerrilla arms ever ready. Wary of the fact that the enemy, the Mexican state, has overwhelming force at their disposal, they have cleverly steered clear of straight-up military confrontation. The antiglobalization movement has been an attentive student of the Zapatistas but has missed some key lessons.

Today in Cancun, February 26, 2001, the numbers are low, only a few hundred protesters, but they climb steadily as the day unfolds. This disappointment is due in part to the location since Cancun is situated at the far end of the Yucatan peninsula, more than 1500 kilometers from Mexico City. The costs of arriving here are huge. As for the local community, the indigenous population of the town is small, as the workforce is, in classic neoliberal fashion, temporary, migratory, and nonunion. Furthermore, most Mexican activists are organizing the mobilization in support of the Zapatista Caravan to Mexico City which unfortunately coincides with this event. Nevertheless the 500 or so who made the journey are aware they represent the millions nationally and globally who are not present.

## A Festival of Resistance, or The Garden of Ghetsemene . . .

The first march on Monday the twenty-sixth is celebratory and peaceful in its manifestation. The protesters are grouped around four main organizations: F-26, Civil Disobedience, the student CGH (the General Strike Council, emanating from the recent marathon strike at the UNAM University), El Barzon (a large debtors union), as well as a bunch of Black Bloc anarchists and a cabal of Maoists. They are predominantly young and radical, dressed in punky and counterculture attire, peppered by the obligatory Zapatista ski masks and scarves. Boisterous and colorful, they march as far as the fortified police cordon at the entrance to the Tourist Zone, where they taunt security forces, a few cheekily exhibiting their backsides to the sullen lines of riot cops. Avenues around the city are lined by loitering police forces and riot squads, some with their gas masks at the ready. The ubiquitous helicopter hovers menacingly overhead. *La Migra* watch out for the participation of foreigners. Agent provocateurs mingle with the marchers, and every inch and every face is monitored and filmed.

Back at the Palapas, a quiet little grass park littered with old mangled trees that functions as base camp for the globophobics, the protesters assemble. Around campfires and a bunch of tents, they meet and organize all evening for the big day tommorow. The mood is intrepid but a little pessimistic. The numbers are dangerously low to attempt the professed aim of the mobilization—to blockade and disrupt the meeting. Rumors abound of the arrival of hundreds more Barzon activists the next day, but this never materializes. Stupendously outnumbered—there are several thousand security elements in Cancun—still the 500 continue with their plans. Rubber inner tubes are inflated and tied together to make mobile barricade defenses. The Civil Disobedience people (with support from F-26 and other people, making them the dominant protest force) are to attempt to break through the police cordon like the Ya Basta! group at Prague, wearing white jumpsuits and fortifying their shoulders and arms with padding, and covering their heads with helmets to protect from beatings. Others plan to enter the convention hotel from the beach, masquerading as tourists, as the main body of the march battles with the police on the main road. Militant Maoists hold their own breakaway meeting, closed to outsiders. They have their own plans, disrupting the unity of the other groups. "Comrades!" screams an older masked man, to the assembled group of about thirty youths, "We are not afraid of the police or jail! Remember the glorious martyrs and prisoners!" The group breaks into another round of ultra-militant chanting about death to this or that. A corrosive assembly the previous night had revealed a serious division between these radicals hell bent on destructive ideas and the majority, who preferred the tactic of nonviolent direct action for the protests.

Despite the industriousness of the preparations, the cheerful hum of the labors, there is an unmistakable mood of foreboding and fear. The local newspapers had contributed to fueling the tensions with their sensational reporting. *They Enter The Ring!* screams one front page accompanied by a photo of masked-up, fist-clenched militants. Others present the protestors as dangerous terrorists—one version (of the police searching arriving buses) indicates that explosives were found, but this can't be confirmed. Complete nonsense, of course, and they forget to inform their readers that the police also stole money and cameras from the buses. "They are going to fuck us up tomorrow!" said one twenty-year-old philosophy student as he tried on his full-face motorcycle helmet. Even with the helmet, all the padding and his white jumpsuit, he still looked terribly small and fragile. (The helmet would be seen the next day lying on the side of the road smashed in half by a police baton, and the youth in jail.) Others spoke confidently of Vicente Fox needing to keep his international image clean hence the police would be on better behavior than usual. Wishful thinking, as the local governor spoke of not tolerating any disorder in the streets of Cancun.

In the shadows of the trees on this warm tropical night, completely surrounded by patrolling cop pickup trucks and undercover agents idling on every corner, they bravely prepare all night for battle, or better, for their suicide mission. Rebel dignity, pride, and courage are the attributes of this raggle-taggle band of Mexican youth.

## Tactics and Spontaneity

The 500 marched tentatively with much noise through the town. They arrived at a wide boulevard with a picturesque park between the two roads in and out of the Tourist Colony. A fortified army of police lines faced them behind two rows of solid metal fencing. This meant the Civil Disobedience plan of pushing through the police lines armed with their rubber tires was thwarted, as those metal fences were not for moving. In the moment's hesitation, the Maoists took the initiative, charging to the front and calling for a storming of the barricades nevertheless. This tactic is fearfully doomed, and the main body of the demonstration regrouped to reconsider strategy, appealing for nonviolence. But already the forces are divided. The Maoists rushed up the police lines full of thunder and fury while the cops laughed. Their assault on the barricades falters a couple of meters short and a standoff for an hour resumes as both sides exchanged insults and an occasional stick flies or a baton is swung. The press horde crowded around with enthusiasm. Tourists stopped to watch. Their plans in disarray, the Ya Basta! grouping failed to come up with a coherent Plan B. They lingered in indecision. The main body of the march, following their lead, stalled and prevaricated. A few disrobed and attempted to dissolve the minor tension between the Maoists and the police lines with their nakedness, while some others decide to stage a sit-down protest to block both sides of the road. After an hour or so, the traffic is held up for miles. Why the police didn't simply divert the traffic from the start is a mystery. Meanwhile a group of thirty had infiltrated the beach as far as the hotel where the forum is held. There they are violently apprehended by a large contingent of riot cops and bundled off to jail. It was when the Civil Disobedience group began to leave, and the majority of people were sitting around the park tired and dehydrated, when the mood had become almost festive as a few hundred tourists and the press corps waited around for the next spectacle, that the barricades suddenly opened up.

## Of Ultraviolence and Brutality

With an unbridled ferocity, the riot squads came storming out at full sprint. Hundreds of them flooded out. They swung wildly and indiscriminately at everyone in their path. First to be pummeled was the isolated group left sitting on the road. The still afternoon air became filled traumatically with screams of panic and pain, and a horrific battle-cry of the marauding cop gangs as they beat their shields . . . People fled hopelessly in every direction as the maddened thugs pursued them relentlessly. There was no resistance because there was none prepared. There was only running in absolute terror. It was simple savage punishment. Scenes of utter vomit-inducing brutality ensued. A tall cop beat a helpless youth on the ground with a three-meter pole while his buddies delivered carefully aimed blows to the victim's head with their batons and boots. A silent couple clutched each other uselessly as a gang of thugs did a Rodney King on them. People with videos and cameras were singled out for beatings. The Civil Disobedience group, encumbered with their absurd rubber tires, got special punishment, while the Maoist contingent abandoned their militant posturing and fled frantically. A few valiant ones went in defense of their bloodied *companeros,* and were beaten heavily for their impudence. Some paltry stones flew and then the menacing sound of gas canisters being shot off was heard. The air filled with the poisonous fumes. The people fled in utter pandemonium. Heavily injured people were carried through the gas clouds. The picturesque grassy knoll resembled a furious medieval battle field. And the beatings went on and on, the cops frantically seeking fresh victims, or else any vanquished body languishing on the ground would do. The blare of ambulances interrupted the din of violence. The rout was complete. The neoliberals had triumphed heroically, their mercenary soldiers delighted with their crusading victory, their little slaughter of the globophobics this sunny afternoon on the Mayan Riviera.

## Tactical Follies

The lessons of Cancun lay in hospital beds and languished in cells around the city that night. With all their creative preparations and aestheticised resistance borrowed from Prague and elsewhere, the facts on the ground announced a grave miscalculation. The group of no more than a few hundred had employed tactics that had been developed, with varying degrees of success, by demonstrations of thousands strong. Massing before a much stronger force of tooled-up cops, and dressed for battle or at least for confrontation, the outcome was surely predictable. With such meager numbers it would perhaps have been wiser to avoid a head-to-head confrontation or the possibility of it in favor of guerilla-style engagement by much smaller groups spread throughout the town. In this way, no group, whether they be the militant Maoists or the peaceniks, are able to determine the fate of everyone. Furthermore it would prevent the police mobilizing their formidable resources in one place and corralling the lambs for slaughter. Five hundred is not enough to close down or disrupt one of these summits if they organize as a bloc; this should have been recognized. But tactical victories could have been won with more mobile, autonomous, and guerrilla-style actions. This would at least have guaranteed fewer injuries and perhaps fewer arrests. Furthermore it would have enhanced the possibility of some people penetrating the cordon and reaching the hotel where the meeting was taking place and so offered the possibility of some disruption, the stated aim of the mobilization.

## The Resurgence of the Struggle . . .

The attempted blockade was defeated but the media coverage was a victory. Images of the unprovoked ultraviolence flashed across the television networks. Newspapers the next day were filled with powerful photos of police violence under headlines of *Brutality! Police Riot!* and *Cowards And Savages*. The resignation of the police chief was demanded. Trolleys filled with food arrived at the protesters' encampment as they bandaged up their wounds and searched to locate the sixty-five prisoners and the fifteen hospitalized about whom the police would release no details. Locals rallied in support and warned protesters of new police movements. A solidarity demonstration was organized in the capital. Even with small defeats, the movement grows. The next day popular pressure helped ensure the prisoners' release, and condemnation of the police came from every quarter, even, opportunistically, from PAN (the governing party) deputies and local representatives. A demonstration was called in front of the town hall. Not one uniformed cop appeared. They were withdrawn in disgrace. The authorities faltered under an avalanche of criticism and the journalists organized their own protest against the police brutality. Fox remained silent, his image tainted, returning a few days later on television to shed apologetic crocodile tears. The World Economic Forum finished up without a peep and the neoliberals hurried away from Cancun without releasing their usual celebratory communiqués. But, no doubt, business continued as usual.

The protesters mockingly charged the undefended town hall, as if to say, "Look! Here we are. . . still!" The message was clear; even if they batter them off the streets, the protesters won't go away. Cancun is a watershed for the movement. New strategies and tactics will emerge, and the neoliberal project continues to retreat under pressure.

# Leticia Velasquez

Bernabe Peréz Gonzaléz, from state of Tabasco, construction worker, Hotel Zone, Cancun, 9/9/03

Construction site, Hotel Zone, Cancun, 9/9/03

Construction workers, from state of Yucatan, Hotel Zone, Cancun, 9/9/03

Beach beyond the construction site, Hotel Zone, Cancun, 9/8/03

# The Charming Outcome of the Cancun Trade Talks
## Writer's Bloc

A few thousand of us maybe. No more. September 10, 2003, and the first "grande manifestacion" was underway as we snaked through the cobbled streets of Cancun, a neoliberal paradise lost. Of the 600,000 people who live there fully two-thirds are transient laborers, many living without water and electricity. Like a large proportion of the world's population, they exist in the twilight zone of mobile capital, industrial tourism and ecological catastrophe.

Cancun was well chosen by the WTO as a site for its fifth ministerial—the city was inaccessible and expensive to reach for many. In addition, the absence of a homegrown social movement translated into an anemic activist infrastructure on the ground. The result: an underlying lack of confidence by those present that any mobilization could be pulled off at all.

The silence from Chiapas didn't help. An inspiration for the antiglobalization movement, the Zapatistas failed to come out early with a call for people to mobilize, nor did they give any indication if they themselves would join us in Cancun. Also, confusion reigned in the USA as a call from prominent NGOs went out early for people to send money rather than be present at the demonstrations.

The presence of just a few hundred Europeans and North Americans underlined the sense that Cancun was shaping up to be a major catastrophe. Having registered criticisms of summit hopping and with a renewed focus on war and US hegemony, the cadres who had beefed up the demonstrations at Seattle and Genoa were not present. Hurdles placed by migration authorities in getting a visa also contributed to the slim representation from the north.

Meanwhile, the Mexican authorities had been very busy trying to dissuade people from attending. The memory of the vicious beating of protesters at the World Economic Forum in Cancun two years prior brought a fear of how the cops would respond this time. Local police forces boasted in the press that they were prepared to "trade an eye for an eye" with protesters, and rumors abounded that the local bullring was being prepared as a gulag. It was a foregone conclusion that thousands of us would be rounded up, the security forces would be out of control, and that we would be lucky to get out of the neoliberal mecca in one piece.

Finally, an awareness of the less than generous human rights record of the Mexican security forces, who brought us Acteal in 1997 and the Tlatelolco massacre in 1968, could not be underestimated. Predictably, as the opening day of the ministerial approached, the climate of intimidation and repression escalated.

## Bienvenidos a Cancun

Spirits were ebullient, however, on September 10 as we approached the fortification—a fence ten feet high reinforced by a matrix of steel and concrete—which prevented us from reaching the convention center where trade representatives were plotting our doom. Behind the fence, thousands of cops. At the front of the march, Mexican campesinos pushed a table displaying a collection of diverse corn strains, altar-like, and were led by one who carried a basket of kernels on his back. The campesinos said that the transgenic agenda of the WTO would mean the end to all this.

From Korea came 200 small farmers and trades unionists. This group knew how to demonstrate. The contingent provided its own free jazz accompaniment; clanging cymbals and the thud of deep drums provided the rhythm for the march complete with banners, costumes and deadly seriousness. They made directly for the front and attacked the fence, their position announced earlier as, "What fence?"

As the barrier began to rock back and forth, the crowd took heart. A few of the Koreans climbed on top to hang banners and led the chants of their comrades below. Lee Kyong Hae led the effort. If there was confusion among the assembled—were we there to take the fence down? Were we there to fight? To go through . . . Lee had the answer—the fence must come down. A sign hung from his neck, "WTO Kills Farmers." He led a chant in English, "Down, Down WTO!" and thousands responded.

Lee, right hand raised, turned away from us, toward the police, the WTO, and the corporate media functionaries who cowered among them. Plunging a knife into his heart, he fell backward from the fence into the waiting arms of his astonished comrades. The protesters were forced to beat back the sickening throng of photographers and journos, three layers thick, who crowded around the body. The *compañeros* kept the vultures at bay, allowing Lee to be carried to a waiting ambulance. The mood quickly altered. The Korean contingent who had carried an ornate paper and wood construction symbolizing the death of the WTO, reassembled. They raised the prop above their heads and ran at the fence, smashing into it. This gesture was repeated three times before they set it alight, sending the crowd into a frenzy of rage and unity.

The crowd joined Lee Kyung Hae and his compatriots in an unscripted but singular objective—to destroy the fence that excluded not just those present in Cancun but 3.5 million Korean farmers and countless others being strangled by the policies of the WTO.

The closest that these Mexican and Korean *campesinos* got to the architects of their doom, convening at the Cancun Convention Center, was seven kilometers. Seven kilometers of smooth concrete highway edged by luxury hotels full of elites from every corner of the world. Seven kilometers of faux *cantinas*, wet T-shirts, cheap labor, liberal investment régimes, and Martha Stewart. Guarded by a mercenary force of tens of thousands, the globalizers came to Cancun to map out the continued imposition of the cash nexus over every aspect of our lives. Some people's dreams are our nightmares.

The closest that Lee Kyung Hae got to deliver his message was that spot seven kilometers from the source of his despair, so it was there that he came to die.

The Koreans were very hardcore and plenty joined in the effort. The fence was assaulted along the line. Over to one side the *campesinos* were hard at work. Meanwhile at another spot twenty meters away, the Korean block made steady progress. Scattered groups of Mexican radicals figured out how best to dismantle the edifice, backed up by squads of stone-throwing fighters. This is the antiglobalization movement, mixed, intuitive, and highly effective

As the Koreans' construction burned, banners hung along the fence were set alight. At two points the fence began to buckle as a second wave of militants appeared from behind. The Koreans split up, some accompanying Lee, in critical condition, to the hospital, while the rest continued to destroy the barricade. A breach was created within a short time and the fence began to be peeled back. The police reinforced the breach and were kept at bay by disciplined gangs of stone throwers and street fighters. Along the 200-meter line the fence continued to be overturned and dismantled, yet the police didn't make a move. Their only attempt to charge the crowd was quickly beaten back under a shower of stones, fists, and appropriated police batons.

Lee Kyong Hae who made the ultimate sacrifice was the leader of a small farmers union; he was fifty-six years old, the father of three daughters, and a militant revolutionary. He was not the first farmer to take his own life in protest and desperation at the policies of the WTO. Later that evening, we tried to figure out what had happened. We tore down the fence; we had beaten back the police and found a way to fight against these pricks in that neoliberal nightmare zone called Cancun. The Koreans stayed overnight at the junction where Lee died, many others joined them. Trying to explain their tactics to us one of them described it thus, "we have specialists here."

Indeed.

## Todos Somos Lee

On September 13, the Global Day of Action Against the WTO, some seven thousand protesters again descended on the newly fortified security barrier near kilometer zero. Members of the resistance—peasants from South Africa, Thailand, Central America, and Korea, with a large crowd of global justice activists still high from the success of the previous days, danced around the fountain. At kilometer zero, the spot where Lee Kyung Hae fell by his own hand, ecstatic celebration mixed with memorial; an American hippie drummer joined the Korean percussionists, Mexican campesinos sported Korean headbands, and a handsome male schoolteacher from Seoul stood slightly apart from the joyous crowd in dark sunglasses and an embroidered ladies' indigenous blouse.

A couple hundred women first massed along the fence and set about it with heavy bolt cutters. Mountains of wire were cut free and discarded by supporters as the women went into the ten-foot-deep no-man's-land, thousands of riot police pressed at the other side. Bolts and chains, which locked the wall together, disappeared in a Fordist destruction line, the chains worn as trophies around the necks of the African women. The notorious Black Bloc displayed a sophisticated and mature reading of the situation—working closely with the women at the front in securing the barricade from nutcases and provocateurs, ensuring the success of the day.

Next up were the Koreans. They had spent the morning weaving rope into long plaits. These were brought forward and attached to the top of the barricade. The throng lined up, took the three lines in hand and began to pull in time with the Korean chants of a work gang. During an incredible three hours the barricade was destroyed and removed from the road by the steady collective action of the crowd. It took several turns and minor adjustments to tear the wall asunder.

Lee's death had an enormously radicalizing effect among those who had come to Cancun. The world was turned upside down. Alone were some Italian Disobedienti who denounced Lee's sacrifice as an individual act. Everyone else understood it as an expression of protest against neoliberalism and of solidarity to those whose way of life is continually being destroyed by the capitalist globalizers. The scattered militancy of the first mobilization evolved over the next few days into a more coherent tactical unity. The affinity between the Korean and Mexican farmers was augmented by the participation of a motley variety of direct action groups, anarchists, Black Bloc–ers, students from Mexico City, and others. The whole was infused with a moral authority engendered by the power of Lee's act. Strengthened by an emotional unity born from the shared grief, the demonstrators were inspired not only by his death but also by its symbolic register of the millions of deaths that his gesture evoked.

At the fence, the atmosphere was otherworldly as the mammoth structure began to buckle and sway. A realization passed through those assembled that this thing was really coming down. The crowd was silent as the drummers accompanied the heaves of those on the ropes and the barricade disintegrated. Like the initial structure, this new fortification had been dismantled by the collective action of the demonstration.

In an unorthodox but tactically genius move, the crowd, flying high on the tremendous group achievement—ready to storm, to riot, to do almost anything—instead sat down. There was a ceremony and a moment of silence for comrade Lee and then the electrifying news that not only had a group of Korean compañeros made it into the convention center, but also the Group of 21 developing nations had rejected the proposals of the USA and EU.

## A Matter of Life and Death

We won in Cancun. However, to compare the collapse of the WTO negotiations in Mexico to the similarly failed capitalist rendezvous of Seattle 1999 is to avoid the true victory that took place. What stood out in Cancun was the leadership of the militant South—the rural farmers of Mexico and Brazil, the unionists of Korea, and the activists from the ghettos of the African continent. Not surprisingly, it was these *compañeros* who brought the vision and militancy to the demonstration's small numbers and lack of focus.

The refusnik delegates of the Group of 21 and the movement's self-appointed NGO representatives were given the political space to resist because of this militancy and the history of opposition to the capitalist project. Far from being altruistic, the G21 was forced to make a decision: sign onto the USA and EU's hegemonic agreement and return home to angry protests, or refuse to play the game. Their decision to refuse proves how strong the movement against capitalist globalization has become.

On the final evening of the demonstrations the mood was triumphant. With tears in his eyes, the president of Via Campesino recounted the words of Lee's daughter when he presented her with a bouquet earlier in the day. "My father is not dead," she said. "He lives in the heart of farmers all over the world." As people gathered around the memorial that had grown up at the junction, Cancunensas brought their children forward to light candles at the memorial, passing vehicles honked their horns in support, and in some of the week's most surreal images, truckloads of Policia Federal gave the thumbs up as local cops tied white flags to the antennas of their cars.

At the fiesta around the memorial that final evening, people from around the world celebrated the death of the WTO and the life of Lee Kyung Hae. His death had crystallized something very important. As one *campesino* woman put it, he has given us a great gift; he has reminded us that the policies of the WTO are a matter of life and death.

# Cancun: The Collapse of the Neoliberal Offensive
# Immanuel Wallerstein

Cancun is more than just a passing geopolitical battle. It represents the interment of a neoliberal offensive that started in the 1970s. To understand the importance of the event, we have to go back to the beginning.

The 1970s mark a turning-point in two cyclical rhythms of the capitalist world-economy. It was the beginning of a long stagnation of the world-economy, a Kondratieff-B phase, out of which we have not yet come. And it marks the moment when the hegemony of the United States in the world-system began to decline. Stagnations in the world-economy mean that the rate of profit has gone down to an important degree, as a result of increased competition in the leading industries and a consequent overproduction. This leads to two kinds of geoeconomic battles: a struggle among the centers of capital accumulation (the United States, western Europe, and Japan/East Asia) to shift the burden of lowered rates of profit to each other. I call this "exporting unemployment," and it has been going on for thirty years, with each of the three centers doing better at different times (Europe in the 1970s, Japan in the 1980s, and the US in the late 1990s).

The second geoeconomic battle however is that between the center and the periphery, the North and the South, in which the North seeks to take back from the South whatever small gains it made during the preceding Kondratieff A-period of expansion (ca. 1945–1970). As everyone knows, Latin America, Africa, eastern Europe, and South Asia all for the most part did poorly after 1970. The only area in the South that did relatively well was eastern and southeast Asia, at least until the financial crisis of the late 1990s. But one area of the periphery always does well in a downturn, since there has to be some region into which declining industries move.

In this difficult period when capitalists were scrambling to maintain their income, partially through relocation of production but more often through financial speculation, they started what can only be called a counteroffensive against the gains of the South and of the working classes in the North in the previous A-period. This came to be called "neoliberalism." The political face of this counteroffensive was to be found first of all in the transformation of the British Conservative Party and the US Republican Party from a party of moderate Keynesians to a party of ferocious believers in the nostrums of Milton Friedman. Mrs. Thatcher's years as prime minister and Ronald Reagan's terms as president of the United States represented a distinct turn to the right in both national and world policy, but even more importantly a transformation of their own party structures, as the basis of pushing the balance-point of internal politics from the center to considerably right of center. The new conservative policy constituted a pushback on all three sources of rising cost for producers: wages, the internalization of costs to reduce ecological damage, and state taxation to finance the welfare state.

There was an attempt to coordinate this policy throughout the countries of the North by creating a series of new institutions, notably the Trilateral Commission, the G7, and the World Economic Forum of Davos. The economic policy that was proposed came to be called the Washington Consensus. First of all, we should note the Washington Consensus replaced something called developmentalism. Developmentalism had been the reigning world economic policy in the previous period (in the late 1960s the United Nations had even proclaimed that the 1970s would be the "Decade of Development").

The basic premise of developmentalism had been that every country could "develop," if only its state would implement appropriate policies, and the end point would be a world of states all looking more or less the same and all more or less equally wealthy. Of course, developmentalism did not work, could not work, which sad reality became clear to everyone in the 1970s.

In its place, the Washington Consensus proclaimed that the world was in the era of "globalization." Globalization was said to be the triumph of the free market, the radical reduction of the economic role of the state, and above all, the elimination of all state-created barriers to trans-border movements of goods and capital. The Washington Consensus ordained that the prime role of governments, especially those in the South, was to end the illusions of developmentalism, and accept the unrestricted opening of their frontiers. Mrs. Thatcher trumpeted that they had no choice. She said: TINA, there is no alternative. TINA meant that any government that did not conform would be punished, first of all by the world market and second of all by interstate institutions.

There has been insufficient attention to the fact that it was only beginning in the 1970s that interstate institutions began to play a significant role in these geoeconomic struggles. The International Monetary Fund (IMF) and the World Bank were turned into very active enforcers of the Washington Consensus. They could play this role because the states of the South, grievously hurt by the stagnation of the world-economy, were short on funds and had to turn constantly to outside lenders to compensate for a negative balance of payments. The IMF in particular imposed drastic conditions on such loans, conditions which generally required considerably reduced social services within the country and gave priority to the repayment of external debt over anything else.

In the 1980s, it was decided to go further. The World Trade Organization (WTO) had been an idea first discussed in the 1940s. But it had foundered on considerable differences among the centers of capital accumulation. What enabled it to proceed in the 1980s was the common agreement of the countries of the North that it could be a very useful tool in furthering the Washington Consensus. In theory, the WTO stands for the opening of frontiers, the maximization of a free world market. The major problem is that the North has never quite meant this. They wanted the countries of the South to open their frontiers, but they didn't really want to reciprocate.

After the United States succeeded in creating the North American Free Trade Association (NAFTA) and Europe had proceeded further in its economic union, the countries of the North decided it was time to implement their program in the WTO. The moment chosen was the Seattle meeting of 1999. The North had however waited too long. The ravages of the Washington Consensus—increasing unemployment, ecological degradation, destruction of food autonomy—led to an unexpectedly strong protest movement which managed to bring together many different kinds of groups from anarchists to environmentalists to trade-unionists. And their combined protests managed to render impotent the meeting. In addition to this, at Seattle, the US and western Europe were at odds with each other because of their respective protectionist policies against each other. So Seattle closed without accomplishing anything.

At this point, two major events occurred. The first was the founding of the World Social Forum (WSF), which held its first three meetings at Porto Alegre, and which constituted a "movement of movements" against neoliberalism, the Washington Consensus, and the forum of Davos. It has been remarkably successful thus far. The second event was 9/11, which led to the proclamation of the Bush doctrine of unilateral preemptive action against anyone the US government designated as "terrorists."

Initially the effect of 9/11 was that of much worldwide support for the fight against "terrorism." And it was soon after this that the next WTO meeting was held in Doha. At that meeting, the North was able to impose on a momentarily intimidated South the acceptance of an agreement to discuss new treaties that would open world economic frontiers considerably further. These treaties were to be consecrated in 2003 at Cancun. Once again, Cancun came too late. Between Doha and Cancun came the invasion of Iraq and its aftermath, which turned world sentiment strongly against the US and exposed the serious limitations of US military power. And in the meantime the world peace movement had considerably strengthened the forces of Porto Alegre, which in turn were able to place considerable pressure on the countries of the South to strengthen their backbone. At Cancun, the more or less united forces of the North pushed their program of opening the frontiers of the South to their goods and capital, while protecting the intellectual property of the North (patents) against dilution or non-respect. The South counterorganized. Brazil took the lead in creating a Group of 21 (including India, China, and South Africa) who said, in essence, that in return the South insisted on an opening of the frontiers of the North to the South's agriculture and manufactures. In this battle, the Group of 21, who were "middle powers," obtained the support of the poorer countries, notably in Africa. Since the North was not willing, for its internal political reasons, to make any serious concessions to the South, the South did not budge. The result was deadlock.

This is seen by everyone as a political victory for the states of the South. It should be clear that this victory was made possible by the conjuncture of US geopolitical weakness and the strength of the forces of Porto Alegre. The WTO is now effectively dead. It will survive on paper, as do many other interstate institutions, but it will no longer matter.

The US hopes to recoup the situation by going unilateral. It will find that it will not be easy to get significant countries in the South to sign one-sided free trade treaties. The South will now move on to challenge the IMF and the World Bank. Indeed, this offensive has already begun, and the strong defiance of Argentina's President Kirchner has shown that such defiance can work. It will not be long before the term "neoliberalism" will represent the almost forgotten follies of yesteryear.

# Something Did Start in Quebec City:
## North America's Revolutionary Anticapitalist Movement
# Cindy Milstein

When thirty-four heads of state gathered behind a chain-link barrier in Quebec City this past April to smile for the television cameras during the Summit of the Americas, it was the tear gassing outside that garnered all the media attention. Those on both sides of the fence jockeyed to put a spin on the meaning of the massive chemical haze that chocked the old city for over two days. The "insiders" claimed that as duly elected leaders of so-called free countries, they were attempting to democratically bring "freedom through free trade," and as such, those on the streets were merely troublemakers without a cause or constituency that needed to be dealt with accordingly. The "outsiders" asserted that those hiding behind the fence were the real source of violence—the tear gas exemplifying what nation-states are willing to do to protect capitalism and the dominant elites—and thus, a certain level of militancy was necessary to tear down the "wall of shame" that many saw as separating the powerful from the powerless.

What got lost in the smoke, however, was the substantive transformation that this particular direct action represented. For Quebec City's convergence, more than anything else, ushered in an explicitly anticapitalist movement in North America—one spearhead-ed by antiauthoritarians (by and large, anarchists). That was our real victory in Quebec. But what caused this sudden sea change?

Serendipitously, one fence; self-consciously, two groups.

It was this movement's collective "good luck" that law enforcement officials and politicians determined on a fence as the heart of their strategy to counter the protests. "It didn't start in Quebec," one could say; last June, in Windsor, Ontario, similar trade dis-cussions went off without a hitch behind chain-link, and barbed wire served nicely to make Davos, Switzerland, an impenetrable fortress this past winter for the World Economic Forum. The state-sponsored prophylactic in Quebec City did in fact ward off unwanted intruders: the summit meetings went on, generally unimpeded. Thus, if the fence had remained merely a physical barricade, it could have been counted as a securi-ty success.

Unfortunately for Jean Chrétien, George W., and their cohorts, the ten-foot fence became a larger-than-life symbolic divide, in essence demanding, "Which side are you on?"

The contrasts could not have been sharper. Closed meetings and secret documents inside; open teach-ins and publicly distributed literature outside. The cynical co-optation of "democracy" via a gratuitous "clause" as a cover for free-floating economic exploitation versus genuine demands for popular control and mutual aid in matters such as economics, ecology, politics, and culture. The raising of glasses for champagne toasts versus the rinsing of eyes from chemical burns.

All of the recent direct actions have, of course, also focused on targets that were figurative to a certain extent. Indeed, the symbolic value of these spectacular showdowns is an essential ingredient in the fight to win the majority of minds over to one perspective or another. But previous focal points, such as the World Trade Organization and International Monetary Fund, have shown themselves to impart somewhat ambiguous messages. The debate stirred up has often centered on how these institutions can potentially be reformed, how the social "good" they do can be salvaged from all the harm they inflict. Besides, some contend, what would replace them? It's proved difficult to move beyond questions regarding the single institution being protested other than to fall back on the buzzword "globalization." And "globalization," while suggesting a wider critique, is just as ambiguous—in no way necessarily underscoring systemic forms of domination that cannot be reformed.

Things were very different in Quebec City. From the vantage point of those on the outside, the fence served no purpose. It not only exemplified a lack of commitment to free expression on the part of the nation-states represented inside but also a further circumscribing of the possibility of freedom itself, and those political leaders trying to allege otherwise were merely revealing their hypocrisy. Hence the heightened level of militancy, illustrative of a movement increasingly intent on fundamental social transformation, directed at tearing the fence down. Yet the fence was crucial for those gathering behind it, too. Beyond providing a literal sense of security, it functioned as a stand-in for the attempt to control the debate around—as well as protect the implementation of—the neoliberal agenda across the Americas. Hence the fiercely fought battle on the part of the police and military in Quebec City to hold the line.

The widespread hatred of the wall and all it embodied meant that those who took a leadership role to bring it down—the libertarian anticapitalists—stepped not only into the limelight but also gained the respect and admiration of other demonstrators, much of the local populace, and a healthy cross-section of the broader Canadian public. Sympathy—for the first time in this North American branch of the new global movement—was largely on the side of those seeking revolution. No longer the pariah or the parvenu at this direct action, the antiauthoritarian contingent was able to come into its own as a strong and visible force, rather than a marginal, marginalized, or even feared element.

To a great extent, credit must be given to two key organizations: la Convergence des Luttes Anti-Capitalistes (the Montreal-based Anti-Capitalist Convergence, or CLAC) and le Comite d'Accueil du Sommet des Ameriques (the Quebec City-based Summit of the Americas Welcoming Committee, or CASA). For starters, it was a brilliant stroke to stake out a nonreformist posture not only in CLAC's name but in the very theme for the summit weekend as well: the Carnival against Capitalism. An opposition to capitalism was openly front and center, both during the many months of organizing leading up to April and at the convergence itself. It was, moreover, an anarchist-influenced version of anticapitalism. As nuanced by CLAC/CASA's short lists of organizational principles, a rejection of capitalism included a refusal of hierarchy, authoritarianism, and patriarchy, along with the proactive assertion of such values as decentralization and direct democracy. There was no mistaking the message at this direct action.

This brand of anticapitalism, in turn, served as the substantive and radical tie that bound Quebec City's many direct action participants together. Those people organizing toward and/or coming to the direct action events could bring along their varied concerns and identities, but they were clearly doing so under the rubric of anticapitalism. A sense of unity was achieved—not through a shapeless tag such as "mobilization," nor by watering down demands until they lose their rebellious edge, nor by ignoring particularity itself. As articulated by CLAC/CASA's "Basis of Unity," "anticapitalism" created a defined and uncompromising space for the multiplicity of individuals who see themselves as part of a revolutionary project.

Crucial in this necessary yet delicate balancing act between a striving for unification and individuation was the strategically smart phrase "diversity of tactics" in CLAC/CASA's statements of principles. Many have written elsewhere that this principle allowed for heightened militancy in Quebec City, or that it diffused the often poorly formulated and argued "violent" versus "nonviolent" debates that seem to fracture this movement internally. Each claim rings partially true, yet both miss the forest for the trees. The diversity of tactics notion helped to unmask the anticapitalism element, and in showing its full face, revealed how influential (and even appealing) it is as a force in this new global movement.

In the recent past, there have been thousands of libertarian anticapitalists at North American direct actions, but they remained separated—and thus largely hidden—by dress, role (such as medic, media, or comm), age, ideological tendency, strategic notions, and so on. Antiauthoritarians "converged" together at mass direct actions, but sadly, the "Revolutionary Anti-Capitalist Bloc" was generally seen as synonymous with the Black Bloc—meaning that a radical political outlook appeared to have minimal support. The blame lies not with the Black Bloc or the fact that many anarchists choose to wear other colors. Instead, the problem has been the inability to combine this spectrum of anti-authoritarian styles under a transparently radical canopy.

The full line in CLAC/CASA's "Basis of Unity" statement on a diversity of tactics altered that equation. It reads: "Respecting a diversity of tactics, the CLAC [or CASA, respectively] supports the use of a variety of creative initiatives, ranging from popular education to direct action." By embracing on an equal footing "education" and "action," thereby also breaking down the supposed theory versus practice divide, the conflation of "militancy" with "radicalism" was shattered. One wasn't a revolutionary because one was a priori a militant; and this indirectly affirmed that not all revolutionaries can afford to take the same risks—just compare a healthy eighteen-year-old to wheelchair-bound octogenarian. (As a corollary, it showed that being militant doesn't necessarily make one a revolutionary, either. There were plenty of disgruntled Quebecois youth on the streets each night during the convergence intent on mischief and it's highly doubtful that they shared CLAC/CASA's principles.)

The diversity clause, in essence, acknowledged that an opposition to systemic domination such as capitalism and nation-states could and should take many forms if a majoritarian movement is to be built. The principle did not make room under the anticapitalist banner for militants; they were there already. What the diversity of tactics stance did do was create a welcoming space for those many more antiauthoritarians who perceive themselves as less militant. It widened the margins not of militancy, in other words, but of what it means to reject capitalism as an antiauthoritarian.

Thus, Quebec's anticapitalist bloc was not one little contingent among many. It was the direct action bloc itself—precisely because it allowed anyone who subscribed to CLAC/CASA's nonreformist stance to march together regardless of how they dressed (or didn't), whether they carried a black flag or a puppet, or whether they wished to avoid arrest or tear down the fence. This was tangibly facilitated, to cite just one example, by the three-tiered color coding of events to indicate varying possibilities of arrest risk and militancy. As the CrimethInc. observes in its "Eyewitness Analysis: Free Trade Area of the Americas Summit, Quebec City, April 19–22," this "served the purpose ahead of time of making everyone comfortable [by] setting their own level of involvement and risk." Instead of 500 or 1,000 people as at past direct actions, then, the ranks of the two anti-capitalist bloc marches during the convergence swelled to 5,000 or more—perhaps the largest in North America in recent memory.

What the diversity of tactics principle translated into was a diversity of people. But this commitment to inclusiveness was only one of the ethical parameters spelled out in the rest of CLAC/CASA's "Basis of Unity." As such, rather than an assertion of difference for difference's sake—potentially implying a diverse movement emptied of content— what emerged in practice was an explicitly radical movement that was diverse. One could argue that the convergence of anticapitalists in Quebec City wasn't diverse enough, of course. Yet it provided the first real guide of how to go about nurturing inclusiveness and unity in a way that is at once qualitative and sincere, and moreover, that allows the particular and universal to complement rather than crush each other as part of a social movement.

To return for a moment to the heightened level of militancy in Quebec City, perhaps the diversity of tactics phrase encouraged a somewhat more confrontational stance. But that pales in comparison to the catalyst exerted by the fence and police tactics as reasons why many people choose to go one step further than they ever thought they would during the direct action. Suggestive of this is a photo that appeared in the 22 April 2001 issue of *Le Journal de Québec*: sporting a Ralph Nader for President T-shirt, a young man lobs a tear-gas cannister back at the police line that just shot it indiscriminately into the crowd.

Care must nevertheless be taken not to let the diversity of tactics principle morph into a code for "anything goes." As noted by L. A. Kauffman in her recent essay, "Turning Point," already "in certain radical circles . . . the militant acts at the front lines are being seen—and celebrated—in isolation, as part of a growing mystique of insurrection." These direct actions are not yet, and perhaps will never become, insurrections. Viewing them as such could lead to the use of tactics that would be potentially suicidal for this still-fledgling movement—as the historical examples of the Weather Underground and Red Army Faction show. Without a bit more definition to the diversity principle, and a way to make people accountable to any parameters decided on, the anticapitalist movement is wide open to stupidity or sabotage—or at least more than it needs to be.

At the same time, it is a positive sign that the diversity of tactics phrase has worked its way into the call for an anticapitalist bloc in DC at the World Bank/International Monetary Funds meetings well in advance of the actual protests this October. For where the tangible commitment to diversity of tactics really shone was in the months of organizational and educational work prior to Quebec City's convergence. Here, the tired bumpersticker phrase, "Think Globally, Act Locally," took on renewed meaning in CLAC/CASA's efforts. While they brought teach-ins to numerous cities across Canada and the United States, and put out their politics on the World Wide Web, the real key to their strategy was the attempt to win over the summit "host" city itself (where many CASA members live and work). Rather than merely organizing a weekend-long direct action, CLAC/CASA used the global and continental issues raised by the Free Trade Agreement of the Americas as a wedge into their own communities, as a way to develop radical resistance for ongoing struggles long after the tear gas clears. These Canadian-based organizers, in short, never lost sight of the need to link the global to the local, and to do such community work openly as radicals. They thereby succeeded in one of the more difficult tasks: bringing anticapitalism home.

A few examples suffice to illustrate the scope of their community activism. For instance, they asked Quebec City inhabitants to "adopt a protester," which meant agreeing to house and hence have relatively intimate contact with an anticapitalist out-of-towner during the convergence. CLAC/CASA's massive leafletting effort in Quebec City, on the streets and door to door, included handing out thousands of copies of a four-page bilingual tabloid that tried to debunk fear-provoking stereotypes and urged townfolks to "unite in one big anarchist contingent on A21." The anticapitalist organizers worked in and with grassroots neighborhood associations, and helped ensure that a no-arrest zone was strategically placed in the residential neighborhood abutting the fenced-in summit meetings to create a sense of security for the locals as well as nonlocals. After the convergence, members of CASA pitched in to help other city residents decontaminate the urban parks affected by tear gas.

This community organizing campaign—slipping into public relations at times—put a positive human face to the negative media (and state/police) portrait of anarchists and gave locals some of the knowledge they needed to begin to judge (and hopefully reject) capitalism for themselves. It probably convinced numerous Quebecois to participate in the days of resistance (or at least provide water and bathrooms, as many did), and much more than that, built a solid foundation of support, sympathy, and trust in the community for longer-term projects. The fact that Laval University gave several of its comparatively luxurious buildings in Quebec City over to CLAC/CASA for such things as a convergence center, sleeping facilities (housing over 2,500 people), and rallying point for the two anticapitalist marches is testimony to these two groups' grassroots efforts. As were the signs in local shopkeepers' windows: "We support you."

CLAC/CASA have proved that it is possible not just to bring thousands into your city but to also work closely with the thousands already there to radicalize and mobilize them for the convergence and beyond. Given that the cities where summits and ministers meet constantly rotate—from Seattle, Washington DC, and Ottawa, to Prague, Genoa, and even Qatar—many anticapitalists will probably get their chance at "hosting" a convergence and could therefore view it as an opportunity to link global concerns to on-the-ground local struggles. Left in the wake of summits and direct actions could be not a small, weary group of anarchist organizers but a large, invigorated radical milieu along with the foundations for resistance attempts in numerous cities across the global.

For it is not a matter of community organizing versus splashy direct actions but how to balance the two so they reinforce, complement, and build on each other in a way that escalates a revolutionary movement globally—as the efforts of CLAC/CASA has shown. While journalist Naomi Klein has been an insightful commentator on this movement, she is wrong in dubbing direct actions as "McProtests." Putting aside the fact that each direct action is not alike but borrows from, rejects, and/or transforms elements of previous actions—that is, there is often a generative, creative process at work—as Quebec City exemplified, mass actions also afford moments of real gain that would otherwise not be possible if resistance and reconstruction were merely parochial affairs. And they give people hope.

The real task of social transformation has only just been glimpsed, of course. Quebec City's convergence felt revolutionary, yet it was by no means a revolution. CLAC/CASA members, like other libertarian anticapitalists globally, are a long way from helping to turn the places they live into free cities in a free society. At least to date, it also appears that they have done little work, much less published thinking, on what a reconstructive vision might look like, as well as how to move toward it in their communities and this movement. Rather than just a Carnival against Capitalism, a carnival for something might have better provided the utopian thrust necessary to sustain and give direction to the difficult struggle ahead.

Nonetheless, by working locally and globally, by nurturing diversity in the arms of an explicitly antiauthoritarian politics, CLAC/CASA, with the help of a flimsy fence that became a mighty symbol, motivated thousands who came to and live in Quebec City to hoist the anticapitalist banner onto center stage. Something did start in Quebec—a distinctly radical movement in North America. Now the hard work of self-consciously shaping and building that movement must begin.

### References:

Comite d'Accueil du Sommet des Ameriques (Summit of the Americas Welcoming Committee), "CASA's Principles." .

Convergence des luttes Anti-Capitalistes (Anti-Capitalist Convergence), "CLAC Basis of Unity."

CrimethInc. Rioters Bloc. "CrimethInc. Eyewitness Analysis: Free Trade Area of the Americas Summit, Quebec City, April 19-22."

L. A. Kauffman, "Turning Point," *Free Radical: A Chronicle of the New Unrest*, no. 16 (May 2001). Available at www.free-radical.org.

Naomi Klein, "Talk to Your Neighbor; It's a Start." *Toronto Globe and Mail*, 2 May 2001.

# And Balanced With This Life, This Death

## Genoa, the G8 and the battle in the streets

## Ramor Ryan

### The Siege of Genoa

The walls went up around the old quarter of Genoa, enclosing the Group of 8 (G8) and their cohorts. Huge heavy walls of concrete and metal, like medieval fortifications or prison fences; walls to keep the people out, the world leaders penned in. Genoa is a beautiful renaissance city carved out of a treacherous mountain slope that seems as if it might slide irrevocably into the sea. Its pulsating streets, the mystery of its dense labyrinth, and the expansive calm of the sea front are a surreal theater for the battle that would consume it.

Leading up to the summit, the authorities had closed down the airport and the main railway stations and severely restricted access by road. Aside from the center of town (the red zone), which was completely forbidden to citizens, the surrounding area (the yellow zone) was also restricted with people enduring random stop-and-searches. Local people fled the town in droves, and most businesses closed for the duration of the summit. The G8 had transformed Genoa from a thriving commercial and tourist metropolis to a war zone under a form of martial law.

As if to justify the extraordinary security measures, the media reported various bomb scares and explosive finds, all of which protesters viewed skeptically. No groups present claimed responsibility. These are not tactics used by the alternative globalization movement. The Italian military brought in an array of defensive missiles. War ships were stationed in the bay. A state of paranoid terror was created to dissuade protesters from coming, and to criminalize those who did.

On the Austrian border, activists from the group "No Borders" were attacked; one woman lost five teeth. A boat full of protesters from Greece was held and the passengers attacked by riot police. Several hundred British protesters traveling by train were detained in France and a group of cyclists were held at the German border. Seventy migrants traveling from Germany to attend the Migrants March on the Thursday prior to the G8 Summit were refused entry into Italy. People disembarking at airports in Milan and Turin were subjected to interrogation and searches. Cars were routinely pulled over and the occupants detained. Nevertheless, tens of thousands of outsiders would make it to Genoa and as many as 200,000 demonstrators attended the final demonstration .

## The Genoa Social Forum—One No, Many Yeses

The logistical setup for the protesters centered around the Genoa Social Forum (GSF), the organizing body representing over 800 diverse groups advocating an alternative to the current corporate globalization. Their slogan was *A Different World Is Possible.* They pointed out that the movement was not antiglobalization, but an alternative vision of globalization, one that does not put profits before people, free trade before free movement; a movement that seeks to eliminate the gap between rich and poor, the powerful and the powerless. In a word, to democratize the process of globalization.

The GSF was based in a huge parking lot on the sea front. From this convergence center, people were dispatched to camp in various stadiums and parks across the city, loosely based on group affiliation. A thriving Indymedia Center was located nearby. There were legal, medical, and administrative centers demonstrating how the movement organizes itself autonomously. Cafe Clandestino provided free food and drink, while Manu Chao played a free late night concert before 25,000 ecstatic revelers the night before the summit began. A message from Subcommandante Marcos was boomed over the PA. How can one town hold so many Che Guevara T-shirts, Zapatista *paliacates*, Palestinian scarves?! The international connection, bridges between First and Thirrd Worlds, North and South, were everywhere to be seen, not just in the presence of Kurdish, African, Russian, or Indian delegates, but also with Europeans who bring their foreign experiences home.

## Gothenburg Revisited

The paramilitary police raided the camping centers at dawn on the twentieth, even before the summit began. From the start it was clear: heavy repression would be used to stifle protest with an iron fist. At the Carlini Stadium, temporary home to the strong Ya Basta! faction, the loudspeakers woke us at 5:30 A.M. "The police have surrounded us, everybody defend the gates!"

Outside, lines of heavily armed paramilitary police stood ready. They demanded to enter to search for arms and explosives. Ya Basta! is a nonviolent direct action organization. "To show we have nothing to hide" and to diffuse the situation, the central committee allowed a delegation of cops in to search the premises. Many activists were furious to have to submit to this search, but the Ya Basta! leaders prevailed. From early on, a split was emerging within the protesters' ranks between those who wished to resist the repression and those who wanted to avoid confrontation. All around the city campsites are raided, causing distress, confusion, fear, and depriving people of sleep. Meanwhile houses of activists preparing to go to Genoa are raided in other cities; doors are kicked down, people detained. Five Germans are arrested while driving in a car close to the red zone.

The first mobilization takes place on Thursday 19 July. About 50,000 people gather for a Migrants' March. The day is warm and sunny and the streets throng with a peaceful, high-spirited multitude. There are no cops in sight, and the mood is light. The first demand—open the borders to people as well as goods. We are not against globalization, but against globalization that criminalizes and marginalizes migrants. Are the G8 listening? Do they care? At least it is reported that they are shifting their agenda to talk about debt relief (for people who never themselves borrowed the money that invariably benefits those nearest to the top of the pyramid) and an AIDS fund for Africa ($10 billion is requested, $1 billion is considered). The media is chocabloc full of street stories, scare stories, spectacular images, all fueling the tension. The stage is set: the New World Order, the Global Empire, protected by 20,000 police and military, besieged by the new global protest movement. Graffiti appears on the walls."They make misery, we make history."

## Death In Genoa

Friday 20 July is a day of civil disobedience. The aim: to shut down the G8 by attempting to breach the fortifications enclosing the summit from a variety of positions. The tactics: direct action. The strongest contingent was the Ya Basta! grouping, numbering more than 10,000 militants . Up at the Carlini Stadium, preparations began early with talks followed by training sessions. Resembling an army preparing for war, men and women, predominantly young and Italian, spent all morning taping up their fragile bodies with foam and padding. The atmosphere was tense, the mood defiant. It really seemed anything was possible. There was an ecstatic mood of celebration when we finally set off on the four kilometer march to the city center. An endless sea of bopping helmets interspersed with a vast array of flags of every hue and color. At the front a long line of Ya Basta! militants pressed forward behind a wall of plastic shields.

News filtered through from around the city. Bad news. The Italian Trade Union group, COBAS, had been beaten badly before they had even gotten close to their target. In another part of the city, the Pink Block, a theatrical and prankster group of several thousand had also suffered heavy repression. A women's pacifist bloc had been attacked from the air by tear-gas firing helicopters. A strong section of anarchists and "Autonomes" had come close to the Red Zone but were now being brutally dispersed. The police were making pre-emptive strikes with tear gas and batons on every block. Only one of the roaming Black Bloc groups was not getting pounded, as they engaged in property destruction aimed at banks and multinational businesses. The only good news: one elderly man had, remarkably, penetrated the Red Zone before been arrested.

Despite all the ominous reports, we swept down the wide boulevard confidently—we were so many! Like an unstoppable river! So many people prepared to use their bodies to break through, to defend themselves, to struggle. *El Pueblo Unido, Jamas Sera Vencido,* they chanted. *Genoa Libera! E-Z-L-N!* Rage Against The Machine blasted from the mobile PA as *Fuck You I Wont' Do What You Tell Me!* was screamed along with by thousands. It was momentarily powerful and wonderful.

Two kilometers from the Red Zone, the police attacked us. First a frantic barrage of tear-gas canisters were lobbed over the front lines, deep into the heart of the demonstration. Nobody here had gas masks. The poisonous gas first blinds you, painfully, then disorientates you. It is immediate and devastating. The people, packed in tightly, panicked and surged backwards. Five hundred heavily armed riot squad cops stormed the front lines. In brutal scenes, the Ya Basta! militants crumbled despite brave resistance. All were battered. People screamed, turned, fled, falling over each other.

We retreated up the road. The sky was heavy with gas and helicopters hovered overhead. A water cannon blasted away, throwing bodies around like paper bags. What now? People looked to the Ya Basta! leadership, but there was no Plan B. The microphone that issued commands during the march was now silent. People retreated further and further, eventually sitting down. Meanwhile the front lines struggled to hold on, and the fighting was intense, the tear-gas volleys raining down, the police hitting out viciously as the plastic shields shattered and the helmets cracked. Bleeding people were rushed to the back with head injuries, including some inflicted when they had been shot in the face with tear gas canisters.

We were defeated before having even begun. The nonviolent direct action tactics, an active defense crushed in the face of decisively brutal police tactics. As the majority of the march sat down further up the road, thousands of others streamed off into the side streets. The right side was blocked by the railway track, while to the left lay a labyrinth of small enclosed streets. *Open new fronts! Break through police lines at 2, 3, 4 different points!* Spontaneous and enraged, thousands ran into the sidestreets. Meanwhile, the Ya Basta! loudspeaker requested people to stay put on the road, far from the Red Zone.

## Rebel Joy and Sorrow

In a beautiful old barrio, the battle raged. Protesters charged up tight streets flinging stones at police lines. The police, protected head to toe, amassed behind shields and flanked by armored vehicles, responded with tear gas and by flinging back the rocks. The ferocious spirit of the protesters more than the paltry stones pushed back the police lines. Barricades were built with dumpsters, cars, anything at hand. The front lines would retreat nursing wounds and poisoned eyes. The more seriously injured were carried to ambulances. New people rushed to the front, while others tore up the pavement for ammunition. A tall gentleman fell back saying, " We almost got through, we almost did it, we just need a few more people!"

Another surge, everyone rushed forward on two or three different streets. Some riot cops got stranded in their retreat and hand-to-hand fighting ensued. Those fighting are not necessarily in black, though some are masked. Some have helmets. It is not the Black Bloc, and there are no agent provocateurs. This is a militant energy driven by people who have said, *Ya Basta! Fuck the police! Rage! Energy! Resolve!*

They move forward. Tear gas is everywhere. The police are retreating. An armored *carabinieri* truck is captured and the occupants flee. It is smashed up and set ablaze. This symbol of the hated oppressive state, is burning and everyone is cheering, filled with rebel joy. Someone sprays "We Are Winning!," the famous slogan that appeared in Seattle on the side of the carcass of the armored beast. Now they are almost in Piazza Alimondo. They are pushing the police back, two blocks, then three, further and further. Protesters are euphoric, storming forward, overwhelming the despised *carabinieri*. Approaching the despised wall of the G8; "*Here we are,*" they chant, "*we resist!*"

Hundreds strong, they poured into the expansive Piazza Alimondo. Two police vehicles drive recklessly into the crowd; one drives away, the other stalls; people rush toward the vehicle. Shots ring out. Rubber bullets? No, the ominous thud of live ammunition. The air heaved. The protesters stopped, reeled around, and fled.

Carlo Guiliani was twenty-three years old. A rebel. The papers belittled him, called him a "ne'er do well," a squatter. But we know him as a comrade and a revolutionary. He fought the paramilitary police bravely, fearlessly, pitting the little streets against the great. He was involved in the Zapata Social Center of Genoa. Carlo's death was not heroic, nor tragic. It was the consequence of his life, how he lived, how he resisted. Moments before he was shot in the face, Carlo probably felt the extraordinary rebel joy of this spontaneous uprising against power in the little side streets of Genoa. He died instantly, or else when the police drove over him, not once but twice, as if to make sure he was dead, really dead. For the police, Carlo had to die. Now they must kill us, because we are beginning to really threaten their power. Carlo was murdered. We are all Carlo.

## The Ghost of Pinochet

Saturday 21 July. This is how the police work . . . It is Saturday afternoon and there are as many as 200,000 people marching on Genoa against the eight most powerful economic powers in the world. It is not a combative march. As they swing onto the sea front, a group of agent provocateurs began throwing stones at the police. These are undercover cops, or secret police, or mercenaries or Nazis. They are used by the police the same way the paramilitaries are used by the state in Chiapas or in Belfast, or even how they used them in Italy in the 1970s. The police want to pick the time and place of the confrontation. They are ready and prepared. This was planned. This is how the police work: a few stones fall harmlessly into their ranks and they open up with tear gas. The canisters fly deep into the multitude, immediately creating panic and chaos. People flee, young and old, parents with babies in their arms. But there are too many people, nowhere to run, they are hemmed in and poisoned from the gas. It is horrific.

This is how the people resist . . . The militants stream through the crowd to the front. There they attempt to build barricades and hold back the advancing cops. The sky fills with stones. They hold the police and those behind them have a few moments more to retreat. Those who needed to get away from the zone could. Communist party stewards directed people away, but many people stayed, indignant that the demonstration could be so brutally dispersed even before it could get to the piazza. Now is the hour of the Black Bloc and the insurrectionary anarchists. All afternoon the streets were mad with tear-gas, with stones, with burning banks, burning cars, barricades. The air was shrill with screams of beatings, violence, and fear.

Eventually the barricades were overrun. The police advanced ferociously, beating people indiscriminately. In a most surreal scene, cops in gray overalls beat up people on the beach, the Italian Riviera, while bathers looked on. Police in small boats launched tear gas onto the beach. A helicopter overhead fired gas into the fleeing hordes. Further up, people jumped off the rocks into the sea. The huge march ended in absolute mayhem. Let it be recorded—200,000 overtly peaceful protesters were not allowed to demonstrate. "The Genoa Social Forum favored and covered the Black Bloc," said Italian Prime Minister Silvio Berlusconi by way of explanation the next day. We are all guilty. We are all Carlo Giulliani.

## Attacking Indymedia

At midnight, the next police operation began. We were eating in a restaurant near the Indymedia Center. The quiet residential street was silent, the neighborhood sleeping. A long line of heavily armored men rushed by, masked and with their batons swinging. In single file, silent but for the thumping of their boots on the pavement. The next moment, a fleet of armored police vehicles rushes by. Suddenly a helicopter shattered the night sky. Finally, a long line of ambulances blasting their sirens passed by. All this in a couple of minutes, a surgical strike on the movement's offices. The police were extracting revenge. They crashed through the front gates of the Indymedia Center in an armored truck, then smashed up the computers, confiscated files and film and broke cameras, terrorizing the journalists inside.

Across the road in the school building being used by the GSF as offices and a dormitory for people who felt unsafe in the camping grounds, the real horror occurred. Police and plain-clothes cops—reportedly from the special paramilitary police unit ,

GOM—burst in and attacked everyone inside. Most were sleeping on the floor. Ninety-three people were injured, as the police closed the door and inflicted heavy punishment. Scores of people were eventually carried out on stretchers. Pools of blood remained on the floor, streaks of blood across the walls. Attacks on property cannot be equated to the legions of broken limbs, broken teeth, broken ribs, and damaged skulls that a squad of policemen inflicted on a somnambulant group of weary protesters as they lay on the floor of a school.

## State-sponsored Terror

These men were following orders. Those who gave the orders get their general directives from a higher authority. The blame for this state terror lies at the feet of Berlusconi's regime, and ultimately, the G8. This is why we protest the G8. This is why comrades move from protest to resistance. The midnight attack on the school and Indymedia, the ensuing torture of the prisoners afterwards, was an attempt to terrorize the movement, to inflict extrajudiciary punishment on activists, and to instill mind numbing fear within the hearts and souls of protesters. In many ways, it was successful. Saturday night in Genoa was one of widespread fear and terror.

At the Carlini Stadium, bastion of the Ya Basta! movement, the officials ordered an immediate evacuation. "Like Saigon," reported one eyewitness. Hundreds of other activists not present at the time were left stranded. Plain-clothes police swarmed in, and criminals were allowed in to rummage through peoples' belongings. That night, all over Genoa people fled from camping sites to roam the streets and alleys and back lanes of the city in fear, hunted like escaped convicts. It was the longest night. Eventually dawn came, but everything had changed.

Genoa was gutted. No city will host the G8 for a while. Thirty-four banks burnt. Eighty-three vehicles both police and civilian, destroyed. Forty-one businesses torched or looted, six supermarkets, twelve government offices illustrating the belief that some protesters have that targeting the economic organs of the enemy is the most effective tactic. (No buses were burnt, apparently because the bus drivers union was in solidarity with the protesters, ferrying everyone around for free the whole week). With Genoa in ruins, the G8 left quietly with a few promises to give some money to Africa (via drug companies). Italian Prime Minister Silvio Berlusconi blamed not just the Black Bloc and the anarchists, but the whole movement, rendering any distinction obsolete.

The GSF has since uncovered damning evidence of police collusion with agent provocateurs, and the inquiries into the night of terror at the school and the denunciations of torture afterwards continues, unrelenting. Two hundred people were arrested, six hundred injured. In the jails, the protesters were tortured while police mocked them with pictures of Mussolini and Nazis. They tortured them, as they have done in Seattle, Prague, and Quebec. They tortured them as they did in Pinochet's Chile, in Argentina; everywhere activists have unsettled power, they terrorize them. They attempt to destroy the movement by spreading panic and fear. To break the back of the militants of this totally unarmed global protest movement.

## A Summer's Day

A lovely tree-filled piazza deep in the heart of Genoa. A pile of flowers. An endless flow of citizens pass by to pay their respects at the site of Carlo's murder. A memorial across the road beside an old church is overflowing with little gifts and offerings. Che Guevara images dominate amidst black, red, and green flags, candles and flowers, cigarettes, beer bottles, tear-gas canisters, Zapatista scarves, sunglasses, gloves. An array of notes and poems and good-bye letters from his friends. A photo of Carlo with his school class. He is the one with the shoulder-length hair and the *Fuck Nike* t-shirt. Politically conscious at sixteen. People weep gently. Two squatter girls tie up a banner with the help of a posh older lady. A Mexican woman offers clasps from her coat to secure the banner. "*We with our hands,*" it read, "*they with their guns.*"

Someone else leaves a poem, Shakespeare's Sonnet No. 18. "Shall I compare thee to a summers day?" On a summers day in Genoa, July 20, 2001, Carlo fell. Let the July 20 Movement flourish.

# Genoa and the Antiglobalization Movement
## Silvia Federici and George Caffentzis

August 2001

### A Citizens' Arrest

These are some reflections on the demonstrations in Genoa during the G8 meetings and the post-Genoa debate. We were not in Genoa on July 19-21, 2001 and were not involved in the process of preparing the demos; thus, there are aspects of this debate we cannot comment upon. We are responding, however, to the widespread realization that the July Genoa days were a turning point for the antiglobalization movement and there are important lessons we in the movement must draw from it.

Two things happened in Genoa that signal the development of a new political reality. First, 300,000 people from every part of Europe came together to challenge the legitimacy of the G8 meeting and practically attempt a citizen's arrest of it. On the first day of the demonstrations, moreover, 70,000 immigrants and supporters marched—an unprecedented feat in Italy where immigrants politically are still relatively invisible.

What also happened in Genoa is that in response to this challenge the Italian government and (more hiddenly) its G8 partners declared war on the antiglobalization movement, first by brutally attacking hundreds of peaceful demonstrators, and then by staunchly defending these attacks as perfectly legitimate, thus de facto backing a strategy of terror and the abolition of all legal, civic, and human rights.

In the days and weeks following the Genoa events, the Berlusconi government has not spared efforts, with the assistance of the many TV channels and newspapers which it now controls, to blame on the antiglobal protesters the violence unleashed on them. Scenes of stone-throwing demonstrators confronting the police or methodically destroying shop windows or putting cars on fire have been broadcast over and over, while the unprecedented sight of the hundreds of thousands who marched with chants and banners have been censored. The goal has been to whip up a wave of moral indignation against the protesters high enough to make people forget the brutality and illegality of the treatment meted out to them.

Thus, it is very important for us, as we reflect on the meaning of the Genoa demonstrations on the fate of our movement, to be clear on one basic fact: *What happened in Genoa reflects a premeditated institutional plan to repress and terrorize the demonstrators, to convince them to never again participate in such protest. This plan was not shaped by how activists behaved.*

This could be seen by the shape of the events. The three days of demonstrations against the G8, July 19–21, were planned, on the one side, by the new Berlusconi government and, on the other, by the Genoa Social Forum (GSF, a network of more than a thousand Italian and international antiglobalization associations, organizations, and groups) and the Tutte Bianche, an Italian organization that has specialized in nonviolent blockades of meetings of the global "leaders." There were a number of meetings between the two sides that supposedly laid the ground rules for the confrontation. Three days of protest were planned. On the first, July 19, there was to be an international demonstration of immigrants; the second day was to be one of nonviolent civil disobedience; and the third day was to be an international mass demonstration.

Even before the first demo, however, it was clear that the government was doing its best to create a sense of panic among the population to prevent people from going to Genoa and to build the image of the antiglobalization demonstrators as terrorists. First there was the "bombs strategy." For a couple of days newspapers and TV news were filled with reports of bombs and/or mysterious packages being found in several parts of Italy, especially in Milan; then letter bombs arrived at the office of the Director of TV 4, one of Berlusconi's channels, and other companies. All in all there were sixty bomb scares(!!).

Meanwhile, hundreds of people were refused entrance at the borders (686 by the eighteenth), a move made possible by the fact that, for the duration of the summit, the Schengen Treaty (which guaranteed EU citizens freedom to cross all EU borders) was suspended. All those who arrived were meticulously screened; three buses of Greek activists, with one of the organizing committees, were prevented from landing from the ship in Ancona. In addition, the gathering places in Genoa were raided; innocuous, defensive material was confiscated and displayed on TV as if they were weapons; airports and train stations were closed.

But the most telling sign of what was to come what was done to Genoa. By the eighteenth, Genoa was a ghost town as the area in which the G8 were to meet—the Zona Rossa—was enclosed in a true iron cage and people were practically forced to leave the city. It is now clear that the government did not want to have witnesses for the "action" planned. As in Prague, workers were forced to take their vacations during the summit, and shopkeepers were told to keep their shops closed and leave because "vandals were coming." One Genovese out of three abandoned the city—in the end the only people left, especially in the Zona Rossa, were some elderly who had nowhere to go and could not even get to the streets because police patrols would push them back inside. Interviewed by the press they looked disoriented, disbelieving. "We look like tigers in a cage," one said. "Not even in time of war we have seen anything like it." Others noted the eerie silence only broken by the buzz of the helicopters and the sound of the boots of the cops on the pavement—"the silence of a city after a coup d'etat," a paper wrote.

Everyone looked dismayed as scores of welders enclosed the Zona Rossa within a gated iron net. "Here democracy ends," "zone with limited rights," read the posters placed on the bars by some activists (and quickly removed by the police). So the signs of what was to come were there.

The next day, July 19, however, passed without incident. In fact it was a glorious day. Immigrant organizations from all over Italy and other parts of Europe marched to protest the treatment meted out to them by the Italian government and the EU, and to present their demands: legal recognition, asylum rights, housing. It was wonderful in Italy, where immigrants are treated like pariahs and made object of a constant persecution, to see immigrants and Italians occupying the streets together, saying no to racism, demonstrating in their lives and struggles the effects of globalization and the political possibilities their presence in Europe opens up. (On the day before in Genoa, a meeting of trade unionists from all over Europe was held, this too a first, and a sign, perhaps, that the trade unions may be beginning to realize the importance of international solidarity and coordination, even though the CGIL has refused to take a position against globalization. "Globalization must be agreed upon (*concertata*)—they said—not fought against.")

The "war" started on Friday, July 20. By this time, despite the raids, the panic disseminated with the "bomb attempts" (a bomb was placed near the entry of the Carlini camp, where the Tutte Bianche and other demonstrators had gathered), despite the high number of people rejected at the borders, the long checks to which individuals and busses were submitted, about 150,000 had assembled. As in the anti–IMF/World Bank demonstrations in Prague, they were to demonstrate in different blocs, coming from the different gathering spots to then converge in the center of the town, where some groups had announced they would try to enter the Zona Rossa. But no one from the main demo made it there. From an early time in the morning a scenario started unfolding that continued through the next day. Demonstrators presumably belonging to the Black Bloc clashing with the police were chased in the direction of the other demonstrators, and soon policemen were attacking with tear gas and batons the whole march with a determination that was almost murderous.

This is no exaggeration and we urge people everywhere to read as many testimonies and reports as they can to verify this statement. Thousands of people, of all ages, peacefully marching were viciously beaten while strange demonstrators, clad in black and moving in paramilitary fashion, were given free reign. For hours they were allowed to move from place to place, destroying things on their way—cars, windows: when the police charged them their goal was to push them towards the march, and in fact, through this tactic, the bulk of the demonstrators were assaulted. It is now agreed and documented that there were provocateurs and members of right-wing Nazi groups among the "Black Bloc" and the other demonstrators. As we heard over and over, a few hundred belligerants were free to move from place to place, rarely pursued by the cops and *carabinieri*, while the mass of the demo was savagely attacked.

That afternoon a policeman in a van shot Carlo Guiliani, a young demonstrator from Genoa, in the head. In the effort to get out of the hands of the furious crowd the driver of the van ran over Carlo's body twice.

As the news of Carlo's killing moved through the streets of Genoa the battles, beatings, and arrests continued. The arrested were sent to a number of jails for booking. One of the most infamous was Bolzenato which was, as one inmate put it, "truly a hell." The police in the prison were special mobile police officers sent from Rome who were trained to put down prison revolts. Cages for torture were built especially for the demo and those arrested were forced to sing fascist songs or little ditties like "1, 2, 3. . . viva Pinochet/ 4, 5, 6. . . kill the Jews/7, 8, 9. . . I don't care about little black kids" (it rhymes in Italian). People who had arrived already wounded were further attacked and women were threatened with rape. Those with dreads had their heads shaved and those with piercings had them ripped out.

The next day was scheduled to be the day of the international mass demonstration. The parade route had been previously announced and no attempt to penetrate the Zona Rossa had been organized that day. Most estimates put the number at about 300,000, one of the largest demonstrations in recent European history. The news of the savage attacks on peaceful demonstrators as well as Carlo Guilaini's killing had spread fast enough that many Italians who had previously planned not to take part in the demos came to protest what had happened the day before.

The GSF organizers were conscious of the danger of the police using the relatively marginal presence of the Black Bloc as an excuse to attack the mass demonstration. They attempted to distinguish the peaceful demonstrators from the Black Bloc by assigning a large number of clearly designated marshals to keep the ones intent on throwing stones at the police and smashing bank windows away from the cortege. This was not an empty gesture. There were times that people in the Black Bloc and the marshals clashed physically.

But these precautions and the previous agreements with the government did not help. The police literally pounced on the demonstrators. Thousands were attacked in the streets; tear gas was dropped on them from helicopters and even launched from boats. Mayhem was the police's order of the day.

With hundreds more arrests, hundreds more wounded, the day ended in the final display of terror: the attack on the Diaz school complex, which had been reserved with the approval of the local government as a place for sleeping. Ninety-three mostly young people were there when the police stormed in and beat most of them there, expertly, often to the edge of their lives. Some G8 leaders had clearly decided that this was to be the antiglobalization movement's Wounded Knee.

## Immovable Objects with Batons: the G8 in Genoa

It would be a mistake to read the police violence unleashed in Genoa as the instinctive reaction of a fascistic government. True, Berlusconi's right-wing political history and the presence in his government of Alleanza Nationale, the modern reincarnation of the Mussulini's party, easily raise the spectre of a fascist coup. But it can be demonstrated that the repression carried out in Genoa was concerted among the G8 leaders who were all present with their security forces during the police attacks, and well aware of it.

*The attacks on demonstrators in Genoa were not the "excesses" of a fascistic government, but a well-calculated strategy, discussed and approved at the highest European and international levels.*

First, the government, as mentioned before, while pretending to dialogue with the movement and expressing concern for the safety of the demonstrators, launched war against them.

Second, the plan for Genoa was quite similar to that implemented in Quebec, and partly in Prague: force the local population to leave, isolate the demonstrators, fence off the meeting's zone, terrorize future demonstrators with preemptive raids, torture the arrested in the jail, scare everyone with heavy sentences and draconian laws. The government created the conditions for confrontation by treating the demonstrators as literal "plague-bearers" and transforming Genoa from the lively city that it is into a military zone where police could operate with impunity.

Third, the complicity of the EU police services and US police has also been documented. We know now that three members of the Los Angeles Sheriff's Department went to Italy in June to give a hand in organizing the police response in Genoa. Also documented is the collaboration between the police of the EU countries and the Italian police. Lists of names were sent to Italy by other EU governments signaling the arrival of certain activists, destined, it seems, to a special treatment; Greek activists believe that the Greek police informed their Italian colleagues about the buses on which the Greek Genoa organizing committee was traveling so that its members could be prevented from landing in Ancona.

Most important, the diplomatic protests that have been presented to the Italian government by other government members of the EU have been totally inadequate considering the gravity of the violations of international law that Italy has made itself responsible for. The behavior of the Italian police and authorities towards foreign nationals has been so abominable that, in other times, it would have been a casus belli. Not only were hundreds and hundreds of peaceful demonstrators brutally beaten in the streets, often in ways that will maim them for life—but, in violation of the Geneva convention on prisoners and the EU convention on human rights, the following occurred:

(a) Demonstrators were mercilessly beaten by groups of policemen even when on the ground, and in no condition to inflict any harm or defend themselves;

(b) On Saturday evening, July 21, when the demos were over, hundreds of policemen conducted a punitive expedition, Chilean style, in the Diaz school complex where participants to the demos were sleeping. Many of them were foreign nationals. Of the ninety-three present, sixty-six exited on stretchers. Wounds inflicted included broken jaws—a young woman lost fourteen teeth—broken ribs and punctured lungs;

(c) Dozens of arrested protesters, including many foreign nationals, were tortured in jail physically and psychologically;

(d) Arrested protesters, again including many foreign nationals, were kept incommunicado up to ninety-six hours—they were literally kidnapped by the Italian state;

(e) The foreign nationals arrested were made to sign statements in Italian (a language many could not read) and beaten when they asked for translators;

(f) Once released, even when cleared of all charges, foreign nationals were still forbidden to remain in Italy. They were taken directly to the airport and put on a plane without documents and their belongings—despite the fact that lawyers and families were waiting for them outside the prisons. They were also informed that (in violation of the Schengen Treaty) they would not be allowed to return to Italy for another five years.

How could the European Parliament and the other government members of the EU have accepted this situation unless they had given it their dispensation? The G8 meeting was not some internal Italian affair; it was the meeting of a club of government leaders. Each of them must be held responsible for what happened there, both inside the Palazzo Ducale and outside. The Security Services of Schroeder, Jospin, Bush, and Blair were in Genoa and must have given them firsthand reports as to what was unfolding. They were not pure bystanders.

Presently, some of the foreign governments are protesting and asking for explanations. But how could all of this have happened to begin with? Why is Italy not being expelled, or at least suspended from the EU? Why is Berlusconi not being denounced as a violator of human rights? And is it imaginable that the Italian government, which rarely acts in an independent fashion and always bends to the powerful, dared so openly to challenge the international agreements it has signed and threaten the lives of hundreds of EU nationals without a prior assenting nod by their governments?

Again, the answer must be *No!* We must make sure that the fact that the Berlusconi government is a right-wing government does not provide an alibi for the other EU countries that are equally responsible but glad perhaps to have the dirty work done by an already tainted partner. Blair publicly signaled his approval of Berlusconi's tactics before Genoa by calling for a "robust" repressive response to the demonstrators. Schroeder called for a vigorous attack on "political hooligans" in the antiglobalization movement in the days after Genoa. Indeed, the focus of the post-Genoa intergovernmental discussion among EU members was of the creation of a EU-wide police body, with a site in every country, that would specialize in responding to the antiglobalization movement, and/or the creation of a special EU investigative corps, again concentrating on the antiglobalization movement.

There are, of course, limits to the EU governmental complicity. Appearances must be saved, and some lip service to human rights must be given. The very use of the human rights strategy as a way of speeding up the globalization process has now created a certain degree of inhibition (at least in Europe) in the use of force. Even the Berlusconi government, after several days of undiluted praise to the police, has had to make some concessions. This is why it has been discovered that some "excesses" occurred, and some heads in the police force have rolled. But, all in all, we are witnessing a great political whitewash.

*The Italian state's reaction in Genoa was so violent and indiscriminate with the blessing of the G8 because the G8 and other globalization planners have nothing to give to the protest movement. They have nothing to negotiate so can only respond with repression.*

That the peaceful were treated as violently as the belligerent is a telling sign that just being against capitalist globalization makes criminals of us. The global leaders cannot afford such a degradation of their legitimacy; they cannot differentiate, and make concessions because they have nothing to concede. The only language they can speak now is that of tear gas canisters, batons, groin kicks, and cigarette burns. The antiglobalization protest is a serious political challenge to their plans on many levels. They disrupts their meetings, give new confidence to Third World politicians who understand that capitalist globalization is a recolonization process, undermine the new international division of labor, and, just a decade after the collapse of communism, repropose the question of an alternative to capitalism as a matter of life and death for the majority of the world population.

The G8 cannot make concessions, since their Genoa meeting occurred under the cloud of a pan-capitalist economic crisis—occurring not just in Asia, Russia, or Brazil, as in previous times, but in the heartland of advanced capitalism with simultaneous profits collapses in the US, Japan, and the EU. This is why, despite the prayers of the Pope and Bono, and despite the condescending invitation to three African leaders, the issue of the Third World debt was not even put on the table. It was replaced by the question of a fund for AIDS in Africa, which is nothing more than a modest donation to the pharmaceutical companies to be administered by the World Bank.

Instead, the main topic of discussion for the G8 was the "economy" in the US, Japan, and Europe. Less than five months before the introduction of monetary unification, few countries in Europe have fulfilled the conditionalities nations must satisfy in order to join the unification stipulated almost a decade ago—few have reduced public spending, or managed to grow within the prescribed limits. Italy in particular has been the object of much deprecation by EU and IMF officers because of its large public debt and its population's resistance to pension and healthcare cuts. Thus, barely three months after the elections, the new government has "discovered" the public deficit is far larger than expected in the very days of the demonstration; as the police were beating and torturing the demonstrators, the government was preparing a legislative packet that is guaranteed to generate much protest and resistance in the fall—a packet which decimates healthcare and reproposes the question of reducing pensions. We can well surmise that the ferocity of the repression in the streets of Genoa and the sadistic behavior displayed by the police were also meant to be a warning for the fall when the truth concerning the price of "European unity" is going to be revealed.

*The state violence in Genoa is an essential part of the devaluation of European labor that is now required by globalization.*

When demonstrators in Genoa said that they felt like they were in Chile or Argentina or they were being beaten like Rodney King in Los Angeles they expressed a deep intuition: *they were being treated by the police as if they were poor people in the Third World or blacks in the US, i.e., people whose labor has been so systematically devalued the police have no inhibitions in killing and maiming them.* This devaluation has taken place in the US and the Third World already (in the US with the quarter-century decline in real wages and the mass incarceration of black and Hispanic youth), but European capital has been hesitant to apply the same "Third World" and "American" methods to their own citizens. At best, this treatment has been reserved for the immigrants from Africa and the Middle East who have found themselves in the clutches of "Fortress Europe." European capital is now being told, however, by the IMF and its own planners that, if European unification is to overcome its own economic crisis, globalization "with a human face" must end. The European working class must be dramatically devalued, and a shortcut to devaluation is to treat anyone who resists the new economic policies not as a legitimate protester but as a criminal. The closest contemporary comparison to the way the Italian police responded to the protesters in Genoa is the violent and unprovoked police behavior against anti–IMF/World Bank demonstrations in Third World nations like Nigeria, Jamaica, and Bolivia.

The killing of Carlo Guiliani in the streets of Genoa must then be seen as the beginning of a campaign intended to degrade and devalue European workers.

## Genoa and the Limits of the Seattle Experience

Even with the inevitable repression and the much grieved for death and maimings, the Genoa demonstrations were in some respects an enormous success for the antiglobalization movement. Hundreds of thousands came from all over Europe to these demonstrations in the face of very open intimidation. Clearly the message of the movement is increasing in its range and power. Moreover, the mass immigrant march was an important first step in tying together the post-Seattle antiglobalization struggle in Europe with the much longer struggle against globalization in the Third World. After all, many immigrants were forced out their homes by the globalization policies they struggled against in the streets of Africa, Asia, and South America.

However, there is no doubt that at the end of the Genoa demonstrations there was an wave of internal criticism and divisiveness within the movement, which for some was much more demoralizing than Carlo's death and the hundreds of broken bones. It is important to voice some of this criticism in order to see that what is being criticized is not due of the personal failings of people of the GSF, the Tutte Bianche, or the genuine Black Bloc (anarchists or autonomist Marxists as opposed to undercover police or neo-Nazi thugs). It arises from a change in the struggle against globalization because a number of the tactics that proved so successful in Seattle are reaching their limit.

The major criticism lodged against the GSF is that it put too much trust in the negotiation with the government, underrating the hostility of the G8 against the antiglobalization movement and the previous examples of Washington DC and Quebec, which testify to the growing tendency toward repression. GSF consequently failed to warn the participants of the risks they ran and to defend the march against surprise attack. The GSF also acted as if it represented the whole movement, which it did not, with the result that again it did not prepare the demonstrators concerning the dangers they ran.

The common criticism lodged against the genuine Black Bloc-ers is that they failed to realize to what extent their tactics exposed them to being used by the government to attack the demonstration. As a result their tactics provoked revulsion among many of the demonstrators who found themselves facing a police charge and being severely beaten on account of both the bloc's belligerence and their readiness to flee after an action.

The main criticism lodged against Tutte Bianche is that they insisted on entering the Zona Rossa even after it was clear that this would not be possible by any sort of civil disobedience, except at an unacceptably high cost. Even if they succeeded in a physical confrontation with the police, they could hardly have counted on the sympathy and applause of the Italian population, especially not the workers who, in Italy, as every other country, have a long history of physical confrontation with the police, but, precisely for this reason, are not likely to appreciate facing the risk of beating or arrest for sake of a purely symbolic gestures.

These criticisms, however just, have arisen, we believe, because two tactics which proved so successful in Seattle are reaching the limit of their effectiveness. First, the flexible, mass nonviolent blockade of globalizers' meetings inaugurated in Seattle—which has been quite successful until recently—is now in a crisis. Certainly as a result of the use of this tactic, the globalizers' meetings since November 1999 cannot be held without the equivalent of city-wide shut-down in order to ensure that the meetings go ahead. At the same time, this type of blockade it is becoming problematic. The globalizers have shown that with thousands of police, tons of iron and barbed wire, and dozens of helicopters, they can have their meetings and make the protestors pay heavily in terms of the arrested, tortured, maimed, and killed. The flexible blockade is not magical. Like any other tactic—e.g., the factory strike or the consumer boycott—it can be thwarted, just as strikes of factory workers can be defeated by the bringing in scabs, as has so often been done in the major factory worker confrontations with capital in the US during the 1980s and 1990s.

The Seattle demonstrations did succeed in disrupting a WTO meeting. But the globalizers are learning, and if their present ruminations are to be realized, they will be soon meet high on the Rockies (the next G8 meeting venue) or (as with the WTO's next shindig in Qatar) similarly inaccessible locations. Under these circumstances the goal of antiglobization demos must be rethought. More emphasis must be placed on the broader political aspects of the convergences—in the same way as in the 1980s, faced by the wide use of scabs by employers, unionists realized that no strike could win without a broad political preparation that often included making connections with workers in Asia or South America. This is being increasingly understood within the antiglobalization movement; it is learning that demonstrations against the WTO in fifty cities around the planet might be more effective than a purely symbolic attempt to blockade the globalizers' meeting in the middle of a desert, on top of a mountain, in the middle of sea, or even in outer space! This does not mean, of course, that large antiglobalization demonstrations on the site of globalizers' meetings will be abandoned. On the contrary, the very possibility that such blockades could be called by the movement will forever change the nature of way capitalist globalizers will meet.

The second way Genoa has also shown the limits of a tactic that proved so successful in Seattle involves the pluralistic approach to demonstrating. The pluralistic style of organizing adopted in Genoa seemed a promising, but ultimately problematic, way of implementing the movement slogan, "One No, Many Yeses" (i.e., we can agree on rejecting capitalist globalization without agreeing beforehand on our alternative ways of fighting it or our postcapitalist ways of living). This approach was tried successfully in Seattle where there were simultaneously nonviolent blockaders, "Black Bloc" assaulters on Starbucks and Nike stores, and AFL-CIO members marching in a huge parade far from the confrontation zone. This model has been refined since then. In Prague pluralism was formalized, with the choice of three colors reflecting different ways of participating in the demonstration, while in Genoa there were five. This choice seemed to imply that there many different ways to confront power and they could coexist and even potentiate each other, as they did in Seattle.

This model assumes, however, that (a) the opposition will accept the rules of the game and modulate its response with respect to individual demonstrators according to the choice s/he made, and (b) that the demonstrators will also play by the rules. But neither assumption worked in Genoa. The police, it appears, clubbed NGOers, feminists, enviromentalists, and Tutte Bianche more than they did Black Bloc-ers. This was not a momentary lapse on the part of the Italian police. It is now clear that from the viewpoint of the authorities all protestors of globalization are criminals.

Demonstrators were also unable to "honor" their colors and moved from one to another according to the situation. For example, many who had come to participate in a nonviolent demonstration physically confronted the police when attacked.

Again, this is not to say that "pluralism" in demonstrations is to be abandoned, but that the movement must be clear as to the extent and limits of this organizational tactic. The policies that govern one's participation in such demonstrations must also be clarified.

For demos are not just to be measured on a utilitarian basis; they are also prefigurations of the future world a movement wants to build and offer protesters an opportunity to show concretely what the alternatives to capitalist globalization can be. This, ultimately, is the most powerful "weapon," the most effective means of consciousness-raising that the antiglobalization movement has, the one that would concretely show not only that this movement is capable of moving an immovable rock, but that it can build a new world. The first thing we can show the world (since it is watching) is that we can engage in common projects without irreducible conflict. If this is not possible, it will be a major defeat for the movment. In that case, the movement will loose its legitimacy as the bearer of alternative to capitalist globalization, a much more dangerous consequence than any police assault. In a word, what is crucial here is not just the police attack on the movement—which was all but inevitable in Genoa given their use of provocateurs, neo-Nazis and preemptive violence—but the movement's relation to itself. The powerful image of a movement that can bring together determined nonviolent blockaders and Black Bloc-ers with unionists, enviromentalists, and NGOers and powerfully say *"No!"* to globalization is now being questioned under the pressure of an intense wave of repression. But the limits of Seattle's tactics are not the limits of the movement.

Finally, we should remember that though demonstrations like those in Seattle, Washington, Quebec, and now Genoa are important, the fate of the movement does not hinge on their success alone. This movement has far deeper and stronger roots in the daily confrontations of billions of people in Africa, Asia, and the Americas against the globalization agenda and its enforcers. A key question on the movement's horizon then is: how can this multiplicity of struggle in the Third World be expressed and amplified by the antiglobalization demonstrations in the metropoles of Europe and North America?

# Growing Through Daring, Forgetting Through Fear

## Celebration and Criticism of the WEF Protests in New York City

## Carwil James

January 2002's protests against the World Economic Forum (WEF) in New York marked the return to large-scale, creative confrontation with the forces of capitalist globalization in the United States. The previous six months had seared two images into the minds of the movement: the point-blank shooting and crushing of G8 protester Carlo Giuliani in Genoa, and the stunning, murderous crash of two planes into the World Trade Center in lower Manhattan.

The first death electrified us with grief, fear, and solidarity. The message was clear: no country, no matter how white or rich (or social democratic, as the live ammunition shootings in Sweden had shown) would spare its citizens if they stood in the way of global corporate rule. As in the days following the Kent State shootings in 1970 or the Sharpeville massacre in 1961, we were a movement overcoming our fear of death, drawing power from our collective vulnerability. Expectations and organizing rose for Washington DC's fall IMF/World Bank meetings.

Then the towers fell. Explosions in quick secession spread across the country: jet fuel, then debris, then intense urban fear, grief, government repression, militarization, media-sponsored patriotism. With a wave of NGOs pulling out and the media tide turning against them, the Mobilization for Global Justice called off its street activities in DC. Seven to ten thousand came to DC anyway. But the strength of maintaining complete commitment despite our fears retreated for much of the movement.

This is what made New York so important. September 11th left behind a triple landscape of fear for activists in New York: the ambient fear of terrorist attack on the very institutions we sought to change with hopeful, creative means; the fear of police repression given strength by the new ultrapatriotism and the public image of police heroism; and the fear that the global destruction of corporate rule would seem incomprehensible to a city still shaken by its own vulnerability. The WEF was hoping to capitalize on these fears by moving the meetings from Davos, Switzerland to New York in a questionable "show of solidarity." Suddenly, in the eyes of the powerful, midtown Manhattan was a safer place than an Alpine resort.

## New Possibilities

From within this atmosphere of anxiety and fear, many participants walked away exhilarated by a week of creative action. For those of us working for radical social change, this mobilization represented not just a return to the barricades, but a number of new and exciting possibilities for the movement.

First, a protest against corporate globalization gained real momentum in the wake of September 11th — something that isn't just a matter of attendance. The decentralized nature of the movement and the lack of any single organization or network that can mobilize huge numbers of people means that we rarely know how large, diverse, or creative a mobilization will be until the week it happens. The mix of hundreds of thousands of activists awaiting proposals that capture their imagination and the unaccountable evaluation of "coolness" of different efforts are part of the magic of the movement's ability to materialize a traveling nonviolent army in different cities. With people still holding their breath about whether we could still make that magic happen, the mobilization surpassed critical mass. A dozen people I know decided in the last week to travel from California, and thousands got on buses and planes to participate in New York.

More importantly, the rush to New York City came off without a well-funded push by American non-governmental organizations (NGOs). Few NGOs made a large public commitment to the week, with many staying away or focusing on policy issues and staying off the streets. It seems that the political and funder backlash that followed Seattle and September 11th finally took its toll. Those that did commit were largely southern NGOs, like the Third World Network, who set the tone at the Public Eye on Davos event and on Pacifica's WBAI, which became the unofficial radio station of the protests.

With the well-resourced NGOs backing off (many of them with plane tickets to the World Social Forum in hand), the radicals, students, and youth who have populated but not always led past mobilizations moved into leadership. Their organizing put anarchism and anticapitalism center stage, spearheaded by the anarchist-leaning Another World is Possible (AWIP) coalition and the Anti-Capitalist Convergence (ACC). The message reverberated from Patrick Reinsborough's keynote speech at the student conference (comparing capitalism to the logic of the cancer cell, and tying it to global environmental collapse) to the simplest slogans confronting the WEF ("Bad capitalist, no martini"). Anarchist puppeteers framed the Saturday and Monday demonstrations; the *Village Voice* ran a cover story on the rise of anarchism within the movement; and even the *New York Times* offered its readers a capsule summary of anarchist politics.

The student presence in New York was also radicalized. The three-day conference at Columbia University was largely organized by anticapitalists and offered a broad systemic critique addressing scores of issues and communities. Regional student organizing in New England often took an anarchist viewpoint and prepared students for participation in the ACC.

The ACC itself moved beyond the tactical focus adopted by past black and revolutionary anticapitalist blocs. It operated as a full mobilizing effort, from educating activists on a regional tour and hosting people in the mobilization, to tactical training and envisioning an ongoing organizing role for the convergence. On the street, it was the basis for phenomenally warm street solidarity, forming large and loud blocs in front of the Waldorf-Astoria and challenging the police mobilization at Sunday's snake march.

The spokescouncil for the mobilization, despite its failure to devise a complete scenario for the massive Saturday rally, provided a powerful forum for coordination. Under massive psychological pressure, it was the smoothest consensus process I've seen at its scale, appearing something like alien parliament with waves of agreement in a sea of hands. An ethic of solidarity with those most vulnerable to arrest and the readiness to flood Grand Central Station with a massive spiral dance are just two of its successes.

Finally, the solidarity offered by this mobilization to struggles overseas turned a corner for the American movement. Rather than vague conceptions like "the Global South" or "the poor," we were rallying for specific people and struggles. Argentina's December revolt inspired many shows of solidarity — the first success in many opportunities for an anti–World Bank/IMF national uprising to take center stage in a US protest. Meanwhile, students at Columbia and the grassroots group SUSTAIN: Stop US Tax Aid to Israel Now put a spotlight on the struggle of Palestinians for freedom. The spirit of the uprising in Argentina, Palestine, and North America was invoked on the streets: "Palestina. Argentina. Viva, viva intifada."

## Lessons Lost

The New York mobilization seemed to prove that the movement against capitalist globalization could bounce back and maintain its creative radicalism. But it also showed that the movement's ability to learn and adapt is not as strong as many of us had hoped. Since Seattle, a series of critiques have helped define the agenda of the movement: Betita Martinez's and Colin Rajah's "Where was the color . . . ?" articles on the persistence of racialized power structures, even in the euphoric togetherness of N30 and A16, sparked movement-wide discussions on racism and culture. The wide range of organizers in the Philadelphia and Los Angeles mobilizations broadened the agenda to issues of poverty in the United States, the criminal injustice system, education, and queer liberation. The summer 2001 gathering of the National Organizers' Alliance acted as an encounter between traditional community organizers and the mobilization-focused activists confronting globalization. The DC mobilization planned for September was putting a spotlight on local issues such as homelessness and hospital privatization.

For some of us, the ability of criticisms to generate real change on these and other issues inside the movement felt as powerful and liberating as seeing street blockades throw off the agenda of the WTO. The movement's ability to grow and learn made it hopeful, made it alive, made it ours, finally. How bitter, then, was our disappointment at seeing lessons we thought had been learned disappear in the rush to respond to the WEF.

Most fundamentally, the anti-WEF mobilization was built from the institution (the WEF) down, rather than from the community up. For the most part, community struggles did not set the agenda of the protests. We were arguing against WEF propaganda ("Corporations come together to solve the world's problems") and chasing the headlines around Enron and Argentina. The net result was that fewer New Yorkers were involved and the protesters had comparatively little interaction with people in the city. People who have massed by the thousands against police brutality and queer bashing, and for workers' rights, access to education, and community gardens, did not see these issues on the agenda of street protests. Labor organizers, who were denied a march permit, limited their outreach efforts and didn't invite their supporters to participate in the rest of the weekend.

This is all unfortunate because New York is one of the strongest North American cities in terms of local struggles. It is truly a world city with exile communities that often become key resistance centers in cross-border campaigns. It is not just an island of corporate skyscraper fortresses, but a landscape of the poor and surviving, the privileged and disillusioned, of communities creating new realities. To walk across the city is to encounter the sites of generations of striving for liberation, the places of inspiration for tens of thousands of artists envisioning a new world, the ground upon which waves of sacrifice have been made in the hope of social change.

We seemed to revert to old ways in dealing with the police, too. As in Los Angeles, Philadelphia, Quebec, and other protests since Seattle, police deployment against the demonstrators was massive and well-publicized. Unlike LA and Philadelphia, where recent episodes of police brutality (the Ramparts scandal and a widely reported brutal beating just weeks before the Republican National Convention) dominated perceptions of the police, the New York Police Department (NYPD) had a heroic image coming out of 9/11.

Press-savvy activists played down confrontation with police, and used a "Don't attack us, we're just protesting" message. The history of police abuse in New York City seemed forgotten: "quality of life" crackdowns on the poor, police shootings of black immigrants, mass searches of tens of thousands of young men of color, the police riot at the Matthew Shepherd memorial march, and the baton-enforced closure of the Million Youth March in Harlem were all absent milestones of cruelty. Also forgotten was a link forged between the anti–corporate globalization movement and the communities targeted by, and organizing against, the police.

Between Seattle and Los Angeles, the movement had seemed to learn a lot. We had gone from a handful of self-appointed "leaders" saying "arrest the rioters, not the protesters" to standing with the neighborhoods at the center of the 1992 riots against police domination. We learned that the police act as a line of social control; that policing dissent is akin to policing race or queerness or cultural conformity; that the people profiled, beaten, and jailed everyday by the police are often allies of—not threats to—the movement. We learned this in convergence centers, on the streets, and in jail. And we worked together, energized by the power of new-found solidarity.

But in New York, seeing ourselves through the eyes of the media, we forgot the lessons we had learned. The streets around the Waldorf-Astoria were ground zero for the "social cleansing" of the homeless by the Grand Central Partnership, an experiment in corporate policing that as spread across Manhattan. The mobilization had nothing to say about this. Haitian immigrant Georgy Louisgene was shot in January by the NYPD, and Brooklyn's Haitian community rallied the week of the convergence, but fewer than a dozen people from the convergence even attended his funeral. And the night of the last WEF demonstration there was a candlelight vigil for the third anniversary of the NYPD murder of Amadou Diallo. I found out about it by the television news.

Finally, there was some slipping backwards in the visibility of antioppression politics. Perhaps strengthened by the "Let's come together as one" message post 9/11, the past emphasis on oppressed groups defining their own liberation seemed absent. No large protest event focused on racism, sexism, homophobia, or adult privilege. The defining role of antioppression trainings, caucuses, and action to transform ourselves (as well as the powerful) is one of the things that makes our movement radical. We ought to strengthen this, and put it at the center of every mobilization.

Perhaps some other shortcomings of the WEF protests can be explained by the rushed nature of the preparations. But this should only remind us of the need to make building from communities out, standing with those most targeted by the state, and dismantling systems of oppression into our goals instead of things to be remembered with each new effort. When we recover these lessons and build on our strengths, we can have the power to take back our world from its corporate masters.

# Contra Cumbre in Quito
# Daniel Burton Rose

*Counterpunch*, November 16–30, 2002

The continental Days of Resistance against the Free Trade Area of the Americas (FTAA) opened with drawers dropping. On the morning of Tuesday, October 29, in front of the Swiss Hotel in Quito, seven pairs of bared buns cried out in opposition: "ALCA NI CAGANDO" ("No FTAA—Not Even Fucking Around"). Inside the seventh Summit of the Business Forum of the Americas, which preceded the seventh Summit of the Ministers and Vice Ministers of Trade for the FTAA with a parallel agenda, was in process.

Conceived in Miami in 1994, the FTAA plans to harmonize the laws of each country in the hemisphere—except Cuba—with the regulations and prohibitions of the World Trade Organization. This includes *über*-national courts, a redefinition of expropriation as an act which prohibits potential profit-making, and the challenging of laws protecting labor, the environment, indigenous sovereignty, and human rights as trade barriers. The US is creating a path of progress with three prongs: diplomatic, infrastructural, and military. These are: the Central America Free Trade Agreement—an extension of NAFTA to Costa Rica, Guatemala, Honduras, Nicaragua, and El Salvador, which US negotiators hope to enact by mid-2003; Plan Puebla Panama, to provide communications, dams, and highways for capitalist integration in Central America; and Plan Colombia, to remilitarize Latin America in the name of "drug eradication" and now, overtly, "counterterrorism."

The message on the streets, in conference halls, among the press, and in cities throughout the continent was as clear as that on the asses: a complete rejection of the proposed accord and of everything the North is trying to impose on the South. The streets themselves cried out against the meeting. Quito is a city of prolific and poetic graffiti. The most prominent are now public displays challenging the FTAA. The FTAA's Spanish acronym, ALCA, lends itself to much creative use: "ALCArajo" ("ALCA go to hell"); "NO ALCApitalismo"; "ALCAquita" ("little shit").

In the Continental Meeting of Parliamentarians on the FTAA, which took place October 28 and 29, Argentinean Nobel Laureate Adolfo Pérez Esquivel denounced the proposed agreement in these terms: "the accord is going to destroy the productive capacity of our peoples, of the national industries and is going to generate dependency; it's a new form of colonization." Thirty-six deputies from fourteen countries attended the *encuentro*, organized by the Quiteñan environmentalist organization Acción Ecológica.

At the simultaneous Continental Gathering of Campesinos Against the FTAA the most prominent voices were indigenous. Leonidas Iza, president of the Confederación de Nacionalidades Indígenas del Ecuador (CONAIE), stated dramatically that the "FTAA would signify the death of the agricultural sector." Abadio Gree of the National Organization of the Indigenous of Colombia said that the FTAA was a struggle for the resources of *Pacha Mama* ("Mother Earth"), and that fighting it was "a war for life."

In Ecuador of the last decade indigenous people are the primary mobilizers. They came onto the political scene as a social force with an uprising in June of 1990, backed by CONAIE. The accumulation of hundreds of disparate land disputes erupted in a cascade of protesters blocking the Pan American highway and demanding the acknowledgment of their cultural identity. Other uprisings followed in '92 and '94, which forged alliances with mestizo *campesinos* and pressed deeper into the country's political process. In 1996 CONAIE founded Movimiento Unidad Plurinacional Pachakutik to insert an indigenous voice into local and national elections. In February of '97 the indigenous movement spearheaded the ousting of cleptocratic President Abdala Bucaram.

The dramatic cresting of this activity came as a response to the overwhelming corruption of President Jamil Mahuad. Over $2 billion dollars were siphoned out, largely from small investors and pension funds, by Mahuad and his cronies. In January of 2000 the president provoked a banking crisis, which more than halved working people's income, then offered dollarization as a solution.

CONAIE marched on Quito and, at the gates of Congress, their several thousand members joined up with a group of disaffected army colonels, among them a Lucio Gutiérrez, who had been sent there to stop them.

Together the group marched into Congress, took over the Supreme Court, and opened the Presidential Palace. A group calling itself the Junta of National Salvation, composed of then-CONAIE president Antonio Vargas, Col. Gutiérrez, and an obscure former Supreme Court Justice named Carlos Solórzano, took control. They ruled for the next few hours until a Colonel Jorge Brito—also involved in the ruling triumvirate—unilaterally ceded control to Muhuad's VP Gustavo Noboa in response to US threats of complete isolation.

The indigenous movement flexed its muscle again when Colonel Gutiérrez decided to run for president. The primary in October of this year placed the colonel. first. A district breakdown of the distribution of votes shows that the indigenous movement provided him with a possible 50 percent of his support.

Gutiérrez is a troubling champion for the indigenous movement. He is said to have served in an elite commando force set up by the León Febres Cordero government (1984–88), which, with the help of Israeli mercenaries, eliminated the small urban guerrilla group *Alfaro Vive Carajo* ("Alfaro Lives Damnit"—a reference to a Liberal reformer and president of the country at the turn of the century). He served as *aide-de-camp* to Presidents Bucaram and Mahuad. Though he says the malfeasance he witnessed in those administrations is the source of his passion against corruption, one of his first actions as a presidential contender was to nominate both his wife and his brother as congressional deputy candidates on his party's ticket.

Col. Gutiérrez spent the week of the antiALCA protests in the United States. There he chummed up to Ecuadorian expat capital in Miami and met with IMF representatives in Washington DC. Though he initially modeled himself after Venezuela's Chávez, he assured all in the US, "I am not Chávez." He threw a bone to protesters Friday November 1: in an interview in New York he said that for Ecuador to join ALCA would be "economic suicide."

The FTAA Ministerial Summit took place in the Marriott hotel in the part of the new city locals call "*gringolandia.*" Five thousand, three hundred and fifty-one police, another 600 military personnel, and a special group of intelligence, rescue, and special operatives, as well as a number of snipers, covered the four-plus blocks in every direction of the massive Marriott complex which were closed to protesters.

CONAIE and CONFEUNASSC-CNC (an organization designed to protect Ecuador's unique *campesino* social security system) organized marches to draw people in from the country to Quito for the *contra ALCA* mobilization. The marches collected down from the Colombian border in the north, up from the Peruvian one in the south; from Esmeraldas, Puertoviejo, and Guayaquil in the west; and El Oriente, the Amazonian provinces, in the east. The trucks and buses began trickling in the night of Tuesday the twenty-ninth, their contents gathering at the downtown Parque El Arbolito in preparation for Thursday's march.

On Thursday protesters began gathering at the park around nine A.M. and pushed off past eleven. Divergent marches 11,000 people strong connected around a circular police cordon. A "ring of diversity" formed to release "the cry of the excluded." One chant went "We Don't Want, and It Don't Benifit us to be, a North American Colony, We Want to be a Latin American Potency"; another, nonsensically, "Bear, Bear, Bear, The FTAA is Rotting" (it rhymes in Spanish!). Indigenous men marched with spears, and incense doused the crowd. Over a hundred *campesino* and indigenous groups were present, as well as queer organizations and those of women. If the Zapatista caravan in 2001 was "the march of the color of the earth," this was a protest of the colors of the rainbow. Vibrant colors and vibrant spirits.

Protest puppets have penetrated South America. Intimidating Uncle Sams loomed, while a gray papier-mâché plane labeled "Plan Colombia" and "DynCorp" weaved through protesters and doused an open fire in the crowd as if it was fumigating coca. Representing the minor whitey bloc, our friend Tristan spray-painted "*Gringos contra ALCA*" on an American flag and set it ablaze.

One major gassing occurred, resulting in the hospitalization of several children and at least one adult (as well as the discomfort of the police, who didn't have masks!). This contained violence was somewhat of a relief, considering that the night before police discharged live ammo into the air in the face of persistent rock throwers.

Representatives of indigenous and *campesino* organizations successfully negotiated a meeting with the ministers. After several days of give and take, one condition remained. Ecuadorian Foreign Minister Heinz Moeller forbade Bolivarian indigenous leader Evo Morales from participating in the group: he feared Morales' presence would push Zoellick over the edge.

The meeting took place Thursday evening at the Swiss Hotel. An estimated sixty-five organizers presented the ministers with a letter three meters wide and a hundred long, a letter which collected the thoughts those in the communities the caravans passed through wished to convey to the Trade Representatives. One barricade broken.

Wiliam Trujillo of CONFEUNASSC-CNC, who participated in the presentation, described what took place. "We broke into their lair and were able to shout at them all what we were feeling. The voices that came with us on the march were turned over to them to hear." After presenting the letter to the ministers the protesters took it back: "We didn't want to leave our story with them."

Protesters counted coup again on Friday when, despite the heavy security precautions, a number of them snuck in through the service entrance and hung an antiALCA banner from the Marriott.

In the face of opposition not only from protesters but from the press and many Latin American Trade Representatives the US delegation made one concession: they agreed to permit the discussion of US subsidies to agro-business in the agricultural working group. The topic of agriculture proved so contentious that it was separated from the eleven other working groups. The next Summit of Ministers is slated for October of 2003 in Miami, about the same time as a WTO ministerial in Cancún. The US is pushing for the enactment of the FTAA on January 1, 2005.

Friday, November 1, with an order prohibiting protests and CONAIE and CONFUNASSC–CNC completing their position paper against ALCA, the presence on the street was light. I marched with a hundred anarkids from Parque El Carolina in a half moon around the Marriott cordon on to the Salesian Polytechnic University, where the conference was wrapping up.

There Trujillo elaborated the future direction of events. The general sentiment among the *contra ALCA* parliamentarians had been to strengthen regional alliances within Latin America—those of the common market of the south, Mercosur (Argentina, Brazil, Uruguay, and Paraguay), and the Andean Community (Bolivia, Colombia, Ecuador, Peru, and Venezuela), and among Central American countries and the Caribbean. (In the case of Brazil, French sociologist Alain Touraine counseled the abandonment of such projects in favor of ALCA because regional alliances would give the country "an image of autonomy.")

The indigenous vision is more constructive. The next step, from the perspective of Trujillo's organization, is a continental wide *consulta* which will ask people what form of integration they would like to see: what would be complementary, instead of dominating. "If things go as planned, the various elements of the *consulta* will allow us to achieve a continental uprising in 2002. A mobilization of everyone who does not want to see this integration of capital take place—from the United States to Argentina and Chile."

Evo Morales concurred with this prognosis in an interview with the Quito daily *El Comercio: ."* . . the International Organizations (such as the IMF and World Bank) need to change their policies before this region turns into a block of rebellion. If they don't change their policies we could go to this."

# Part III:
# We Are Everyone? Organization and Representation within the Movement

# This Is What Bureaucracy Looks Like

## NGOs and Anti-Capitalism[1]

# James Davis

*"I'm aware that it's a lot more glamorous to be on the barricade with a handkerchief around your nose than it is to be at the meetings with a briefcase and a bowler hat, but I think that we're getting more done this way"* [2]

—Bono

This essay takes a critical look at the role Non Governmental Organizations (NGOs) play in the growing movement against global capital. The movement, which made its spectacular US debut in Seattle, has lent NGOs unprecedented political influence. Leading thinkers and institutions of capitalist planning are desperate for allies to appease their critics. As we will see the impulses of the NGOs and those of the movement are politically at odds. While much discussion has concentrated on tactical differences, a more profound problem lies beneath. Lacking in imagination and caught between the many-headed street movement and an impulse to negotiate directly with power on its behalf, the specter of NGOs, as a device for the containment of political dissent, arises.[3]

## The Government's Friend

There is no doubt that NGOs do vital work in any number of places around the world.[4] From famine relief to bringing clean water to rural communities throughout the South many such groups are at the front line of people's struggles to survive and gain a modicum of political rights. NGOs have inherited a tradition of charity work that has been around since the earliest days of colonialism. More and more of them have abandoned the sorry history of proselytism and missionary work in favor of a human rights agenda and, more recently, a clear political and economic critique. In this regard the contribution of NGOs to the creation and maintenance of a space for political discourse in many places is inestimable. The experience of Chiapas is one example where NGOs, among others, organized in support of the Zapatistas and made an overt military solution an untenable option for the Mexican State. In Seattle and Quebec groups like Public Citizen and Global Exchange made enormous organizing contributions, mobilized formidable resources and infiltrated the corporate media with articulate and provocative spokespeople and sound bites. But it is precisely for groups like this that the contradictions of institutionalized radicalism become most apparent. To understand why this is the case we must consider the changes in the terrain of struggle that Zapatismo and Seattle have wrought.

After having been denounced in the South for decades as an incubus, the World Bank the IMF, and their even more nefarious offspring the WTO, are now pilloried even in the business press, which feels it must distance itself from them, or risk contagion. The WTO has effectively put the overdeveloped countries on notice that their turn to be 'structurally adjusted' has come and hence expanded resistance to the 'first world' also. George Soros, the swashbuckling knight-errant of speculative financial flows, has criticized the institutions and neoliberal ubereconomist Jeffrey Sachs is back-pedaling madly. A legitimation crisis is brewing for international capital. The only question is, who will save them and how? Recent demonstrations in Seattle, Prague, Davos, D.C., Melbourne, and Genoa, escalating in fierceness, and increasingly articulate, have left the capitalist planned *coup du monde* a shambles.

To the media it seems that NGOs and protestors are interchangeable and synonymous. In reality elite decision-makers evaluate the NGO world with a quick and pragmatic eye and see potential allies in the delicate work of diffusing this new opposition. *The Economist* took note of this in pointing out that when "assaulted by unruly protestors, firms and governments are suddenly eager to do business with the respectable face of dissent." Legitimation strategies are everywhere. In *Business Week* , "A double backlash is generating skepticism about the ability of globalism to do good."[5] All of a sudden we witness the recruitment of a moral philosophy absent from the economist's dictionary since the nineteenth century and along with it a pantheon of do gooders to show the way.

Among the re-imagers we find Bono, narcissistic Irish pop star, cultural carpetbagger, and supremely cynical carer whose current promotions include a campaign to 'forgive' Third World debt. He has become a roving ambassador for Jubilee 2000,[6] an NGO that advocates debt relief as good business. Bono (born again) has met the pope (a fan), Jesse Helms and Bushman Paul O Neil. Columbia's Jeffrey Sachs has coached him in the intricacies of global capitalism. In recent years Sachs has changed his colors and jumped ship from his hard line of the '80s and early '90s. Having factored in political crisis he is now the 'sustainable' neoliberal barely recognizable as one of the primary architects of 'shock therapy.' That policy succeeded in prising the collective wealth of Russia away, laundering it through the Mafia and the banking system, and recycling it as investment dollars in the US and Western Europe. The shock has contributed to a fall in the life expectancy of Russian men by six years in the '90s, among other calamities.[7]

Bono is an extreme example of those with whom the institutions would like to be associated. His naiveté about why he was at the Prague WTO meeting is almost endearing; at least other opportunists in the NGO industry appreciate that without the demonstrations and the ensuing legitimacy deficit there would be no seats at the table for any of them. Some of them will have read as much in *The Economist* who was in no doubt as to why "groups such as Oxfam were all but co-opted into designing debt relief strategies."[8]

The ideal for capitalism would be to create and co-opt a "responsible" leadership who could then negotiate on behalf of the hordes and diffuse the movement while recuperating it. "Horst Kohler, the IMF's new boss has been courting NGOs. Jim Wolfensohn, the [World] Banks boss, has long fawned in their direction"[9]. Surely, they imagine, there are some reasonable types who understand that we can't go back to the Stone Age and that progress will continue. The World Bank successfully recruited Stephen Hellinger, president of Development Gap,[10] one of the organizing NGOs of the "Fifty Years is Enough" campaign.[11] He works with them to review the effects of Structural Adjustment and reflects on his experience in the *Financial Times*. "Wolfensohn has yet to take the critique that is coming out around the world," he says and adds that, "It has been six years, the hopes we had for him have yet to materialize."[12] Incredibly Hellinger finds Wolfensohn to be the impediment to change, a different boss and perhaps we could get somewhere.

Is it mere coincidence that the implementation of the neoliberal project in the form of privatization, trade feudalism and the attempted elimination of the welfare state occurred simultaneously with the emergence of NGOs[13] as central to its explanation and narrative? While neoliberalism as conceived by the Chicago boys (Sachs among them) Thatcher, Reagan et al, was a strictly conservative strategy, its execution and implementation is a Clintonian liberal project. "The principle reason for the recent boom in NGOs," according to *The Economist*, "is that Western governments finance them. This is not a matter of charity but of privatization."[14] In Africa and elsewhere Western governments routinely recruit NGOs to distribute aid and administer development projects.[15] Indeed *The Economist* claims that governments rely to a greater and greater degree on "useful information" that NGOs can provide. By way of example they state: "the work of Global Witness[16] is actually paid for by the British Foreign Office."[17]

## Supply and Demand

More profoundly NGOs can often be found in control of services formerly provided by Third World Governments until debt and restructuring eliminated them. Caroline Fetscher[18] has written of the situation in Bangladesh where up to 5,000 NGOs are involved in literacy programs. Alex Demirovic points out that due to their mistrust of Southern governments, Northern NGOs can become shadow bureaucracies parallel to Southern Nation State administrations. These NGOs "often work as public service contractors with headquarters in the large cities, far removed from the problems of the population, sturdily professional and apolitical. The agenda for the aid is, in fact, frequently determined by the self-interest of these organizations."[19] As these relationships become more institutionalized the implications for democracy among the recipients, i.e. the poor of the Global South, are fairly clear.

If Bono's elite power is exclusively to do with the image then the NGO's can more powerfully claim to be the real fake. As Antonio Negri and Michael Hardt describe it, "these NGOs conduct just wars without arms, without violence, without borders. Like the Dominicans in the late medieval period and the Jesuits at the dawn of modernity, these groups strive to identify universal needs and defend human rights."[20] In the new framework of legitimacy that Negri and Hardt describe as "Empire" (and which the Zapatistas, among others,[21] recognize loosely as neoliberalism), "new articulations of the exercise of legitimate force"[22] are demanded. The pattern is a familiar one with the shibboleth of morality wheeled out to underline the economics of war and intervention. As such, Negri and Hardt point out that NGOs, in this case Oxfam, Medicins Sans Frontieres and Amnesty International, are enablers and perpetuators of imperial intervention. Kosovo is one example where liberals cheered as Luftwaffe planes supported American bombing of defenseless Serbs. And this after multiple fabrications announced by NATO and the CIA but dutifully reproduced, reported and spectacularised by the media.[23]

To simplify with a metaphor, NGOs are to imperialism what artist bohemians are to urban gentrification. For NGOs authenticity is derived from their branding, or more accurately from the composite of their brand identity. As is the case with the more traditional corporate brands authenticity remains a holy grail. Nike and Benetton derive theirs from 'Blackness,' diversity and the urban street credibility of their billion dollar illusions. NGOs generate their authenticity from compassion extraction activities. For them cultural otherness and the mediation of abject desperation is the foundation of moral authority. This is most obvious in the Fair Trade game, whereby NGOs import, distribute and sell crafts and produce from the South. "Buy a basket from a typical crafts importer and the peasant artisan receives a tiny fraction of what you pay. At the Global Exchange Fair Trade Craft Stores, you know the producer got her or his fair share, around 15-30% of the retail price."[24] Like World Bank and IMF activities, the currency of fair trade is market rather than social relations.

As is the case with most valuable raw materials such extractions are located most often in the south. And like gold and diamonds, 'compassion' and 'authenticity' mined in the South are most profitably consumed in the North. And as with gold and diamonds the scarcity of compassion must be carefully managed owing to its natural abundance. The compassion market is notoriously inelastic as was evidenced by the 'compassion fatigue' crisis suffered by NGOs during the second Ethiopian famine of the 1980s. But as brands go, the NGO sector has succeeded in accumulating that most scarce of resources, compassionate capital. Like Lady Diana's landmine campaign, their moral appeal is absolute.

## Movements . . .

Elsewhere in this collection the notion of revolutionary prefiguration[25] is discussed. It is relevant to any discussion of NGOs also. The movement against global capitalism is marked by political evolution from those movements that have gone before. In its style it owes a debt to the women's movement and its rejection of hierarchy and charismatic oratory, to the peace movement of the seventies in its mass non-violent demeanor; to the European black bloc of the eighties in its tactical probing for the weaknesses of a jack booted foe and to the radical environmental movement for the joy with which it goes about its work and its emphasis on changing everyday life for the better. The radically democratic nature of the movement is its strongest suit. Perhaps this is a lesson that NGOs are incapable of learning if we consider that NGOs were granted a seat at the UN as consultants and fundraisers when the charter was written at the dawn of the post colonial era. There is a political difference between the movement described and the manner with which the majority of NGOs organize themselves, particularly those with the profile and organizational ability to seize the moment.

## And Miners

Hierarchical in structure and often led by careerist NGO celebrities, the industry is degenerate in its industrial relations and, as is often the case with countercultural outfits, relies to an outrageous degree on volunteer labor. In this arena too NGOs find ways to profitably invest political rhetoric. They exploit their workers using the goodfight jargon just as sweatshops use motifs of 'familia' or nationalism to justify injustice or as IMF officers argue for particular environmental or labor abuses by reference to general growth rates and so on.

NGOs might indeed operate in the moral economy ignoring the dictates of the surplus value theory of labor. One can't accumulate compassion in this manner without exploiting workers. Along these lines Ralph Nader, Trojan corporation killer and the Elvis of reformism, has stated that the NGO business has no need of trade unions. Back in the eighties at *Multinational Monitor*, a magazine he owned, he expressed the opinion that workers at the magazine had no right to unionize. The editor, Tim Shorrock, was fired for attempting to organize. The following is extracted from an essay by Nick Mamantas published by the *Greenwich Village Gazzette* (New York). "Public interest groups are like crusades, Nader explains, you can't have work rules, or 9 to 5." Workers should be treated equitably, using the resources the "crusade" has, but anyone in a public interest firm in Washington "can leave and double their income by going across the street. Shorrock, with his "union ploy," became an "adversary" according to Nader. "Anything that is commercial, is unionizable," but small public interest organizations "would go broke in a month," Nader says, if they paid union wages, offered union benefits and operated according to standard work rules, such as the eight-hour day.

No surprise then that the majority of NGOs and Unions are reluctant to embrace street demonstrations and risk the contagion of radical democracy infecting their workers and members. The crucial moment in Seattle came when Union leaders steered the rank and file away from sites where demonstrators confronted police and succeeded in derailing the meetings,[26] a tactic employed once more by Canadian Trade Union leaders at the FTAA demonstrations in Quebec City in April 2001.

Discord between the streets and NGO's was clear during February 2002 in New York City. At least 15 000 demonstrators turned out to greet the World Economic Forum who had been driven from Davos, Switzerland by fierce opposition the previous year. The absence in NY of Global Exchange and The Sierra Club, among others, represented their retreat from both street confrontations as a tactic and popular opposition as a strategy in this instance. Instead the NGO's attended the World Social Forum in Porto Allegre, Brazil, their rationale echoing that of the WEF; the Forum invoked the dead of September as the pretext for coming to NY and the NGOs as a pretext for staying away.

The Social Forum has grown as a model in parallel with the growth of the anti capitalist globalisation movement and following the Zapatista inspired series of Intercontinental Encuentros which happened during the '90s. Both the Encuentros and Social Forums represent a move towards a model of dual power, the creation of 'open spaces'that operate as sites for the development of alternative ideas and practices. Yet there is a distinction between the two, which articulates the tensions between traditional and new or radical definitions of what social movements are and what contemporary movements might achieve. The Social Forums were proposed by ATTAC, a French NGO committed to introducing the Tobin Tax, essentially a levy on international financial flows and a means of shoring up the sovereignty of countries exposed to the vagaries and whims of financial and currency speculators. The tax would be partly distributed among NGOs and so enjoys their support. ATTAC are oddly constituted with a founding group who retain control of the franchise. According to Bernard Cassen, one of the founders, "there are more than 200 local committees all over France, constituted as legal bodies—ATTAC-Pays Basque, ATTAC-Touraine, ATTAC-Marseilles, and so on—in their own right, with democratic rules that we impose on them, in exchange for use of the acronym."[27] These democratic rules are imposed by a ruling oligarchy who dominates the main bureaucratic level as a defense against any kind of sectarian penetration.

Following on from this, verticality is inscribed in the social forum through a corporatist organizing method. The social forums are far more than a conference of left parliamentary celebrities and prominent NGO's, but they are formally dominated by these elements. Organizers have purposely marginalized radical voices and assemblies, for example the Life after Capitalism assembly was moved to a suburban country club in Porto Allegre and proved difficult for many people to attend. Similarly in Florence at the European Forum the Intergalactica and HUB meetings were dislodged to tents equally impossible to locate. These events specifically were designed to address some of the problems that a growing democratic movement faces; truly horizontal organising, breaking out of the traditional conference model and a serious consideration of social disobedience as practice. These tensions symbolise the fundamental democratic problem facing this, or any, putative social movement. The issue at hand is representation and what can replace it. Networked groups functioning on the basis of accountable exercises of power are just incredibly hard work to maintain, particularly when the participants are as dispersed as they are. During the current period of formulating these networks the vacuum is filled by cash and resource rich groups who can seize the apparatus unencumbered by the luxuries of democracy.

In this regard the Forums offer a disturbing tableau of Leninist intrigue. The International Organizing Committee responsible for organizing continental forums is impossible to identify online, much less to establish how the group formed. The World Social Forum enjoys the largesse of the Ford Foundation, The German Green Party and the Canadian Government. So much for their commitment to non violence. ATTAC, essentially a front for the Fench Parti Socialiste, seems to be a major influence and power broker at all the planning levels of the Fora. Indeed such is the willingness of some of these forces to ingratiate themselves with the neoliberals that one could have read in TerraViva, the so called daily of WSF3, how George Soros, Michael Orizek (the WEF's press man) and Bernard Cassen, the 'head' of ATTAC France, are in perfect harmony regarding the Tobin Tax. In a similar vein Klaus Schwab, founder of the WEF, lauded the 'leaders of the twenty-first century,' in reference to the 'social entrepeneurs' who grace the Social Forum. Other media outlets, not being official organs of the WSF, were more candid about who was important, listing various NGO attendees and other 'progressive celebrities.'

The elite within the social forum movement, like those within the NGO's, are clear in their wish to move into a more formal political role, whether it be via the UN, the European Commission or some of the various institutions of capital who have been targets thus far of the movement. Kenneth Roth, the head of Human Rights Watch, was first invited to the WEF the year following Seattle where the role of the NGO's was marginal, but the following year at Davos was "quite different," he adds "we (were) not as mainstream as we would like, but our concerns dominate(d) discussions."

While the WSF is formally closed to political parties it is dominated by the Lula led Workers Party of Brazil (PT). Lula himself attended both Davos and Porto Allegre in 2003, offering Davos, on the social forums behalf, that the essential demand of the movement was the removal of trade protectionism by the Western governments. This so called bridge was celebrated internationally as the big news from Porto Allegre.

Yet the Forum was far more varied than any organising bureaucrat might wish. In Porto Allegre there were demonstrations against parliamentary participants who voted in favour of the Iraq war as well as a youth camp of some 15000 participants. In Florence the Euraction hub, a self-organised creation of a dozen Italian and European groups, was conceived as a space both outside, and interlocutor to, the 'main event,' where horizontal and ludic actions could find expression. In Porto Allegre the Youth Camp represented a cauldron of dissent. They took off on the last day on a sponti nude demonstration, clashed with cops and many got arrested, and none of this was reported by the NGOs or the PD, the workers party. Only on indymedia.

So these kinds of actions also represent the social forum, or indeed are the real heart and soul of it. It's clear that the Social Forum has not been conceded as an organisational and inventive locus by the more democratically inclined elements of the movement. An activist example of this being the invasion of the Forum Area proper by a 150 or so Hubbies on the Friday—under the banner: Stop the World! Another War is Possible!—to raise the profile of the Hubspace and speak with people to convince them to come down and participate. The results were immediate and that night thousands converged on the hub for dinner, dancing and polymorphous pleasure in general. A lucid debate has been taking place on these issues around the world and it is clear from a survey of it that few if any protagonists suggest abandoning the Social Forums, instead its obvious that a battle will be joined between the luxury hotel suite crowd and the larger number who expect, well, everything.

The closing plenary in Florence was the moment for candid recognition of the danger posed by an institutional enclosure of the Social Forum. Several speakers also articulated concern at the process of recuperation of creative social tensions by mainstream political forces who seek to collapse this desire and anger under their representative umbrella. Others underlined the need to understand that during the previous twelve months the initiative behind the international dynamic has shifted from the grassroots formations to the forces around the Social Forum. In the shadow of ultra violence after Genoa, there has been a general retreat from direct action and a corresponding return to mass mobilisations which in concrete terms achieve little apart from temporarily allaying sentiments of isolation and impotence.

Regardless of the impulses of some in favour of hierarchical forms and elite monopoly of power the Social Forums are one of the most potent tools the movement has created and employs. It remains the case that anyone can call or constitute a forum while no one (Lula being the excepted proof) can speak in their name. The use of tactical media, existing and new networks along the ley lines of social and political solidarity and the abandonment of traditional forms of 'representative' organising all conspire to make this movement vastly more powerful than any troupe of professional bureaucrats or green parliamentarians.

While the street movement in Seattle drew together a wide range of issues into a generalized critique, many NGOs seem fixated with specialization. Salaried professionals rely on teams of researchers, media spinners, accountants, import/export consultants, tax lawyers and all the poorly paid but very committed staff one would expect from a professional operation. And incredibly they actually refer to these people, the majority of whom are motivated young idealists, as 'our staff.' "The danger of yuppie-NGOs (a jet-set civil society) forming at the global level is not insignificant."[28] This leadership of professional reformers acts as if in the belief that the head and the feet are separate. A morbidity pervades this division of labor where everyday is casual Friday.

In part because they organize as businesses in a manner determined by capitalism, this is all they can do. A brand will suffer in the market place if it lacks focus; the specialized niche is life or death. What is generalized is their moral appeal and that is packaged as pity, condescension, remorse and self-righteousness.[29]

Shortly after Seattle, *The Economist* bemoaned that in France, where blockades were happening over fuel prices, politics was again being conducted in the streets. *The Economist* was remembering the derailment of the MAI, the ritual slaying of the WTO, the incineration of French plans to get rid of guaranteed pensions through general strikes in 1996 and 1997 and a litany of other 'setbacks' due to people power. They recalled the chaos of the sixties when it was impossible to make 5 year business plans, when social movements in France and elsewhere were 'out of control' and the demands on capital were intolerable. *The Economist* was one of the first to identify the NGOs as potential allies in the war for globalization. Open any page of *Foreign Affairs*, read the output of the British Treasury Department, or even The World Bank's own literature and it will be found now as doctrine. Indeed on the World Bank's homepage NGOs appear in the `partners' window alongside business and bond investors.[30]

We are not without historical precedents, for it is the history of resistance and social movements, which gives capitalism many of its great ideas. A look back at the civil rights movement and the manner in which it was co-opted and neutralized is indicative of the dangers now. And few will need to be reminded of the serial sell -outs in the chilling history of trade unionism, usually by its own leadership. The trouble with trade unionism, remarked Winston Churchill at a cabinet meeting at the end of WW1, is that there is not enough of it—that is, of the sound patriotic kind at least.[31]

A further trait of the contemporary movement is that it levels its demands against capital in isolation rather than against the state. Historically the state has mediated between the two, closeting its loyalty to employers behind a rhetorical or legalistic impartiality. But the state has shored up its own position via a host of institutional defenses, welfare and social work among them. In part globalization is the end of these as capital transcends its perceived need for the state brokered compromise. Privatization was the answer to which a question had to be found and simultaneously the discourse of entitlement was replaced by that of 'responsibility.' In abandoning any notion of social contract and by evacuating the space of 'public good,' capital, via the state, has created a subtle symbiosis whereby charity is the new welfare and NGOs are the new social workers. Structural adjustment has achieved this in the South while Bush's state sponsored religious volunteerism, combined with the philanthropic experimentalism of Bill Gates, Ted Turner and George Soros, are its latest expressions in the North. The market economy and the market society are indistinguishable . . . compassion in all things. "The international institutions, which clearly recognize the problem of internationally controlling the financial and capital markets...are also aware of the need for intermediary organizations. With NGOs they form complex political networks and negotiation systems. The result can be described as global governance."[32]

The implications for the movement are predictable. Those who most loudly condemned the militants of Prague and Seattle are most likely to have their loyalty to the politics of the negotiating table rather than the street rewarded. Indeed the more sober among them speak of 'reforming' the institutions rather than their abolition. Like Bono's generosity in 'forgiving' debt to those who never borrowed, not to mention reparations, among the NGO's the language of forgiveness is abject. Thus can Kevin Danaher,[33] cofounder of Global Exchange and prominent critic of the World Bank intone that "If we really care about the future of the planet, we must struggle to transform the World Bank."[34] What we would transform it into is left unsaid.

## The Last Bureaucrat

This posture, assumed by most of the leading NGO's concerned with trade in particular and globalization in general, belies a fascination they share with a gamut of capitalist functionaries throughout the West. Mainstream economics is in theory as imperialist as capitalism is in reality. It has in the last generation become a theology. Academically the discipline is contained within a system of imposed ignorance, its most interesting challenges are excluded as 'externalities' (famine, pollution) or more glaringly as 'market failures,' "Land has no production cost, it is a free and unreproducable gift of Nature"[35] proclaims a basic introductory textbook. War, the great engine of accumulation, is dismissed as outside its remit though without it there would be no property, or at least no destruction and regeneration of it. The contemporary economist is a number cruncher obsessing over the harmony of equations as the bodies pile up around him. Yet NGOs, particularly their intellectual elites, remain under the spell of professional economics, convinced that more sensible theories will prevail and that the World Bank needs to reorient itself towards 'micro loans' to better deliver the theology of the market to those as yet 'underdeveloped.'

NGOs, however well intentioned many may be, are not a substitute for real social and political movements. Above all, neither capital, the state, nor the NGOs should be allowed dictate who the movements' leaders are. It should be remembered that the Seattle victory was revised by many NGO and union leaders as the outcome of a great collaboration between them. This clearly overstates the case and purposely overlooks the tensions between them and the 'street warriors' who did the heavy lifting.[36] But pragmatically many NGOs have valuable research and mobilizing resources and, like the media, any serious political or social movement cannot ignore its relationship with them. For the first time in 20 years real radical possibilities have opened up. Where once the committed had few options but a professional NGO track there is now the inkling of a truly global anti capitalist movement to work towards. Essentially the NGOs are a class of professional activists with whom the movement has a relationship. They are often strong critics of the excesses of capitalism and are willing to commit resources and considerable ability and talent to the creation of a just order. What is demanded of them will determine whether their political choices have to do with the movement's agenda or that of capital.

It can go either way. The following from Lori Wallach, a prominent researcher, writer and director of Public Citizen in Washington DC, in a *Foreign Policy* interview, illustrates the contours of this political divide. She described her work in Seattle; "[T]hese anarchist folks marched in there and started smashing things. And our people actually picked up the anarchists. Because we had with us longshoremen and steelworkers who, by their sheer bulk, were three or four times larger. So we had them just literally sort of, a teamster on either side, just pick up an anarchist. We'd walk him over to the cops and say, this boy just broke a window. He doesn't belong to us. We hate the WTO, so does he, maybe, but we don't break things. Please arrest him."[37] This behavior is premised on a tactical assumption that reassuring capital is "getting more done."

Wallach's remarks underline a very important point. The conditions of negotiation between capital and the NGOs are the unilateral disarmament of the movement's tactics. This is the only thing the NGOs have to offer neoliberalism; a special sort of police power and movement sabotage. In other words, the promise (articulated, indicated or simply understood) that the politics of the street will be replaced by the politics of 'heated' negotiation. But the potential exists for a genuinely radical movement to grow in opposition to capital *itself,* which has nothing to do with this sort of politics. The movement in the streets has made apparent capital's inherent irrationalism. In going on a new offensive without first seeing to it that a spurious opposition existed it has overplayed its hand and its vulnerability is exposed. It is now fighting a rearguard action to create one. NGO's, who couldn't get their calls returned five years ago, can now write their own contracts and are privy, finally, to policy making at the highest levels. For Lori Wallach and her crowd it is almost like being a real cop.

1. Thanks to Christian Parenti, Ramor Ryan, Juliana Fredman and the editors of this collection for their close and insightful readings.

2. Susan Dominus, "Relief Pitcher," *New York Times Magazine*, September 8, 2000

3. James N. Rosenau, "Governance, Order, and Change in World Politics," James N. Rosenau and Ernst-Otto Czempiel, *Governance without Government: Order and Change in World Politics* (Cambridge: Cambridge University Press, 1992)

4. *Globalization: Lessons Learned*, Business Week, Editorials, June 11 2000. http://www.business-week.com/common_frames

5. http://www.jubilee2000uk.org/

6. Laurie Garrett, *Chronic Diseases, Depression, Stress, Cut Life Short for Russians*, Seattle Times, March11, 1998.

7. *Angry And Effective*, September 21, 2000. The Economist, http://economist.com/search/search.cfm

8. ibid

9. http://www.igc.org/dgap/index.html

10. http://www.50years.org/

11. Carola Hoyos, *James Wolfensohn's self-created storm*, Financial Times, Jan 30, 2001 http://globalarchive.ft.com/globalarchive/articles

12 There were 176 NGOs in 1909 , by the 1990s the UN estimated that 250 million people were involved.

13. *Sins of the secular missionaries*, The Economist, Jan 27, 2000

http://economist.com/search/search.cfm

14. Tessa Morris-Suzuki, *For And Against NGOs*, New Left Review 2, Mar Apr 2000, p. 69. See Carino Constantino-David, '*Intra-Civil Society Relations: An Overview*' in Miriam Coronel Ferrer, ed., *Making Civil Society*, (Vol 3, Philipine Democracy Agenda), Quezon City 1997, p. 26.

15. Global Witness is a prominent NGO in the campaign to end the traffic in 'conflict diamonds.' http://www.oneworld.org/globalwitness/

16. *Sins of the secular missionaries*, The Economist, Jan 27, 2000

http://economist.com/search/search.cfm

17. Caroline Fetscher, *"Der Mythos, Greenpeace und das Lob der privaten Helfer,"* Kommune, H.6, p.44

18. Alex Demirovic, *NGOs and Social Movements: A Study in Contrasts*, Capitalism Nature Socialism, 11. 04, December 2000, p. 138

19. Antonio Negri, Michael Hardt, *Empire*. (Harvard) p. 36

20. See Gustavo Esteva and Madhu Suri Prakash, *Grassroots Postmodernism*, (Z)

21. ibid *Empire*

22. See Massimo Di Angelis & Sylvia Frederici. The war in Yugoslavia: On Whom the Bombs Fall. In *Aurora of The Zapatistas*. Midnight Notes. Autonomedia pp. 203-215

23. http://www.globalexchange.org/stores

24. See Eddie Yuens introduction to this book

25. See Alexander Cockburn, Jeffrey St. Clair, Allan Sekula, *5 Days That Shook the World*, (Verso 2001), pp. 62-69, for a devastating account of this betrayal and the rhetorical attacks on demonstrators by NGO leaders.

26. New Left Review. Issue number 19. Available at http://slash.autonomedia.org/print.pl?sid=03/02/17/1931213

27. Alex Demirovic, *NGOs and Social Movements: A Study in Contrasts*, Capitalism Nature Socialism, 11 (4), Dec. 2000, p.137

28. See Gustavo Esteva, Madhu Suri Prakash, *Grassroots Postmodernism*, (Z), pp 110-146

29. http://wbln0018.worldbank.org/essd/essd.nsf/NGOs/home http://63.236.1.211/Search/document.asp?i=2000101FAESSAY2001010114.XML

30. David Mitchell, *1919 Red Mirage*, (Macmillan 1970) p. 125. It is worth recalling too Tony Blair's outburst during recent fuel blockades by truckers in Britain where he rejected any negotiation on principle with those pursuing extra parliamentary tactics.

31. Alex Demirovic, *NGOs and Social Movements: A Study in Contrasts*, Capitalism Nature Socialism, 11 (4), Dec. 2000, p.138

32. His more recent suggestion of the Global General Strike is a more serious proposition.

33. Kevin Danaher, "*Why and How to Pressure the World Bank*," in.Robert Burbach, Kevin Danaher, eds., *Globalize This! The Battle against the World Trade Organization and Corporate Rule*, (Monroe: Common Courage Press, 2000)

34. See John Bellamy Foster, *Marx's Ecology*, (Monthly Review Press 2000), p. 167.

35. Alexander Cockburn, Jeffrey St. Clair, Allan Sekula, *5 Days That Shook the World*, (Verso 2001), pp. 62-69

36. Moises Naim, *Lori's War*, Foreign Policy, Spring 2000. http://www.findarticles.com/m1181/2000_Spring/61640248/p1/article.jhtml

# Another Forum is Possible

## Whose Bridges Are We Building? Do We Need a New International?

# Ezequiel Adamovsky

*ZNet | VisionStrategy*
February 6, 2003

It was the first World Social Forum (WSF), 2001. The teleconference between representatives of the WSF and the World Economic Forum in Davos was already tense, when Hebe de Bonafini—the spokesperson of the *Madres de Plaza de Mayo*—told George Soros, "I actually have nothing to talk with someone like you." She meant, of course, that Soros and the like were the enemy, and that the WSF was there, well, to oppose them. Wasn't it?

Two years later, newly elected President Lula da Silva announced his intention to visit both Forums. For some of us, this sounded a bit weird, to say it softly. But despite complaints from a few personalities, most progressive people in Porto Alegre decided to give him a chance in Davos, after he swore that he would be "the same Lula" in both places. I even heard people recalling the example of Che Guevara's disrupting speeches at the UN, back in the 1960s.

Lula finally delivered his speech in front of the rich and powerful in Davos. But he found no anxiety-ridden faces in the audience, and certainly no disruption occurred. On the contrary, Davos was delighted by him. After all, Lula's only criticism, voiced politely, was that rich nations should stop protecting their agriculture with high tariffs. In other words, Lula advised them to stick to their own neoliberal dogmas and embrace real free trade, all the way. And it shouldn't be forgotten that he also proposed the creation of an international fund to help undeveloped countries—a commonplace that makes people smile in Davos, IMF, World Bank, and G7 meetings. Meanwhile, our people demonstrating outside were facing severe repression. Well done, Mr. Lula!

I don't know if Lula's misleading performance means, as Argentinean sociologist Pablo Bergel put it, "the end of the WSF." But it was irritating indeed to see how, right after Lula's appearance in Davos, Brazilian newspapers started to celebrate the "bridge" that Lula had built between the two forums, a "space for dialogue." Thousands of copies of *TerraViva*, the self-proclaimed "independent daily of the WSF III," were distributed for free, featuring well-intentioned articles by members . . . of the World Economic Forum! You can read there how Bernard Cassen—head of ATTAC France—George Soros, and Michael Orizek—WEF's communications director—are in perfect agreement with applying the Tobin Tax. Or take the contribution by Klaus Schwab, founder and president of WEF, in which he celebrates the emergence of a new type of "leaders for the 21$^{st}$ Century." Strangely enough, he does not refer to businessmen or neoliberal gurus, but to the "social entrepreneurs" of the like that meet in Porto Alegre every year. In his piece, Schwab explains how his own foundation is offering funding for such "social entrepreneurs" to attend to Davos. But, hey! Excuse me, weren't we activists committed to changing the world, rather than "entrepreneurs" willing to become the "new leaders"? You can also read in the same newspaper the proposal to institutionalize the WSF by transforming it in "UN's second Chamber." That would surely contribute to re-legitimate an institution that, like WEF, represents everything but the people. Wouldn't it be perfect for the constitution of the Empire—to put it in Michael Hardt and Antonio Negri's terms—to make a little room for the world's "civil society" (that is, some NGOs and representatives of unions and some well-mannered social movements)? In view of this obvious move to co-opt the WSF and destroy its radical potential, Lula's "bridge" to the WEF seems to me not only misleading, but also a major threat to the global movement (especially if one takes into account the fact that the PT is one of the few organizations that control the Organizing Committee of the WSF).

And this takes us to my second question. It is well known (and has been repeatedly pointed out lately) that the way the WSF functions is far from transparent, not to mention open and horizontal. The decision-making body of the WSF—the Organizing Committee (OC)—is controlled by a bunch of people no one really knows—not even the members of the International Council of the WSF, so far a rubberstamp appointed by the OC itself.

It is about time the OC adopts more transparent procedures and transfers the decision-making process to social movements. But far from that, some of the same organizations that control the WSF to a great extent—ATTAC France, CUT and MST (Brazil), Focus on the Global South (Thailand), and the World March of Women (Quebec)—have engaged in the creation of a Social Movement's World Network (SMWN).

The idea to coordinate social movements "on a more permanent basis" is undoubtedly important. Too important to be left in the hands of such few organizations, if it is to represent nothing less than the social movements of the whole world. But who wrote the statements of the SMWN? Who decided how it is going to organize? And more important, who elected the Secretariat, or even decided that a Secretariat was needed? Certainly not the movement I belong to, or any of the movements in Argentina, or most of the movements of other countries, as far as I know. Did the *piqueteros*, the Bolivian *cocalero* peasants, European No Border activists, South-African Anti-Eviction campaigners, etc. discuss the issue? I would be surprised if they knew what I'm talking about. Grassroots activists of real social movements were simply not there at the meetings. And no substantial effort was made to make sure the initial proposal was available in advance, so that the movements could at least discuss it at home and send their opinions.

In Porto Alegre, I had the chance to attend the meeting to organize a "Network of the Youth of the WSF," a sort of "youth chapter" of the SMWN. To my surprise, the members of hierarchical political organizations and NGOs, who had called for the meeting, tried to convince the rest of us that the network they were trying to set up was going to be horizontal and decentralized. But if they now suddenly believe in horizontal organizing, why don't they start by reforming their own organizations?

The proposal for the SMWN is written in the same nonhierarchical language. Networks, after all, are decentralized and horizontal by definition, right? But one gets a little suspicious when new funky language seems to be there only to conceal the old political forms and practices. Networks are made of loose, informal, and voluntary links between different groups. That is why no organization and institution can claim to represent a network. A certain number of groups can indeed form a coalition, but it would never encompass a whole network. And networks definitely don't have Secretariats; that's the very essence of a network.

Needless to say, this debate goes far beyond the issue of how we organize the WSF; it has to do with the future of our movement as a whole. The question at stake is, are we really committed to the nonhierarchical bottom-up politics of the new social movements?

I personally have no objections to the creation of a new International—a project that, by the way, is being put forward by some of the same Trotskists who also proposed the SMWN. I don't think it will work this time either, but if they want to try again, well, it's their business. But, please, don't call it a "network," and don't claim it represents the "social movements of the world."

Unfortunately, this is not the only example of traditional left-wing agendas in WSF 111. Shall we let political parties in, as some of the members of the Indian Organizing Committee of the next WSF are demanding? Must we all join those parties, as member of WSF International Council Roberto Savio suggested? Is getting more Lulas and Chavezes elected the way for the movement of movements to move forward, as the huge rallies organized by the WSF seemed to imply? We should all have say on these issues, if we are to have a real debate. And we need to think very carefully, as Indian activist Jai Sen said, if we shouldn't establish some rules to keep the WSF as an open space.

In conclusion, there are moves from the right wing and from the politics of the traditional left wing to domesticate and co-opt the movement of movements. I'm afraid the lack of transparency and real participation in the WSF makes those attempts more likely to succeed.

In view of this, it is not the time to build bridges, but to strengthen the fortress.

# On Populism and the Antiglobalization Movement
## James O'Connor

*Capitalism, Nature, Socialism,* October 15, 2000

## Poverty[1]

Nobody *defends* mass poverty in the world because there is no defense. Yet mass poverty persists. Most economists believe that the cure for poverty is faster economic growth. An increasing rate of growth in the US in the last half (compared with the first half) of the 1990s reduced the percentage of American families living in poverty. A century and a half of industrial capitalism in the North (neoliberal economists argue) has reduced poverty to "manageable" levels. This means, first, that the poor have become politically manageable, and, second, that poverty is no longer a scandal. Hence no special programs are needed to elevate families economically beyond welfare reform.

Until the appearance of the antiglobalization movement—to some the "anti–corporate globalization" movement—the World Bank and IMF were confident that increased economic growth in general and in the South in particular would reduce poverty in the latter, as US growth has decreased poverty here.[2] Everyone knows that they failed miserably, that conditions in the South beginning with the debt crisis and structural adjustment programs in the late 1970s/early 1980s have deteriorated badly compared with the "golden age" of nationalist, semisocialist development during the 1950s and 1960s. Exactly how much the Bank/IMF are to blame for the disasters in Latin America in the 1980s and in Africa during the 1980s and 1990s no one can say. But the antiglobalist movement is predicated on the fact that the Bank and the Fund (and US foreign policy) soon became a big part of the problem, not the solution.

The movement has increasingly protested IMF and World Bank policies that movement leaders rightly believe increase, not decrease, world poverty. This movement is wel organized and tenacious and has good leadership; the movement is also growing in numbers and militancy and has become global in scope. In the US, politically, it is a populist movement, not a class-based movement, which is probably a plus at the moment.[3] The movement, finally, has become influential enough to force the World Bank to change its theory of poverty and its alleviation. The Bank today still regards economic growth as indispensable to "poverty reduction" and still rejects the radical idea that poverty can be reduced by redistributing wealth and income. Their new idea is that a larger share of the increments to growth (the extra capital that growth produces) should be allocated to targeted antipoverty projects. Most movement leaders would reject this theory or policy as too timid. They are rightly convinced that any significant reduction of poverty presupposes a redistribution of wealth and income, from the North to the South, from local corrupt elites to local workers, small farmers and unemployed, and from global corporations to the hundreds of millions of people living in poverty today.

Movement leaders are quite clear that the redistribution of wealth and income presupposes a redistribution of political power, which, of course, is where the Bank, IMF, and WTO draw the line. Thus the ongoing struggle against global political elites, global corporations, and global institutions such as the Bank. This struggle is bound to continue until the movement has achieved a national and international power shift in its favor.

At this point movement folk whose stock in trade are ideas have different visions for the future. Some stress bulking up the UN to give it real power over the global corporations and elites. Some want to reform the IMF et al, while others want to abolish the international economic agencies. Some want "people-centered alternatives" while many in the South want better terms of trade, market opening in the North, technology transfer, and so on. Some imagine a global Keynesianism while others stress international labor solidarity. Whatever the envisioned future, movement spokespeople seem to agree on one thing—they won't quit until wealth and income have been redistributed to the point at which world poverty is or nearly is abolished. In CNS (Capitalism, Nature, and Socialism)-talk, they are "reds" because they demand that wealth be redistributed but not yet "green" because they don't also demand that at the same time wealth be systematically *redefined*— from commodity wealth to ecological production, distribution, and consumption.

Meanwhile the global corporations (and financial markets and other basic features of capitalism about which populists say little) and the US imperialist state which stands behind the corporations and markets, and the IMF et al, which serve this state—all these forces will fight the movement tooth and nail. If history is any guide, popular power comes after World Wars and during economic crises and hard times—and nobody wants either war or depression. But just because something has never happened before doesn't mean that it can't happen, or be made to happen in the future.

## Populism and Globalization

The antiglobalization movement wears many political and ideological masks, so many that "movements" might be more accurate than "movement." In the South the movement is often nationalist, often radically so. At home US nationalism is another name for

US imperialism, which the antiglobalist movement in North America does not yet explicitly acknowledge. Yet while the slogan "end US imperialism" has been conspicuously absent at protest demonstrations, most in the US movement oppose the US–dominated IMF, WTO, and World Bank and also support market opening, improve terms of trade, technology transfer, and more radical demands (such as the decommodification of water and other basics) placed on the North by the movement (and by many governments) in the South.

North and South, the movement today is fundamentally populist (as noted). This means among other things that it is not (yet?) based on the interests and demands of any one economic class or alliance of classes. While global capital plays the "class card" at every turn, antiglobalization sentiment is divided into (among other ways) left-populist and right-populist castes. In the US, left populism (secular and internationalist) is organized within the movement itself while right-wing populism (antisecular and nationalist) is not internationally organized. In the South, right populism, fundamentalism, and nationalism (i.e. anti–US imperialism) are much better organized. This is particularly true in Saharan Africa and the Middle East, on the edges of prosperous Europe, and in South Asia on the border of the Southeast Asian "emerging market economies." Right-wing populism in the South seems to be weakest in Brazil and South Africa—big industrial countries distant from the North and also from regions where fundamentalism is strong—where class-based antiglobalism (which for obvious reasons is also powerfully antiracist North imperialism) is relatively well organized. European right populism—anti-immigrant nativist workers, tradespeople, truckers, open racists, and political extremists, et al—is better organized than in the States but not as well as in the countries and regions in the South where right populism is a factor. The South, of course, has tens of millions of left populist villagers, fisherfolk, landless movements, workers' movements, women's movements in towns and countryside, indigenous peoples, scientists, intellectuals, and others under attack on two fronts: first, by the forces of neoliberal globalism, and second, by local right-wing populist parties and movements. My own opinion is that at some point most everybody will be taking sides on globalization (for or against, reform or revolution) and hence that antiglobalist politics North and South (and East) are likely to be difficult (to put it mildly) for some time to come.

One important fact of life in antiglobalist politics is that right populists in the South are anti-imperialist while their opposite numbers in the North are pro-imperialist. Of equal importance, right populists in the South are people of color and antiracist while their counterparts in the North are (often proudly) racist. In most countries I would guess that right populists regard themselves as patriotic. This all means that the likelihood of a right-wing global populist movement is zero while the odds are much better for an international populism of the left. This is important because the political terrain of both capital and antiglobalist movements is itself global.

One globalist (imperialist) project is to create a strong globalist comprador bourgeoisie in as many countries in the South as possible; thus one reason for the urgency often expressed by the globalizing elites. The means of implementing this project are many and varied. Tying a country's currency to the dollar is one way. Structural adjustment programs (SAPs) are another, as they change not only economic structures in the South but also the class composition and political alignments in SAPed countries. A successful SAP project helps transform a local business class into a globalist comprador class, which is best able to rule or govern a country the way that the US wants the country to be ruled (without the need for obvious or dramatic interventionism on the part of the US government and military). Neoimperialist political rule involves above all destroying all traces of older models of nationalist economic and social development in the South and also opposing new regionalist models based on political economic polycentrism (Samir Amin's term). It should be clear to everyone at this point that the purpose of US policy as outlined by neoliberal globalists is to replace any and all national projects with the single globalist development model organized by Washington and Wall Street (see "House Organ," *CNS,* September 2000).

Unfortunately for the latter there is no way that the US imperial state (or national security state) can expand and evolve in ways that will allow it to keep up with (much less regulate) the expansion of global capital, on the one hand, and the growing antiglobalist movement, on the other. This is indicated by the short life of the Washington Consensus (unrevised version); the attacks on neoliberal thinking from outside and inside the major international institutions; the inability of the World Bank and IMF to hold their hardline stances when confronted with major economic crises (e.g. 1997–1998) and the loss of legitimacy they suffered when their crisis-management policies were exposed as recession-producing policies; the confession that free markets alone aren't able to do away with mass poverty in the South; and the pathetic yet dangerous attempts on the part of big corporations to make money off global warming and ozone depletion (and the rest) instead of confronting the environmental (social) crisis directly. Recall it took a landed gentry, the stewards and trustees of yore—FDR being the best-known—to confront the Great Depression on a broad front, and only near the end of FDR's first term at that.

The fact that neoliberal practice has slipped away from neoliberal theory shouldn't be underestimated. This and other failures of empire create good chances for left antiglobalism since they put into question the legitimacy of the hegemonic or ruling ideas of our time, as well as the real intentions of the globalists (make money and more money into infinity). As I wrote in a previous article, "High Stakes," neoliberalism is a castle in the air. Harmless economic nonsense on paper, neoliberal economics becomes a psychotic enterprise when the globalists try to occupy the castle and make it home. This is what Emma Bovary did, in her own way, which ended in her painful suicide. This will also be neoliberal globalism's fate absent some very (unlikely?) deep reforms of the system. As noted, some put forth the idea of a global New Deal, which for me is harder to imagine than systemic crisis and collapse.

Yet the failures create openings for left antiglobalist forces. Perhaps most important is to heed the call of the nationalist, left populists in the South: continue to attack the Washington consensus and neoliberal model of global development; help breathe new life into older models of nationalist development and newer models of regional polycentric development; support trade and investment rules, technology transfers and other South demands that will help restore or reinvent nationalist socio-economic, ecological development; demand that ecological rationality, equity, and social justice come before efficiency and profit. Abolish the WTO and radically reform the IMF and World Bank, possibly via UN General Assembly control of these and other global institutions.

Every country has the right to develop its resources, human and ecological, in accordance with its own needs and desires. No country should be forced into the monocultural model of globalist development, as designed by Wall Street and the US Treasury. Not even our own country. That should be basic. As history has shown, self-determination is a very imperfect solution; however, it's a better solution than neoliberal imperialism and its castles in the air.

## Potted History

The antiglobalization movement has a short and as yet unrecorded history. Some say that the movement began in the late 1970s, at the birth of neoliberalism, in the first stage of the Third World debt crisis, IMF structural adjustment programs (SAPs), and the IMF riots in Africa, Latin America, and Asia. The word "globalization," however, wasn't commonly used until the late 1980s and early 1990s. Others seem to date the origins of the movement to the alternative summit in Rio 1992, but this was a meeting of NGOs, not a protest demonstration by social movements.[4] The genesis of the movement might be dated to any one (or all) of a dozen major protests at IMF, World Bank, G7, and other international meetings during the 1990s, the Madrid "Fifty Years are Enough" demonstrations arguably the most successful. In almost all accounts, however, Seattle 1999 appears time and again as a real turning point, the first movement victory in the streets.[5]

This reading of the 1990s risks missing the movement's two significant victories against MAI internationally and "fast track" at home (the latter being antiglobalist, if not anticorporate),[6] which were achieved by a combination of NGO lobbying, pressure group politics, internetworking, and street protests, together with some inside deal-making between organized labor and the Clinton administration with respect to "fast track." Historians may see these victories as the real precursors of the antiglobalization movement, first, because they were victories and second, because they were accomplished by the vanguard of the movement, those who could see further into the future than anyone else at the time.

Yet my own favorite origins story is Seattle if only because the media still systematically lies about what actually happened on the streets and in the jails of that fabled city late last year. Most Americans doubtless believe that the Seattle demonstrators fomented a "riot," when in fact most confined their participation to a peaceful march. The "rioters" were police beating up militants engaged in nonviolent resistance (a few dozen self-described anarchists could not be said to be "rioting" when they broke a few windows). Shades of the early civil rights movement, when nonviolent sit-ins, marches, and demonstrations were met by spontaneous and organized police brutality, which time and again came back to haunt the forces of racism during the later stage of the movement culminating in the Civil Rights Act of 1964.

Since Seattle, antiglobalist (and anticorporate) demonstrations have multiplied in number and also with respect to the targets demonstrators choose to protest. In Washington DC, Philadelphia, Los Angeles, Bangkok, Formosa, Melbourne, and Prague (among other places) there was a kind of wedding (if not a wedding, an engagement) between antiglobalist forces, on the one hand, and civil rights, welfare rights, anti-police brutality, feminist, environmentalist, and other domestically-oriented movements, on the other hand—ad hoc as these were. For example, organized groups from the nominally domestic environmental justice movement protested in Seattle and antiglobalist forces showed up in Philadelphia and Los Angeles, where environmental justice issues were among the most paramount ("nominally domestic" because the movement—called by some the movement for environmental and economic justice and by others the movement for environmental and social justice—has been working with EJ groups in other countries for some time). The Independent Media Centers, established in dozens of cities, exemplified what a truly democratic, yet organized and professional, media could look like. More than making up for the absence of big labor and mainstream environmental organizations in Philly and LA were living wage, welfare rights, and other local groups and movements (noted above).

The result has been that more people doubtless understand in various ways the linkages or internal relationships between the big corporations and globalization, and between global and local issues, American foreign and domestic policy, and economics and politics, generally. The drum beat faster in Seattle and half a million or more demonstrators around the world have picked up the beat since Seattle.

Antiglobalization protests have paid dividends, at least a down payment on a long overdue debt by global corporations and elites to the world's poor, small farmers and tradespeople, sweatshop workers, unemployed, village women, countless others. Or if not a down payment, the promise of one. As noted above, World Bank and IMF chiefs and others who constitute the global elite are acting as if the movement has caused them to see the light and undergo a change of heart. Suddenly, "poverty reduction," "living wages," "an end to sweatshops," "better health care and education," and a World Bank one-billion-dollar AIDS relief project for Africa and other movement causes are proposed by the elites as their very own aims or goals ("House Organ," *CNS*, June 2000). As also noted, neoliberal economists in power are finding more exceptions to the policy implications of monitarist/neoclassical economic theory than Alfred Marshall ever dreamt of, while second-tier global officials whisper about the need to reintroduce capital controls to prevent another financial crisis of the 1997–98 type. Sometimes it seems that half of the entire French establishment is wondering if globalization is worth the candle.

In practice, there has been more pleasing rhetoric than plausible policy changes: this despite the facts that two billion people live on less than two dollars a day worldwide and the elite's discreet admission that the rising tide lifts all boats theory of development has badly designed rigging and leaky logic. In practice, also: more militarized police trampling more boldly on the civil liberties of protest demonstrators here and abroad have mocked the basic tenets of liberal democracy.

For their part, the individuals and groups and NGOs who have organized a decade or more of protests, and the ideologies which movement rhetoric is based upon, all speak to one central point: world economy and politics as we know them are much too important to be left to the economists and politicians—unecological, inequitable, unjust, and undemocratic as these economics and politics are. More people here and elsewhere increasingly regard the world that global capital is making as a hopelessly alienated and reified place unfit for real human beings. The economists' language of efficiency, profits, and "consumer choice" is no match for the best ideals and practices of the antiglobalist movement. And more women and oppressed minorities are especially adamant in their opposition to the world that ideologues of global capital imagine as some kind of New Jerusalem.

For their part, despite stated good intentions, sincere or not, global corporations and financial groups and institutions and political elites will do everything and anything they think is necessary to preserve the "global way of life"—the totalitarianism of the single globalist development model, which most in the ruling class and political elite probably regard as the culmination of the idea of Progress, invented hundreds of years ago by their real and imagined North European forerunners. Not merely their profits but their whole way of life is at stake. They believe that this way of life is the best possible way and hence regard anyone who opposes it not only as a political enemy but also as suffering a mental or moral disorder. This is a dangerous group of people: unable to grasp neoliberal globalization as a castle in the air which will drive more people mad, they label "insane" those who refuse to live in their dream world.

## Politics and Populism Revisited

I think that we can expect (and should encourage) the antiglobalist movement to become more political, not only with respect to (as at present) political *means* to ecological, economic, and social goals, but also with regard to political *ends*. Since Seattle, in less than a year, movement issues and demands are becoming more multidimensional and all-inclusive, presented as ensembles of problems and solutions interrelated in various ways, unable to be resolved at any other level than the political (which, dialectically, makes local experiments in alternative working and living all the more important). This is especially so given that domestic issues of racism and police brutality are connected in more people's minds with global issues arising from corporate rule, the rule of international finance markets, and the subordination of use value by exchange value. The difference between what corporate and political elites say they will do (reduce poverty) and what they actually do (increase poverty), will also help to politicize the movement (in the sense of developing political goals). The fact that antiglobalization protests of traditional and new types engender more police violence and suspension of civil liberties, is also a politicizing factor. Because many mainstream North NGOs seem to want to believe elite promises and also seem to downplay police brutality, there might possibly occur a split between NGOs (especially government-sponsored, corporate-funded NGOs) and movement organizers and activists who are less credulous and more intellectually sophisticated (in the critical thinking sense) than the typical NGO official. I think this can be regarded as a good rather than bad thing, a positive development, because NGOs are by definition already compromised in various ways while the movement itself may be likened to a flow of creative and critical human energy, thinking and doing, directed at what most see as an oppressive and exploitative system of corporate/US Treasury/central bank/IMF et al, rule. I don't believe that the elites see the NGOs as the real threat to their world capitalist project, but rather the unpredictable, centerless movement. Alex Demirovic's theory of NGOs and social movements is important precisely because of the kinds of distinctions he finds between the two four years ago, Alex denoted theoretically what today is working itself out in different variations in practical terms, for everyone who cares to see.

There are reasons why the idea of debating, developing, and adopting political goals will be regarded by all kinds of people as unrealistic, falsely utopian, and possibly harmful or dangerous. There are many differences between the antiglobalization movements in the South and the North in terms of what they want, how they organize themselves, and the language and goals of resistance. There are the different relationships that different parts of the movement have with the existing political systems worldwide, including different assessments of the possible scope and limits of liberal democracy, and different definitions of the word "democracy" itself. There is the awful deadening effect of bourgeois politics as usual in today's world of neoliberal globalization. Above all, there is the terrible fear of any action or organization that proposes any "totalizing" solutions to the problem of globalization. To say that the movement's political aims will be democratic, pluralistic, anti-sexist, pro–oppressed minorities, ecological ad infinitum would be (and is) seen in many circles as a bad joke. Yet I think that the movement itself will be forced to adopt a project with definite political ends, an international and internationalist project as the only viable way to oppose globalization successfully, including defining and implementing as much as possible independent alternatives.

The last problem I'll mention seems to be more intractable than it really is. This is the division, noted above, between right-wing populism and the populism of the left in the US. I have often read that on the subject of foreign trade and investment right and left populism speak the same language—that both are antiglobalist in the sense that both reject "free trade" and liberalized foreign investment. Superficially, the fit between right populists and US organized labor seems even tighter: American workers tend to support the regulation of international business and also to be socially conservative. This is Pat Buchanan's political formula and on the surface not so distant from Ralph Nader's political positions in 1996.[7]

In fact the similarity between right and left populists begins and ends with the slogans "Stop the export of jobs" and "Fair trade not free trade" (although most right populists seem to be self-defined protectionists while left populists are not, or if they are they keep it to themselves). Right populists around the world, including in the US, are cultural reactionaries and, unlike many if not most populist small farmers a century ago, left populists today are mainly cultural liberals. For right populists, cultural conservatism fits nicely with their uncritical nationalism, while left populists tend to be multicultural and internationalist. Right populists are often small-businesspeople being squeezed by big corporations and left populists (exceptions are noted above) are militantly anticorporate, but the former ally themselves with the latter only when the labor or trade union issue is tabled. Right populist businesspeople are as anti-union as left populists are pro-union (thus the only question of interest in any coalition of the two in relation to a particular issue, say, "free trade," is, which side has the power to dump the other side from the coalition when the stakes change and the issue of unionism and worker power comes up, as it always does). Right populists hate the WTO and IMF because they appear to represent a shift of power from the American nation-state to international bodies; left populists feel the same way not because the WTO and IMF are international bodies but because they make US foreign policy more undemocratic than it already is and because they exploit and oppress the South. In sum, there are not a lot of things that right-wing nationalists and left-wing internationalists and democrats (small "d") can or do agree on. This is partly because of differences in ideology and political sensibility and partly because their constituencies are very different: the right speaks to small business under attack from big business (for example, small farmers in the US today who have to sell their crops to one of a handful of giant food companies) while the left speaks more to the poor, the unemployed, workers getting less than a living wage, and some trade unionists (for example, public sector unions under attack by top elected officials who are paid to organize workforce downsizing or to prepare a public utility or social service for privatization). Populism of all kinds appeals to the little guy against the big guy but today the little guy has many names, including (as noted) public sector workers. In sum, left populism and right populism are very different with respect to the issues of nationalism vs. internationalism, cultural conservatism vs. social liberalism, and business vs. labor. Right populism isn't a terribly big danger in the US for the simple reason that the US is the imperial hegemon, that is, nationalism equals imperialism under the stars and stripes.

Circling back to the subject of political goals for the antiglobalist movement: the Green Party? the US Labor or Socialist parties? a fifth international of red-green organizations and parties? a movement to split the US Democrats into center-left and center-right components? an IMF-LEFT, established by South countries organized regionally or in polycentric forms, financially backed perhaps by . . . ? a World Forum for Capital Controls, which repoliticizes international capital movements? a World Collective of farmer-to-consumer networks, explicitly seeking to reduce and eliminate the power of the US–based global food companies? a Global Counsel on Immigration that politically eliminates the superexploitation of immigrant workers employing the immigrants' own organized political power? a reconstituted UN, in which the Security Counsel is confined to administrative tasks, politics the monopoly of the General Assembly?

So many political goals have been cited, trial ballooned, mentioned in passing, received scholarly attention, etc. thats I don't know what they will be, but I think I know what they in fact are today, whether the participants are aware of it or not: the idea that capital today is politicized, that the WTO, for example, is a political form of capital (and a big capitalist mistake, as Nader said years ago, since it makes what is fundamentally a private relationship—capitalist free trade—into a public and political relationship which needs to legitimize itself to the global public, and thus presents itself as a political target).

It's clear that all movement struggles pertaining to the conditions of production (health and education, the use of place and space, environment, community, etc.) are by definition political struggles. This is so because the state either produces or regulates the conditions of production (because these conditions are not produced as commodities, only treated as if they are commodities). This is the idea, in short, of struggles within and against the state, to democratize the state, an idea shared by some theory-minded radicals, while ridiculed as an oxymoron by more traditional leftists. I'm not sure that the antiglobalist movement will acknowledge that much of its activity aims to democratize (or abolish) the state, e.g. the WTO, and I'm even less sure that the movement will some day choose other, perhaps more politically potent or interesting, political goals. I am pretty sure that without such goals, there will be lots more corporate and state greenwashing, today compounded by World Bank "redwashing," or the make-believe that this eminently capitalist institution either wants to or is able to abolish poverty worldwide.

This is not such a difficult task as the World Bank and IMF make it out to be. What's difficult is to prioritize "economic growth"—capitalist accumulation—as the indispensable condition for "poverty reduction," as the World Bank and IMF do and will continue to do. Translated, this means that "there will be no redistribution of wealth, monetary, physical, ecological, or any other kind; the best we can do is to increase growth rates then target the poor for a goodly share of the increments to growth." How? Of course, by turning the poor into human capital! However, if you think about it, poverty can be abolished in a few months, assuming the political will and the economic and ecological resources. First step, make poverty abolition the basic goal of international politics. Second step, allocate some billions of dollars of World Bank, IMF, regional development bank, and other monies to the task at hand. Third step, employ these monies, not for human capital or any other kind of capital, but to use local biomass for building homes, schools, and the rest; paying (well) public health and medical technicians, teachers of the "pedagogy of the oppressed" variety, psychologists of the Fanon-type, planners of the Kerala or Gaviota variety, and organizers of the type presently engaged in the antiglobalist movement (including NGO people of course). And more, but you get the idea. *Then,* choose investment projects, not in terms of EIRs that seek to minimize damage to local or regional ecologies but rather to *maximize* ecological values, community values, cultural values, public health values, and so on: a simple reversal of existing capitalist values and investment criteria. Not "safe food" but "nourishing food." Not "adequate housing" but "excellent housing." Not "mass transport" but "public transit of different types that are a pleasure to utilize." Obviously, not "chemical-laced" agriculture but "pesticide-free agronomy." Not "food monopolies" but "farm-to-market global distribution." The tragedy is that so many people *know* "what is to be done," based on tens of thousands of local and regional experiments and practices, from the allocation of water to the production and allocation of steel (in the US during WWII, for example), yet we can do little to make a world in which use value subordinates exchange value (and concrete labor subordinates abstract labor) given the present-day monopoly of power by capital, capital markets, the capitalist state, and capitalist international agencies. Just suppose the IMF, World Bank, et al, were reduced to the status of the IHO, ILO, and other branches of the "international peoples' state," while the latter's power was expanded to the level of the present-day World Bank and IMF. That would be something, wouldn't it? The problem of course is not a technical one, a practical problem, but a political problem, the problem of capitalist power, in and outside the markets. No movement can challenge capitalist power with success without adopting its own political aims and socio-economic alternatives.

There is every need for an internationalist political terrain, an anti-imperialist terrain (which in our world means an antiwhite rule terrain, as the North Europeans here and overseas still rule the world). World War I broke up their continental empires, Russia's excepted, and WW II broke up their overseas empires, the US's remains. Not yet has domination by European whites remains and the white settler capitalist powers been overthrown by the "lesser" ethnicities and people of color.

1. This is the fourth of a series of sketches on "global capital and its antimonies." All four can be found on the CNS/CPE website: http://gate.cruzio.com/~cns/.

2. The "anti–corporate globalization" movement because US movement leaders (theorists? spokespeople?) seek an alliance between organized labor and the big environmental organizations. Neither organized labor nor mainstream environmentalists are "anticorporate," the first because labor needs corporations for jobs, good wages and benefits, and so on, the second because so many enviro leaders are connected to the big corporations as well as dependent on big money for project grants, etc. Both, however, are anti–corporate globalization, labor because corporate globalization policies mean job losses and lower pay, and the enviros because they oppose many types of corporate investments and production systems in the South as harmful to the environment.

3. How do you know a populist declaration or document when you see one? My own method is to look for key words. Most if not all documents originating within the populist antiglobalist movement use expressions such as "global corporations," "undemocratic and elitist" (applied to the IMF, et al), "peoples of the world," "non-governmental organizations," and "people-centered alternatives." These same documents don't use words such as "capitalism"

and "capital" and "finance capital" and "capital markets" (that discipline the corporations). The word "exploitation" (e.g., of labor) is used to apply to the South but not the North. "US imperialism" is taboo outside of sectarian party circles, as is "imperialism" of any type. In movement analyses and declarations from the South, "nationalism" is used, not so in statements from the North. Finally, movement publicists fail to distinguish between NGOs and social movements. The above is, of course, a personal reading.

4. For the differences between NGOs and social movements, see Alex Demirovic, "NGOs and Social Movements: A Study in Contrasts," *CNS*, 9, 3 September 1980.

5. More precisely, the conflicts within the WTO (US versus Europe, South versus North) combined with the street protests (which older participants say they hadn't seen the likes of since the anti-Vietnam war movement in the late 1960s) to produce a stalemate in WTO member negotiations. Stymied on the agricultural and some other fronts, the WTO is at present cooking up even more outrageous trade rules in Geneva, in secret, pertaining to global trade in services and intellectual property rights.

6. Much of organized labor in the US, for example, is definitely antiglobalist but hardly anti-corporate, as noted above.

7. Black and feminist groups put Nader on the carpet for ignoring civil right issues and women's issues such as abortion rights four years ago. Nader's standard response to civil rights questions has been, "Ask my running mate." When last September he was attacked by the National Organization of Women (NOW) for neglecting women's issues (obviously a Gore-inspired move to stop women from voting for Nader in 2000), Nader reminded everyone of his political support of women, including abortion rights. As two major campaign speeches in Santa Cruz made clear, Nader is obviously no social conservative and just as obviously plays up his main theme of corporate greed and corruption and the role of the "public citizen" in fighting the same. Nader is thus a left populist with nothing in common with the likes of Buchanan, yet his machine will seek votes among small businesspeople in the heartland who seem to agree with him on economics, even though they no doubt disagree with him on most social issues. The question is, do they really agree on economics or does it just seem that they do? (see above).

# Seattle '99

## Wedding Party of the Left and the Right?

# Eric Krebbers & Merijn Schoenmaker

(De Fabel van de Illegaal)
Some editing of the English translation by Alain Kessi

At the end of November the members of the World Trade Organization will discuss their new Millennium Round in Seattle. The North American city will see a whole series of demonstrations, actions, and discussion meetings. By now a very diverse mixture of activists, lobbyists, and politicians are gathering under the vague banner of the anti-globalization movement. Both the left and the right are joining and seem to have put their quarrels aside.

"A historic change is under way at the very heart of the globalization process: millions of people are mobilizing. Tens of thousands of them will be in Seattle,"[1] says lobbyist Susan George. "The fight against the WTO and all it stands for is in my view the main one. There is even a chance of winning this fight."[2] George is one of the foremost European lobbyists against "globalization."

Many lobbyists seem to somewhat overrate the movement. "Seattle will be the protest of the century," some of her colleagues say, without much knowledge of history. "The bosses are scared," others add. But who are they supposed to be scared of? The left has not been a very strong force since the fall of the Berlin Wall, and it hardly exists nowadays. That's why the lobbyists are no longer exclusively looking to their left. They have started to actively build a new worldwide movement in which not only left-leaning people, but also conservatives, nationalists, and even the New Right must be able to feel at home. The extremely unclear concept of "globalization" comes in handy. Political activists of all creeds can project their own problems on it.

George and some sixty other lobbyists, researchers, and opinion leaders and their NGOs are members of the International Forum on Globalization (IFG), an elite think tank. They organize a congress in Seattle and never tire of repeating that they expect some twenty-four hundred participants. IFG members often participate at meetings all around the world. They are the main driving force behind the campaigns against "globalization," and they initiated the actions against both the MAI and the WTO.

They want to bring the Left and the Right together in one big movement, and they seem to be successful at it. Therefore the IFG lobbyists cherish their somewhat progressive image and at the same time try to remain acceptable for the Right. But after reading their articles and books it becomes very clear: the IFG is politically right wing and very conservative.

By criticizing "globalization" and multinationals they try to use the remaining left-wing activists to further their own conservative goals, and also try to influence them ideologically. Therefore the IFG are a danger to the already vulnerable left.

In the Netherlands, a lot of left-wing activists are also enthusiastically participating every time the IFG members initiate a new campaign. They are also organizing actions at the end of November, taking part in the worldwide coordinated protests. In the beginning of this year the Dutch organization De Fabel van de Illegaal, together with some other groups, was still actively asking organizations to sign the NGO declaration on the WTO, which was written by some IFG members. When the ideas of the IFG became clearer to them, De Fabel decided to stop, although other groups continued.

## French Culture in Danger

Seattle prepares for the reception of activists from many countries. Peoples' Global Action (PGA) this time organizes two action caravans to the WTO meeting. One across the US includes activists from Chiapas, Mexico, and another one from Canada, ending at the elite IFG meeting. It is a strange choice, for the PGA is known as a left-wing grassroots movement. Also expected in Seattle are eco-activists, union members, steelworkers, lorry drivers, farmers, fisherfolk, postal workers, women's rights activists, artists, students, gay and lesbian activists, and pacifists. Only a small minority will want to get rid of capitalism altogether. The rest will rather aim at an international regulation of "the economy" or will opt for a nationalist future.

The French farmer and leader of the Confederation Paysanne (CP), José Bové, no doubt belongs to the nationalist category. The farmers of the CP are angry with the US government, which doubled the import tariffs on French chees, in retaliation for the decision of the EU to put a ban on meat with hormones coming from the US. The farmers immediately started a dynamic campaign against McDonald's, which is, after all, an American multinational.

The angry farmers organized many actions, and even broke down a McDonald's restaurant in Millau. Last June farmers from India, arriving with the PGA action caravan, came to help a bit. At home they also have a tradition of attacking American companies. The French farmers also disturbed an American film festival because they are very much worried about their own French culture. Bové got arrested but was released shortly after. He sent his regards to the French premier and president for their support and received a ticket to Seattle from the ministry of agriculture to defend the French interests there. Besides the French Communist Party and the Front National, some Dutch antiglobalization activists also reacted very positively to the farmers' actions. They called for solidarity with Bové.[3]

## Supporting Working Families

"The Seattle summit will be a historic confrontation between civil society and corporate rule," says Mike Dolan. He works for the American consumer watchdog group Public Citizen founded by Ralph Nader. Public Citizen is connected to the IFG and initiated the campaign against the MAI treaty. Dolan now acts as the great coordinator and spokesman of the countermovement in Seattle. Not everyone seems to be happy with him, but little can be done about his presence. He sits in the middle of the web, like a spider. On the one hand Dolan supports the American PGA caravan with several thousand dollars; on the other he speaks up for the extreme-right Pat Buchanan, now a candidate for the American presidency, representing the Reform Party. "Whatever else you say about Pat Buchanan, he will be the only candidate in the 2000 presidential sweepstakes who will passionately and unconditionally defend the legitimate expectations of working families in the global economy," Dolan writes.[4] Indeed, Buchanan supports American workers, as long as they are conservative and obedient and not unemployed, black, gay, female, lesbian, or Jewish. He's also not particularly fond of left-wing workers. Buchanan on Argentina: "With military and police and freelance operators, between six thousand and one hundred fifty thousand leftists disappeared. Brutal: yes; also successful. Today peace reigns in Argentina; security has been restored."[5]

## Closed Eyes

Former Republican big shot Buchanan is known for his sharp attacks on international trade treaties like GATT, NAFTA, MAI, and now the WTO. "Traditional antagonists as politically far apart as Ralph Nader and Pat Buchanan are finding some common ground on trade issues," says IFG member Mark Ritchie.[6] He is also director of the American Institute for Agriculture and Trade Policy, which supports small farmers. Reform Party spokesman in New Hampshire John Talbott agrees with Ritchie. "If you close your eyes, it is difficult to hear much of a difference between Ralph Nader on the left and Pat Buchanan on the right when they talk about the devastating effect of free international trade on the American worker and a desire to clean big money and special interests out of Washington."[7] According to Buchanan this big capital is mainly in the hands of "the Jews." He presents himself as "the only leader in this country who is not afraid of fighting against the Jewish lobby."[8] Buchanan calls Hitler "an individual of great courage" and doubts whether the holocaust really was that big an event.[9] But "Jewish capital" isn't the most important reason why Buchanan wants to be a candidate for the presidency. No, in the first place he wants to end "illegal immigration," that is, according to Buchanan, "helping fuel the cultural breakdown of our nation."[10]

The populist Buchanan is probably the foremost representative of the extreme right in the US. His constituency consists of Christian fundamentalists, militia members, and neo-Nazis. These millions of people might explain Dolan's flirt with Buchanan. Together with his enthusiastic commentary Dolan sent around a newspaper article in which Buchanan openly says: "American workers and people first."[11] But Buchanan is not alone with that opinion. Also the big right-wing trade union AFL-CIO wants to make "the rights and interests of US workers a priority."[12] The union also mobilizes their rank and file for the demonstrations in Seattle.

## The Government Is Not the Enemy

When Dolan's work and ideas were criticized from the grassroots level, the coordinator of the American PGA caravan immediately took his side. "Let's work together when we can, work in parallel when we must, but never work against each other when our goal is the elimination of the WTO and its corporate benefactors."[13]

While organizing, Dolan keeps repeating his mantra: "Remember, for us, the enemy isn't these governments that comprise the WTO. The enemy is the transnational corporate, free trade lobby."[14] Consequently Dolan can perfectly work together with the right-wing Republican council member Derdowski, who earlier initiated plans for a Seattle MAI-free zone. Also according to Derdowski the discussion around the WTO transcends the old borders between the left and the right. "The issue for conservatives is the sovereignty of America, the Constitution. State and local authority are in danger of being eroded through international treaties ceding authority to foreign regulatory bodies."[15] Together with the Republicans Dolan organizes a demonstration in Seattle.

On a meeting they brainstormed on how to get the conservative inhabitants of the affluent districts of Seattle to also take to the streets. They decided to put IFG member David Korten on the task. They assumed this former businessman would easily connect to the rich.[16] Shortly after, Korten showed up at the grassroots level. He acted as the most important guest lecturer at a strategy meeting on nonviolent direct action. Korten would very much like to return to the '50s, when the economy was, according to him, still local and capitalism was not yet "perverted." His second hang-up is neo-Malthusian. He wants to reduce the world population from six to one billion. How? That he has, wisely, not revealed yet.[17]

## Crucial Battles

Susan George also believes that "state sovereignty" is "under threat."[18] Therefore she wants us to strive for the "greatest possible unity."[19] The need for that also became clear to George in the US fight against fast track, a special presidential authority to push through trade treaties. "The anti-NAFTA and anti-WTO forces of the left defeated fast-track authority for the president only with the help of the far right. It was still a good thing to defeat fast track."[20] Ritchie, her colleague at the IFG, also has a good deal of experience in working together with the extreme right. "Aside from Nader and Buchanan, the anti-GATT and NAFTA trade alliance include a wide spectrum of what would have previously been called left and right elements. This diversity of views and constituencies gave the campaigns much of their strength."[21]

De Fabel van de Illegaal, on the other hand, fights the coming together of the left and the right. Whoever starts working with the right automatically drops migrants, women, and gays as potential allies, for they are always under attack from the right. The last couple of months De Fabel have heavily criticized collaborations with the right. Articles have been written on the ideas and activities of the New Right ideologist Goldsmith, who is also an important IFG member and sponsor of the think tank.[22] George got very angry about the criticism. De Fabel was splitting up the movement, she wrote. And because of that "we" would lose the "crucial battles" that "will be fought" in Seattle.[23]

1. Susan George, "Seattle Prepares for Battle," *Le Monde Diplomatique,* November 1999.

2. Susan George, "Letter to De Fabel van de illegal," 21 September 1999.

3. Kees Stad, "Dolle toestanden in Frankrijk," 7 September 1999.

4. Michael Dolan, e-mail, 2 March 1999.

5. Chip Berlet and Margaret Quigley, "The Right Wing Revolt Against the Modern Age," *The Public Eye* Vol. VI, No. 1 (December 1992).

6. Mark Ritchie, "Cross-border Organizing," in *The Case Against the Global Economy and for a Turn Towards the Local,* Jerry Mander and Edward Goldsmith, eds., 1996.

7. Chip Berlet, "Right wing populism/Reform Party," Public Eye Homepage, 11 July 1999.

8. Bert Lanting, "Kritiek op Buchanans kijk op nazi-Duitsland," *De Volkskrant,* 25 September 1999.

9. "Pat Buchanan in His Own Words," *Fair Report,* 26 February 1999

10. Leonard Zeskind, "Free Trade and Foul," *Searchlight,* October 1999.

11. Edward Walsh, "Buchanan Dumps on Clinton Steel Policy," *Washington Post,* 2 March 1999.

12. Tom Gilroy, "Gephardt Calls for a Seat at the Table for Labor, Environmentalists in WTO-Talks," *Washington Post,* 13 October 1999.

13. Michael Morrill, e-mail, 13 October 1999.

14. David Postman, "Protesters Busily Practice for WTO Meeting," *Seattle Times,* 10 September 1999.

15. Geov Parrish, "Shutting down Seattle," *Seattle Weekly,* 19 August 1999.

16. Helene Cooper, "Globalization Foes Plan to Protest WTO's Seattle Round Trade Talks," *Wall Street Journal,* 16 July 1999.

17. Doug Henwood, "Antiglobalization," *Left Business Observer* No. 71, January 1996.

18. Susan George, "State sovereignty under threat-globalizing designs of the WTO," *Le Monde Diplomatique,* July 1999.

19. Susan George, "Letter to De Fabel van de illegal," 21 September 1999.

20. Susan George, e-mail, 17 September 1999.

21. Mark Ritchie, "Cross-border organizing," in *The Case Against the Global Economy and for a Turn Towards the Local,* Jerry Mander and Edward Goldsmith, eds., 1996.

22. Eric Krebbers, "Millionaire Goldsmith Supports the Left and the Extreme Right" and "Goldsmith and His Gaian Hierarchy," *De Fabel van de Illegaal* No. 36, September 1999.

23. Susan George, "Letter to De Fabel van de illegal," 21 September 1999.

# Fascists for Che
## White Supremacists Infiltrate the Antiglobalization Movement
# Nick Mamatas
*In These Times*

Neo-Nazi rallies in America's urban centers are most often the tiny affairs of a few racists, and are often drowned out by massive counterprotests. But on August 24, hundreds of followers of the National Alliance and other neo-Nazis, under a front called Taxpayers Against Terrorism, held their fourth and largest anti-Israel event in Washington DC since September 11.

The racist National Alliance and other white supremacist and neo-Nazi groups are piggybacking on antiglobalization and anti-Israeli occupation movements with a new enthusiasm by adopting anticorporate and pro-Palestinian rhetoric, hoping to recruit young activists drawn to the post-Battle of Seattle political milieu.

Neo-Nazis "are definitely gaining confidence," says Zein El-Amine, who helped recruit progressive Arabs to the rally's counterprotest. "They are getting more sophisticated with their organizing. ... They had Arabic signs at this demo that said 'Zionism is terrorism.'"

The confidence shows in numbers. The rally of more than 300 on August 24 was significantly larger than its counterpart on May 11, thanks to online organizing and a new tactic of holding a "Rock Against Israel" concert featuring hate rock acts Brutal Attack, Celtic Warrior, and Intimidation One at a "secret location" after the protest. Only those who attended the rally were allowed entry to the show, which was held at a National Guard armory in White Marsh, Maryland.

The progressive-sounding Web site www.g8activist.com is home to the so-called Anti-Globalism Action Network (AGAN), another front for the National Alliance. At first blush, the group sounds legit. The URL is designed to resemble www.g8activist.ca, a real antiglobalization site, and AGAN claims to stand against the Bush administration's imminent war on Iraq. The site has reposted an article by David Finkel from the socialist magazine *Against the Current* that criticizes Israeli Prime Minister Ariel Sharon. National Alliance members and supporters often post to the boards at www.indymedia.org to hype forthcoming events; others make dubious free speech pleas "towards a broadening of the anti-globalism movement to include divergent and marginalized voices," as the AGAN Web site puts it.

While the tactics are new, the strategy isn't. According to Finkel, a longtime pro-Palestinian activist: "Fascists and racists of all stripes usually strike a pose of 'anti-globalism' and sometimes even 'anti-capitalism,' and anti-Semites in particular pose as friends of the Palestinian people when they feel it will advance their real agenda of promoting hatred of Jews."

In the United States, groups like the White Aryan Resistance and followers of Lyndon LaRouche tried to join coalitions against the Gulf War in 1991, and modern-day "Third Position" groups who claim to be "neither left nor right" simultaneously claim both Che Guevara and Benito Mussolini as inspirations. A few dozen members of Nazi and white-supremacist groups skirted the edges of the anti-WTO protests in Seattle in 1999, managing to conflate themselves with the antiracist anarchist militants of the "Black Bloc" in the minds of mainstream anti-hate organizations like the Southern Poverty Law Center and the Anti-Defamation League. Implying cooperation between the two groups, the SPLC asked in a 2000 report, "How is it that members of the far 'left' and 'right' found themselves facing down police together?" The ADL continues to list the circle-A symbol of anarchism as a "general racist symbol" on its Web site.

The National Alliance is also working to exploit continuing fear of terror attacks with a new community-based "terror-free zone" campaign, which calls for an end to US aid to Israel alongside a return to pre-1965 US immigration regulations. The National Alliance leaflet, being distributed in working-class neighborhoods, says the group will collect names of neighborhood signatories and pass them on to nations in the Middle East. This will ensure, the group claims, that communities signing on will be "declared terror-free zones" and will "not be targeted for reprisals."

Of course, the pro-Palestinian gloss is just that. Before his death earlier this summer, William Pierce, the leader of the National Alliance, told Michelle Cottle of the *New Republic*: "My primary concern is not really for Palestinian freedom or how they run their lives over there—or for the Iraqis." The National Alliance sees Arabs in France and Germany as little more than subhumans who need to be removed from the continent. The post-9/11 shift represents nothing more than the dovetailing of interests of white supremacists and the most extreme Muslim fundamentalists: the elimination of multiculturalism, extreme nationalism, and vicious anti-Semitism.

It is unlikely the Nazis will be able to recruit sizable numbers with this latest scheme. "These loathsome neo-Nazi cults are small in numbers and influence," Finkel says, "which is why they act in this parasitic fashion."

# Shutting Us Out

## Race, Class, and the Framing of a Movement

# Kristine Wong

From October 1997 to August 2000, I worked as the community organizer for the Community Coalition for Environmental Justice (CCEJ). Seattle-based and people of color–led, CCEJ waged local battles that furthered the global struggle for environmental justice. One of our most successful efforts was our Stop the Burning! campaign. In 1998, the campaign successfully pressured the local Veterans' Administration hospital to shut down a medical waste incinerator that was releasing dioxin into the Beacon Hill neighborhood, an area where the majority of the residents were low income and people of color. CCEJ's Stop the Burning! campaign organized Seattle residents against a global problem—the incineration of medical waste, which produces dioxin, one of the most toxic chemicals known. Dioxin migrates across countries, continents, and cultures, poisoning our bodies, food supply, and environment. Incinerators all over the world are operated by transnational corporations (TNCs), primarily located in low-income communities and communities of color. These facilities have also been supported by international institutions such as the World Bank, which has promoted hospitals that incinerate their waste, rather than use safer disposal methods. Consequently, our local victory had global impact.

By the end of summer 1999, organizing against the WTO Ministerial Meeting was accelerating. The mobilization provided an opportunity for collaboration among local activists, and to build an inclusive movement that linked the struggle at a local and on a global level. My concern was that the great majority of anti-WTO forces were not addressing the connections between WTO policies and the daily lives of the working class and communities of color, much less recognizing or including grassroots groups as an integral part of their leadership.

Whether or not the protests succeeded in shutting down the WTO, local campaigns like CCEJ would still exist. To be a genuine victory, the protests would have to broaden and unite existing grassroots movements, not recreate the oppressive structures they attempt to replace. A successful shutdown of the WTO would be an incredible victory for low-income communities and communities of color around the world, especially for countries in the Global South. However, it would limit the potential of such a movement if those most affected by globalization were unrepresented.

Riding on the golden waves of Seattle, activists have flocked from one protest to the next, hoping to pressure international institutions like the World Bank and IMF, and the US presidential election conventions to reconsider their financial ties to TNCs. At all these events, protesters of color have been outnumbered by whites.

Since Seattle, there has been a dialogue about the role people of color play in this movement. In this essay, I write about how people of color have been marginalized in the antiglobalization movement due to their absence in the movement's leadership and practice, and how the media has compounded this problem.

## Elite Supergroups: Framing "Fair Trade, Not Free Trade" for the Masses

While the marginalization of people of color in the antiglobalization movement can be attributed to a number of factors, the manner in which the elite "supergroup" leadership articulated and marketed the "fair trade, not free trade" demand is one of the main reasons. While smaller groups are the backbone of the movement, it was financial and political muscle that put Public Citizen, organized labor, and the Sierra Club in some of the key positions of power, influence, and recognition in the months leading up to the WTO.

After the WTO announced that Seattle would be the site of its Millennium Round Ministerial, Public Citizen, a well-established, non-governmental organization (NGO) based in Washington DC, set up an office downtown for their anti-WTO organizing arm, called People for Fair Trade (PfFT). Though the operations were lean in Seattle, it had a full-time staff working on trade issues through Public Citizen's Global Trade Watch program in DC. Moreover, PfFT's Seattle staff alone was larger than that of most other grassroots organizing groups in Seattle, including CCEJ, and employed mostly whites within its ranks.

In the fall of '99, I attended an educational presentation sponsored by PfFT about the WTO. The meeting was held in Rainier Valley, one of the largest communities of color in Seattle. As soon as I entered the room, it was clear that, despite the demographics of the neighborhood, the atmosphere was not inviting to a variety of races and ethnicities. Hand-painted cardboard cut-outs depicting a sea turtle, a loaf of bread, and a tree were propped against the wall. Seats were arranged lecture-style, facing a blackboard.

The presentation was devoid of anything that could resonate with most working-class people of color, focusing on three cases showing how the WTO had the unprecedented power to rule against countries' ability to make their own laws. This was illustrated by three WTO rulings. The first ruling sacrificed a sea turtle protection law for the shrimp fishing industry, while the second forbade the United States from enforcing its own gasoline quality laws. The third had to do with food quality—the prohibition of banning hormone-injected beef in the European Union.

A few other people of color were present at the Rainier Valley event—I watched their reactions closely. A middle-aged African-American woman and a Latina with two young children stared at the presenters blankly. The presentation favored passive learning through listening rather than active learning through educational exercises and activities that draw upon the interest and experience of the participants. For entertainment, two young white women with facial piercings and matted hair earnestly led the attendees in a folk song against free trade accompanied by an instrument resembling a ukulele. The women said they were going on a national tour to spread the message of why people should take action against the WTO. Both women of color politely gathered up their belongings and left the room.

BAYAN, an international Filipino organization, was also at the event. They were convening a People's Assembly in late November, consisting of delegates from the Global South opposed to WTO policies. Their lead organizer in Seattle, Ace Saturay, had a few minutes to speak at the end of the meeting. Yet by that time, almost all of the other people of color had left. After the event I approached one of the presenters with my concern about the style and content of the presentation. She mentioned that a curriculum addressing globalization and its impact on health care was being developed. While she was open to my suggestions, she did not address my concern.

People for Fair Trade's presentation was a replica of an educational brochure about the WTO, published by the Working Group on the WTO. Titled "A Citizen's Guide to the World Trade Organization," the brochure was one of the first and most widely distributed publications, and played a key role in articulating the issues around the WTO to the activist public, as well as to the mainstream media. An analysis of its content easily illustrates how the antiglobalization movement has not engaged people of color.

The brochure addressed democracy but did not use language or content applicable to many people of color, beginning with its very title. Many people of color are immigrants or refugees, and not all are "citizens." The most pressing issues for the majority of the world's people go beyond consumerism: access to a living wage, privatization of traditionally public sector services, disproportionate exposure to toxic pollutants, police brutality, and the rise of the prison-industrial complex. The brochure referred to none of these. Instead, they were labeled as "environmental" and "health" issues, even though the gasoline and beef cases were environmental health issues.

While choosing to describe the issues as "environment," "health," and "labor" rather than the complex "public health and environmental justice" may appear to be splitting hairs, the simplification had its consequences. As a result, people of color–led grassroots groups in the environmental justice movement, such as CCEJ, whose work was already challenging the root causes of globalization, were not viewed as key players who should have been included in the public discourse about globalization's effect on "environmental" issues. While the International Forum on Globalization's "Invisible Government" report and the Earth Justice Legal Defense Fund's "Trading Away Public Health" more accurately described the WTO as having an impact on public health issues, they also neglected to term them as environmental justice issues.

## Environment and Health Day: Dioxin or Sea Turtles?

Around October, I heard that the organizers of the protest were planning a different theme for each of the five days of the ministerial. The first day, Monday, November 29, was to be "Environment and Health Day." I contacted the main coordinators for that day, senior staff at Public Citizen and the Sierra Club, to talk to them about including a section about dioxin in the day's events. My intention was to make sure that a race, class, environmental health, and justice analysis would be included in the day's proceedings. My experience is a perfect example of the power dynamic that white groups have wielded over smaller, community-based people of color groups in the antiglobalization movement.

While I did not receive a return call from the Sierra Club, I did get a response from the staffperson at Public Citizen. She acknowledged that race and class dimensions were of concern, informing me that people of color would be represented in the day's events. She said I could participate in the planning group for Environment and Health Day, and that she would add me to the email list of organizers. This never happened. When I realized that she was not including me in the group, I decided to plan a separate environmental justice event about dioxin that would illustrate how local environmental justice struggles are connected with global ones. All I needed was to find a space downtown to hold the event. However, after contacting United Methodist Church, one of the few non-business spaces downtown open to renting space for anti-WTO events, I found that Public Citizen had already rented it for the day. This left me with no choice but to again ask Public Citizen if I could reserve some part of the facility for about one to two hours, so that the dioxin event could take place. The fact that I had to ask a Washington DC–based group for permission to get access to space to educate others about local struggles in my own city of residence was ironic and disturbing.

When I asked the Public Citizen staffperson for access to the space, I informed her of my plans for the dioxin event. She let me know that she could not give me an answer, as plans for Environment and Health Day had not been finalized. About a month later, she contacted me to let me know that the planning group had decided to hold a march featuring protesters dressed as sea turtles for the day. The group's decision was exactly what

I had feared. The sea turtle march was the day's main public event. A march full of sea turtles would send out an extremely limited message to the public—that the WTO hurt endangered species and the environment, but not the health and welfare of people around the world. I could picture the media images already—turtle-protesters splashed in newspapers and magazines all over the world, permanently branding the WTO in people's minds as just another environmental issue.

The Public Citizen staffperson added that she knew people who could explain to me the connections between CCEJ's local struggle and the policies of the WTO. I found this to be extremely condescending and insulting, as the scope of the event I was planning should have indicated to her that I was aware of the connections between local and global environmental justice. Soon after, an organizational ally asked the Public Citizen staffperson via email to include CCEJ in the planning committee, a completely unsolicited request. The staffperson replied that I had been included in the planning for Environment and Health Day.

## Exclusionary Images: The Sierra Club and the American Revolution

The Sierra Club's anti-WTO materials defined fair trade with exclusionary imagery. A postcard by the club's Seattle chapter clearly targeted mainstream white environmentalists. "We can make trade clean, green, and fair," it proclaimed. Calling for "Clean air standards, Food safeguards, and Wildlife protections," against a blue and green background, it featured three colonial-era men marching defiantly, one brandishing an American flag. At the bottom of the postcard ran the slogan, "No globalization without representation." The Sierra Club's intent was for the trio to be viewed as American revolutionaries on their way to the Boston Tea Party, protesting taxation without representation. Rather than choosing an image that reflected the global implications of the issue, the Sierra Club chose a nationalistic approach that glorified the American Revolution. An African-American friend remarked to me that the picture reminded her of the days of slavery.

Fortunately, not all of the local events excluded people of color. Teach-ins organized by BAYAN, the People's Assembly, and Seattle Central Community College students provided a few opportunities for participants to learn about the connections between local and global issues. Coordinated by Lydia Cabasco, student organizers of color gave presentations in local high schools. At the Seattle Central teach-in, I gave my local-global dioxin, environmental justice, and global waste trade presentation. Yalonda Sindé, of CCEJ, gave a presentation about how corporate globalization both causes and perpetuates poverty. The International Forum on Globalization's Seattle teach-in on November 26 and 27 featured a selection of well-known speakers from across the Global South, while Seattle's Workers Voices' Coalition and the Northwest Labor and Employment Law Office

(LELO) sponsored events and a December 4 workers' conference focused on immigration, women, and the global economy.

## Seattle and DC Media Spin: Manufacturing White Identities; People of Color Ignored

### Part I: Seattle

Despite wholehearted efforts by people of color to get the word out to the community and the media about the way local issues are affected by globalization, the supergroups' agenda prevailed. The media fashioned these groups into an activist family of identities: fair trader/anticorporate crusader, labor loyalist, and environmentalist. These identities were prized by the mainstream media for providing the official advocacy position of the protesters. Their "newfound" alliance was neatly packaged in the nickname of "Teamsters and Turtles," a sound bite that described labor and environmentalists "together, at last." On the other hand, the Direct Action Network and the great majority of peaceful young protesters were portrayed as rebellious and irresponsible. They were good for action-packed photo opportunities with shock value—white youth with matted hair and piercings who either ravaged downtown stores, occupied the streets in droves to make political statements, or were hauled off to jail in handcuffs.

While the media's fixation on "Teamsters and Turtles" and white youth was easily digestible by the public, it completely eclipsed the problems of the people most affected by globalization. Similarly, media promotion of white activists gave power to these groups to define the antiglobalization movement: who are the experts, what are the issues, and where will it head next.

Worst of all, the media completely ignored the participation of people of color in the protest. The People's Assembly march of international delegates and local activists of color marched from Seattle's International District to Fourth and Pine Streets downtown. There it converged with the student march coming from Seattle Central Community College, and the labor march coming from Memorial Stadium. CCEJ organized an environmental justice contingent as part of the march, and marched alongside representatives from the Southwest Network For Environmental and Economic Justice, and later with the Indigenous Environmental Network. At Fourth and Pine, the People's Assembly held a participatory rally, among the most powerful images of the week, that welcomed any protester to take their turn addressing the crowd. The result was an exhilarating, electrifying mix of everyday people with an international perspective, mostly women of color, who spoke from their hearts on the impact of globalization. Their words, full of raw energy, vision, and power, never reached the ears of the larger public. As noted by Yalonda Sindé, who monitored television media during the week, the coverage of people of color was largely reduced to images of African American youth looting stores whose windows had already been broken during the November 30 march.

The domination of "Teamsters and Turtles" and white youth in the media was no surprise. True to form, the corporate media followed the lead of the "supergroups" and presented the issues in safe, clichéd terms. Just as I had predicted, the sea turtles hit the pages of the *Seattle Post Intelligencer* on Tuesday, November 30; were splashed across a two-page photo spread in *Newsweek*'s "Battle of Seattle" issue; and were placed atop a *New York Times* op-ed about the protests. "Teamsters and Turtles" and young white demonstrators became the universal symbols of the antiglobalization movement, rather than the numerous communities around the world who have resisted globalization.

## Part II: Washington, DC

The next major protest that I took part in was "A16"— a protest against the World Bank and IMF in Washington DC. As in Seattle, I was also a print journalist with the Independent Media Center (IMC). Connecting with and interviewing activists of color in the streets, I found them to be well informed, committed, and inspiring. They had traveled from all around the United States and all over the world to be a part of the protests, and hailed from different generations, faiths, sexual orientations, and economic backgrounds. They spoke passionately about how the policies of the World Bank and IMF were responsible for gentrification, sweatshop labor, environmental racism, the global trafficking of women, poor access to HIV/AIDS treatment, police brutality and racial profiling, and the rise in the prison-industrial complex at the cost of education.

Another priority of mine was to seek out local organizers and events that made the connection between the policies of the World Bank and IMF and the current state of affairs in the low-income communities of color in Washington DC. In the Columbia Heights neighborhood, I attended an antigentrification rally that stopped at several apartment complexes. At each stop, black, Asian/Pacific Islander, and Latino immigrant residents who were being evicted came outside to tell the crowd the unjust circumstances of their displacement. Many of these residents tied their situation to those around the world who have also been displaced from their homes by World Bank and IMF-funded development projects.

Just as in Seattle, I found nothing of these experiences in the mainstream media accounts of the A16 protests. With labor withdrawing its support from the D.C. protests, and sea turtles nowhere to be found, the *Washington Post* focused on pierced, alternative-looking white youth as the new American revolutionary icon, showcasing them as the main participants engaging in this social movement. Although people of color did not constitute a majority of the protesters, this does not mean their presence was not worth mentioning. Ignoring their presence rendered their participation invisible to mainstream society. This dynamic seriously impacts the relationship of people of color with this growing social movement.

The media's elimination of people of color from coverage of the Seattle and DC protests created a public perception that these people had not participated. The media then used this representation to criticize white activists for expressing anger toward policies that do not (as the corporate pundits see it) directly affect them. In their view, if a critical mass of people who were most affected by globalization weren't out in the streets protesting the event, then how valid could the concerns be?

What the media ignored was that the numbers of protesters of color present were not necessarily indicative of popular opinion in those communities. Several factors influenced the numbers of people of color at these protests. Due to the cost of travel and accommodation, as well as the luxury needed to take time off work and family responsibilities, it was less likely that working-class people of color would have been able to come. Secondly, in light of widespread brutality to people of color by police and in the prison system, especially African Americans, it was clear that protesters of color risking arrest was an entirely different prospect than those in the Direct Action Network (DAN) with white skin privilege. Additionally, many immigrants of color who were not legal residents were not in any position to risk arrest. Others may have been discouraged from protesting, whether it be through painful memories of the way protesters were treated by the political regimes of their home countries, or through the stories of family members who had witnessed or experienced violent repression of those who spoke out against unjust policies.

Finally, media coverage may have affected the way people of color perceived the globalization issue due to its focus on the protesters and not on the real issues at hand, much less the local-global connections. Predictably, this only exacerbated the racial imbalance by sending out messages to people of color that the WTO, the World Bank, and the IMF had nothing to do with their lives.

## Whose Independent Media?

In the months preceding the WTO Ministerial Meeting, the IMC in Seattle was founded to give the underrepresented greater access to the media during the protests. The IMC was a work and resource space for independent media, and a website where anyone could contribute up-to-the-minute audio, video, or print news on the webcast. The IMC's print team produced a daily paper for distribution on the streets of Seattle, titled the *Blind Spot*. While the IMC has stimulated a grassroots independent media movement and challenged the corporate media, it has difficulties in determining how it can work with local community-based organizations and the ethnic media.

During the WTO and DC protests, I doubled as a print journalist for the *Blind Spot*. As a local activist who knew a few other locals in the space, I was able to find out what the writing, editing, and printing processes were, even though I had to push my way through various channels to get that information. However, had I been a person of color from out of town, it would have been more difficult to determine how to get involved. The atmosphere was chaotic and not very welcoming to people of color, as there were so few around. Although a workspace had been set aside for people of color, I was not aware of it at the time. Evaluative meetings between the Seattle IMC and local activists of color took place in the winter and spring following the WTO. While I was unable to attend all the meetings, I took part in some, letting others know that the IMC needed to meet with local community groups and the ethnic media before determining their place in the Seattle landscape. Others had recommended antiracism training. While a good group of IMC staff, cofounders, and activists were committed to moving in the direction of these recommendations, the overall membership was divided on how best to proceed.

After the WTO protests, activists in DC began to organize an IMC for A16. As a print reporter, I focused on stories about people of color that made the local connections to globalization, writing a story for the *Blind Spot* about the Columbia Heights evictions/anti-gentrification rally on April 15 and turning it in that night. Earlier, I also sent them my interview with a Malaysian-born activist from JustACT, the San Francisc—based group who had brought a number of youth activists of color to the protest. The interview had an international perspective about the repression of Asian/Pacific Islander student activists and linked US youth of color's struggle against police brutality and the prison system with globalization and privatization.

At the editorial meeting that night, I was told that both pieces were slated to be published the next day, the April 16 edition of the *Blind Spot*. On that day, I marched with the People's Assembly, this time as a reporter as well as an activist. To meet the *Blind Spot* deadline, I headed back to the IMC later that afternoon.

While I was writing my story, the *Blind Spot* arrived. Neither of my pieces had been published. Reading the issue, I found the content to be problematic. It was closer to the mainstream media than to the voice of the underrepresented. None of the articles provided perspectives outside those centered around white protesters and their efforts to represent people of color struggles. For example, instead of printing an article focused on the evictions rally in Columbia Heights, editors of the *Blind Spot* chose to include an article about a group of squatters that took over a house as their way of protesting on behalf of the residents being evicted. The story that should have gotten printed was the Columbia Heights rally that covered affected residents who were speaking out for themselves.

The content that did involve stories mentioning the struggles of people of color failed as substantive analyses of the issues. Rather, it appeared to have been placed there for token value. Someone without much exposure to these issues might look at the April 16 issue and think that it covered a diverse range of perspectives, simply because the code words "race," "Mumia Abu-Jamal," and "class" appeared in the stories. The lack of analysis could have been avoided had people of color with an understanding of and experience with these issues been part of the editorial team.

However, while the IMCs have challenges ahead of them regarding people of color issues, they have succeeded where the mainstream media have failed, giving the world first-person, unedited coverage of what really happened on the streets of Seattle. They should be commended for that, and for creating a worldwide movement of IMCs, one of the lasting contributions of the WTO protests.

## Recommendations and Conclusion

While people of color in the Global South have been fighting against globalization for decades, the WTO protests have given the spotlight to the post-Seattle antiglobalization movement. In contrast to movements in the Global South, the post-Seattle movement has spawned a new group of activist nomads, involving thousands protesting international trade and lending policies at events all over the world. Ironically, these event-based convergences that have built the post-Seattle movement are the very same events that have dissipated it, by encouraging activists to protest so globally that many forget the importance of acting locally. A year later, the movement has reached a turning point in its evolution. If it is to survive, it must look to people of color–led groups fighting globalization on a local level to build its own leadership, foundation, and direction.

Looking to these groups for leadership and direction means acknowledging the disproportionate effects of globalization on low-income communities and communities of color, especially in the Global South, and how people of color–led movements have fought back. This means acknowledging grassroots community organizations that are the movements' backbone and giving them the space to frame globalization in a way that resonates with the daily lives of low-income communities and communities of color around the world.

However, while this is an approach that will build the movement, it will fail unless the Northern, mostly white leadership is committed to using its power and resources to make this vision become a reality. True sharing of leadership would require elites to sacrifice some of their organizations' power and funding. While seemingly unrealistic, this is what is necessary if the movement is to mature and develop into one that can build a truly globalized movement for social justice.

The media has an integral role in the future direction of the movement. Media images, whether they are mainstream or independent, need to go beyond the protests and focus on the real issues of corporate-led globalization. The images must include people of color in the struggle, draw from multiple sources, and dispel stereotypes. Likewise, the IMCs must find a place in the community through collaborating with grassroots groups and the ethnic media to determine what their role will be.

I look forward to an antiglobalization movement that is collective in scope, where people of color and community-based organizations are recognized in the fight against globalization.

A community resource guide on environmental justice is available from the Community Coalition for Environmental Justice. Write to: CCEJ, 105 14th Avenue, Suite 2C, Seattle, WA 98122; call (206) 720.0285; or check out http://www.ccej.org.

# Peoples' Global Action
# Sophie Style

*Z Magazine,* January 2002

Cochabamba, the third-largest city in Bolivia, is best known as the "city of eternal spring." But, as Oscar Olivera, a factory laborer and spokesperson for *la Coordinadora* (the Coalition for the Defense of Water and Life) reminded us at the beginning of the third Peoples' Global Action (PGA) conference, it wasn't the pleasant climate that drew grassroots movements from all over the world to this highland city for a week in September 2001. The year before, Cochabamba became a key symbol of the struggle against global capitalism, when tens of thousands of local people took to the streets against the privatization of their water supply by the US transnational Bechtel—and won.

As a powerful and unique coalition of peasant irrigation unions, coca growers, labor activists, local professionals, young people, and street children, la Coordinadora was able to overturn the contract signed under World Bank pressure and have control of the water returned to the people of Cochabamba, although not without costs. At the third massive mobilization in April 2000, where 30,000 people shut down the city center for five days, the president sent in military units, including a sharpshooter trained at the School of Americas who gunned down a seventeen-year-old protestor. Months later, though, and spurred by their victory, Olivera says, "the water is sweet."

News of the water wars in Cochabamba spread quickly via the internet, and the web of international solidarity—which is at the heart of the PGA network—sprung immediately into action. On April 23, 2000, for example, the front three pages of the local paper in Cochabamba carried stories of a protest in New Zealand by activists known as "The Water Pressure Group" who hosed down the Bolivian consulate in Auckland from a bright red fire truck, bearing placards reading "Bolivia, the World is Watching You."

## Transnational Resistance

This exhilarating feeling of international solidarity began to dawn on me in 1997 as I sat in the blazing heat on a squatted farm in Andalucia, southern Spain. Inspired by the Zapatistas, I attended the second *encuentro* "for Humanity and Against Neoliberalism," which gathered together around 4,000 women and men from around the world—trade unionists, peasants, indigenous peoples, feminists, anarchists, ecologists, students, unemployed, fisherfolk, writers, artists, and poets. Conversations that had begun the previous year in Chiapas at the first *encuentro* were continued; people listened to each others' stories of hunger strikes, seed saving, dancing on motorways, blockading nuclear convoys, squatting land, being teargassed, and reclaiming tribal languages. In spite of vastly different contexts, we discovered that our struggles are increasingly similar in every part of the global empire, and that a new, horizontal form of solidarity is emerging.

## A Brief History Of PGA

It was immediately after this gathering, at a meeting with representatives of grassroots movements from the South and North, that the idea for PGA was born. It is hard to define exactly what PGA is. In many ways it doesn't really exist. PGA is not an organization; it has no members or constituted legal identity, no central funds, leaders, or spokespeople. Instead it is more of a tool or a fluid network for communication and coordination between diverse social movements who share a loose set of principles or "hallmarks." Even these have been continuously modified or expanded over the past three and a half years reflecting the dynamic, evolving process, which is central to the philosophy of PGA.

The hallmarks were first drafted at the launch of this worldwide network in Geneva, from February 23-25, 1998, and attended by over 300 people from seventy-one countries. A similarly eclectic international gathering took place in Bangalore, India in August 1999, home to the Karnataka State Farmers Association (KRSS) who, in Gandhian style, have cremated fields of GM cotton and dismantled Cargill's seed factories. These conferences, including this latest one in Bolivia, have been organized, at least in theory, by a rotating group of conveners drawn from all continents and social sectors, and a floating support group. Parallel to these, PGA meetings have also been organized at a regional level (South Asia, Latin America, Europe) and on specific topics (gender, Plan Colombia).

Since February 1998 then, PGA has evolved as an interconnected web of very diverse groups, with a powerful common thread of struggle and solidarity at the grassroots level. These gatherings have played a vital role in face-to-face communication and exchange of experiences, strategies, and ideas. From the G8 Summit meeting in Birmingham in 1998, which was accompanied by over sixty-five demonstrations worldwide, these have multiplied to encompass the growing list of now household names: Seattle, Prague, Quebec, Genoa.

## Delegates in Bolivia

The diverse groups that make up the PGA network are a striking aspect of the conference in Cochabamba, a richness that brought with it tensions and contradictions. Not surprisingly, the largest contingent came from Latin America. This included representatives of some of the most powerful social movements, such as the Ecuadorean peasants confederation, landless peasants in Brazil, the Zapatistas of Chiapas, and the Six Federations of the Tropics of Cochabamba. The latter group, representing over 35,000 subsistence farmer families in the tropical coca growing area of Chapare, was one of the hosts of the conference; the other was the National Federation of Domestic Workers of Bolivia (FENAETROB), who organize for the rights of domestic workers throughout the country, ninety-nine percent of whom are women. There was a strong presence of organizers from women's movements in Latin America, in particular from Colombia, Nicaragua, and Mexico, some of whom are equally active in trade unions, working on gender issues. Similarly strong was the presence of indigenous peoples or *pueblos originarios*: Quiché of Guatemala, Kuna of Panama, Mapuche of Chile and Argentina, Quechua and Aymara from the Andean region, and Quichua from Ecuador.

Many of the Brazilian and Argentinean delegates were from a new network of young, mostly urban organizations that have specifically organized around global days of action such as May 1, the Prague World Bank meeting, or around the Free Trade Area of the Americas. Equivalent in a lot of ways to these groups were those present from Europe, North America, and Australia who have mobilized in the streets of London, Prague, Quebec, Melbourne, Gothenburg, Genoa, Barcelona, and Davos. Delegates came, for example, from Ya Basta! in Italy, the Movement of Global Resistance (MRG) in Catalonia, the Swiss anti-WTO coordination, London Reclaim the Streets, and the Comité de luttes Anti-capitalistes (CLAC) from Canada. (Airline chaos stopped almost all the United States participants from coming.) Also present were ecological activists from the Rainbow Keepers in Russia and the Ukraine and a delegate from the Canadian Union of Public Employees (CUPE), the largest and one of the most progressive unions. Two delegates from Aoteroa Educators, the training branch of the intertribal Maori independence movement called Tino-Ranga-tiratanga, were involved from the start.

In spite of huge visa complications and delayed flights, a small delegation from Asia and the Pacific arrived towards the end of the meeting. From India, there were representatives of the National Alliance of People's Movements (NAPM) and BKU, the national farmers' federation. From Bangladesh, the General Secretary of the Krishok Federation of peasants and landless agricultural workers attended, as did a woman from the Aboriginal Association. One of the walls in the main meeting area was draped with banners from the Movement for National Land and Agricultural Reform from Sri Lanka (MONLAR). Among the new groups attending were three representatives of the huge Indonesian farmers federation and a representative of the Nepal peasants association, both with over 10 million members.

Since the launch of PGA, there has been a very obvious underrepresentation of social movements from both Africa and the Middle East. Unfortunately, neither of these imbalances was rectified at this conference, partly as a result of visa restrictions, but primarily due to a lack of links in these regions. However, four delegates from the new popular movements in South Africa—landless peasants, Forum Against Privatization, and urban struggles against evictions and service cut-offs—were able to make it immediately after the mobilizations at the Durban conference on racism. Other groups from Africa who have been part of the PGA process are the Ogoni and Chikoko movements in Nigeria and peasant groups in Senegal and Mozambique. Important discussions about the broadening of the PGA network in these areas are still to be had. Only a few weeks after the meeting in Cochabamba, for example, Lebanese and Palestinian organizations sent out a call to diverse groups in the Middle East to launch a grassroots antiglobalization movement, spurred by the WTO conference in Qatar.

## Criminalizing the Movement

Even in the run-up to the conference, we had been witnessing a steady build-up of new antiterrorist laws by governments worldwide that are broad enough to include protest groups such as the PGA network. This issue was already high on the agenda for discussion, but with the meeting starting only days after the suicide attacks on the World Trade Center and the Pentagon, it gained a renewed sense of urgency. The implications of these attacks on the antiglobalization movement could be felt immediately. The local and national media declared that suspected terrorists were taking part in the meeting. Interpol paid a visit to the conference site. The border was practically sealed to delegates trying to get to Cochabamba, including a busload of people from Colombia and Ecuador whose entry was denied. At the opening assembly, the Bolivian press crowded the panel, waiting for our response to the attacks.

Although no one person or group can speak for PGA, a multitude of voices from around the world expressed a sharing and identification with the sudden suffering and pain of ordinary people in the US These voices equally spoke out against the absurd use of military power against civilian populations in retaliation for these attacks and against the double standards of the US government. Many groups had a very intimate experience of the darker side of US foreign policy. Only a few hours away in the Chapare region, for example, poor peasant farmers come face to face with a US military base as part of the aggressive coca eradication program in Bolivia, much like Plan Colombia.

I found it difficult not to be overtaken by fear in this newly tense situation, but the fearlessness of those around me was overwhelming—people who are already engaged in a battle for life or death in a much more direct way than I have ever experienced. It soon became clear that the rapidly unfolding responses to the attacks only affirmed the importance and relevance of two major themes of the conference, ones that had been proposed long before that fateful September day.

## Opposition To Privatization And Militarism

The first of these themes was about strengthening campaigns against privatization and militarism. In the US and Britain, political figures have tried to justify the war on Afghanistan with revived rhetoric about economic development as a panacea, particularly in the run-up to the WTO trade negotiations in Qatar.

In the workshop on land, delegates from Brazil, Colombia, Mexico, South Africa, and Asia described the same stories of lands taken over by agribusiness, either directly or subcontracted to locals, and the subsequent escalation of landlessness, hunger, and urban slums. This rapid privatization of traditional communal lands has intensified with regional free trade agreements such as NAFTA. There was much discussion on the devastating implications of the Free Trade Area of the Americas (FTAA) and the regional development plans in South America.

Similarly, at another workshop on water, people shared stories of their struggles against World Bank-driven privatization plans in Canada, Sri Lanka, South Africa, Spain, and Bangladesh. These discussions culminated in the decision for a worldwide campaign against the privatization of the global "commons," which includes market-based "solutions" to climate change such as carbon trading. For indigenous peoples at the meeting, this was framed in terms of an all-encompassing struggle for territory and sovereignty and the right of communities to freely organize their societies, livelihoods, and relation to nature.

The discussions around a sustained campaign against militarism were only tentative, but a later meeting of many PGA delegates in Ecuador came up with some more concrete proposals. These included organizing a specific gathering on this issue, inviting movements struggling for autonomy in the context of heavy militarization in areas of strategic geopolitical importance that are rich in natural resources (for example, Afghanistan, the Andean region, Central Africa, the Middle East, East Timor, West Papua, the Balkans, Turkey, and South Asia). Broader links for this campaign will also be made with groups working against the arms industry, the prison industry, police brutality, religious fundamentalism, with antiwar groups, women's peace groups, and migrants. One of the most memorable days of the conference for most people was a trip to the heavily militarized Chapare region where the group was welcomed by over 10,000 cocaleros waving hundreds of rainbow-colored *huipil* banners, the indigenous flag of diversity.

## Decentralizing

The second major theme of the conference was a general agreement that we need to localize antiglobalization actions and decentralize the network. We had all witnessed the incredible energy and concentration of efforts in recent years at mass actions like Seattle that brought previously obscure institutions like the WTO and the G8 into the public consciousness. But the growing repression of these mobilizations, manifested in Genoa, and the cowardly retreat of the WTO to the desert of Qatar and the G8 to the remote Canadian mountains resort of Kananaskis in June 2002 has raised wider questions about where and how we organize actions.

Issues came up around the burn-out people had felt after spending up to a year planning for one or two days of actions, the increasing logistical problems of crossing borders to reach the meeting places of these summits, and the drying up of many sources of funding for antiglobalization movements. In any case, this move towards decentralized mobilizations was perfectly illustrated by the response of groups around the world to the WTO Ministerial in Qatar. Reports have come through Indymedia websites, for example, of over 120 actions in towns and cities in over forty countries between 9-13 November 2001.

These same questions also relate very closely to future international PGA conferences. It was decided in Cochabamba not to hold the fourth one for at least the next two years and, instead, to focus on regional meetings to strengthen and broaden the network at the regional and local level. Also, there were various discussions about having exchanges between movements, where one or two people would travel to another country and take part in a specific campaign with another group, learning from each others' strategies and forms of organizing. Another similar proposal was a variant of the "caravan" formula, where, for example, one participant from each continent would travel in a small group to a specific region to meet with groups and research a specific issue, and then feed back to the network as a whole.

A further proposal revolved around the idea of popular education campaigns or *consultas*, which have been used very successfully by the Zapatistas across Mexico, la Coordinadora in Cochabamba, and in Spain earlier in 2001. After two massive mobilizations, for example, 'la Coordinadora' held a popular consulta in the area served by the water company, asking people whether they wanted these services to be privatized. Fifty thousand people voted, and between ninety-four and ninety-eight percent of the people said no. The basic idea is to build coalitions of social movements in towns, cities, and villages, and together to explore creative ways of getting direct participation, feedback, and debate from a wide cross-section of society. This could be on a range of global issues (e.g., militarism, economic globalization, labor rights, immigration, the environment, women's rights, and democracy) and their implications at a local level. People were already starting to work on popular consultations in Brazil in March 2002 to coincide with Inter-American Development Bank meeting, and in Europe in 2004 during elections for the European Parliament in June.

Imagine for a moment a room full of 200 people from around thirty-five different countries, who speak about as many languages (although translations are only made between Spanish and English in the large group discussions). Some are representatives of movements with 10 million members while others are from smaller autonomous collectives. All come from a wide range of political cultures with strategies that range from working within political parties to direct action outside the system (or both).

There were moments of tension and frustration during the week, some of which raised important issues for the network. One of these, for example, touched on power relations between North and South. The role of facilitator, and with it a particularly Western-style of consensus decision making, was on balance taken on more often by people from the North, and it emerged that many from the South felt unhappy with what was seen as an obsession with time keeping and with people being interrupted in order to keep to the timetable. The problem partly stemmed from not having adequate time to agree on a process that everyone felt happy with and understood and that reflected cross-cultural differences and decision-making styles.

Another key issue was that of gender, which it was felt had been neglected as a central theme in previous meetings. A number of women also made it clear that they felt that sexism was still very much a problem within the movement and that this has to be addressed.

By far the best part of the week in Cochabamba were the informal conversations, one-to-one or in small groups, over mealtimes or in the evenings over the local Bolivian home-brew *chicha*. It was here that we discovered the most about each other in the midst of laughing, singing, and dancing together. "What actually came out the meeting?" I'm often asked. I think above all it has strengthened connections between people and the movements they are part of, encouraging real horizontal solidarity and renewed hope in a time of many shadows. Above all, we made new friends.

For more information on PGA see www.agp.org.

# Anti-Europeanism and Anti-Americanism
# Michael Hardt

5 February 2003

There is a new anti-Europeanism in Washington. The United States, of course, has a long tradition of ideological conflict with Europe. The old anti-Europeanism generally protested against the overwhelming power of European states, their arrogance, and their imperialist endeavors. Today, however, the relationship is reversed. The new anti-Europeanism is based on the US position of power and it protests instead against European states failing to yield to its power and support its projects.

The most immediate issue for Washington is the European lack of support for the US plans for war on Iraq. And Washington's primary strategy in recent weeks is to divide and conquer. On one hand, Secretary of Defense Rumsfeld, with his usual brazen condescension, calls those European nations who question the US project, primarily France and Germany, "the old Europe," dismissing them as unimportant. The recent *Wall Street Journal* letter of support for the US war effort, on the other hand, signed by Blair, Berlusconi, and Aznar, poses the other side of the divide.

In a broader framework, the entire project of US unilateralism, which extends well beyond this coming war with Iraq, is itself necessarily anti-European. The unilateralists in Washington are threatened by the idea that Europe or any other cluster of states could compete with its power on equal terms. (The rising value of the euro with respect to the dollar contributes, of course, to the perception of two potentially equal and competing power blocs.) Bush, Rumsfeld, and their ilk will not accept the possibility of a bipolar world. They left that behind with the cold war! Any threats to the unipolar order must be dismissed or destroyed. Washington's new anti-Europeanism is really an expression of their unilateralist project.

Corresponding in part to the new US anti-Europeanism, there is today in Europe and across the world a growing anti-Americanism (or really anti-USism). In particular, the coordinated protests on February 15 against the war will be animated by various kinds of anti-Americanism—and that is inevitable. The US government has left no doubt that it is the author of this war and so protest against the war must, inevitably, be also protest against the United States.

This anti-Americanism, however, although certainly justifiable, is a trap. The problem is not only that it tends to create an overly unified and homogeneous view of the United States, obscuring the wide margins of dissent in the nation. The real problem is that, mirroring the new US anti-Europeanism, it tends to reinforce the notion that our political alternatives rest on the major nations and power blocs. It contributes to the impression, for instance, that the leaders of Europe represent our primary political path— the moral, multilateralist alternative to the bellicose, unilateralist Americans. This anti-Americanism of the antiwar movements tends to close down the horizons of our political imagination and limit us to a bipolar (or worse, nationalist) view of the world.

The globalization protest movements were far superior to the antiwar movements in this regard. They not only recognized the complex and plural nature of the forces that dominate capitalist globalization today—the dominant nation-states, certainly, but also the International Monetary Fund, the World Trade Organization, the major corporations, and so forth—but they imagined an alternative, democratic globalization consisting of plural exchanges across national and regional borders based on equality and freedom. One of the great achievements of the globalization protest movements, in other words, has been to put an end to thinking of politics as a contest among nations or blocs of nations. Internationalism has been reinvented as a politics of global network connections with a global vision of possible futures. In this context anti-Europeanism and anti-Americanism no longer make sense.

It is unfortunate but inevitable that much of the energies that had been active in the globalization protests have now at least temporarily been redirected against the war. We need to oppose this war but we must also look beyond it and avoid being drawn into the trap of its narrow political logic. While opposing the war we must maintain the expansive political vision and open horizons that the globalization movements have achieved. We can leave to Bush, Chirac, Blair, and Schröder the tired game of anti-Europeanism and anti-Americanism.

# Interview with Barbara Epstein
# Douglas Bevington & Chris Dixon

*With the Seattle WTO protests, we saw the growth of widespread mass actions in the US. Yet in the wake of September 11, 2001 many stepped back from mass action. Recently, however, we have seen the return of mass protests in opposition to the war against Iraq. What kinds of connections and continuities do you see between the movement challenging capitalist globalization and the antiwar movement?*

Since the fall of 2002, in the US, much of the activist, radical current within the antiglobalization movement has shifted into the antiwar movement. I suspect that the same has happened elsewhere as well. If the US continues on its present course of attempting to establish itself as unchallenged world power, it seems likely that this will not be a temporary detour for the antiglobalization, or anti-neoliberal, movement. One of the debates within the anti-neoliberal movement has revolved around the question of whether transnational capital is truly transnational or not, what the relationship is between transnational economic power and particular nation states, especially the US. Michael Hardt and Antonio Negri's book *Empire* argues that the phase of US imperialism is over and we are now in a Foucaultian phase in which power is everywhere. Hardt and Negri refer to this phase as that of "empire" and suggest that spontaneous mass mobilizations could transform it into a worldwide system of decentralized networks.

I think it has become clear that the US remains the center of power in the world. On the basis of US economic and military power, the Bush Administration aspires to world dominance. This problem is not likely to go away soon. It certainly would be best for the US and the world if Bush were defeated in the next election, but even if this were to happen US imperialism would not go away: we would only have a milder, less aggressive version of it. In its first few years the movement challenging capitalist globalization focused on the power of the transnational corporations and their ability to dominate international organizations such as the World Trade Organization, the World Bank, the International Monetary Fund. These issues are still important but it is the US that poses the greatest threat to peace, international stability, and democratic rights in the US and elsewhere. Challenging capitalist globalization continues to be important, but I think it has become clear that it is so intertwined with US imperialism that the two issues have to be addressed together. The Bush Administration will undoubtedly continue its efforts to extend US power, and these efforts are likely to be a major focus of activists concerned with capitalist globalization.

People outside the US tend to be much more aware of the dangers posed by US imperialism than the US public is. But a movement inside the US would have more leverage than movements outside it. So it's extremely important that we try to build a strong movement against US aspirations toward world power. Such a movement has to have a radical edge, involving people willing to take risks by expressing views that challenge mainstream opinions and by engaging in civil disobedience and possibly going to jail. Such a movement also has to have room for people who oppose US power grab but who are not willing to take such risks, at least, not yet. The role of radicals in the movement involves not just doing the riskiest things, but providing the kind of leadership that will make it possible for a broad movement to develop, in which people with different kinds of commitments, perspectives, willingness to take risks, can work together. Since 9/11 the right has gained enormous public support based on its claim that it can make the US secure. On the whole the left has ignored the issue of security. This isn't a good idea. We have to address the issue of security. We can begin by pointing out that as long as the US behaves like a bully toward the rest of the world there can be no security. We could then have a discussion of what the US should stop doing and also what positive steps it might take to promote peace. Such steps would surely include a commitment to no more preemptive, unprovoked military strikes, obeying international laws, respecting the authority of the United Nations, ceasing to support aggressive military actions on the part of US allies (Israel, for instance), and beginning to reverse global discrepancies of wealth and power.

*In your recent talks, you have highlighted the problematic role of socialist sectarian organizations in the US antiwar movement. Could you elaborate on this concern?*

Left-wing sects played a large role in the recent antiwar movement. The two major organizations sponsoring the large antiwar demonstrations were United for Peace and Justice, a broad, nonsectarian coalition of groups that opposed the war; and International ANSWER (Act Now to Stop War and End Racism), which was organized by the highly sectarian Workers' World Party (WWP). Other left-wing sects as well played roles in the antiwar movement. In the San Francisco Bay Area, the February 16, 2003 demonstration was sponsored by four groups or coalitions, which included ANSWER and NION (Not in Our Name, a group organized by the Revolutionary Communist Party).

The large role of such groups in the antiwar movement had to do with the weakness of the peace movement and the virtual nonexistence of a nonsectarian socialist left in the US. The first Gulf War, in 1991, demoralized the US peace movement. There was a great deal of public dissent over that war before it broke out, and many antiwar activists hoped that it would be possible to prevent it from starting, or, once it began, hoped to build a strong enough movement to stop it. But almost as soon as the war began the media, and public opinion, shifted overwhelmingly to support of the war. The quick US victory, and the near absence of protest after the first few weeks of the war, constituted a major defeat for the antiwar movement.

During the '90s both the peace movement and the socialist left, in the US, were very weak. At the end of the decade the antiglobalization movement seemed to promise a revival of left protest, but in the wake of September 11, 2001, it too pulled back. The result was that when the Bush administration began warming up to attack Iraq, the first to respond were Workers' World Party activists; they created ANSWER out of the International Action Center (another WWP project). ANSWER sponsored the first large antiwar demonstrations on both coasts, and remained a major force in the antiwar movement even after the organization of United for Peace and Justice, which drew together peace groups, churches, trade unions, and many other groups.

ANSWER performed an important service for the antiwar movement by mobilizing large demonstrations when no other organization was ready to do this. But ANSWER's prominent role in the movement also caused problems. The Workers' World Party is a Trotskyist group which, at the time of the Sino-Soviet split, supported the Chinese Communist Party not only in its rejection of the Soviet policy of peaceful coexistence, but also in its identification with the legacy of Stalin. Since then the WWP has supported other dictators including Milosevic and Saddam Hussein. The vast majority of those who attended antiwar rallies sponsored by ANSWER probably had no idea of the political positions taken by the activists at the center of ANSWER. But they were subjected to the speeches given by many of those whom ANSWER activists chose for their rallies. Many protesters were dismayed by the angry, haranguing style of these speeches, and by the large number who spoke on issues that had little to do with the war in Iraq, and which in some cases seemed much more likely to divide than unite opponents of the war.

The more space sects take up within a movement, the less room there is for the development of the broad, democratic organizations that a movement needs in order to sustain activity beyond immediate crises. There was a kind of division of labor during the protests against an attack on Iraq: many of the demonstrations were organized by sects; those opposing the war attended the demonstrations, but most didn't even think of joining any ongoing antiwar organizations. As long as opposing the war simply meant going to demonstrations, most people didn't care very much about the political positions held by those who organized the demonstrations, beyond the fact that they opposed war on Iraq. The political positions of those taking the lead in organizing demonstrations were much more of an issue in regard to forming coalitions of organizations to sponsor those demonstrations, and for the prospects of forming an ongoing antiwar organization. United for Peace and Justice was formed by antiwar activists concerned about the limitations of ANSWER. It became a broad coalition of some 200 organizations that opposed the war, including churches, trade unions, social justice and peace organizations. But due to the pressures of mobilizing demonstrations, and no doubt the difficulties of functioning in an environment already dominated by sects, United for Peace and Justice did not take steps toward forming a broad based antiwar organization during the war, but is now moving in that direction.

Traditionally sects have been understood, on the left, as small organizations with rigid and doctrinaire views, organizations whose members regard themselves as possessors of truths which others fail to understand, or understand only incompletely. Some sects do have some ideas that are worth taking seriously, but many hold views that will not withstand the light of day, and are sustained within the sect only as a result of the continual reinforcement of these ideas by members of the sect. Sectarian thinking is not necessarily limited to small, isolated organizations. Many communists, for instance, believed that the Soviet Union was a democratic society long past the time when it had become obvious to virtually everyone else that this was not the case. The issue is not so much the size of the organization in question but the degree to which it becomes self-enclosed and self-justifying.

The more confusing the world becomes, and the more the left is thrown on the defensive, the more attractive sectarian thinking becomes, because it creates at least a temporary refuge from uncertainty and turns a sense of defeat into a belief in one's moral or intellectual superiority. In the late seventies, as many of the mass movements of the sixties dwindled, some sects sustained themselves. But they were built on the willingness of members to refrain from questioning beliefs whose distance from reality was becoming more and more apparent. Ultimately many of these sects exploded. Some, like the sects that played a role in the antiwar movement, have sustained themselves to the present. Sectarian dynamics are not limited to organizations. There is a lot of sectarian thinking in the academy, especially in academic currents associated with the left. For a time poststructuralism provided the vocabulary for what amounted to a sectarian set of beliefs. "Political correctness" refers, in a half-joking way, to the related problem, on the left, of seeing the world through ideological categories designed to give one the moral high ground. The problem with sectarianism is that it convinces only those who are inside the circles that it creates, and even they are likely to eventually lose patience with it. Many people who join sects become burnt out and flee from left activity as a whole. It seems to me best to acknowledge that we don't have all the answers. We can argue for what we are reasonably certain of (for instance, that US aggression is sure to create enemies) while recognizing that no ideology, left wing or otherwise, can be counted upon to prevent mistakes.

*What other kinds of fissures and challenges do you see facing the antiwar movement?*

The antiwar movement was lopsided in relation to both race and age. The movement was overwhelmingly white, despite the fact that African Americans in particular opposed the war in very large numbers. Figures varied, but on the whole African Americans tended to oppose the war in about the same percentages as whites supported it. At one point, according to polls, two-thirds of African Americans opposed the war while two-thirds of whites supported it. The relatively low participation of African Americans and other people of color in the antiwar movement was the movement's most glaring weakness. Whatever ongoing movement emerges to oppose US efforts toward world power is likely to be similarly unbalanced in relation to race. Activists can rectify this balance to some degree through hard work: outreach to organizations and communities of African Americans and other groups of color, efforts to address whatever obstacles there may be inside the movement to the participation of African Americans and other people of color. But it would be a mistake to think that such efforts can resolve the problem overnight.

The racial imbalance of the antiwar movement was rooted in the deep racial divisions that exist in US society. Most African Americans are probably not going to rush into a predominately white movement under any conditions. The danger is that activists will regard the movement's racial imbalance as the fault of someone in the movement and throw accusations of racism at each other. There are very few progressives who are racists in the conventional sense of that term: people who believe that whites are superior to people of color. White progressives can be ignorant or insensitive, but these issues are not usefully addressed by accusations of racism. (The same goes for accusations of anti-Semitism: there is no quicker way to make progressive non-Jews uncomfortable around Jews and, perhaps, reluctant to work with them, than by throwing around accusations of anti-Semitism.) In addition to putting effort into outreach, antiwar activists should encourage autonomous antiwar activity within the African American community, as within other communities.

The antiwar movement was also lopsided in relation to age, though not as badly as in relation to race. There were large numbers of young people in antiwar protests; young people were particularly important in civil disobedience actions. It was a good thing that older people were also involved in the movement. One of the weaknesses of the movement against the war in Vietnam was young people dominated it to such a degree that older people often had a hard time finding a way of participating in it. But it would have been better if there had been more young people in the recent antiwar movement. The young people who participated in it were a small fraction of their generation. Most campuses remained relatively quiet. Polls reported that people in their twenties and early thirties were more likely to support the war than any other age group. One reason that the young generation as a whole did not turn against the war was that there was no draft. Beyond this, the generation now in their twenties grew up in a period in which conservative ideas have been ascendant and in which, for most people, collective action for social change has been a dim memory. The young people who formed the anti-corporate globalization movement rebelled against these values. But most young people have been affected to one degree or another by the dominant values of the last quarter century.

*As a historian of social movements in the US, do you see parallels between the conditions facing movements currently and those of other times in history? What would you suggest we can learn from such parallels and the ways in which movements responded in the past?*

I see parallels between the rise of fascism in the late twenties and early thirties and the readiness of the Bush administration to attack other nations in order to extend its own power, in the process breaking international laws and disregarding world opinion. Some people on the left worry about a drift toward fascism internally. I am concerned about domestic repression and the erosion of civil liberties, but there are many obstacles to imposing anything that could be called fascism in the US. Internationally, however, the parallels between the behavior of the US and the behavior of Nazi Germany are hard to ignore.

The rise of fascism transformed radical politics in the US and elsewhere in the thirties. It led to a shift away from a politics oriented toward revolution toward a politics oriented toward the defense and extension of democracy. In 1928 the Communist International had predicted a period of worldwide crisis in capitalism which would make socialist revolutions possible. Communists were instructed to leave liberal or socialist-led trade unions and organize explicitly revolutionary unions instead. Communists were encouraged to denounce liberals and socialists. In the US, the revolutionary orientation of what was called "the Third Period" also had a more positive side. Breaking away from the AF of L enabled communists to organize unions along industrial lines. Focusing on the possibility of revolution encouraged communists to organize those most sharply affected by the depression, blacks and the unemployed.

By the mid-thirties, however, it had become clear that socialist revolution was not on the immediate agenda, that there was nothing communists could do that would bring it about, and that continued insistence upon it would only marginalize communist parties. The rise of fascism, not in the US but internationally, required opposition from all those opposed to it, not just communists but also the socialists and liberals whom Communists had been instructed to denounce as part of the revolutionary orientation of the early thirties. In 1935, the Communist International shifted from the policy of the Third Period to that of the Popular Front against fascism. This meant shifting the focus of communist activity from promoting revolution to creating alliances against fascism and for democracy. It was this shift that enabled communists, in the US and elsewhere, to play leading roles in progressive movements with mass constituencies.

The Soviets promoted the shift from the Third Period to the Popular Front for its own reasons. Realizing that Soviet Union was the primary target of Nazi aggression, the Soviets wanted an alliance with the western European powers. But the Soviets' concerns about the danger of fascism coincided with the concerns of socialists and liberals elsewhere in the world. In the US, communists were shifting away from the sectarian politics of the early thirties, towards more mainstream or popular efforts, even before the Communist International changed its line.

The left might take a lesson from the shift that the communist movement made in response to the rise of fascism in the thirties. We are again facing a very serious threat from a resurgent extreme right, this time centered in the US. Whether we call it fascism or not, is not the issue. The left cannot defeat it alone, but neither can liberals, who are likely to focus all their efforts on replacing Bush by someone only slightly better. They are unlikely to raise such issues as the growing disparity of wealth and power between the US and the rest of the world, and the influence of the corporations that seek to extend that discrepancy, perhaps through more subtle policies than those pursued by the Bush administration.

*What relations do you see between academics and current movements? How useful is contemporary scholarship and theory to these movements?*

There are probably more people with progressive opinions in the academy than in any other single institution in the US. As mainstream politics in the US shifts toward the right, it is important to have spaces where left and progressive discussion can take place. There are many universities that help to provide these. But progressive thinking in the academy tends to be disconnected from action; faculty, in particular, are often reluctant to do anything that might be seen as rocking the boat. Two issues that might be good places to start in reversing this trend are the impact of the Patriot Act on the universities (along with the influence of the Department for Homeland Security more generally) and in university involvement in military research, especially that related to nuclear weapons.

In regard to contemporary scholarship and theory relating to social movements: there is a long tradition of valuable studies of social movements; excellent histories and sociological studies continue to appear. Unfortunately the field of theory of social movements is not doing as well. Much current theory is so detached from the concerns of social movements that it is of little if any use to those engaged in these movements. This is a pity because activists need theory, not only about society and how to change it, but also about how social movements function and how progressive movements can best be built. In the past productive theories of social change have come mostly from those at least to some degree involved in efforts toward social change. Good theoretical work on social movements seems most likely to come from those with at least one foot in social movements.

*In your article "Anarchism and the Anti-Globalization Movement," in the September 2001 issue of* Monthly Review, *you write: "If a new paradigm of the left emerges from the struggle against neo-liberalism and the transnational corporate order, it is likely to include elements of anarchist sensibility as well as of Marxist analysis." Do you see such a paradigm emerging and, if so, how do you see it mixing these elements?*

Many anarchists and socialists are more open toward at least some of each other's positions than they might have been in the past. Anarchists in the anti-corporate globalization movement tend to be very critical of capitalism and open to a Marxist analysis of class. Most socialists and Marxists are more skeptical about the state than many of their predecessors were. Few believe that seizing the state will in and of itself solve very many problems. But major differences between socialists and anarchists remain, over such issues as the usefulness of electoral activity in the present, and the shape of a future non-capitalist society. So far there is no common paradigm.

*What would you say are necessary elements for building a vibrant left in the US?*

The Communist Party, in the thirties, and the New Left, in the sixties, gained audiences and inspired people to action because they named problems that were central and obvious but which were not supposed to be publicly acknowledged. The Communist Party pointed out that the functioning of the economy could not be left to the capitalists, or even to a state willing to act only on behalf of the capitalists, but required the intervention of a state acting on behalf of ordinary people. Communists also pointed out that Nazi aggression was a threat to the rest of the world, and had to be stopped, long before it was considered politically acceptable to say this. The New Left pointed out that the US, which claimed to lead the forces of peace and democracy, violated the latter by its support of racism at home and the former by its actions in Vietnam. The left has an equally clear and compelling message today: by acting as the world's bully, the US threatens peace, democracy, the natural environment, and possibly the survival of the human race. The discrepancy of wealth and power between the US and the rest of the world should not be extended or defended, but undone.

The left too often weakens this clear and compelling message by engaging in actions, and using language, that look and sound to anyone outside the left like those of a cult. Too many people on the left understand politics as a public expression of one's feelings or one's moral sensibility rather than as an effort to bring about change. At its extreme, this can lead to an equation of radicalism with the violent expression of rage. Too many people on the left confuse left discourse with dogmatism, and think that being a radical means imposing a set of ideological frames on reality, acknowledging whatever seems to fit those frames and leaving out what seems not to. The problem of "political correctness" or "the language police" is real, and undermines the potential influence and attractiveness of the left.

The left also has a problem of credibility based on the dismal failure of socialist revolution in terms of democracy and basic human rights, in the Soviet Union and elsewhere. It seems to me crucial that the left should identify itself with both these values, and behave in ways in accord with them. This means, among other things, that debate inside the left, while it can be sharp, has to take place in ways that are considerate and respectful. A culture has to be promoted in which differences are addressed by examining them, not by denunciation, implicit threats of ostracism, or other forms of bullying. In the past, movements of the left have grown not only due to the appeal of the positions that they took, but because people found life inside these movements more fulfilling than life outside them.

# Part IV:
# Facts on the Ground—The Hidden Topography of Revolt

# Why Not Show Off About the Best Things

## A Few Quick Notes on Social Conflict in Italy and the Metaphors Used to Describe It

# Wu Ming

December 1, 2002

> *A match used to show off like this: I'm able to set a barn on fire! I can set fire to a petrol tank, the seat of a ministry, an Etruscan museum, whatever! Why not just say you're able to light the gas and boil the soup? We always show off about the worst things.*
> —Gianni Rodari, "Minimal Fables"

Some people have called the Italian insurgence of 2000-02 *la primavera dei movimenti*, the springtime of movements. That is also the title of a video documentary that was sold in newsstands enclosed with *L'Unità* daily paper.

In 1969 the biggest struggles of factory workers were described as *autunno caldo*, the hot autumn. Recently, it's become quite normal to hear such comments as: "It's like the hot autumn!" or "It's the hot autumn again!."

Social conflict is endemic and "natural," thus it is quite appropriate to use seasonal metaphors to describe it. Nobody can deny that Italy is living in a new, hot season of struggle and social turmoil. Conflict is multilayered and manifold: there is a "molar" aspect related to huge mass mobilization, involving the biggest general strikes in Europe and the biggest political demonstrations ever. Perhaps more important, there is a "molecular" aspect, related to everyday activism, hacktivism, guerrilla communications and the building of direct democracy—social forums at municipal and regional levels, independent media projects springing up like mushrooms, the hard battle on copyright and intellectual property and so on.

It is impossible to give a full account of what is going on, and I won't even try. I am neither a political theorist nor a social scientist. I am a storyteller. I belong to a permanent workshop on genre fiction and popular culture. Our stance on the Italian social movements stems from that: we are interested in "mythopoesis," i.e. the social process of constructing myths, by which we do not mean "false stories," but rather stories that are told and shared, re-told and manipulated, by a vast and multifarious community, stories that may give shape to some kind of ritual, some sense of continuity between what we do and what other people did in the past. A tradition: in Latin the verb *tradere* simply meant "to hand down something," it did not entail any narrow-mindedness, conservatism, or forced respect for the past.

Revolutions and radical movements have always found and told their own myths. They often got trapped in the iron cages of their own myths: their traditions and rituals became alienating, the continuity between past and present was imposed on the people instead of being proposed.

Radicals of all ages overreacted to that situation by becoming iconoclastic, by trying to "de-mythologize" the imagery and discourse of the movement. By doing that, they simply replaced one alienating imagery with another. Iconoclasty soon became a new iconophilia. The pro-situs who adore St. Guy of Paris are only one of the most striking examples of this.[1] As a consequence, misery and impotence rule, bitter nihilism and defeatism replace theory, and fools rush into the nearest dead-end street (primitivism, technophobia etc.).

Myths are necessary. We couldn't live together without stories to tell and listen to, without "heroes" whose example we can follow or reject. Our language, our memories, our imagination, and our need of forming communities are the things that make us human beings, and stories keep them all together. There is no way we can get rid of myths, and why the fuck should we? Instead of wasting our time listening to some bullshitter who poses as the most radical of all, we ought to understand the way actual social movements want to fulfill their need for myths and mythologies, and help them keep mythologies lively, flexible and in motion.

As far as this kind of experimentation (radical "mythopoesis") is concerned, Italy has always been an exciting laboratory. For many historical and social reasons, the Italian social movements were able to emerge as multitudes of people describing themselves through an endless, lively flow of tales, using those tales as weapons in order to impose a new imagery from the grassroots. When we talk about "myths", we mean stories that are "tangible," made of flesh, blood, and shit. As we tried to explain several times to people who live in other countries, "mythopoesis" is what enriches the Italian movements.

## Italy from a Bird's Eye View

Not even Italians are able to fully understand Italy's political history, because we are talking about total chaos, mayhem, black operations by the intelligence [actually, counterinsurgence] services, and almost constant rioting in the streets. Italy was one of the most important outposts of the cold war, because it bordered with Yugoslavia, had the most powerful and influential Communist Party in the Western hemisphere (mainly because communists had led the armed resistance and helped kick the Nazis out of the country) and was (nay, still is) at the center of the Mediterranean Sea, therefore "dangerously" close to Libya, the Middle East, and so on. Hidden powers of all sorts fought dirty wars in this country since the fall of the Fascist regime. In 1948 the CIA and the Vatican did all they could to make the Christian Democrat Party win the national election; they even staged "appearances" of the Virgin Mary all across southern Italy. It goes without saying that Our Lady warned people to vote against the People's Front [the coalition of socialists and communists].

That was the beginning of the so-called "K Factor," which meant the Italian Communist Party (PCI) and its allies had to be kept out of national government, in spite of getting more than the thirty percent of votes (and keeping them well into the 1980's).

The PCI was not an uptight Stalinist party, or rather, it had unmistakable Stalinist features, but it also was a popular party that shared some features with North-European social democracy and based its politics upon "cultural hegemony," a concept devised by the party's founder Antonio Gramsci, one of the most brilliant and inspirational Marxist thinkers of the Twentieth-Century, who died in a Fascist penitentiary in 1937. The PCI, unlike its brother parties in Western Europe, tugged sharply at the umbilical cord and got ever more independent of the USSR. This process started in the late 1960's and ended in 1982 with what became known as *lo strappo*, the tearing.

At least one-third of the country, including my native region Emilia Romagna, whose capital is Bologna, had communist local administrations. The biggest Italian trade union, CGIL [Italian General Federation of Labour, which still has a membership of five million workers], was very close to the PCI. Everything that happened in Italy in the past fifity years had to do with America's necessity to "tame" the left, the unions, and the movements. The US kept in office a ludicrously corrupted Christian Democrat government, which was continually thrown into legitimacy crises because of scandals, strikes, and mutual back-stabbing within the coalitions.

In the summer of 1960 the situation had grown so unstable that the Christian Democrats endeavored to prop up their government by involving the Italian Social Movement, i.e. the neo-fascist party. As a consequence, riots flared up in many cities, especially in Genoa, where young workers fought the police and prevented the fascists from holding their party congress in a town that was awarded with the gold medal of resistance. The prime minister Fernando Tambroni ordered the police to fire. Several demonstrators were injured and killed in Reggio Emilia and Licata. Tambroni was forced to resign and was replaced by a less reactionary premier. Since striped t-shirts were in fashion among the youth and all the Genoa rioters happened to wear them, that battle made history as "the revolt of striped t-shirts." As to the political situation, it continued to be very unstable:

from 1948 to 1989 Italy changed prime ministers about fifty times.

The most difficult times were after the hot autumn, when incredibly huge and radical mass mobilizations faced the fiercest repression by the powers-that-be. A brief history of this is in the Introduction to Luther Blissett's essay, "Enemies of the State." The 1969-80 campaign of black operations against the left—the so-called "strategy of tension"—was possibly the darkest period for Italian public life.

Because of general and unstoppable corruption, the whole political system sort of "collapsed" in the early nineties, when the amount of scandals and investigations piled up out of sight and the ruling class understood that a political change could not be delayed. The Christian Democrats, the "socialists" (which actually had become a right-wing party, and the most corrupted of all) and all the major parties were beheaded and then disbanded.

Silvio Berlusconi, whom corruption and political alliances had turned into one of the biggest tycoons, was running the risk of being thrown to jail, thus he decided to build a big political machine and take the field directly. He started to support and fund the old Italian Social Movement (i.e. the old-fashioned fascist party), the only right-wing party untouched by the campaign for "clean hands" (mainly because it always was too dirty to be involved in any level of government). The fascists put some make-up on their ugly faces and became Alleanza Nazionale, which describes itself as a "center-right conservative party," but actually little has changed in their ideological DNA.

Berlusconi and his gang won the national election for the first time in 1994, but that administration was brought down by a general strike less than six months later. The government was replaced by a *governo dei tecnici*, a temporary coalition formed mainly by non-professional staff, like economists, social scientists, professors, and businessmen. In April 1996 a center-left coalition called "the Olive Tree" defeated Berlusconi's coalition and governed the country until Berlusconi used all his wealth and any kind of dirty tricks to win again in 2001.

The current government is a bunch of mafiosi, corporate managers, lawyers of the Mob, racists, neofascists, old-time fascists, "postfascists," and every other brand of right-wingers and nutters. The majority of the Italian population never ceased to share this view. We ought to keep in mind that Berlusconi won the election also thanks to a somewhat tricky law, as well as the ineptitude of the other coalition. As a matter of fact, the majority of voters didn't choose the rightwing. This is one of the reasons why, only a few months later, the government was already surrounded by dissent, social conflict, workers' strikes, and the rise of a new leftist movement from the grassroots of society.

Actually, "resistance" preceded Berlusconi's take-over: it can be traced back to the legendary "Battle of Seattle," 30 November 1999. That was a very inspirational event.

When Berlusconi won the election, Italian society was already seething with big demonstrations, meetings everywhere, clashes with the police and so on. What happens in Italy is certainly peculiar, but it is also linked with a planetary struggle against neoliberal warmongering capitalism and the US iron heel.

The government (and the forces behind it) tried a blind counter-insurgence strategy in Genoa during the G8 summit (July 2001), where the *carabinieri* (the military police) murdered Carlo Giuliani, a twenty-three-year-old demonstrator, beat the shit out of marchers, and tortured several of them in police stations. That was a boomerang, for it didn't stop the growth of the movement, and the 300,000 demonstrators of Genoa became the 400,000 of the Perugia-Assisi march against the war on Afghanistan. Then three million people took part in the biggest demonstration in European history (Rome, 23 March 2002, I was there, and it was absolutely amazing!) and twenty million people joined the general strike on April 16, to which some hidden power tried to respond by reviving the old "strategy of tension": mysterious murders, bombings, and death threats started to hit the headlines and fill the TV news. However, it will take more than that to stop the shoulder push.

## The Shoulder Push

21 July 2001, Genoa: The day after the police murder of Carlo Giuliani, a few dozen thousand activists were caught in a mousetrap but the multitudes came to rescue them. Three hundred thousand people of all kinds marched to challenge police repression.

14 October 2001, Perugia: Half a million people marched for thirty-three kilometers against Italian involvement in the imperial war on the Afghanistan populace.

10 November 2001, Rome: One hundred thousand people demonstrated again against the war.

23 March 2002, Rome: Three million people marched against the Berlusconi government. The biggest demo I ever saw. The biggest "anybody" saw, I guess.

16 April 2002, all across Italy: The general strike to stop the government attack on workers' rights was unbelievably successful: ninety-eight percent of industrial workers walked out and filled the streets and squares of every city.

20 July 2002, Genoa: In the first anniversary of Carlo Giuliani's death, about fifteen hundred thousand people gathered in town and proved that the movement is alive and kicking.

14 September 2002, Rome: more than half a million people demonstrated against Berlusconi's attempt at passing laws (on the appointment of judges and internationa) judicial inquiries] that make impossible his prosecution (for corruption, counterfeited balance, negotiations with the mob and so on).

18 October 2002, all across Italy: A further general strike, although it was promoted only by the left-wing unions, almost equalled the success of the previous one.

6-10 November 2002, Florence: Despite the fact that the corporate media spread moral panic about riots and vandalism, the European Social Forum was a big success. After four days of overcrowded meetings and conferences, almost one million people demonstrated against neoliberalism and the plans of preventive war on Iraq.

November-December 2002, all across Italy: FIAT (the biggest Italian automobile firm) went bankrupt and decided to sack thousands of workers all over the country, both white and blue collars. The workers alone were supposed to take it upon themselves to save the bosses and managers from the ruinous decadence of unsustainable development. The unions went to war, there were strikes and demonstrations everyday, plants were occupied to the bitter end. Sicilian FIAT employees even started Telefabbrica, a pirate TV station to inform the public of their reasons.

All this turmoil is sometimes called *la Spallata*, the shoulder push. That's because Silvio Berlusconi himself, on March 2, gave vent to his feelings by stating: "All around me there is a worrying wish to overthrow the government by pushing with the shoulder. The wind of Jacobin hatred is blowing, I see demonstrators shouting insults and slandering me. Those under the illusion that demonstrators and magistrates can give us the final shoulder push must know that this shall not take place in Italy, because the majority of citizens are able to tell love from hate" (see *Corriere della Sera* of 3 March 2002).

To tell the truth, the right-wing, mafia-fuelled Berlusconi regime has started to feel the pressure and get extremely nervous. In June 2002 the government lost the "midterm" election of governors and mayors: the rightwing even lost in Verona, the most right-wing and racist city in the whole country. The coalition is slowly decomposing, the moderate Center Union Party is seriously thinking of slipping away, and internal conflicts take place continuously (since the beginning of its mandate, the government had to get rid of two ministers and two vice-ministers). There have been too many scandals and court trials, too many mistakes and arrogant statements. There is too much inflation and economic depression, as well as too much obligingness towards the US and, what's more, too much class war: ever more sectors of the *confindustria* (the powerful Italian Manufacturers Association) are beginning to regard this government as highly dysfunctional from a capitalist point of view. Berlusconi is losing all his popularity.

## Sedimentation

People use to ask me: "How can there be such a turmoil in Italy, if the national media is under complete control of Berlusconi?" Well, there is much more communication in heaven and earth than is dreamt of in your theory. Of course Berlusconi owns Mediaset, the private television network, and now controls RAI, the public television network. This can't help but "foster" self-censorship among journalists, although not everyone complies. However, the movement and grassroots opposition rely especially on the Internet, independent radio stations, pirate TV neighbourhood channels, real time "oral history" and the existence of a big alternative public space.

An alternative public space began to form in the second half of the Seventies, when the first *centri sociali* were occupied (Milan's Leoncavallo, still one of the biggest in the country, was occupied in 1975). There are more than a hundred *centri sociali* in Italy, most of them are former Fordist-Taylorist factories or warehouses. They are usually managed by leftists, anarchists, and/or members of urban countercultures. Social centers are not mere "squats": some of them are nearly as big as little villages and contain concert halls, radio stations, even community kindergartens. You happen to enter a room and bump into a theater company or a big brass band rehearsing; in the next room you may find people training in capoeira or ethnic vocals; you may attend the presentation of a book, a video festival, a free jazz jam session, a chill-out DJ set or the weekly meeting of the local Social Forum. There are about twenty places like this in Rome. Since the 1970's the social centers have been one of the main infrastructures of the "movement of movements": during the 1980's they were the epicenters of punk culture and gave hospitality to groups and individuals challenging repression, yuppie culture, and institutionalized boredom; in the early 1990's they were affected by cyberpunk culture, started to host national meetings of hackers (and later hosted those that would become the Indymedia collectives), then they hosted raves etc. They accompanied any transformation in youth culture and radical politics.

In the past ten years, in some of the most important Italian cities, the social centers won their battle against repression and got rid of any sword of Damocles: they forced city councils to acknowledge their existence and now they are "legal" (which caused a lively and polemic debate between the activists who pursued "mass illegality" and the ones whom were accused of being "reformist"). However, in many cases repression goes on, and some places are still provocatively searched or even vacated by force, and activists keep facing court trials.

The social centers can thrive on Italy's peculiar cultural atmosphere. As one "Luther Blissett" wrote a few years ago, peculiar events in Italian history blurred the distinctions between "serious culture" and "popular culture" long before the debate on postmodernism, trash culture, etc. Since 1945, conforming to the Gramscian strategy of cultural hegemony, the *Partito Comunista* placed the right men in such "right places" as cinema, academic circles, and publishing houses. These people loosely followed the policy of the party until 1968, when some of them backed the new class struggle as *engagés* intellectuals. During the 1960's, cultural studies were partially emancipated from elitist snobbery after the publication of Umberto Eco's *Apocalittici e integrati*, which investigated the way intellectuals would look at mass culture products (comics, TV etc). In the following decade, the PCI definitively sided with the state: socialdemocracy chose not to fill the empty spaces of "youth culture" and "alternative" behaviors, which became a land of conquest for radicals. The 1977 students' movement roused interest in "counterculture": punk and the world of zines became subjects of media investigation and cultural studies. At the same time, the military repression of the movement forced many comrades to go "underground" in the media and cultural institutions. ("Mondo Mitomane 1994-96").

You can find people who have an experience in activism and/or countercultures even working in the official, mainstream media. Some of them "conformed" and settled on the other side of the barricade; many more of them think theirs is a shitty job (complying with the requests of their bosses and so on) and are sympathetic to the movement. In the early months of 1990, during the long occupation of nearly all Italian universities to stop an act of reform that students charged with paving the way for the "Berlusconization of the university," the *Il Manifesto* daily paper published an open letter by some veterans of the former movements. They called on "the ten thousand zeligs[2]" i.e. their old comrades now working in the mainstream media and the communication industry to raise their heads, reconnect with the latest generations of radicals and either work as "fifth columns" of the movement in the media, or cut loose and help to found new realms of communication. Both ways were (and still are) very hard, long and winding, yet that open letter made a good point and is still very far from being out of date.

Among the many metaphors used in the left's public discourse (the hot autumn, the springtime of movements, the tearing, the shoulder push, the ten thousand zeligs, etc), two are used to describe the "continuity of past and present" I hinted at in the premise: Italy as "the great laboratory" and the decades-long experience of the movements as "the sedimentation." The former does not need an explanation, since a laboratory is where experiments take place; the latter refers to the process of depositing sediment, that is, according to the Oxford Dictionary, "sand, stones, mud, etc carried by water or wind and left somewhere, e.g. at the bottom of a lake, a river, the sea, etc." The waters and winds of social conflict have carried and left us plenty of experiences and examples. Among the sand and the stones are so many nuggets that it would be absurd not to keep digging. Stories are shovels. That's the way we use them.

1. Guy Debord and the Situationist International.

2. From Woody Allen's *Zelig*, in which the title character was the epitome of conformism.

# Confronting Empire
# Arundhati Roy

Porto Alegre, Brazil
27 January 2003

I've been asked to speak about "how to confront empire?" It's a huge question, and I have no easy answers.

When we speak of confronting "empire," we need to identify what "empire" means. Does it mean the US government (and its European satellites), the World Bank, the International Monetary Fund, the World Trade Organization, and multinational corporations? Or is it something more than that?

In many countries, empire has sprouted other subsidiary heads, some dangerous by-products—nationalism, religious bigotry, fascism and, of course, terrorism. All these march arm in arm with the project of corporate globalization.

Let me illustrate what I mean. India—the world's biggest democracy—is currently at the forefront of the corporate globalization project. Its "market" of one billion people is being prized open by the WTO. Corporatization and privatization are being welcomed by the government and the Indian elite.

It is not a coincidence that the prime minister, the home minister, the disinvestment minister—the men who signed the deal with Enron in India, the men who are selling the country's infrastructure to corporate multinationals, the men who want to privatize water, electricity, oil, coal, steel, health, education, and telecommunication—are all members or admirers of the RSS. The RSS is a right-wing, ultranationalist Hindu guild which has openly admired Hitler and his methods.

The dismantling of democracy is proceeding with the speed and efficiency of a structural adjustment program. While the project of corporate globalization rips through people's lives in India, massive privatization, and labor "reforms" are pushing people off their land and out of their jobs. Hundreds of impoverished farmers are committing suicide by consuming pesticide. Reports of starvation deaths are coming in from all over the country.

While the elite journeys to its imaginary destination somewhere near the top of the world, the dispossessed are spiraling downwards into crime and chaos. This climate of frustration and national disillusionment is the perfect breeding ground, history tells us, for fascism.

The two arms of the Indian government have evolved the perfect pincer action. While one arm is busy selling India off in chunks, the other, to divert attention, is orchestrating a howling, baying chorus of Hindu nationalism and religious fascism. It is conducting nuclear tests, rewriting history books, burning churches, and demolishing mosques. Censorship, surveillance, the suspension of civil liberties and human rights, the definition of who is an Indian citizen and who is not, particularly with regard to religious minorities, is becoming common practice now.

Last March, in the state of Gujarat, two thousand Muslims were butchered in a State-sponsored pogrom. Muslim women were specially targeted. They were stripped, and gang-raped, before being burned alive. Arsonists burned and looted shops, homes, textiles mills, and mosques.

More than a hundred and fifty thousand Muslims have been driven from their homes. The economic base of the Muslim community has been devastated.

While Gujarat burned, the Indian prime minister was on MTV promoting his new poems. In January this year, the government that orchestrated the killing was voted back into office with a comfortable majority. Nobody has been punished for the genocide. Narendra Modi, architect of the pogrom, proud member of the RSS, has embarked on his second term as the chief minister of Gujarat. If he were Saddam Hussein, of course each atrocity would have been on CNN. But since he's not—and since the Indian "market" is open to global investors—the massacre is not even an embarrassing inconvenience.

There are more than one hundred million Muslims in India. A time bomb is ticking in our ancient land.

All this to say that it is a myth that the free market breaks down national barriers. The free market does not threaten national sovereignty, it undermines democracy.

As the disparity between the rich and the poor grows, the fight to corner resources is intensifying. To push through their "sweetheart deals," to corporatize the crops we grow, the water we drink, the air we breathe, and the dreams we dream, corporate globalization needs an international confederation of loyal, corrupt, authoritarian governments in poorer countries to push through unpopular reforms and quell the mutinies.

Corporate globalization—or shall we call it by its name?—imperialism—needs a press that pretends to be free. It needs courts that pretend to dispense justice.

Meanwhile, the countries of the North harden their borders and stockpile weapons of mass destruction. After all they have to make sure that it's only money, goods, patents, and services that are globalized. Not the free movement of people. Not a respect for human rights. Not international treaties on racial discrimination or chemical and nuclear weapons or greenhouse gas emissions or climate change, or—god forbid—justice.

So this—all this—is "empire." This loyal confederation, this obscene accumulation of power, this greatly increased distance between those who make the decisions and those who have to suffer them.

Our fight, our goal, our vision of another world must be to eliminate that distance. So how do we resist "empire"?

The good news is that we're not doing too badly. There have been major victories. Here in Latin America you have had so many—in Bolivia, you have Cochabamba. In Peru, there was the uprising in Arequipa. In Venezuela, President Hugo Chavez is holding on, despite the US government's best efforts.

And the world's gaze is on the people of Argentina, who are trying to refashion a country from the ashes of the havoc wrought by the IMF.

In India the movement against corporate globalization is gathering momentum and is poised to become the only real political force to counter religious fascism.

As for corporate globalization's glittering ambassadors—Enron, Bechtel, WorldCom, Arthur Anderson—where were they last year, and where are they now?

And of course here in Brazil we must ask ...who was the president last year, and who is it now?

Still ... many of us have dark moments of hopelessness and despair. We know that under the spreading canopy of the war against terrorism, the men in suits are hard at work.

While bombs rain down on us, and cruise missiles skid across the skies, we know that contracts are being signed, patents are being registered, oil pipelines are being laid, natural resources are being plundered, water is being privatized, and George Bush is planning to go to war against Iraq.

If we look at this conflict as a straightforward eyeball to eyeball confrontation between "Empire" and those of us who are resisting it, it might seem that we are losing.

But there is another way of looking at it. We, all of us gathered here, have, each in our own way, laid siege to "Empire."

We may not have stopped it in its tracks—yet—but we have stripped it down. We have made it drop its mask. We have forced it into the open. It now stands before us on the world's stage in all it's brutish, iniquitous nakedness.

Empire may well go to war, but it's out in the open now—too ugly to behold its own reflection. Too ugly even to rally its own people. It won't be long before the majority of American people become our allies.

Only a few days ago in Washington, a quarter of a million people marched against the war on Iraq. Each month, the protest is gathering momentum.

Before September 11th 2001 America had a secret history. Secret especially from its own people. But now America's secrets are history, and its history is public knowledge. It's street talk.

Today, we know that every argument that is being used to escalate the war against

Iraq is a lie. The most ludicrous of them being the US Government's deep commitment to bring democracy to Iraq.

Killing people to save them from dictatorship or ideological corruption is, of course, an old US government sport. Here in Latin America, you know that better than most. Nobody doubts that Saddam Hussein is a ruthless dictator, a murderer (whose worst excesses were supported by the governments of the United States and Great Britain). There's no doubt that Iraqis would be better off without him.

But, then, the whole world would be better off without a certain Mr. Bush. In fact, he is far more dangerous than Saddam Hussein.

So, should we bomb Bush out of the White House?

It's more than clear that Bush is determined to go to war against Iraq, regardless of the facts—and regardless of international public opinion.

In its recruitment drive for allies, the United States is prepared to invent facts.

The charade with weapons inspectors is the US government's offensive, insulting concession to some twisted form of international etiquette. It's like leaving the "doggie door" open for last minute "allies" or maybe the United Nations to crawl through.

But for all intents and purposes, the new war against Iraq has begun.

What can we do?

We can hone our memory, we can learn from our history. We can continue to build public opinion until it becomes a deafening roar.

We can turn the war on Iraq into a fishbowl of the US government's excesses.

We can expose George Bush and Tony Blair—and their allies—for the cowardly baby killers, water poisoners, and pusillanimous long-distance bombers that they are.

We can reinvent civil disobedience in a million different ways. In other words, we can come up with a million ways of becoming a collective pain in the ass.

When George Bush says "you're either with us, or you are with the terrorists" we can say "No thank you." We can let him know that the people of the world do not need to choose between a malevolent Mickey Mouse and the mad mullahs.

Our strategy should be not only to confront empire, but to lay siege to it. To deprive it of oxygen. To shame it. To mock it. With our art, our music, our literature, our stubbornness, our joy, our brilliance, our sheer relentlessness—and our ability to tell our own stories. Stories that are different from the ones we're being brainwashed to believe.

The corporate revolution will collapse if we refuse to buy what they are selling—their ideas, their version of history, their wars, their weapons, their notion of inevitability.

Remember this: We be many and they be few. They need us more than we need them.

Another world is not only possible, she is on her way. On a quiet day, I can hear her breathing.

# Out of the Ordinary
# Naomi Klein

*The Guardian*
January 25, 2003
Additional research by Dawn Makinson and Joseph Huff-Hannon

How do you celebrate the anniversary of something that is impossible to define? That was the question faced by tens of thousands of Argentinians on December 20, 2002, as they marched from all corners of Buenos Aires to the historic Plaza de Mayo. It was a year to the day since the first *Argentinazo*, a word that is completely untranslatable into English or, for that matter, Spanish. The *Argentinazo* was not a riot exactly, although it sure looked like one on the television, with looters ransacking supermarkets and mounted police charging into crowds; thirty-three people were killed across the country. It wasn't an ordinary revolution, either, although it sort of looked like one on the face of it, with angry crowds storming the seat of government and forcing the president to resign in disgrace. But, unlike a classic revolution, the *Argentinazo* was not organised by an alternate political force that wanted to take power for itself. And, unlike a riot, it pulsed with a unified and unequivocal demand: the immediate removal of all the corrupt politicians who had grown rich while Argentina, once the envy of the developing world, spiralled into poverty.

In reality, the *Argentinazo* was just what the word itself sounds like: a chaotic explosion of Argentinian-ness, during which hundreds of thousands of people suddenly and spontaneously left their homes, poured on to the streets of the capital, banged pots and pans, yelled at banks, fought police, revved motorcycles, sang football anthems, and managed to send the president fleeing his palace in a helicopter. Over the following twelve days, the country would go through five presidents and would default on its ninety-five billion-dollar debt, the largest default in history. (The fifth, "caretaker" president Eduardo Duhalde, is still hanging on to power, and elections are planned for April.)

Now, one year on, as enormous crowds fill the Plaza de Mayo once again, it is clear that this is a significant day - but what, exactly, is it marking? Is it a celebration of a national revolt against corporate globalisation, a mood that seems to be spreading across Latin America, with the Workers' Party taking power in Brazil, and privatisation programmes stopped in their tracks from Mexico to Peru? Is it the beginning of *Argentinazo: The Sequel*, a forward-looking movement that will replace the failed recipes of the International Monetary Fund (IMF) with something better?

In the end, December 20, 2002 is not a day of jubilant celebration or of particularly convincing fist waving. The mood, instead, is one of mourning, nowhere more so than at the corner of Avenida de Mayo and Chacabuco, in front of the headquarters of HSBC Argentina, a hulking twenty-eight storeys of Darth Vader-tinted glass. It was on this same piece of asphalt that twenty-three-year-old Gustavo Benedetto fell to the ground exactly a year earlier, killed by a bullet that came from inside the bank. The man charged with the murder—who had been in a group of police officers caught on video shooting through the bank's tinted glass—is Lieutenant Jorge Varando, chief of HSBC's building security. He is also a retired elite military officer who was active during the 1970s, when 30,000 Argentines were "disappeared," many of them kidnapped from their homes, brutally tortured, and then thrown from planes into the muddy waters of the Rio de la Plata.

From the mid-1950s to the early 1970s, Argentina was a profoundly undemocratic place, ruled by a succession of juntas who, even when they did allow for limited elections, barred the populist Peronist party from putting up candidates. It was in this context that left-wing students and workers first began organising themselves into guerrilla armies. Many of these activists thought that they were starting a socialist revolution, though for Juan Peron, who prodded them on from his exile in Spain, the militias were just a means with which to expedite his glorious return as paternalistic leader. The largest armed faction of this growing opposition was the Montoneros, a youth movement that borrowed its populist politics from Evita and its guerrilla warfare theory from Che Guevara. Though such cells never posed a serious threat to national security, the Argentinian army used a series of guerrilla attacks on military and corporate targets as an excuse to declare an all-out campaign against the left - the generals called the action a "war on terror," but the name that has stuck ever since has been the "Dirty War."

Between 1976 and 1983, Argentina was ruled by a twisted military regime that combined fundamentalist Catholic social control with fundamentalist free-market economics; it banned rock music while it raked in billions of dollars worth of loans and investment from foreign banks and multinational corporations. The generals saw it as their mission to cleanse Marxist and other "subversive" thought from every school, workplace, church, and neighbourhood. At the same time, they also saw it as their right to profit personally from this crusade, not only skimming from public coffers but also stealing private houses, possessions, and even children from the people they tortured and killed (the state was eventually forced to pay compensation to many of the victims' families).

To this day, the generals deny almost everything and, thanks to an official state pardon, the killers of that time now walk free—the despised Leopoldo Galtieri, who led Argentina into the disastrous Falklands war and who died earlier this month, took many of his secrets with him to his grave. Since the end of the military dictatorship, however, several exhaustive fact-finding investigations have gathered evidence about abuses during and after the Dirty War. It was by combing through these investigations that Argentinian human rights groups discovered that Varando, the man whom the HSBC had put in charge of its security operations, was one of a group of military personnel accused by relatives of the disappeared of war crimes during an attack on the La Tablada military barracks in 1989. A report by the Organisation of American States' Inter-American Commission on Human Rights, completed in 1997, states that two prisoners at the La Tablada base, Ivan Ruiz and Jose Alejandro Diaz, were "disappeared" under the watch of Major Jorge Varando. Varando says that he transferred Ruiz and Diaz to another officer, and when that officer was later killed in the action, he believed the prisoners had escaped. Because of a subsequent amnesty, however, there was never a full criminal investigation into the events at La Tablada. Today, in connection with a separate incident, Varando is awaiting trial for the murder of Gustavo Benedetto.

At the corner of Avenida de Mayo and Chacabuco, where the HSBC's plateglass facade is now encased in reinforced steel as impenetrable as the mirrored sunglasses on the police officers standing guard outside, Argentina's past and present have come crashing together. Benedetto's alleged killer worked for a foreign bank, one of the very same foreign banks that swallowed the savings of millions of Argentinians when the government declared a freeze on bank withdrawals in early December 2001. While the accounts were locked, the peso was "unpegged" from the US dollar and the currency went into freefall. When the banking freeze was partially lifted a year later and customers could once again get at their money, their savings had lost two-thirds of their value.

Though banks such as HSBC blame the government for the freeze, the measure was in fact a response to the fact that private banks had helped their wealthiest customers to whisk roughly twenty billion dollars out of Argentina over the previous year. At the time, there was no ban on taking capital out of the country. A particularly dramatic moment came last January, when police raided an HSBC branch, as well as several other banks, searching for evidence that hundreds of armoured vehicles had been used to transport billions of undeclared US dollars to the Ezeiza International Airport in cash. The foreign banks claimed that the authorities were looking for scapegoats to blame for the economic crisis, and HSBC Holdings Ltd. says that its locally incorporated subsidiary has always acted in accordance with Argentinian laws. It is not aware of any evidence that its subsidiary participated in flight capital.

According to the prosecuting attorney in the capital flight case, the investigation into allegations of "fraud against the state, and illegal association" is ongoing, and so far no charges have been laid.

At the core of the allegations against the foreign banks is the timing: the exodus of cash took place only days before the government froze all withdrawals, leading to a wide-spread belief that the banks—unlike regular Argentinians who were taken by surprise—had been tipped off that the freeze was imminent. This is an important point, because for many of Argentina's richest families and businesses, the banking fiasco and devaluation has actually made them richer than they were before: they now pay their employees, their expenses, and their debts in devalued pesos, but—thanks to the banks—their savings are safely stored outside the country in US dollars. It's a highly profitable arrangement.

After the twenty billion dollars in "disappeared" capital was discovered, there was so much public outrage that several foreign bankers faced charges under Argentina's "economic subversion" law, which prohibits acts that sabotage the country's economy. This obstacle was neatly dealt with last May, however, when a coalition of banks, headed by HSBC, successfully lobbied to have the law struck down.

This incident has been linked to yet another controversy, this one involving bribery, legislators, and foreign banks. In August, the *Financial Times* published allegations made by bankers and diplomats that Argentinian legislators had solicited bribes from foreign banks in exchange for offers to vote down several pieces of legislation that would have cost the financial institutions hundreds of millions of dollars a year. The banks reportedly turned down the offers. After the article was published, several banks were again raided by Argentinian police—among them HSBC's headquarters and the private residence of a senior HSBC spokesperson—this time to search for evidence of the reported bribe solicitation and to discover the source of the allegation.

There has been speculation that the raids were politically motivated, to get back at the banks for going public with the bribery allegations. When Mike Smith, president of HSBC Argentina, testified at a legal hearing about the scandal, he said that he had no specific knowledge of the incidents described in the *Financial Times* and denied HSBC paid any bribes. He also said that soliciting bribes in exchange for favourable laws was common practice in Argentina. This investigation, too, is ongoing.

Benedetto was only one of the thirty-three people who died violently during the *Argentinazo* of 2001. But his story, haunted by the ghosts of history, yet so unmistakably modern, has become a symbol for a country now trying to make sense of its unrelenting economic crisis. How can twenty-seven children die of hunger every day in a country that is so naturally abundant that it once fed much of Europe and North America? How can a nation where factory workers used to buy homes and cars on the highest wages in Latin America now have the highest unemployment rate on the continent and an average wage lower than Mexico's? Benedetto thought that his government owed him answers to those questions, which was why he went to the plaza that December day.

"Once upon a time there was a country called Argentina," writes journalist Sergio

Ciancaglini, "where many people disappeared and where, years later, the money disappeared, too. One thing is related to the other." Ciancaglini argues that anyone who wishes to understand what happened to Argentina's missing wealth must first journey back into its past, to find out what happened to its missing people. Since the *Argentinazo*, there has been a grassroots explosion of groups embarking on precisely such a journey, a kind of national forensic detective mission that is linking the economic interests of the generals' dictatorship with the policies that drove the economy into ruin years later. The belief–the hope–is that when these pieces are finally put together, Argentina may finally be able to break the cycle of state terror and corporate plunder that has enslaved this country, like so many others, for far too long.

Benedetto loved reading books about history and economics. According to his older sister, Eliana, "he wanted to understand how such a great country could have ended up in such a mess." Bennedetto dreamed of being a professor of history, but that was a goal for a more optimistic time. When his father died in March 2000, Benedetto had to find a job, any job, with which he could support his mother and sister. It was a bad time to be looking for work. In La Tablada, the postindustrial suburb where the Benedettos live, most of the factories were already boarded up. The best job he could find was as a supermarket clerk in a nearby mall.

But at least he had work. Though the world's press discovered Argentina's economic crisis only relatively recently, it had been a fact of life in neighbourhoods such as La Tablada for at least six years. In the mid-1990s, when the IMF was still holding up Argentina as a miracle of economic growth, as a model of the riches that awaited poor nations who fling open their doors to foreign investment, unemployment was already reaching crisis levels. It's a pattern that has been replicated many times across Latin America, in countries who have followed similar free-market reforms; today, only Chile survives as a putative "success story," while more than fifty percent of Argentina's population has fallen below the official poverty line.

Oddly, when Argentina had less wealth on paper, fewer Argentinians went hungry. Many complex economic factors contributed to this shift, from changes in agricultural export crops to falling wages in the industrial sector. But there were some simple changes that played a part, too, such as the fact that small neighbourhood markets used to sell food on credit during difficult times, a little bit of grace that disappeared when Argentina became a globalisation showcase and those small shops were replaced by foreign-owned hypermarkets the size of Aztec temples, with names such as Carréfour, Wal-Mart, and Dia, the Spanish-owned chain where Benedetto finally managed to get a job.

So it probably wasn't a coincidence that, in the days leading up to the *Argentinazo*, many of the hypermarkets found themselves under siege, looted by mobs of unemployed men, their faces covered by t-shirts turned into makeshift balaclavas. When Gustavo showed up for work at Dia on December 19, the atmosphere was unbearably tense: no one knew whether this concrete castle was about to be the next stormed by hungry, angry mobs. At noon, the manager decided to end the suspense and close early.

When Benedetto arrived home, he turned on the television. What he saw was a country in open revolt, with protests erupting everywhere. All day and all night, he flicked from one station to the next, but by 10:40PM every station was showing the same image: President Fernando de la Rua, his face clammy with sweat, stiffly reading from a prepared text. Argentina, he said, was under attack from "groups that are enemies of order who are looking to spread discord and violence," He declared a state of siege.

For many Argentinians, the president's declaration sounded like a prelude to a military coup—and that was a fatal mistake for the de la Rua government. Benedetto watched live images of the Plaza de Mayo filling up with people. They were banging pots and pans with spoons and forks, a wordless but roaring rebuke to the president's instructions: Argentinians would not give up basic freedoms in the name of "order," they declared. They had tried that before under the junta, and it had ended badly. And then a single rebellious cry rose up from the crowds of grandmothers and high-school students, motorcycle couriers and unemployed factory workers, their words directed at the politicians, the bankers, the IMF, and every other "expert" who claimed to have the perfect recipe for Argentina's prosperity and stability: "Que se vayan todos!"—everyone must go!—they said.

Benedetto slept fitfully that night. When he arrived for work the next morning, the store was completely boarded up, so he went back home and turned on the television again. It was then that he felt an impulse he had never had before—he wanted to join a political demonstration. All of a sudden, Benedetto, an easy-going guy who had not protested against anything in his life, leapt up from the couch, flicked off the TV, and told his mother that he was going downtown.

On his way to the bus stop, Benedetto asked several friends from the La Tablada neighbourhood if they wanted to come along with him—to be part of this history they were seeing unfolding on their television screens. But he couldn't find any takers: most people in La Tablada had had enough of history. During the 1970s and 1980s, this working-class neighbourhood was literally caught in the crossfire between the army and the guerrillas; several leftwing cells were active in the area at the time, and it was also home to Infantería Mecanizada No 3 de La Tablada, a large military base that was the site of alleged human rights abuses. In La Tablada, the Dirty War was even filthier than it was elsewhere, with parents bumping into their children's killers at the corner shop. And since any kind of contact with a leftist was enough to get you branded a collaborator, the safest course of action was to retreat into your home: doors were closed on former friends looking for sanctuary, blinds were hastily drawn when there was a commotion outside, the radio was turned up to drown out screams from neighbouring apartments. In La Tablada, as elsewhere in Argentina, residents learned to live faithfully by the philosophy of the terror times: "No se meta"—don't get involved. It's an attitude that has survived to this day. Gustavo, however, had decided to break with that tradition. He had no way of knowing that the tactics of the dictatorship were about to return to the streets of Buenos Aires. During the two hours it took him to get from the suburbs to downtown Buenos Aires, the chief of police had sent down an order to "clear the Plaza de Mayo." At first, the riot squads used rubber bullets and tear gas; then they switched to live ammunition.

The police pushed the crowds on to Avenida de Mayo and the crowds pushed back. At around 4PM, a group of around twenty police officers were looking for a safe place to take refuge and reload their weapons. They chose the lobby of the HSBC, one of the most secure buildings in the city, because it also houses the Israeli embassy. A handful of demonstrators—fewer than five, according to court documents—broke away from the streams of people heading for the Plaza de Mayo and began throwing stones at the bank. One man shattered a pane of glass with a metal bar.

The police and private security guards inside panicked and opened fire. According to evidence heard later in court, in just four seconds a hail of at least fifty-nine bullets was fired on to the packed street outside. Just then, Gustavo Benedetto, walking on his own and having been downtown for less than an hour, happened to turn on to Avenida de Mayo. He was many yards from the bank when a lead bullet, fired from a 9-mm weapon, caught him in the back of the head. He fell to the ground; in an instant, he was dead.

The HSBC may have been a good place for the police officers to find sanctuary during the chaos of the Argentinazo, but when it comes to a murder allegedly committed from its lobby, a bank, with its security cameras monitoring every angle, offers little by way of cover. The HSBC's own surveillance cameras, since entered as court evidence, clearly show police and bank security officers aiming and firing their weapons through the plate-glass window. This evidence has led to a rare event in the annals of Argentinian justice: the arrest of a former military officer on a charge of murder.

Jorge Varando is a graduate of the School of the Americas, a "counterinsurgency" training camp based in the southern US. He has testified that he did not shoot Benedetto and argues that he acted properly as a security officer defending the bank. In a recent radio interview, he is quoted as admitting to firing his gun, saying that he did so "in total tranquillity" and "to stop those trying to enter the building."

HSBC has so far refused to comment on the case because of the ongoing legal proceedings, except to note that its employee Varando has steadfastly maintained his innocence. It's not yet clear whether Varando will be represented by an HSBC lawyer when the case goes to trial, but the bank had its own counsel at the pretrial hearings.

HSBC is inevitably involved in some part, because the shooting took place from its premises and its security cameras offer crucial evidence. But that evidence has proved problematic. When the court staged a reconstruction of the murder, matching the videotape of Varando firing his weapon with the site where Benedetto was killed, it became clear someone had changed the angle of the key security camera, making it extremely difficult to match the re-enactment with the original footage of Varando shooting through the glass. Bank personnel said the camera angle had been changed accidentally during routine cleaning.

And the case has attracted even more widespread interest because every month since the murder, friends and family have placed a makeshift memorial to Gustavo Benedetto in front of the bank—and every month the memorial has been mysteriously removed and Benedetto's name erased. This practice finally stopped last November, when a television crew that had been staking out the HSBC building at 3am filmed as two federal police officers pulled up outside the bank in an unmarked car and destroyed the concrete and ceramic monument with crowbars. The officers have since been suspended.

Up until quite recently, Argentina pursued a policy of official amnesia when it came to the crimes of the Dirty War. Sure, the human rights nongovernmental organisations still issued numerous scathing reports, the Mothers of the Plaza de Mayo still marched and the children of disappeared parents still showed up, from time to time, outside the homes of ex-military figures to throw red paint. But before the *Argentinazo*, most middle-class Argentinians regarded such actions as macabre rituals from a bygone era. Hadn't these people received the memo? The country had "moved on"—or at least it was supposed to have done, according to former president Carlos Menem. Menem, a Ferrari-driving free-marketeer who is Argentina's very own morphing of Margaret Thatcher and John Gotti, was first elected in 1989, with the economy in recession and inflation soaring. Claiming that many of Argentina's economic troubles stemmed from botched attempts by his predecessor to bring to justice the generals of the Dirty War, Menem offered an alternative approach: instead of going backwards into the hell of unmarked graves and the lies of the past, he said, Argentinians should wipe the slate clean, join the global economy, and then put all of their energy into the pursuit of economic growth.

After pardoning the generals, Menem launched a zealous programme of what here in Latin America is called "neoliberalism": that is, mass privatisations, public sector layoffs, labour market "flexibilisation," and corporate incentives. He slashed federal meals programmes, cut the national unemployment fund by almost eighty percent, laid off hundreds of thousands of state employees, and made many strikes illegal. Menem dubbed this rapid free-market makeover "surgery without anaesthesia", and assured voters that, once the short-term pain subsided, Argentina would be, in the words of one of his advertising campaigns, "born again."

The middle-class residents of Buenos Aires, many of them ashamed of their own complicity or complacency during the Dirty War, enthusiastically embraced the idea of living in a shiny new country without a past. "Don't get involved," the mantra of the terror years, gave way seamlessly to "Look out for Number One," the mantra of high capitalism, in whose cause neighbours are competitors and the market is put before all else, including the quest for justice and the rebuilding of shattered communities. In the years that followed, 1990s Buenos Aires went on a career and consumerism jag that would put the most shopaholic, workaholic New Yorker or Londoner to shame. According to government data, between 1993 and 1998, total household spending increased by forty-two billion dollars, while spending on imported goods doubled over the same high-rolling five years, from fifteen billion dollars in 1993 to thirty billion dollars in 1998.

In the swanky neighbourhoods of Recoleta and Palermo, residents bought not only the latest imported electronics and designer fashions, but also new faces and new bodies—Buenos Aires soon rivalled Rio de Janeiro as a capital of cosmetic surgery, with one plastic surgeon alone boasting 30,000 clients. Argentinians clearly wanted to be remade, just like their country—and like their president, who himself disappeared periodically, to reappear later with his face stretched taut and claiming that he had been stung by a bee.

The masks and disguises of the 1990s looked remarkably lifelike for a while. The national GDP increased by sixty percent over the decade and foreign investment poured in. But, just as Enron's stockholders did not care to look too closely at the books so long as their profits were going up, Argentina's foreign investors and lenders somehow failed to see that Menem's lean, mean government was eighty billion dollars deeper in debt in 1999 than the 1989 government had been. Or that, thanks largely to layoffs at privatised firms, unemployment had soared from 6.5% in 1989 to twenty percent in 2000.

In short, "Menem's Miracle," as *Time* gushingly called it, was a mirage. The wealth flowing in 1990s Argentina was a combination of speculative finance and one-off sales: the phone company, the oil company, the rails, the airline. After the initial cash infusion and greased palms, what was left was a hollowed-out country, costly basic services, and a working class that wasn't working. It also left behind it a wild west-style deregulated financial sector that allowed Argentina's richest families to move 140 billion dollars in private wealth into foreign bank account—more than either the national GDP or the foreign debt.

As Argentina's wealth disappeared, destined for bank accounts in Miami and stock exchanges in Milan, the collective amnesia of the Menem years wore off, too. Today, almost twenty years after the junta's dictatorship ended and with the old military generals dead or dying, the ghosts of the 30,000 disappeared have suddenly reappeared. They now haunt every aspect of the country's present crisis. In the months after the *Argentinazo*, the past seemed so present that it was as if time itself had collapsed and the state terror had been committed only yesterday. In the courts and on the streets, a national debate erupted not only about how so many had got away with murder, but also about the reasons why the terror had occurred in the first place: why did those 30,000 people die? In whose interest were they killed? And what was the connection between those deaths and the free-market policies that had failed the country so spectacularly?

Back when students and union members were being thrown into green Ford Falcons and driven to clandestine torture centres, there was little time for such questions about root causes and economic interests. During the terror years, Argentinian activists had a single overarching preoccupation—staying alive. When groups such as Amnesty International began to intervene on their behalf, they, too, were preoccupied with day-to-day survival. Investigators would trace the missing people and then petition for their release, or at least for confirmation of their deaths.

There were, however, a few exceptions, individuals who were able to see that the generals had an economic plan as aggressive as their social and political ones. In 1976 and 1977—the first two years of junta rule, when the terror was at its bloodiest and most barbaric—the generals introduced an economic "restructuring" programme that was to be a foretaste of today's cut-throat corporate globalisation. The average national wage was slashed in half, social spending drastically reduced, and price controls removed. The generals were rewarded handsomely for these measures: in those same two years, Argentina received more than two billion dollars in foreign loans, more than the country had received in all of the previous six years combined. By the time the generals gave back the country in 1983, they had increased the national foreign debt from seven to forty-three billion dollars.

On March 24, 1977, a year after the coup, Argentinian investigative journalist Rodolfo Walsh published an "Open Letter from a Writer to the Military Junta"—it was destined to become one the most famous pieces of writing in modern Latin American letters. In it, Walsh, a member of the Montoneros youth movement, broke with official press censorship by launching a righteous and detailed account of the generals' terror campaign. But there was a second half to the "Open Letter" which, according to Walsh's biographer, Michael McCaughan, was suppressed by the Montoneros leadership, many of whom, though militant in their tactics, were not as focused as Walsh on economics. The missing half, just published in McCaughan's book, *True Crimes*, shifted the focus from the military's human rights abuses to its economic programme, with Walsh declaring—somewhat heretically—that the terror was not the "greatest suffering inflicted on the Argentinian people, not the worst violation of human rights which you have committed. It is in the economic policy of this government where one discovers not only the explanation of the crimes, but a greater atrocity which punishes millions of human beings through planned misery."

Walsh once again offered a catalogue of crimes: "Freezing wages with rifle butts while prices rise at bayonet point, abolishing all forms of collective bargaining, prohibiting assemblies and internal commissions, extending working days, raising unemployment . . . an economic policy dictated by the International Monetary Fund, following a recipe applied indiscriminately in Zaire or Chile, in Uruguay or Indonesia." Minutes after posting copies of his letter, Walsh was ambushed by police and shot dead on the streets of Buenos Aires.

Harder to kill, however, has been Walsh's description of an economic logic that outlived the dictatorship, a logic that guided the scalpel of Menem's surgery without anaesthesia and that still continues to guide every IMF mission to Argentina, which always seem to call for more cuts to healthcare and education, higher fees for basic services, more bank foreclosures on mortgages. But Walsh didn't call it "good governance" or "fiscal prudence" or "being globally competitive"—he called it "planned misery."

Walsh understood that the generals were not waging a war "on terror" but a war on any barrier to the accumulation of wealth by foreign investors and their local beneficiaries. He is proved more prescient every day. Civil trials continue to unearth fresh evidence that foreign corporations collaborated closely with the junta in its extermination of the union movement in the 1970s. For example, last December a federal prosecutor filed a criminal complaint against Ford Argentina (a subsidiary of Ford), alleging that the company had inside one of its factory compounds a military detention centre where union organisers were taken. "Ford [Argentina] and its executives colluded in the kidnapping of its own workers and I think they should be held accountable for that," says Pedro Troiani, a former Ford assembly-line worker who has testified that soldiers kidnapped and beat him inside the factory walls. Mercedes-Benz (now a subsidiary of DaimlerChrysler) is facing a similar investigation in both Germany and Argentina, which stems from allegations that it collaborated with the military in the 1970s to purge one of its plants of union militants, giving names and addresses of sixteen workers who were later "disappeared," fourteen of them never to be seen again. Both Ford and Mercedes-Benz deny that their executives played any role in any of the deaths.

And then, of course, there is the case of Gustavo Benedetto. On the face of it, there is nothing to connect Benedetto's murder to the past and there is no comparison between the repression during the *Argentinazo* and the terror of the Dirty War. Yet the Benedetto case highlights the changing role of the military, the state, and financial interests, and the current role of ex-military officers.

In the 1970s, Jorge Varando, the man accused of Benedetto's murder, worked for a military regime that opened up Argentina's banking sector to private banks. In 2001, with the military downsized along with the rest of the public sector, he worked directly for one of those very banks. The fear is that the grand achievement of two decades of democracy is only that the middleman has been cut out and that repression has been privatised. Now Argentina's banks and corporations are guarded by units of armed former military officers, who protect them against public protesters, raising difficult questions about the compromises that were made in the country's transition from dictatorship to democracy.

Today, the history of that transition is being rewritten on the streets. There is no neat "before" and "after" the dictatorship. The dictatorship's project is instead emerging as a process: the generals prepped the patient, then Menem performed the "surgery." The junta did more than disappear the union organisers who might have fought the mass lay-offs and the socialists who might have refused to implement the IMF's latest austerity plan. The great success of the Dirty War was the culture of fear and individualism that it left behind in neighbourhoods such as La Tablada, where Gustavo Benedetto grew up.

The generals understood that the true obstacle to complete social control was not leftist rebels, but the very presence of tight-knit communities and civil society. Which is why they set out to "disappear" the public sphere itself. On the first day of the 1976 coup, the military banned all "public spectacles," from carnivals to theatre to horse races. Public squares were strictly reserved for shows of military strength and the only communal experience permitted was football. At the same time, the military launched a campaign to turn the entire population into snitches: state-run newspapers were packed with announcements reminding citizens that it was their civic duty to report anyone who seemed to be doing anything "subversive."

And when the population had retreated into their homes, the economic project of the dictatorship could be continued and deepened by successive civilian governments without even having to resort to messy repression—at least until recently.

In the 1970s, when the Mothers of the Plaza de Mayo began searching for their missing loved ones, it was common for these brave women to say that their children were innocents, that they were "doing nothing" when they were taken. Today, the Mothers lead demonstrations against the IMF, talk about "economic terrorism," and proudly declare that their children were indeed doing something when they were kidnapped—they were political activists trying to save the country from the planned misery that began under the dictatorship and only deepened under democracy.

In the rubble that was left of Argentina after December 2001, something extraordinary started to happen: neighbours poked their heads out of their apartments and houses, and, in the absence of a political leadership or a party to make sense of the spontaneous explosion of which they had been a part, they began to talk to each other. To think together. By late January 2002, there were already some 250 *asambleas barriales* (neighbourhood assemblies) in downtown Buenos Aires alone. The streets, parks, and plazas were filled with meetings, as people stayed up late into the night, planning, arguing, testifying, voting.

Many of those first assemblies were more like group therapy than political meetings. Participants spoke about their experience of isolation in a city of eleven million. Academics and shopkeepers apologised for not watching out for each other, publicity managers admitted that they used to look down on unemployed factory workers, assuming that they deserved their plight, never thinking that the crisis would reach the bank accounts of the cosmopolitan middle class.

And these apologies for present-day wrongs soon gave way to tearful confessions about events dating back to the dictatorship. A housewife would stand up and publicly admit that, three decades earlier, when she heard yet another story about someone's brother or husband being disappeared, she had learned to close her heart to the suffering, telling herself "Por algo será"—it must have been for something.

Most assemblies began, in the face of so much planned misery, to plan something else: joy, solidarity, another kind of economy. Soup kitchens were opened, job banks and trading clubs formed. In the past year, between 130 and 150 factories, bankrupt and abandoned by their owners, have been taken over by their workers and turned into cooperatives or collectives. At tractor plants, supermarkets, printing houses, aluminium factories, and pizza parlours, decisions about company policy are now made in open assemblies, and profits are split equally among the workers.

In recent months, the *fabricas tomadas* (literally, "taken factories") have begun to network among themselves and are beginning to plan an informal "solidarity economy": garment workers from an occupied factory, for example, sew sheets for an occupied health clinic; a supermarket in Rosario, turned into a workers' cooperative, sells pasta from an occupied pasta factory; occupied bakeries are building ovens with tiles from an occupied ceramic plant. "I feel like the dictatorship is finally ending," one *asamblista* told me when I first arrived in Buenos Aires. "It's like I've been locked in my house for twenty-five-years and now I am finally outside."

Rodolfo Walsh estimated that it would take twenty or thirty-years before the effects of the terror campaign would wear off and Argentinians would at last be ready to fight for economic and social justice again. That was a little more than twenty-five-years ago. So I couldn't help thinking of Walsh when I met Gabriela Mitidieri, a self-confident high-school student who, except for her politics, would fit right in at an audition for Fame Academy 2. Mitidieri was born in 1984, the first full year of elected government in Argentina after the dictatorship. "I am the daughter of democracy," she says, with a slight edge of 18-year-old sarcasm. "That means I have a special responsibility."

That responsibility, as she sees it, is vast—finally to free the country from the economic policies that survived the transition from military to civilian rule. Yet she seems undaunted by the task, or at least unafraid. Gaby, as she is called by friends and family, charges off to demonstrations wearing low-slung cargo pants and her brother's Blink 182 knapsack; she holds placards with black-painted fingernails and she stares down police lines with eyes dusted in blue sparkles. Her parents don't share her fearlessness. When the streets of Buenos Aires exploded in the 2001 *Argentinazo*, the modest Mitidieri home was experiencing an explosion of its own. The conflict was over whether or not the then seventeen-year-old Gaby would be allowed to join the demonstrations. Gaby was determined to go to the Plaza—"I just couldn't stand to be one of those people who watches the world through a TV screen," she says today. Her father, a survivor of the Dirty War, during which he had been kidnapped and tortured, physically blocked Gaby's way to the door, while she shouted that he, of all people, should understand why she needed to be in the streets. Sergio Mitidieri was unmoved—he had been Gaby's age when he first got involved in student politics and his youth hadn't saved him or his friends, many of whom were killed in the concentration camps.

Like many of his generation, Mitidieri did not return to political activism after the generals retreated. The terror of those years stayed with him, robbing him of the outspoken confidence of his student days—for years, he told Gaby that the scars on his back and shoulders were from sporting injuries. Today, he still doesn't like to talk about the past; he keeps his head down and works hard to support his wife and four children. Gaby says that her father's fear—"He lives with the idea of death hanging over his head"—means that the dictatorship, whether imposed by external terror or internal fear, is still gripping the country. "When I first found out about what happened to my father," Gaby says, "I kept asking myself, 'Why did he live? Why did they let him survive?' Then I read 1984 and I realised that he and the others survived to keep the fear alive, and to remind the entire population of the fear. My father is living proof of that."

But sitting in the Mitidieri home on the first anniversary of the *Argentinazo*, it struck me that Gaby, the self-proclaimed daughter of democracy, might just be underestimating democracy's contagious power. In 2002, when she announced on the morning of December 19 that she was joining the anniversary demonstrations, her mother quietly helped her pack her knapsack: water, a cellphone, a lemon (it helps mitigate the effects of teargas). She even lent Gaby a headscarf. And Gaby's father watched them pack, looking worried, but also proud.

That evening, the local neighbourhood assembly called for everyone to come out of their houses with their pots and pans to celebrate the day, one year earlier, when something happened to change Argentina (though still no one can explain exactly what that was). And a strange thing happened: Gaby's parents showed up. They hung around on the edges of the gathering, they didn't talk to anyone—but they were there.

"We still have fear," Sergio Mitidieri told me, "but we have anger, too. It's better to fight in the streets than to be quiet at home. Gaby taught me that."

# Resistance in Peru
## Eric Schwartz

*Z Magazine,* June 2001

As Peru lurches out of a decade of state repression and crushing neoliberal reforms, most international attention celebrates the country's "transition to democracy" and upcoming elections. From Peru, the view is different: the elections offer only slightly more choices than our own presidential elections, and the fight for democracy is far from over. But there is a lot more happening in Peru than elections. There is constant invisible struggle, creative resistance against home-grown dictators and globalized capitalism.

One night in early February I was driving through Cusco, in southern Peru, at midnight when I saw about eighty riot police near several earth-mover machines. On the opposite side of the street, scattered fires lit a large crowd made up of vendors from the Contra- bando, Cusco's massive street market. The vendors, who are mostly indigenous and about two-thirds women, were gathered to prevent the city's sneak-attack effort to dig huge holes at each end of the market. The vendors believed the pits were the first step toward their displacement from the downtown tourist center. Later that night, the vendors were on the losing end of a fairly serious rock-and-tear gas confrontation. The hole was dug and no cars entered the Contra the next day. But when the sun came up the following morning, the hole had somehow been filled and traffic continued as normal.

A few days later, three to four-thousand Contrabando vendors were hanging out, drinking tea, and snacking on ice cream cones on Cusco's major downtown road. Traffic was completely blocked. When the news rushed through the crowd that their representatives had been unsuccessful at the public works office, the vendors rose up and continued to the mayor's office, confusing and alarming dozens of tourists as they flooded across the central plaza.

At City Hall, a representative of the mayor came out to scold the crowd. Apparently his message wasn't exactly what the vendors were looking for, because he had to retreat into the building under a light rain of pebbles, fruit, and empty water bottles. He made several more attempts at "dialogue" over the next hour, but the vendors stayed firm in their demand to talk to the mayor. In a message that seemed to be directed at the line of riot police guarding the mayor's office, the vendors chanted, "Here. There. The fear has ended." When the well-dressed vendors association leaders came out to urge their com-

pañeros to go home and wait for the mayor to issue a preliminary report, they were rejected with the same fury that had met the mayor's spokesperson. The vendors finally headed
home, but their mobilizations continued until the city finally offered them a new home
near the city center.

Peruvian politics is in a funny place right now. Alberto Fujimori, the country's US-
backed dictator for ten years, has fled to Japan. Fujimori is happily enjoying the wealth he
plundered from a decade of shady arms deals and IMF-mandated privatizations in a ten-
thousand dollars a month apartment in downtown Tokyo. His security chief, Vladimiro
Montesinos, the real power for at least the last three years and a friend of the CIA, was last
spotted having plastic surgery to change his face in Venezuela. All of the country's elites
except a small band of insanely loyal congresspeople, who insist the transitional president
is in league with the terrorists (obliterated after a decade of anything-goes counterinsurgency), are scurrying to distance themselves from the criminal "Chino."

But there's one inconvenient detail—Montesinos recorded over two-thousand tapes
of his let's-make- a-deal sessions with the country's elites. Millions of Peruvians have seen
grainy footage revealing the owner of one of the leading newspapers personally accepting
three million in US cash and the country's most powerful businessperson, Dionisio
Romero, urging Vladimiro to scrap the second round of elections to let Fujimori win in
2000. The Peruvian Rasputin talks about his great relationship with US Ambassador
Hamilton, buys judges to rule in favor of a US mining company, and plots his media campaign to destroy opposition politicians.

Montesinos's spying mania has opened a window onto the most intimate and ugly
machinations of state power. The TV reveals one corrupt politician after another pleas-
antly inquiring about Montesinos's family and his health for several minutes before finally cutting to the chase: "Vladimiro, I'm having financial problems…" Jose Crousillat, the
owner of a major TV channel, tells Montesinos, "I await your orders," then turns to count
the towering stacks of Peruvian *soles* in front of him.

The problem, of course, is that the so-called "mafia" that supported Fujimori for ten
years is doing everything they can to stay in power. The "vladivideos" trickle out, slowly,
ensuring that only a fraction will be seen before the election. Some of the implicated
politicians and military officials, whose crimes weren't erased by the 1985 amnesty law, are
placed under house arrest. Others, including Dionisio Romero, are pardoned without
explanation by the vast network that Vladimiro created in the judicial system. Protesters
against mafia politicians are regularly taunted or attacked by small, well-organized gangs
of "counter-protesters."

But in spite of the same old grim scene in electoral politics, Peru offers a much
more hopeful picture at the grassroots level. In Peru, anti-neoliberalism struggles of amaz-

ing creativity and militancy explode into view every week, in communities across the country. Grassroots struggles that would be considered incredible examples of coalition-building and tactical success in the US are granted a paragraph in the national left-wing newspaper *Liberacion* or aren't mentioned at all. Coming from the belly of the beast, the sheer frequency with which these struggles erupt is astounding.

A lot of these struggles are focused on efforts to oust the corrupt fujimorista gang that brought neoliberal "reforms" to Peru. As the most visible symbol of the "mafia," Lourdes Flores has been chased out of town on several campaign stops. In March, protesters disrupted newly ordained Cardinal Cipriani's first mass. This is the man who has defended disappearances, attacked human rights groups as terrorists, and called human rights "bullshit"—and those are just his public statements. Also active in the anti-Mafia struggle, the Lima-based Civil Society Collective performs symbolic actions like burying the houses of Fujimorista "trash-politician's" in garbage and covering Fujimorista banks and TV stations with white- paint handprints. The group has a broad, diverse base of support and calls itself leaderless and nonviolent.

Much of the struggle is directed at mafia-dominated TV stations and media stars. When the arrogant pop star Raul Romero recently shrugged off the 1992 La Cantuta student massacre as an "acceptable social cost," several hundred family members showed up the next day and forcefully turned back his car from a Fujimori-friendly TV station. For several days, Raul's fans had to settle for reruns. When he finally attempted to "clarify" his comment for the public, he had to do so over the phone.

Years of bitter struggle have taught millions of Peruvians from all backgrounds that it's necessary to disrupt business as usual to create social change, that dialogue alone just doesn't work. In recent months, squatters in Lima, flood victims in Puno, and countless other groups have forced the authorities to resolve their problems by blocking major roads. In several towns south of Lima, residents frustrated by empty campaign promises and angry at Peru's mandatory voting laws recently staged a forty-eight-hour general strike and blocked highways to prevent the delivery of voting booths and ballot boxes.

In the agricultural community Tambo Grande in northern Peru, farmers recently broke through police lines to torch a Canadian mining facility that would have permanently poisoned agriculture in the area. Between the million dollars of damage caused by the fires, a two-day general strike, and several days of blocked highways, the Manhattan Sechura company is finally considering pulling out. Tambo Grande also chased out another foreign mining company in the early 1980s.

In March, hundreds of residents of the desperately poor "young towns" surrounding Arequipa in southern Peru peacefully invaded City Hall to demand more public services. Deep in the interior of the country, indigenous farmers fiercely resist the army's efforts to destroy their coca crops. The unprocessed coca leaf is central to traditional Andean culture and is used to treat everything from headaches to morning sickness. US-imposed eradication efforts rely in part on a genetically engineered herbicide that leaves the soil barren and causes unknown ecological damage.

After ten years of outright repression and legal "reform," Peru's labor movement yields a shadow of the power it held in past decades. Yet in spite of these setbacks, labor in Peru is far ahead of US labor in its independence, its coalitions with other social movements, and its militancy. The majority of the county's unions and labor federations have refused to back any of the presidential candidates, attacking the bland similarity of their economic plans. Peruvian bus drivers routinely demand legal reforms by blocking vehicular access to municipal buildings with their buses. In Cusco, owner-operator drivers put one-hundred buses up on jacks so they couldn't be towed and stayed in them for several days.

In Lima, health workers have protested unjust firings by chaining themselves to the gate of the health ministry building. In cities across the country, teachers embarked on hunger strikes against the same "temp-worker-ization" that is devastating private sector unions and making a mockery of labor laws in the United States. If the FTAA and similar institutions bring Latin-American style "flexible" labor reforms and privatization home to the US, even more American workers may find themselves in a similar situation.

In Cusco alone, there have been three general strikes in the past year. The most recent one, on March 14, was a powerful display of how different social movements can fight together around shared —and bold—demands. Local media reported 20,000 people in the streets on the morning of the strike, protesting the ongoing privatization of the Inca ruins at Machupichu and the planned privatization of the electric company and airport. Union members were only a part of the strike: banner-carrying contingents of teachers, bus drivers, and sanitation workers marched with farmer's groups, mothers who run the low-income feeding centers, market vendors, and neighborhood associations.

There wasn't any main rally or preplanned march route, just an immense wave of people flooding the downtown, stopping traffic, and shutting down noncooperating businesses. Marches spontaneously split apart into different directions, only to meet up with other masses of people a block away. Kids played soccer and volleyball in the middle of car-free streets. The strikers transformed the streets into the kind of liberated community spaces that groups like Art and Revolution have tried to create during the mass antiglobalization actions. Near Machupichu, tourist porters who haul inhumanly heavy loads for hikers on the Inca Trail successfully blocked the railroad going to the trailhead.

Even after a decade of repression has reduced the organized left to a shell of its former strength, Peruvian popular movements remain astonishingly vibrant. Whichever candidate wins the upcoming elections, Peruvians will resist the neoliberal regime with creativity, militancy, and most of all, tenacity. The best way North Americans can support these struggles, besides challenging the FTAA negotiations and the IMF, is to bring the lessons learned from our Peruvian compañeros into our own organizing.

Of course, capitalism in North America, with a sizable middle class and a sophisticated propaganda system, is very different from the crude and brutal form capitalism takes in Peru. Peruvians turn to militant solutions because poverty and state oppression rule out any other path. Yet Peru's powerful militant spirit, built over decades of struggle, gives us a vision of the broad-based culture of resistance we need to create here at home—a culture where most working people understand that nothing changes without political struggle and are willing to take militant action to solve the problems they face; a culture where people don't fight for causes or issues, but for themselves and their communities; a culture that will sustain us through the same kinds of crushing defeats that have battered Peruvian social movements, with our hope and our will to take to the streets intact. If we can learn from the powerful example our Peruvian friends offer us, we can cause a fierce enough rumbling here in the belly of the beast to return the favor.

# Standing Challenges to Capitalism in the Balkans
## Shon Meckfessel

The countries of the Balkan peninsula are in a unique position in the global economy. One resident of Sarajevo described this role as the "burning trashcan of globalization." Their convulsions and failures are incessantly posited as "other" to the adjacent West, their dysfunction cited as inherent proof of Western functionality. Greece is the poorest member in the European Union; Romania, Bulgaria, and Albania are still reeling after their severe dictatorships; Yugoslavia, once a relatively prosperous and open alternative to the East/West cold war dichotomy, has broken into five countries too traumatized to preserve their independence. Yet as one of the last areas of eastern Europe to face privatization and be sold off to foreign interests, people in the Balkans are largely critical of the effects capitalism has brought to its neighbors. In most of these countries, popular reluctance to playing this role has manifested in a resurgence of nationalism—itself such an unworkable alternative that neoliberalism soon follows in a philanthropic guise. But in scattered instances, resistance to the false choice between neoliberal invasion and regressive nationalist isolation has flourished. As the situations in these countries vary, so do the ways people resist. However, all share a rejection of their "burning trashcan" role, of the supposed necessity of capitalism as a solution. Below are four of many such instances.

### Slovenia
Slovenia is a place of contradictions. Its standard of living is the highest in eastern Europe, its citizens travel more than Australians, and the capital city of Ljubljana seems perversely cheery, yet Slovenia often charts the highest suicide rate in Europe. Slovenia was the first country to break away from Yugoslavia in pursuit of a place in western markets, and has been touted as the success story of post-communism: low unemployment, steady growth, low inflation, a balanced budget and manageable debt. Yet the population is noticeably nostalgic for communism: partisan statues still everywhere stand proudly, and kids sport hammer-and-sickle "CCCP" shirts. More surprisingly, the infrastructure of social support from the old days has somehow withstood, so far, the massive influx of foreign capital. Wages are relatively high, university and health care are largely state-provided, pensions

and welfare are good, the gap between rich and poor is small. The biggest complaint most people have is the boredom of living in a small country.

The contradictions of Slovenia are inherited from the contradictions of Yugoslav communism. Yugoslavia emerged ravaged from World War II. Tito, its beloved dictator, brought immense wealth and development into the country by keeping a diplomatic foot on each side of the Iron Curtain, ideologically expressed as "market socialism." It developed trade links with world markets while maintaining some sort of socialist distribution of wealth at home. The country also received massive foreign loans as Tito courted both sides in the cold war, incurring a debt that later brought about a total economic collapse; many cite this collapse as a central cause for the war in the 1990s. However for four decades Yugoslavia enjoyed a standard of living better even than Greece or Spain. Slovenia, once the richest republic in Yugoslavia, was not as devastated by economic collapse in the early 1990s as the others; it was the only republic to escape war, hyperinflation, and nationalist isolation in its secession.

While traveling in Slovenia, I found widespread appreciation of the old Yugoslav principle of self-management. Most people admitted the faults of single party rule within Yugoslavia—Slovenia broke away largely in reaction to the conservative dominance of the Communist Party and of the army—but still spoke warmly of the successes of self-management. Every workplace had a workers' council, in which every worker had at least a nominal say in the way the factory was run. One essay published in Ljubljana even argues that the war was made only by those sectors of society that were not reorganized by self-management: military, police, politicians, and peasants in rural isolation.[1] Many have dismissed Yugoslav self-management as merely tokenistic—including massive student revolts in Belgrade in 1968, demanding self-management and workers' councils worth the names—but its memory holds enough sway in Slovenia to make people wary of capitalist methods of organization.

One Slovenian friend, an economics student and anarchist antiglobalization activist, once told me she had few worries about Slovenia's integration into the global economy. "We're just too small, there's not enough here to justify the effort to conquer us." But Slovenia's future isn't necessarily so promising. "If Slovenia wants to join the European Union, it will have to drop a lot of protectionist and nationalist rules of its own… there is not enough shock in Slovenia's economic therapy," chides the *Economist*.[2] It is also playing bridge troll to fortress Europe, the last line of the Balkan "sanitizing corridor," which Croatian Prime Minister Racan boasted negotiating with Western diplomats. Slovenians and internationals have formed "no border camps" a number of times in protest. Slovenia's politicians, lusting for the self-importance conferred by EU and NATO memberships, have begun to implement neoliberal, militaristic reforms. Polls show the public to be divided about these changes.

With such a mixed situation, it's not surprising that radicals try unique approaches. The first resistance movement appeared soon after the Yugoslav military withdrew from their massive base in the center of Ljubljana. An army of activists, artists, punks, and miscellaneous miscreants organized a successful takeover of the base, dubbing the entire multiblock complex "Metelkova Mesto," or Metelkova Town. The city government laid siege to the center, and began demolishing it with bulldozers and wrecking balls while the occupants refused to leave. The media moved in and embarrassed the city by granting interviews with the occupants. Finally, the city retreated and granted the squatters control. Presently, after over ten years of existence, Metelkova is home to three concert halls and clubs, a skate park, an anarchist reading room, scores of art studios and practice spaces, three galleries, two drama theaters, offices for numerous activist groups, and four bars, two of them for gay and lesbian bargoers. Around 150 groups and individual artists are based in the complex.

Unfortunately, the present success of Metelkova has come with some sacrifices. The city, after abandoning the wrecking-ball approach, has become an ominous benefactor. First the municipal government insisted on paying for the center's electricity, and soon gave them the dubious gift of a twenty-four-hour security guard. The mysterious guard hasn't offered to stop nazis on the occasions they've attacked the space, but occasionally harasses drunk Metelkovites. This year, the city is demolishing a block of studios in which free community art classes have been taught for years, in order to build a large for-profit youth hostel complex in its place. The skate park is closed for construction, but no one seems to know for what end. Some of the older Metelkovites now refuse to frequent the town, frustrated with the commercialism that they claim has destroyed it as a truly autonomous public space.

Some of the dissenting ex-Metelkovites have gone on to more militant, explicitly political, and uncompromised organizing through the takeover of another space, named "Molotov." Unlike Metelkova, which hasn't housed any residents for several years, Molotov is home to a dozen or so activists. Social events revolve around the communal kitchen or living room, or an intermittent bar and concert space. The building was owned by the state railroad company, which astoundingly granted use of it to the squatters after they took it over. But after the city suspected the squat as a base for anti-NATO organizing, believe the residents, it moved in with a bulldozer, cut off their electricity and water, and began midnight raids of the center to intimidate them into leaving. The city seemed angered after the anti-NATO campaign helped turn public opinion against NATO membership, from a minority of dissenters into a majority of the country's populace. An initial siege, during which no one entered or left the center, lasted two weeks; the city has pulled back its bulldozers and riot police, and hired a twenty-four-hour private security guard. Local media was at first very sympathetic in their coverage, which forced the question of the preservation of public space in the face of capitalist development into wide discussion. But as Molotov refuses to accept gifts of the Metelkova sort from the city, the press has increasingly dismissed them as intractable radicals. A legal battle has kept the city from evicting them so far, but Molotov's future is as precarious as its flickering power supply.

## Croatia

A few years ago, discussion of political and social alternatives in Croatia was nearly impossible. Even in areas such as the capitol city Zagreb, which was mostly spared from direct destruction during the war, an atmosphere of fear dominated everyday life. Any public critic of state policies would risk being labeled a "bad Croat," a censure seen as treacherous and villainous as being in the attacking army. Dubravka Ugresic, a courageous and brilliant author critical of nationalism, was exiled to Austria. The *Feral Tribune*, a brilliant award-winning independent satirical magazine, was only able to survive the regime's endless lawsuits and tailored tax assaults with sustained support from international journalistic associations. Even punk rock culture, which had previously enjoyed mainstream success, became suspect. Police routinely arrested kids on the street for rebellious dress. Friends told me of one punk concert outside Zagreb, which was suddenly broken up by police firing shotguns over the heads of attendees. Protesters wishing to retain a memorial square to the victims of fascism were annually tear-gassed and assaulted by fascist counterprotesters, with police cooperation. This year, the country's first gay pride march was greeted with tear gas and hundreds of *seig heiling* protesters, determined to keep "bad Croats" out of public life. Criticisms of the state's neoliberal agenda have received a similar reception.

A casual visitor to Zagreb today might never suspect such tendencies. Thanks to the heroic efforts of groups such as "Attack!" (Autonomous Culture Factory), Croatia boasts one of the most inspiring liberatory movements in Europe. Attack! now resides in a gigantic factory building granted by the city after activists squatted it two years ago. On any night, the center might be hosting a naked fashion show in mud and twig, a Serbian dance party, a book release of the latest Emma Goldman translation, a touring Ukrainian folk-punk band, or an anarcha-feminist discussion group. Hundreds of young people are involved in the center's activities. In a country still emerging from nationalist isolation, the center hosts many visitors from the east and west, and serves as a regional hub for transnational organizing.

In April 2002, organizers from the center arranged a conference and series of actions called *Drugacije Svijet Je Moguc!* ("Another World is Possible!"). The conference included workshops on "Globalization, Privatization, and Women—the case of Croatia," "Agents for sustainable development in Croatia," and organic farming, self-management, participatory economics, revolution, and antimilitarism. Remarkably, mainstream media covered the event fairly and with considerable interest. As the participants took to the streets, more and more passersby took up signs and joined the marches. World War II-generation veterans led chants of "Death to Fascism—Freedom to the People!" Several hundred marched to the IMF office and met with lines of riot police. Other marches against genetic engineering and war were equally successful. Organizers were particularly proud of the "Take It or Leave It" fair, in which hundreds of residents freely donated and took from a large store of goods, and "exchange doesn't have to be one thing for one thing." At first people were confused, but soon happily seized on some things, and ran home to offer unneeded goods for others. Nearly 1000 people participated.

"We're in a radical situation here," explained one anarchist publisher and organizer. "People relate to radical solutions."

## Serbia

Because of the isolation of the sanctions, Serbian underground culture has had little chance to develop perspective. A strong culture of resistance to Milosevic's rule appeared, particularly in Belgrade and Vojvodina, which ultimately resulted in a mass popular overthrow of the regime in October 2000. Unfortunately, this culture was defined by opposition to the monstrous rule of Milosevic, which left Serbs poorly prepared for a critical response to the neoliberal invasion that has taken its place. People are still generally strongly anticapitalist in ideals, yet impatient for recovery of the economy. After police arrested a protester at an anti-G8 march recently, they apologized, "We're only arresting you because you blocked the street, but we hate capitalism too." However, Belgrade is littered with billboards such as, "Why privatization? To get new machines!" Serbia is now in a similar situation to Bosnia, in which a friend lamented, "We can't build our own factories, and nobody's going to donate $200 billion. Donations are nice—but $200 billion?" As I write, Pizza Hut has just bought out my favorite traditional café in Belgrade, where drinkers and diners of all ages and sorts got together and discussed the day's events around its tables.

In the midst of this despair and the apparent necessity of compromise, a few instances of determined anticapitalist resistance have arisen. In Bor, a town in eastern Serbia, the subject of Makavejev's film *Man is Not a Bird*, some 12,000 miners and processing workers provide an suggestive model. For decades, the wealth of the copper mine, the largest open-pit mine in Europe, has escaped the workers and found refuge in the pockets of local and national politicians. The average monthly wage of a full-time Bor miner is currently thirty-five dollars, a third of the Serbian average. Life expectancy in Bor is absurdly low, thanks in part to unregulated burning of wastes, some of which the company obtains at a profit from other countries. The miners and process workers have been fully aware of the cause of their plight, and have tried a number of redresses: their union has filed numerous grievances, courts have ruled that the politicians must return the money to Bor, the press has extensively reported on the situation and infuriated the public, but nothing has gotten close to bringing change.

Last summer, two members of Anarcho-Syndicalist Initiative, a group recently started by college students and punks in Belgrade, went to Bor to meet its occupants and give a talk. The hall was packed, the audience excited, the question-and-answer period heated. Participants took home every copy of *Direkt Akcion*, ASI's paper, which speaks of gender liberation, surrealism, and alchemy alongside classical anarchist unionism and antinationalism. Two weeks later, the president of the current union, himself a miner, called up ASI's general secretary. "We've all been passing around the papers, talking about the ideas from the meeting, and I think we'd like to dissolve our union and form a chapter of ASI." Reformist measures had so far gotten them nothing, he said, and the radical approach of an anarchist union, with its focus on direct action, sabotage, and class warfare seemed their last option. Soon after, the former president announced on television that they'd dissolved their union, and that the country should expect massive civil unrest if Bor was not given satisfaction. ASI has mailed their statutes to Bor, and the workers are discussing membership. "This week, we're fifty punks," smiled one member of the anarcho-syndicalist union. "Next week, fifty punks and 12,000 miners."

Meanwhile, the minister of privatization delivered an address on television, saying that things in Serbia are improving, privatization is progressing, but there has been some setback due to certain subversives, anarchists even, who have been distributing antiprivatization propaganda in front of factories in Belgrade. Some foreign investors have already pulled out due to this threat.

One week before I left Serbia, an American prospector satellite surveyed Bor's deposits, and discovered not only massive veins of top-quality copper remaining, but perhaps the largest gold deposits in Europe, running underneath the entire city. An American mining company immediately expressed interest in buying Bor. The miners have made no offers of concession.

## Albania

Albanians are used to living under and fighting against exploitation and imperialist dominance. A century ago they overthrew Ottoman imperial rule, enjoying two years of independence before being invaded in turn by Italy, Serbia, Montenegro, Greece, Austro-

Hungary, and France. National liberation forces drove out invader after invader; in Benito Mussolini's words, "Several thousand Albanians, without artillery, ejected us by force from Valona, and to escape being thrown into the sea, we began negotiations, but to no avail."[3] Soon the newly independent country found itself under its own fierce dictator, King Zog, who sold off the country's wealth to Italy. When Zog fled to London with all the country's gold at the outbreak of WWII, Albania was invaded in force by the Italians and later the Germans. The Albanian partisans drove out the fascists while abolishing the dictatorship to establish communism, which quickly evolved into the most oppressive of its manifestations. Enver Hodxa soon broke with the USSR for being too reformist, and ruled through an intense regime of extreme isolationist paranoia and unthinkable repression—every block had a "neighborhood watch" to make sure no one went anywhere but to work, and one in three people was a police informer. Then, in part thanks to an Italian television station boosting its signal to reach more of Italy, the allure of Western prosperity encouraged Albanians to overthrow the rule of the Communist Party in 1991.

As one of the last of the communist countries to revolt, Albania implemented widespread economic reforms with haste; people burned the greenhouses for their communist taint. Ideologues of capitalistic progress held it up as a model:

" . . . since communism was peacefully overthrown five years ago, the country has experienced more good than bad. . . . progress has been fast if inevitably patchy. Albania's cocoon of isolation was shed. Land was made private, state dinosaurs sold off or killed, small businesses allowed to sprout, and politics and religion freed. From the rockiest bottom, growth, albeit alongside much crookery, was the most rapid of all the ex-communist countries.[4]

After five years of utopian capitalist transition, the economy utterly collapsed and the entire country exploded in violence. Albania's miraculous growth had depended on a group of seven or so pyramid schemes, which suddenly vanished with eighty percent of the country's wealth. The population, furious after losing its life savings on the president's advice, arose in spontaneous revolt, raiding police and military armories, and set about destroying every police station, government building, and factory which could possibly be associated with the investment schemes or the government. The events are ambiguous and invite various readings. Traditional rivalries and blind panic erupted in widespread violence, with at least 2,000 deaths. Some participants, however, insisted that their reaction was not senseless. "We are not crazy rebels, we are people fighting together against a dictatorship," insurrectionists told the *Economist* reporters in the south of the country." English missionary Ian Loring, in his firsthand account of the events, explains, "The feeling among many was that capitalism as well as communism had now failed them."[5] Soon the uprising spread north through the entire country, and for two years furiously persisted. Greece and Italy invaded with international sanction to establish order, but were repulsed with a force reminiscent of that in Mussolini's quotation. No organized groups have claimed leadership of the uprising.

The *Economist* explains that, despite the liberalization of the economy, the system collapsed because of Berisha's corrupt political practices, and the appearance of pyramid schemes that he apparently encouraged. But hasn't political corruption and mass theft of public wealth always accompanied rapid growth and the privatization of the economy, its panicked movement of wealth and lack of social control? Has the *Economist* forgotten the plight of privatized Russia, where all social wealth found its way into a "New Russian" handful, where everyone not lucky enough to be a select millionaire has been left selling pencils, where life expectancy has fallen ten years in the last ten years?

In the north of Albania, where the government has abandoned control, the situation is difficult for an outsider to judge. Outside researchers have avoided traveling through the north, so information is scarce. Rumors abound of mafiacracy, banditry, and famine. In two short trips through the area, I saw contradictory indications. Shells of iron refineries tower over mountains of grass-covered top-quality ore, hollow factories teeter, weeds devour once collective-cultivated farms under tatters of burned-out greenhouses, people in small towns leer with desperation. Scattered mines and small factories, however, seemed to be working. In the city of Shkoder, alongside signs of deep disturbance, young people laughing, dancing, drinking, flirting, and eating pizza flood the promenades deep into the night. I wondered if they would have been any better off cooperating with international forces and their own government, adopting the IMF austerity measures that reduced Romania to a poverty even worse than under communism, or opening their doors to the foreign investors that have quickly robbed Czech Republic of so much natural wealth. Soon after Albania's rebellion, both of those countries elected nominally protectionist left-wing governments, even a leader of the old Communist Party in Romania's case. Perhaps Albania's rebellion was prudent; after losing eighty percent of their savings to progress, could Albanians be blamed for guarding the little they still have? The tragic lack of available productive alternatives little diminishes the strength of the Albanian's collective act of negation. The new economic order's effect on eastern Europe as a whole has, if anything, affirmed the foresight of the uprising.

After both World Wars, much of Yugoslavia, Albania, and the rest of the Balkans was leveled by protracted battles among local factions, ambitious neighbors, and sprawling empires. Yet, due perhaps to their pivotal geopolitical location, these countries rebuilt themselves and maintained relative independence. Their political approaches were innovative and unique, if not always admirable. Today, as they find themselves in radically different situations from each other, the roles they take within the global context will also vary widely. No partisans espousing grand humanitarian ideals of have come into power from the last decade's convolutions. But in the various resistance movements to capitalist hegemony, possibilities for political and economic alternatives are emerging. As the Balkans have been the location of notorious harbingers of world conflict in the past, the very insecurity of their situation may allow the articulation of new global precedents. Perhaps they are doomed to integration as a dysfunctional corner of the global order; the growth of resistance, however, gives a reason for hope. In the necessarily global context of current struggle, the success of these movements depends largely on global developments. Will the world provide a means of inclusion for Albania with greater appeal than nationalist isolation? Will the ex-Yugoslav microstates fall inevitably into a situation akin to Latin America's: neighbors shut off from each other and forced to deal individually with a distant master? Will resistance thrive as part of a growing worldwide movement, or be marginalized in favor of successors to the authoritarian structures so entrenched by the past?

For information on anarchism in eastern Europe, contact wielkowitsch@hotmail.com for subscription to the excellent bimonthly newsletter *Abolishing the Borders from Below. Zaginflatch*, the newsletter of the Zagreb Anarchist Movement, can be ordered from markos@zamir.net or Knjizara Konzor, Ilica 42, 10000 Zagreb, Croatia. Metelkova's website is www.metelkova.org. For Serbian/Bosnian/Croatian speakers, check out www.kontra-punkt-online.org.

1. Miroslav Stanojevic, "Regulation of Industrial Relations in Post-selfmanagement Society," Kuzmanic & Truger ed., (Ljubljan: Peace Institute Ljubljana, 1993).

2. Quoted by Michael Parenti, "Slovenia, Somewhat Out of Step," *Z Magazine.*

3. Ramadan Marmullaku, *Albania and the Albanians*, (London: Archon Books London: 1975), pp. 33-34.

4. *Economist*, March 8, 1997.

5. Ian Loring as told to Muthena Paul Alkazraji, *Christ and the Kalashnikov*, (London: Marshall Pickering, 2001).

# Apology for the Algerian Insurrection
# Jaime Semprun

*Edition de l'encyclopedie des Nuisances*, 2001
Translated by Kari, al-Majnun

Quevedo said about Spanish people: "they haven't been able to be historians but they deserved to be." This is still right concerning the 1936 Spanish revolution; others have written the history of the events. It's too early to write the history of the insurrection that started in Algeria during the spring of 2001, but it's not too late to defend it; in other words, to fight the deep indifference, puffed up with historic recklessness, as we see it in France.

To illustrate the importance and significance of this uprising, one just need to relate the acts and declarations of the insurgents. Put together according to their most universal and true meaning the facts give a picture of the situation from which a terrible morality is emerging: the dignity, the understanding, and the courage of the Algerian insurgents condemns the abjection in which people of the modern countries are living, with their apathy, their petty worries, and their sordid hopes.

The young rioters fought police and *gendarmerie* (military police) forces during several weeks shouting: " You cannot kill us, we are already dead!" Treated as half-dead by Algerian society, they knew that they had to destroy it to start living. ("Our answer to the nothingness will be to destroy its sire," declared one of them in July). Since April 21$^{st}$, mainly in Kabylie, but also since June 10$^{th}$ in Kenchela (in the Aures), the 11$^{th}$ in Skikda (north of Constantine) and the 16$^{th}$ in all the eastern part of the country (at Oum El Bouaghi, Batna, Tebessa, Biskra, El Tarf, etc.), they erected barricades, cut roads, and assaulted *gendarmerie* and police stations. They attacked a prefecture headquarters (in Tebessa, two ministers were inside the building), burned or vandalized many courthouses (in Ouacifs the "Justice Court," recently built, was reduced to ashes), some tax offices, post offices and state corporation offices, political party headquarters (at least thirty-two), banks, social security offices, communal parks, etc. The list is of course incomplete, and even if it were complete, it would only give a vague idea of the scale of the movement. At least we see that the insurgents undertook to clear the land from all "material expressions of the State." (*Monde Diplomatique* had the civic stupidity to suavely blame the rioters for finishing off the "public services," and asked if, by doing so, the "crowd of the castoffs of society" is not participating in "its own weakening.")

When peoples are recovering from submission, things that used to be supported are not anymore. After many other killings committed by police and the military, the murder of the student in Beni Douala, on April 18th, provoked the first riots three days later. In Amizour, near Beja'a, the population started an insurrection on the twenty-second after the arbitrary arrest of three students. In Khenchela, on the tenth of June, an officer who shows off, driving a large car, called to a young woman with contempt. Attacked by the young people who ran to defend the women, he cried out: "But what is going on with you today?" and the answer is "Everything changed." He got a good hiding, and his car was destroyed. One hour later, he came back with thirty soldiers dressed in civilian clothes, armed with automatic rifles. After a pitched battle, the soldiers had to retreat, but the riot spread in the whole town: barricades were erected, the city hall, the tax office, Sonelgaz corpoorate headquarters, the prefecture, and two chain stores are turned upside down by the people shouting: "This is the way for Chaouis!" The whole city is devastated.

When the routine of oppression is not tolerated anymore, the extraordinary becomes normal. During these weeks, these months, nearly everyday a *gendarmerie* brigade was attacked or harassed; and usually several at the same time. Military barracks were besieged; a blockade was imposed on the *gendarmes* who were then forced to launch raids for supplies. Those who admittted to having any relation with them, even strictly commercial, were boycotted, put in quarantine, and punished. Some hotels were burned, as well as villas, cafes, restaurants, and stores, targeted because they belonged to dishonest officials or various wheeler-dealer-businessmen. There were numerous destructions but it seems that there has been little looting. Thus, for example, in Kherrata on May 23rd the large stock of goods found in the house of a *gendarmerie* ex-officer were immediately burned. Everyone expressed their grievances, concerning housing, water, industrial nuisance, and monopolizing of all sorts; the corrupted were systematically exposed to public condemnation and treated as scoundrel. To start dealing with the problems posed by dilapidated state of the country, it was necessary to fight firstly those who prevent the people from taking care of these problems.

The population settled the authority hash; with officials close at hands, mainly the mayors were targeted. Beyond those skirmishes, the project of a complete expropriation of the expropriators was taking shape. Still marked by ambiguities that ended when the movement broke with the labor unionists, a declaration of the popular comity from Beja'a's Wilaya (prefecture) declared to the political power on July 7th: "Your gendarmes, symbols of corruption, are only useful to kill, repress and traffic. That is why they have to leave immediately. Concerning our security, our brave vigilance committees are perfectly dealing with it: they are our pride." The declaration goes on, reminding that the citizens' problems "are assumed by our neighborhood and villages' delegates and by labour unionists delegates who are working in an assembly called popular comity. Isn't it Direct Democracy? "

The insurrection, or at least its more advanced organization, was limited to Kabylie. Nevertheless, it has to be called Algerian insurrection because the Kabyle insurgents themselves called it Algerian and tried to extend it, and they refused the berberist identity argument in which their enemies wanted to disguise them.

# Flare Up! Niger Delta Women Take on Oil Companies
## Erin Volheim

*Earth First! Journal*
September-October 2002

"We are all women here. We are angry and grieved—that is why we have come together. We cannot rely on our husbands anymore for this fight, because they are not giving us the desired results. Moreover, these days you know that it is the women that take up most of the responsibilities.

Me, I am a fisher woman. My only occupation is fishing. But nowadays, when I go to the riverine areas, there are no fish. Oil pollution and gas flaring have killed all the fish. The farmers who farm the land cannot get anything from their land anymore because of environmental degradation. Oil spillages have destroyed their lands.

As a result of all this, we are hungry. Our children are suffering. This gas they are flaring is causing so many of us to die prematurely. Three days ago, I lost my sister. She died from suffocation. She was just crying "My throat, my throat," and she died within thirty minutes.

They do not give our women employment, we are jobless and have no money because our means of livelihood have been destroyed. We are hungry—that's why we came here. Gas flaring has destroyed our lives."

—Elizabeth Ebido, Itsekiri protest leader

On an American television, the camera pulls back its focus from a scene of parrots chattering in lush green surroundings. Our viewing experience of this tropical environment widens, as we gain an aerial scope. From up high, we are looking down on an island. The pattern of tropical vegetation now reveals the ominous symbol of the Shell Oil corporation.

This thirty-second commercial of US televised green wash is supposed to make us think that Shell is environmentally friendly. In fact, it holds a deeper, more insidious message reflected in the political reality of the oil-rich Niger Delta. Shell and ChevronTexaco have made a devastating imprint on this watershed and the indigenous Urhobo, Itsekiri, Ijaw, Ogoni, and Ilaje peoples who depend upon it. Against tremendous odds, these people have met multinational corporations with resistance for the past thirty-five years. Pipeline sabotage, protest and nonviolent hostage-taking are as common as company oil spills.

Nigeria is the world's sixth-largest oil exporter, accounting for approximately one-twelfth of the oil imported by the US. Sales of crude oil account for more than eighty-five percent of the Nigerian government's revenue. Five companies tower over Nigeria—the British/Dutch Shell, the Italian AGIP, the French Elf-Aquitaine, and US giants ChevronTexaco and Mobil. Each operates in partnership with the Nigerian National Petroleum Company, a government-run corporation.

These oil companies claim that their activities are conducted under the highest environmental standards and that the impact of oil on the environment of the delta is minimal. The late Ken Saro-Wiwa, former spokesperson for the Movement of the Survival of the Ogoni People until he was unjustly hanged in 1995, maintained that Ogoniland has been "completely devastated by three decades of reckless oil exploitation."

In 1956, the discovery of oil in the Niger Delta triggered a chain of events that led to the political and economic marginalization of its inhabitants. Rivers, forests, mangrove swamps, farmland, and fishing creeks have all experienced devastation.

Oil has been more of a curse than a blessing for the people. Nigerians once believed that corporate promises of economic prosperity would come true. Instead, they have been at the receiving end of horrendous government repression and brutality. Indigenous youth have been shot or wounded routinely during protests. Environmental Rights Action in Nigeria calls for a complete withdrawl of multinational oil companies for these reasons and more.

This summer, actions were organized by indigenous women working together for their survival. These actions were unique because they were carried out by women who were united in protest despite a history of long-term intertribal strife. Nigeria, like all of Africa, is comprised of a glorious patchwork of indigenous cultures. Nigerians represent more than 250 different ethnic groups, whose relations have been strained by more than a century of British rule. To add insult to injury, the economic disparity forged by oil corporations has increased the intertribal tension as they each vie for a small bit of prosperity.

It is in this complex political climate that 3,000 Ijaw, Itsekiri, and Ilaje women took everyone by surprise by working in unison to confront Shell and ChevronTexaco. Nigerian writer Blessyn Okpowo witnessed on August 8, "As early as five a.m., the quiet waterfronts in Warri came alive. Special boats and passenger vessels of various shapes and sizes began to arrive at the waterfronts. Each boat was full to capacity with women singing solemn songs in the various dialects. Their songs were sorrowful dirges lamenting the pitiful conditions of the Niger Delta."

They seized the Ogunnu operational headquarters of ChevronTexaco and Shell by nonviolently overpowering the security guards and entering before the shift change. They carried placards accusing the companies of polluting their environment, and they forced work to stop. Women and children barricaded the gates and setup canopies. They brought food and bedding and were prepared to stay as long as needed. Ilaje leader B.I. Ugbasanin vowed, "All will not be well for the oil companies in our areas until they start treating us as human beings that deserve a good life."

Soon after, the women had a face-off with security agents, armed soldiers, and police. Scores of women were seriously injured as soldiers used wire whips and kicked them. Four soldiers and three policemen beat Alice Youwuren, a widow and mother of seven, unconscious. She was admitted to a Shell clinic in Warri. According to newspaper reports, another woman was shot dead after a soldier fired into the crowd to disperse the protesters. Shell and ChevronTexaco deny the reports of injuries and murder. They say the women were hired by the union to do a counter-protest and create negative publicity.

They do corroborate that the remaining women were teargassed and that the situation was quelled the following day.

From August 14-23, one hundred Ilaje women took over a smaller Ewan oil platform. After nine days, ChevronTexaco decided to ignore this smaller group and wait them out. When the Ilaje women realized that they were not perceived as a threat to business as usual, they left on their own accord.

These protests were the latest in a month of all-women demonstrations that began July 8 with a ten-day siege of ChevronTexaco's offices in Escravos near Warri. The Itsekiri women, after taking over an offshore oil terminal, used a potent cultural shaming tactic: they threatened to remove their clothes. Public nudity, a local taboo, would have embarrassed the 1,000 oil workers on the terminals who regard these older women in high esteem.

On July 16 Ijaw women took over four oil flow stations, fifty miles southeast of Escravos. These combined July actions cost ChevronTexaco three million dollars in lost revenue. Talks with ChevronTexaco ensued and both parties came to an agreement that temporarily satisfied the Ijaw and Itsekiri women. However, the communities near Escravos received no sign that the company would follow through. No hard copies of the agreement were provided, nor did they sign any. This led them to commit to the actions last month.

The public role of women in the Nigerian political arena has great potential. Their willingness to work together is a powerful antidote if it can be sustained. Matters will only become more complicated as George Bush Jr. wars with other oil nations.

The US is looking into doubling its oil imports from Nigeria in an effort to be less reliant on the Middle East. Nigeria's military government seems happy to further develop and destroy the region for short-term profit and greater political power on the international front.

In solidarity with the people of Niger Delta, take on a Shell or ChevronTexaco near you. Contact: ChevronTexaco, 575 Market St, San Francisco, CA 94105; (415) 894-7700.

For more information, contact Project Underground, (510) 705-8981, www.moles.org.

# Testimonies and Declarations
# Women Speak Out

In July and August of 2002, hundreds of women from Itsekiri, Ilaje, and Ijaw communities came together to demand environmental and economic justice from ChevronTexaco and Shell, two corporations that have been operating in the Delta since the early 1960s. In July, women occupied ChevronTexaco's Escravos facility and at least four other flow stations. The women, numbering 3000 demanded an end to pollution, economic reparations for damages, support for local economic development, and jobs for their sons. The women stalled ChevronTexaco's operations, leading to negotiations and concessions by the company. About two weeks after the demonstrations ended, the women went to the offices of ChevronTexaco and Shell in Warri to demand that they follow through with their concessions. Carrying only protest signs, the women were confronted by the dreaded "kill-and-Go" mobile police.

The following testimonies were taken by Environmental Rights Action (ERA), with women who participated in the demonstrations and community leaders.

**TESTIMONIES** From Women Demonstrating Against ChevronTexaco and Shell operations in the Niger Delta, July-August 2002.

## ENVIRONMENTAL TESTIMONIES
### Delta State–ChevronTexaco and Shell

"SHELL and CHEVRONTEXACO gas flare and oil spills has polluted our river and atmosphere. For the first time women from Itsekiri, Ijaw, and Ilaje decided to put an end to these predicaments. We went there to ask for help not to fight but we were maltreated. We Itsekiri, Ijaw, and Ilaje are one no division, no divide and rule."
—*Bimpe Ebeleye*
*Awoye Community, Ilaje Woman*

"Chevron has neglected us. They have neglected us for a long time. For example, any time spills occur, they don't do proper cleanup or pay compensation. Our roofs are destroyed by their chemical. No good drinking water in our rivers. Our fishes are killed on daily basis by their chemicals, even the fishes we catch in our rivers, they smell of crude oil. Chevron know the right thing to do, they intimidate us with soldiers, police, navy and tell us that

cases of spill are caused by us. We are tired of complaining, even the Nigerian government and their Chevron have treated us like slaves. thirty years till now, what do we have to show by Chevron, apart from this big yard and all sorts of machines making noise, what do we have? They have been threatening us that if we make noise, they will stop production and leave our community and we will suffer, as if we have benefited from them. Before the '70s, when we were here without Chevron, life was natural and sweet, we were happy. When we go to the rivers for fishing or forest for hunting, we used to catch all sorts of fishes and bush animals. Today, the experience is sad. I am suggesting that they should leave our community completely and never come back again. See, in our community we have girls, small girls from Lagos, Warri, Benin City, Enugu, Imo, Osun, and other parts of Nigeria here everyday and night running after the white men and staff of Chevron, they are doing prostitution, and spreading all sorts of diseases. The story is too long and too sad. When you go (to ERA) tell Chevron that we are no longer slaves, even slaves realize their condition and fight for their freedom."
—*Voice of Mrs. Felicia Itsero, 67,*
*Ijaw mother and grandmother (translation from Ijaw by Ms. Fanty Waripai)*

"Our problem with Chevron stared on June 10 in our river. We sent a delegation to see Chevron and complain about our plight as a neglected oil producing community. Instead of Chevron to listen to us, the women, they phoned soldiers from Escravos tank farm. The soldiers who numbered up to fourteen, met us at the river and rough handled us. They destroyed five of our boats and wounded our people. We were tortured. When they saw that we were prepared to die, Chevron later called us and promised to listen to our demand. From that June 10, 2002, we waited and nothing was done. So on July 17, 2002, we decided to enter the Abiteye flow station and peacefully protest. Our demands are genuine, even the soldiers who Chevron sent to torture us can tell you that we are not violent, so nobody can use violence against us. We are mature people and we are protesting in a matured manner. Most times Chevron signed memoranda of understanding (MOU) with us and they refused to meet the conditions. Even the environmental problems from Chevron's facility are threatening us, and they have not done anything for our local fisher women. If you want to catch fish now, you really have to go into the deep sea and we don't have such equipment. In fact, I want to say that Chevron in insensitive and callous to our plight. Out problem is caused by them and we are now living in abject poverty. When we protest like this, they just give money to few greedy individuals and they think that they have solved the problems. We are prepared to die."
—*Voice of Mrs. Lucky Murade, 30-year-old and mother*
*(Translated from Pidgin English by ERA's Patrick Naagbanton)*

"We went to Shell's office to protest the sufferings and degradation we get from the operations. As we arrived their premises we shared ourselves into groups (CHEVRON + SHELL), they invited FIRE FOR FIRE (Policemen) to use horsewhip on us, beating women, spraying tear gas. We were treated roughly, even old women were treated like goats, and my back was thoroughly wiped.

After running from their premises we advance to DBS (Delta Broadcasting Service) to tell the world of our sad experiences with SHELL & CHEVRON. The same security men that maltreated us also came to DBS, we were also beaten and all staffs of DBS also got a piece from the security agents. We want them to go from our land we need them no more. This time we are ready to die."

—*Rose Jemeigbe*
*Itsekiri woman*

"Chevron is deceitful. They have deceived us several times and we know them better now. We won't leave this place till our demands are met."

—*Voice of Mrs. Juliet Tomfawer, 39 years old and mother.*
*(Translated from Pidgin English by ERA's Patrick Naagbanton)*

For the past thirty-six or thirty-seven years they have been operating in our area, most of the pipes in our area have not been changed. They decided to leave them until they burst in different places, and pollute the river, because to avoid payment or compensation to the host community they will say it is sabotage, the government comes into their rescue. No truth in what they are saying (sabotage), it has been pipes not changed, joints in the wells not attended to."

—*Hon Dele Jombai (a community leader)*
*Tsekelewu community, Warri North L.G.A., Delta State*

The Ijaw women are complaining they (CHEVRON) may please the government; they may please other people, but we want the international community to know that the Ijaws, Itsekiris, and other peoples of the Niger Delta have been oppressed seriously. The Ugborodu people are suffering, we the Ijaws are in perpetual slavery. Apartheid is in Ogborodu community, apartheid is in the whole Delta State.

Our condition as Itsekiri people is growing worse every second. We visit other places and we see development. We have (crude oil) what it takes for development but we are despised. We cannot even train our children in school, we have been experiencing different kinds of ailment never known to us. Sickness and premature death is sweeping our land because frequent oil spills, gas flares, and other activities related to oil exploration. These are the reasons why the women are provoked; no water, good roads, nothing at all. We the women have decided to die at CHEVRON and SHELL's gate instead to die instal-mentally from gas flares and frequent oil spills.

Women numbering about 3,000 stormed their premises on a peaceful protest. We have now decided that we are going there with our husband and children so that the elimination process will be easier for them."

—*Mrs. Kate Ajagbawa*

*Itsekiri woman (Tebu & Igboko)*

*Mother of five children*

# Rattling the Chains of Global Apartheid
# Jeff Conant

January 2003

## W$$D

The growing social movements in South Africa refer not so much to the vague and all-encompassing term "globalization" as they do to a more specific term whose usage is on the rise: global apartheid. These words were especially in evidence during the spectacle known as the World Summit on Sustainable Development (WSSD), held in Johannesburg from August 26 to September 4, 2001. The WSSD, though largely ignored by both mainstream and alternative media, may have been a crystallizing moment both for the "movement" and for the global institutions that sponsored, financed, and ultimately hijacked the event. It was certainly a moment in which the words "global apartheid" came vividly to life for a massive gathering of people originating in the far-flung quarters of the earth, from fortress Europe to occupied Palestine to war-torn Colombia to famine-stricken East Africa to the Great US of A. On a local level, from the perspective of the disenfranchised and bitterly disillusioned social movements of the "new South Africa," the words *global apartheid* serve as a reminder that the mechanisms of neoliberalism are not new, and in fact, that the new world order is the old world order with its boots polished.

The WSSD, also known as Rio-Plus-Ten, was organized as an attempt to assess the achievements of the Rio de Janeiro Earth Summit ten years earlier, and to build on those achievements. The stated goals of WSSD were poverty reduction and environmental conservation—"people and planet." But the achievement of these goals was doomed from the outset. The Rio Summit, a landmark gathering of environmental groups, government officials, and heads of business, had given rise to such international agreements as the Kyoto Protocol on Climate Change and the Convention on Biodiversity. It also gave rise to a decade of corporate green washing and a successful campaign to define sustainable development on terms favorable to corporate capital; that is to say, development that sustains a healthy profit margin, a cheap labor force, and an invisible fist to keep the market in balance.

In the run-up to the WSSD it was noted that one key event had perhaps the largest impact on thwarting any positive outcome from the original Rio summit process. That event was the creation of the World Trade Organization.

Locally, in the new South Africa, the key event of the previous decade was, of course, the nation's overthrow of the apartheid regime and its mythic reintegration into the "world community." Thabo Mbeki, who followed Nelson Mandela as chairman of the African National Congress (ANC) and president of South Africa, was eager to use the WSSD as a showcase for his country's democratic advances, just as he had during a slew of other global gatherings he had recently hosted—the World Conference Against Racism, the World Aids Conference, and the World Economic Forum. But, unfortunately for those interested in showing the world that South Africa was free and that development, as such, was truly sustainable, the spectacle of the Summit failed to mask two ugly truths: the fact that the democratic opening in South Africa had been soundly defeated by neoliberalism, and the fact that the multilateral institutions most invested in "development"—the World Bank and the IMF—have no interest in either alleviating poverty or conserving the environment. A third grisly truth was also confirmed at WSSD—the United Nations is powerless to stop the global race to the bottom.

If these facts are common wisdom by now, it is largely because of the tireless mobilization of civil society activists to pull back the curtain at the most revealing moments. In Johannesburg during two weeks in 2002 the curtain was pulled back by the united efforts of South African social movements and the stalwart ad-hocracy of "antiglobalization" activists together taking to the streets of Johannesburg. To illustrate, let me tell one small part of the story of those two weeks in Johannesburg.

## White Candles and Stun Grenades

*"We will dismantle the World Bank and IMF*
*Enough, it's really enough."*
— Chorus sung by thousands in unison in the streets of Johannesburg

Two nights before the Summit was to open at the posh Sandton convention center, local organizers from the Landless Peoples' Movement and the Anti-Privatization Forum invited foreign activists to join them in a peaceful candlelight march. The march was to go from Witwatersrand University, site of a two day teach-in on local and global issues, to the city jail, where seventy-three members of the Landless Peoples' Movement had been locked up since a fray at the home of Johannesburg's mayor several months before. Trevor Ngwane, chairman of the Anti-Privatization Forum (APF), offered an explanation of the events leading up to the arrests, and assured the foreigners that the march would be peaceful. "We are only going to visit our brothers in the jail," he said. "We welcome your solidarity."

As night fell a crowd of some 700 people—mostly black South Africans in their red APF shirts—carried candles through the street leading from Wits University towards the city jail. Among the crowd were several dozen foreigners, from veteran antiglobalization activists Vandana Shiva, Maude Barlowe, and Oscar Olivera to new students of the movement attending the Summit to get an inside look at the UN process. They were to get more than they bargained for.

Only two blocks into the march, without a moment's notice, sudden explosions rocked the night and smoke choked the street. Amid a mass of shouting and confusion the entire throng turned and stampeded in the opposite direction. Through the smoke a police blockade appeared, as APF members recovered their posture and assured the foreigners that these were only stun grenades, not live ammo.

"This happens all the time," I was told by a stranger. "We know what to do."

As the smoke settled, the booming voice of Trevor Ngwane called out to the crowd, "Down, down, sit down." Soon the street was blocked on the one side by thirty or forty police in riot gear with teargas guns and clubs, and on the other by a seated mob holding candles. The crowd began to sing Zulu songs of protest as Ngwane, Maude Barlowe, and others negotiated with police. Two women injured in the action—one burned by a stun grenade and the other trampled by the crowd—were removed back to the university.

The next day, the small but potent vigil and the violent repression it received made headlines not only in South Africa, but throughout Europe. Foreigners visiting the country for the first time got a quick and dirty lesson in South African political process, and the tone of the events surrounding WSSD was set. Even for foreign activists unfamiliar with the South African scene it was immensely clear that this march and the street-level power struggle it represented was no isolated event. It was set in a history of such actions—sit-ins, wildcat strikes, industrial sabotage, spontaneous and strategic visits to the homes of local politicians, and more proactive strategies like the famous reconnections of water and electricity to those in the townships too poor to pay.

In the weeks to come, events outside the convention center were a mix of spontaneous protests and strategically planned, highly visible actions. Manifestations of the globally marginalized, from Tibetan Buddhists and Palestinian Muslims demanding recognition of their homelands, to networks of environmental justice activists and land rights groups, gathered everywhere mixing their chants with the near-constant singing of Zulu war songs that brought the history of colonization and resistance to the ears of summit delegates in the streets and meeting halls of the city. Much of the organizing was done under the auspices of the Anti-Privatization Forum, an umbrella coalition made up of socialist militants, radical students, the Landless People's Movement, independent intellectuals , and smaller issue-based groups. The name "Anti-Privatization Forum" speaks to the depths of South Africans' grievances with neoliberalism. It also celebrates one of its key component organizations, the heroic Soweto Electricity Crisis Committee (SECC), which responded to the privatization and cut-off of services by teaching families how to recon-nect their power in what they called Operation Khanyisa, meaning "light up" in Zulu. What all of the groups that make up the APF have in common is their opposition to the ANC government. Trevor Ngwane, a former ANC representative from Soweto, has gener-ously noted, "We cannot blame the entire ANC just like that for all of our problems. But we should blame Mandela and Mbeki because they eagerly, willingly, even keenly embraced capitalism."

As it became clear throughout the 1990s that the new South Africa was worse off even than the old South Africa, the movement grew organically and coalesced under the banner of the Durban Social Forum during the World Conference Against Racism. To trace the lineage of resistance one step further, the Durban Social Forum, which staged its first mass rally on August 31, 2001, took its name from the Genoa Social Forum, the gath-ering that sparked the most riotous uprising Europe had seen in three decades.

A year later, on August 31, 2002, the largest march since the end of apartheid danced and sang and shouted and sweated its way through the streets of Johannesburg and straight into the history of global anticapitalist resistance.

## Landless People's March: a Kick in the Milk White Teeth of Sandton

The decision to hold the world summit in Sandton, outside of Johannesburg, was indica-tive. A posh suburb and commercial hub, Sandton is known as the wealthiest square mile in all of Africa. In a nation that, more than any other, represents staggering divisions of race and class, the choice to hold a summit on issues of poverty and development at the Sandton convention center was a slap in the face of the social movements. And the social movements wanted nothing more than to slap back.

Ten kilometers or so from Sandton lies Alexandra, the poorest of Johannesburg's townships. Alexandra, an overcrowded, underserviced, violent, and totally polluted infor-mal settlement, was home to some of the ugliest apartheid repression, and the fiercest anti-apartheid resistance. As such, it was historically a strong center for the ANC. So the decision by the Anti-Privatisation Forum to stage a march from Alexandra to Sandton was both symbolically brilliant and politically risky. If the people of Alexandra did not back the APF it would weaken their standing among the poor throughout the country. If they did, it would prove that the ANC had truly lost its popular footing. Perhaps equally important, by gathering in the township the march would give thousands of foreigners attending the summit an opportunity to witness firsthand the misery caused by apartheid.

The march was scheduled for Saturday, August 31, halfway through the summit. Although there were several days of official discussions still to come, the previous week left even the more optimistic NGOs frustrated and disillusioned with the summit. Sixty-four thousand people had registered and paid to participate in the summit. On arrival, it was discovered that the Sandton convention center could only hold 6000. After the large government delegations, many of which hosted handfuls of corporate CEOs and industry reps, there was little room left for "civil society." Those who managed to bear the humiliation of long lines and security checks did so only to find that the negotiating sessions were closed and the key meetings were "full." Worse, rumors had begun to circulate and later were confirmed that inside decisions had been made to ensure that the language of multilateral environmental agreements would, from now on, be made consistent with the trade rules of the WTO. By the end of the first week, Saturday's Landless People's march came to look like a good forum for everyone on the "outside" to protest whatever was happening on the "inside."

The ANC tried to outlaw the march. When it saw that this would only result in mass civil disobedience, it opted to organize its own march for the same time. The ANC march was billed as the "legitimate" march where conference attendees could hear speeches by President Thabo Mbeki and other world leaders. Hugo Chavez, Fidel Castro, and even Yassir Arafat were rumored to be on the bill. With this lineup, the landless peoples' march would truly represent a radical fringe.

At the end of the day, after the two marches had run their course, the numbers told the story. Legitimate march: 1000 attendees. Radical fringe: 20,000.

With scores of armored personnel carriers barricading intersections, helicopters circling above, and parades of riot police on motorcycle, horseback, and foot, marchers gathered on a hill overlooking both Alexandra and Sandton. Student-types from Europe and North America, NGOs from across the global South, Korean peace activists, Japanese antinuclear activists, and German greens mixed with indigenous peoples from all nations, Palestinians in their *khaffias* and even a handful of globe-trotting Black Bloc anarchists. But by far the largest showing was black South Africans, many in their red APF shirts bearing a logo of mama Africa and a raised fist. Many also wore headbands condemning NEPAD—the New Economic Program for African Development, a continental scheme spearheaded by Mbeki that would unite Africa under a common bond of structural adjustment, export production, and trade liberalization. "Phansi NEPAD!" the headbands declared—down with NEPAD.

The march was not a march at all but a sea of dancing and singing, a joyful gathering of the vibrant human tribe across boundaries of race, class, ideology, and nation. During the six or so hours in which the march snaked ten long kilometers from the miserable shantytown of Alexandra to the gleaming malls of Sandton there were no nations, no color lines, no doubts about who one was marching with and, despite the constant presence of police helicopters and tanks, no fear. This parade against global capitalism had been brewing for decades, and nothing was going to stop it.

The march remained peaceful even as thousands gathered outside the Sandton convention center to listen to speeches by Ngwane, Virginia Setshedi, and other movement leaders. As the afternoon waned and the exhaustion of the dry ten-kilometer trek under the African sun set in, a proud glow arose over the crowd. It must have been clear to everyone present that, as the invisible barrier between Alexandra and Sandton was broken down by an unstoppable mass mobilization a decade after the fall of apartheid, a new turn had been taken, and a movement that had been building organically for years had suddenly come into its own.

### Sources:

The history and background of the South African social struggles in this essay are largely gleaned from the writings of Patrick Bond, especially his *ZNet* commentaries and his book *Against Global Apartheid*; and the writings of Ashwin Desai, especially his book We Are the Poors: Community Struggle on Post-Apartheid South Africa. Additional history and quotes are from personal interviews with Trevor Ngwane that I conducted during the course of the World Summit.

# Insurgent Chinese Workers and Peasants:

## The "Weak Link" in Capitalist Globalization and US Imperialism[1]

# John Gulick

The attacks of September 11 forced the worldwide movement against capitalist globaliza-tion into temporary retreat. But as the Bush II regime parlayed the mini-horror of cold war-blowback into the mega-horror of US imperial conquest in Central and West Asia, savvier elements of the movement against capitalist globalization quickly regrouped. While the Cheney-Perle-Rumsfeld-Wolfowitz axis in Washington plotted the invasion and occupation of Iraq, these elements of the movement appropriately preoccupied them-selves with how to theoretically link capitalist globalization and US imperialism, and how to recompose the movement accordingly. Given the urgency with which this reorientation had to be effected, and the tremendous stakes involved, it is no mystery why relatively obscure events unfolding in the "rust bowl" of northeast China in the spring of 2002 were missed by most opponents of capitalist globalization and US imperialism. Yet these events that took place in the cities of Daqing and Liaoyang crystallized a much vaster pattern of events that may seriously wound both capitalist globalization and US imperialism.

In March 2002, up to 50,000 workers cut loose by the Daqing Petroleum Administration Board (DPAB) protested in broad daylight against the Board's capricious slashing of their severance pay. For over a week some of these workers overran and occu-pied the headquarters of the DPAB, a subsidiary of China's leading oil transnational, the public-private PetroChina.[2] During the same month, up to 40,000 furloughed and sacked workers electrified Liaoyang with a sequence of high-profile protests held in front of the city hall.[3] Coming from several local state-owned enterprises (SOE's) that had failed to pony up wage arrears and pension installments,[4] the demonstrators were catalyzed to action when the city's mayor shamelessly remarked to reporters, "There is no unemploy-ment in Liaoyang."[5] Banners proclaimed such militant slogans as "The army of industrial workers wants to live!" and "It is a crime to embezzle pensions!"[6] The Daqing and Liaoyang protests were probably the largest authentically independent workers' demonstrations in the history of the People's Republic of China (PRC).[7]

When the worldwide mobilization against capitalist globalization hit its pre-September 11 stride, some of its partisans characterized it a "movement of movements," arguing quite cogently that one of its virtues and trademarks is its decentralized, networked, and pluralistic character.[8] According to this formulation, the movement as a whole consists of parallel initiatives and struggles within and across the global South and global North. While these parallel campaigns are animated by the same, or at least similar, principles (i.e., against the depredations of global neoliberalism), they are also unshackled by a concentrated, top-down structure of command and control. Curiously, however, one of the most pivotal movements in objective opposition to the imperatives of capitalist globalization was not and is still not conventionally regarded as part of the broader movement: the movement (informal, localized, and episodic though it may be at present) of insurgent Chinese workers and peasants resisting the assorted hardships imposed on them by the Chinese Communist Party (CCP)'s accelerated implementation of its "economic reform" and "opening up" policies, epitomized by China's November 2001 accession to the World Trade Organization.

Scattered outbursts of worker and peasant protest have been on the dramatic upswing in China since 1998.[9] Demonstrating workers are aggrieved by the downsizing, closure, and privatization of SOE's and by brutal exploitation in subcontractor sweatshops while demonstrating peasants are aggrieved by plunging crop prices. Both workers and peasants are absolutely exasperated by and fed up with the venality of local party-state officials. Consequently the number of reported worker and peasant protests has metastasized at a dizzying pace. According to the Chinese Ministry of Public Security (a state entity usually inclined to downplaying the extent of social unrest), the year 2002 constituted a high-water mark for worker and peasant demonstrations.[10] Whereas an average of eighty daily "incidents" occurred in 2001, by December 2002 this figure had swelled to 700.[11] The CCP's experiment with "socialist market economy with Chinese characteristics" has entered some kind of watershed crisis, one that its newly installed "fourth generation" leadership is trying to address with short-term palliative measures.[12]

This momentous development of the past five years seems to have eluded the attention of many activist-theoreticians close to the movement against capitalist globalization. Whatever their tactical and programmatic differences concerning the how and the where of the movement, French socialist intellectuals and Italian anarcho-communist militants, US environmental radicals and Chiapan Zapatistas, Brazilian landless laborers and South African municipal activists alike share at least one thing in common: theorizers of and spokespeople for the movement against capitalist globalization recognize each and every one of them as participants in this amorphous but definable movement. Generally speaking, the same recognition has not been extended to Chinese workers and peasants courageously fighting the multiple and intertwined evils associated with CCP-engineered neoliberalism and global capitalist integration. This failure to characterize current-day Chinese worker and peasant protest (and, in some cases, outright insurrection) as part of the worldwide refusal against capitalist globalization stems partially from the reality that neither rebellious Chinese workers and peasants, nor representatives democratically elected by them, have actively taken part in those events customarily associated with the broader global movement—the successive street demonstrations staged alongside the summit meetings of the WTO/IMF/World Bank/G7, or the respective World Social Forums in Porto Alegre and Florence, and so on. A salient cause of this absence is that the CCP remains dead-set against the licensing of independent popular organizations that could potentially contest the prerogatives of the party-state, and coercively suppresses their very existence.

One irony of overlooking the historic Daqing and Liaoyang protests, and thousands of comparable protests, is that the trajectory of capitalist globalization and of the US imperialist quest for planetary dominance rests largely upon the disposition and the action of ordinary Chinese workers, peasants, and rural-to-urban migrants. Although the claims they make upon party-state officials may deal mostly with hand-to-mouth issues, the Chinese demonstrators unwittingly endanger the smooth functioning of a Pacific Rim accumulation regime critical to the prolongation of US imperial power.

Despite a host of imagined and genuine geopolitical frictions between nominally "communist" China and the US, the mutual destinies of the CCP elite and US ruling groups are becoming inextricably wedded to one another. US big business direly needs China as an outlet for exports, as a theater for financial speculation, and as a supply platform for the production of cheap parts and components. As long as China continues to hold the lion's share of its voluminous currency reserves in dollars, stabilizing the privileged status of the US currency as "world money," the hawks and neocons in Washington can live with China's emergence as the "workshop of the world."[13] The CCP's acquiescence to this arrangement is virtually guaranteed by the staking of its legitimacy and sheer survival on an economic model dependent upon huge flows of US-led foreign direct investment and parity access to US markets.[14] And by decisively tying its political future to an emergent mainland Chinese capitalist class whose fortunes are entwined in the trans-Pacific commodity chain, the CCP all but confirmed this dependence at its 16th National Congress held in November 2002.[15] To the extent that the CCP tries to waver from the implied terms of this marriage, the US Departments of War and State have various tools at their disposal - arms transfers to Taiwan, leverage over the oceanic conduits of oil transport, coy complaints about human rights abuses, all buttressed by post-911 encirclement—

to force China back into line, overblown proclamations about its high-tech military buildup notwithstanding.[16]

At the risk of oversimplifying, US ruling groups need a "socially stable" China as much as the CCP does. The structural arrangement between a deepening of neoliberal reform in China and the putative reinvigoration of US hegemony thus frames the backdrop in which the gathering storm of Chinese worker and peasant resistance is taking place. Besides the fact that the segment of the Chinese populace suffering from the CCP's latest concessions to capitalist globalization makes up roughly one-eighth of humanity, this equation is precisely why partisans of a recomposed "global justice" movement should train their sights on increasingly agitated and unruly Chinese workers and peasants. Bearing this in mind, myriad aspects of the recent worker and peasant mobilizations warrant closer inspection.

Ever since it broke up the agricultural communes and announced "market socialist" economic reforms more than twenty years ago, the post-Mao CCP has based its claim to authority on its ability to hasten the growth of the productive forces while keeping a lid on domestic disarray.[17] CCP ideologists have cast the rapid development of manufacturing, science, and technology, and the maintenance of civil order, as worthy projects in themselves and as preconditions of one another. Additionally, the CCP has stressed two rationales for this combination of high growth and social stability: boosting the "standard of living" and enhancing China's power in the international system. Arguably, the CCP emphasized the former rationale before the Tiananmen Square protests, and the latter afterwards. It can also be said that large swathes of the Chinese population—regardless of social class, age, region of residence, or ethno-racial identity (i.e. Han or "minority")—have in principle embraced these ideals.[18] The party has kept its grip on power over the past two decades in large part because its "market socialist" policies have contributed to remarkable gains in the average standard of living and a more prominent role for China on the world stage.[19]

However, six years after the 15th National Congress of the CCP, economic growth can no longer obscure the sharpening of social inequality in China. Tens of millions of SOE workers and hundreds of millions of land-poor peasants and landless migrants now face the end of all minimal welfare guarantees and destitution. China's official income disparity surpasses that of famously polarized India, Indonesia, Egypt, and Pakistan, according to the World Bank (whose SOE bankruptcy and buy-out prescriptions are partially responsible for engendering the very conditions it decries).[20] In the last half-decade, around fifty million SOE toilers have been sacked, demoted, or furloughed with little or no living allowance.[21] A large number of the millions recorded as reemployed by the CCP barely subside peddling plastic novelties and other consumer wares on the street. During the same period, peasant incomes have flatlined while school and other rural public service fees have escalated. More recently, courtesy of WTO entry, corn, sugarcane, soybean, tobacco, and wheat prices have been pressed downward. Meanwhile, the army of rural migrants (also known as the "floating population"), its members often condemned to virtual forms of bonded or sweated labor, numbers nine figures.[22]

Hard and comprehensive data on the frequency, size, and type of worker demonstrations, as well as data concerning trends, are difficult to come by. But statistics issued by the Ministry of Public Security make it clear that there has been a dramatic swell in the number and intensity of worker demonstrations, as do warnings about "social instability" sounded by eminent Chinese academics and top CCP officials. Moreover, Ministry of Labor and Social Security reports indicate that heightened worker insubordination behind factory walls was the harbinger of heightened worker protest in the streets. In the last few years, these shop floor actions have spilled into local public arenas and assumed multiple forms: pickets with speeches, marches on labor bureau and government offices, and physical blockades of road and rail traffic.

Production stoppages, work-to-rule strikes, and other incidents involving the total or partial withholding of labor rose by 900 percent between 1992 and 1998, and by an additional twenty percent between 1998 and 2000.[23] These wildcat actions afflicted SOE's, joint ventures, and Chinese capitalist-owned enterprises alike. Undoubtedly this explosion in spontaneous shop floor revolt is rooted in the conversion of the Chinese labor force into so much variable capital. Party-state edicts of the past fifteen years have progressively scrapped the Chinese working class' social wage (work unit-based education, heating fuel, housing, medical, transportation, and other subsidies) and empowered SOE managers and private sector bosses to hire and fire with impunity and peg pay scales to worker productivity.[24] While Chinese workers must foreswear the "iron rice bowl" and ramp up their work intensity, neither SOE managers nor private sector bosses are required to sacrifice anything. No matter their incompetence at bringing enterprises up to capitalist world market standards of efficiency, unaccountable SOE managers amass wealth by skimming rescue loans tendered by state-owned banks and illicitly transferring public property to personal cliques at rock-bottom prices.[25] And, of course, the new generation of mainland Chinese capitalists gets rich the old-fashioned way—not by brokering the looting of the enfeebled public sector, but by appropriating a hefty share of the value produced by their fellow countrymen and countrywomen.

Northeast China, once the robust heartland of Chinese state-owned heavy industry, has been the epicenter of demonstrations staged by SOE workers. In Liaoning province more than half a million SOE employees were thrown out of work in 2002 alone, and the real unemployment rate in the province's hardest-hit cities now tops twenty-five percent.[26]

In Heilongjiang province, where SOE's absorb seventy percent of the labor force, 500 SOE's were merged, privatized, or shuttered between 1998 and 2002, leading to a net loss of some 1.2 million jobs.[27] Vast numbers of northeast China's idled SOE workers, especially the middle-aged with no saleable skills in an overcrowded labor market, now face out-and-out penury.[28] In many cases, SOE managers have embezzled pension funds that laid-off workers counted on for a dreary subsistence.[29] In other cases, managers have refused to ante up severance packages and back wages owed to unemployed SOE workers.[30] By the end of 2000, the tally for wage arrears in Liaoning and Heilongjiang combined was an estimated one billion dollars.[31] The central government has done little to attend to the pressing social security needs of northeast China's laid-off. Despite bombastic promises the nationwide unemployment insurance system remains desultory.[32]

Because of their size, durability, and magnitude, the demonstrations in Daqing and Liaoyang garnered a fair amount of attention from workers' rights NGOs and the international press. But the Daqing and Liaoyang demonstrations are not exceptional. In early 2000, for example, 20,000 downsized mineworkers and their relatives staged a three-day riot in the Liaoning town of Yangjiazhangzi. Demonstrators smashed windows and vandalized police vehicles.[33] In mid-2001, as many as 10,000 coal miners from the Jilin province town of Jishu, inflamed by wage arrears and corruption in the local mining bureau, blocked northeast China's most central rail line for more than three days.[34] Slightly more than a year later, another coal mining town in Jilin, Taonan City, was wracked by worker demonstrations. Livid about withheld pay, faulty mining equipment, and hazardous work conditions, 2,000 miners marched on the offices of the city party committee and shouted incendiary slogans that the CCP could interpret as treason: "Overthrow the dark government and put the evil-minded mining bureau on trial!"[35] In December 2002, 2,000 chemical plant workers owed several years' back pay formed a human chain across the Avenue of the Red Flag in the Liaoning district of Shuangtaizi.[36] In the same month, 2,000 unemployed paper-mill workers in Jiamusi, Heilongjiang barricaded the city's two primary national transport conduits, the rail line to Beijing, and the road to the airport. Stirred to action by the usual dose of local state venality—in this case officials helping themselves to the mill-workers' living allowance fund—the Jiamusi demonstrators refused to back down even when military police arrived on the scene.[37] Most alarmingly for the CCP, in January 2003 textile workers robbed of their retrenchment entitlements took to the streets in Dandong, a city in Liaoning that had already witnessed protests by defrauded investors and demobilized soldiers in the same month.[38]

The upsurge in SOE worker demonstrations has not been confined to northeast China alone. In July 2001 more than 1,000 furloughed sugar-mill workers from the inner Mongolia city of Linhe assembled in front of the local CCP office to protest the failure of their employer to deposit its revenues into an unemployment insurance fund.[39] In April 2002, a thousand laid-off steelworkers in the southeastern province of Guizhou impeded traffic on two highways to protest insufficient redundancy benefits.[40] Beginning in September 2002 and extending several weeks thereafter, more than 500 retrenched oil workers from the massive inland city of Chongching staged daily sit-in demonstrations outside the headquarters of Chuandong Oil Exploration and Drilling Company (COEDC), demanding lower pension premiums, higher unemployment allowances, and job placement for those not nearing retirement age.[41] Coming on the heels of the 16th National Congress of the CCP, the month of December 2002 was marked by an explosion of SOE worker demonstrations all across China. In the gritty Shanxi province city of Datong, a motley contingent of more than 10,000 idled workers expressed their disgust with social security arrears and party-state corruption by burning a Japanese luxury sedan driven by a provincial cadre (a vehicle worth the combined annual income of fifty to eighty employed workers).[42] In the Hebei province city of Shijiazhuang, a 5,000 person-strong crowd of laid-off workers and their dependents surrounded municipal government offices, demanding explanation for why money had been collected for a social security fund which never materialized.[43] Finally, in Piangxiang, Jiangxi province, 5,000 miners facing termination besieged the town's civic center. Particularly galled by the Pingxiang City Mining Bureau's heavy-handed attempts to get its workforce to quit "voluntarily," which would have spared the Bureau social security obligations, the miners displayed a banner that perfectly encapsulates their class situation in the bureaucratic capitalist PRC: "Ask heaven and earth, who controls whether we float or sink? It is the corrupt officials and privileged class!"[44]

At present, the panoply of SOE worker demonstrations comprises the primary front of Chinese popular protest. But ever since Deng Xiaoping's famous tour of the special economic zones in 1992, when he implored party bosses to accelerate the most neoliberal aspects of the economic reform program, domestic and foreign private capitalist investment has been the basis of industrial accumulation in China. At the same time, coastal metropolises (especially in the south) have been the leading crucibles of working class formation. This is precisely why workers' resistance to superexploitation in the subcontracting sweatshops of Guangdong and other coastal provinces can be considered the cutting edge of Chinese popular struggle against capitalist globalization.

The political economy of urban coastal China is multifaceted and complex, but nonetheless it is possible to distill a few essential features. While the transnational corporations of the US, Europe, and the rich countries of East Asia turn to the export platforms of urban coastal China in order to defend and extend their profits, the means by which they do this are multiple. Fixed investment in plant and equipment, with or without a local public or private partner, in order to directly employ cheap labor and thus slash production costs, is one. The global companies also slough off routine stages of industrial production to Chinese capitalist suppliers and then purchase components, parts, semi-finished, and finished goods from them. Subcontracting arrangements allow the transnationals to unburden themselves of immobile commitments that carry a high risk factor, and to take advantage of a special attribute offered by local capitalist jobbers: their capacity to rapidly mobilize reserves of labor-power when the global companies need orders filled quickly and just as rapidly demobilize (*i.e.*, lay off) these reserves when external demand slackens.[45] The structural condition of the sweatshop proletariat of urban coastal China thus involves both a high rate of exploitation and profound employment insecurity, the latter reinforcing the former.

Mainland Chinese-owned suppliers, joint ventures, and even foreign-owned firms attain these high rates of exploitation through absolute surplus value extraction. Mandatory overtime is standard in the export platforms, and work weeks in excess of 110 hours are not unheard of.[46] Factory managers have an array of soft and hard power techniques at their disposal to force a desperate labor force to work intensively for long periods. Quite regularly bosses will shortchange workers for overtime or withhold several months of pay, deliberate ploys to keep workers in a suspended state of semi-peonage.[47] In some instances, forms of physical intimidation, such as compulsory (and illegal) body searches, are used to underscore absolute control.[48] What is more, the demographic makeup of the export platform workforce boosts the effectiveness of these types of coercion. Many are migrants from the rural interior who lack both local residency permits and local support networks, and their fear of being deported tends to dampen their resistance to super-exploitation. Needless to say, sweatshop workers are prohibited from forming any kind of defensive or mutual aid organization independent of the government apparatus. Party-state corruption further amplifies abusive managerial practices in the export zones. A strong corpus of statutes exists to protect workers from the most heinous kinds of workplace maltreatment, but party-appointed judges under the sway of local "red capitalists" rarely make rulings injurious to their benefactors.[49]

It is both astonishing and inspiring, then, that a burgeoning fury of worker demonstrations has shaken multiple Chinese capitalist worksites, many of them deeply tied into world circuits of production and exchange. For example, in July 2001, in the very crown jewel of Chinese capitalism—the special economic zone of Shenzhen—migrant workers at the Baoyang Industrial Corporation responded to illegal body searches by staging a day-long protest at the local township courthouse.[50] In April 2002, in the nearby Guangdong province city of Dongguan, 1,500 former employees of a Hong Kong-based supplier of US transnationals (among them, Mattel and Wal-Mart) violently butted heads with factory security personnel while protesting their summary dismissal.[51] In October 2002, in Lingchuan of neighboring Guanxi province, 200 employees of a fertilizer factory subcontracted to a Shanghai capitalist held a sit-in demonstration to protest eight months worth of wage arrears.[52] And in January 2003, hundreds of grubby migrant construction workers plied wooden planks in front of a Beijing luxury residential compound, refused to let the compound's well-heeled residents cross, and demanded immediate delivery of a year's back pay owed by the compound's contractor.[53]

Apart from its sheer magnitude, the most noteworthy feature of this insurgent workers' movement is its demographic composition. For the first time in at least two decades, there exists a dynamic, militant, and independent Chinese workers' movement that is spearheaded not by sympathetic intellectuals but by members of the working class directly wounded by the CCP's neoliberal economic reforms.[54] The movement's nominal leaders are organically emerging from the rank-and-file on the basis of concrete contributions and sacrifices made to their local struggles and the resulting trust and respect they garner from their rank-and-file peers. What is more, not only are the movement's leaders evolving from organic settings and processes rooted in local working-class civil societies, but it is their shop-floor mates who actually comprise the shock troops of the demonstrations and protests.[55] A study conducted by researchers at the Chinese Academic of Social Sciences in 2002 indicated that a majority of Liaoning's unemployed were willing to publicly express sympathy with demonstrating workers and more than one-quarter were willing to join them in direct action.[56] Finally, the grassroots origins of the movement's leaders and the fluid boundaries between them and their rank-and-file constituencies suggests that it is difficult for the CCP to suppress the movement by decapitating its leadership, whether by bribery or by personal harassment, mock trials or hard time.

Peasant protest in the contemporary PRC is a dark continent of sorts, unknown and unknowable in its dimensions and scope. Mounting discontent in the countryside has commanded the attention of the CCP's "fourth generation" leaders, even as their unflagging commitment to the market rationalization of agriculture, per the terms of WTO entry, feeds this mounting discontent.[57] The bulk of peasant protest has been directed against grasping rural cadres who subject peasants to all manner of illegal fees, surcharges, and taxes. For example, in December 2002, a huge crowd of 80,000 peasants turned out in Shaanxi province to demand that the party-state clamp down on exorbitant taxation at the local level.[58] More recently, however, peasant protest has been generated by the global law of value: plunging crop prices. For example, in fall 2002, 30,000 sugarcane-growing tenants in Guanxi province took over a local government building in demonstration against dropping sugar prices, or, as the protestors put it, against "exploitation and squeeze" by the procurement agencies.[59] And in December 2002, 10,000 tobacco farmers from Yunnan province converged on the provincial capital, Kunming, to demonstrate against falling purchase prices paid by the tobacco bureau.[60]

In and of itself, the increasingly squalid circumstances of many Chinese workers and peasants is not sufficient to provoke them to petition officials, block roads and railways, and occupy government buildings. They do not protest primarily because the depth of their immiseration leaves them no other choice. Rather, what prompts them to demonstrate is the piquing of their sense of injustice. They realize that clearly recognizable others, especially SOE plant managers, local and regional party-state notables, and rural cadres, flagrantly prosper in inverse proportion to their own suffering.[61] Moreover, they also recognize that this inverse relationship is often oiled by flagrant corruption and outrageous abuses of authority—the illegal stripping and pawning of SOE assets, the looting of temporary social insurance stipends fronted by Beijing, the extortion of phony taxes and surcharges, and so on.[62]

Central government crackdowns on crooked bureaucrats, managers, and officials may assuage some protestors' sense of being wronged.[63] But to a large degree it is the CCP's liberalizing and globalizing economic policies that spawn the opportunities for the ethically impaired to milk public property for private enrichment. What is more, no matter how much China's party-state adopts the "rule of law," the underlying drift of the CCP's reconciliation with capitalist globalization is more social polarization, not less. Today's protests aimed at local party-state venality contain within them the seed of tomorrow's protests against central party-state policy.[64] This is all more the case because significant numbers of Chinese workers and peasants, especially SOE workers, still take seriously the CCP's anachronistic claim to rule on behalf of all Chinese people, including those strata whose class interests were theoretically privileged in the heyday of Maoist state socialism. Thus even at this stage of the transition to capitalism, when the culture of possessive individualism has allegedly swept over all of Chinese society, the party's redrawing of the old social contract still has the capacity to trigger a sense of betrayal and outrage. Workers march to protest lay-offs and peasants riot to protest illegal taxation in part because many of them still regard job security and low-cost medical care and primary schooling as inalienable rights, and such convictions pose big trouble for the legitimacy of the CCP, given the neoliberal bent of its economic policy.[65]

Convinced that "there is no alternative" and certain that China's destiny is full neoliberal integration into the global capitalist order, the "China hands" of the mainstream Western media assume that the current wave of Chinese worker and peasant protest will die down and fade into history, thus mimicking the pronouncements of PRC ideologists. In the short term, so the argument goes, the social engineers now at the helm of the CCP will calm the demonstrations by buying off the protestors—that is, by partially meeting the protestors' monetary demands for wage arrears, social insurance payments, and the like—when possible, and by selectively using repressive force when necessary. While CCP leaders buy time with carrots and sticks, over the medium run they will devise and implement policies to attend to the welfare of China's "disadvantaged groups," Hu Jintao's term for tens of millions of structurally unemployed workers and some 150 million uprooted peasants with no place to go.[66] Setting aside the fact that bigger and better neoliberal globalization may well aggravate both environmental degradation and mass destitution in China, it serves well to remember that many of the same commentators who optimistically herald technocratic solutions today were recently convinced that state-controlled media blackouts would prevent local autonomous workers' movements from horizontally communicating with one another. Among others, the protesting Chongching oil workers who consciously followed in the footsteps of their brothers and sisters in Daqing put the lie to this notion.[67] The more Chinese workers and peasants augment their independent strength, the more the architects of bureaucratic capitalism in Beijing are put on notice—and the more the US imperialist project of a "New American Century" in East Asia and elsewhere suffers setbacks.

1. The author would like to thank Jim Davis and Eddie Yuen for their editorial suggestions, Reigan Robbins for her research assistance, and Hou Xiaoyang for her moral and material support.

2. John Chan, "Workers' Protests Continue in Northeast China," *World Socialist Web Site*, May 25, 2002, www.wsws.org/articles/2002/may2002/chin-m25.shtml; Trini Leung, "The Third Wave of the Chinese Labour Movement in the Post-Mao Era," *China Labour Bulletin*, June 2, 2002.

3. While the Liaoyang demonstrations were brought to a temporary halt when local officials met some of the protestors' demands halfway, the alleged "leaders" of the demonstrations, Yao Fuxin and Xiao Yunliang, were arrested and detained without being accused of any specific crime. Yao and Xiao were ultimately put on trial, something of a ritualistic proceeding in which they were not allowed to verbally defend themselves, and charged with "subverting state power," a serious offense that could lead to lifetime prison sentences. At the time of writing, court officials had yet to formally announce a verdict. For information on how you can assist Yao, Xiao, and other independent workers' movement activists in China, visit the website of China Labour Bulletin (www.china-labour.org.hk/iso). In the view of this author, China Labour Bulletin is subtly animated by a syndicalist perspective and is free of the

"human rights imperialist" agenda of many of the global North-based human rights NGOs.

4. Eric Eckholm, "Corruption Protest in China Leads to Charges, Top and Bottom," *New York Times*, September 12, 2002; Micheal Lev, "7,000 Chinese Workers Unite in Daring Protest," *Chicago Tribune*, March 13, 2002; Philip Pan, "Three Chinese Workers: Jail, Betrayal and Fear," *Washington Post*, December 28, 2002.

5. Lev. The real unemployment rate in Lioayang actually hovers somewhere around the forty-percent mark. See Katherine Arms, "China Workers Protest Amid Leadership Move," United Press International wire service, November 5, 2002.

6. Pan, Lev.

7. Leung.

8. Perhaps the Canadian author-activist Naomi Klein is most closely associated with the appellation "movement of movements," although it is unclear and unimportant who initially coined it. See, for example, Klein, "Reclaiming the Commons," *New Left Review*, May-June 2001, www.newleftreview.net/NLR24305.shtml.

9. Tim Pringle, "Industrial Unrest in China—A Labour Movement in the Making?" *China Labour Bulletin*, January 31, 2002; Elisabeth Rosenthal, "Workers' Plight Brings New Militancy in China," *New York Times*, March 10, 2003.

10. "Containing Unrest," *Economist*, January 18, 2003.

11. *Cheng Ming*, January 3, 2003, pp. 17-19.

12. On December 12, 2002, the new president of the CCP, Hu Jintao, assented to a state council directive restraining local and military police from using brute force against worker and peasant protestors. See *Cheng Ming, ibid.,* and Hamish McDonald, "Why China is Allowing Dissent," *The Age*, January 31, 2003, p. 11.

13. Liu, Henry, "China *vs.* the Almighty Dollar," *Asia Times Online*, July 23, 2002, www.atimes.com/atimes/China/DG23Ad04.html

14. Scott B. MacDonald, "China not immune to U.S. woes," *Asia Times Online*, July 27, 2002, www.atimes.com/atimes/China/DG27Ad01.html.

15. John Gittings, "China Turns Its Back on Communism to Join Long March of the Capitalists," *Guardian*, November 9, 2002.

16. Antoneta Bezlova, "Why China Doesn't Mind the War in Iraq," *Asia Times Online*, March 26, 2003, www.atimes.com/atimes/China/EC26Ad03.html; David Murray, "Challenge in the East," *Guardian*, January 30, 2002.

17. Maurice Meisner, *Mao's China and After* (New York: The Free Press, 1999).

18. At the peril of generalizing, few among the Chinese are romantic, black-green, or red-green critics of modernity, although a significant portion of older-generation workers (especially SOE workers) lament the erosion of collectivist values. See Robert Weil, *Red Cat, White Cat* (New York: Monthly Review Press, 1996).

19. C. P. Chandrasekhar, "A Challenge in China," *Frontline* 19(7), March 30-April 12, 2002.

20. Tim Pringle, "The Path of Globalisation: Implications for Chinese Workers," *Asian Labor Update* 41, October-December 2001.

21. John Chan, "Beijing to Prosecute Leaders of Workers' Protests," *World Socialist Web Site*, April 20, 2002, www.wsws.org/articles/2002/apr2002/chin-a20.shtml.

22. Ibid., "The Legacy of Retiring Chinese Premier: Social Inequality and Unrest," *World Socialist Web Site*, March 19, 2003, www.wsws.org/articles/2003/mar2003/chin-m19.shtml; Christopher Horton, "Changing of the guard: Exit Zhu, Enter Wen," *Asia Times Online*, March 18, 2003, www.atimes.com/atimes/China/EC18Ad01.html.

23. Pringle, "Industrial Unrest in China—A Labour Movement in the Making?"

24. Chen, "Wage Arrears Fuel Discontent," *China Labour Bulletin*, August 31, 2002, www.china-labour.org.hk/iso/article.adp?article_id=3016; Pringle, "The Path of Globalisation: Implications for Chinese Workers."

25. Chen, "Wage Arrears Fuel Discontent."

26. Chan, "Workers' Protests Continue in Northeast China,"

27. "Chinese Province Grapples with High Jobless Rate," *Straits Times*, February 6, 2003.

28. Julie Chao, "China's Labor Unrest not Likely to Lead to Reforms," Cox News Service, July 8, 2002.

29. "Chinese province grapples with high jobless rate."

30. Ibid.

31. Chen, "Wage Arrears Fuel Discontent;" Chan, "Workers' Protests Continue in Northeast China."

32. Chan, "The Legacy of Retiring Chinese Premier;" Pringle, "Industrial Unrest in China."

33. Erik Eckholm, "A Mining Town's Sullen Peace Masks the Bitter Legacy of China's Labor Strategy," *New York Times*, April 14, 2002.

34. Pringle, "Industrial Unrest in China."

35. *Cheng Ming.*

36. "Chinese Labourers Protest Corruption and Unpaid Wages," Agence France Press wire report, December 30, 2002.

37. Chrostopher Bodeen, "Protesting Workers Arrested in Northeast China," Associated Press wire report, December 11, 2002.

38. McDonald.

39. Pringle, "Industrial Unrest in China."

40. Chan, "Beijing to Prosecute Leaders of Workers' Protests."

41 *China Labour Bulletin,* September 17, 2002.

42. *Cheng Ming.*

43. Ibid.

44. Ibid.

45. Chen, "Wage Arrears Fuel Discontent."

46. Pringle, "Industrial Unrest in China"; Chan, "Beijing to Prosecute Leaders of Workers' Protests."

47. Remarkably, one academic study concluded that *eighty percent* of foreign-financed firms in Dongguan, Guangdong illegally retained workers' wages for between one and three months. See Chen, "Wage Arrears Fuel Discontent."

48. Pringle, "Industrial Unrest in China."

49. Philip Pan, "Chinese Workers' Rights Stop at Courtroom Door," *Washington Post,* June 28, 2002.

50. Pringle, "Industrial Unrest in China."

51. Chen, "Wage Arrears Fuel Discontent."

52. "Two Hundred Workers in Southern China Protest Over Unpaid Wages," Agence France Presse, October 8, 2002.

53. "Hundreds of Workers Protest at Luxury Compound in Beijing," Agence France Presse, January 17, 2003.

54. Leung.

55. Ibid.

56. "Containing Unrest."

57. Chan, "The Legacy of Retiring Chinese Premier."

58. *Cheng Ming.*

59. Arms, *Cheng Ming.*

60. *Cheng Ming.*

61. Pringle, "Industrial Unrest in China."

62. Chao.

63. Eckholm, "A Mining Town's Sullen Peace Masks the Bitter Legacy of China's Labor Strategy"; McDonald.

64. See analysis in Rosenthal.

65. Pan, "Three Chinese Workers: Jail, Betrayal and Fear."

66. McDonald; Rosenthal.

67. Leung.

# Part V: Articulating Resistance

# Activistism:

## Left Anti-Intellectualism and Its Discontents

# Liza Featherstone, Doug Henwood, and Christian Parenti

"We can't get bogged down in analysis," one activist told us at an antiwar rally in New York in the fall of 2001, spitting out that last word like a hairball. He could have relaxed his vigilance. This event deftly avoided such bogs, loudly opposing the US bombing in Afghanistan without offering any credible ideas about it (we're not counting the notion that the entire escapade was driven by Unocal and Lockheed Martin, the "analysis" advanced by many speakers). But the moment called for doing something more than brandishing the exact same signs—"Stop the Bombing" and "No War for Oil"—that activists poked skywards during the Gulf War. This latest war called for some thinking, and few were doing much of that.

So what is the ideology of the activist left? Socialist? Mostly not; it's too state-phobic. Some activists are anarchists—but more out of temperamental reflex than rigorous thought. Others are liberals, though most are too confrontational and too skeptical about the system to embrace that label. And many others profess no ideology at all. So, overall, is the activist left just an inchoate, "postideological" mass of do-gooders, pragmatists, and puppeteers?

No. The young troublemakers of today do have an ideology and it is as deeply felt and intellectually totalizing as any of the great belief systems of yore. The cadres who populate those endless meetings, who bang the drum, who lead the "trainings" and paint the puppets, do indeed have a creed. They are activismists. That's right, activismists. This brave new ideology combines the political illiteracy of hypermediated American culture with all the moral zeal of a nineteenth-century temperance crusade. In this worldview, all roads lead to more activism and more activists. And the one who acts is righteous. (To clarify, we're talking about the global justice, peace, media democracy, community organizing, financial populist, and green movements—leaving aside feminist, labor and mainstream civil rights groups, many of which are currently afflicted by "inactivism," which is of course far worse). The activismists seem to borrow their philosophy from the factory boss in a

Heinrich Boll short story who greets his employees each morning with the exhortation, "Let's have some action." To which the workers obediently reply: "Action will be taken!"

Activists unconsciously echoing factory bosses? The parallel isn't as far-fetched as it might seem, as another gloomy German, Theodor Adorno, suggests. Adorno admittedly doesn't have the last word on activism; he called the cops on University of Frankfurt demonstrators in 1968. Nonetheless, he had a good point when he criticized the student and antiwar movement of the 1960s for what he called "actionism." In his eyes this was an unreflective "collective compulsion for positivity that allows its immediate translation into practice." Though embraced by people who imagine themselves to be radical agitators, that thoughtless compulsion mirrors the pragmatic empiricism of the dominant culture "not the least way in which actionism fits so smoothly into society's prevailing trend." Actionism, he concluded, "is regressive, it refuses to reflect on its own impotence."

It may seem odd to launch such a critique, just when activistism seems to be working. Protest is on an upswing; even the post 9/11 frenzy of terror baiting didn't shut down the movement. Demonstrators were out in force in early February to protest the World Economic Forum, with a grace and discipline that buoyed sprits worldwide. The youth who are getting busted, gassed, and trailed by the cops are putting their bodies on the line to oppose global capital. They are brave and committed, even heroic.

But is action enough? We pose this question precisely because activism seems so strong. The flipside of all this agitation is a corrosive and aggressive anti-intellectualism. We object to this hostility toward thinking, not only because we've all got a cranky intellectual bent, but also because it limits the movement's transformative power. Our gripe is historically specific. If everyone were busy with bullshit doctrinal debates we would prescribe a little anti-intellectualism. But that is not the case right now.

## The Real Price of Not Thinking

How does activist anti-intellectualism manifest on the ground? One instance is the reduction of strategy to mere tactics, to horrible effect. Take for example the largely failed San Francisco protest against the National Association of Broadcasters (NAB), an action which ended up costing tens of thousand of dollars, gained almost no attention, had no impact on the NAB, and nearly ruined one of the sponsoring organizations. During a postmortem discussion of this debacle one of the organizers reminded her audience that: "We had three thousand people marching through [the shopping district] Union Square protesting the media. That's amazing. It had never happened before." Never mind the utter non-impact of this aimless march. The point was clear: we marched for ourselves. We were our own targets. Activism made us good. Thoughtless activism confuses the formulation of political aims. One of us was on a conference panel during which a prominent activist lawyer went on about the virtues of small businesses, and the need for city policy to encourage them. When it was pointed out that enthusiasm for small business should be tempered by a recognition that smaller businesses tend to pay less, are harder to organize, offer fewer fringe benefits, and are more dangerous workplaces than larger businesses, the lawyer dismissed this as the "paralysis of analysis." On another panel, when it was pointed out that Saul Alinsky-style community organizing is a practical and theoretical failure whose severe limitations need to be recognized, an organizer and community credit union promoter shut down the conversation with a simple: "I just don't want to discuss this."

The antiwar "movement" is perhaps the most egregious recent example of a promising political phenomenon that was badly damaged by the anti-intellectual outlook of activistism. While activists frequently comment on the success of the growing peace movement—many actions take place, conferences are planned, new people become activists, a huge protest is scheduled for April in Washington DC—no one seems to notice that it's no longer clear what war we're protesting. Repression at home? Future wars in Somalia or Iraq? Even in the case of Afghanistan, it turned out to be important to have something to say to skeptics who asked: "What's your alternative? I think the government should protect me from terrorists, and plus this Taliban doesn't seem so great." The movement failed to address such questions, and protests dwindled. On some college campuses, by contrast, where the war has been seen as a complicated opportunity for conversation rather than sign waving, the movement has done better. Students at University of Massachusetts, Cornell, and elsewhere have fasted and held teach-ins to call attention to hunger in Afghanistan, while at other schools, "tent cities" have become meeting places for students of varying viewpoints to discuss the war.

But nationwide, the unwillingness to think about what it means to be against the war and how war fits into the global project of American empire has also led to a poverty of thinking about what kind of actions make sense. "How can we strategically affect the situation?" asks Lara Jiramanus of Boston's Campus antiwar Coalition. "So we want to stop the humanitarian crisis in Afghanistan—what does it mean to have that as our goal? I don't think we talk about that enough." We're not arguing for conformist ideologies. The impulse to resist hierarchy and mind-control is one of the more appealing and useful facets of the new activism. Consider the campus anti-sweatshop movement, which includes members of the International Socialist Organization, SDS-type radical democrats, anarchists, and plain-vanilla liberals. This movement's willingness to embrace radicals and non-radicals alike has been a strength, attracting both policy wonks and people who like to chain their throats to the dean's desk. Such flexibility is usually commendable. What bothers us about activistism as an ideology is that it renders taboo any discussion of ideas or beliefs, and thus stymies both thought and action. Many activists agree. Jiramanus, who is also involved in the Harvard Living Wage Campaign, says that some in that group believe that the fight for a living wage is part of a "larger ideal" while others don't. "But if your analysis is not broad enough," she points out, "you're not much different from those groups that do charity work." In her campus labor solidarity group, "people will say, 'I'm not progressive, I just care about this issue.' There's a failure to think of our work in a larger context, and a reluctance to ask people what they believe. There needs to be a venue for talking about alternative economic systems." But she says these questions don't get talked about, and people who do think about them are afraid to bring them up in meetings. "It's like, 'there's no time for it, we need to win the living wage campaign right now.'"

Thoughtful people find this censorious hyperpragmatism alienating and can drop away from organizing as a result. Even more often, without an analysis of what's really wrong with the world—or a vision of the better world they're trying to create—people have no reason to continue being activists once a particular campaign is over. In this way, activistism can end up defeating itself. Activistism is tedious, and its foot soldiers suffer constant burnout. Thinking, after all, is engaging; were it encouraged, Jiramanus pleads, "we'd all be enjoying ourselves a bit more."

Increasingly, there are activists who treat ideas as important. "We need to develop a new rhetoric that connects sweatshops—and living wage and the right to organize—to the global economy," says the University of Michigan's Jackie Bray, an antisweatshop activist. Liana Molina of Santa Clara University agrees: "I think our economic system determines everything!" But about the student movement's somewhat vague ideology, she has mixed feelings. "It's good to be ambiguous and inclusive," so as not to alienate more conservative, newer, or less politicized members, she says. "But I also think a class analysis is needed. Then again, that gets shady, because people are like, 'Well, what are you for, socialism? What?'"

The problem is that activists who, like Molina, are asking the difficult questions that push into new political terrain are very often forced to operate in frustrating isolation, without the support of a community of fellow thinkers.

## Whence Came This Malady?

Steve Duncombe, a NYC-DAN activist, author, and NYU professor, says his fellow activists "think very little about capitalism outside a moral discourse: big is bad, and nothing about the state except in a sort of right-wing dismissal: state as authoritarian daddy." Activistism is intimately related to the decline of Marxism, which at its best has thrived on debates about the relations between theory and practice, part and whole. Unfortunately, much of this tradition has devolved into the alternately dreary and hilarious rants in sectarian papers. Marxism's decline (but not death: the three of us would happily claim the name) has led to woolly ideas about a nicer capitalism, and an indifference to how the system works as a whole. This blinkering is especially virulent in the US where a petit-bourgeois populism is the native radical strain, and anti-intellectualism is almost hard-wired into the culture. And because activistism emphasizes practicality, achievability, and implementation over all else, a theory dedicated to understanding deep structures with an eye towards changing them necessarily gets shunted aside. Marxism's decline isn't just an intellectual concern, it too has practical effects. If you lack any serious understanding of how capitalism works, then it's easy to delude yourself into thinking that moral appeals to the consciences of CEOs and finance ministers will have some effect. You might think that central banks' habit of provoking recessions when the unemployment rate gets too low is a policy based on a mere misunderstanding. You might think that structural adjustment and imperial war are just bad lifestyle choices. Unreflective pragmatism is also encouraged by much of the left's dependency on foundations. Philanthropy's role in structuring activism is rarely discussed, because almost everyone wants a grant (including us). But it should be. Foundations like focused entities that undertake specific, politely meliorative schemes. They don't want anyone to look too closely at the system that's given them buckets of money that less fortunate people are forced to bay for.

Activistism is contaminated by the cultural forms and political content of the nonprofit sector. Because nonprofits are essentially businesses that sell press coverage of themselves to foundation program officers, they operate according to the anti-intellectual logic of hyperpragmatism and the fiscal year short-termism generated by financial competition with their peer organizations. When nonprofit businesses lead, the whole left begins to take on the same obsessive focus with "deliverables" and "take-aways" and "staying on message." For many political nonprofits, actions—regardless of their value or real impact—are the product, which in turn promise access to more grants. Nonprofit culture fosters an array of mind-killing practices. Brainstorming on butcher paper and the use of break out groups are effective methods for generating and collecting ideas and or organizing pieces of a larger action. However when used to organize political discussions these nonprofit tools can be disastrous. More often than not, everybody says some thing, break out groups report back to the whole group, lists are compiled and nothing really happens.

What is to be done? Our point is not that there should be less activism. The left is nothing without visible, disruptive displays of power. We applaud activism and engage in it ourselves. What we are calling for is an assault on the stupidity that pervades American culture and we are particularly concerned about is when this nonthinking pervades activist culture and in turn, left culture. This implies a more democratic approach to the life of the mind and creating spaces for ideas in our lives and political work.

We're not calling for leadership by intellectuals. On the contrary, we challenge left activist culture to live up to its antihierarchical claims: activists should themselves become intellectuals. Why reproduce the larger society's division between mental and physical labor? The rousing applause for Noam Chomsky at the World Social Forum in Porto Alegre (a yearly gathering of activists from around the world) was hardly undeserved, but ideas don't belong on pedestals. They belong in the street, at work, in the home, at the bar, and on the barricades. We put out this call—to indulge a bit of activistism lingo—because the current moment demands some thinking. With overwhelming approval for Bush and his endless war, bland moralism and tired slogans won't win the day: "War is Not the Answer" is little better than "War is the Answer"—recently spotted on a Manhattan counterdemonstrator's placard.

The movement is also undergoing a fascinating rhetorical shift, as activists reject terms like "antiglobalization," which emphasized—not very lucidly—what they're against, in favor of slogans like "Another World is Possible" which dare to evoke the possibility of radically different economic arrangements. What would that other world look like? Activists must engage that question; to do so, they have to do a better job of understanding how this world really works. Intellectuals briefing activist groups on some aspect of how things are often face a tediously reductive question: "That's all very interesting, but how can we organize around that? What would be the slogans?" None of us were in Genoa or Porto Alegre, but we're told that there was plenty of serious discussion of both this world and the better one. But Americans shouldn't have to go all the way to Brazil or Italy to talk and think about this stuff. Unfortunately here at home, those with the confidence to discuss such questions are too often the ones with the silliest ideas: at the "Another World Is Possible" rally during WEF weekend, speakers waxed hopefully of a world in which all produce will be locally grown. That's absurd, unless you're planning to abandon cities, give up on industrial civilization, and reduce the world's population by ninety-five percent. But we're barely acknowledging these issues, much less debating them. The spirit we wish to inspire was expressed a few years ago by a Latin American graduate student. Seeing one of us holding a copy of Aijaz Ahmad's *In Theory*, he exclaimed with all seriousness: "That book is like having an intellectual grenade in your hand. Hasta la Victoria." In many other countries, activists' tiny apartments are stacked with the well-thumbed works of Bakunin, Marx, and Fanon. We'd like to see that kind of engagement here. And judging at least from the European experience, it would pay off even in activistism's own pragmatic terms: protests in major European cities routinely dwarf our own, and activists there have far more influence on mainstream discourse and even government policy. In the long run, movements that can't think can't really do too much either.

# Josh MacPhee

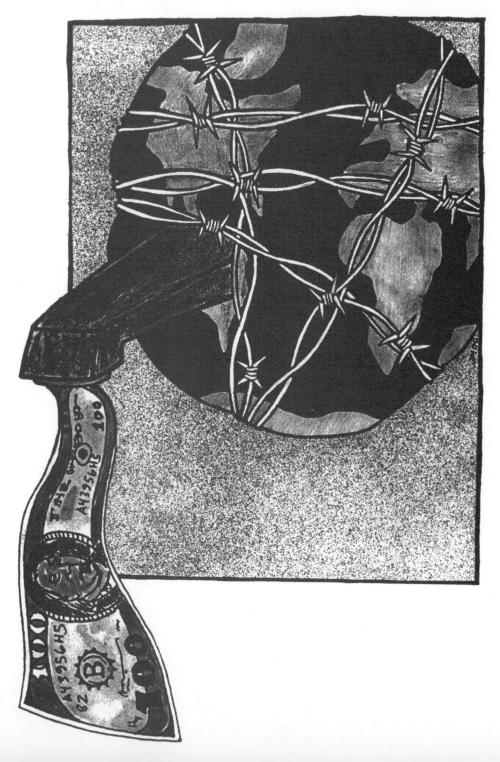

# The Meaning of Seattle
# Noam Chomsky

Interviewed by David Barsamian
February 23, 2000

*Let's talk about what occurred in Seattle in late November/early December around the WTO ministerial meeting. What meaning do you derive from what happened there?*

I think it was a very significant event and potentially extremely important. It reflected a very broad feeling which has been pretty clear for years and has been growing and developing in intensity around a good part of the world. It is opposed to the corporate-led globalization that's been imposed under primarily US leadership, but the other major industrial countries, too. It is harming a great many people, undermining sovereignty and democratic rights, and leading to plenty of resistance. What was interesting in Seattle was several things. First of all, the events reflected very extensive programs of education and organizing, and it shows what can be achieved by that. It wasn't just that people suddenly showed up. Secondly, the participation was extremely broad and varied. There were constituencies brought together that have rarely interconnected in the past. That was true internationally, Third World, indigenous, peasant, labor leaders, and others. And here in the US, environmentalists, large labor participation and other groups, which had separate interests but a shared understanding. It's been pretty evident before. That's the same kind of coalition of forces that blocked the Multilateral Agreement on Investment a year earlier and that had strongly opposed other so-called agreements like NAFTA or the WTO agreements, which are not agreements, at least if the population counts. Most of the population has been opposed to them. It has reached a point of a kind of dramatic confrontation. Also it will presumably continue and I think could take very constructive forms.

*Are there any lessons to be derived from Seattle?*

One lesson is that education and organizing over a long term, carefully done, can really pay off. Another is that a substantial part of the domestic and global population, I would guess probably a majority of those thinking about the issues, range from being disturbed by contemporary developments to being strongly opposed to them, primarily to the sharp attack on democratic rights, on the freedom to make your own decisions and on the general subordination of all concerns to the specific interests, to the primacy of maximizing profit and domination by a very small sector of the world's population. Very small, in fact. Global inequality has reached unprecedented heights.

*The United Nations Conference on Trade and Development meeting has been going on in Bangkok. Andrew Simms, writing in the* Guardian Weekly *in mid-February, says that "UNCTAD, given the right power and resources, could help overcome failings in the international system" and it has "the confidence of developing countries." Any comments on that?*

That's a bit of an exaggeration. UNCTAD first of all is basically a research organization. It has no enforcement powers. It does reflect to some extent the interests of the so-called developing countries, the poorer countries. That's the reason why it's so marginalized. For example, there was very little reporting of the UNCTAD conference in the US apart from the business press here and there. It has Third World, South participation. And when UNCTAD does reflect the concerns of the great majority of the world's people, it is generally ignored. One example with substantial contemporary repercussions is the UNCTAD initiative to stabilize commodity prices thirty years ago, so that poor peasant farmers would be able to survive. Agribusiness can handle a collapse in prices for a year; a poor farmer can't tell his kids to wait until next year to eat. The proposals conformed to policies routinely adopted in the rich countries, but were blocked by the rich, following the advice of "sound liberal economists," as political economist Susan Strange puts it—advice that is followed when it contributes to profit and power, ignored otherwise. One consequence is the shift from production of "legitimate crops" (coffee, etc.) to coca, marijuana, and opium, which are not subject to ruinous price fluctuations. The US reaction is to impose even harsher punishments on the poor, abroad and at home, sharply intensifying next year if current proposals are implemented. It's not the only case. UNESCO was undermined for rather similar reasons. But to speak of "confidence of developing countries" would be overstating it. Have a look at Third World-based publications, say from the Third World Network in Malaysia. One of their important publications is *Third World Economics*. A recent issue has run several very critical reports of the UNCTAD conference because of its subordination to the agenda of the powerful. It's true that UNCTAD is more independent and more reflects the interests of the developing countries than, say, the WTO, which is run by the industrial states. So yes, it's different. But one shouldn't exaggerate.

*The issue of inequality, not only in the US but around the world, as you just mentioned, is certainly hard to ignore. Even the* Financial Times *recently commented that "At the start of the nineteenth cen-*

*tury, the ratio of real incomes per head between the world's richest and poorest countries was three to one. By 1900, it was ten to one. By the year 2000 it had risen to sixty to one."*

And that is extremely misleading. It vastly understates what's going on. The real and striking difference is not the difference among countries but the difference within the global population, which is a different measure. That's risen very sharply, which means that within countries the divisions have sharply risen. I think it's now gone from about something like eighty to one to about 120 to one, just in the last ten years or so. Those are rough figures. I'm not sure of the exact numbers. But it's risen very sharply. The top one percent of the population of the world now probably has about the income of roughly the bottom sixty percent. That's close to three billion people.

*And these outcomes are not the law of some natural force.*

Those are the results of very specific decisions, institutional arrangements, and plans which can be expected to have these effects. And they have these effects. There are principles of economics that tell you that over time things ought to even out. That's true of some abstract models. The world is very different.

*Thomas Friedman, writing in the* New York Times, *called the demonstrators at Seattle "a Noah's ark of flat-earth advocates."*

From his point of view that's probably correct. From the point of view of slave owners, people opposed to slavery probably looked that way. If you want some numbers, I just found some. The latest issue of Doug Henwood's invaluable *Left Business Observer* gives the global facts. This is a recent estimate by a World Bank economist. It actually only goes as far as 1993. In 1993, the richest one percent of the population had as much wealth as the bottom fifty-seven percent. So that's 2.5 billion people. The ratio of average incomes from the world's top five percent and the world's bottom five percent, that's the one that increased from seventy-eight to one in 1988 to 114 to one in 1993, and probably considerably more since. The inequality index, the Gini index, as it's called, has reached the highest levels on record. That's world population. One might argue that this doesn't matter much if everyone is gaining, even unequally. That is a terrible argument, but we don't have to pay attention to it, because the premise is incorrect.

Going back to Friedman, from his point of view, it's correct. For the one percent of the population that's he's thinking about and representing, the people who are opposing this are flat-earthers. Why should anyone oppose the developments that we've been describing?

*Would it be fair to say that in the actions in the streets in Seattle, mixed in with the tear gas was also a whiff of democracy?*

I would take it to be. A functioning democracy is not supposed to happen in the streets. It's supposed to happen in decision making. This is a reflection of the undermining of democracy and the popular reaction to it, not for the first time. There's been a long struggle, over centuries, in fact, to try to extend the realm of democratic freedoms, and it's won plenty of victories. A lot of them have been won exactly this way, not by gifts but by confrontation and struggle. If the popular reaction in this case takes a really organized, constructive form, it can undermine and reverse the highly undemocratic thrust of the international economic arrangements that are being foisted on the world. And they are very undemocratic. Naturally one thinks about the attack on domestic sovereignty, but most of the world is much worse. Over half the population of the world literally does not have even theoretical control over their own national economic policies. They're in receivership. Their economic policies are run by bureaucrats in Washington as a result of the so-called debt crisis, which is an ideological construction, not an economic one. That's over half the population of the world lacking even minimal sovereignty.

*Why do you say the debt crisis is an ideological construction?*

There is a debt, but who owes it and who's responsible for it is an ideological question, not an economic question. For example, there's a capitalist principle which nobody wants to pay any attention to, of course, which says that if I borrow money from you, let's say, I'm the borrower, so it's my responsibility to pay it back and you're the lender, so it's your risk if I don't pay it back. That's the capitalist principle. The borrower has the responsibility and the lender takes the risk. But nobody even conceives of that possibility. Suppose we were to follow that. Take, say, Indonesia, for example. Right now its economy is crushed by the fact that the debt is something like 140 percent of GDP. Trace that debt back. It turns out that the borrowers were something like a hundred to two hundred people around the military dictatorship that we supported and their cronies. The lenders were international banks. A lot of that debt has been by now socialized through the IMF, which means Northern taxpayers are responsible. What happened to the money? They enriched themselves. There was some capital export and some development. But the people who borrowed the money aren't held responsible for it. It's the people of Indonesia who have to pay it off. And that means living under crushing austerity programs, severe poverty, and suffering. In fact it's a hopeless task to pay off the debt that they didn't borrow. What about the lenders? The lenders are protected from risk. That's one of the main functions of the IMF, to provide free risk insurance to people who lend and invest in risky loans. That's why they get high yields, because there's a lot of risk. They don't have to take the risk, because it's socialized. It's transferred in various ways to Northern taxpayers through the IMF and other devices, like Brady bonds. The whole system is one in which the borrowers are released from the responsibility. That's transferred to the impoverished mass of the population in their own countries. And the lenders are protected from risk. These are ideological choices, not economic ones. In fact, it even goes beyond that. There's a principle of international law which was devised by the US over a hundred years ago when it "liberated" Cuba, which means conquered Cuba to prevent it from liberating itself from Spain in 1898. At that time, when the US took over Cuba, it cancelled Cuba's debt to Spain on the quite reasonable grounds that that debt was invalid since it had been imposed on the people of Cuba without their consent, by force, under a power relationship. That principle was later recognized in international law, again under US initiative, as the principle of what's called "odious debt." Debt is not valid if it's essentially imposed by force. The Third World debt is odious debt. That's even been recognized by the US representative at the IMF, Karin Lissakers, an international economist, who pointed out a couple of years ago that if we were to apply the principles of odious debt, most of the Third World debt would simply disappear. These are all ideological decisions. They're not economic facts. It is an economic fact that money was lent and somebody owes it, but who owes it and who takes the risk, those are power decisions, not economic facts.

*To return briefly to the events at Seattle,* Newsweek *had a cover story on December 13 called "The Battle of Seattle." They devoted some pages to the anti-WTO protests. There was a sidebar in one of the articles called "The New Anarchism." The five figures the sidebar mentioned as being somehow representative of this new anarchism are Rage Against the Machine and Chumbawamba. I don't suppose you know who they are.*

I know. I'm not that far out of it.

*They're rock bands. The list continues with the writer John Zerzan and Theodore Kaczynski, the notorious Unabomber, and then MIT professor Noam Chomsky. How did you figure into that constellation? Did* Newsweek *contact you?*

Sure. We had a long interview. [chuckles]

*You're pulling my leg.*

You'd have to ask them. I can sort of conjure up something that might have been going on in their editorial offices, but your guess is as good as mine. The term "anarchist" has always had a very weird meaning in elite circles. For example, there was a headline in the *Boston Globe* the other day in a small article saying something like "Anarchists Plan Protests at IMF Meeting in April." Who are the anarchists who are planning the protest? Ralph Nader's Public Citizen, labor organizations, and others. There will be some people around who will call themselves anarchists, whatever that means. But from the elite point of view, you want to focus on something that you can denounce in some fashion as irrational. That's that analog to Thomas Friedman calling them flat-earthers.

*Vivian Stromberg of Madre, the New York-based NGO, says there are lots of motions in the country but no movement.*

I don't agree. For example, what happened in Seattle was certainly movement. Just a couple of days ago students were arrested in protests over failure of universities to adopt strong antisweatshop conditions that many student organizations are proposing. There are lots of other things going on which look like movement to me. While we're on the Seattle matter, in many ways what happened in Montreal a few weeks ago is even more dramatic.

*That was the Biosafety Protocol meeting.*

That wasn't much discussed here, because the main protesters were European. The issue that came up was clear and important. A kind of ambiguous compromise was reached, but the lineup was very sharp. The *New York Times* report stated it pretty accurately. The US was virtually alone most of the time in the negotiations leading to the compromise. The US was joined by a couple of other countries which would also expect to profit from biotechnology exports. But primarily the US against most of the world over a very significant issue, the issue that's called the "precautionary principle." That means, is there a right for a country, for people to say, I don't want to be an experimental subject in some experiment you're carrying out? At the personal level, that is permissible. For example, if somebody comes into your office from the university biology department and says, You're going to be a subject in an experiment that I'm carrying out. I'm going to stick electrodes into your brain and measure this, that and the other thing, you're permitted to say, I'm sorry, I don't want to be a subject. They are not allowed to come back to you and say, You have to be, unless you can provide scientific evidence that this is going to harm you. They're not allowed to do that. But the US is insisting on exactly that internationally. That's the precautionary principle. In the negotiations at Montreal, the US, which is the center of the big biotech industries, genetic engineering, and so on, was demanding that the issue be determined under WTO rules. According to those rules, the experimental subjects have to provide scientific evidence that it's going to harm them, or else the transcendent value of corporate rights prevails and they can do what they want. That's what Ed Herman calls "producer sovereignty." Europe and most of the rest of the world insisted on the precautionary principle, that is, the right of people to say, I don't want to be an experimental subject. I don't have scientific proof that it's going to harm me, but I don't want to be subjected to that. I want to wait until it's understood. That's a very clear indication of what's at stake, an attack on the rights of people to make their own decisions over things even as simple as whether you're going to be an experimental subject, let alone controlling your own resources or setting conditions on foreign investment or transferring your economy into the hands of foreign investment firms and banks. Those are the issues that are really at stake. It's a major assault against popular sovereignty in favor of concentration of power in the hands of a kind of state-corporate nexus, a few megacorporations, and the few states that primarily cater to their interests. The issue in Montreal in many ways was sharper and clearer than it was in Seattle. It came out with great clarity.

*Food safety, irradiation, and genetic engineering seem to touch a deep chord in people and also to cross traditional what's called left-right, liberal-conservative lines. For example, French farmers, who are fairly conservative, are up in arms around these issues.*

It's been interesting to watch this. In the US there's been relatively little discussion and concern about it. In Europe and India and Latin America and elsewhere, there's been great concern and a lot of very activist popular protest. The French farmers are one case. The same is true in England and elsewhere, quite extensively. There's a lot of concern about being forced to become experimental subjects for interventions in the food system, both in production and consumption, that have unknown consequences. That did cross the Atlantic in a way that I don't entirely understand. At some point last fall the concerns became manifested over here as well, to the extent that something quite unusual happened. Monsanto, the major corporation that's pushing biotechnology and genetically engineered crops, their stock started to fall notably. They had to make a public apology and at least theoretically, maybe in fact, cancel some of their more extreme projects, like terminator genes, genes that would make seeds infertile so that, say, poor farmers in India would have to keep purchasing Monsanto seeds and fertilizers at an exorbitant cost. That's quite unusual, for a corporation to be forced into that position. It reflected in part the enormous protests overseas, primarily Europe, which is what mattered because of their clout, but also a growing protest here.

On the other hand, we should also take account of the fact that in the US it's essentially a class issue. Among richer, more educated sectors, there are tendencies which amount to protecting themselves from being experimental subjects, for example, buying high-priced organic food.

*Do you think the food safety issue might be one around which the left can reach a broader constituency?*

I don't see it as a particularly left issue. In fact, left issues are just popular issues. If the left means anything, it means it's concerned for the needs, welfare, and rights of the general population. So the left ought to be the overwhelming majority of the population, and in some respects I think it is. There are other related matters that are very hard to keep in the background. They're coming to the fore all over the place, dramatically in the poorer countries again, but it's showing up here, too. Take, say, the price of pharmaceuticals. They are exorbitant. In the US they're much higher than in other countries. Drugs in the US are twenty-five percent higher than in Canada and probably twice as high as Italy. This is because of monopolistic practices that are strongly supported by the US government and were built into the WTO rules—highly protectionist devices called intellectual property rights—so huge megacorporations that produce pharmaceuticals are allowed to stay off the market, and charge what amounts to monopoly prices for a long period. This is being very strongly resisted in Africa, in Thailand, and elsewhere. In Africa, the spread of AIDS is extremely dangerous and may lead to a major health catastrophe. Here, when Clinton or Gore makes a speech, they talk about the need for Africans to change their behavior. Well, OK, maybe Africans should change their behavior. But the crucial element is our behavior of guaranteeing that the producers, mainly, though not entirely, US-based, be able to charge prices so high that nobody can afford them. According to the latest reports, about six hundred thousand infants a year are having HIV transmitted to them from the mother, which means they'll probably die of AIDS. That's something that can be stopped by the use of drugs that would cost about a couple of dollars a day. But the drug companies will not permit them to be sold under what's called compulsory licensing, that is, allowing the countries to produce them themselves at a much cheaper rate than the drug companies charge under the monopolistic conditions. We're talking about huge numbers of people. There may soon be forty million orphans just from AIDS alone in Africa. Similar things are going on in Thailand. And they're protesting. They have their own pharmaceutical industries in Thailand and Africa, particularly trying to gain the right to produce generic drugs which would be far cheaper than the ones sold by the major pharmaceutical corporations. This is a major health crisis. There are tens of millions of people involved. The same is true in other domains: malaria, tuberculosis. There are preventable diseases that are killing huge numbers of people because the means of prevention are kept so expensive that people can't use them. That's not as much of a problem in the rich countries. Here there's a problem of getting the pharmaceutical companies to permit Medicare to provide prescriptions for the elderly. That's a problem, and it's a real one. But in the poor countries, and not so poor, like Thailand, for example, Africa, South Asia, we're talking about the deaths of tens of millions of people in a few years. Why do drug companies get this enormous protection and in effect monopolistic rights? They claim that they need it because of the costs of research and development. But that's mostly a scam. A substantial part of the costs of research and development is paid by the public. Up until the early 1990s, it was about fifty percent, now maybe it's forty percent. Those numbers much underestimate the actual public cost because they don't take into account the fundamental biology on which it's all based, and that's almost all publicly supported. Dean Baker, a very good economist who has studied this carefully, asked the obvious question. He said, OK, suppose the public pays all the costs, double the public cost, and then insists that the drug simply go on the market. His estimates are a colossal welfare saving from this. We're now talking about not abstract issues. We're talking about the lives and deaths of tens of millions of people just in the next few years.

*Returning to the US, talk more about the student sweatshop movement. Is it different from earlier movements that you're familiar with?*

It's different and similar. In some ways it's like the anti-apartheid movement, except in this case it's striking at the core of the relations of exploitation that are used to reach these incredible figures of inequality that we were talking about. It's very serious. It's another example of how different constituencies are working together. Much of this was initiated by Charlie Kernaghan of the National Labor Committee in New York and other groups within the labor movement. It's now become a significant student issue in many areas. Many student groups are pressing this very hard, so much so that the US government had to, in order to counter it, initiate a kind of code. They brought together labor and student leaders to form some kind of government-sponsored coalition, which many student groups are opposing because they think it doesn't go anywhere near far enough. Those are the issues that are now very much contested. Last I heard, I don't know the details, there was a big demonstration in Wisconsin with students arrested.

*Aren't the students asking the capitalists to be less mean?*

They're not calling for a dismantling of the system of exploitation. Maybe they should be. What they're asking for is the kinds of labor rights that are theoretically guaranteed. If you look at the conventions of the International Labor Organization, the ILO, which is responsible for these things, they bar most of the practices, probably all of them, that the students are opposing. The US does not adhere to those conventions. Last I looked, the US had ratified hardly any of the ILO conventions. I think it had the worst record in the world outside of maybe Lithuania or El Salvador. Not that other countries live up to the conventions, but they have their name on them at least. The US doesn't accept them on principle.

*Comment on an African American proverb that perhaps intersects with what we're talking about: "The master's tools will never be used to dismantle the master's house."*

If this is intended to mean, don't try to improve conditions for suffering people, I don't agree. It's true that centralized power, whether in a corporation or a government, is not going to willingly commit suicide. But that doesn't mean you shouldn't chip away at it, for many reasons. For one thing, it benefits suffering people. That's something that always should be done, no matter what broader considerations are. But even from the point of view of dismantling the master's house, if people can learn what power they have when they work together, and if they can see dramatically at just what point they're going to be stopped, by force, perhaps, that teaches very valuable lessons in how to go on. The alternative to that is to sit in academic seminars and talk about how awful the system is.

*Tell me what's happening on your campus, at MIT. Is there any organizing around the sweatshop movement?*

Yes, and on a lot of issues. There are very active undergraduate social justice groups doing things all the time, more so than in quite a few years.

*What accounts for that?*

What accounts for it is the objective reality. It's the same feelings and understanding and perception that led people to the streets in Seattle. Take the US. The US is not suffering like the Third World. In Latin America, after by now twenty years of so-called reforms, they haven't moved. The president of the World Bank has just reported that they're where they were twenty years ago. Even in economic growth. This is unheard of. The whole so-called developing world, I don't like the term, but it's the one that's used for the South, is pulling out of the 1990s with a slower rate of growth than in the 1970s. And welfare gaps are increasing enormously. That's in the rest of the world. In the US, there's also an unprecedented development. Economic growth, by all macroeconomic measures, growth of the economy, productivity, capital investment, in the last twenty-five years has been relatively slow compared with the preceding twenty-five years. Many economists call it a "leaden age" as compared with the preceding golden age. But there has been growth, even though slower than before. However, it's accrued to a very small part of the population. For the majority of nonsupervisory workers, which is the majority of the workforce, wages are maybe ten percent or more below what they were twenty-five years ago. That's absolute level. Relative, of course, much farther below. There has been productivity growth and economic growth during that period, but it is not going to the mass of the population. Median incomes, meaning half below, half above, are now barely getting back to what they were ten years ago, well below what they were ten and fifteen years before that. This is in a period of reasonably good economic growth in the last two or three years. They call it amazing, but the last two or three years has been about what it was in the fifties or sixties, which is high by historical standards. It's still left out most of the population. The international economic arrangements, the so-called free trade agreements, are basically designed to maintain that. They undergird what's called a "flexible labor market," meaning that people have no security. The growing worker insecurity that Alan Greenspan once said was one of the major factors in the fairy-tale economy. If people are afraid, they don't have job security, they're just not going to ask for better conditions. If they have a fear of job transfer, which is one of the consequences of the mislabeled free trade agreements, and there's a flexible labor market, meaning you don't have security, people are not going to ask for better conditions and benefits.

The World Bank has been very clear about the matter. They recognize that labor market flexibility has acquired a bad name as a euphemism for pushing wages down and workers out. That's exactly what it does. It acquired that bad name for a good reason. That's what labor market flexibility is. They say it's essential for all regions of the world. It's the most important reform, I'm quoting from a World Bank development report. It calls for lifting constraints on labor mobility and on wage flexibility. What does that mean? It doesn't mean that workers should be free to go anywhere they want, say, Mexican workers come to New York. What it means is they can be kicked out of their jobs. They want to lift constraints on kicking people out of their jobs and on wage flexibility, which means flexibility down, not up. People are at some level aware of this. You can hide a lot under glorification of consumption and huge debt, but it's hard to hide the fact that people are working many more hours a week than they did twenty-five years ago just to keep incomes from stagnating or declining.

# From Carnival to Commons:

## The Global IMC Network

# Dorothy Kidd

May 30, 2003

## Introduction

I first encountered the Indymedia Center (IMC) in downtown Seattle, in late 1999, a whiff of tear gas away from the demonstrations against the World Trade Organization (WTO). Even then I was in awe. While earlier networks of radical media also countered the messaging of the dominant corporate and state media, the scope and scale of the IMC's information-circulation capacities surpassed them.[1] The enormous costs and difficulties of production and distribution faced by earlier media activists like me were minimized by the digital platform. As well, Open Publishing, the software innovation introduced by the Community Activist Technology group in Sydney, Australia, allowed anyone with a modem to upload their real-time audio, video, texts, and photos to circulate almost instantly with a global reach. There are now over 110 IMC sites, operating in twenty-two languages and in thirty-five countries around the world, taking the project of amplifying the voices of under-represented groups to a whole new plateau.

The strength of the global IMC network was not just its command of powerful technologies. As one of the cofounders, Jeff Perlstein, described in the *The Battle of Seattle*, the IMC was also an "experiment in media democracy," in which local crews operating autonomously and collaboratively, enabled "actual" community newsrooms with "virtual online counterparts" as spaces for organizing, participatory media-making, and circulation. This model of do-it-yourself reporting not only challenged the hierarchies and gate-keepers of mainstream journalism production, but also the conditions of reception. Instead of passive consumers of information, audiences can actively surf the site's extraordinary bounty of first-person narratives, news reports, longer analyses, links to activist resources, and interactive discussion opportunities, becoming their own news editor.[2]

The flexibility of the network of autonomous sites quickly led, according to Eddie Yuen, to the IMC becoming the trademark of the anti-corporate globalization movement. While the "carnivals of resistance" momentarily took down the fences of global capital in the streets, the global IMC seized electronic and cyber space, going around the corporate and state media blockade to create a carnival of representation, a plurality of perspectives, images, and modes of address.

Since Seattle, I have been following the IMC through their online presence, interviews, and participation in off- and online discussions. The IMC Network continues to lead with almost-instant stories from protest movements around the world. However, since Seattle, the geopolitical context has changed enormously. The surprise and revelry of the carnivals of resistance has often been brutally set aside by the postmodern press gangs, dragooning governments, and peoples around the world into the empire's order. Indymedia offices have been raided by national and international security agencies in the US, Canada, Italy, and Spain, and their websites spammed by hackers from state security forces, right-wing organizations, and individuals. As well, the initial cohesion of collaboration during protests has led to some dissension over goals, and the exacerbation of power differences between women and men, techies and non-techies, and sites in the southern hemisphere and the north.

The IMC Network's rapid growth and draw on resources, pace of production, and dependence on volunteers is increasingly hard to sustain. What about the long haul? How can the high-energy carnival of protest-based communications contribute to a longer-term communications commons, autonomous in ownership, direction, form, and content, from the dominant corporate and state media. What lessons might we learn from earlier radical media, the precursors to the IMC?

## Press Conferences Versus Minicam Witnesses

In Seattle, two distinct radical media paradigms had diverged. One was best represented by the nongovernmental organizations (NGOs) such as the International Forum on Globalization, Global Alliance, Corporate Europe Observatory, Friends of the Earth, Public Citizen, Sierra Club, Oxfam, and the Institute for Agricultural and Trade Policy. These mostly Anglo-US NGOs were funded by foundations such as Ford, Charles Stewart, and Solidego, and operated with a reformist agenda, arguing for "fair trade not free trade" (Wall, 2003:5). While some of these NGOs had emerged from the professionalization of the environmental movements, others had always been elite "thinktanks." With some differences among them, the overall intention of the NGOs was to "be at the table" to reform the process.

The NGO communications teams offered "alternative" proposals to the neoliberal programme of the WTO, but their style of production, and their relationship with their audiences, was not unlike the mainstream. Trained professionals would use rational arguments to appeal to the WTO, other multilateral organizations, national governments, and the mainstream media through press conferences and the operations of a mainstream media press centre, advertisements in the mainstream media, and the circulation of reports and analyses via their own websites. Their public communications forums also followed the vertical, rational model, with websites and two days of teach-ins presenting briefs from international experts about the trade was already schooled in many of these issues but had few opportunities for their own expression or for dialogue and discussion.

In contrast, the Seattle IMC articulated a very different communications strategy and practice. They did not prep professional communicators to counter the status quo inside formal meetings or press briefings. Instead a motley crew of several hundred volunteers took their cameras, microphones and writing implements to the streets to bring witness from the demonstrators, which other crews then rapidly edited and circulated to a global audience on the web. Their production logic emphasized the flatness of a do-it-yourself approach, in which a diversity of perspectives, from a range of tones and registers, would stream out to a networked audience, using a media circuit primarily outside government and corporate media. Rather than the singular focus on "alternative content," the network acted to change relations of production and reception, too.

The IMC was not only independent of the ownership of global corporations and governments, but also of the logics and languages of the mainstream stenographers to power.[3] This qualitative shift from a praxis of media "alternatives" to an "autonomous communications" grew from the combined experience of a number of social movements, and the collective intelligence of several generations of old and new media producers, who shared their technologies and techniques. This kind of autonomous communications did not begin with the IMC, but followed a centuries long trajectory of radical media.

## The Electronic Fabric of Struggle

Let's make a network of communication among all our struggles and resistances. An intercontinental network of alternative communication against neoliberalism and for humanity. This intercontinental network of alternative communication will search to weave the channels so that words may travel all the roads that resist. It will be the medium by which distinct resistances communicate with one another. This intercontinental network of alternative communication is not an organizing structure, nor has a central head or decisionmaker, nor does it have a central command or hierarchies. We are the network, all of us who speak and listen.

From the 1996 First Intercontinental Encounter for Humanity and Against Neoliberalism, in Chiapas, Mexico. Ruggiero and Duncan, cited in Rodriguez, 2001:155

Many of the first IMC builders cite the Zapatistas as a major influence. On January 1, 1994, the Zapatistas in Chiapas, in southern Mexico, had courageously taken on the Mexican Army, in protest against a key agreement of the global capitalist program, the North American Free Trade Agreement (NAFTA). However, unlike earlier revolutionary armed movements in Central America, the Zapatista's political objective was not the seizure of state power, but the establishment of political, economic, and cultural self-determination of their own territories. A central element of this new politics was controlling the production and circulation of their images: representation was as important to their sovereignty as the rifle.

The sophisticated communications strategy of the Zapatistas itself owed to an earlier "electronic fabric of struggle." As Harry Cleaver has documented, the Zapatista network built on earlier webs of trade unionists, and women's and environmental groups in Mexico, the US and Canada, Latin America and Europe, started in opposition to NAFTA and other capital friendly agreements. Several of these movements met again in Seattle. While the meeting between trade unionists and ecologists, symbolized by Teamsters and sea turtles, has been well documented, Seattle also convened a meeting of global feminists; the popular assembly of BAYAN, an international Filipino organization, involved in earlier struggles against International Monetary Fund (IMF) policies in the Philippines and throughout Asia; and two contingents from South Korea, fresh from battles against the IMF during the Asian economic meltdown.

Each of these networks had their own global communications networks that, like the Seattle IMC, combined the internet with earlier forms of old and new media. Below, I discuss one of the long-term feminist projects. Among the smaller contingent from Korea were representatives from Jinbonet, a site set up in late 1997 to host a number of Korean labor movement and activist websites, and provide technical services and an interactive news service. These earlier networks, with extensive experience campaigning against neoliberalism, were largely shifted aside, sidelined by the much younger, whiter, and wealthier US crowds. The heritage of their earlier organizing, and their communications strategies, have all but been erased.

## Recovering The Heritage of Seattle

While Seattle was a culmination of two decades of mobilizing against neoliberalism, the composition of the Seattle street was much different than Chiapas or other southern centers such as Caracas, Santo Domingo, Lagos, or Manila, where protests against the World Bank and IMF's structural adjustments programmes (SAPs) started in the 1980s. Unlike Seattle, the earlier wave of anti-corporate globalization movements in the streets of the South, had often been led by poor, indigenous groups, among whom were many women. Their primary communications instrument had been word-of-mouth and radio, and not the Internet. And while many did take to the streets, carnival-like, to resist their further immiseration, they also acted in many other ways to collectively create and regulate common resources, of water, electricity, healthcare, food, and education.

Communications was key to the repertoire of the pre-Seattle social movement groups. The histories of most of these initiatives are usually coloured with struggles to survive against severe censorship, external constraints, lack of resources to produce and distribute, and internal power struggles, but also include some critical lessons. Many of the campaigns against neoliberalism and for more democratic communications began in Latin America. For example, the miners of Bolivia started the world's first community radio station in the late 1940s, mixing experiences of short-term "tactical" uses of radio against army incursions with long-term media institution building.

During the 1970s and 1980s a proliferation of "alternative media" groups, often with short lifespans, adapted the available old and new communications technologies, of print, radio, video, and internet newsnets to provide alternative content. They usually countered the imperialist message from the US, whether that of the US government or of entertainment corporations such as Disney. Some also experimented with ways to involve local people in new kinds of production and reception. For example, the Sandinista radio network in Nicaragua recognized the need to facilitate the direct and unmediated expression of the "voiceless," the workers, peasants, indigenous people, and urban wageless who were usually excluded from mainstream discourse of the media, the Church, and government.

In the later 1980s and 1990s, several global alliances formed, such as the World Community Radio Association (AMARC), the Videazimut video network, and the Association for Progressive Communications computer networks, partly in recognition of the need to connect wider struggles of social movements in favor of human rights, racial equality, the rights of women, ecology, and liberty of sexual preferences, regionally and globally. In the beginning, they primarily shared a political orientation against the emerging plans of neoliberalism; however they gradually exchanged operational knowledge and discussions about approaches, and bicycled a little programming. By the 1990s, a small number of programming exchanges began, using the internet for distribution. For example, Pulsar, a project of AMARC, circulated news and other scripts via the internet, which local stations could download and reproduce in their own local languages and program formats.

Many of these projects challenged the power structures of trade union leadership, the Catholic Church, or the revolutionary party to involve the poorest and most marginalized. During the late 1980s and 1990s, the traditional movement leadership was often set aside by a new sector of nongovernmental organization professionals, as the neoliberal structural adjustment bullying took effect and Southern nation-states began to off-load public services onto the churches and NGOs. This new cadre of NGO professionals also developed among the alternative media where nongovernmental organizations and Northern aid organizations began to fund and routinely recruit NGO-type professionals to administer communications projects throughout Latin America.

## Radio Fire

"I was listening to San Francisco Liberation Radio covering the anti-Iraq-war protests downtown and it reminded me of Radio FIRE. One person would call in on their cell phone from the demonstrations, and then another, just talking about what was happening. It had the same immediacy and informality."

*Personal conversation, March 2003.*

In 1996, Commandante Marcos was retreating from the Mexican Army, checking the shortwave radio to find out what was going on around him when he tuned into an interview with Marcela Lagarde, a Mexican feminist, about the struggle women in Latin America had to make inside the left movements. Marcos tracked down Lagarde through the originators of the broadcast, the Feminist International Radio Endeavor (FIRE), and invited Lagarde to come to meet the FZLN and become their "gender advisor." FIRE is a member of a loose network of alternative media that is part of the global women's movement. Operating on shortwave radio out of Costa Rica since the late 1980s, in Spanish and English, they now combine a local FM radio service with an internet site. FIRE was started as a result of the international networking speeded up by the United Nations Forums on Women, and particularly the 1985 Forum in Nairobi, Kenya. Much like those organizing the protests against the WTO, the feminists of that era recognized the strategic importance of directing and producing their own media to counter the mainstream patriarchal discourse. Just as importantly, their aim was to facilitate women to speak directly, without mediation, from their own experience; to share and connect this with other women; and to create alternative visions and analyses. And finally, the women's movement recognized it would need flexible communications instruments responsive enough to take action quickly on issues that transcended borders, but that were often considered unrelated such as waged and unwaged work, violence against women, reproductive rights, children's welfare, prostitution, and peace and international development.

Much like the IMC, the FIRE network also dealt with questions of autonomy from the mainstream media, as well as the movement media. FIRE's first decision was to work with existing feminist networks rather than starting a new one. They also described themselves as activist/communicators, as do the IMC activists. However, what FIRE cofounder Maria Suárez Toro describes as "interactive autonomy" is not the same as the "independence" or "separateness" used by IMC proponents. FIRE recognized a level of reciprocity with the movement organizations with whom and for whom they worked. Unable to be self-sustaining, they ackowledged that their programming content, and their financial support was in turn dependent on their inclusion in the activities of women's networks, the support in kind from women's groups, and funding from women's foundations. And in turn, their role was to facilitate the communications among the networks., and particularly the horizontal connections South-South between activists within Latin America and with those in Africa and Asia.

FIRE also used media "tactically." For example, they broadcast popular tribunals against violence against women, in which the Costa Rican women's movement held the Government of Costa Rica to account for international agreements brokered at the UN, or the Organization of American States. They have also covered campaigns against neoliberalism, including the second *encuentro* of the Zapatistas in Spain in 1997, and the World Social Forum in Porto Alegre.

Like the IMC, FIRE has been very inventive with technology. Drawing from her experience in the Sandinista literacy campaigns in Nicaragua, Suárez told me that the group's goal is to use whatever communications instruments are most widely and popularly available. "Too many people think that the technology is the communication… But we have to liberate the technology to put it into the hands of the women where the action is." For example, they created a portable radio set-up with phone hook-up to produce inexpensive live programming. They also designed their website to distribute material to and from women's groups around the world. Their tinkering has allowed them to show that women could not only "control" the medium, but shape it to their own needs."

FIRE grew out of the earlier generation of global social justice movements and communications networks. They rely for their support from some of the same Northern government agencies and private foundations as many other international NGOs. While providing reports from social movements of poor and indigenous women, they also circulate within the orbit of INGOS in the women's, environmental, and human rights movements. Nevertheless, their communications paradigm was not the didactic, counterhegemonic one of many "alternative media" of the 1980s and 1990s, but much more spontaneous and participatory, matching the events which they covered. Their participation in South-South networks, and their nuanced conception of interactive autonomy, which recognizes their dependence on movements and on Northern funders, has allowed them to straddle these two sets of institutions and communications paradigms.

## A Social Network

"We need a new understanding of how our solidarity can create a network. A lot of time [people] think of [Indymedia] as a digital network—a digital network is not going to be a threat to the status quo and corporate power. Where the threat is is that we are organizing a coordinated social network and that means improving our communications from the many to the many and to all the nodes."

*Sheri Herndon, Seattle IMC, Madison-Wisconsin IMC Broadcast, 2002*

In the streets of Seattle were groups protesting the slashing of three sets of social contracts: the wage, the social wage, and the communications contract. There were trade unionists whose waged livelihoods were threatened by corporate restructuring involving runaway jobs; social movements concerned about the erosion of the social safety net for themselves and their living environments; and high tech information workers and DIY media makers no longer content, or even needing, to allow corporate newsmedia to dominate the public airwaves and technologies. For while the neoliberal project fosters the extension of capital and the logic of accumulation worldwide, it also creates conditions of radical possibility. Corporate globalization contributes to extending the technical and social networks of information and interpersonal communications technologies around the world, including similar systems of representation and communications.

While the IMC derives its strength from its birth among those three multitudes in Seattle, there is a tension between the three. Nurtured by the new strata of techies, whose skills and adaptability keep many of the internet sites going day by day, and jolted forward by the protest focus and the young lords of carnival, too often women, workers, and poorer people of colour have been marginalized. This real tension, exacerbated by the gendered, class, and racialized divisions of labour among media and internet aficionados, has been noted and debated since the opening of the IMC site in Seattle. However, the reality remains that those people able to volunteer, and to work within the existing social milieu, tend to represent a small minority of young, white, male North Americans and Europeans.

In response, several sites around the world have begun to work outside the nexus of the white and/or professional class circles of the global justice movement and techie crowd. For example, the New York IMC features the work of activists involved with the Diallo police brutality case, housing, and AIDS. The Los Angeles IMC works in collaboration with Latino community groups, on and off the net. In San Francisco, the site owed its origins to our initiative to bring together activist groups working on the regional housing crisis, the prison industrial complex, and a protest against the National Association of Broadcasters, the US corporate media trade organization. Since then, the local group has developed a number of special series in collaboration with groups organizing around issues in the forest, antiwar, energy, and labor. In the most recent wave of peace organizing in the spring of 2003, the San Francisco IMC have become a community fulcrum enabling real-time discussion of movement and media issues in street demonstrations, public events, on microradio, and online. Creating a live loop with cell phones, the internet, video cameras, and a pirate radio station, a tactical media squad linked commentaries from demonstrators in the street to audiences in the downtown area and around the world

In Latin America, the IMC groups are even more closely connected to existing social activist groups, and thus use the available technologies and means of communications. Computers, telephone lines, and internet access are usually limited to a tiny fraction of urban middle, professional, and upper classes. Tim Russo of Chiapas Media told me in 2002, "The internet just doesn't cut it for getting information back to the communities. What is important in solidarity in the South is not so much how to produce information, but how to train people to produce information for themselves, and this is different than what a lot of other Indymedia's [in the United States] think." The Chiapas IMC produces and distributes much of their content using radio, audio cassettes, and video, using the internet primarily for national and international distribution.

In Brazil, they also mix earlier kinds of media production with internet distribution. In Rio de Janeiro, the IMC has taken video documentaries from *favela* to university to foster discussion of the upcoming Free Trade of the Americas (FTAA) agreement. In Porto Alegre, they use the internet to gather and circulate news, which is then sent to a network of free-and community-radio stations. In Sao Paolo, the IMC set up a free internet center to enable poor people to access it. They also take the video of demonstrations, or of land occupations, to the neighborhoods, setting up monitors outside for everyone to watch. Almost all of the IMC centers also distribute printed newssheets that are photocopied and posted in walls all over the city, because of lack of funds for printed copies.

The Buenos Aires IMC intervenes in the public spaces of the movements of unemployed and neighborhood assemblies. They not only go to *assambleas* in the neighborhoods and factories to report on campaigns, but also to actively recover their collective historical memories through reflections and poetry. Their videos document the contemporary use of the *escrache*. Begun as a technique used by the Mothers of the Plaza de Mayo, to denounce the generals and officials responsible for the disappearance of thousands during the "dirty war," the same technique is now used to target government and corporate officials as well as the mainstream media.

## Conclusion

The challenge of the global IMC is to move beyond the protest-based news site to an ongoing operations of autonomous communications amidst the growing enclosure of the internet and repression from the police and reactionary groups and individuals. Most production collaboration is still carnival-like, via hyperlinks during major demonstrations and mobilizations, or one-off projects between radio and video crews. While the techie crew meet on-line regularly, there is much less ongoing meeting and global decision making among other constituencies on a global basis. Some of this is beginning to happen at the regional level, in North America, Europe, and Latin America, or among particular production groups, such as video or radio.

This necessarily will involve creating a different relationship with audiences and with social justice movements. Open Publishing elicited a cornucopia of work, but also led to serious problems. In April 2002, a decision was made to replace the open newswire with a center page of the most significant stories from around the world. While partly due to the need to feature global stories, it was also a response to the serious spamming suffered by some sites. As Australian media critic, Graham Meikle has argued, this could lead to a professionalization of new writing and editing, not unlike the same trend among the "alternative" community media of the earlier generation. Or, it could contribute to the development of a new kind of software and social relation between the site crew and audiences, in which audiences were more involved in curating and editing stories. All the IMCs need also to learn about working more closely with ongoing social movements.

The real tragedy of the European commons was not the need for stricter central regimes to curb the commoners. Instead, the tragedy was the commoner's lack of productive resources and capacity for self-defense against the first generation of capitalist agribusiness. The size and active number among the IMC network, their flexibility and technological adaptability, should make the IMC network much more resistant to enclosure. However, it will require a commitment to build a news commons, shared by news producers, audiences, and movements alike, to help foster communications among all the social networks organizing for a different world vision.

1. For accounts of earlier media networks from around the world, see the first and second volume of John Downing's *Radical Media*, Clemencia Rodriguez's *Fissures in the Mediascape*, Alfonso Gumucio Dagron's *Making Waves: Stories of Participatory Communication for Social Change*, Dee Dee Halleck's *Hand-held Visions: The Impossibilities of Community Media*, and Nick Dyer-Witheford's *Cyber-Marx*. See also the edited collections: Pilar Riaño (ed.) *Women's Grassroots Communication*, Bruce Girard, (ed.) *A Passion for Radio*, Alain Ambrosi and Nancy Thede, (eds.) *Video: The Changing World*, and Bosma et al (eds.) *Read Me! Filtered by Netttime*.

2. For discussion of the IMC, see Luciano Alzaga, "Rebellion Among the Surveilled Webs." *Znet interactive*, 2002, www.zena.secureforum.com/interactive/content/display; 2002, Matthew Arnison "Decisions and Diversity: Sydney Indymedia volunteer" (Version 0.2) www.cat.org.au/maffew/decisions.html, June 2001, Matthew Eagleton-Pierce, "The Internet and the Seattle WTO Protests." *Peace Review*. Special Issue: Social Justice Movements and the Internet 13:3, (Sept. 2001), 331-338; Dee Dee Halleck, *Hand-Held Visions*. (New York: Fordham University Press, 2002); Madhava, "Reclaim the Streets, Reclaim the Code: An Interview with Matthew Arnison of Community Activist Technology and One of Indymedia's Original Coders," *Punk*

*Planet* #43 (May/June 2001); Omar Pahati, "Digital Pirates and the "Warez' Wars," *Alternet*, Jan. 24, 2002.

Dean Paton, "War of the Words: Virtual Media Versus Mainstream Press," *Christian Science Monitor*. Dec. 3, 1999; Theta Pavis, "Modern Day Muckrakers: The Rise of the Independent Media Center movement," *OnLine Journalism Review*, 2002; USC Annenberg, Bryan Pfaffenberger "In Seattle's Aftermath: Linux, Independent Media and the Survival of Democracy," *LinuxJournal*, (13-Dec.1999); Elinor Rennie, "Community Media: Fenced Off or Walled Out? Finding a Space for Community in the New Media Environment" Presented at IAMCR, Barcelona, 2002; Chris Shumway, "Participatory Media Networks: A New Model for Producing and Disseminating Progressive News and Information," www.reclaimthemedia.org, Rachel Rinaldo, "Pixel Visions: the Resurgence of Video Activism," www.lip.org, 2000; John Tarleton. "Protesters Develop Their Own Global Internet News Service," *Mark Nieman Reports*, Winter 2000.

3. See Scott Uzelman, "Catalyzing Participatory Communication: Independent Media Centre and the Politics of Direct Action, MA thesis, Simon Fraser University, Burnaby, Canada.

# The Direct Action Dividend
# Rachel Brahinsky

*San Francisco Bay Guardian,* April 16, 2003

Nine people drift through the Financial District with chalk-white, dazed faces. It's lunchtime, and their clothing is torn and doused in fake blood. They aren't actors or stuntmen. Part of an ongoing antiwar statement, these grim figures are protesters trying to bring stark images of Iraqi deaths home to San Francisco's streets.

The country hasn't seen such widespread direct action protests in many years. Demonstrators have shut down corporate lobbies, performed sidewalk political theater, and put their bodies in the middle of streets to draw attention to their cause.

The wave of direct action protests—which are done without permits, unlike typical mass marches—has sparked harsh criticism locally from elected officials and the *San Francisco Chronicle* and *San Francisco Examiner*, which have emphasized in numerous stories that blocking traffic drains the city treasury. Other critics say they don't understand direct action, arguing that there's no way such tactics—like physically barring ChevronTexaco Corp. or Bechtel Corp. employees from working—could stop a war.

But now, just as the invasion of Iraq is becoming the occupation of Iraq, there are signs that direct action is actually beginning to change the way people think, talk, and even act.

The sheer volume of protest has forced increased press coverage, and corporate entities that most people have never heard of—such as the Carlyle Group and Autonomy Corp.—are now slipping into the public eye. On the ground the movement has coalesced remarkably quickly and has been able to shift tactics nimbly, in large part because of the internet.

Whereas a few weeks ago the rhetoric sharply focused on Iraq, now organizers are turning their assessments inward and making connections between the war abroad and the wars at home—over economic equity, environmental justice, and racism. It's a move that's essential if the left is to build strong coalitions that could transcend the Iraq war and could help generate momentum for a regime change at home in 2004.

## Burning up Iraqi crude

In the dark, early hours of the morning April 14, demonstrators drove an old station wagon to the main entrance of ChevronTexaco headquarters in suburban San Ramon. They slashed all four tires and formed a human chain, with arms linked through the car with PVC pipe, barring the main entrance to the sprawling compound.

Accusing the massive oil conglomerate of "toxic terrorism," demonstrators took on a company whose refineries have been polluting the low-income city of Richmond for years. When they learned that ChevronTexaco has been refining millions of gallons of Iraqi crude in that city, organizers smelled an opportunity to publicly emphasize the connections between the company's involvement in the Middle East and its Richmond pollution. Carla Perez, with the Oakland-based Communities for a Better Environment, said the ChevronTexaco action naturally fit into her organizing work. "Our members are mostly low-income people of color. They know this war," Perez said. "They live this war everyday. They don't have to think twice about war with Iraq." Yet their concerns about poisoned East Bay air have been largely left out of local news of late. "When the media and the government conspire to fixate on one issue," she said, referring to the long media buildup to the Iraq invasion, "they are successful at taking attention from injustices back home." The demonstration was a good example of how activists are using the surge of political involvement sparked by the war to raise awareness of local concerns. Long after the bombing ends in Iraq, the oil issue will linger, and Richmond residents will likely still have to deal with the environmental fallout from accidents and fires at the refinery.

Meanwhile, ChevronTexaco and the rest of big oil will keep pressing US leaders to force open the Middle East oil economy. The bonds formed between Richmond environmental justice activists and antiwar organizers are key and could become the glue that holds together a new, broader social justice effort. As they blocked the gates of California's largest corporation, Perez and company took a page from an old book. Street agitation was a cornerstone of the civil rights movement, and even earlier, won Americans the right to an eight-hour workday. The current wave of direct action—married with recent worldwide mass protests, internet-centered social change lobbying campaigns like MoveOn.org, and more aggressive activity by Black Bloc-type activist groups—is a foundational part of the new peace and justice movement.

## Regime change for the White House

Already the rhetoric of the peace movement has begun to slip into the national parlance. In an April 2 speech to New Hampshire Democrats, Massachusetts senator John Kerry—who did not oppose the war—took a political risk by echoing a call that has become popular among peace activists. "What we need now is not just a regime change for Saddam Hussein and Iraq, but we need a regime change in the United States," said Kerry, who is seeking the Democratic nomination for president.

Such moments, when mainstream Democrats are pulled to the left—even if it's simply rhetorical—inspire organizers, many of whom tell us they've felt an unusual surge of motivation lately. Part of that comes from seeing that direct action works because of the movement's unique structure: a decentralized coalition of community-based affinity groups. The affinity group form (named for the nonhierarchical anarchist affinity groups active during the Spanish civil war) was picked up by feminists and antinuclear activists in the 1970s and has been used since for lower-profile yet persistent activity—notably by anti-militarism groups and radical environmental organizations like Earth First! "The way we organize reflects a new form of politics within the long tradition of nonviolent direct action," protest veteran David Solnit told us. "We're looking for shifts in consciousness. We're looking for people to become self-organized" rather than being led by a central command. Dozens of collectives have sprung up. Many are named to make a point (like the Global Intifada or Freedom Uprising); others are more free spirited (such as Guerrilla Gardening or the Dot.commies). Each group has its own goals and makes its own decisions but can also join others for specific actions or campaigns. Many send representatives to a regular "spokescouncil" meeting of the umbrella coalition Direct Action to Stop the War (DASW). There they offer support for each other's actions and plan collaborative events, such as the March 20 shutdown of the Financial District.

There are also possibly dozens more that function independently. "We're amazed all the time at actions going on that we don't know about," said Patrick Reinsborough, part of the DASW media group. Many hope each cluster will foster new leaders who will stay committed and will turn their energies toward pushing for real leadership change in next year's national elections, while building local power over community concerns.

## Looking ahead

In the coming months, there's some work to be done to broaden and strengthen the peace coalition. Case in point: the April 7 demonstration at the Port of Oakland, which was marked by extreme police violence. Direct action organizers called for the shutdown of the docks used by Stevedoring Services of America, which won the contract to manage the port in Um Qasr, Iraq.

Unfortunately, they demonstrated on a day when there weren't any ships to block, according to Steve Stallone, spokesperson for the International Longshore and Warehouse Union, which represents dockworkers.

Because of that, "it was always only going to be symbolic," Stallone told us. "Their real idea was to highlight that these companies are making money off the war. Certainly they did that. But it's not a substitute for the real work of organizing the workers to stop work and really shut down the war." In terms of the power and threat of direct action, the

# Neither Their War Nor Thier Peace

## Retort

Febnauy 15, 2003

Last week, at American insistence, the copy of Picasso's Guernica in the anteroom to the UN Security Council Chamber was curtained over—not "an appropriate backdrop" it was explained, ror official statements to the world media.

## WE HAVE NO WORDS FOR THE HORROR TO COME,

for the screams and carnage of the first days of battle, the fear and brutality of the long night of occupation that will follow, the truck bombs and slit throats and unstoppable cycle of revenge, the puppets in the palaces chattering about "democracy," the exultation of the anti-Crusaders, Baghdad descending into the shambles of a new, more dreadful Beirut, and the inevitable retreat (thousands of bodybags later) from the failed. McJerusalem.

## WE HAVE NO OLYMPIAN PREDICTIONS.

We do not know what happens next. We shall not ape the ludicrous certainty of the CIA hacks on the news, trotting out tonight's "analysis" (tonight's excuses for a half-million dead and wounded in a single laser-guided week).

## THE BEST WE CAN OFFER IS NEGATIVE WISDOM,

addressed to comrades in a dark and confusing time.

- **The answer to War is not Peace.** "War is the health of the state," as Randolph Bourne indelibly put it, but so is the so-called Peace that the state stage-manages for us - the peace of cemeteries, the peace of "sanctions" and "containment," the peace of the "Peace Process" (photo-opportunities on the White House lawn plus gunships and bulldozers in Jenin), the decade of Iraqi deaths unseen on your TV screens. "Neither their War nor their Peace" should be our slogan.

- **It is time to make War on the Warmongers.** Which means a struggle waged across long years, a campaign of attrition and demoralization. It matters greatly that already, before the war begins, millions of people are in the streets. But marching is no substitute for Mario Savio's call to "put your bodies upon the gears, and upon the wheeJs, upon the levers, upon all the apparatus." Don't mistake the elation of the stroll down Market Street for the painful, dangerous, month-by-month business of sapping the will of the political-military machine. We know that its will can be broken. We know that a time can come when the customary ignoring of the ruled by the rulers becomes dysfunctional, and leads the state to catastrophe. "Vietnam" is the word for that twilight of the gods. Cheney and Rumsfeld blurt it out every night in the small hours, and wake with their pacemakers knocking.

- **Terror too is the health of the state.** Underneath the absurdity of the duct tape and plastic sheeting advisories lies a serious policy, which our present leaders seem poised. to pursue to the bitter end - the fomenting of a permanent culture of Terror, sealing each of us into a pod of fear and isolation, and feeding our every movement into the Total Information Awareness databank. We are already in a spiral, where Terror and the State embrace more tightly each day. And the target is us - our freedoms, our common resources, our possibilities of invention and ease.

- **Don't put your faith in the blood-stained "intemational community."** Remember the U. N.'s record through the years as hand-wringing frontman for any and every initiative of power. Remember Kofi Annan's role as chief blind eye to the Rwandan genocide. Don't think that Swiss banker Blix will fail to do his masters' bidding in the end. Don't mistake the German government, which happily goes on hosting 100,000 American troops, for a real opponent of the U. S. Reich. The dogs will all want their share of the spoils. And even if, at the last minute, a nauseous "diplomatic solution" is cobbled together, have we any doubt who will go on paying the costs? The curtain could be rolled back again to reveal *Guernica*, the suits could make speeches congratulating themselves on the triumphs of military humanism, and still the shit-smeared 3-year-olds in the hospital beds in Baghdad would be writhing in agony—under Blix's well-fed gaze. For such is the price of containment.

- **Look through the mind-numbing speeches in the Security Council to the real pressure, the mass disaffection that is making the present prewar scenario unlike any other.** This is the real ground for optimism, we believe—limited optimism—in an otherwise night-marish situation. The dreary ghost of "public opinion," which the states of the world are normally so adept at conjuring and pretending to obey, has suddenly become a destabilizing factor in the final arrangements for war. Schroeder thought he could call the pacifist beast into the streets strictly in order to take the Reichstag, and then retreat gracefully to the usual politics of "meeting our international obligations." Blair thought the eternal British love affair with "their finest hour" would steer him past the familiar shoals of anti-Americanism. It has all turned out to be more difficult than Straw and Chirac ever dreamt. **Let as keep up the cruel pressure of refusal. Let uskeep on setting the diplomatic lapdogs at each other's throats.**

- **This is a war for Global Capitalism. not for Oil alone.** The annals of oil are an unin-terrupted 'chronicle of violence, genocide, and the cynical lawlessness of the cor-porate frontier. Iraq itself was born from this vile trinity. Now oil men parade the corridors of the White House. All five permanent members of the UN Security Council speak obediently for oil companies that have proved themselves specialists over the years in 'regime change,' whenever it suits their interests. Nobody, not even Bush, contests the fact that the US industrial-military machine is a hopeless oil junkie. War is inevitable, it is said, not because of American imperialism but because of its addiction to the automobile. Dirty mobility is what America means by freedom. All of which is true. Petroleum is global capitalism's great lubricant, its key means of production. But the case is not proven that Iraqi oil, specifically, is a necessary part of the world picture. In hard cash terms, the Iraqi embargo matters little for cor-potate profits. Pay heed to the yearly reports and 'position papers' churned out by Haliburton and Shell. What they truly covet is not sabotaged wells in the desert, but the deep-water fields beneath the warm seas of the Bight of Benin, the Gulf of Mexico, and coastal Brazil. So let us not see in the slaughter of Iraqi civilians *only* the murderous logic of the S.U.V. It is not oil capital but capital in general that we must confront. Look around as you march up the Boulevard of Shame, at the bland headquarters of Bechtel, Esprit, and Chevron. Which of the three has the cleaner hands worldwide? To fixate on a single commodity and its detritus obscures the full horror and ruthlessness hidden by the word 'globalization': primitive accumulation.

predatory and profligate, careering forward on a planetary scale.

- **In the destruction of Baghdad resides the logic of empire.** Oil is a metaphor for something more lethal, more destructive. What is at stake is the true madness of the world market, the hubris of an imperial "grand design" intended to make the world safe, once and for all, for capital The map of the oil-rich Middle East will be redrawn, but that will be only the beginning. "'American internationalism reflects . . . our national interests . . . a single sustainable model for national success": such is the breathtaking monism of the new National Security Strategy. Is it any wonder that the costs of empire mount? More than half of all Fed.eral funds flow to the military. American "'bases" metastasize across the planet—in 130 countries by the last count, and rising steadily. The homeland economy is bloated and debt-ridden.

- **As for the miserable fantasy of the war as a blow strack in.the name—the Iraqi people apinst their oppressor—"mercy by all means necessary" thesis—**the best we can do in the face of such Looking Glass politics is go back to Edmund Burke. Long ago he had this to say about the sudden discovery of human wickedness that regularly precedes an invasion: "It is not with much credulity I listen to any, when they speak evil of those whom they are going to plunder. I rather suspect that vices are feigned. or exaggerated, when profit is looked for in their punishment. An enemy is a bad witness: a robber is a worse." These are words for the times. The earth is crammed full of atrocities, and tyrants are always the hue humanitarians.

- **What matters on a march is speecb, not speeches,** the centrifuge of voices, rhythms, and banners, not the hectoring of stale celebrities. Least of all does it matter what CNN makes of the occasion. We recognize that, whether we like it or not, part of what's happening here is a numbers game, a counting of heads. But don't expect the stenographers of power to do anything else than traduce what you see.

- **Trust your senses.** A march, among other things, *materializes* the dead percentages in the polls, and takes life for a moment off the flickering screen. It is a reminder— a fleeting and artificial one, but nonetheless welcome—of what the public realm could be.

# The Revenge of the Concept

## Artistic Exchanges, Networked Resistance

## Brian Holmes

### I.

Among the events of recent history, few have been as surprising, as full of enigmas, as the coordinated world demonstrations known as the Global Days of Action. Immediately upon their appearance, they overflowed the organization that had called them into being: the Peoples' Global Action (PGA), founded in Geneva in February of 1998. This transnational network of resistance had adopted a new concept of solidarity advanced by the Zapatistas, who encouraged everyone to take direct action at home against the system of exploitation and oppression that they described as neoliberalism. As early as the month of May 1998, the PGA helped spark demonstrations against the WTO whose effectiveness lay both in their simultaneity and in their extreme diversity: street parties in some thirty cities around the world, on May 16; four days of protest and rioting in Geneva, beginning that same day; a 50,000-strong march that reached Brasilia on May 20; protests all over India after a huge demonstration in Hyderabad against the WTO on May 2. The following year, London Reclaim the Streets threw out the idea of a "carnival against capital" in financial centers across the world for the day of the G8 summit, June 18: there were actions in over forty cities, including a ten-thousand-strong "carnival of the oppressed" by Niger Delta peoples against transnational oil companies. In the face of transnational capitalism, a networked resistance was born, local and global, tactical and strategic: a new kind of political dissidence, self-organized and anarchistic, diffusely interconnected and operating only from below, yet able to strike at the greatest concentrations of power. What is the strength of such movements? The improbable and serious appeal to a "do-it-yourself geopolitics": a chance for personal involvement in the transformation of the world.

These kinds of actions are about as far as one could imagine from a museum, yet when you approach them, you can feel something distinctly artistic. They bring together the multiplicity of individual expression and the unity of a collective will. That is their enigma, which sets up a circulation between art and solidarity, cooperation and freedom. But this enigma stretches further, into the paradoxes of a networked resistance. Because since their surprising beginnings, we have seen the movements change, we have seen them globalize. Activists from the South and the North travel across the earth in jet planes, to demonstrate next to people without money, without work, without land or papers—but who may know the same writers, the same philosophers, the same critiques of contemporary capitalism. The intensive use of internet by the movement of movements means that dissenting messages take the pathways used by financial speculation. Sometime you wonder whether the two can even be distinguished. What are the sources of this networked resistance? And what exactly is being resisted? Is revolution really the only option—as one could read on a banner at the carnival against capital, on June 18, 1999, in the financial center of London? Or do we not become what we resist? Are the "multitudes" the very origin and driving force of capitalist globalization, as some theorists believe?[2]

Two British critics, Anthony Davies and Simon Ford, posed exactly those questions, with direct reference to art. They pointed to the way that artistic practice was tending to integrate with London's financial economy, particularly through the vector of specially designed "culture clubs" where artists sought new forms of sponsorship and distribution, while businessmen looked for clues on how to restructure their hierarchical organizations into cooperative teams of creative, autonomous individuals: "We are witnessing the birth of an alliance culture that collapses the distinctions between companies, nation states, governments, private individuals—even the protest movement," the two critics claimed.[3] They perceptively drew a link between contemporary artistic experiments—those dealing with the use and appropriation of complex signs and tools, or with the catalysis of interactions between free individuals—and the politicized street parties of the late 1990s. But their analysis opposed these new movements, not to transnational capitalism, but to the outdated world of pyramid-shaped hierarchical organizations. Thus their image of the June 18 carnival: "On the one hand you have a networked coalition of semi-autonomous groups and on the other, the hierarchical command and control structure of the City of London police force. Informal networks are also replacing older political groups based on formal rules and fixed organizational structures and chains of command. The emergence of a decentralized transnational network-based protest movement represents a significant threat to those sectors that are slow in shifting from local and centralized hierarchical bureaucracies to flat, networked organizations."

Conceived at the outset of the year 2000, this alliance theory was mainly concerned with distinguishing a "new economy" from the old one. It combined a network paradigm of organization, as promoted by Manuel Castells, with a description of the culturalization of the economy, as in British cultural studies. But what it demonstrated was more like an "economization of culture." Everything seemed to be swirling together: "In a networked culture, the topographical metaphor of 'inside' and 'outside' has become increasingly untenable. As all sectors loosen their physical structures, flatten out, form alliances and dispense with tangible centers, the oppositionality that has characterized previous forms of protest and resistance is finished as a useful model."

These kinds of remarks, which came from many quarters, were already confusing for the movements. But they took on an even more troubling light when the al Qaeda network literally exploded into world consciousness. On the one hand, the unprecedented effectiveness of the S11 action seemed to prove the superiority of the networked paradigm over the command hierarchies associated with the Pentagon and the Twin Towers. But at the same time, if any position could be called "oppositional," it was now that of the Islamic fundamentalists. Their successful attack appeared to validate both the theory of a decisive transformation in organizational structures and Samuel Huntington's theory of the "clash of civilizations." Suddenly the protest movement could identify neither with the revolutionary form of the network, nor with the oppositional refusal of the capitalist system. Loud voices from the right immediately seized the opportunity to assimilate the movement to terrorism. And to make matters worse, the financial collapse that the movement had predicted effectively happened, from the summer of 2000 onwards, casting suspicion over everything associated with the dot-com bubble—including all the progress in democratic communication. At the same time, the secret services of the most powerful countries, and especially the US, declared themselves ready to meet the challenge of the networks, by giving themselves new capacities for autonomy, horizontality, interlinkage.[4] The difficulty of situating a networked resistance to capitalism within a broader spectrum of social forces thus became enormous—as it still is today.

Now, this difficulty has not stopped the mobilizations, particularly in Europe. What has come to a halt, or rather, splintered into a state of extreme dispersal, are the theoretical attempts to explain them in a way that can contribute something both to their goals and to their capacities of self-organization. What I want to do here is to make a fresh try at this kind of explanation, from the viewpoint of an economic anthropology that can distinguish between the fictions of a "self-regulated market" and the reciprocities and solidarities that make it possible to live together as human beings. So we'll begin with a social and economic study of the vital need for resistance to the crises of capitalism. We will then see this resistance develop within the contemporary technical environment, without accepting any form of technological determinism. And finally, returning to the question of alliance or opposition, we can grasp some of the contributions that artistic practice makes to this networked resistance, by rediscovering languages that seemed to have been consigned to the museum. I am thinking primarily of conceptual art: a practice that doesn't produce works, but only virtualities, which can then be actualized, at each time and in each place, as unique performances.

## II.

Following the Zapatistas, people in the movement of movements tend to call the current economic structure "neoliberal." But this word evokes a political philosophy stretching back to the eighteenth century. One can speak instead of *flexible accumulation*, which describes the computer-linked, finance-driven, just-in-time model of the globalized economy.[5] By subordinating the other spheres of social life—education, science, culture, etc.— this organization of production and consumption produces a veritable hegemony, a mode of regulation for society as a whole. To grasp the way this hegemony is experienced by individuals, I have proposed the notion of the *flexible personality*.[6] It is an ambiguous notion: because although it primarily designates the managerial culture that legitimates the globalized economy, and that renders it tolerable or even attractive for those who are its privileged subjects, it also recalls the profound opportunism that this organization demands, as well as the "flexible" nature of the workforce that it subjects to increasingly individualized forms of exploitation. The flexible personality designates the lived experience of a relation of domination. It is essential to define its limits.

One can begin to do so by pointing to the different kinds of social struggles that have intensified over the last ten years. Ecological struggles, against resource waste, polluting industry, invasive infrastructures. Workers' struggles, against falling wages, worsening labor conditions, insufficient health coverage or unemployment benefits. Struggles against the privatization of medical and scientific knowledge, against the control of the university and of cultural production by business. And finally, struggles against the preponderance of the financial sphere in the taking of democratic decisions. This list of different fields of struggle refers us, in a more abstract way, to four "fictive commodities": land, labor, knowledge, and money. That is, four major articulations of social life that capitalism claims to treat as things to be sold, confiding their destiny to the operations of a self-regulating market.[7] The problem being that the basic conditions under which these "things" are produced do not all have a price tag, and so escape any monetary regulation. These four major articulations of society exist at least partially outside the market: they are "externalities."[8] And the maintenance of their fictive status as commodities implies a perpetually deferred cost, which in the long run can only manifest itself in a phenomenon outside any imaginable accounting. This is the phenomenon of systemic crisis. Its looming shadow has motivated the increasing levels of social struggle.

It was an anthropologist, Karl Polanyi, who provided the most striking description of a systemic crisis, in a book called *The Great Transformation*, published in 1944. The story begins with the enclosure of community pasture lands in England, known as *commons*, which were transformed with fences into private property. This privatization of resources led to the appearance of rural poverty in the course of the eighteenth century. The threat of famine then made possible an unprecedented exploitation of labor power, which former peasants were compelled to sell for a bare minimum in the new factories of the Industrial Revolution. In this way, the owning class accumulated great fortunes, which split away from the nationally instituted money to employ the international currency of gold bullion. Polanyi pays special attention to demonstrating the directive role that independent bankers played in the creation of the gold standard, which served as a universal but legally private equivalent between all the different national currencies. He shows that a cycle of three privatizations—land, labor, and money—leads finally to the worldwide market of the nineteenth century.

For a hundred years, gold served as a coherent and relatively stable language of exchange for commercial transactions; and the profits were a powerful argument in favor of peace, or at least, against generalized warfare. It was the gradual abandonment of the international gold standard under the pressure of repeated financial breakdowns that led, in the 1930s, to the reconstitution of strictly national economies, closed in on themselves and subject to various forms of central planning (ranging from the relatively benign New Deal, to Nazism and Stalinism). But Polanyi, writing in 1944, did not suggest anything as simplistic as restoring the gold standard. His strongest argument was that the violence of free-market exchanges, when "disembedded" from their place within the larger social structure of reciprocities and solidarities, was finally what destroyed the *laissez-faire* system itself, provoking the fascist reaction. The fundamental problem therefore lay with the very notion of the self-regulating market. The last chapter of *The Great Transformation* predicts the opening of a new era in the history of humanity. It calls for the institution of a mixed economy, broadly regulated within a national framework and yet also highly respectful of individual rights, able to guarantee what the author describes as "freedom in a complex society"—that is, in a society which has recognized the limits of the free market.

The Keynesian welfare state of the postwar period could appear as an answer to Polanyi's vision. It submitted industrial and financial activity to a social regulation, conceived within each national framework in a more or less democratic fashion. But the dynamics of capitalism rapidly overflowed this national frame, as one can see in the evolution of the world monetary system. After the war, the Bretton Woods treaty tied signatory countries into a system of relatively stable exchange rates, whereby all the currencies were pegged to the dollar, which in turn was convertible into gold. But this system proved untenable, and after the United States suspended convertibility in 1971, the currencies began to "float" against each other; since the outset of the eighties they have been subject to the fluctuations of a highly speculative exchange market, operating at the speed of computers and telecommunications. At the same time, controls on crossborder investments have gradually been lifted, and many state services and industries, considered as unfair competition with the private sector, have been suppressed. In a world which no longer erects any significant barriers to the directive capacity of money, capital flow into the stock markets now commands the majority of productive investments everywhere; and every material reality comes to be dependent on highly volatile financial information. In this way there arises what Rem Koolhaas has called "the world of ¥ $": a world-economy built around the incessantly changing equivalence of the yen, the euro, and the dollar, representing the three major poles of world prosperity. One can see the convertibility of these three currencies as a new kind of economic language, serving primarily to convey the opportunistic speech of private investors, indeed, of a transnational capitalist class. ¥ $ is the monetary language of the flexible personality.

The last twenty years have seen the incredible inventiveness of this worldwide language, which has generated a myriad of private dialects: stocks, futures, options, swaptions, floaters, hedges, and so on through the endless list of derivatives. Despite their appearance of total autonomy, of absolute disconnection from the solid earth, these forms of privately managed credit money have directed the productive apparatus of the world's countries, ever more radically since 1989. In parallel to these developments in the private sphere, a new type of postnational state has slowly come into being, abandoning the former emphasis on social security and public welfare, and seeking instead to encourage the insertion of its most innovative citizens into the worldwide information economy.[9] And the language of ¥ $ has also taken on cultural, intellectual, organizational, and imaginary forms, giving rise to artistic productions, managerial techniques, modes of behaviors, desires and dreams that have served to legitimate the regime of flexible accumulation, while continually feeding it with new innovations. But this very inventiveness, this speculative confidence, has also gnawed away at the ecological, social, political, and financial foundations of the system. We went through the Asian crisis of 1997, which spread to Russia and Brazil, threatening even the American economy; then we saw the crash of the NASDAQ in spring 2000, with a continuing plunge of the world's stock markets that has not yet stopped at the date of writing, three years later. The possibility of a systemic crisis, which could be seen on the horizon throughout the 1990s, has rushed suddenly closer at the outset of the new millennium.

What are the effects of the crisis as it stands today? One can draw a few insights from recent developments in Argentina. In the late 1990s the Argentine state, under pressure from the IMF, desperately attempted to maintain the value of the peso with respect to the dollar, and more broadly, with respect to the standard of prosperity represented by the currencies of ¥ $. A series of structural adjustments were supposed to improve the economy's health, and insure the continuing parity of the peso and the dollar; but their effect was to exclude increasing numbers of Argentines from access to employment, basic services, food, and finally even to their money, when bank withdrawals were frozen in late November 2001. Thus the state's maintenance of the peso's exchange value, insuring the integration of the country's elite to the world economy, no longer permitted any use value on the local level. Resistance now became a question of sheer survival, and some Argentines spoke of a crisis in the very process of civilization: "The new state project implies, in the short term, an abrupt cut-off . . . of the systems of social reproduction: the state gradually detaches itself from the populations and the territories; and finally, from social cohesion itself."[10] But this detachment only gives the state the power of an empty affirmation, an entirely formal language of exchange, which is valid in theory but not in fact. And the void calls out either for a democratic invention, or for an authoritarian solution.

This situation of suspended crisis appears likely to spread, leaving open, at least for a time, the possibility of very different responses. The illusions of the 1990s, however, are definitely over. The collapse of the stock markets, and the economic slowdown that has followed, brings a threat of deflation, unemployment, and exclusion to bear on most of the world's populations. Under current political conditions, the only possible response seems to be a strengthening of the barriers that separate the privileged classes from all the others—and this, even within the richest countries. The new military posture of the United States, while directly motivated by the September 11 attacks, and foreseen long in advance by the neoconservatives, also represents an attempt to restructure society, and to institute a new form of discipline in the face of the void that has been left by the collapse of the speculative bubble. It is in this way that the ideological version of economic flexibility meets its own limits. This shift toward heightened military and police control takes away much of the legitimacy that flexible modes of management were able to confer on capitalist society. Still the opportunistic model of the flexible personality will probably continue to orient the behavior of privileged individuals for years yet to come, even as it subjects them to strong contradictions. Under such conditions, the various forms of resistance to capitalism will clearly intensify, not least because they find a vital energy in the feeling of absolute necessity brought on by the crisis. Now I want to deal specifically with one such form of resistance: the resistance to the privatization of knowledge, the fourth "fictive commodity" whose importance Polanyi had not yet measured. It is through the cooperative production of immaterial knowledge that we will rejoin the enigma of the networked protests.

Just one more thing. I do not want to accord any privilege, in what follows, to that supposedly more "advanced" fraction of the world population which is so deeply involved with electronic networks. I think that the opposition established by Manual Castells, between the "net" and "self," between modern abstraction and regressive identity, is simply false.[11] Much more interesting is the divide between the possessive individualism of the flexible personality and a concern for human coexistence. As we saw above, the movement of movements found one of its beginnings in a concept of solidarity arising from the Zapatista struggles, which have fundamentally to do with questions of land. But the meaning of these survival struggles of the Mayan peoples could only reach the subjects of the developed world through the nternet, where the fundamental stakes concern the treatment of cultural and scientific knowledge. Here the essential struggle is to overtake and dissolve the language of ¥ $, not through a return to the closed, bureaucratic frameworks of the Keynesian state, but instead through the *political* development of new principles of exchange and reciprocity. Thus this fourth field of resistance, which touches closely on human language but also on technical development, seems destined to furnish elements of articulation for other struggles in a shared search for alternatives to the systemic crisis.

## III.

It is well known that the Linux operating system kernel, and free software generally, is made cooperatively without any money changing hands. This is something that quickly caught the attention of artists and culture critics, with the result that in the early days of the Nettime mailing list, for example, there were a lot of discussions about what Richard Barbrook called the "high-tech gift economy."[12] The expression recalls an anthropologist, not Polanyi but Marcel Mauss, the author of the famous essay on *The Gift*. His essential contribution was to underscore, at the very heart of modern economic exchange, the presence of motives irreducible to the calculation of the value of material objects, and also of the individual interest one might have in possessing them. As Barbrook points out, the heritage of Mauss was very much alive in alternative circles, his ideas having inspired the situationists, who passed them on to the do-it-yourself media ethic of the punk movement. But mostly what fueled the discussion of the internet gift economy was not theory, but the simple practice of adding information to the net. As Rishab Ghosh explained, "the economy of the Net begins to look like a vast tribal cooking-pot, surging with production to match consumption, simply because everyone understands—instinctively, perhaps—that trade need not occur in single transactions of barter, and that one product can be exchanged for millions at a time. The cooking-pot keeps boiling because people keep putting in things as they themselves, and others, take things out."[13] By placing the accent on the overflowing abundance and free nature of the available content, Ghosh responded implicitly to one of the most contested themes in Mauss's essay, which cast each gift as the deliberate imposition of a debt on the receiver, instating hierarchies which were quite foreign to the practice of networked information exchange.

Today, with the popular explosion of Gnutella and other peer-to-peer file-sharing systems, these notions of the high-tech gift economy have begun to form part of common sense. It seems to admit at least a few new things: that the coded creations circulating on the internet are never "consumed" like a cigarette would be; that use by some people in no way limits their availability for others; and that certain kinds of exchanges therefore have nothing to do with rarity and are quite possible without money. What is less often remarked, because of a denial which is characteristic of free-market rhetoric, is the fact that nonmonetary models of exchange have been operating on a very large scale for as long as one can remember, for instance in the realm of academic publishing, where information is shared not for monetary value but for the recognition it brings—which itself is at least partially dependent on the feeling of contributing something to humanity or truth. In fact there exists quite a large movement in the domain of scientific publishing aiming for online release of all the articles carried by specialized journals, in order to make the results universally accessible despite the increasing cost of many essential print publications.[14] Recently, an author by the name of Yochai Benkler has taken the twin examples of free software and academic publishing as a foundation on which to build a general theory of what he calls "commons-based peer production," by which he means nonproprietary informational or cultural production, based on materials which are extremely low cost or inherently free. This voluntary form of self-organized production depends, in his words, "on very large aggregations of individuals independently scouring their information environment in search of opportunities to be creative in small or large increments. These individuals then self-identify for tasks and perform them for complex motivational reasons."[15] Benkler's first aim, however, is not to explain peoples' motivation, but simply to describe the organizational and technological conditions that make this cooperative production possible.

Four attributes of the networked information economy appear as preconditions of commons-based peer production. First, information must be freely available as inexhaustible raw material for products which, in their turn, will become inexhaustible raw materials for further productions. Second, potential collaborators must be easily able to find the project that inspires them to creativity and labor. Third, the cost of production equipment must be low, as is now the case for things like computers and related media devices. Fourth, it must be possible to broadly distribute the results, for instance, over a telecommunications net. Under these conditions, quite complex tasks can be imagined, divided into small modules, and thrown out into the public realm where individuals will self-identify their competency to meet any given challenge. The only remaining requirement for large-scale production of cultural and informational goods is to be able to perform quality checks and integrate all the individual modules with relatively low effort into a completed whole—but these tasks, it turns out, can often be done on a distributed basis as well. The fact that all of this is possible, and actually happening today, allows Benkler to contradict Ronald Coase's classic theory, which identifies the firm, with its hierarchical command structure, and the market, functioning through the individual's quest for the

duction, these mobilizations begin and end with the fabrication of publicly available texts. For example, the People's Summit in Quebec City in April 2001 began long in advance, with many different studies of the consequences to be expected from the future agreement on the Free Trade Area of the Americas. These studies led to the drafting of a remarkable document, "Alternatives for the Americas," which is a countertreaty of great precision, composed through a process of knowledge exchange and political coordination on the scale of the American hemisphere.[16] It's also true that as a direct consequence of the massive demonstration that took place during the summit, the official working draft of the FTAA treaty was made public for the first time; until then it had not even been available to elected representatives of the American peoples, but only to executive negotiating teams (and scores of corporate "advisers"). In this way the counter-globalization movements constitute a public archive. And yet between the fundamental landmarks represented by these text publications, how many face-to-face debates took place, how many moments of singular or collective creation, how many acts of courage and solidarity? And how many emotions, images, memories, and desires were created and shared during the days of action in Quebec City?

The spectacle of these great gatherings, overflowing with freely given creations, could appear like a new form of the potlatch ceremonies described by Marcel Mauss, a gift-giving ritual where the demonstrators try to outdo their adversaries through open displays of generosity. No doubt there is something of that, which explains why the words "free" and "priceless" have been so important in these demonstrations. But what seems more interesting in the reference to Mauss is his way of perceiving gift-giving rituals as "total social facts," bringing all the different aspects of social life together in a system of complex and indivisible relations. Whoever saw the extraordinary symbolic transactions between pacifists, ecologists, unionists, anarchists, spirtualists, delinquents, reporters, by-passers, cops, and politicians at the G8 summit in Genoa, in July of 2001, can find a real resonance in what Mauss says about the Melanesian gift-giving ceremonies, the American Indian potlatch rituals, and the "market-festivals of the Indo-European world":

"All these phenomena are at once legal, economic, religious, and even aesthetic, morphological, etc. They are legal, including public and private law, diffuse and organized morality; they are strictly obligatory or simply praised and blamed, political and domestic at the same time, involving the social classes as well as the clans and families. They are religious: including strict religion and magic and animism and diffuse religious mentality. They are economical: because the idea of value, of utility, of interest, of luxury, of wealth, of acquisition and accumulation as well as consumption and even purely sumptuary expenditure are everywhere in them, even though these are all understood differently than by us today.

What is more, these institutions have an important aesthetic side to them . . . the dances that are carried out alternatively, the chants and parades of all kinds, the dramatic performances . . . everything, food, objects, and services, even "respect," as the Tlingits say, everything is a cause for aesthetic emotion."[17]

There is no nostalgia for a primitive life in the fact of quoting Mauss, nor any facile admiration for the "revolutionary fête." Things are much more complex. On the one hand, the contemporary quest for "direct action," for "direct democracy," finds an initial realization in the collective, cooperative production of these public events, which bring together all the rigorously separated aspects of modern social life. Indeed, the very aim of such events is to criticize certain fundamental separations, like the one that amputates any basic concern for life from the laws of monetary accumulation. But that doesn't mean that the event, the ecstatic convergence, is a total solution: instead it is a departure point for a fresh questioning of the social tie, at times when its deadly aspects become visible, as they are today. The protestors' claim, not just to the occupation but to the *creation* of public space, with all the conflicts it brings in its wake, offers society an occasion to theatricalize the real in order to replay the meaning of abstractions that are no longer adequate to the needs and possibilities of life. The "total social fact" of the contemporary demonstration is, at its best, a chance to relearn and recreate a language for political debate, which isn't just about money, and doesn't only have "¥ $" in its vocabulary. And the networked protests we are speaking of, including those of the peace movement in 2003, have produced the first chances to do this at the scale of the globalized economy and of global governance.

Artistic practice has been one of the keys to the emergence of these "global social facts"—not least because artistic practice has also been one of the ways to hold off group violence, to open up a theatrical space that doesn't immediately become a war zone. This is obviously something that contemporary society risks forgetting, and that particular risk is reason enough in itself to go beyond the specialized, disciplinary definition of art, to try to relocate art within a much broader political economy. Before I do that, however, I want to draw one last group of ideas from Yochai Benkler. His paper closes with the problem of what he calls "threats to motivation." One of these comes from the failure to integrate the results of commons-based peer production into usable wholes which can make a project successful. Translated into political terms, this would mean the failure of the networked movements to change any tangible aspect of social life. That is a real threat to motivation; and I think it's vitally important to keep offering practical ideas and proposals about possible changes on all the scales of governance and existence, from the neighborhood to the world level, at every new demonstration. Benkler points to different strategies for putting together the results of common effort. These strategies range from self-organization of the integration process, to the delegation of this tricky point to hierarchical structure a or a commercial enterprise. Again the translation into our terms is obvious, and it has begun to become visible at events such as the European Social Forum, held in Florence in November of 2002. Just when the networked struggles get big enough to succeed, they can be handed over to a traditional politburo supported by professional media people. The problem with such expedient strategies is that they risk giving participants the impression that the voluntary production of political culture with their peers is being confiscated by somebody in a directive position. A fantastic example of this is the thirty-thousand member ATTAC association in France, which, to many members' discontent, is in fact a strictly controlled, hierarchical organization at the national level. However, for ATTAC to have the social power it does, it has had to also produce a decentralized network of local committees, which operate very differently from the national bureau and regularly criticize or contradict its decisions. The tension you can see there in a very real situation, between collective process and effective decision, is at the heart of the democratic experiment today. You might even say that working though that kind of tension is the art of politics.

## IV.

So now we return to the language of art, and to an art whose very essence is language. Obviously I'm talking about conceptual art. But today this most revolutionary of all art forms is considered a failure. The "escape strategies" that Lucy Lippard talks about in her famous book on *The Dematerialization of the Object of Art* were intended to free artists from dependency on the gallery-magazine-museum circuit. It was thought that artists could motivate people to use their imagination in completely new ways, by giving them linguistic suggestions, virtual proposals that they could actualize outside the specialized institutions. But exclusive signatures rapidly took precedence over the infinite permutation of the works in the lives of the viewers/users. The necessary corollary was that the concept should refer primarily to itself, as in a famous piece composed of a chair, a picture of a chair, and a dictionary definition of the word "chair" (Joseph Kosuth, *One and Three Chairs*, 1965). Such a work, completing itself in a tautology that required no transformative activity from the public, could easily be presented within the existing system. Thus the conceptual escape attempt only led from market-oriented New York to the museums of Europe, then finally back to the market. In 1973, Seth Siegelaub said in an interview: "Conceptual art, more than all previous types of art, questions the fundamental nature of art. Unhappily, the question is strictly limited to the exclusive domain of the fine arts. There is still the potential of it authorizing an examination of all that surrounds art, but in reality, conceptual artists are dedicated only to exploring avant-garde aesthetic problems . . . . The economic pattern associated with conceptual art is remarkably similar to that of other artistic movements: to purchase a work cheap and resell it at a high price. In short, speculation."[18] Lucy Lippard, for her part, wrote in 1973 that the "ghetto mentality predominant in the narrow and incestuous art world . . . with its reliance on a very small group of dealers, curators, editors and collectors who are all too frequently and often unknowingly bound by invisible apron strings to the 'real world's' power structures . . . make[s] it unlikely that conceptual art will be any better equipped to affect the world any differently than, or even as much as, its less ephemeral counterparts."[19]

These admissions of defeat are well known. But recently, another history of conceptual art has been coming back to light. It is a history that unfolds in Latin America, and particularly in Argentina, in the cities of Buenos Aires and Rosario. It would seem that here, in the context of an authoritarian government and under the pressure of American cultural imperialism, conceptual art could only be received—or invented—as an invitation to act antagonistically within the mass-media sphere. Certain Argentine pop artists considered that the commercial news media could actually be appropriated as an artistic medium, like a canvas or a gallery space. To do this, Roberto Jacoby and Eduardo Costa created an artificial happening, one that never really happened, and they stimulated the media with information about it, so as to achieve specific fictional effects.[20] But this attempt was only a first step towards a fully political appropriation of the communications media by artists. The most characteristic project was *Tucumán Arde*, or "Tucumán is Burning," realized in 1968.[21] The military government was attempting to "modernize" the sugar-cane industry in the province of Tucumán, with a shift from small, locally owned businesses to larger factories owned by foreign capital; at the same time, the official media painted an idyllic picture of a region which in reality was wracked by impoverishment and intense labor struggles. So a group of some thirty artists and intellectuals from Buenos Aires and Rosario researched the social and economic conditions in the province, carrying out an analysis of all the mass-media coverage of the region, and going out themselves to gather firsthand information and to document the situation using photography and film. They then staged an exhibition that was explicitly designed to feed their work back into the national debate, so as to counter the media picture. Yet the project, although it did not shy away from advertising techniques, could not be reduced to counterpropaganda. As Andrea Giunta writes: "In many of its characteristic traits—such as the exploration of the interaction between languages, the centrality of the activity required from the spectator, the unfinished character, the importance of the documentation, the dissolution of the idea of the author, and the questioning of the art system and the ideas that legitimate it—*Tucumán Arde* maintains a relation with the repertory of conceptual art. But not with the tautological and self-referential form of conceptualism, in which, from a certain viewpoint, one finds a reconfirmation of the modernist paradigm. Language does not refer back to language, to the specificity of the artistic fact; instead, the contextual relations are so strong in this case that reality ceases being understood as a space of reflection and comes to be conceived as a possible field of action oriented toward the transformation of society."[22]

*Tucumán Arde* is extremely interesting to consider from the contemporary viewpoint of tactical media practice, which in many respects has been one long effort to research, expose, and go beyond the idyllic picture of globalization being painted by the corporate media.[23] But to understand the major differences from today's situation, one must realize that *Tucumán Arde* was done with the support of the Argentine CGT, that is, a radical labor union, and the exhibition was shown in a union hall. In other words, to obtain the funding and distribution of practices that would not be supported by the market, the Rosario group had to collaborate with a bureaucratic structure, which is essentially an outgrowth of the capitalist firm. And that is almost impossible today, at least in the overdeveloped countries. For complex reasons which have to do both with the antibureaucratic bias of the New Left, and with the heightened integration of labor unions to the state after the crisis of 1968, it has become very difficult for social movements, let alone artists, to collaborate with official structures such as parties, unions, etc. The motivation just isn't there. This is why the use of carefully conceived linguistic formulas, of oriented but open signifiers, would become a far more effective means of mobilization in the late 1990s, when ideas could be distributed and constantly transformed through the proliferation of connections offered by the internet. In this way one achieved a nonbureaucratic capacity for subversive political action on a large scale, outside any compulsory framework. A new kind of conceptualism began to emerge, in which "attitudes become forms," as the curator Harald Szeeman said in the 1960s. An idea or phrase could become a worldwide event, in which every individual performance was different. Just as in Lawrence Weiner's famous prescription, the action could be carried out by the originators of the ideas, or realized by others, or not done at all. In the late 1990s, this revolutionary promise was realized. Thirty years after experiments such as *Tucumán Arde*, the counterglobalization movement burst onto the world scene as the revenge of the concept.

The examples of this could be as numerous as there are experiences. That is why I want to talk about an event in which I was personally involved: the carnivalesque performance and riot in the City of London on June 18, 1999. Before it took place, this day was intensely dreamed by a multiplicity of actors, sometimes connected in constant dialogue and exchange, sometimes affected at a distance by signs that promised to break their isolation and unleash their agency. The inspiration first emerged, at least in certain versions of the story, during the summer of 1998 in conversations between members of London Reclaim the Streets and the London anarchist group Greenpeace (not the famous

NGO).[24] It spread through the networks of Peoples' Global Action, drawing on the suggestive potency of two key ideas. One was the "street party," as a form of direct democracy which refused the domination of the city by the automobile, but also the traditional procedures of party politics. The other was the phrase "Our resistance is as transnational as capital": a return of twentieth-century internationalism in red, black, and green, after a long trip through the jungles of Chiapas where the Zapatista uprising began on January 1, 1994 (the day NAFTA came into being). A complex circulation through time and space, where solidarity means respect for local autonomy and differing motivations for struggle, was encapsulated in these two key ideas. A call to action, distributed widely through the Internet, put it like this:

"The proposal is to encourage as many movements and groups as possible to organize their own autonomous protests or actions, on the same day (June 18th), in the same geographical locations (financial/ corporate/ banking/ business districts) around the world. Events could take place at relevant sites, e.g. multinational company offices, local banks, stock exchanges. Each event would be organized autonomously and coordinated in each city or financial district by a variety of movements and groups. It is hoped that a whole range of different groups will take part, including workers, peasants, indigenous peoples, women, students, the landless, environmentalists, unwaged/unemployed and others . . . .everyone who recognizes that the global capitalist system, based on the exploitation of people and the planet for the profit of a few, is at the root of our social and ecological troubles."[25]

J18 in London was the most exquisitely planned and spontaneously realized artistic performance in which I have taken part, an awakening to new possibilities of political struggle that would be echoed throughout the world. Thousands converged in the morning at the Liverpool tube station in the city, receiving carnival masks in four different colors that encouraged the crowd to split into groups, outwitting the police by following different paths through the medieval street plan of Europe's largest financial district, then coming together again in front of the LIFFE building, the London International Financial Futures and Options Exchange, which was the symbolic and real target of this protest against the global domination of speculative exchange. The choice of site was essential. Long years of effort by far-flung organizers and intellectuals had been required to understand and describe the ways in which capital had escaped its former national bounds, in order to redeploy itself transnationally in new oppressive systems; yet until the late 1990s, that knowledge remained largely abstract, floating in a deterritorialized space like the financial sphere itself. Here it was translated into tangible forms of embodied expression: transgressive dancing, defiant music, a verbal and visual poetics of resistance. For once, individual pleasure once did not appear as the negation, but rather as the accentuation of collective struggle, confronting financial abstractions which could be understood by the participants through the immediate experience of the stone-and-glass architecture, while the significance of each of their acts was multiplied by the knowledge that other, similar events were occurring all over the planet. Spontaneous invitations for passing traders to come join the party were combined with sudden attacks on private property, generating an unexpected, threatening, sympathetic, and immensely confident image of revolt—a way to finally start answering the decades-old pleas for help from oppressed peoples in the South, while also responding to the unbearable social divisions that transnational capitalism imposes on countries like Britain. Of course this carnivalesque outburst was just one moment in a longer process of struggle, prepared by untold numbers of people under far harsher conditions. But the language of protest that emerged here nonetheless marked a turning point. It was the immediate inspiration for the larger and more complex confrontation in Seattle, six months later, which finally forced the messages of the global resistance movements through the frosty screens of the traditional media, opening the political crisis of global capitalism's legitimacy. A crisis which has not ceased to morph and mutate into the increasingly violent forms that it is taking today.

From my point of view there can be no mistake. The revenge of the concept is the reappearance, in broad daylight, of the global class struggle: a political struggle over to right to share in the fruits of technological development and to guard against its many poisons. But if this re-embodiment of class struggle can also be an artistic experience—and an experiment that reverses and transforms the concept of art—it is because the articulation of the old divides has radically changed. In the face of an all-dominating capitalist class which has imposed a global division of labor, and extended its ideological grip over core populations through the devices of popular stockholding, speculative pension funds, and the seductive traps of consumer credit, the focus of struggle is no longer so much the rate of the industrial wage as the very existence and production of that which lies outside the cash nexus: land in the sense of a viable ecology; labor as the energy of life from its beginnings in travails of birth; knowledge not as fragmented commodities but as an overarching question about meaning; trade and exchange as an institution of human coexistence. Arising within these fields of struggle are new desires and political designs, irreducible to the organizing schemes of capital and state. In the best of cases, opposition becomes a prelude to radical invention.

Still the tensions have increased dramatically in all these domains, under the advancing pressure of systemic crisis. As the techniques of mass-mediated control ratchet up toward overt fascism, in the wake both of September 11 and of the stock market failures, the improbable meeting of teamsters and turtles in Seattle and the naked life dancing in front of the LIFFE building in London might seem to recede into some distant past.

It is certain that the power of surprise was soon lost, as every international summit became an overwhelming protest, and the ruling oligarchies found new courage to ignore the democratic expressions of the citizens. Broader and deeper revolts must now be invented. But these were among the early experiments in a rearticulation of struggles, whose destiny is to cross all the borders. For the artists of another world, wherever they live and however they understand themselves, let these moments be counted among the seeds of the future.

## Notes

Thanks to participants of the WorldInfo Con in Amsterdam, December 2002, for ideas, and to Felix Stalder, Ken Wark, and Keith Hart, for critiques of an initial version circulated on the electonic mailinglist Nettime.

1. There is no "history" of these movements, but information and stories can be found at www.agp.org.

2. This is the thesis of Negri and Hardt's *Empire* (Cambridge: Harvard University Press, 2000); also see Yoshihiko Ichida, "Questions d'Empire," *Multitudes* 7, December 2001, online at www.multitudes.samizdat.net.

3. Anthony Davies and Simon Ford, "Art Networks," www.societyofcontrol.com/research/davis_ford.htm. Further quotes are from this article and "Culture Clubs," www.infopool.org.uk/cclubs.htm.

4. See Defense Advance Research Projects Agency, "Terrorism Information Awareness System," www.darpa.mil/iao/TIASystems.htm. Also see military strategist Thomas Barnett: ""If we live in a world increasingly populated by Super-Empowered Individuals, then we field an army of Super-Empowered Individuals," www.nwc.navy.mil/newrulesets/ThePentagonsNewMap.htm.

5. Cf. David Harvey, *The Condition of Postmodernity* (Oxford: Blackwell, 1990), pp. 141-48.

6. Cf. Brian Holmes, "The Flexible Personality," *Hieroglyphs of the Future* (Zagreb: Arkzin, 2003), online at www.geocities.com/CognitiveCapitalism/holmes1.html.

7. Cf. Bob Jessop, *The Future of the Capitalist State* (Cambridge: Polity, 2002), pp. 12-14.

8. For example, a government "Superfund" program was deemed necessary in the United States in 1980, to clean up toxic waste on land that companies had used as

free dumping grounds. Since 1995 corporate taxation for this fund has been stopped, and since 2002 the Bush administration, hostile to the expense, is curtailing federal funding. As though the ecological balance were at once priceless and impossible to pay for.

9. Cf. Jessop's treatment of the "Schumpeterian Postnational Workfare State," in *The Future of the Capitalist State*, op. cit.

10. Colectivo Situaciones, *19 y 20. Apuntes sobre el nuevo protagonismo social* (Buenos Aires: De Mano en Mano, 2002).

11. The opposition structures his work on the "information age": *The Rise of the Network Society* and *The Power of Identity* (Oxford: Blackwell, 1996 and 1997).

12. Richard Barbrook, "The Hi-Tech Gift Economy," in *ReadMe, Filtered by Nettime* (New York: Autonomedia, 1999), online at www.firstmonday.dk/issues/ issue3_12/barbrook.

13. Rishab Aiyer Ghosh, "Cooking Pot Economy," in *ReadMe*, op. cit., online at www.firstmonday.dk/issues/issue3_3/ghosh/index.html#SEC5.

14. See, for example, the Budapest Open Access Initiative, www.soros.org/openaccess.

15. Yochai Benkler, "Coase's Penguin, or Linux and the Nature of the Firm," www.benkler.org/CoasesPenguin.html.

16. "Alternatives for the Americas," www.web.net/comfront/ alts4americas/ eng/eng.html.

17. Marcel Mauss, *Essai sur le don* (1923-24), online at www.uqac.uquebec.ca/ zone30/Classiques_des_sciences_sociales/livres/mauss_marcel/socio_et_anthropo/2_essai_sur_le_don/essai_sur_le_don.html.

18. Michel Claura and Seth Siegelaub, "L'art conceptuel," in *Conceptual Art: A Critical Anthology*, eds. A. Alberro and B. Stimson (Cambridge: MIT Press, 1999), pp. 289-90.

19. Lucy Lippard, "Postface," *Six Years: The Dematerialization of the Art Object from 1966 to 1972* (New York: Praeger, 1973), p. 264.

20. Cf. E. Costa, R. Escari, and R. Jacoby, "A Media Art (Manifesto)," in *Conceptual Art: A Critical Anthology*, op. cit., pp. 2-3.

21. A description of *Tucumán Arde* (including the relation to Jacoby's work) can be found in Marí Carmen Ramírez, "Thriving on Adversity: Conceptualism in Latin America, 1960-1980," in *Global Conceptualism: Points of Origin, 1950s-1980s*, exhibi-

tion catalogue, Queens Museum of Art, 1999, pp. 66-67. Also see M.T. Gramuglio and N. Rosa, "Tucumán Burns," in *Conceptual Art: A Critical Anthology*, op. cit., pp. 76-79.

22. Andrea Giunta, *Vanguardia, internacionalismo y política: arte argentino en los años sesenta* (Buenos Aires: Paidós, 2001).

23. Cf. D. Garcia and G. Lovink, "The ABC of Tactical Media," www.waag.org/tmn/abc.html. Also see the wide variety of projects that have made it into the "Next 5 Minutes" festivals, www.n5m.org. Today, indymedia.org is considered (by some) as the broadest expression of tactical media.

24. Cf. "Friday June 18th 1999: Confronting Capital and Smashing the State!" in *Do or Die* 8, London, online at www.eco-action.org/dod/no8/j18.html.

25. See www.corporatewatch.org.uk/magazine/issue8/cw8glob6.html.

# Kevin Harris

# Spiritual Warfare
# Hakim Bey

November 2000

## 1

As I understand it, corporate law is based on the ancient legal fiction of the King's Two Bodies. The individual king dies but the KING never dies, and certain properties belong to the archetype but not to the mortal sovereign. For example, the mortal king cannot sell or alienate lands belonging to the immortal king, the realm itself. But the mortal king partakes of the unique rights of his immortal doppelganger, for instance, in the privilege of granting monopolies. The monopolies (such as the East India Company or the Chinese salt monopolies) formed the germs of the modern corporation. But the truly modern corporation could only come into being when the concept of the monopoly was opened up and combined with the concept of the royal body in a single entity. Thus in law a corporation enjoys far more privilege and far less responsibility ("limited liability") than any mere fleshly human being. A corporation would seem rather to be a discorporation, a spiritual disincarnate undying being with vast powers on the material plane. Sounds like a demon, doesn't it? In a single century corporation law has succeeded in pulling off an occult stunt that makes Satanism look like a harmless hobby for disgruntled employees.

Banking is another highly spiritual activity, rooted in the fact that the original banks were temples. In the late fourth millennium Sumerian temples were loaning money-commodity currencies: cattle, barley, silver—at rates as high as 33.3% per year. The tradition of the Jubilee (known to the Bible), the periodic forgiveness of debts, appears first in Sumeria. The economy would have collapsed without such safety valves. The modern bank solved this problem by obtaining the monopoly on moneycreation. The invention of coins in Lydia, 7th-century B.C.E., facilitated this fiat magic. By lending (at interest) ten times its reserves, the bank simply creates the money needed to pay off the debts owed to it. The Federal Reserve Bank (a private bank with a monopoly) actually coins money and lends it to the government. Most states have been in debt to private banks for centuries.

The key to such magic was to cut off all connection between commodities (e.g. barley or silver) and money. Money freed of its anchor in real goods can float upwards forever, compounding itself unto eternity. The history of money reveals an ever-more-attenuated connection with gross materiality, till in 1973 even the (highly magical) link with gold was dissolved by the alchemist Nixon. At this point money began a wild spiralling apotheosis that still goes on. At present over ninety-five percent of all money has no actual connection with any material substance. It is not productive capital but "pure" capital—not wealth, only money. Money begets money, as Ben Franklin gloated—the sexuality of the dead. Pure spirituality, and yet endowed with absolute power over materiality and life itself. Money: not just the "bottom line" but the only line, the final enclosure—the disappearance of the outside.

In short, money is another demon. The landscape of our tired old Enlightenment indeed seems haunted by spectres (or "hobgoblins," as in the first English translation of the *Communist Manifesto*). Corporations and banks need to be understood in the light of the history of religions. Strange spooks inhabit the belfry of "neoliberalism" in its amok triumphalism. We need a hermetic critique of institutions. We want a science of hieroglyphics to help us penetrate the tranced labyrinth of text and image that conceals (at its center) the sheer nonbeing of corporations and banks, and the purely magical nature of money.

Ideology now appears to us as yet another spook. Ideology betrayed us, not (like banks and corporations) by winning, but by losing the struggle for paradigmatic hegemony in the last millennium. If the dialectic is going to be kick-started again in the twenty-first-century, ideology's not going to be doing the kicking. The movement of the social needs to be resurrected, not just resuscitated. Something miraculous is demanded. Something "impossible."

## 2

Biotechnics presents yet another scary supernatural scenario. But "Frankenfoods" and six-toed babies or any possible failure of genetic manipulation frighten me far less than its actual successes. In a world where every decision made by science is determined (predetermined) by "money interests" (i.e. the interests of money and the interest on money), then we have a world where science and humanity retain no interests in common. Who precisely is going to "benefit" from the imminent end of human reproduction as we've known it? What three percent of the world will look like movie/TV stars (who already look like mutants)—and what ninety-seven percent will resemble unsuccessful graduates of Chernobyl's Wormwood High?

And why do Americans seem to care so much about who owns what piece of recorded music (recordings which are nothing more than the digital tombstones of once-live performances), and so little about who owns the "intellectual copyright" of the DNA of, say, rice? Bioengineering in alliance with pure capital has already reshaped our lived reality; the "killer apps" and "terminal genes" are mere details. This is the future; we're living in it now. And not one scifi writer predicted it.

## 3

Nothing's happening. As I write we have a Schrodinger's President situation here in the

US We can't open the box because it might kill the cat; but we can't not open the box. There are ever thinner and thinner slices of unreality. What you see happening is what's actually happening—i.e. nothing. No conspiracies, no depth, no illusions. Nothing is hidden, no datum goes unprocessed. All information, all the time; infinity-wide and a micron deep. All light, no shadow.

The medium for this ecstasy of information is of course the media. Unified on a global scale for the first time since writing was invented around six thousand years ago, the media—TV, radio, movies, print, internet, image-commodities, education, music—all propagate the same sameness, the same hysterical greed for an ever-less-seductive fetishism, the same thin scrim over an abyss of boredom. And the boredom itself is the flimsy curtain that only barely contains our terror, anger, shame. Thinner and thinner slices.

"Alternative media" means stuff that can't compete in the free market. Governments are no longer interested in subsidizing it, and in fact it has near-zero influence on what passes for the consensus. The whole vitality of an avant-garde depends on the existence of an outside toward which it strives. But there is no more outside. Only failure. Do we have to make failure our outside?

This would constitute a way of renunciation and even asceticism: a deliberate unknowing or refusal of knowlege. The monasteries of the Dark Ages were points of light on a map of sepulchral gloom. A crisis of epistemology was overcome by keeping knowlege secret. Maybe in these Lite Ages we need monasteries of darkness to tide us over and preserve our last secrets till the unending day of the plague has passed. If ever. No doubt a counsel of despair. But I can't see any way to avoid the work of negativity. If not the monastery then. . . the barbarian horde.

# 4

The First World and the Second World have both collapsed; Capitalism died at the same moment as communism. Only pure capital survives. There is no Third World and there is no third way. On the one side, humanity; on the other side, money. This is no longer a question of mere tactics, "molecular" or otherwise. Conceptually this is confrontation, strategy, war.

But how do you wage war against disincarnate entities? Malay Black Djinn curse? Exorcism? Probably futile. Could there exist some form of warfare capable of being waged on the invisible plane? A guerilla response to the pure war of pure capital? A strategy, yes—but what? As F. Jameson says, it appears to be "impossible to imagine an alternative" to capital. Perhaps we have less need for a new Marx or Kropotkin, and more for a new von Clauswitz or Sun Tzu.

# 5

I can't help thinking that somehow or other luddism still has a role to play. The original luddites were not primitivists; they wanted a technology that could support the social relation, not destroy it in the name of profit and/or efficiency. What we used to call "appropriate technology" in the 1960s and '70s. In the intoxication of the internet and other groovy new technologies a great many radicals appear to have abandoned their old commitment to such "machine smashing" notions as renewable resources, biodiversity, or the social responsibility of science. It's not theory but personal experience that forces on me the impression of the "best minds" of the era slumped before the screen, lost in cyberspace, tranced into the belief that what happens there is really happening. And yet already the market is bored with its new toys; NASDAQ trembles and even biotech stocks are looking dull. Nothing's happening—except for drifts of dead daytraders falling like November leaves. Boring, boring. Not even money is interesting anymore.

Despite the fact that luddism is historically a movement of the left, some ideologues have dismissed it as reactionary because it is not a "progressive" movement. Indeed if "left" demands the Enlightenment and its "cruel instrumentality of reason" (i.e. not rationality but rationalism), if "left" implies a single world culture based on the machine and its demands, then some might say the time has come to move "beyond left and right" and even to look for allies amongst other so-called reactionaries. It's hard to find common ground with the left these days because it's hard to locate any left at all. (The Green Party doesn't count; does the Green Party have a coherent critique of capital?) Left would be nice. Hell, even "young" Marx looks good now that all the old marxists are dead. As for the right, is it possible that there may exist some true conservatives who are not racists, chauvinist nationalists, apologists for neoliberalism, fashion fascists, nor heavy-metal diabolists? Conservatives interested in the conservation of things like wilderness and farms, human values, community, and other such old fashioned virtues? Maybe both Left and right are empty categories, null sets. Can biophilia unite humans against the frigid antibiosis of capital's machinery? I have my doubts but I'm trying to resolve them and find a way out of despair. Meanwhile could we finally just forget the ancient floor plan of the French Assembly and simply address ourselves instead to those remnants who still feel that humanity is something more than a dwindling market niche?

# 6

According to P. Virilio, a globe united by one technology, one economy, one image, has become a setting for the one big accident. Maybe it's already happened: the failure of ideology, of the movement of the social—the end even of the spectacle and its replacement by sheer simulacrum. If not the end of history then the idea of the end of the idea of history. Theology and materialism both in the trashbin; physics and metaphysics alike—6000 years of immiserabilism—culminating in the victory of those "other bodies," alien and inhuman, demons of our inner emptiness. Any strategy of resistance then—however "impossible"—would have to develop a kind of rough empiricism capable of transcending the false consciousnesses of both materialism and immaterialism. This process of discovery might provide useful tasks for those monasteries of darkness where hermetic critique and hieroglyphic theory will be studied—tasks of both negation and creation.

From my perspective religion and spirituality are two different things. Religion in Sumer and Egypt appropriated spirituality from shamanism and neolithic paganism. Religion used its supposed monopoly of grace to reinforce separation and hierarchy. From this point of view ideology might appear simply as secularized theology, since its end result is the same.

Spirituality (for want of a better word) strikes me as an empirical thing, since—like countless others—I've experienced it through psychotropic plants and chemicals, and by other means no less natural or unnatural. I find it interesting that global capital seems unable to digest and commodify the "power plants" and phantastica; over and above the economic advantages of the war on drugs there remains a residue of sheer psychic hysteria about the repression that somehow suggests real power is at stake. And real power is rare outside the sphere of money. We should take note of such esoteric power flows. We need every possible advantage.

A resistance based on empiricism, it seems to me, will have to consider the apparent actuality of spirit. At this point I must admit that I'm waiting for a sign, like some very minor Old Testament prophet. I can't predict, but I have the feeling that this sign will somehow involve what I'm calling spirituality. For this reason I expect the sign to appear not in America or any of the other "included zones" but perhaps in what used to be called the Fourth World, the world of tribes, foresters, and peasants (and shamans and pagans), the excluded zones where the frontline battles of global capital are being fought. If both religion and ideology have betrayed us then the sign cannot take the form of religion or ideology. Somehow the sign will combine elements of difference and also solidarity, and present a real opposition to sameness as well as separation. This sounds quite paradoxical, and therefore suggests the spirituality of the sign. Above all I believe the sign will arise spontaneously, and that it cannot be cooked up as an intellectual exercise or artwork. And I have absolutely no idea what it will be. Or if it will be.

## 7 (addendum)

What does all this mean in terms of possible strategy—or even tactics—"after Seattle," etc., etc.? How does this "waiting for a sign" relate to the struggle against the WTO, IMF, World

Bank, NAFTA, GATT, major corporations, superfunds... not to mention the usual old straightforward enemies like governments and armies? and new ambiguous enemies like the NGOs?

I'd like to make a plea for theory, which doesn't by any means imply ideology. Theoria originally signifies "vision," and includes both sight and "visionary experience." Since the decay of postdeconstruction, postmodernism, and post-everything else, theory has fallen on hard times. Theory now requires the kind of empiricism evoked in the previous paragraphs; it needs psychotropic madness and spontaneity as well. But above all theory needs to clarify the issue of capital, and this is a work of negation. The protesters in Seattle or Prague are by no means united in their understanding of capital. The reformist element actually believes in "capital with a human face," and shares no common language with the anarchists, etc. As a result alliances made around the emotions of confrontation tend to dissolve when strategic issues are raised. Populism would be a welcome phenomenon, and might have some appeal to reform and even to productive capital, as well as to the resistance. But populism in the Green Party style has no future except lost elections. Until a viable form of populism appears I think nonauthoritarians might as well work on sharpening their theory of capital.

Another crying need is for real strategic thinking. New and unusual forms of the old "demo" caught the Seattle police by surprise, but the actions against the Democratic and Republican conventions were failures because these tactics were anticipated by police. (The anticonvention actions also failed, I suspect, because no one really cares about politics. The best tactic would have been to deliberately stay away from the conventions, not to demonstrate at all, but to denounce them as boring shams.) Each move on the part of capital's forces requires a new tactical response from the resistance, and these new tactics can only arise out of strategic thinking. Elementary von Clausewitz.

Meanwhile, in closing, a salute to French farmer José Bové. He did more for the cause by driving his tractor into a McDonald's than all web pages and NGOs combined. And hail to Vandana Shiva as well. She and her Indian women are very nearly a "sign" in themselves.

# A Short Personal History of the Global Justice Movement

## From New York's Community Gardens, to Seattle's Tear gas, Quebec's Fences, the 9/11 Backlash, and Beyond

## L.A. Kauffman interviewed by Benjamin Shepard

"All War, All the Time?" asked the small pink and black stickers, encouraging people to sign up for Mobilize New York's antiwar email alerts. They were the first in a series of stickers that suddenly appeared on the streets of New York in late 2002. In the four weeks before the February 15, 2003, antiwar protests, you couldn't go anywhere in New York City without seeing bright blue stickers that featured a flag flying above the globe, bearing the slogan, "The World Says No to War." It seemed like every phone booth, subway car, and mailbox sported one of these stickers. Highly stylish, yet concise and action-oriented, the stickers were designed by L. A. Kauffman, a longtime activist and writer whose specialty is effective movement mobilizing and organizing.

I met Kauffman on February 8 at the offices of the United for Peace and Justice coalition on West Forty-second Street. The space was packed with the stickers, buttons, and posters she created to promote the February 15 "World Says No to War" protest, and filled with the hustle-and-bustle energy of a convergence center. More than a hundred volunteers were just finishing a morning meeting before heading out on the streets for an afternoon of leafleting, stickering, and wheatpasting. By the time the five-week campaign was over, UFPJ distributed more than 1.1 million pieces of literature. More than fift-five thousand of Kauffman's leaflets were downloaded off the Internet for photocopying. During the weekend of the interview alone, more than two hundred fifty people handed out leaflets in all five boroughs of the city.

Kauffman, wearing her trademark fedora hat and dark horn-rimmed sunglasses, plus a Green Bay Packers T-shirt from her beloved home state of Wisconsin, discussed her journey from public space/community garden activism in Manhattan's Lower East Side, to the Seattle WTO protests, through the peak years of global trade summit protests, to September 11 and its aftermath, and finally to the staff of United for Peace and Justice.

Just the day before, UFPJ had gone to court to challenge the NYPD's rejection of a parade permit for February 15. At issue was the core principle of the right to march, as well as to rally, to express opposition to the Iraq war. The themes that run through the interview mirror the issues raised by the march permit fight: the project of building a robust and colorful public commons, and a pulsing democratic politics that arises from the street.

*Benjamin Shepard: Do you want to explain what you are planning for next week, what the conditions are right now?*

L. A. Kauffman: Well, right at this moment, you and I are sitting down to have this conversation in the middle of a huge firestorm of controversy over the February 15 protest. We're in court and fighting for the incredibly basic right to get a march permit from the City of New York and the New York Police Department. They're saying that—because of "security concerns"—they will not allow us to march anywhere in the city. They'll allow us to have a "stationary event," a rally. But they won't allow us to march. The federal government sent an attorney to stand with the city today at our court hearing and support their case.

For me, having spent much of the previous five years doing direct-action organizing, this is a very peculiar position to be in. I never really imagined that I'd find myself organizing a classic mass march and rally, much less embroiled in a dispute over getting a permit from the police. The groups that I've been part of over the years have never asked for permits. We just do what we want to do. If you have enough people, the police usually accommodate you, and you usually end up with fewer barricades and restrictions on your movement.

But while I cringe at the idea of asking the police for permission to exercise my rights, I also think the reasons why UFPJ applied for a permit were good ones. We're making a real effort to bring in lots of people for February 15 who are first-time protesters, and to bring in a more racially diverse group of people than have historically been involved in the peace movement. We want it to be a safe place for old people, children, immigrants, everyone.

The irony is, having a simple, permitted march and rally—the type of protest that, five years ago, seemed so dull and tame and circumscribed from the perspective of the direct action global justice movement—has now become a dramatic act of defiance. The political space for dissent has shut down so dramatically that merely gathering in large numbers has become a bold move.

## The Struggle for Community Gardens in New York's Lower East Side

*BS: Let's go back to five years ago, when that political space was opening up. When I first met you, you were planning for the big April 1999 civil disobedience around the community garden issue, which was another public space struggle. We were fighting for another set of spaces that were getting squeezed and homogenized and globalized.*

LAK: The fight over community gardens in New York City in some ways was a very local community fight, with purely local relevance, and yet it was more than that, too. From 1997 to 1999, that campaign pulled a lot of new people into activism and, as far as the East Coast was concerned, was a real incubator for the kinds of creative political energies that were expressed in the Seattle WTO protests, and in the big trade summit protests from November 1999 until September of 2001. Many of us who were working on the garden fight took inspiration from ACT UP and a lot of other direct action movements that had come before us.

*BS: The West Coast Earth First! stuff, too, right?*

LAK: Yes, definitely. There were people who shuttled back and forth between the New York City community garden fight and old-growth forest blockades in remote Oregon. The New York City community garden fight was one of the first times that Earth First!-style blockading techniques were used in an urban context.

Those tactics are often most effective for groups whose numbers are small but whose appeal is broad. And they worked really well here, putting the gardens issue onto the agenda, making the controversy something that everyone knew about, and helping transform what was a very small movement into a relatively large movement.

The action you are talking about took place when the movement had grown a fair bit, it was a civil disobedience action with something like fifty arrests. These were people from all over the city, many of whom had never done anything like that before, sitting in the street, breaking the law to defend public space in New York City.

## Fall of 1999—An Expanding Movement Space

*BS: The space for people to do all sorts of things, including organize and build communities. By the fall of that year, you started hearing rumblings about Buy Nothing Day, which we were working on in New York City, and people were starting to buy tickets out to Seattle. When did you first start hearing about what was happening?*

LAK: I don't remember when I got the sense that Seattle was going to be huge. The word was spreading that it was going to be bigger and size and different in character from anything we'd been seeing in recent years. It grew out of a deep political radicalization that was happening in a lot of movements, like the garden movement, that were working on local issues or what people might write off as "single issues." People were coming to see the connections between all these local and particular fights, finding a common foe in corporate globalization.

Obviously, the global justice movement had been building throughout the Global South long before Seattle and there were major, important protests around the world long before Seattle. We were just about the last country in the world to have a vibrant movement around these issues.

I'll never forget the chills that went down my spine in Seattle—I was in a joyous crowd that was blocking the streets in the face of riot gear, tear gas, and pepper spray—when I first heard the chant "This is what democracy looks like." There was this immediate sense that a new force was on the scene. Within the United States, Seattle opened a huge political space for dissent overnight. It was a period of incredible creative energy, where huge numbers of new people—especially young people—were coming into activism, were questioning the structures of global power, were experimenting with art and culture and decentralized forms of organizing. And the global justice movement as a whole around the world was doing something that was very extraordinary, which was putting big issues about power and wealth, about the organization of the global economy, onto the agenda. We were making our critiques part of the global discourse about trade policy and development.

I hadn't seen that before in my lifetime, a movement that was managing to alter the terms of the debate at such a high level, at such a large scale. And all of that together just created such a sense of possibility and momentum. The phrase "another world is possible" seemed not to be an empty slogan at all. Large numbers of people were not only envisioning another world, but also acting in creative ways to bring it about.

*BS: What happened over the two years after Seattle? How were people building on that beyond the protests?*

LAK: Those were incredible, chaotic, whirlwind years, marked by a series of big actions: Seattle WTO in November 1999; the A16 IMF/World Bank protests in Washington, D.C. in April 2000; the Republican and Democratic Conventions in summer 2000; the Quebec City Free Trade Area of the Americas protest in April 2001.

There were two major dynamics in play during those two years between Seattle and September 11 that were in some respects at cross purposes.

One dynamic was the broadening of the global justice movement. Faith-based activists, organized labor, and big national progressive organizations were putting more and more resources and energy into the global justice movement. But simultaneously, there was a dynamic in the direc- action end of the movement toward more and more tactical militancy. Outside of the Seattle WTO protests, there wasn't all that much actual property destruction in those years, but there was a move toward more and more militant tactics and toward direct confrontation with the police.

The notion of "diversity of tactics" emerged as an attempt to reconcile these two dynamics. Some people took the phrase simply as a synonym for property destruction. But the idea behind it was more complex. It was a way for all wings of the movement to work together, without flattening out their differences in the name of some false "unity." Those who were going to engage in direct action of whatever kind would agree to make sure that their tactical choices did not endanger other people, especially those who wanted to engage in safe and legal forms of protest. Those who were organizing safe and legal forms of protest would agree not to publicly denounce others for their tactical choices, especially in the media.

The IMF/World Bank protests that were slated for September 29–30, 2001, were really going to be a watershed moment. There were going to be simultaneously broader and more militant than anything we had seen before. There were going to be very large numbers of people who were going to be engaging in quite militant tactics with the hope of shutting the meetings down. But there was also a major mobilization happening by church groups, by the AFL-CIO, by more politically mainstream forces. And there were discussions, productive discussions taking place behind the scenes among all these different forces about how to coexist in a single protest, how not to denounce each other to a media, but also not to endanger each other—so that, for instance, the folks who were mobilizing their churches knew they could ask people to come without putting them in danger of arrest.

## Quebec City and the Need for an Aesthetic Intervention

*BS: When you say more militant tactics, I have an image of people locking down. I have an image of people blocking streets, and occasionally people will break a window . . .*

LAK: And fighting with cops.

*BS: Like the Days of Rage, 1969.*

LAK: Actually, on a far bigger scale. The Days of Rage was just a few hundred people engaging in an isolated protest. Compare that to the April 2001 summit protest in Quebec City, which was the apex of that tactical radicalization on the North American continent.

Quebec City was absolutely insane. It was a protest against the Free Trade Area of the Americas, a trade agreement that would expand NAFTA to the entire of hemisphere and push forward the agenda of corporate globalization. There was a gathering of political leaders from the hemisphere to negotiate the agreement and a huge protest gathering outside. The summit protests were making world leaders increasingly nervous, and they were responding with over-the-top security measures. For the FTAA summit, the entire downtown area of Quebec City was closed down and fenced off.

People were really angry, and they attacked the fence. The police responded by barraging us with just a staggering amount of tear gas and pepper spray—big, poisonous clouds of it. There were long standoffs, lasting hours, with police in riot gear shooting off canister after canister while the crowd did its best not to back down.

There were tens of thousands of people, and easily hundreds of them fought back against the police. Now, in most contexts, I think that fighting the police is stupid and counterproductive; it's not something I would do. But in this case, I felt like, this is a meeting of illegitimate authorities who have retreated into a fortress, the police are reacting to our righteous anger by absolutely barraging us with tear gas, and so fair enough: I cheered every person who threw a tear gas canister back at the cops. *Return to sender.*

But at the same time, I had a big problem with the aesthetics of the Quebec City protest, and with the aesthetic drift of the global justice movement more generally. Our side was becoming more and more militaristic. All those people—mainly, but not exclusively, young men—dressed in black, looking all menacing and ominous, getting off on confrontations. They had unwittingly become almost a mirror image of the repressive forces that they were up against. And the spirit of carnival that had been so striking in Seattle, that sense of a carnival of resistance, was getting lost.

A friend and I, as we drove back down to New York, started talking in a culture-jam way about, What would it have been like if the people who were throwing back the tear gas canisters had been wearing pink ball gowns instead of black hoodies? Or if everybody were wearing pink ball gowns, would the police still attack them with tear gas? We started talking about, okay, how can we make an aesthetic intervention into what's going on, influence the tone and look of the next big summit protest? And how might that affect the success of the event?

BS: *I don't want to interrupt, but can you explain what is the metaphor of the carnival at a protest? And why is that effective?*

LAK: Well, the central idea behind the carnival is that protests gain in power if they reflect the world we want to create. And I, for one, want to create a world that is full of color and life and creativity and art and music and dance. It's a celebration of life against the forces of greed and death. And it's a way of protesting that gets out of the angry shouting shrill position that you can get put in when you're just simply saying no. Having a carnival is a way of saying yes. In a funny way, it's not unlike creating a community garden. It's a way of saying, we not only oppose what's happening now but we have a vision of a different moral order, in which people are free to express their creative energies to the greatest extent, a world where public space is dedicated to community-building and fostering public expression, instead of given over to commercial expression.

*BS: OK, so back to the IMF/World Bank protests . . .*

LAK: There was a real sense heading into the IMF/World Bank protests that there was the potential for a level of repression that was similar to Quebec City. So a few of us started a group called the Masquerade Project. We raised a bunch of money and bought hundreds and hundreds of gas masks, because we thought the police were likely to be using tear gas against us down in D.C. And we got all these huge boxes of rhinestones and glitter and feathers and sparkles and paint, everything you can think of, and we starting throwing gas mask–decorating parties. We decorated all of these fabulous gas masks and gave them away to people. We were giving them away well in advance of the protest because we were afraid of them being confiscated if we kept them in one place. So there were already hundreds of them out in the world before September 11.

The idea was that people were going to need to protect themselves. Tear gas is no joke, it can have very serious health consequences, and a vinegar-soaked bandanna just isn't adequate. We felt really strongly that we wanted to protect people, but if you are wearing a regular old gas mask you look scary and ominous, even if you are just protecting yourself. It all changes when the gas mask has been transformed to look like a bug or a psychedelic flower or what have you—that was the aesthetic intervention we were after.

We were planning a fundraiser at a nightclub—we were going to have a gas mask fashion show and walk the catwalk showing off our fabulous creations. That fundraiser was scheduled for September 12.

Needless to say, we canceled it. A day later, a call went out via the local media that the rescue workers needed additional respirator devices—and we immediately decided to donate our gas masks. One of my most surreal memories of that period was the night, I guess it was September 13, when a couple of folks and I sat up until something like four in the morning un-decorating the gas masks. We were prying off the rhinestones with kitchen knives, peeling off the paint, picking off the sequins, and then we took them down to somewhere on the edge of the frozen zone around Ground Zero and donated them to the rescue workers. We were quite aware of the irony: some of the gas masks that we had purchased to protect people *from* the police ended up being worn *by* the police, and that was okay with us.

*BS: I saw you on September 12 at about noon in Union Square, the day after the attacks. We were sitting in the park. There was a huge cloud of smoke coming up behind us. Everybody was shell-shocked. And you said, "The global justice movement has got to become a global peace and justice movement." It was the first time I'd thought of, wow, I guess this is where we are going to have to take this thing.*

LAK: Yeah, I remember saying that. That was such a haunting meeting. A bunch of us— thirty people, maybe, or more—were sitting in a big circle in the grass, in a place that until the day before had been a prime spot for viewing the World Trade Center. The smoke from Ground Zero got closer and closer until that horrible stench surrounded us and we had to flee. We went and reconverged in the back of the New York City Independent Media Center because you couldn't breathe.

*BS: I remember the week after 9/11 you were in a frenzy of organizing. I was in my apartment with my sheets over my head. That was a horrible time. And you were out leafleting. Tell me about that.*

LAK: We all had our ways of coping with the initial shock. Mine was that I just threw myself into organizing, printing up thousands of leaflets and just handing them out on the streets for the peace vigils we were having in Union Square. That first week was such an extraordinary time in terms of the atmosphere in the city, in the way people related to each other in New York. People were devastated, and yet there was this amazing gentleness in people's demeanor. For me, I didn't want to be in my apartment looking at the television set, I wanted to be out on the street talking to people. I wanted to do something.

There was an extraordinary protest shortly after September 11 that got virtually no media coverage. I think it was on the Friday night after the Tuesday attacks. It was a nearly spontaneous march that went from a candlelight vigil in Union Square up to Times Square. It was very emotional, and very non-ideological. It wasn't about the intricacies of interventions and imperialism, it was just all these people who did not want to see mass slaughter committed in our name as revenge for the mass slaughter that had just happened in our city.

But then each succeeding protest became less interesting and compelling. It felt like all the nuance and emotion was drained out, as more and more people—people from the global justice movement, people from the anti-authoritarian left—pulled back out of ambivalence, and all that remained were the sorts of groups that have ideological certainty no matter the circumstances. Out came the boring old "Money for Jobs, Not for War" signs that you see at every fucking demo—I always paraphrase that one as "Money for Soul-Draining Wage Slavery, Not for War"—with fewer and fewer homemade or heartfelt signs.

*BS: I remember on October 7, 2001—the day the bombing of Afghanistan began—we were at a march that went from Union Square to Times Square. You were getting more and more pissed off by the signs and the speeches, and you said, I'm getting really bored with this knee-jerk anti-imperialist politics. And you just walked off.*

LAK: Yeah, I was disgusted. I decided on the spot, I'm not going to another one of these things. And I didn't.

You know, the people who destroyed the World Trade Center were attacking many things. They were attacking the United States as a symbol of global imperialism and global might. But they were also attacking the United States as a symbol of religious tolerance, of cultural diversity, the emancipation for women and gay people. A good deal of what al Qaeda and the Taliban sought to destroy were things that we progressives had fought dearly to create.

Not everything, it was a very complex situation. It absolutely had to do with U.S. military aggression throughout the world, but it wasn't just that. And you didn't hear anybody at the protests talking about the religious fanatics who oppose all those aspects of a diverse, secular society that we treasure. You didn't hear anybody talking about much of anything outside of a crude anti-imperialist analysis, in which you quickly get backed into the "enemy of my enemy is my friend" corner. People did not have a way of talking about how ambiguous the situation was.

The politics felt very cold, cerebral. And it made me sick. It made me physically sick to think that the movement that I was part of was merely showcasing the shrill and the simplistic, was dominated by people with cold and creepy politics. I had this very strong sense after September 11 that if you do not have humanism and a genuine love for other human beings at the core of your politics, I don't want to work with you. I don't want to be in coalition with you. If you could not genuinely mourn and grieve for the thousands of people who were slaughtered in our city, forget it. I am certainly not marching with you.

It was a very clarifying political moment. I happened to get an insurance settlement from a car accident around that time, and I retreated to a house on a mountain hours from New York City and pulled out of activism completely for most of a year. I stopped writing, stopped organizing, just needed time and space.

*BS: That was a hard space to work in after that. We always do a permitless parade in December, and I wanted to do a dance party for a world without war. But people said we couldn't do it. People were mourning. It was like that old Larry Kramer argument that you can't tell a joke in a world with AIDS, which I really disagree with. You have to.*

LAK: But there was a period of such extreme mourning that you really couldn't dance. There was certainly a sense within our circles, among people who had embraced that carnival model, of where does this go. It was certainly not relevant for that moment. It's like any other tactic or mobilizing style—context is everything.

## One Year Later—Global Justice Meets Antiwar

*BS: There was a moment after the first anniversary of September 11 when spaces started to get opened up again. I think that is worth talking about.*

LAK: The one-year anniversary was absolutely a turning point emotionally and politically, for many people, including myself. It was only after the anniversary that I felt free to start organizing again. I was at a writer's colony, and every day in the newspaper the Bush administration was threatening war with Iraq, and I started feeling that drive to do activism.

As you know, I came back to New York and said, "Let's get an antiwar group going," and pulled together a lot of the people who had been in the community garden fight and Reclaim the Streets and the Carnival Bloc to say, okay what can we do and how can we come together and have an impact?

We created a couple of different groups. And we turned back to that carnival model. We formed what we called An Absurd Response to an Absurd War to go down the October 26, 2002, ANSWER march in Washington, D.C. We decided after great debate that we would indeed go down and participate in a Worker's World event—that was my quota, one Worker's World event is all I can stomach in my lifetime—and we had what we called a "Party for Perma-War." People loved it and responded really well to reintroducing satire, humor, color, dance, music into the movement. It helped that some of the satire was directed *toward* the movement: When we'd pass, say, an ANSWER sound truck, we'd switch from our exaggerated pro-war chants like "We need oil, we need gas, watch out world we'll kick your ass" to things like, "March march, chant chant, rhetoric rhetoric, rant rant."

*BS: Playfulness. That's where creativity comes. So now you are working with dovetailing the global justice and the antiwar movements, working towards February 15. What has that been like?*

LAK: The global justice movement—at least in the United States, it was different elsewhere in the world—really went quiet after 9/11. That was part of my sense of mourning for that whole year, the fact that one of the most promising and innovative movements of my lifetime had been seemingly destroyed overnight.

But there was a network of connections in place, a whole infrastructure, which people were able to reactivate pretty quickly after September 2002. The whole global character of February 15 has everything to do with the global justice movement and the institutions it created: the date was selected at a November 2002 meeting of the European Social Forum, and then was really picked up by activists all over the world after the World Social Forum in Porto Alegre, Brazil, which was in late January 2003.

The antiwar movement is, of course, much larger in terms of numbers than the global justice movement was. It contains a lot of forces that were just beginning to become active in the global justice movement. But the infrastructure that the global justice movement built meant that people have been able to go mobilize much faster that they perhaps have ever been. February 15 is likely to be the single largest day of protest in world history. Obviously, the Internet has greatly facilitated this mobilization, but without the foundation built by the global justice movement, it simply wouldn't have happened on anything like this scale.

Working here in the United for Peace and Justice office has been just amazing. We can't print enough stuff. We print a half a million pieces of literature and they just fly out the door. More than three hundred people are out on the streets of New York leafleting this weekend. The scale of the thing is incredible. People's level of motivation is incredible.

And I think it's especially extraordinary given the degree to which the political space for dissent in this country shrank in the wake of 9/11. Mobilizing this number of people, getting people out on the streets on this scale, is a very radical act at this moment. That's why we're having such a huge fight over the permit, over our right to have an antiwar march in New York City. Tactics that a lot of people wrote off as too tame or uninspiring or ineffective during the peak years of the global justice movement have a different significance now.

I think one of the real weaknesses of the global justice movement—and of direct action movements more generally—is the tendency to confuse tactics with strategy, and to see tactics as principles. For a while there, a lot of people had the attitude that if you weren't doing the most in-your-face kind of direct action, you weren't doing anything at all.

This period is an object lesson in the point that tactics are tools. And just as you don't use a hammer when a screwdriver is what you need, different tactics have different effects at different times. The classic march and rally is a very powerful way of expressing dissent right now, a powerful way of opening up political space. Is that same style of protest going to be effective five year from now? Who knows. But I think one of the real lessons of this chaotic five years, from an organizer's point of view is that you absolutely have to keep strategy front and center. And strategy means assessing real world conditions.

*BS: So where are you at today after having gone through all of this?*

LAK: Well, I'm organizing full-time-plus again, after a long hiatus. And I don't think I'm alone in that. I think there are a lot of people who pulled back after 9/11 and now are back organizing more than ever. We are in a movement-building, movement-expanding phase again. And while I'm very alarmed by the direction that the country is taking and the world is taking, very apprehensive, I'm also very hopeful about the scale and commitment of this burgeoning movement. There was certainly a setback, a period of mourning and shock, a period of reflection and reassessment, but now activism is back big time and—at least for the foreseeable future—is only going to grow.

## Afterword

This interview was completed on February 8. As the week before the February 15 protest progressed, things only got weirder. The Bush administration sent attorneys from the Justice Department to file a friend of the court brief backing the City of New York's case that the march represented a security threat. After the Office of Homeland Security put the country on "orange" terrorist alert, the *New York Daily News* ran a headline with an ominous black cover with the words, "SHOW OF FORCE, Officials warn stepped-up security will jam city streets, crossings, subways," on February 10. By Tuesday, the *New York Times'* cover showed a picture of police officers with automatic rifles in Times Square (where some activists planned to converge after the rally) with the headline, "Alert on Terror." The paper reported that courts had rejected United for Peace and Justice's appeal for a permit, arguing that a "Stationary Rally Poses Less Risk." The same edition published the administration's guide to preparedness for a chemical attack: duct tape, plastic sheeting, and fresh water, in a message that seemed reminiscent of the Cold War warnings for school children to hide under their desks if attacked by an atomic bomb. The following day, papers showed long lines of people stockpiling duct tape, as hysteria took hold nationwide. In the meantime, Fox News ran "Homeland Security: Terror Alert High" graphics during evening programming about a new bin Laden tape broadcast around the world; silly putty in his hands.

As the week progressed, news became more and more Orwellian. Protesters at the rally responded to the sentiment. "We're already at War with Iraq. We've always been at war with Iraq. War is Peace!" one placard read. Riffing on *1984*, another stated, "Support the Military Tribunals. If you've done nothing wrong, you have nothing to fear." Countless others played on the duct tape warnings. It was clear that amid the warmongering, a backlash was unfolding. The Saturday march offered its culmination. By Saturday, the administration was acknowledging that the information they had about an imminent attack was not quite as solid as first thought and was backpedaling, saying it didn't really wanted people to start duct taping their homes just yet.

The day of the rally, despite the state-imposed barriers, activists from all walks of life descended on the city. The day of the protest, the police sent horses to break up feeder marches heading to the rally, sought to separate crowds from each other, pushed marchers off sidewalks with batons, and arrested nearly three hundred people.

My father, a sixty-six-year-old retired pastor who was in town over the weekend, observed, "We started out at 51st St, then 57th, then 62nd, and then 68th up 2nd Avenue. At 68th Street, we realized we were being pushed out of town. Every time we'd try to turn down to go to the rally, the police would push us up away from the rally. It was perfectly clear that was what they were trying to do. It was crowded like a VE day. They brought out batons to push us and we chanted, 'Let us through!!! Let us through!!!' Every time it would calm down, the police would try . . . to stop us, yet most of us broke through anyway. I was just a citizen trying to gather with other citizens to have a conversation with the President. I was trying to communicate how I felt about this. I'm a citizen. I pay for this war. My friends are going to go get shot for it. I'd like to have a say so. I don't want to have my head patted or told what to think, being told my opinion doesn't count. Being told to pay attention to people who know what they are doing like Kenny Boy and Dick Cheney, the important people. We're going to war. Bush says, Trust me. I've got a memory long enough to remember the last time a president said, trust me, I have a secret plan. Nixon's secret plan to get us out of Vietnam was to invade Cambodia. All Saturday, it was quite clear they were running the marchers out of the streets, like a defense used to run Tony Dorsett out of bounds. They were running people away from the rally." By the end of the day, this sixty-six-year-old retired pastor had engaged in direct action, working with a crowd to push up through a police line to get past police to get to the rally. And he was not alone.

Over a half a million marched through the streets of New York, in coordination with protests in a staggering eight hundred cities and towns around the world; seven hundred thousand mobilized in London, one million in Rome. All weekend long, the protests were the top news story. Many described the day as the largest day of simultaneous peaceful protest in world history. Two days later, the *New York Times* cover story compared the weekend's mobilization with the Velvet Revolution of 1989 and the revolutions of 1848. "The fracturing of the Western alliance over Iraq and the huge antiwar demonstrations around the world this weekend are reminders that there may still be two superpowers on the planet: the United States and world public opinion. In his campaign to disarm Iraq, by war if necessary, President Bush appears to be eyeball to eyeball with a tenacious new adversary: millions of people who flooded the streets of New York and dozens of other world cities."

L. A. and I spoke again on Monday, two days after the protest. Chills ran through my body as we spoke about the possibility that the weekend had created. Seattle was no longer the baseline for protest. Out of the ashes of an extraordinary backlash, we'd created a new organizational possibility, in many ways, thanks to the ambitious work of organizers such as Kauffman.

*February 17, 2003*

# Glossary
## Iain A. Boal

The compiler salutes that small band of writers drawn to the critical glossary as a literary form: first, contrarian lexicographers such as Ambrose Bierce (*The Devil's Dictionary*) and Charles Bufe (*The Heretic's Handbook of Quotations*); poets, too, of a committed imagination with an accurate ear for the demoralization of the dialect of the tribe—and here I think, for example, of Benjamin Péret, W.H. Auden, Allen Ginsberg, and Tom Paulin; but most to the purpose, a pair of critics, one American and the other Welsh—Kenneth Burke and Raymond Williams—who composed what the former called a "dictionary of pivotal terms" and the latter dubbed a "vocabulary of culture and society." These glossators were far from nostalgic for some Adamic speech, for the "true meaning" of a word; nor did they intend to combat, in the manner of reactionary linguistic watchdogs, loose usage with precision, let alone vulgarisms with a style book. It is, in fact, the active *range* of meanings that matters, since the immense complexity and contradiction within terms like "environment" and "violence" register deep conflicts in the social order.

Language, on this view, does not just label things in the world; it helps to constitute it. The naming of parts, the framing of questions, the refusing to explain, are at once the prerogative and the springs of power. Much more crucial to the powerful, however, than their assertions—that, say, a fugitive was "suffering from drapetomania"—are the presuppositions that underlie discourse. It was one thing, in the antebellum South, to query the medical diagnosis of drapetomania, defined as a "pathological propensity to attempt to escape"; it was quite another to challenge the institutions of slavery and medicine that conspired to pathologize the seeking of freedom. Defunct vocabularies, and labels such as drapetomania, abandoned by the classifying classes as either obsolete (vis-à-vis some new regime of stigmatization) or embarrassing (after a struggle by those so labeled), are particularly revealing of the strategic links between language and institutional sites of power. The anticapitalist movement, standing on terrain not of its own choosing, too often retorts in an idiom satisfactory to the sovereign.

Raymond Williams' explorations in historical semantics are much the better known, but his *Keywords* was anticipated, a generation earlier, by Kenneth Burke when he launched a critique of the left's political lexicon in the face of corporate-fascist reaction to capital's big twentieth-century emergency. Burke recommended "intellectual vagabondage" that would constitute a "grave interference with the cultural code" of industrial modernity; he proposed sabotage of the system by defending inefficiency, pessimism, dissipation, mockery, distrust, hypochondria, and treason. One communist called Burke's negative aesthetic the "philosophy of the petit bourgeois gone mad," and Burke didn't much disagree. In view of the millennial coronation of business culture Kenneth Burke's 1931 "Program" in *Counter-Statement* repays a fresh reading.

Then in April 1935, at the time of the popular front and the *bienio negro* in Spain, Burke gave a brief address to the first American Writers' Congress in New York on "Revolutionary Symbolism in America." He told his audience that, when they weren't talking into the mirror, they were using a patronizing language that was sure to fail, simply because idealizing "the workers" in the same breath as insisting on the absolute degradation of work under capitalism was a rhetorical disaster. Burke went on to recommend "the people" rather than "workers" as a mode of address, even though he was aware that, in a society riven by hierarchies of class, gender, race, and the rest, "the people" has its own problems, to say the least; any totalizing term is necessarily ideological. So hostile was the reaction—he was accused of proposing the rhetorical methods of Hitler—that Burke later hallucinated excrement dripping from his tongue.

Another totalization—there is none greater—stamped the days of Seattle and since, both on the streets and in the suites. I mean, of course, the "globe" (and its derivatives), under which sign the committees of capital and their opponents converged. "Globalization," which began as business school jargon, became a cant word during the nineties, but students of imperialism were frankly unimpressed by the purported novelty of the phenomenon; already in 1848 two pamphleteers had remarked that the "need of a constantly expanding market for its products chases the bourgeoisie over the whole surface of the globe. It must nestle everywhere, settle everywhere, establish connections everywhere." Actually, the connections are still distinctly patchy; much of Africa lies unwired, and one in three people in the world have never yet heard a phone ring.

But this is just to rehearse the banality that capitalist development is uneven. More to the point is the fact that structural adjustment at home in the US has been dismantling the remains of the New Deal compromise, as well as the dividends of the civil rights, feminist, peace, and environmental movements. The pattern of events has confounded the rump of professional revolutionaries, stranded since the mock-epic of the cold war, no less than the stenographers of power in the accredited media. Not that the program of the liberal NGOs—"Reform the corporations!" "A place at the table!"—is other than in bad taste. Still, it would be wise to hear the critic who observed that, although political writing is always instrumental, its time of instrumentality—its time as a weapon—sometimes lies a little in the future. As to what might be entailed in the forging of a political language adequate to the matters currently at hand, the following glossary is offered as a gesture, though readers should bear in mind that its remit is the vocabulary of capitalist globalization and its detractors.

> "It is not only by shooting bullets in the battlefields that tyranny is over-thrown, but also by hurling ideas of redemption, words of freedom, and terrible anathemas against the hangmen that people bring down dicta-tors and empires."
>
> —*Emiliano Zapata*

**Activist** Label used, often without qualification, by those campaigning for "social change," suggesting a liberal confidence in the general direction of history, as if the Pol Pots and Kissingers of the world weren't themselves active in the business of social change. The bane of hard-core activists is "passivity" in their targeted communities and the ivory tower; anti-intellectualism is the theory, activism the practice. Still, they have a point: "doing theory" in the academy can be a nasty sight.

**Anarchist** Pierre-Joseph ("property is theft") Proudhon was among the first to embrace this term of abuse—Roget's *Thesaurus* places it in the company of terrorist, savage, and fanatic—but anarchists in the tradition of William Godwin, Pietr Kropotkin, and Emma Goldman have greatly outnumbered advocates of "negotiation by dynamite," which remains the specialty of governments. Still, anarchists have understood that, however much they carry in their hearts a world organized on principles of mutual aid and free association, the current owners show no signs of leaving quietly, and for that reason Buenaventura Durruti once remarked: "The bourgeoisie may blast and ruin their own world before they leave the stage of history. We are not in the least afraid of ruins." If the tactics of anticapitalist *enragés* – the symbolic breaking of corporate property - showed one (masked) face of anarchism, the other was the classic anarchist organizational form of nonhierarchical affinity groups.

**Autonomy** A term with wide currency among the opposition to capitalist globalization—cf. Italian *autonomia*, German *autonomen*, Zapatista *autonomismo*, and "temporary autonomous zones" (TAZ). Not to be understood in the abstract formalist Kantian sense of autonomy as obedience to reason, but in Cornelius Castoriadis' sense of movement away from heteronomy in general ("being in someone else's project," whether state, par-ent, or boss) towards self-activity—of a collective kind, rather than the "independence" of loners, self-made entrepreneurs, and authoritarians in flight from mother.

**Biopiracy** Athough the term slanders pirates (see Marcus Rediker's *Between the Devil and the Deep Blue Sea*) it is intended as a corrective to what the genetic-industrial complex (Monsanto et al.) calls bioprospecting. Refers to the privatization of plant and other organic material (fungi, animal DNA, human body and blood products, etc.) from the global South, home to ninety-five percent of the world's genetic resources, by way of the Northern patent mills. There is a deep continuity with the post-Columbus plunder of specimens by naturalist agents of empire and the nineteenth-century global system of botanical laboratories (e.g., Kew Gardens, *Jardin des Plantes*).

**Biotechnology** The new frontier whose salesmen and stock analysts glimpse whole continents of (com)modified life waiting to be staked out. The synergy between DNA technologists, silicon robotics, and venture capital produced a preemptive patent rush, rapid monopolization of life forms licenced by the courts, and a Niagara of hype (Green revolution redux and even immortality). These new enclosures (q.v.) are meeting popular resistance worldwide; the struggle is on to prevent the privatization of the world's germplasm (the essential means of production for farmers), not to mention the viralization of life by the vectors of transgenic DNA.

**Black Bloc** The roving, uncivil, complement to sit-down protest, sharing a commitment to direct action in the streets, but viewing sedentary disobedience as privileged, moralizing, and needlessly sacrificial. Named for the black clothing, a parody of the dress code of solemn bourgeois ritual. Its origins lie in European anarchist and autonomist tendencies, removed from the American legacy of civil rights (Gandhian and Quaker-style) pacifism. The tactic of corporate property damage and open masquerade has made the Black Bloc grist for the mills of the spectacle and, apparently, *agents provocateurs*.

**Borders** Be careful what you ask for. "World without borders" has now joined those other countercultural bumper slogans— "Think globally, act locally," "Flexible work hours!"—as the basic vocabulary of neoliberalism. The hip academy's love affair with "transgressing borders" has put them in interesting company—the German *Wehrmacht* and the WTO. The dismantling of barriers is, of course, highly selective in favor of goods and capital rather than people, a fact well understood by workers trying to enter fortress Europe or to cross the Rio Grande from the South, and by travelers to G8 summits.

**Capitalism** From Latin root *capit-* "head"; for connections not merely etymological between capital punishment and the punishment of capital, see Peter Linebaugh's *The London Hanged.* The economic order that, like its ruling class, will rarely speak its name, preferring the codewords "market," "democracy," and "freedom." Capitalist exploitation is organized around the production of commodities by commodities, from which follows the subversion of markets, the annulling of democracy, and the subordination of freedom.

**Civil Society** "Community," "stakeholder," "participation," "transparency," "empowerment"—these are the grisly fetish words of foundation officers, non-profit apparatchiks, and boardrooms everywhere, echoed in the field by the NGO cadres busy producing "locals." These liberal shibboleths, that cluster under the heading of "civil society," name simulacra of the social and disclose only its disappearance. Not for the first time; at the turn of the nineteetn-century, romantic schoolmasters and antiquarians—the clerisy of European nationalisms—celebrated the "folk" at the very moment its extinction was assured by enclosure of the commons and the criminalization of custom. It was the protoromantic Rousseau who remarked: "The first person who, having fenced off a plot of ground, took it into his head to say this is mine and found people simple enough to believe him, was the true founder of civil society."

**Coase's Theorem** The notorious December 1991 World Bank memo, written by Lawrence Summers, later US Treasury Secretary, argued that the "economic logic behind dumping a load of toxic waste in the lowest wage country is impeccable" because "under-populated countries in Africa are vastly *under*-polluted, their air quality is probably vastly inefficiently low compared to Los Angeles or Mexico City." Brazil's secretary of the environment wrote to Summers about the leaked memo: "Your reasoning is perfectly logical but totally insane" and was fired soon after. The reasoning referred to was in fact a pure example of the logic behind Coase's Theorem, which relates market efficiency, property, transaction costs, and "exernalities," and underpins much of neoliberal legal and economic doctrine, as well as WTO and IMF policies. Ronald Coase is the economist responsible for tradeable pollution rights by dreaming of a world of zero transaction costs where everything can be smoothly brought to market, and no ethical distinction made between the harm done by an oil refinery to those living downwind and the harm done to its owners by downwinders being in the way; it's just a cost-benefit matter requiring only clear and absolute private property rights (no common goods) and enough police to enforce them. The World Bank's "impeccable" Coasian logic means that there is no right to clean water, air or soil but merely the right to pay to keep them clean or to be compensated for their fouling. Too bad about those not at the bargaining table—above all, the unborn (or still-born) generations. Luckily economists have long prepared us to discount the future;

Coase once said that the future valuation of property was put at risk by "such cataclysmic events as the abolition of slavery." Coase won the Nobel Prize for Economics in 1991.

**Commons** See under "Enclosure."

> The law locks up the man or woman,
> That steals the goose from off the common,
> But lets the greater felon loose,
> That steals the common from the goose.

**Community** The maximum shibboleth. A mantra used affirmatively across the entire political and cultural landscape; NPR once interviewed a spokesman from the "organized crime community." There is an implied antithesis to "the state" (with its suggestion of power, authority, and central decision) in favor of the local and the face-to-face. The results can be grotesque: the release of asylum and hospital inmates to "the community" often means, in reality, warm ventilation grates. The "communitarian" right would rather nobody noticed that the shattering of communities is a direct effect of capital moving away in obedience to the logic of the very system they endorse.

**Corporation** From *corpus*, "body." The body of the Catholic Church was the ur-corporation, as the monastery was the prototype for other key institutions in the West—the asylum, the hospital, the university, the factory. By a legal fiction the business corporation was given a deathless personality—an idea related to the theory of the "divine right of kings" by which the monarch has two bodies, one that decays, one that doesn't ("The king is dead; long live the king"). The laws of the corporation inversely mirror the laws of criminal conspiracy. When individuals combine *in pursuit of* capital, they are afforded more protection than they enjoy in their own persons (e.g., limits to both civil and criminal liability, special treatment re taxation); when individuals combine *against* capital, they have less protection than they have on their own—mere association is criminalized, since the very act of combining is seen as a threat. That is, two or more people agreeing to commit a misdemeanor—whether or not they ever go through with it—is considered by the state a felony, because the greater threat is the sheer coming together in opposition to those interests the state serves.

**DAN** Direct Action Network. Emerged from the direct action training camp two months before Seattle, organized by the Ruckus Society, offspring of Greenpeace commando training crossed with Earth First! forest defense techniques, and adapted to nonwilderness, urban contexts—street blockades, lockdowns, tall building banner-hangs—combined with political puppetry, street theatre, culture-jamming, and net-based bypassing of capitalist media. See under "Direct action."

**Democracy** System of periodic ratification of political masters by ballot; meanwhile, the major decisions — who whom, for what, how — remain in the hands of the few. Democracy is the ideological keystone of the West's charter myth, and historically consistent, by its own account, with slavery (Athens), monarchy (England), and plutocracy (United States).

**Development** Perhaps *the* key term of modernity, drawing into a single nexus the discourses of real estate, childhood, and colonialism, for the future realization of added value. By the colonization of infancy and the infantilization of the colonies, labor and land (human and natural capital) are made ready for "improvement," the older word that "development" replaced, etymologically derived from *pros* "profit."

**Direct Action** A mode of politics that tactically—and for some, strategically—shortcircuits official channels of "representation," often by interrupting business as usual, and deploying a variety of means, open and clandestine: street manifestations, blockades, trespass, sit-ins, banner hanging, squatting, sabotage, croptrashing, piethrowing. The debate since Seattle about property damage and the activity of the Black Bloc—whether it is tactically effective ("helps break the spell of the commodity" versus "allows demonization of the movement as mindless vandalism") and whether it constitutes violence ("to treat property as sacred and inviolable is to think like the state, and anyway what about the silent violence of structural adjustment or redlining") rehearses old tensions between pacifist and "physical force" traditions in abolitionist, nationalist, and anticolonial struggles.

**Diversity** The key term of US multiculturalism, a liberal doctrine endorsed by big business and government for the management of "difference" in response to the civil rights, feminist, and gay liberation movements. The doggerel read at Clinton's first inauguration, "On the Pulse of Morning," confirmed the ascendancy of multicultural nationalism; contrast the previous inaugural verse (at Kennedy's induction), "The Gift Outright," Robert Frost's white puritan poem of blood sacrifice and western conquest. Although capitalist globalization is spoken of as a homogenizing force (viz. extinction of languages and species, death of customary lifeways, Weberian harmonization), it co-opts and even encourages the proliferation of identities—gender, ethnic and consumer—consistent with profit taking. Biodiversity, that mantra of environmentalists, is, to say nothing of its merits, multiculturalism projected onto the realm of nature; by the same token, the native plant movement draws, willy-nilly, from the wellsprings of xenophobia and anti-immigrant rhetoric. To speak of nature is always already to be in the space of the social.

**Economy** The alpha and omega of our epoch. The mere utterance of the words, the "bottom line," is supposed to halt discussion. The disembedding of the "economy" from its social and moral matrix has been a long and savage process; its first paid professor was the Reverend Malthus in 1800. As often, it was in a work of imagination, not theory—in Daniel Defoe, rather than Adam Smith—that one encounters the first classic projection of *homo economicus*. What is Robinson Crusoe, that lonely, primitive accumulator and idol of economists, but a cost-benefit calculating machine? Such is the neurotic Protestant imago that the technicians of the WTO dream of universalizing.

**Enclosure** The exclusion (sometimes physically by hedges and fences) of commoners and peasants from the means of life, in order to "free" them for wage labor under capitalist modernity. Enclosure meant not only the extinction (by force and later by acts of parliament) of customary "rights of common" to soil, grazing, firewood, timber, and the cultivated and uncultivated bounty of the earth, but, at least as important, the breaking of communal consciousness and autonomy. The commodification of land and labor was capitalism's essential founding process, written "in letters of blood and fire." The buying and selling of commodities could then be generalized; property and price come to mediate all relations with nature and humanity. The structural adjustment programs of the IMF and the WTO's intellectual property regimes amount to new (as well as old) forms of enclosure—privatization of water and public land, auctioning of the electromagnetic spectrum, the patenting of seeds, etc.

**Environment** When taken to mean *external* surroundings, "environment" reinforces the old split between humanity and nature, between inside and outside, which at least has the merit of not positing a fascist metaphysics of identity (blood and soil, thinking with the body, woman equals nature). Environments are constituted by the life-activity of their inhabitants; without the active involvement of its denizens, no expert has any business claiming even to identify an environment.

**Environmentalists** Corporate capital's stormy petrels, warning of bad weather. That Mobil and environmentalists both like to operate under the sign of NASA's " whole earth" image reveals how green politics is a version of global managerialism. The Malthusian assumptions and the eugenic and racist roots of environmentalism (population control, native plant fanaticism, defense of wilderness that was someone else's home) are barely below the surface.

**Fair trade** The alternative to "free trade" on offer from the loyal opposition, led by Global Exchange, a San Francisco travel agency and crafts importer.

**Free trade** Traditional slogan of imperial monopolists and protectionists...for export only.

**Gibson's Law** "For every PhD there is an equal and opposite PhD." Scientists flatly contradicting each other became a common sight during the mad cow outbreak, and caused a crisis of legitimacy in Europe, which will only deepen with each surprising plague. Because scientists are increasingly licensed by industry, we are bound to hear more kitsch assertions like "The chances of GM pollen drift are zero," and "There can be no prions in the milk."

**Global South** The old West/East division, based on the political geography of the capitalist-communist bloc system, is giving way to North/South terminology, reflecting the post-cold war configuration of a Northern capitalist core (to use the metaphor of world-system theory) and a Southern periphery. The obvious limitations of these hemispheric spatial terms led, in the first case, to the coining of *tiers monde*/"third world" for countries "nonaligned" with the two blocs, and recently to the attachment of "global" to "South" to capture the fact that capitalism's uneven development creates conditions typically associated with the South inside the Northern heartlands.

**Globalization** Business school jargon that gained general currency in the 1990s, to describe the dismantling of barriers to the movement of capital and the loss of local and national sovereignties to the interests of transnational firms, helped along by developments in telecommunications and the collapse of the two-bloc world. Globes were originally "emblems of sovereignty" (1614) that became playthings of merchant princes and navigators, familiar as props in Renaissance portraiture. It was the task of cartography to project the globe into two dimensions; without the resulting maps and charts the business of empire and planetary capitalist hegemony would be literally unthinkable.

**GMO** Genetically modified organism. See under "Biotechnology."

**Human rights** Liberal discourse lately favored by the managers of the new world order, not least the military humanists of NATO and the Pentagon who use it, arbitrarily of course, as a trojan horse for intervention worldwide, by land, sea, air and, soon no doubt, space—mercy by any means necessary.

**IMF** International Monetary Fund. Created by the US and Britain at the 1944 Bretton Woods conference to provide loans to countries with short-term liquidity problems, and to buffer the irrationality of markets by enshrining capital controls in Article VI. Since the defeat of this original scheme of John Maynard Keynes and Dexter White, the IMF has been turned into a major global instrument for the disciplining of movements toward local autonomy by savage "conditionalities" on loans.

**Independent Media Center** Hub of noncorporate news gathering and dissemination, taking advantage of the new technics of communications (digital cameras, satellites, wireless telephony, the internet). The mushrooming of IMCs ( or, Indymedia Centers), modeled on the Seattle experience, is a response to the continuing enclosures and concentration of the capitalist media.

**Internet** The child of Victorian telegraphy, even down to the utopian hype—in 1852 a Saint-Simonian disciple announced: "A perfect network of electric filaments will afford a new social harmony." The space-pulverizing machinery of the virtual brings, along with new connections, intensified separation, plus low-grade depression and digital palsy, that nasty relative of the televisual body ("couch potato"). Its liberatory refunctioning as a tool for "organizing from below" flourishes in the shade of its dominant use as essential support for the global transmission of administrative, military, and commercial intelligence, and the enhanced surveillance of labor.

**IPR** Intellectual property rights. Their origins lie in the history of the printing press and questions of copyright ownership; the new technologies of communication, replication, and the rise of corporate patents and branding have brought trade-related intellectual property rights (TRIPs) sharply into focus, and onto the main agenda of the WTO. It is symptomatic that the fortune of today's Croesus is amassed by licensing intellectual property (software, patents) rather than by owning oil wells or steelmills, in the style of nineteenth-century robber barons. The managers and brokers of capital prefer these purified forms of property; they can circulate at the speed of light.

**Libertarian** Historically the contrast was with "determinist" (*vis-a-vis* free will); later used by anarchists (e.g. Noam Chomsky) to distance themselves from authoritarian socialists in their various guises (Stalinist, Leninist, Trotskyist, Maoist, Castroite); recently the party of market fetishists, automatic weapons collectors, and the antitax lobby.

**Luddite** The most powerful swearword of capital ("mindless, destructive, resister of progress"), now doing double-duty since "communist" has, for the moment, lost its charge. Still, all the sabotage in history would not even register in the scales compared to capitalism's scheduled destruction. Both the left and the right told the same lie about the historical luddites, that they were primitivist and backward looking, as if those skilled weavers at the dawn of industrial modernity were against the future rather than its foreclosure by immiseration, factory discipline, and the gallows.

**Market** More accurately described by the French historian Braudel as the "anti-market." Capitalism from its birth has been about oligopolies and monopolies. The necessary contrast to the glory of old marketplaces, fairs, bazaars, and agoras is the "container," the tilt-up warehouse, and the supermarket.

**Multitude** Key term of the philosopher Spinoza, the anti-Hobbes of early modernity, now dusted off for the digital epoch by certain critics of globalization. The argument goes: if capitalism at its dawning produced a multitude, and the factories of the industrial revolution a proletariat, the social factory of the cybernetic economy is producing a new (global, wired) multitude. Some in the current anticapitalist movement recognize themselves in this neo-Spinozist scheme, and hope that the power of the new antinomian multitude will constitute the gravedigger this time.

**Neoliberalism** Post-sixties version of classical liberalism's gospel of the market and the "hidden hand." For forty years the strategy developed during the crisis of the 1930s to prevent anticapitalist movements from taking power—national Keynesianism—was hegemonic in the West, in the form of welfare safety nets, income redistribution, domestic industry protection, state-financed public works, and capital controls. The assault on national Keynesianism came in the shape of globalizing neoliberalism, propagated in reactionary think tanks (funded by oil and armaments fortunes) in response to the revolutionary events of the sixties and the falling rate of profit. The immediate intellectual roots lay in the work of an English accountant Ronald Coase (q.v.), with von Hayek the bridge to classical liberalism, the University of Chicago its academic home, and Thatcher and Reagan its door-to-door salesforce. Neoliberals wish to bury the memory of their system's savior—"capitalism in itself," observed Keynes in 1924, "is in many ways objectionable"—by claiming that "there is no alternative" to unregulated global flows of money and goods, the sale of public assets, the overriding of workplace and environmental protections, and a recomposed planetary division of labor; in sum, the removal of any fetters on the rate of exploitation.

**NGOs** Nongovernmental organizations. The mendicant orders of late capitalism, as

Antonio Negri put it. By one calculation they numbered a mere nine in 1907, most famously the Red Cross. The Biafran famine in the mid-1960s, where international state action proved spectacularly inadequate, was the watershed, and by the late nineties NGO's numbered in the thousands. They are thriving on famine, disease, and war, and in the spaces (North as well as South) created by structural adjustment—forced privatization, market deregulation, and the hollowing out of state agencies.

**NVDA** Nonviolent direct action. See under "violence" and "direct action."

**Pacifism** The rejection of all forms of organized violence. Dismissed right, left, and center—by generals, revolutionaries, and pragmatic liberals alike—as hopelessly unrealistic, though pacifists are unimpressed by what passes for political realism and look for routes to a peaceable world that interrupt the codes of violence. The "peace process," however, usually means war by other means, and pacifists operating under its banner might reflect on Tacitus' remark about the fate of Carthage: the Romans "made a desert and called it peace."

**Police** Institutionalized by Napoleon in France and by Robert Peel in nineteenth century London to enforce the wage form and the criminalization of custom. The more modern the police force, the more medieval-looking the body armor—though the weaponry is the scientific fruit of corporate laboratories.

**Policy** Etymological variant of "police."

**Primitivism** A branch of Romanticism (Enlightenment's unruly sibling) having deep American roots, with recent developments in Detroit and Eugene. Rejects industrial civilization and, in austere versions, even agriculture; in the limit case, human language itself is considered a technology of alienation. Associated in the public mind with the Unabomber, whom the press portrayed as society's mad outcast, but his manifesto reveals not only a widely held apocalyptic view of modern science and technology, but in some ways a traditional white American male profile, viz. anti-urbanism, misogyny, and a fascination with violence and homemade explosives.

**Privatization** Etymological kin to "deprivation," though any memory of why that might be—namely, that "privacy" was a prideful abstention from a life in common—is long gone. The transvaluation has taken four hundred years, and can be marked by the junkbond artist Ivan Boesky's notorious speech to Berkeley's Haas (Levi Strauss) Business School when he announced "Greed is good," and was cheered to the rafters. The privatization of everything is often imagined to be the ideal of free marketeers, but their real game involves the maximum socialization of costs in the sink of nature and labor.

**Risk** The entry under "risk" in the *Dictionary of the Social Sciences* has a single crossreference, to "profit." That is at least honest, since the rhetoric of risk, which now drives medicine, law, portfolio management, criminology, social welfare, education, public health, technology impact, environmental policy, banking, industrial hygiene, urban planning, military strategy, and genomics, emerged during the seventeenth century in the milieu of Lloyd's coffeehouse, where the new capitalist dealers in risk (sale of annuities, stock jobbing, marine insurance) were busy undermining the moral economy with the logic of the market and the counting house. Modern apologists of risk, such as Tony "Third Way" Giddens, inform us that new technologies make for an unavoidably dangerous world, and therefore the real menace comes from riskophobes and untrusting luddites facing backwards.

**Seattle** Poster city, during the Clinton years, of the "new economy," home of Microsoft, Boeing, and Starbucks, the firms that connected its workforce, flew the top layer around, and kept them awake and flexible. Seattle is a classic example of the denaturing by containerization of the old waterfronts of the Atlantic and Pacific littoral, whose passing has been recorded in Alan Sekula's photodocumentary *Fish Story*. Since 1999 the Chamber of Commerce knows that the name of their city conjures up, not so much a vision of the new economy, but its nemesis.

**Science** Since harnessing fundamental chemistry to colonial warfare and atomic physics to state arsenals, science seems more menace than hope, the scientist more Frankenstein than Prometheus. Industry science is often intended actually to produce ignorance— about cigarettes, asbestos, global warming, GM crops—turning the skepticism of critical inquiry to corporate advantage, in order to buy time; a Brown and Williamson (tobacco company) memo admitted: "Doubt is our product." Science, once (and still) emancipatory vis-à-vis the mystification of clerics, has become capital's way of knowing the world.

**Sixties** The long shadow of that crowded decade continues to haunt both the *soixante-huitards* and those who insist it was all a chimera. That it was a revolutionary conjuncture, and a global one, should be of interest this time around. For evidence see Ronald Fraser's *1968*, Sonya Sayres et al. *The Sixties Without Apology*, Michael Watts' *1968 and All That*, and Chris Marker's two-part documentary *Le Fond de L'Air est Rouge*.

**Sovereignty** Supreme authority. The parcellized power of feudal lords became absolute under monarchical and nation-state systems; late capitalism is reparcellizing and punching holes in state sovereignty (e.g., Native American casino enclaves) in the interests of flexible accumulation. Most conspicuously, the sovereignty of WTO rules now trumps national laws enacted for the protection of the environment and workers.

**Terrorism** The strategic use of violence against civilians—typically by states but also by those thinking like a state, however marginal and poor in resources. Terrorism seeks to kill and maim, but also more widely to demoralize, to spread the message that no one is safe. Terrorism is an act of communication. It aims to breed rumor, grab headlines, burn an image of pain and horror into the citizenry's collective skull. The tactic is costeffective, and has had successes. Colonial occupiers have given up and gone home in the face of it. Whether victimization and the sowing of mass paranoia can ever provide the basis for a "revolution"—that is, the release and refocusing of repressed social energies—is another question. Whereas terror is often disavowed (though inherent to rapine, slavery, inquisitions, and colonialism), terror*ism* lives on the oxygen of publicity. It took modern form with the Jacobins' spectacular use of Dr. Guillotin's enlightenment machine for rational decapitation. The next *fin-de-siècle* burst of "propaganda by the deed"—political assassinations, bombings, and incendiarism, often in fact the work of *agents provocateurs* in the service of the state's need to justify the deployment of its hegemonic violence—turned out to be just a curtain-raiser for the twentieth century which witnessed the apotheosis of terrorism. Its emblematic instruments have been, in the industrialized North, the carbomb, and, in the Third World, disappearances and the death squad. But twentieth-century terrorism's hallmark was bombardment from the air, the Damoclean threat of mass death aimed at the inhabitants of cities—Guernica, London, Dresden, and the ground zero of globalized atomic terror, Hiroshima. For keepers of nuclear stockpiles to declare a "war on terrorism" places them very deep in Orwell's debt. In political rhetoric, the epithet "terrorist" is projected only onto others—enemies so designated by authorities wherever; in the US, the term has proliferated to implicate all resistance to capitalist globalization, foreign and domestic. Thus fast-track WTO legislation, corporate bail-outs, and environmental deregulation are called "counterterrorism" measures. Not for the first time is "terrorist" (cf. "Luddite" and "communist") being forged as a weapon in capitalism's arsenal.

**Utopia** Thomas More's sixteenth-century book forever lent its name to projections of an ideal world. They are, typically, static blueprints—More's original *Utopia*, though it contained a savage critique of early capitalist enclosures, was really a nostalgic retrospect for a dying patriarchal feudal order. We are currently living in the utopia of 1930s automobile company executives, who gave us fair warning in the GM pavilion of the 1939 World's Fair.

Although Ursula Le Guin's *The Dispossessed*, P.M.'s *Bolo Bolo*, and William Morris's *News from Nowhere* shine out as beacons in a dismal genre, it is hard to envisage the far side of capitalism, the more everyday life has been colonized by the imagineers of the commodity world.

**Violence** Chief of the state monopolies—indeed, no state is conceivable without it, though it will be called "force," not "violence." The stenographers of domination systematically invert necessary ethical distinctions between the violence of the oppressor and the oppressed, between harm to persons and harm to property, between institutionalized violence (right and left) as opposed to the improvised violence of insurrections. Violence routinized is a mirror of the state, as nonviolence advocates are quick to point out; on the other hand, nonviolence fetishized is often a mark of privilege.

**Virtual** The electronic sublime heralded fifty years ago by the barkers of the cybernetic revolution have finally arrived under the sign of the "virtual." Video screens constitute the myth space of modernity, which thus far mostly offers playworlds where wargaming meets Fordist speed-up. It is no surprise that relationships at a remove are often welcomed when the spaces of everyday life—depending on gender, race, class, and age—are surveilled, dangerous or denatured, with the chances of pleasurable encounters close to vanishing. The virtual life is, however, always on the cusp of boredom, which is fascination's other face.

**War** The health of the state, in the indelible phrase of Randolph Bourne (1917).

**World Bank** Emerged out of the International Bank for Reconstruction and Development (IBRD), set up at the Bretton Woods meeting in 1944 to funnel low-interest loans for the rebuilding of war-ravaged Europe, and to head off communism. It later evolved into the prime agency for Third World aid and development, or what the *Wall Street Journal* called "promoting socialism." During the 1970s McNamara oversaw a massive growth in the World Bank's resources; on his watch the "structural adjustment" loan was devised as a vehicle for imposing, as they say, "free-market liberalization." In recent years, by hiring on some of its milder critics, the World Bank is able to play good cop to the IMF's bad cop.

**WTO** World Trade Organization. 1995 successor organization to GATT (General Agreement on Tariffs and Trade). Its early origins lie in the ITO (International Trade Organization) set up in 1948 in Havana to coordinate the international trading system in the wake of the crisis of the 1930s. GATT was a system of member-state negotiations ( "rounds") concluding in contracts that fixed tarrifs in industrial products at national borders. The Uruguay Round ended in 1995 with the establishment of a permanent international bureaucracy, the World Trade Organization (WTO), having a much larger scope that does not stop at borders, and includes agriculture, intellectual property rights (IPR), trade in services, and investment measures. It is structured in the image of the private tyrannies it serves, capitalist firms.

# Notes On Contributors

**Ezequiel Adamovsky** is an anti-capitalist activist and writer, and a member of the movement of Neighbour's Assemblies in Buenos Aires.

**Katherine Ainger** is an editor of the *New Internationalist*. She is a member of an editorial collective writing *We Are Everywhere: The Irresistible Rise of Global Anti-Capitalism* (Verso).

**Stanley Aronowitz** is a distinguished professor of sociology at the Graduate Center, City University of New York. Long involved in the labor movement and in education, he is founder of the Center for Worker Education at the City College of New York. He is the author of over eighteen books, including, *The Knowledge Factory: Dismantling the Corporate University and Creating True Higher Learning* (Beacon, 2000).

**Hakim Bey** is the author of *Temporary Autonomous Zones* and *Millenium* (Autonomedia, 1996), among other books.

**Iain Boal** teaches in the geography department at the University of California at Berkeley. He is the co-editor, with James Brook, of *Resisting the Virtual Life* (City Lights, 1995) and the author of *The Long Theft* (forthcoming from City Lights).

**Rachel Brahinsky** reports on local politics, homelessness, labor, and energy for the *San Francisco Bay Guardian*.

**Daniel Burton Rose** is an activist and writer based in the East Bay. He is the co-editor of *The Celling of America: An Inside Look at the U.S. Prison Industry* (Common Courage Press, 1998). An award winning journalist, he has written for *Vibe, Z Magazine, San Francisco Bay Gaurdian, Dollars and Sense, Middle East Report,* and the *Multinational Monitor,* among other publications.

**George Caffentzis** is a coordinator of the Committee for Academic Freedom in Africa, a member of the Midnight Notes collective, and coeditor of *Auroras of the Zapatistas: Local and Global Struggles of the Fourth World War* (Autonomedia, 2001).

**Manuel Callahan** is a member of Accion Zapatista (www.utexas.edu/students/nave/), a collective dedicated to supporting the Zapatista struggle and promulgating Zapatismo as a revolutionary project. He lives in Austin, Texas.

**Noam Chomsky** is a longtime political activist, writer and professor of linguistics at MIT. His latest books include *The Common Good* (Odonian Press, 1998) and *The New Military Humanism* (Common Courage Press, 1999).

**Jeffrey St. Clair** is the author of *Five Days that Shook the World* (Verso, 2000). He edits the radical muckraking newsletter *CounterPunch.com.*

**Thatcher Collins** is a freelance writer and activist who has written for *Dollars & Sense,* mytwobeadsworth.com, KPFK Radio, and many other publications.

**Jeff Conant** is a writer and activist living in the San Francisco Bay Area. He has written about struggles for social and environmental justice from Chiapas, Honduras, Ecuador, Mozambique, and elsewhere. This research is part of his work as coordinator of a popular education project on grassroots environmental health initiatives for the Hesperian Foundation, a publisher of materials on health and social justice.

**James Davis** is an Irish filmmaker living in New York. His most recent work is *Safety Orange,* a documentary about the U.S. criminal justice system.

**Eric Drooker** is an award-winning author/artist. His paintings are often seen on the covers on the *New Yorker,* the *Progressive,* and numerous other magazines. His latest book, *Blood Song: A Silent Ballad* is a companion to his earlier volume, *Flood!: A Novel in Pictures.* (www.Drooker.com)

**Barbara Ehrenreich** is the author of numerous books, including *Nickel-and-Dimed: On (Not) Getting By In America* (Metropolitan Books). A social critic and journalist, she has written for a wide array of newspapers and magazines, and is currently a columnist for the *Progressive.*

**Barbara Epstein** teaches in the history of consciousness program at UC Santa Cruz. She is the author of *Political Protest and Cultural Revolt: Nonviolent Direct Action of the 1970s and 1980s* (University Of California Press, 1991).

**Liza Featherstone** is a Manhattan-based journalist. She is the co-author of *Students Against Sweatshops: the Making of a Movement* (Verso).

**Silvia Federici** is a coordinator of the Committee for Academic Freedom in Africa and a co-editor of *A Thousand Flowers: Social Struggles Against Structural Adjustment in African Universities* (Africa World Press, 2000).

**John Gulick** is an assistant professor of sociology at the University of Tennessee, Knoxville. He is currently conducting research on the socioecological contradictions of China's development and intra-imperialist competition over the natural resources of the Russian Far East. He can be reached at jgulick@utk.edu.

**Michael Hardt** is an associate professor of comparative literature at Duke University. Among his publications are *Gilles Deleuze: An Apprenticeship in Philosophy* (1993) and, together with Toni Negri, *The Labour of Dionysos: A Critique of a State-Form* (1994) and *Empire* (2000).

**Kevin Harris** is an illustrator, graphic artist, and printer. He's influenced by deerpahts and detritus. Kevin@cea.edu.

**Doug Henwood** is the editor of *Left Business Observor* and author of *After the New Economy* (Verso, 2003).

**Brian Holmes** is a cultural theorist, art critic and member of the French activist association Ne pas plier (Do not bend). He is also member of the French magazine *Multitudes*.

**Andrew Hsiao** is an editor with the New Press and a writer with the *Village Voice*. He lives in Brooklyn.

**Carwil James,** an Oakland-based activist speaker, poet, and researcher, has been organizing for radical social change since 1993. His recent work includes nonviolent direct actions in solidarity with Iraq and Palestine, co-writing a theater piece on oil, environmental destruction, and war, and designing a series of posters challenging American and Israeli militarism.

**Boris Kagarlitsky** is a political scientist and activist living in Moscow. He was a political prisoner under Brezhnev (1982–83), a member of the Moscow City Soviet (1990–93), advisor to the chair of the Federation of Independent Trade Unions of Russia (1992–94), and is now a senior research fellow at the Institute of Comparative Political Studies of the Russian Academy of Sciences. His books include *Return of Radicalism* (Pluto Press, 2000) and *Twilight of Globalization* (Pluto Press, 2000).

**George Katsiaficas** is the editor of *New Political Science*. He is the author of *The Imagination of the New Left: A Global Analysis of 1968* (South End Press, 1987), *The Subversion of Politics: European Autonomous Social Movements and the Decolonization of Everyday Life* (Humanities Press, 1997), and, with Kathleen Cleaver, edited *Liberation, Imagination and the Black Panther Party* (Routledge, 2001). He is currently based at Chonnam National University in Kwangju, Korea.

**Eliot Katz** is the author of *Unlocking the Exits* (Coffee House Press, 1999) and a coeditor of *Poems for the Nation* (Seven Stories Press, 2000), a collection of contemporary political poems compiled by Allen Ginsberg.

**L. A. Kauffman's** column on radical activism, *Free Radical: Chronicle of the New Unrest,* is on the web at www.free-radical.org. She's writing a history of radical direct action movements from the early '70s to the present.

**Dorothy Kidd** has been involved in community and social justice media since working in neighborhood video projects in Toronto, Canada, in the early 1970s. In the 1980s and 1990s, she worked as a producer and chronicler of community radio in Canada and internationally. Her current work looks at the developing international movement for media democracy.

**Naomi Klein** is the author of *No Logo* and *Fences and Windows*. She is working on a documentary in Argentina. Additional research for this piece by Dawn Makinson and Joseph Huff-Hannon.

**Eric Krebbers** and **Merijn Schoenmaker** are members of the Dutch organization De Fabel van de Illegaal.

**David Kubrin** has been a political activist and organizer since the late 1950s. He has taught history at Dartmouth College and the University of Wisconsin, and currently teaches science at a San Francisco middle school. During the '80s he was a member of Matrix, an anarchist, pagan affinity group involved in actions at Diablo Canyon, Vandenberg Force Base, Livermore labs, and elsewhere.

**Mark Laskey** is an anarchist activist from Boston, Massachusetts. He's a member of the Northeastern Federation of Anarcho-Communists and works in the Sabate Anarchist Collective, the editorial collective for NEFAC's theoretical and agitational magazine.

**Josh MacPhee** is a Chicago-based artist and the author of *Stencil Pirates* (Soft Skull, 2004).

**Nick Mamatas's** work on politics, publishing, and fringe cultures has appeared in the *Village Voice, In These Times, Clamor, Razor, Silicon Alley Reporter, Artbyte,* and the Disinformation Books anthologies *You Are Being Lied To, Everything You Know Is Wrong,* and *Abuse Your Illusions.* His short novel *Northern Gothic* (Soft Skull Press, 2001), a tale of the Civil War draft riots and twentieth-century gentrification was nominated for the Bram Stoker Award for achievement in horror fiction.

**Shon Meckfessel** is an independent author and activist residing in both Sacramento, California, and Belgrade, Serbia. He is currently writing a book on resistance movements in the Balkans entitled *Suffled How It Gush.*

**Cindy Milstein** is a faculty member at the Institute for Social Ecology, a board member for the Institute for Anarchist Studies , and a columnist for *Arsenal* magazine. She can be reached at cbmilstein@aol.com.

**Wu Ming** (formerly the Bologna scene of the Luther Blissett Project, www.lutherblissett.net) is a collective of novelists and mythographers, whose books are translated and published all across the planet (as yet, except for the U.S.). For further details, visit www.wumingfounda-tion.com.

**James O'Connor,** a professor emeritus at the University of California at Santa Cruz, is a co-founder and editor of *Capitalism, Nature and Socialism: A Journal of Socialist Ecology.* He's the director of the Center for Political Ecology, also in Santa Cruz. He is the author of six books, including *Natural Causes: Essays in Ecological Marxism* (Guilford Press, 1998).

**Christian Parenti** is the author, most recently, of *The Soft Cage: Surveillance in America From Slavery to the War on Terror* (Basic) and a fellow at City University of New York's Center for Place, Culture, and Politics. His forthcoming *Empire of Chaos: Tripping Through Occupied Iraq* will be published this fall by the New Press.

**Retort** can be contacted at P.O. Box 9699, Berlceley, CA 901709 retortsf@yahoo.com

**Arundhati Roy** is the author of the novel *The God of Small Things*, for which she received the Booker Prize. Her latest book, a *Los Angeles Times* bestseller, is *War Talk*, published by South End Press. She is also the author of *Power Politics* (South End Press, 2002) and *The Cost of Living* (Modern Library, 1999). In 2002, Roy was awarded the Lannan Foundation's prize for Cultural Freedom for her "extraordinary and courageous work [celebrating] the human right to freedom of imagination, inquiry, and expression."

**Ramor Ryan** was born in Dublin town. In keeping with old Irish traditions of rebellion and exile, he now lives between Chiapas, Mexico, and New York City. He is working on a book chronicling his travels.

**Eric Schwartz** is a former member of the Amalgamated Transit Union in Portland, Oregon.

**Sophie Style** is a writer and activist based in the U.K.

**Erin Volheim** is a writer and environmental activist.

**Immanuel Wallerstein** is a senior research scholar at Yale University, Director of the Fernand Braudel Center at Binghamton University, and author of *Utopistics: Or Historical Choices of the Twenty-first Century*. He chaired the international Gulbenkian Commission for Restructuring of the Social Sciences, whose report is *Social Sciences*. A collection of his work appears as *Essential Wallerstein*.

**Kristine Wong** is a Chinese-American activist and writer. A longtime environmental justice and community health organizer, educator, and trainer, she has lived and worked in the San Francisco Bay Area and Seattle.

**Retort** is a collective of anti-capitalist dissidents that includes James Davis, Rob Eshelman, Juliana Freidman, David Martinez, and Ramor Ryan, among others.

**Eddie Yuen** is the co-editor of *The Battle of Seattle: The New Challenge to Capitalist Globalization* (Soft Skull Press, 2002). He is on the faculty of the activism and social change program at New College of California in San Francisco.

# Editors' Acknowledgements

**Eddie Yuen** thanks Laura, Iain Boal, James Davis, Scott Fleming, David Martinez and Ramor Ryan. Dedicated to Betty Yuen and to the memory of my father, Hoh-Kun Donald Yuen.

**Daniel Burton-Rose** would like to thank: Candace, Bo, Punani, my mother and father and Billy for support; Ronica, Sonja, Pol, Jess, Laura, Clea, and Georgia for camaraderie; Trevor, Tiffany, Crystal, Alexis and Erik for your help—without you I couldn't have done it, really, and Scott Fleming and the people at the Prison Activist Resource Center (www.prisonactivist.org) for letting me in their space.

**George Katsiaficas** thanks Allison, Brian, Joe, David and EPICA for their continuing commitment, Kwangju people for their sacrifice and optimism, Billy for his friendship and engouragement, and Daniel and Eddie for staying focused in the trenches.